A MISSION OF HONOUR

The Royal Navy in the Pacific, 1769-1997

John McLean

DEDICATION

This book is dedicated to the memory of my late uncle, John Cope, who served as a lieutenant on *HMS Illustrious* during the Battle of Okinawa.

Published by Winter Productions. Printed through Colorcraft Ltd., Hong Kong, for Winter Productions:
48 Crompton Street, Derby DE1 1NX, United Kingdom, and
27 Euston Road, Wadestown, Wellington, New Zealand.
Copyright © John McLean 2010
ISBN 1 872970 23 0

ACKNOWLEDGEMENTS

I wish to thank Dr. Murray Bathgate of Wellington, New Zealand, Mr. Iain MacKenzie of the Admiralty Library in Portsmouth, and Lt.-Cdr. Stewart Hett of London for the helpful suggestions that they have made during the writing of this book.

I also wish to thank the Royal New Zealand Navy Museum at Devonport, Auckland, and Mr. Paul Restall in particular for their generous help in providing many of the photographs. Thanks also to Mrs. Chris Jones for typographical editing and my sister, Mrs. Jane Stirrat, for her computer work.

ABOUT THE AUTHOR

After taking the degrees of Master of Arts in History and Bachelor of Laws, John McLean studied at Gray's Inn and was called to the English Bar. He is the author of thirteen books – both fiction and non-fiction. He is also a former officer of the Royal New Zealand Naval Volunteer Reserve.

INTRODUCTION

In welcoming the reader on board I wish to stress that this is not a definitive history of the Royal Navy in the Pacific since such a work would require many volumes and half a lifetime to complete. It is an attempt to describe some of the many and varied activities that the Navy carried out in the world's largest ocean between Captain Cook and that sad and poignant moment when *HMY Britannia* and *HMS Chatham* sailed away from Hong Kong in 1997, having handed this British created jewel over to China.

Each of the chapters is a subject in itself and so it is not absolutely necessary to read them in sequence. Where possible, the participants have been allowed to tell what happened in their own words.

The Pacific Command (or "Squadron") was established in 1819 by Captain Thomas Masterman Hardy ("Kiss Me Hardy"). Its headquarters were at Valparaiso in Chile, which had recently gained its independence from Spain with help from Britain, not the least being that of Lord Cochrane, formerly of the Royal Navy, who landed at Valparaiso in November, 1818, and assumed the position of Vice-Admiral of Chile and Commander-in-Chief of its armed forces.

Valparaiso, although an important commercial centre, was not the sailors' favourite port-of-call – at least not at first sight. "Few places strike a newcomer with so strong an impression of ugliness as Valparaiso and, as we shot round Coramilla Point and a gust of wind nearly ripped out our topmasts, the impression I can vouch was universal....The cliffs form an amphitheatre reaching to the height of eight hundred or a thousand feet; they display no beauty of either form or colour," wrote Lieutenant Hon. Fred Walpole[1] after arriving there on *HMS Collingwood* in 1844. However, after four years on the station and getting to know both the Chileans and the English merchants of the city, the same officer wrote, "Four years ago we were sad to come, now we are equally sorry to go." [2]

For the first few decades of the nineteenth century Royal Navy warships in the eastern Pacific operated mainly off the coast of South America, whose young republics were developing a growing trade with Britain which, at the time, was the largest trading nation in the world. And the Navy's function was to support that trade by keeping the seas clear of pirates and privateers, which latter were mainly American, and to survey the coasts and sea lanes to make them safe for commercial shipping.

It was not until later in the century that California, Oregon and British Columbia made their presence felt, and the changing situation was recognised by the Royal Navy in the 1860s when it transferred its Pacific Command to Esquimalt on Vancouver Island.

On the other side of the great ocean the emerging lands of Australia and New Zealand were initially served by the Royal Navy's East Indies station, whence ships sailed occasionally to the Antipodes and the South Pacific to show the flag and to try to bring some law and order to places that desperately needed them.

In 1859 the work of the East Indies station in southern Pacific waters was taken over by the establishment of the Australia station, based at Sydney. This covered Australia, New Zealand and the islands of the South Pacific at a time when so many of these places were being opened up to trade, shipping and settlement.

In 1865 the China station was created out of part of the East Indies station and so the Pacific now had three commands, the Pacific based at Esquimalt, the Australia based at Sydney and the China station based at Hong Kong.

After Australia set up its own Navy in 1913 the Royal Navy left Sydney and created the New Zealand station to serve that country as well as the islands of the South Pacific, so many of which were British colonies.

CAPTAIN COOK

"The winds and waves are always on the side of the ablest navigators".

- Edward Gibbon, *The Decline and Fall of the Roman Empire* [1]

On Thursday, 26th January, 1769, the Royal Navy entered the Pacific when *HMS Endeavour*, under the command of the then Lieutenant James Cook, sailed past Cape Horn, at the bottom of South America, and into the limitless waters of the world's largest ocean, which is bigger in area than all six continents put together. In the strong southerly winds there were sporadic squalls of rain as the 106 foot long vessel, with eighty-five men on board, ploughed her way west, a flock of albatrosses flying with her and adding to the noise of wind and wave.

Although armed with six 4 pound carriage guns and eight swivel guns the *Endeavour* was not one of the Navy's fighting ships. She was formerly the *Earl of Pembroke* and had been built three years earlier at Whitby in Yorkshire where Cook had lived for some years. Drawing about fourteen feet of water when fully laden, she was purchased by the Navy Board specifically for this voyage.

Her commander, the son of a Yorkshire farm labourer, had risen through the ranks of the Navy on merit and in the next few years would literally put the Pacific on the map and carve his name in history as the greatest oceanic explorer, discoverer, navigator and cartographer that the world has ever seen.

The purposes of this history making voyage were to observe the transit of Venus in Tahiti and to try to ascertain whether or not the fabled southern continent existed in that part of the planet that lies between Tahiti and New Zealand.

The former purpose was at the behest of the Royal Society, the body that founded modern science, and there were both scientists and naturalists on board. Thus, from the very beginning, the Navy's role in the Pacific was essentially one of peace – discovery of new lands, people, flora and fauna, surveying the seas, coasts and harbours, and opening up these distant parts of the world to British trade and enterprise by keeping them free from pirates and slavers. These were to be the dominant roles of the Navy in Pacific waters until the terrible wars of the twentieth century.

Since Cook was the founding figure in the Royal Navy's relationship with the Pacific the best way to begin this great story is by way of a brief account of his voyages.

The First Voyage

From Cape Horn the *Endeavour* sailed north-east to Tahiti, which was reached on 13th April, 1769, when she anchored in Matavai Bay for a three months stay. It had been eight months since they left England and, despite having sailed through one and a half oceans and experienced several climate changes, all were in good health. This was to be a feature of all of Cook's voyages and was not unconnected with the attention that he paid to the food and health of his men.

Cook issued rules of behaviour for his crew in their dealings with the natives in this new ocean, the first being "To endeavour by every fair means to cultivate a friendship with the natives and to treat them with all imaginable humanity". Another rule enjoined those going ashore to look after their personal weapons and tools and not let them be stolen. This was particularly important as throughout the Pacific they were to find that the natives were, almost without exception, inveterate thieves, and much of the trouble with the local people was to revolve around trying to get back what had been stolen.

Cook had brought beads, red cloth, nails and pieces of iron to trade with the islanders for fresh food so that the *Endeavour* could live off the land as much as possible without dipping into its own supplies of preserved food and this was to be a hallmark of Royal Navy ships in the Pacific during the eighteenth and nineteenth centuries.

In the unknown and possibly dangerous land of Tahiti Cook and his men built an establishment ashore that was part fortress and part observatory for all the instruments – quadrant, telescope, astronomical clock, etc. – that were required for recording the transit of Venus. Named "Point Venus", it was surrounded by an earthen bank and a ditch, while four pounder guns were mounted on some old casks. There were also six swivel guns, and the forty or so men inside it carried small arms. Further accoutrements were a forge for the armourer to shape iron and an oven for the cooks to prepare the food.

The purpose of this fortification was to enable them to observe the transit of Venus safe from the thieving hands of the natives but one Tahitian did manage to get in and steal the heavy and valuable quadrant. After the offer of a reward and through the good offices of a chief, it was retrieved. Captain Cook even had his stockings swiped from under his pillow while he was lying there awake.

The 2nd of June, the day of the transit, was particularly clear and they were able to watch Venus, surrounded by a penumbra described as a "dusky shade", pass over the Sun.

Having fulfilled one object of the voyage, it was now time to move on to see if any land lay between Tahiti and New Zealand. The west coast of the latter had been discovered by the Dutchman, Abel Tasman, in 1642 but how far its land extended east was still unknown.

In the event they found only sea until on 6th October a sharp-eyed boy seaman up the mast, Nicholas Young, called out the magic words "Land ahoy!" and they pulled into a bay on the east coast of New Zealand's North Island which, due to the hostile reception from the Maoris, Cook named Poverty Bay. And, in honour of the observant lad, he named a nearby cape Young Nick's Head.

The Maoris were Polynesians but they were not indigenous to New Zealand; their forebears had sailed there some generations earlier from islands near Tahiti and had taken possession of the place by exterminating and eating the original inhabitants, the Moriois and others. Not all the Maoris were hostile and even those who were could sometimes be brought round to respect and even friendship by a demonstration of firepower from the *Endeavour's* guns.

Further north Cook found a harbour suitable for landing and for observing the transit of Mercury, which he wanted in order to get a more accurate idea of his longitude. He named the place Mercury Bay and for eleven days his men went ashore there in wooding and watering parties while others cleaned the ship and surveyed the bay. Before leaving he took formal possession of the place in the name of George III.

He then sailed up the east coast to the top of New Zealand, giving names that were to endure such as Cape Colville (after his friend, Lord Colville, under whom he had served on *HMS Northumberland*), Bream Bay (because of the abundance of fish), the Bay of Islands (an abundance of islands), the Hen and Chicken Islands (a big one and lots of little ones) and North Cape.

The *Endeavour* then sailed round the top of the North Island where she encountered a succession of gales which, for the first time since arriving in New Zealand, blew her out of sight of land and tore one of her sails. From there she passed down the west coast, with Cook observing that the land looked more fertile than in the far north. Upon sighting the island's most majestic snow capped peak, he named it Mount Egmont after the Earl of Egmont, a former First Lord of the Admiralty (1763-6). We "saw a very high mountain, and made very much like the Peak, Teneriffe," wrote the observant Cook, "....it is of a prodigious height and its top is covered with everlasting snow." [2]

It was now time for repairs and recreation and, as if by Providence, they found a deep inlet in the Queen Charlotte Sound, which Cook named Ship Cove, just as he named the Sound after his Queen. This was an ideal anchorage in almost every respect as the ship could be secured to the steep banks by cable, there was a stream of fresh water, birdsong in the forest, and at first there did not seem to be any Maoris in the area. However, they soon appeared and the first ones that the sailors saw greeted them with a hail of stones.

While watering parties were sent out and carpenters got to work on the much travelled ship Cook and Joseph Banks, the botanist, visited a nearby cove where they saw the remains of a cannibal feast. Shortly afterwards some Maoris came to the ship with pieces of partly defleshed bones that they were chewing. There were four heads that had not been touched, one of which a curious Sir Joseph Banks bought from them – "both the hairy scalps and skin of the faces were on" wrote Cook [3] – one of the many preserved heads that found a peace and quietness in the country houses and museums of England and Europe that was denied to them in the last hours of their lives by their own people.

During his stay at Ship Cove Captain Cook climbed a mountain from which he saw the strait that was to be named after him (but not by him). By the time he came back down he was convinced that New Zealand consisted of two main islands, something that the earlier exploration in 1642 by Abel Tasman had left undecided.

Cook continued his mapping of the New Zealand shore line by sailing down the east coast of the South Island where he made two famous mistakes; he drew Banks Peninsula as an island and

10

Stewart Island as a peninsula. But, compared with the whole, these errors were minor indeed.

He continued his circumnavigation of the South Island, noting positions and features on his developing chart and giving appropriate names such as Dusky Bay, Doubtful Harbour (later Sound), Cascade Point, Cape Foulwind, Admiralty Bay and Cape Farewell. Not only had he made a remarkably accurate chart of New Zealand's coastline but the *Endeavour's* botanists had taken on board more than four hundred new plants. The vessel had landed at a total of eight places in both islands and altogether the men had spent more than seven weeks ashore in a land that one day would provide a home for so many British people.

Cape Farewell was the final piece of land that he saw before crossing the Tasman Sea to discover the east coast of Australia, which was then called New Holland since whatever exploration that had been done on its northern and western coasts had been done mainly by Dutchmen operating from the Dutch East Indies.

Just as Nicholas Young had been the first to sight New Zealand it was Lieutenant Hicks who first saw Australia and so Cook named this historic spot in the south-east of the continent Point Hicks (now Cape Everard).

From here Captain Cook proceeded north where, in the course of the next few months, he would chart two thousand miles of a coast line that had hitherto been unknown to civilised man.

He made his first landfall in Australia at Botany Bay where, with a typically gracious gesture, he let his wife's cousin, young Isaac Smith, be the first white man ashore on a coast that would never be the same again. The exact spot, just inside the bay on its southern head, is to-day the Captain Cook Landing Place Historic Site. The easternmost point of this head is Cape Solander, named after one of the *Endeavour's* botanists, Doctor Solander, while the cape on the northern head of the bay's entrance was named after Joseph Banks, who now had his name bestowed on geographical features in both Australia and New Zealand. To these would later be added the Sydney suburbs of Bankstown and Banksia as well as Revesby, after Banks' home town in Lincolnshire, the Canberra suburb of Banks, and Banks Island off north-western Canada.

While water, wood and fish were being collected by the sailors their ever energetic commander surveyed both the bay and the surrounding land. Because of all the plants that the botanists collected the place was named Botany Bay.

Unlike the Maoris when he first arrived in New Zealand, the natives around Botany Bay were not hostile but nor were they particularly welcoming. They were darker and in some ways more primitive than the Maoris and were completely naked. For them this arrival of white men from across the sea would be the greatest challenge that their race ever faced.

Of Australia's aborigines the observant Cook wrote, "They may appear to some to be the most wretched people upon earth but in reality they are far more (sic) happier than we Europeans, being wholly unacquainted not only with the superfluous but the necessary conveniences so much sought after in Europe; they are happy in not knowing the use of them. They live in a tranquillity which is not disturbed by the inequality of condition." [4]

Cook was never one to let the grass grow under his feet and, after a week at Botany Bay, he put to sea again to continue his survey of eastern Australia. He sailed past the entrance of Sydney harbour although he noted it as a prospective good anchorage. He named it Port Jackson after George Jackson, the Secretary of the Admiralty.

Up the coast he went, observing, noting tides and weather, charting and sounding. He named Cape Byron after Captain John Byron, R.N., the grandfather of the poet, and Cape Morton and Morton Bay after the Earl of Morton, who was the President of the Royal Society, under whose auspices the *Endeavour* carried out the Transit of Venus. The spelling of these two places was later wrongly altered to "Moreton". His first landfall after Botany Bay was for a day and a night at a place that he called Bustard Bay for it was here that his men shot and ate a bustard, which weighed seventeen and a half pounds. It is situated south of the later town of Gladstone in Queensland.

When the *Endeavour* got among the islands of the Great Barrier Reef the bottom was often shoaled with only a fathom or two between the ship's bottom and the seabed. So small was the margin of safety that the *Endeavour's* cutter would go ahead, taking soundings. That she never struck a shoal in this maze of islands and coral reefs was a measure of the seamanship of her captain. He gave names to Cape Capricorn, which he calculated to be directly under the Tropic of Capricorn, Cape Townshend (after Lord Charles Townshend, who had signed Cook's commission as a lieutenant), Whitsunday Island (discovered on Whit Sunday), Dunk Island (after George Montagu Dunk, Earl of Halifax and First Lord of the

Admiralty), Cape Upstart (sticking up cheekily from low lying land), Thirsty Sound (no fresh water), Magnetic(al) Island (where his compasses played up, hence the name), Trinity Bay (discovered on Trinity Sunday), Green Island ("low, green and woody") and Cape Tribulation ("because here begun all our troubles" [5]).

It was the night of Trinity Sunday, 10th June, 1770, when the seabed suddenly rose and "before the man at the (sounding) lead could have another cast the ship struck and stuck fast". [6] They were on a coral reef at high tide.

Sails were hauled in and about fifty tons of gear were jettisoned, including the six guns and carriages as well as ironwork and rotten food.

The sharp coral made a hole in the vessel which had to be plugged with wool and oakum while pumps dealt with the inflow of water. Fortunately a piece of coral had got stuck in the hole and this reduced the volume of water getting through.

The stricken ship did not come off on the next high tide but did so on the following one – some twenty-three hours after the accident.

Because of the need to get her ashore for repairs boats were sent forth to try to find a suitable landing place in this distant and remote land. After six days she limped into the mouth of what is now known as the Endeavour River. Stores were taken off the ship and tents were set up ashore for the sick and to protect the provisions from the heavy rainstorms of that area.

For the next six weeks this would be their home. To avoid having to dip too deeply into the ship's food stock (down to provisions for only another three months) they lived off the land and the sea as much as they could – fishing with the seine, eating clams, turtles and wild beans. It was here that Joseph Banks shot a wallaby. It was then skinned, taken on board the *Endeavour* and, upon reaching England, stuffed by a taxidermist.

The stores were taken ashore, the sick were put in tents on the beach, the carpenters got to work on the hole, and those masters of iron work, the armourers, began making whatever nails and bolts that were required to secure the new planks.

All was ready by 4th August when the *Endeavour* put to sea again but she was still amongst all those shoals and islands. By a combination of excellent seamanship and good luck she continued her voyage up through what later became known as the "Inner Route" of the Great Barrier Reef to the north-eastern point of

Australia, which Cook named Cape York after the Duke of York, the brother of George III, who had died three years earlier. Then, on nearby Possession Island, he took formal possession of the whole east coast of Australia in the name of the King of England. He named it all New South Wales even though in later times that name would apply only to the southern state of which Sydney is the capital.

The *Endeavour* then sailed up to New Guinea, where Cook made a brief landing, and then it was back to England via Batavia (Jakarta). On this first and most important voyage to the Pacific Captain Cook and his lively and hardworking crew had paved the way for the addition to the British Empire of a continent far larger in area than the thirteen colonies across the Atlantic that were about to be lost in the War of Independence.

The Second Voyage

Captain Cook was given two ships for his second voyage – the *Resolution*, under his own command, and an escort vessel, the *Adventure*. The *Resolution* had a hundred and twelve men on board, the *Adventure* eighty-one.

Cook had already shown that there was no southern continent between Tahiti and New Zealand and the purpose of this second voyage was to ascertain whether or not this fabled piece of land existed further south, i.e. in the higher latitudes towards the South Pole.

From England he sailed to Cape Town and then south towards the Antarctic continent where he found that navigating among the icebergs in temperatures below freezing point was every bit as dangerous as negotiating the reefs, shoals and islands of the Great Barrier Reef in temperatures that were at the other end of the thermometer. He got as far south as 71° latitude – further than any known voyager before.

From the southern latitudes he sailed up to Dusky Sound in the south-west of New Zealand, arriving there on 25th March, 1773. After months in sub-Antarctic waters it was time for repairs, replenishment and recreation.

A forge was set up on the shore for the armourers to go about their skilled metal work while the sailmakers, carpenters and watering and wood parties were no less occupied. Cook released some live geese that he had taken on board in Cape Town and which had survived the freezing temperatures among the icebergs. Here also he made a beer with the leaves of the rimu tree and manuka in what would be New Zealand's first "home brew" experiment. Most of the men liked it although one of them had to enhance the taste with some rum and sugar.

After six weeks in the Sound they sailed up to Ship Cove, Cook's favourite haunt on his earlier voyage. Then it was time to winter in Tahiti where the *Resolution* anchored in Matavai Bay before going on to Huahine and Raiatea. While at Raiatea Captain Cook tasted kava for the first time.

He then sailed to Tonga by way of the Hervey group in the lower Cook Islands, which he named after his friend, Captain Augustus John Hervey, R.N. From Tonga he returned to what was now his South Pacific headquarters, Ship Cove in New Zealand, where the *Resolution* was repaired and caulked. From here he explored and charted the strait between the North and South Islands but weather prevented him from entering Wellington harbour. As with Sydney harbour, he just looked up through its entrance and noted that it looked promising.

Some of the officers went walking in the area of Ship Cove and, as had happened when the *Endeavour* was there, they found the remnants of a feast, which showed that not only were the locals cannibals but also they didn't bother to clean up after a meal for, strewn over the ground were the victim's bowels and untouched head while his heart was on the end of a stick that was attached to a canoe. Those who had partaken of the meal were still hanging around and so one of the officers, Lieutenant Pickersgill, whose horror was matched by his curiosity, purchased the severed head (still with the flesh on it) for two nails. What happened next is an event unprecedented in the annals of the Royal Navy.

Pickersgill took it on board the *Resolution* and showed it to those on the deck, among whom were several Maoris who had not taken part in the feast. Their eyes lit up. Charles Clerke, a young officer, asked one of them if he would like a piece. Answer: yes. Clerke thereupon cut a slice from the head and broiled it. When ready, the Maori gobbled it down.

At this moment Captain Cook arrived on the scene and wondered what all the commotion was about. The great man, always with his eye to science in all its many forms, was both revolted and fascinated. No white man had ever witnessed an act of cannibalism in New Zealand and, despite strong evidence, there were those who doubted that these things actually happened. Maybe the Maoris were just pretending.

If Cook required evidence it came a few moments later when another piece was broiled by Lieutenant Clerke and the Maori again ate it – this time in front of Cook and the entire crew. Some of the sailors were so sick that they had to rush for the gunwales to vomit over the side at what must surely be the only occasion on which an act of cannibalism was ever carried out on board a ship of the Royal Navy.

From Ship Cove the *Resolution* did another tour of sub-Antarctic waters – this time to the east of New Zealand – before visiting Easter Island and then Matavai Bay, Tahiti, again for a three week stay. From there she sailed up to Niue, which Cook named Savage Island since a native threw a spear that just missed his shoulder.

The ship sailed on to Tonga, which, for obvious reasons, they named the Friendly Islands, and then the New Hebrides, which Cook named since they reminded him of the Hebridean islands in Scotland. Here he found a good harbour, which he named Port Sandwich after the First Lord of the Admiralty, just as he would name the Sandwich Islands (Hawaii) after him too.

He then sailed to New Caledonia, naming it too, and had difficulty getting through the reef, which almost totally surrounds this large island and which hardly ever rises above the level of the sea. Cook spent twenty-seven days here, charting much of the coast but not all of it. He then sailed back to Ship Cove, discovering and naming Norfolk Island on the way.

From this second voyage he returned home via Cape Horn, having discovered hundreds of new islands in the South Pacific and proving that there was no great southern continent apart from Antarctica, which is too far south for any purpose other than scientific.

The Third Voyage

When a nation finds itself with a person of Captain Cook's unique capabilities it is foolish not to take the utmost advantage of them and for this reason the Admiralty sent him out to the Pacific on a third voyage for the purpose of finding out whether the fabled North-West Passage, linking the Pacific with the North Atlantic, actually existed. Again there were two vessels, the *Resolution* of the

16

The eastern Australian mainland and south coast
of New Guinea.

North Cape

Bay of Islands

Auckland

Manukau Harbour

Coromandel
Peninsula

Rangiriri

Tauranga

Poverty
Bay

Mt. Egmont

Cape Farewell

Ship
Cove

Wellington

Cape Foulwind

Nelson

Cook Strait

Lyttelton

Banks Peninsula

Mount
Cook

Dusky
Sound

Dunedin

Stewart Island

New Zealand

Nootka
Sound

Vancouver
Island

Jervis
Inlet

Strait of Georgia

Vancouver
Fraser
River

Juan de Fuca Strait

Esquimalt

Cape Flattery

Whidbey
Island

Puget
Sound

Bainbridge
Island

Seattle

Columbia
River

Part of west coast of North America

Port
Arthur
Wei Hai Wei

Peking

Tientsin

Port Hamilton

Chin-kiang
Quelpart

Nanking

Woosung

Shanghai

Yangtse
River

Ningpo

Amoy

Canton

Swatow

Formosa

Bias Bay

Hong Kong

Macau

China

previous voyage, and the escort *Discovery*. Cook was in command of the former.

They left Plymouth on 11th July, 1776, and sailed to Cape Town and thence through the sub-Antarctic ocean to Ship Cove, stopping for three days in Adventure Bay, Tasmania, to get wood and water as well as grass for the live cattle that they had on board. Here Cook came across a different type of native – the Tasmanian aborigine (now extinct). Despite Tasmania's cold temperatures they too were naked except that the women wore a kanagaroo skin over their shoulders for carrying their babies.

From Ship Cove the two vessels sailed to Tonga and then to Tahiti. From there they went north, spending the anniversary of the birth of Christ on an island which Cook called Christmas Island.

On 18th January, 1778, they sighted the east coast of the Hawaiian island of Kauai. Thus did these beautiful islands become known to the wider world. In Cook's words, "At this time we were in some doubt whether or no the land before (us) was inhabited, this doubt was soon cleared up by seeing some canoes coming off from the shore towards the ships. I immediately brought to to give them time to come up, there were three or four men in each and we were agreeably surprised to find them of the same Nation as the people of Otahiete (Tahiti) and the other islands we had lately visited. It required but very little address to get them to come alongside but we could not prevail upon any one to come on board. They exchanged a few fish they had in their canoes for anything we offered them, but valued nails or iron above every other thing. The only weapons they had were a few stones in some of the canoes and these they threw overboard when they found they were not wanted." [7]

Cook and his ships stayed for a fortnight off a village called Waimea and then sailed for five weeks across an empty ocean to Nootka Sound on the western side of an island, now called Vancouver Island after a young officer on the *Discovery* whom we shall meet in the next chapter.

The island had an abundance of wood and water and they made the acquaintance of the natives, who dressed in animal skins. Unfortunately, like so many other natives that they had encountered, these ones were also enthusiastic thieves. The sailors didn't have to put up with them for long as they began their exploration and mapping when they sailed up the west coast of the island and then along the deeply indented coast of what is now British Columbia, giving names such as Mount Edgecumbe and Cape Fairweather,

17

which latter was the diametric opposite of the names he gave to Cape Foulweather in Oregon and Cape Foulwind in New Zealand.

They stopped at Cape Hinchinbrook, at the entrance to Prince William Sound, where the Indians were even more brazen in their thievery than their counterparts in the south. One night, while the sailors on the *Discovery* were having their evening meal below and the deck was all but empty, a group of Indians came on board for plunder. They drew their knives and began to steal everything that wasn't bolted down.

The sailors swapped their cutlery for their cutlasses and rushed on to the deck to defend their ship and its possessions. The Indians jumped or were pushed overboard into the freezing sea but then, seeing some men out taking soundings in one of the *Resolution's* boats, they paddled their canoes in that direction.

The boat returned in a hurry to the *Resolution* and the surveyors climbed on board. Next thing the Indians overpowered those who were guarding the boat, cut it loose and began to take it away. However, upon the *Resolution's* guns being manned, they changed their minds. Thus was averted a situation that might have got very ugly since no captain could tolerate the theft of a boat which, in the event of shipwreck, could be the means of saving the lives of the crew.

On this northern voyage Captain Cook sailed right round the Gulf of Alaska as far as the Aleutian island of Unalashka, keeping the coast in sight but finding no North-West Passage. In a letter to the Admiralty, he said that he would sail south to Hawaii and then return in the summer to explore the Bering Sea in a further attempt to find that elusive passage.

In Hawaii he anchored in Kealakekua Bay, on the west side of what is known as the Big Island (Hawaii itself). The natives thought that Cook was the god, Lono, who had departed long ago and was expected to return about this time. There was an elaborate ceremony with a rotting pig and human skulls which Cook was forced to attend. In this heady and volatile atmosphere there were the usual thefts of tools and other equipment culminating in the stealing of the *Discovery's* cutter – its biggest boat – during the night of 13th-14th February. 1780.

As with the attempted theft of the *Resolution's* boat by the Indians, this latest theft was obviously one that could not be tolerated and so Captain Cook went ashore with a party of marines to try to recover it while his sailors blocked the entrance to the bay.

18

There was an argument on the beach and a Hawaiian threatened Cook with a dagger whereupon Cook fired at him, the shot barely affecting him as he was well covered with a thick cloak. A chief then tried to stab one of Cook's men and the frenzied mob started throwing stones.

The marines were ordered to fire at the gathering war party and a general melee ensued in which Cook momentarily turned his back on the frenzied Hawaiians so that he could signal his boats to come closer to the shore. It was at this moment that he was struck with a club from behind. Then, after being stabbed in the neck with a dagger, he fell face down in the shallow water. The mob held him under the sea and smashed him to pieces with their blunt clubs and sharp daggers. Captain Cook, at the age of fifty, died in the ocean that he had largely discovered and charted and whose people he had befriended on hundreds of islands and recorded their customs in his Journal.

The Hawaiians then cut up his body, which they later claimed to have burned. There was no evidence of this apart from their own word and the people of this island were not known for their truthfulness. It is believed that they ate him.

Some days later they returned a small piece of flesh from his thigh but, significantly in view of the rumoured act of cannibalism, this was the only piece of his flesh that they returned although they did also return several defleshed bones – those of the thighs, legs, arms, feet and skull. These were put into a coffin by his grieving sailors and consigned to the deep.

During Captain Cook's second voyage he wrote in his Journal, "for we can by no means tell what use future ages may make of the discoveries made in the present". [8] To find the real memorial of this greatest of discoverers and navigators one only needs to go to any of the places that he discovered and apply those noble words that grace Sir Christopher Wren's tomb in London's Saint Paul's Cathedral – *Si monumentum requiris, circumspice* ("If you want his memorial, look around you"). Look at the size and magnificence of Sydney, the prosperity of British Columbia, the vast pineapple and sugar plantations of coastal Queensland, all the cultivated farm lands of New Zealand, and the ocean trade of the Pacific. All these and much more stem from the ground breaking discoveries that were made by Captain Cook.

CAPTAIN GEORGE VANCOUVER

Among those who witnessed the murder of Captain Cook was a young midshipman, George Vancouver, who, on the day before Cook's death, was himself stoned and beaten by the hostile Hawaiians when he was in a cutter chasing a native thief.

Young George had joined Cook's second expedition in 1772 at the age of fifteen and so received his training in navigation, seamanship and surveying from the great master himself. When Cook set out on his third voyage Vancouver, by now a midshipman, was appointed to the escorting vessel, *HMS Discovery*.

After arriving back in England in 1780 George Vancouver was promoted to the rank of lieutenant and he served on the West Indies station for five years.

The advance of British and American fur traders across the North American continent all the way to the Pacific irked Spain, which claimed sovereignty over the whole coast of North America from its base in Mexico, a claim that was not recognised by Britain.

A Spanish force had built a fort in Nootka Sound on what is to-day Vancouver Island and seized three British ships there and so the Admiralty appointed George Vancouver to go back to the North Pacific to assert Britain's interests, which were mainly in the fur trade. More specifically, Vancouver was to meet the Spanish commissioner at Nootka Sound to settle the damages claims arising out of the seizure of the three British merchantmen, he was to make a detailed survey of the coast all the way from California to Alaska, and, like Cook, he was to try to ascertain whether the long imagined North-West Passage really did exist. Of these three assignments the most important was the survey of the long coastline and it would take him three seasons for, as Captain Cook had found out, it was only practicable to survey these cold, northern seas in the summer months. For the purpose he was given two ships, *HMS Discovery* (not Cook's ship but another of the same name), and its armed tender, *HMS Chatham.*

It took them a year to get out there by way of the Cape of Good Hope, Australia (where Vancouver was the first to explore its south-west corner), New Zealand, Tahiti and that place of most unhappy memories, Hawaii.

In April, 1792, they reached the Californian coast near Cape Cabrillo, north of the Golden Gate. On Saint George's Day (23rd April) they found and named Point Saint George.

Continuing up the coast, Vancouver sailed past the mouth of the great Columbia River without entering it. His instructions from the Admiralty were not to waste time going up rivers that could not be safely navigated by ships of a size that were capable of making the journey to the Pacific. He was not there for the benefit of native canoes but for that of naval vessels and merchantmen. Anyway the shallow bar of the Columbia would have been difficult to cross.

From its delta he proceeded up the coast, exploring, charting and naming places such as Point Grenville and Destruction Island, until he reached Cape Flattery.

From this point Captain Cook had gone up the west side of Vancouver Island whereas George Vancouver went the other way – under the island and into the maze of islands, channels and inlets that a couple of centuries later would become one of the industrial powerhouses of the planet.

His aim was to trace every foot of the shoreline, not only in the straits and sounds near the 49th Parallel but also further up the Alaskan coast so that, if a North-West Passage did exist, he would find it.

After refitting at Port Discovery (named by Vancouver after his ship but now called Discovery Bay) and taking on fresh water and wood, the two ships passed through the entrance to a great Sound, which their small boats would spend a month surveying in detail. It was found that this intricate waterway, with deep inlets, many islands and narrow channels, extended south for about a hundred miles. They named it Puget Sound after Peter Puget, Vancouver's chief surveyor on the voyage. Another surveying leader in the Sound was the Master of the *Discovery*, Joseph Whidbey, whose name was given to the big island at its entrance, Whidbey Island, which he circumnavigated.

It was here that Vancouver established the procedure for the rest of the voyage by keeping the two big ships in a safe anchorage, where an observatory could be set up ashore to check longitude and the rate of the chronometers, while the actual survey would be conducted by means of small boats. This was wise as, with the strong winds that blow down from the steep mountains and the difficulties of anchoring due to the great depths of water even close to the shore, the Sound could not be surveyed adequately by ships as large as the *Discovery* and the *Chatham*.

In Vancouver's own words, "I became thoroughly convinced that our boats alone could enable us to acquire correct or satisfactory information respecting this broken country; and although the execution of such a service in open boats would necessarily be extremely laborious and expose those so employed to numberless dangers and unpleasant situations that might occasionally produce great fatigue and protract their return to the ships, yet that mode was undoubtedly the most accurate, the most ready, and indeed the only one in our power to pursue for ascertaining the continental boundary." [1]

While *HMS Chatham* went north to trace the San Juan Islands, which could be seen in the hazy distance, Captain Vancouver took the *Discovery* to the tip of Bainbridge Island (opposite the future site of Seattle), which he named Restoration Point since he anchored there on the anniversary of the Restoration of Charles II. From here two boat expeditions, one led by Vancouver and the other by Peter Puget, set off in a southerly direction to trace the various inlets and passages into which the Sound divides.

During the survey there was a lot of rain and this made conditions in the open boats rather uncomfortable. The *Chatham's* cutter was twenty-two feet long and her launch nineteen feet and it appears that the *Discovery's* boats were slightly longer. The usual complement of a boat was one officer, a midshipman, some marines and a team of oarsmen.

In case of trouble the boats were armed with swivel guns, muskets and small arms. In addition some of the officers and midshipmen had sporting guns for shooting birds.

The boats were provisioned for up to two weeks and, besides rations, they also carried tents for the men to sleep in at night and a marquee for the officers, as well as trinkets to trade with or give to the Indians.

The surveying day began at 4 a.m. and they worked until dusk and sometimes later. Meals were short and were usually taken ashore, the main meal being at the end of the day. If the banks were too steep for pitching tents, they would sleep on the boat but this was both uncomfortable and unpopular.

In their dealings with the Indians Vancouver insisted that they take every possible care to avoid disputes and to make sure that, in any trade, the Indians were satisfied with what they got in return, which was usually pieces of iron. On only one occasion did they meet hostility but, after Puget ordered a swivel gun to be fired over the Indians' heads, the latter unstrung their bows and even offered to trade them to the sailors.

22

Vancouver and his surveyors were impressed by the beauty of the Sound, which, when the boats were away beyond their provisions, provided them with extra food in the form of fish and birds. They took to eating crows, of which, in Peter Puget's words, "we could always procure plenty". [2]

After the *Chatham* returned from her exploration of the San Juan Islands Captain Vancouver did what all naval captains loved doing; he took possession of the recently surveyed Sound and surrounding countryside in the name of King George III at a spot that he later named Possession Sound. Thus was Puget Sound made known to the wider world.

After leaving their newly discovered Sound the ships put into Birch Bay, just south of the 49th Parallel, so that the carpenters and blacksmiths could do what had to be done to the ships after their long survey. Then, on 12th June, 1792, Captain Vancouver set out on another history making exploration that, unbeknown to him, would lead to a great city taking his name.

On his way up the coast he came across the Fraser River with its large and shallow delta, and he bypassed it for the same reason that he had bypassed the Columbia. The details of rivers were for later surveyors.

The shoals hindered the ships' boats, which had to keep well out. "These can only be navigable for canoes," wrote Vancouver, "as the shoal continues along the coast to the distance of seven or eight miles from the shore." [3]

After noting the two openings of the Fraser River into the sea, Vancouver sailed up to English Bay and around what is now Stanley Park into what he named Burrard Inlet after a naval friend, Sir Harry Burrard, but which is to-day Vancouver Harbour. Here, on Wednesday, 13th June, 1792, Captain Vancouver passed beyond the First Narrows into a large, safe anchorage.

As he passed through the First Narrows to explore the inner harbour he met about fifty Indians in their canoes "who conducted themselves with the greatest decorum and civility, presenting us with several fish cooked, and undressed," wrote Captain Vancouver. "….These good people, finding that we were inclined to make some return for their hospitality, showed much understanding in preferring iron to copper.

For the sake of the company of our new friends we stood on under an easy sail, which encouraged them to attend us some little distance up the arm (the inner harbour). The major part of the canoes

23

twice paddled forward, assembled before us, and each time a conference was held. Our visit and appearance were most likely the object of their consultation, as our motions on these occasions seemed to engage the whole of their attention." [4]

They "gradually dispersed as we advanced from the station where we had first met them, and three or four canoes only accompanied us up....We landed for the night about half a league from the head of the inlet (the Port Moody arm)....Our Indian visitors remained with us until by signs we gave them to understand we were going to rest and, after receiving some acceptable articles, they retired. A great desire was manifested by these people to imitate our actions, especially in the firing of a musket, which one of them performed, though with much fear and trembling. They minutely attended to all our transactions and examined the colour of our skins with infinite curiosity....

The shores in this situation were formed by steep rocky cliffs, that afforded no convenient place for pitching our tent, which compelled us to sleep in the boats. Some of the young gentlemen, however, preferred the stony beach for their couch, without duly considering the line of high water mark, found themselves incommoded by the flood tide, of which they were not apprised until they were nearly afloat." [5] Thus ended the first day in the story of the city of Vancouver.

At 4 a.m. the next morning "we retraced our passage in, leaving on the northern shore a small opening extending to the northward (Indian Arm)" [6] and then, "under sail, with a fresh favourable breeze", [7] they sailed out through the harbour and back into the Strait of Georgia.

"The shores of this channel (the harbour)....may be considered on the south side of a moderate height and, though rocky, well covered with trees of large growth, principally of the pine tribe. On the northern side the rugged, snowy barrier...rose very abruptly, and was only protected from the wash of the sea by a very narrow border of low land. By seven o'clock (a.m.) we had reached the north-west point of the channel, which forms also the south point of the main branch of the (Howe) Sound." [8] He named this Point Atkinson (to-day Lighthouse Park).

Captain Vancouver thus became the first Western explorer to discover this magnificent, land-locked harbour which, in an act of historical aptness, was later named after him.

24

After leaving Burrard Inlet Captain Vancouver proceeded north, exploring Howe Sound and Jervis Inlet. It was slow work as each inlet had a narrow entrance but went deep into the mountains. For example, Jervis Inlet was fifty miles from its entrance to its head. But Vancouver had set out to make a methodical survey and such annoying terrain would just have to be traced. One of these inlets might even have been the entrance to the North-West Passage.

As he moved up the Strait of Georgia he was looking out for a tide coming down from the north as that would show that the tree covered land mass on his port side was an island and not part of the North American continent.

They made their way up the ever narrowing stretch of water between what we now know as Vancouver Island and the mainland and into the Queen Charlotte Strait where they found the main navigation channel near the south-west shore. A fog came down, rendering the survey of this area less reliable than elsewhere; the surveyors missed the entrance to both Seymour Inlet and Belsize Inlet. However, they added other waterways to the map, including Smith Sound, Rivers Inlet and Burke Channel.

As the season progressed and they got further north the weather deteriorated and it was particularly hard for those in the open boats, who were out on their own for up to two weeks at a time. Archibald Menzies, the surgeon-botanist, wrote of these crews, "enduring at times the tormenting pangs of both hunger and thirst, yet on every occasion struggling (as to) who would be the most forward in executing the orders of their superiors to accomplish the general interest of the voyage." [9] Ever careful of his men's welfare, George Vancouver tended to worry if the boats were overdue.

The happy result of this summer surveying season was that the two ships rounded the top of Vancouver Island and sailed down its western coast to Nootka Sound. Thus Vancouver became the first man to circumnavigate the island that would be named after him.

The Spanish commandant of the area, Senor Juan Francisco de la Bodega y Quadra, was at Nootka and so he and Vancouver settled down to negotiate the problem of the Spanish interfering with British ships in the area. Although the talks did not really get anywhere a firm friendship developed between the two officers. On one occasion they went together to pay a visit to Maquinna, the Indian chief at Friendly Cove, and on the way back Quadra asked Vancouver to name some place after them both. Vancouver replied by suggesting that the big island they were on be named Quadra's and Vancouver's Island – a cumbersome name that in the fullness of time became known as Vancouver Island.

Also at Nootka Sound was the storeship, *HMS Daedalus*, which had brought them supplies. That was good news but it was overshadowed by the tidings that en route the vessel had put into Oahu in the Hawaiian group where its commander, Lieutenant Hergest, and the astronomer, William Gooch, and a seaman had been murdered. Hergest had been on the *Resolution* when Captain Cook was clubbed to death at Kealakekua Bay and he was also a friend of Vancouver's.

With the winter setting in and the survey completed for the season it was now time to head for warmer waters, viz. Hawaii. where Vancouver set himself two tasks: punish the murderers of the *Daedalus* men and try to make peace among the warring chiefs and, if possible, get them to cede their beautiful islands to Britain. He could see that, by virtue of their situation, they would grow in importance as the trade of the North Pacific developed.

On the way down the coast they passed again the Columbia River and this time *HMS Chatham* managed to get across its bar. Once inside, she anchored in a safe place and sent her boats up the swift flowing river. They traced and charted it for about a hundred miles and the furthest point they reached they named Port Vancouver (to-day the small American city of Vancouver, opposite Portland, Oregon). It would not be long before the Columbia would be an important route for the fur traders, who were moving ever westwards.

While the *Chatham* was mapping the Columbia Vancouver's *Discovery* was entering the Golden Gate where she anchored in Yerba Buena Bay (to-day San Francisco). This was the first visit to this Spanish settlement by a foreign ship and during her ten day stay the Spaniards were most hospitable.

Vancouver had taken Captain Broughton off the *Chatham* and despatched him to London with all the charts and reports of this first season of surveying. The advantage of having an officer accompany the documents was that he could explain matters to the Admiralty where necessary.

On 12th February, 1793, Vancouver arrived at the island of Hawaii and the two ships set off to make a survey of this biggest of the Sandwich Islands. They met at Captain Cook's graveyard of Kealakekua Bay, having between them circumnavigated the island. At this bay of unhappy memories Vancouver put his field pieces on the deck and kept about four hundred stand of arms loaded and under guard on the quarter deck. Since they clubbed Captain Cook to death these volatile natives had started to obtain European firearms from visiting trading vessels.

At the time the Hawaiian islands were divided between two powerful chiefs, Kamehameha, who was the lord of the island of Hawaii, and Kahekili, whose writ covered Maui, Oahu, Kauai and many smaller islands.

Captain Vancouver probably knew more about the native politics of Hawaii than any other European and, despite witnessing the murder of his hero, Captain Cook, he had a genuine affection for the islands and their people. However, he was unsuccessful in his attempts to end the civil war and nor would Kamehameha cede his lands to Great Britain on the very sensible grounds that Britain at that time could not protect him from his enemies, viz. Kahekili and his warriors.

Vancouver was more successful in bringing the murderers of Lieutenant Hergest to justice; three had already been killed before his arrival and their fellow murderers were executed after Vancouver involved himself with the case. He wanted the islanders to understand that "no distance in time would in future secure any from detection, or prevent the punishment which such crimes demand." [10]

On 20th March, 1793, *HMS Discovery* anchored off Waikiki Beach. She left four days later and sailed a short distance along the south coast of Oahu where a team under Joseph Whidbey made the first ever survey of Pearl Harbour.

The *Discovery* and *Chatham* returned to America's north-west coast in May, 1793, for a further surveying season of four months. They would continue north from where they left off the previous year and, following Vancouver's usual custom, the two big ships found suitable anchorages and sent the small boats out to do the survey.

In this colder climate the boats now had an awning to protect them from rain while Vancouver issued them with extra wheat and portable soup so that they could have two hot meals a day. The officer in charge of each boat was given extra spirits which he could give out at his pleasure.

They made their way up the coast, naming Cascade Inlet for all the waterfalls along its sides, and circumnavigating the island of Revilla Gigedo.

It was on this voyage that Captain Vancouver had his only real trouble with the Indians. Relations had been so good that he seems to have dropped his guard when he went ashore to make the necessary observations. A crowd of Indians gathered round him in a threatening manner and he managed to get away in the pinnace but the Indians followed in their canoes. Things became nasty when they snatched some guns from his boat. He managed to ward them off until Puget arrived. The order was then given to fire and the Indians at once headed off for the shore but not before about nine of them had been killed and two of Vancouver's men wounded. To make sure that no one ever forgot it Vancouver named nearby features Traitors Cove, Escape Point and Betton Island (after one of the wounded sailors).

This was the only time that blood was shed in a dispute with the natives in all three of Vancouver's voyages. The tribe involved was the Tlingit Indians, who were known for their aggression. In their war canoes there was usually an old hag in the stern who urged the young men on to ever more bloody deeds.

Vancouver and his men were repelled by the Tlingit women, who had a horizontal slit across their lower lip which, stretched with ornaments, made it look like the opening in a post box. These slits extended the full length of the mouth. Vancouver described these original punks as having "hideous appendages" [11] and being "an instance of human absurdity that would scarcely be credited without ocular proof". [12]

Because of the preponderance of skins that they wore the Indians of the north were regarded as dirty and smelly by the sailors, who compared them unfavourably with the Polynesians who, being almost naked and swimming in the sea, did not give out such a stench.

Vancouver's second surveying season ended at Port Protection, Alaska. Because of the many deep inlets progress had been slow. He had taken the survey from 52° latitude to 56° 30 but this represented a direct distance of only just over three hundred miles.

This time on the voyage down the Californian coast on his way to winter in Hawaii Captain Vancouver and his ships received a less friendly welcome from the Spanish officials at San Francisco and Monterey. Although Spain claimed a paper sovereignty over the whole north-west coast of America they knew that they were powerless to stop Vancouver who, with the power of England behind him, went wherever he liked unmolested by the puny forces of Spain. He shared with them his charts, which were far superior to any that the Spanish ever produced. All this made them feel their inferiority all the more; hence the churlish attitude that was ordered by the new commandant of Alta California, Jose Joaquin de Arrillaga.

Fortunately the local officials at Santa Barbara ignored their commandant's wishes and extended a friendly hand to the *Discovery*, *Chatham* and *Daedalus* (which had recently returned from Sydney with more provisions) when they anchored off Santa Barbara's beautiful coast line. Vancouver and his officers went riding and shooting and the Spanish priests extended their usual hospitality. One of the missionaries was visiting Santa Barbara from Buena Ventura further south and so Vancouver gave him a ride back on the *Discovery*. A very good way of repaying missionary kindness.

Vancouver continued his survey of the California coast down as far as latitude 29° 54' north (near the present Punta Baja on Mexico's Baja California peninsula). This was a remarkable achievement as in only two relatively short summer seasons he had completed a thorough survey from latitude 29° 54' to north of latitude 56° - a distance of more than 1,700 miles, not counting the thousands of extra miles of deep inlets and islands that had been traced, sounded and charted by the boats' crews. This was the most extensive marine survey that the world had ever seen.

Although the Spanish claimed sovereignty over much of this coast they had never done anything with it or even surveyed it properly, and what was one day to become the United States' largest and richest state was made known to the world by Captain Vancouver through his charts and published descriptions.

Vancouver's small fleet sailed on to Hawaii where they refitted their vessels and moved the stores from the *Daedalus* on to the other two. They spent six weeks at Kealakekua Bay where a portable observatory was set up ashore. It might be thought strange, if not macabre, that out of the many bays in the Hawaiian islands Vancouver should keep returning to this place of bitter memories. However, it did have an excellent anchorage and he took the precaution of allowing only armed working parties to go ashore and to receive only chiefs on board.

Vancouver continued to press the suit of a marriage of the islands to Britain by means of their cession to King George III but this time it was the unimaginative British government that poured cold water on the idea and not Kamehameha. The great Hawaiian leader was concerned at the impact that trading vessels and other indicia of the Western world were having on the islands and he wanted a powerful protector. Because of the traditional structure of Hawaiian society he naturally preferred a monarchy like that of Great Britain to the alien republican values of the United States.

In the cabin of the *Discovery* Kamehameha and his chiefs agreed to cede the islands to Britain in return for protection but the British government, engaged in a bloody struggle with France, turned them down – much to Vancouver's chagrin. Nevertheless the Union Jack, with the Christian crosses of Saint George and Saint Andrew, continues to adorn the state flag of Hawaii – a sign of what might have been and a reminder of the early links that they had with the Royal Navy in the Pacific and its great commanders, Cook and Vancouver.

Had the Sandwich Islands become a British colony, as so many other groups of Pacific islands would, then their history during the nineteenth century and the first few decades of the twentieth would probably have been far happier as the British were better colonisers than the Americans, whose clumsiness and inexperience in places like the Philippines led to much warfare and bloodshed.

The Hawaiians, like those of Britain's other Pacific colonies, would have been well governed with a light touch by incorrupt and fair-minded administrators while the natural riches and attractions of Hawaii would have ensured a high level of prosperity in addition to the good order and personal freedom that are the hallmarks of British rule.

However, despite these advantages there is little doubt that the Hawaiians were better off under the American flag, as in 1958 the British Conservative government, in order to join the wretched European Common Market, made its treacherous decision to shed virtually all its colonies as quickly as possible and without regard to the welfare and interests of the people, most of whom were handed over to local dictators.

The British were the best colonisers that the world has ever seen but, with the exception of Belgium, the worst decolonisers, leaving a mess behind in virtually every one of their colonies that they had ruled so successfully and humanely for centuries but then left in such haste. Thus the Hawaiians would have been thrown to the wolves by a cold, uncaring and selfish government in London. It

30

was fortunate for Captain Vancouver that he could not foresee all this.

During their sojourn in Hawaii Archibald Menzies, the surgeon-botanist on the *Discovery*, together with another officer, Joseph Baker, a midshipman named McKenzie and a native, climbed to the top of Mauna Loa (13,680 feet), one of the two highest peaks on the island of Hawaii. This is believed to have been the first ever ascent of the mountain since the natives, used to their tropical climate, never went above the snow line.

However, life was not all play during this last Hawaiian winter and Captain Vancouver managed to complete his charting of the islands by surveying the north coast of Maui, the east coast of Oahu to Kahuku Point and then round to Waimea where the steep and powerful waves are to-day the greatest challenge for the world's top surfers. Simultaneously the *Chatham* surveyed the north coast of Kauai and this was the last piece in the jigsaw puzzle of the chart of the Sandwich Islands.

For his last surveying season on the north-west coast of America Vancouver chose to begin at Cook's Inlet, Alaska, the last place that Captain Cook explored before he sailed down the coast of the Alaska Peninsula en route to his tryst with destiny at Kealakekua Bay. From here Vancouver would move down in a south-easterly direction to where the *Discovery* and *Chatham* had finished their survey of the previous year at Cape Decision.

Vancouver's instructions were to take his survey as far north as 60° latitude and this ran through Cook's Inlet which, because of its width, was thought by the Admiralty to be a possible entry to that elusive North-West Passage.

In these high latitudes floating ice was a problem and so was fog, extensive shoals and swift currents. In fog the *Discovery* and *Chatham* kept in touch by firing their guns.

The land was almost uninhabited although there were a few Russian fur posts. During their boat survey of approximately 400 miles of coast in Prince William Sound Whidbey and his men saw no more than a dozen Indians.

One of the last achievements was Whidbey's discovery of the Chatham Strait, which enabled Vancouver to put the huge land mass of Chichagof and Baranof on his charts as islands rather than part of the mainland. Then, as the icing on the cake, Whidbey traced Stephens Passage northwards and found that the expanse of land on its west was also an island, which Vancouver named Admiralty

Island. With the end of the survey approaching no doubt his thoughts were very much on his seniors at the Admiralty and how they would receive his charts and reports. In fact, he named Stephens Passage after Sir Philip Stephens, the Secretary of the Admiralty, to whom his reports were sent.

On the last day of this three year survey – 17th August, 1794 – all of the four boats returned to the *Discovery* and *Chatham* at the same time, the crews wet, tired, hungry but exhilarated at what they had achieved. The cheers of the sailors rang across the bay as they realised that their task, sometimes monotonous but always exacting, was at last completed after three arduous seasons of braving ice, Indians and isolation.

As the expedition's commander Vancouver could be proud of the lack of accidents and the general good health of the men, experiencing as they did extremes of climate from the heat of Hawaii to the ice of Alaska. He had given place names to more than four hundred features on the north-west coast of America and there was hardly anyone of importance in the Admiralty who hadn't had his name given to some peak, point, island, bay or mountain.

More importantly, Vancouver had, by his persistence, method, science and the quality of his charts, put this part of the world on the map. *HMS Discovery* and *HMS Chatham* were the trailblazers that paved the way for British rule on the west coast, thereby giving Canada a trans-continental character that it otherwise would not have had.

It would be neat and facile to describe this survey as Captain Cook's fourth voyage since Vancouver was continuing the survey of the north-west coast of America that Cook had been prevented from completing by his death, and Vancouver was doing it to the same high standards and showing the same consideration towards the natives. However, it would be unfair to Vancouver to describe his work by reference to someone else – even though that man was his hero. If Captain Cook was the Great Navigator, George Vancouver is equally deserving of the title of the Great Surveyor. His work speaks for itself in a field in which he has neither superiors nor equals.

CAPTAIN BLIGH AND THE BOUNTY

Awake, bold Bligh! The foe is at the gate!
Awake! awake! – Alas it is too late!
Fiercely beside thy cot the mutineer
Stands, and proclaims the reign of rage and fear.

The Island, Byron

Another protégé of Captain Cook was William Bligh but unfortunately his reputation is quite different from that of George Vancouver. Cook had appointed him Sailing Master on the *Resolution* for the third voyage and he, like Vancouver, was present on that terrible last day in Kealakekua Bay.

In 1787 Bligh was appointed commander of *HMS Bounty* and was instructed to sail her to Tahiti to acquire breadfruit trees and then take them to the Caribbean.

The *Bounty* was an armed transport vessel (four 4 pounders and two swivel guns) with a ship's company of forty-two (including two gardeners for the breadfruit) and she was stored and victualled for eighteen months. Breadfruit was eaten by the natives in Tahiti as a substitute for bread and the planters and merchants of the West Indies believed that it would be a cheap source of food for the slaves. Bligh was instructed to take half of the breadfruit trees to His Majesty's Garden at Saint Vincent and the rest to Jamaica.

The *Bounty* sailed from Spithead on 23rd December, 1787, but she couldn't get around Cape Horn because of the westerly winds and so she had to cross the Atlantic to Cape Town, then sail through the Indian Ocean and half of the Pacific to get to Tahiti. A very long voyage – especially for the seamen who had to put up with the arrogance, insults and temper of their captain. In an act of personal spite Bligh demoted the Sailing Master, John Fryer, and replaced him with Fletcher Christian.

The ship pulled into Adventure Bay, Tasmania, which Bligh knew from his service with Captain Cook. Of the now extinct natives of Tasmania Bligh wrote, "we heard their voices, like the cackling of geese, and twenty persons came out of the woods. We threw trinkets ashore, tied up in parcels, which they would not open until I made an appearance of leaving them. They then did so and, taking the articles out, put them on their heads...They spoke so quick that it was impossible to catch one single word they uttered." [1]

33

Sailing to the east of New Zealand, they discovered – in Bligh's words – "a cluster of small rocky islands, which I named Bounty Isles." [2] Many years later, on 9th July, 1870, Captain George Palmer of *HMS Rosario* took possession of them for the Crown and to-day they are owned by New Zealand.

They reached Cook's old haunt of Matavai Bay, Tahiti, on 25th October, 1788, after a voyage of 27,086 nautical miles from England that had taken just over ten months – an average of 108 miles a day under sail.

The *Bounty* spent twenty-three weeks in Tahiti where its crew collected 1,015 breadfruit plants. However, the trade was not all one way as they also brought orange and lime trees to Tahiti. Citrus fruit was considered useful for combating scurvy and, with the Royal Navy taking an ever greater interest in the Pacific, it was felt desirable to have a stock of the fruit in the islands. So successful was the experiment that within a few decades Tahiti was exporting large quantities of oranges and lemons to Auckland, New Zealand.

The *Bounty* sailed from these beautiful islands at sunset on 4th April, 1789. Twenty-four days later, when she was near Tonga, a section of the ship's company mutinied against their obstreperous captain.

This rebellion was led by Fletcher Christian, whose relationship with Bligh was every bit as bad as Fryer's had been, and he was supported by another eighteen of the crew of forty-two. In Bligh's words, "He (Fletcher Christian) with several others came into my cabin while I was asleep and, seizing me, holding naked bayonets at my breast, tied my hands behind my back and threatened instant destruction if I uttered a word.....I was now dragged on deck in my shirt and closely guarded." [3]

Fletcher Christian ordered the boatswain to hoist out the longboat. Then the boatswain and the other seamen, who were to be put into the boat, were allowed to collect some twine, canvas, sails, a 28 gallon cask of water, 150 pounds of bread and a small quantity of rum and wine – so at least the sailors would still get their tot (or at least a part of it). They were also allowed to take a quadrant and a compass but no maps or any of Bligh's surveys and drawings. And no weaponry apart from four cutlasses.

The mutineers, described by Bligh as a "tribe of armed ruffians", [4] put in the boat all those whom they wanted to get rid of, viz. those who were not part of the mutiny. These included all the midshipmen as well as the carpenter, who was allowed to take his tool kit.

When Bligh was making a last remonstrance with the mutineers he was told, "Come, Captain Bligh, your officers and men are now in the boat and you must go with them; if you attempt to make the least resistance, you will instantly be put to death." [5] Bligh got into the boat and, in his own words, "we were at length cast adrift in the open ocean." [6] Indeed they were – all nineteen of them in a boat that was only twenty-three feet long from stem to stern.

Although unskilled in the art of managing men Bligh was nevertheless an exceptionally talented navigator and he took this small, open boat, so heavily laden that its gunwales were only a few inches above the water, the rest of the way across the Pacific without charts to Dutch Timor, which was the closest European settlement of which he was aware since, when he left England, the First Fleet had not yet arrived in Sydney.

There was little wind so they rowed the boat to the low lying island of Tofua in the Tonga group in the hope of getting provisions but they were attacked by natives and one of them, John Norton, the quartermaster, was killed. With the longboat thus lightened they set off again into the vast and limitless ocean. Without the guns of a warship there was little security for British sailors in the South Pacific of the pre-European era and Bligh decided that there would be no more pulling into islands for provisions as it was just too dangerous. Instead he put everyone on survival rations of an ounce of bread a day and a quarter of a pint of water. These were supplemented occasionally by a sliver of pork and a teaspoonful of rum.

On one occasion, in Bligh's words, "some noddies came so near to us that one was caught by the hand. It was about the size of a small pigeon. I divided it, with its entrails, into fifteen portions." [7]

In stormy weather, of which there was a lot, the waves would wash over the stern and the men would bail it out with whatever strength they had. Rain meant that they could replenish the cask and in one squall they caught twenty gallons for drinking purposes. "Our limbs were dreadfully cramped, and the nights were so cold, and we so constantly wet," wrote the deposed captain. [8] However, on one day they managed to advance 102 miles.

Sailing through the islands of the New Hebrides they saw the smoke of the natives' fires but they dared not land.

They managed to find their way through the Great Barrier Reef at a place that is to-day called the Bligh Entrance. They caught three booby birds, the presence of which always indicates the vicinity of land, and "the stomachs of two of them contained several flying fish and small cuttle fish, which were all saved for dinner." [9] They added them to their small ration of bread and dipped the resulting savoury into the sea to salt it.

By now the men were suffering from giddiness, weak joints and acute constipation and so they landed on a few islands, mostly uninhabited, near Torres Strait. Bligh named one of them Restoration Island since they were there on the anniversary of the Restoration of Charles II (25th May). So, with George Vancouver's naming of Restoration Point in Puget Sound, the Pacific was to have two features to honour the Restoration, which was probably the happiest day in our history. Bligh and his men reached another island on the Sabbath and so that was named Sunday Island.

After escaping into their boat from an attack by spear wielding aborigines, they landed on Booby Island and then headed through the tropical waters of the Arafura Sea and the Timor Sea to Timor. They knew that there was a Dutch settlement on the island but didn't know where it was and so they landed at a native village and took a guide on board to direct them. They finally landed at the Dutch headquarters of Kupang after a forty-seven day voyage in the tropical heat over 3,618 nautical miles. This was a feat of seamanship for which Bligh deserved – and received – the highest praise.

Fletcher Christian and his mutineers also had their problems. They initially sailed the *Bounty* to a nearby island where they were attacked by cannibals. They then returned to Tahiti where two of them suffered violent deaths. Then *HMS Pandora*, which had been despatched from England to search for both the *Bounty* and the mutineers, arrived in Tahiti and fourteen of the mutineers were arrested and put in a wooden cell on the quarterdeck. This five foot high cage measured only eighteen feet by eleven feet – a very uncomfortable journey in the extreme heat and a dangerous one too. For four months they were manacled hand and foot to an iron bar that ran along the inside of the cage. On 29th August, 1791, as the *Pandora* was going through the Great Barrier Reef near Torres Strait she hit a reef and sank in fifteen fathoms of water. Thirty-one of her ship's company and four of the mutineers went down with the ship to their watery grave.

All the mutineers would have perished but for the presence of mind and humanity of a boatswain's mate, William Moulter, who unlocked their cage at the last minute, thereby enabling most of them to jump off the sinking vessel. Ninety-nine of them managed to reach a sandbank four miles away and there they remained for four days before setting off for Timor in the ship's boats – just as Bligh did.

At their court-martial on board *HMS Duke* in Portsmouth harbour four of the mutineers were acquitted, two were found guilty but escaped serious punishment, another was pardoned and three (John Millward, Thomas Birkett and Thomas Ellison) were found guilty and hanged aboard *HMS Brunswick* on 29th October, 1792. One of those found guilty but pardoned was Peter Heywood, who later became a naval officer and a distinguished surveyor of the South American coast. At one stage he was even offered the position of Hydrographer of the Royal Navy but he declined.

Meanwhile the mutineers who remained in the Pacific (Fletcher Christian and eight others) plus eighteen Tahitians (mainly to provide them with womenfolk) set off from Tahiti in the *Bounty* to search for a home where they could live undisturbed by such annoyances as being arrested by a visiting British warship.

On 15th June, 1790, they found Pitcairn Island which, having been fortuitously misplaced on Royal Navy charts, seemed to be ideal – good soil, warm climate, plenty of water and, most important of all, very remote and inaccessible.

The island had been named by Captain Philip Carteret, R.N., who sailed around the world in 1766-9 on *HMS Swallow*. After entering the Pacific through the Straits of Magellan he offered a bottle of brandy to the first of his men to sight land. The lucky winner was fifteen year old Midshipman Robert Pitcairn, whose sharp eye detected the small, high island that Carteret named after him.

The mutineers unloaded their livestock and other provisions and then burned the *Bounty* so as to remove the evidence of their crime and prevent anyone escaping on it. Pitcairn might have been paradise but it was also their prison. In fact, it was worse as by 1800 all the mutineers had died except one, "Alexander Smith" whose later name was John Adams, and most of them had died from bloody causes.

Adams was the only man left and he shared the island with nine Tahitian women and dozens of children. However, he was a good man and instructed them in the Bible with the result that ever since the Pitcairners have been known for their adherence to Christian values (Christian as in Christ and not Fletcher!). In 1825 John Adams was given an amnesty for his part in the mutiny, which marked the closing of the page on this unfortunate affair.

In 1831 the people of Pitcairn were moved by the British government to Tahiti (before it became a French colony) as it was feared that the small island of Pitcairn, only two square miles in area, would not be able to provide enough food for the increasing population.

The result of this early example of "social engineering" was that they were afflicted by sickness in their new home and twelve of them died. Not surprisingly, the survivors chartered a vessel to take them back to Pitcairn, which in 1838 became part of the British Empire when the Union Jack was raised there by Captain Elliot and the men of *HMS Fly*.

This was a fitting climax to the drama as the mutiny had been against Bligh and not against the Crown – just as Mr. Ian Smith's Rhodesian "rebellion" in 1965 was against the British government, which was lying to the Rhodesians and leading them to their destruction, and not against the Queen, to whom the Rhodesians remained loyal in spite of the sanctions and other shenanigans of Whitehall.

Nevertheless, there was a problem of so many people living on such a small island and so in 1856 a section of them moved to Norfolk Island, east of Australia, when it ceased to serve as a penal settlement. If they were to move, they wanted an empty island where they could continue to keep the world at bay. They did not want a repeat of the Tahiti experience.

Meanwhile back in England William Bligh was busy proving the old adage that "nothing succeeds like failure". Overlooking his appalling record of man management, which had led to the loss of one of His Majesty's ships, the authorities continued to give him command of vessels. They compounded their folly in 1805 when they appointed him Governor of New South Wales – largely on the basis of his reputation as a "firm disciplinarian", which they thought would be useful in a convict colony.

It didn't take him long to antagonise almost all sections of society, including some very influential settlers, officials and soldiers. These people all had experience of the difficult task of running a colony that was populated mainly by potentially dangerous convicts, and Bligh's manner was so overbearing and offensive that on 26th January, 1808, the King's soldiers in the form of the New South Wales Corps, under Major George Johnston R.M., marched on Government House and arrested the Governor – something that has never happened before or since in the history of the British Empire. This was known as the "Rum Mutiny". The arrest of Bligh was celebrated by all night partying in Sydney.

A rebel government was installed in Sydney and Bligh was put on a ship for Hobart where he tried to gather support to take back control of his former fiefdom but nobody was prepared to help him and he was effectively a prisoner on board *HMS Porpoise* for two years.

When he returned to England he busied himself with the court-martial of his arrestor, Major Johnston, but in the event Johnston was merely dismissed from the Royal Marines and was allowed to return as a free man to New South Wales where he had a farm at Annandale, to the south-west of the small settlement of Sydney and to-day one of the inner suburbs of the big city of Sydney.

By now the Admiralty had at last got the message and Bligh was never given another important command. These were the two most significant mutinies in the British Empire in the Pacific in the period from Captain Cook to the present day and that they were both mounted against the same man speaks volumes about his lack of skill in handling men, which in the Navy is every bit as important as handling a ship, which latter Bligh could do very well.

By the standards of the time Captain Bligh was not unduly cruel with the lash but he was certainly one of the nastiest men ever to command a naval vessel. His arrogance and stupidity prevented him from understanding that insults could be just as wounding as lashes. Unlike Captain Vancouver, he seems to have learned nothing from his time with that most humane and efficient commander, Captain Cook.

****

In view of the genesis of the Pitcairn community, viz. a mutiny against lawful naval authority and the burning of one of His Majesty's ships, it is remarkable to record that over the years the Navy was to take a paternal and sympathetic interest in Pitcairn and its people. A report in the *Panama Star* of 1853 stated, "The island has been constantly visited by English and other men-of-war and by whalers but happily no Colonial Office has interfered to interrupt the harmony which prevails in this community." [10] Between 1814 and 1892 Royal Navy vessels are known to have visited Pitcairn on forty-three occasions; [11] this was a very large number for such a small and remote island.

When *HMS Seringapatam* (Captain Hon. William Waldegrave) arrived off Pitcairn on 15th March, 1830, she brought a present of clothing and agricultural tools for the islanders. An even more welcome visitor was *HMS Curacoa* in 1841; she arrived at the height of an influenza epidemic and her surgeon spent three days on the island, treating the sick.

When *HMS Virago* arrived there in 1853, the first of three of Her Majesty's vessels to visit the island that year, it was the first time that the islanders had seen a steamship and so the captain took them on a trip around the island.

When the flagship of the Australia station, *HMS Portland*, visited the island in 1852 it brought a much needed bull and some cow calves. The admiral on board, Fairfax Moresby, "took so much interest in the welfare of the islanders that he undertook, at his own expense, to send the pastor, Mr. Nobbs, to receive ordination from the Bishop of London." [12] To fill the gap while he was away Admiral Moresby left the *Portland's* chaplain on the island. He stayed until the following year when Nobbs – now the Rev. Nobbs – arrived back on the *Portland* with his daughter.

Mr. Nobbs had arrived on the island independently in 1828 and married Sarah Christian, the grand-daughter of Fletcher. The most common opinion held by those who visited the island was the high moral tone of the settlement. One of these, Walter Brodie, who was stranded there from his ship in 1850, wrote, "there never was...another community who can boast of so high a tone of morality or more firmly rooted religious feelings" [13] while Lieutenant Hon. Fred Walpole of *HMS Collingwood* wrote in the 1840s, "nor has her gracious Majesty any more devotedly loyal subjects....The people spoke of the kindness shown to them by the (naval) vessels that had visited them." [14]

When *HMS Icarus* visited Pitcairn in 1901, its captain, Commander Knowling, in his report to the Colonial Office, wrote that, "an almost utopian state of existence prevails amongst its inhabitants...No one smokes or drinks intoxicants, and each adult man works from 5 a.m. to 2 p.m. for the public good, directed by the local parliament. Two p.m. is the dinner hour and the remainder of the day the people employ themselves about their own businesses. The women of the family do all the housework." [15]

After the Pitcairners moved to Norfolk Island the Navy often stopped there and relations between the sailors and the descendants of the mutineers were never anything short of excellent. At this distance in time it is hard to compile "league tables" but, from the comments of both officers and men, it would appear that there was no place where they looked forward to shore leave more than Norfolk. This was not for reasons of wine, women and song as of that there was comparatively little but the warm-heartedness, hospitality and sheer decency of the people meant more than that. The continuing warm and happy relations between the Navy and these people, who were descended from those who mutinied and burned a naval vessel, would have to be the final insult to the memory of Captain Bligh.

CAPTAIN PHILLIP AND THE FIRST FLEET TO AUSTRALIA

True patriots all, for be it understood,
We left our country for our country's good.

- A Convict Couplet

From the earliest days of American settlement convicts were sent from Britain to work on the Virginian plantations and elsewhere but this ceased after the War of Independence when the architects of American "freedom" sanctimoniously declared that they would no longer dirty their hands by being party to the transport of convicts. After all, black slaves were cheaper.

This coincided with the explosion of the prison population in Britain which soon outgrew the gaols and so the prisoners were incarcerated on hulks in the rivers. In such insalubrious conditions typhoid broke out periodically and the government was under pressure from those who lived near the hulks to get rid of them.

As the need to remove criminals "beyond the seas" became more urgent the government looked round for a new dumping ground and eventually selected Botany Bay on the east coast of Australia, which had been visited by Captain Cook not all that long ago and was spoken highly of by Joseph Banks, the botanist on the *Endeavour* who had been impressed by its profusion of plants.

However, sending convicts to such a place would be very different from sending them to America where, as soon as they landed, they had been indentured to free settlers for work on their plantations and so they were no longer a charge on the British government.

Since there were no free settlers in Australia it would be nothing more than a gaol with the entire cost of convicts' food and upkeep being a continuing drain on the British exchequer. Nevertheless the plan moved to action and Captain Arthur Phillip R.N. was chosen to lead this historic First Fleet to Australia.

Phillip had joined the Navy at the age of fifteen and served during the Seven Years War. When it ended he was put on half-pay so he and his wife went farming in Hampshire. He saw further naval service between 1779 and 1784 and was then put back on half-pay.

His tryst with destiny came in October, 1786, when he was appointed captain of *HMS Sirius* and governor-designate of the new penal colony of New South Wales, his commission being described at the time as "a more unlimited one than was ever before granted to any Governor under the British Crown". The choice was made by the Home Secretary, Lord Sydney, since the entire transportation of convicts, which would continue over several decades, was under the auspices of the Home Office. Lord Sydney was rewarded for his efforts by having the main town in the new colony named after him.

It was never easy to start a new colony but this one was to be far more distant than any other while the founding bloodstock was about as bad as one could get. Phillip was obviously a naval officer who liked a challenge or maybe he was just happy to do anything to get back in command of a ship.

The *Sirius* was a vessel of twenty-four guns, and Captain Phillip had as his second-in-command Captain John Hunter, who would later succeed Phillip as Governor of New South Wales. The lieutenants were William Bradley, Philip Gidley King and G.W. Maxwell. King would become the third Governor of New South Wales while Bradley was to survey Sydney harbour, give his name to one of its features (Bradley's Head), become a rear-admiral and then, in an amazing twist of fortune, was himself sentenced to transportation for a postal fraud which he committed while mentally unstable. However, he did not return to Sydney in chains as the sentence was reduced to exile in France. A much more appropriate sentence for a rear-admiral.

The "Botany Bay fleet", consisting of *HMS Sirius* (flagship), its tender *HMS Supply*, the convict transports (converted merchantmen) *Alexander*, *Charlotte*, *Friendship*, *Lady Penrhyn*, *Prince of Wales* and *Scarborough*, and the storeships *Golden Grove*, *Fishburn* and *Borrowdale*, sailed from the Mother Bank, Isle of Wight, on the morning of Sunday, 13th May, 1787, with a total of 736 convicts (548 males and 188 females). Most of them were petty thieves and forgers as for more serious offences the penalty was death by hanging.

One poor old lady, Dorothy Handland, was eighty-two at the time of sailing; she had been sentenced to seven years for perjury. The journey was too much for her and she hanged herself from a gum tree at Sydney Cove shortly after arrival, thereby earning the further "distinction" of being the first person to commit suicide in Australia.

There was also a guard of 212 marines and some of their wives and children, as well as other officers, making a total of around 1,030 people. The marines were distributed among the convict vessels, with a heavier concentration on those that contained a lot of male prisoners. The only trouble occurred on the *Scarborough* where there was a plot by some of the men to rise up and take over the ship but it was thwarted in time and the ringleaders were rounded up and distributed among the other vessels.

It took more than eight months for the Fleet to reach Australia. They stopped at Santa Cruz, on the Canary island of Tenerife, because Phillip wanted more water and fresh vegetables. The only vegetables that were available there were figs and mulberries "but these were plentiful and excellent". [1]

From there this history making fleet sailed down to Rio de Janeiro, taking advantage of the stronger winds that blow in the western Atlantic. Here the port officials tried to levy the standard charge of £3-12-0 per ship but Phillip retorted that they were loaded with "the King's stores" and so the Portuguese waived the fee. At Rio the provisions were cheap and so they took on stocks of rice, meat and more vegetables.

They had an easy passage to Cape Town where they stayed a month. This was as far as European settlement had so far reached and therefore, before venturing into the unknown, they took on board a veritable farmyard consisting of two bulls, three cows, three horses, forty-four sheep, thirty-two pigs and a flock of hens. Some of the officers bought their own animals in Cape Town, which was a wise precaution since eighteenth century Australia was a barren land and it was not long before food became scarce.

The ships were crowded, verminous and filthy. The holds in which the prisoners were confined had no ports for reasons of security; it was pitch dark down there as they were not allowed lanterns or candles for fear of starting a fire. Fresh air was at a premium and it was a great credit to Captain Phillip and his organisation that the death rate was kept to about 3% which, for any passenger vessel in the eighteenth century, was exceptionally low.

At sea the convicts were brought up in batches under guard to exercise on the deck. Phillip tried to keep them as fit and well fed as conditions allowed since their labour would be needed upon landing and weak people are not good workers.

Applying the same high standards of care for those on board as Captain Cook did, Phillip allowed each convict a daily allowance of three quarters of a pound of bread and the same quantity of beef, while each marine received a pound of each of the same products plus a pint of wine a day.

The ships reached their destination between 18th and 20th January, 1788, after the longest sea voyage in history with so many people on board – "a proof of the flourishing state of navigation in the present age" according to Phillip.[2] This was no mean achievement but the hard part was yet to come for this versatile officer.

As soon as they landed they met some aborigines, who no doubt had been following with their sharp eyes the large and very visible sails of Phillip's ship, *HMS Supply*, as she entered the bay. Because he believed that the *Supply* was a faster vessel than *HMS Sirius* Captain Phillip had boarded her at sea a few miles out of Cape Town but in the event she reached Botany Bay only a few hours ahead of the others.

The aborigines were, in Phillip's words, "perfectly devoid of clothing".[3] They were probably not expecting visitors – especially ones so heavily clad as British naval officers. Despite their aversion to clothes they did, however, seem "fond of ornaments, putting the beads and red baize that were given them on their heads or necks and appearing pleased to wear them".[4]

It did not take Captain Phillip long to realise that Botany Bay did not live up to its praises by Captain Cook and Joseph Banks. However, it should be remembered that Cook required only shelter and refreshment for a relatively small vessel whereas Phillip had to provide a permanent home for more than a thousand people.

Of Botany Bay Phillip wrote, "Though extensive, it did not afford a shelter from the easterly winds and that in consequence of its shallowness ships even of a moderate draught would always be obliged to anchor with the entrance of the bay open, where they must be exposed to a heavy sea that rolls in whenever it blows hard from the eastward....No place was discovered in the whole circuit of Botany Bay which seemed at all calculated for the reception of so large a settlement."[5] There was a dearth of fresh water and the soil around Point Sutherland was damp and apparently unhealthy.

On 22nd January – six days after landing - Captain Phillip sailed a short distance up the coast and into the harbour that Captain Cook had named Port Jackson but which he did not enter. Captain Phillip did enter it and so became the first white man to discover what is probably the finest harbour in the world, with its thirty-six coves and bays that stretch several miles inland.

On first laying eyes on this jewel Captain (now Governor) Phillip described it as "the most valuable acquisition Great Britain ever made". He reported to Lord Sydney that it was "the finest harbour in the world in which a thousand sail of the line may ride with the most perfect security". [6]

Phillip and his officers examined several of the coves and chose one "which had the finest spring of water, and in which ships can anchor so close to the shore that at a very small expense quays may be constructed where the largest vessels may unload. This cove is about half a mile in length and a quarter of a mile across at the entrance." [7] Thus began the city of Sydney.

On 26th January, 1788, the fleet left Botany Bay and sailed up to the newly discovered harbour – a day that has ever since been celebrated as Australia Day since it marks the beginning of the story of European Australia.

Describing this historic event, Captain Collins, the Judge-Advocate of the new colony, wrote, "In the evening of this day the whole of the party that came round in the *Supply* were assembled at the point, where they had first landed in the morning, and on which a flag-staff had been purposely erected and a Union Jack displayed, when the marines fired several volleys...the Governor and the officers who accompanied him drank the health of His Majesty and the Royal Family and success to the new colony. The day, which had been uncommonly fine, concluded with the safe arrival of the *Sirius* and the convoy from Botany Bay, thus terminating the voyage with the same good fortune that had from its commencement been so conspicuously their friend and companion." [8]

The male convicts were unloaded first and were brought ashore from their transports in longboats. "The confusion that ensued will not be wondered at, when it is considered that every man stepped from the boat literally into a wood," wrote Captain Collins. [9] "Parties of people were everywhere heard and seen variously employed – some in clearing ground for the different encampments, others in pitching tents or bringing up such stores as were more immediately wanted, and the spot which had so lately been the abode of silence and tranquillity was now changed to that of noise, clamour and confusion." [10]

On 6th February it was the turn of the female convicts, many of whom were petty thieves or prostitutes. It was the first time that the men convicts had seen any women since leaving England and not surprisingly a general debauch ensued, with a great

46

thunderstorm adding to the confusion and excitement of the night. The next day Governor Phillip called them all together and gave them a good telling off.

Phillip was faced with building a settlement out of nothing. The trees came right down to the water's edge so that ground had to be cleared first for habitation and gardens. Furthermore not all the convicts were willing or able to work. Many were lazy and others were sick with scurvy and dysentery. Why, Governor Phillip asked them, should the industrious carry the idle – something that has been an issue in Australia ever since.

A portable canvas house, which had been put on board in England, was erected on the east side of Sydney Cove for the Governor, the convicts were in tents on the other side of the Cove while the marines were camped at its head.

Land was cleared at the adjoining cove to farm the livestock that had been brought from the Cape and this was called Farm Cove. Vegetable gardens were established but there was so much stealing from them that it became necessary to utilise an offshore island which the thieving convicts could not reach and this was called Garden Island. It later became a base for the Navy and was eventually linked with the mainland by reclamation.

By its nature the regime at Sydney was a harsh one; convicts were flogged and so were errant marines, the latter usually receiving more lashes for the same offence than the former. When food ran short Phillip put everyone on short rations, convicts receiving the same amounts as the highest officials.

Governor Phillip's instructions were to show friendship to the local aborigines as it was thought that a settlement of convicts would pose enough problems without having native troubles as well. Phillip practised what he preached and, should a convict try to escape, the aborigines would often catch him and hand him back in return for a reward. Convicts and marines were punished if they harmed the local Iora people but things did not always go well. On one occasion Governor Phillip had a spear put through his shoulder at Manly Cove; nevertheless he declared that the natives there had a "confident and manly bearing" [11] and for this reason he gave Manly Cove its name. When he returned to England he took two aborigines with him but one died during the freezing English winter.

When it became clear that the colony was not supporting itself Phillip began the practice of granting free land to convicts whose time was up and who wanted to stay in Australia rather than undergo the long voyage back to Britain. This was greatly expanded by one of his successors, Governor Lachlan Macquarie and was a big factor in getting Australia going. But the idea came from Phillip.

The first four governors of New South Wales were naval captains, and the transport of convicts remained a task for the Navy for many years. For example, in 1836 no fewer than twenty-one ships of the Royal Navy were hired by the British government to take convicts to Australia, the Home Office paying all the costs for the voyage out while the Admiralty paid for the return voyage.

The transport of these wretched and unfortunate people was distasteful to the naval mind since young men join the Navy to fight the nation's enemies and not to lock up their fellow citizens. Too often the Government have regarded the Navy as an extension of their policing operations and the Admiralty has not always been strong enough to resist it.

There is a world of difference between a sailor's mentality and that of a cop or a prison guard and it is foolish to confuse their very different roles – as is still happening with the Royal Navy being forced to waste its scarce resources on chasing small boats in the Caribbean that might be carrying marijuana or cocaine, each of which is less harmful than alcohol.

After returning to England from his Australian mission Captain Phillip retired to Bath where he died in 1814. He is buried in Saint Nicholas' church in the nearby village of Bathampton. Each year on the Friday closest to the anniversary of his birth (11th October) a ceremony is held at his tomb where a wreath is laid by the Australian High Commissioner to Britain. In the Antipodes his name is remembered in Melbourne's Port Phillip Bay as well as two Phillip Islands, one in Victoria and the other off Norfolk Island. In Sydney his statue stands in the Royal Botanic Gardens overlooking the harbour that he chose with such wisdom and foresight as the site for the first settlement. Saint Phillip's, the oldest church in Sydney, is also named after him.

In Bath Abbey there is a memorial plaque to Governor Phillip which reads, "To his indomitable courage, faith, inspiration and wisdom was due the success of the first settlement in Australia at Sydney, 26th January, 1788". A fitting epitaph for the naval captain who is rightly regarded as the Father of Australia.

SURVEYING AND CHARTING

After the defeat of France in the Napoleonic Wars the Admiralty decommissioned a large number of its fighting ships; in 1814 there were 713 naval vessels in commission and approximately 140,000 sailors whereas six years later the Navy had diminished to 134 ships and 23,000 men.

The diminution in fighting ships was accompanied by a rise in the number of survey ships to trace and chart all the new lands that were being opened up, mostly in the Pacific Ocean. This process had been going on since Captain Cook's time but it was in the years after Waterloo that it became the Navy's chief task in the Pacific.

Since Britain had the largest empire, the biggest share of world trade and the largest number of merchant ships, it had a greater need than other powers for accurate charts of the sea lanes, harbours and rivers.

Hydrography was a never-ending process as, besides charting new islands and coast lines, older surveys had to be updated with new and better equipment and in the light of changing conditions, such as moving shoals and channels at the entrance of harbours and even changes caused by volcanic or seismic activity. The quality of the charts advanced simultaneously with improvements in the arts of navigation.

The Royal Navy carried out the surveying and mapping of the world's greatest ocean virtually single-handedly and for this reason no account of Britain's Navy in the Pacific would be complete without a due account of its hydrographic activities.

We shall start with the eastern and northern coasts of Australia, the two sides of the southern continent that are part of the Pacific littoral.

Australia

Captain Flinders and HMS Investigator

Shortly after the founding of Sydney in 1788 Captain John Hunter R.N., with the help of Lieutenant William Bradley and James Keltie, the master of *HMS Sirius*, the ship on which Captain Phillip had sailed, made the first ever survey of Sydney harbour, with Bradley drawing the original chart. This was more in the form of a "sketch" than the more informative charts of later times. Bradley also made a chart of Norfolk Island.

The first systematic survey of Australia after Captain Cook was carried out by Captain Matthew Flinders, R.N., a Lincolnshire lad who, in his own words, "was induced to go to sea against the wishes of my friends by reading Robinson Crusoe". The main reason why the Admiralty was beginning to take an interest in Australia was the fear that the French might try to establish themselves on some uncharted and unsettled part of this newly found continent.

Matthew Flinders joined the Royal Navy in 1789 at the age of fifteen and in 1792 he sailed in the waters of Torres Strait on *HMS Providence* where he assisted his commander, the notorious Captain Bligh, with the map work. In 1795 Flinders made another voyage to Australia on *HMS Reliance*. He was only a midshipman but he and the ship's surgeon, George Bass (also from Lincolnshire), did some survey work in an open boat to the south of Sydney.

In 1798 Flinders, by then a lieutenant and in command of the sloop *HMS Norfolk*, made a voyage in Australian waters that established for the first time that a wide strait existed between the bottom of the Australian continent and the big island which was then known as Van Diemen's Land but is now called Tasmania. He named this stretch of water Bass Strait after his friend and surveying colleague from the earlier voyage. The largest island in the Strait is called Flinders Island. The *Norfolk* also surveyed up Australia's eastern coast as far as Hervey Bay in Queensland, which, like the Hervey group of islands in the South Pacific, was named after Augustus John Hervey, Earl of Bristol, who was a Lord of the Admiralty from 1771 to 1775. While on the subject of names it should be pointed out that the reason for the change of name from Van Diemen's Land to Tasmania was that the former had too many convict connotations and so the settlers opted for a new name in order to improve their island's image – just as the convict name of Botany Bay also fell into disuse. In the nineteenth century the Australian colonists could be very touchy about their convict origins whereas to-day many of them pester genealogists in order to find a convict ancestor.

After returning to England in 1800 Flinders was given command of the 334 ton sloop, *HMS Investigator*, with instructions to explore and survey the entire Australian coast line – something that Captain Cook had never done. As with Cook's voyage on the

50

Endeavour, the *Investigator* was also to collect specimens of plants and for this purpose she had on board a naturalist, twenty-seven year old Robert Brown, and two botanical artists to collect and record what was discovered.

After surveying Australia's southern coast the *Investigator* arrived at Sydney on 9th May, 1802. "The officers and crew were, generally speaking, in better health than on the day we sailed from Spithead, and not in less good spirits," wrote Flinders at the time.[1] This was partly due to "a strict attention to cleanliness and a free circulation of air in the messing and sleeping places". [2]

At Sydney the *Investigator* took on the brig *Lady Nelson* as its tender for the survey work to come. This small, 60 ton vessel was especially adapted for going up rivers and over other shallow areas. She drew only six feet of water and her crew were mostly convicts.

The *Investigator* was given a place at Castle Point, on the east side of Sydney Cove, and the men set up camp on shore where they lived in tents, the sailmakers working on the canvas, the coopers on the casks, and the astronomers on their time-keepers and other instruments from a makeshift observatory. Since the convict colony was not all that safe the Governor assigned a party of marines to guard the *Investigator's* tents and equipment.

Of Sydney Captain Flinders wrote, "The number of inhabitants was increasing rapidly…The seal fishery in Bass Strait was carried on with ardour, many boats were employed in catching and preparing fish along the coast, sloops and schooners were upon the stocks, various detached settlements were in course of establishment and more in project….The commerce carried on from Sydney to Parramatta and the villages at the head of the port, and to those on the rivers falling into Broken and Botany Bays, made the fine harbour of Port Jackson a lively scene of business." [3]

From Sydney Captain Flinders sent the charts that he had already made of southern Australia to the Admiralty together with a statement of the principal astronomical observations hitherto made.

During her survey of southern Australia the *Investigator* lost eight men in an accident at the entrance to the Spencer Gulf and in Sydney she was looking for another fifteen men. She could find only six seamen and so she took on nine convicts to make up the difference. The deal was that, upon their return at the end of the voyage, they would receive conditional emancipations or full pardons depending on their service as recommended by Captain Flinders. In the event of a full pardon they would be free to return to

Britain, which for other transported convicts would have meant the death penalty upon detection. Not surprisingly, there were many applications from sea minded convicts for these positions. Several of the chosen nine had been seamen and all were healthy. In Flinders' words, "I considered them a great acquisition to our strength." [4]

At the end of the journey seven of them received their emancipation. One had died during the voyage and the other had behaved so badly that Flinders could not give him a recommendation. Of the seven who were emancipated, Flinders took four of them on his next surveying voyage but, in his words, "I am sorry to add that the subsequent behaviour of two was different to what it had been when their liberty was at stake and that a third was condemned to the hulks not very long after he reached England." [5]

There was also a party of marines on the *Investigator* – ostensibly to protect the tents and other equipment when the men went ashore but no doubt also to protect the ship from any untoward behaviour by the convicts; in distant waters, with no settlement or other ship within hundreds of miles, nine convicts might very well have been able to take over the vessel – as happened with Captain Bligh.

Captain Flinders also took with him a couple of aborigines to act as interpreters – Bongaree and Nanbaree. Bongaree, the chief of the Broken Bay tribe near Sydney, had extremely sharp eyes and from the *Investigator* far off shore he was able to tell whether there were any aborigines lurking in the long grass or trees.

After twelve weeks at Sydney *HMS Investigator* and her tender left on 22nd July, 1802, for Torres Strait at the top of Australia. As Flinders made his way up the east coast he was checking – and amending where necessary – earlier observations and positions made by Captain Cook. "From Port Jackson (Sydney) to Sandy Cape, Captain Cook's positions had been found to differ from mine not more than from 10' east to 7' west, which must be considered a great degree of accuracy considering the expeditious manner in which he sailed along the coast and that there were no time-keepers on board the *Endeavour*, but from Sandy Cape northward, where the direction of the coast has a good deal of westing in it, greater differences began to show themselves," wrote Flinders. [6]

The aborigines seemed to be quite numerous. "Our course at night was directed by the fires on the shore," wrote Flinders.[7] To facilitate communication with the natives they would send Bongaree ashore but, the further north they went, the more difficult it was for him to make himself understood since the dialects of the aborigines were many and varied.

On board the *Investigator* Bongaree and Nanbaree wore European clothes but, when they went ashore to deal with the natives at places like Sandy Cape in Queensland, they stripped off their clothes and went naked like their fellow aborigines in order to create empathy and understanding as an inducement to friendly relations. [8] "It is scarcely necessary to say," wrote Flinders, "that these people are almost black and go entirely naked since none of any other colour or regularly wearing clothes have been seen in any part of Terra Australis." [9] In similar vein Captain Cook, while sailing in the same waters, had written of an aboriginal woman standing on the shore, ".... We could see very clearly with our glasses that the woman was as naked as ever she was born, even those parts which I always before now thought nature would have taught a woman to conceal were uncovered." [10]

Among the places that Flinders named as he sailed up the coast was Port Curtis, a harbour which he examined and named after Vice-Admiral Sir Roger Curtis. He proclaimed it "the only harbour that is of use to shipping north of Byron Bay".

Inside the Great Barrier Reef the *Lady Nelson* was damaged and so she returned to Sydney by means of a passage through the Reef to the open sea. The tides run with great violence through these narrow passages with their coral bottoms and she was lucky to make it.

The *Investigator* reached the waters at the top of Australia and lay off Murray Island where the natives' dialect was so different from that of the Sydney area, whence Bongaree and Nanbaree hailed, that they could not make themselves understood. But language difficulties never got in the way of trade.

After passing through Torres Strait Flinders made his way around the shore of the Gulf of Carpinteria in the sticky, tropical heat. He gave to the large island at the bottom of the Gulf the name of Mornington Island after the Duke of Wellington's older brother, the Marquess of Wellesley, who was currently Governor-General of India and one of whose titles was Earl of Mornington. The group of islands of which Mornington forms a part was named the Wellesley Islands after the same man.

Flinders also named the Sir Edward Pellew group of islands after a distinguished naval commander, and he ascertained that the land known as Cape Van Diemen was actually an island thirty-five miles long.

The two original charts that Flinders made of the Gulf of Carpentaria in 1802 continued to be issued by the Admiralty until 1929 when they were superseded by a more up-to-date chart, but even that was based on Flinders' old survey.

One of the more interesting findings of this voyage to the north coast of Australia was near Cape Wilberforce when the *Investigator's* men came across a fleet of *praus*, in which were "Malays" from the Indonesian island of Macassar. Altogether there were about sixty of these boats, divided into six groups, each with a commander, the whole fleet being under the direction of the Raja of Boni. They sailed to Australia each year to collect trepang (sea cucumber), a Chinese delicacy and aphrodisiac which they took back and sold to Chinese traders; it was, in fact, the Dutch East Indies' largest export to China.

The six commanders came on board the *Investigator* but, as Moslems, they were horrified to see hogs in the ship's launch. Nevertheless they drank port wine and even asked for a bottle to take away with them.

They all wore the short, curved dagger, known as a *kris*, by their side. Fortunately the cook on board the *Investigator* was a Malay and so was able to translate. Because of their daggers, not to mention the muskets in their *praus*, Captain Flinders kept all his men under arms and half the crew were at quarters all night to guard against any attempted attack. These were wise precautions since the ship's company of the *Investigator* was outnumbered, each *prau* containing about twenty-five men.

The fleet had left Macassar in the Dutch East Indies two months earlier during the westerly monsoon and had made its way to Australia by going from island to island until they reached the north-eastern tip of Timor whence they steered in a south-easterly direction, which carried them to the coast of northern Australia.

In Australia the fleet divided into sections so that they could spread out and dive for the precious sea cucumber. They usually dived in six to eight fathoms of water and a good dive could bring up eight to ten cucumber at a time. A thousand of them made a picol and a hundred picols was a cargo for a *prau* to take back to Macassar to sell to the Chinese traders, who exported it to Canton.

Their navigation aid was a single pocket compass of Dutch manufacture which was carried only by the raja, thus giving him full control over the whole fleet. They carried their water supply on the *praus* inside the joints of bamboo, which they could easily refill in the monsoon. Their food consisted of rice, coconuts and dried fish.

They had been coming to Australia for many seasons and, since the *Investigator* was the first ship they had ever encountered, the leader of the fleet begged Captain Flinders for an English flag, which was given to him to fly at the head of his *prau*.

Sixteen years later Captain Phillip King, a successor surveyor to Flinders, came across another group of Malays who were there for the same purpose. On this occasion they sailed out to his vessel, *HMS Mermaid*, in canoes that were rowed by a man and five boys. Communication was through sign language and a smattering of Malay on King's part, and the "Malays" made it plain that they disliked the aborigines, whom they called "Maregas". They alleged that the Australian natives were both treacherous and hostile and the two sides were always quarrelling. In the words of Captain Keppel, who had a lot to do with both races during his service on the East Indies station, "The Malay who, in addition to his natural haughtiness, assumes the importance to which he imagines his religion (the Mahommedan) entitles him, looks down on the native of Australia as little better than a wild hog, and would thrust his *kris* into him with less ceremony, inasmuch as he could not touch the unclean beast without being defiled. The native, however, true to his own creed, has life for life. The Malay, being aware of this, endeavours to smother his hatred until just about to depart; but the native neither forgets nor forgives. It is immaterial to him who his victim is, so that it often happens on the arrival of a *prau*…that the native has a score to wipe off." [11]

It was around this time that some of the *Investigator's* timbers were found to be rotting and so Captain Flinders had to terminate the survey and return to Sydney, which he did by way of the west coast of Australia, thereby becoming the first man to circumnavigate the southern continent

Another historical service that he performed was to promote the name "Australia" in his charts and communications rather than "New Holland", the name by which it had hitherto been known. He is widely credited for giving Australia its name. He also named the Coral Sea, beyond the Great Barrier Reef, for its profusion of coral atolls.

Captain Phillip Parker King and HMS Mermaid

With the end of the Napoleonic Wars the British government regarded it as a priority "to explore, with as little delay as possible, that part of the coast of New Holland...not surveyed or examined by the late Captain Flinders" and the man they appointed for the task was Captain Phillip Parker King R.N., the son of Captain Philip Gidley King, the former Governor of New South Wales. He was further instructed to find out if there was any great river leading into the Australian interior while the Colonial Office asked him to collect information about Australia's climate, topography, fauna, flora, timber, minerals and natives to help it decide whether it was worthwhile to establish a regular trade between Britain and Australia. A further part of Captain King's extensive brief was to look for fertile areas with natural harbours with a view to settlement, and he was also to discover and give names to bays, rivers, channels, islands, etc.

Captain King arrived in Sydney in September, 1817, and he was provided with an 84 ton cutter by the Governor, Lachlan McQuarrie, which was christened *HMS Mermaid.* She had been built of teak in India only a few months earlier. At 56 feet in length she drew only nine feet of water when fully laden and so was excellent for shoal waters and rivers.

Sydney had grown since Flinders' time but it was still a rough and brutal place where both male and female ex-convicts and aborigines drank and swore, fought and gambled. On market day, when produce was sold in an open field just south of Sydney on the road to Parramatta, the patrons had the added spectacle of convicts being hanged while still in their chains on a small mound overlooking the stalls, for Market Day was also Hanging Day and both were crowd pullers.

The *Mermaid* left Sydney on 22nd December, 1817, with a crew of nineteen, including Flinders' helpful native, Bongaree. Instead of going north Captain King took the *Mermaid* around the southern and western coasts of Australia and began his survey at North West Cape, about half way up the coast of Western Australia.

On the north coast of the continent Captain King discovered and named the Sir George Hope Islands after a late Vice-Admiral, and also the Coburg Peninsula, which was named after Prince Leopold, the future King of the Belgians. The nature of the survey was expressed by Captain King as follows: "Our object was not so much to lay down the extent of the banks and directions of the channels as to find rivers and trace the coast line." [12]

While surveying a big river in the Van Diemen Gulf "we encountered several large alligators and some were noticed sleeping in the mud….and, as they appeared to be very numerous and large, it was not thought safe to stop all night up the river." [13] So that was another thing that they could note down for the Colonial Office.

Captain King named Bathurst Island after the Earl of Bathurst, the current Secretary of State for the Colonies who had taken an interest in the voyage, while Port Hurd was named after the late Captain Thomas Hurd, Hydrographer of the Admiralty. The *Mermaid* then returned to Sydney, putting in at Kupang in Dutch Timor for provisions.

The chart that Captain King drew in 1825 of Arnhem Land and the area around the future city of Darwin was still being used in the Second World War when Darwin found itself in the front line of Australia's defence. It had, however, been emended through eight editions but was still based on King's survey since no other survey had been done.

Captain King's next survey, again with the *Mermaid* and *Lady Nelson*, left Sydney on 8th May, 1819, for the north with Lieutenant Oxley R.N., the Surveyor-General of New South Wales on board. Now that the Hunter Valley was being settled, the old convict colony at Newcastle, where the prisoners mined coal and loaded ships, was no longer as isolated as it had been and it was becoming easier for prisoners to escape. Oxley accompanied the voyage to look for a new site further north and more isolated, that could be used as a penal colony with less chance of escape and Port Macquarie seemed to be the answer.

The two vessels anchored off this lovely spot and a whale boat was sent out to examine the entrance to the harbour. "In pulling in we got among the sand rollers on the north side, on which the sea broke so heavy as at one time to endanger the boat but fortunately we escaped with only the loss of an oar," wrote Captain King. [14] "After contending for some time against the tide, which was ebbing with great strength, we landed on the south side." [15] It was those strong waves that in later times has made Port Macquarie such a mecca for surfers. "We climbed the hill to observe the channel over the bar, the water of which was so clear that the deepest part was easily seen," wrote Captain King. [16] They then sounded the depth both on the bar and in the channel, and made a plan of the harbour.

The next day they rowed four miles up the Hastings River and spent two days examining it. "We landed at Point Elizabeth and walked a mile back through a fine open country, well timbered and richly clothed with luxuriant grass, and apparently much frequented by kangaroos. In the morning, before we embarked, our barica was filled at a water hole." [17]

The banks on both sides of the river were thickly wooded. "There is a great extent of brush land, in which the soil is exceedingly rich and in which the trees grow to a large size, these being covered with parasitical plants and creepers of gigantic size...it is in these brushes that the rosewood and cedar trees grow and also the fig tree," wrote Captain King. [18]

The natives helped them launch the boat into deeper water and the sailors gave them fish hooks and lines in return. "Everything we said or did was repeated by them with the most exact imitation: and indeed they appeared to think they could not please us better than by mimicking every motion that we made. Some biscuit was given them, which they pretended to eat, but, on our looking aside, were observed to spit it out," wrote Captain King. [19]

When they left Port Macquarie on 20th May the *Mermaid* found eleven feet of water when she went out over the bar whereas the *Lady Nelson*, on the north side of the channel, had only nine feet.

Once outside the bar the two vessels parted company. Lieutenant Oxley had to get back to Sydney on the *Lady Nelson* to start planning his harsh new settlement which, in 1821, replaced Newcastle as a penal colony for those who had committed secondary crimes after arriving in New South Wales.

Free settlers were not allowed as far north as Port Macquarie but, with an eye to the future, Captain King wrote, "When this is allowed, it will, from the superiority of its climate and the great extent of fine country in the interior, become a very important and valuable dependency of the colony of New South Wales." [20]

He was proved right when, in 1830, Port Macquarie was opened to settlers, many of whom grew sugar cane. In the late 1830s Port Macquarie was closed as a penal colony, the prisoners being sent even further north to Moreton Bay in Queensland as, with the advance of settlement, it was too easy for convicts to escape. Some found their way back to Sydney even though the local natives were bribed by the authorities with tobacco and blankets to hand any runaways in.

The *Mermaid* sailed on to the Great Barrier Reef, all the way looking for and taking bearings from geographical features mentioned by Cook and Flinders. At some islands the natives would come on board and the sailors would dress them in old shirts and trousers, etc. but it was noticed that, as soon as the aborigines got back to the beach, they would take all the clothes off, sometimes experiencing difficulties with straps and buttons. They preferred to go naked and did so until a different species of white man (and woman!) arrived on the scene – the missionaries, with a bible in one hand and a pair of trousers or a skirt in the other.

Forty-nine years after Captain Cook the *Mermaid* also put in at the mouth of the Endeavour River and, just as Cook had trouble there with the "simple savages", who tried to take turtles from the deck of the ship, so too did the *Mermaid*. One of the *Mermaid's* sailors was particularly fair headed and light skinned and the aborigines believed that he was really a woman and, to satisfy their curiosity, they asked him to take his clothes off. He took off his shirt but refused to go any further whereupon they became very angry and hostile.

The *Mermaid* left the thick mangroves of this river and headed up to Cape York, which they identified from a distance by the prominence of its Mount Adolphus. It had taken eleven weeks to reach Cape York from Sydney. "I had been able to lay down the different projections of the coast and our track within the barrier reefs between the Percy Islands and Cape York, besides having surveyed Port Macquarie, examined Rodd's Bay and constructed our boat at Endeavour River," wrote Captain King proudly. [21]

Upon the *Mermaid's* return to Sydney she was freshly coppered, caulked and otherwise repaired at her berth on the east side of Sydney Cove. While this was happening the ship's company lived on board a hulk that was rented for the purpose. She was then secured alongside the hulk and was stripped and immersed under the water for several days in an effort to get rid of all the rats and cockroaches with which she was infested.

Upon being raised, the water was pumped out and her sailors thought that they now had a clean ship but, before leaving Sydney, it was again infested with rats "and we had not been long at sea before the cockroaches also made their appearance in great numbers." [22] During the *Mermaid's* time under the sea only the living stock of cockroaches had been destroyed while their many eggs, deposited in recesses and cracks in the timber, "proved so

59

impervious to the sea water that, no sooner had we reached the warmer climate, than they were hatched and the vessel was quickly repossessed by them, but it was many months before we were so annoyed by their numbers as had been the case during the last voyage." [23]

For the *Mermaid's* third surveying voyage Captain King requested a surgeon and he was given Doctor James Hunt, who had just arrived in Sydney as the doctor on a convict vessel.

Leaving Sydney this time on 13th July, 1820, the old girl proceeded north again, sometimes landing to get bearings from a hilltop by means of a theodolite and to obtain sights on the beach for the time-keepers.

On this voyage Captain King was able to assert the superiority of the Inner Route, between the reefs and the mainland. The Outer Route by contrast, although having a clear passage between sixty and a hundred miles wide, had many detached reefs on both sides – both known and unknown. The sea of the Outer Route was of almost unfathomable depth, making it difficult to anchor and so a ship "must keep under sail till she come up to the edge of the Great Barrier and pass through one of its openings into the comparatively shallow and sheltered water inside of it". [24]

On the Inner Route the weather was better, the seas calmer – "only the surface ripple flaked with spray" [25] – and there was easier access to the all important wood and water on either the mainland or any of the multitude of islands, whose high green tops rose above the turquoise sea. The Inner Route contained safe anchorages at night under the lee of an islet or reef where the ship could stay if the weather turned dirty. Furthermore, if a cargo consisted of horses, cattle or sheep, forage could be obtained for them near at hand along the Inner Route.

There was clear water on the Inner Route, making navigation easier. In the words of the naturalist on a later surveying vessel, Mr. Jukes of *HMS Fly*, "Although there is not much variety there is considerable beauty in a small coral reef when viewed from a ship's mast-head at a short distance in clear weather….It is this perfect clearness of the water which renders navigation among coral reefs at all practicable, as a shoal with even five fathoms of water on it can be discerned at a mile distant from a ship's mast-head in consequence of its greenish hue contrasting with the blue of the deep water. In seven fathoms water the bottom can still be discerned on looking over the side of a boat...but in ten fathoms the depth of colour can scarcely be distinguished from the dark azure of the unfathomable ocean." [26] However, the glare of the sun on the water could affect visibility.

After this third voyage the *Mermaid* was pretty worn and so back in Sydney Captain King was given a bigger vessel, *HMS Bathurst*, which had more boats than the *Mermaid* and a ship's company of thirty-two. These were the commander (King), a surgeon, two master's mates (assistant surveyors), a botanical collector, steward, boatswain's mate, carpenter's mate, sailmaker, cook, sixteen seamen and five boys. This time there was another aborigine, Bundell, as Bongaree, after three voyages on the *Mermaid* as well as several with Captain Flinders, had decided to stay on land this time.

They left Sydney on 26th May, 1821, but after three days at sea a young girl aged about thirteen was discovered concealed among the casks. She had hidden herself there so that she could accompany the boatswain to sea. When she was brought on to the deck it was found that her appearance and clothes were filthy as she had been four days in a dark hold. Although she knew quite a few of those on board they could scarcely recognise her as she had been dreadfully seasick.

Under questioning she claimed that her boatswain knew nothing of her scheme before the ship sailed and Captain King, not wanting to waste time going back to Sydney, allowed her to remain on board provided that the boatswain would share his rations with her. This he agreed to do and so the *Bathurst* had an extra person as she made her way up to Torres Strait to explore, trace and chart more of the thousands of islets and reefs that make up that unique phenomenon, the Great Barrier Reef. The stowaway would not have been the most popular person on board as a woman on a ship was believed to bring bad luck to the vessel.

At the end of this voyage Captain King was able to write, "Such then are the first fruits of the voyages I have had the honour to direct. Much however of the coast yet remains to be examined and, although for the general purposes of navigation it has been quite sufficiently explored, yet there are many spaces upon the chart left blank, that would be highly interesting to examine and really important to know. We have a slight knowledge also of the natural history of the continent; slight however as it is, no country has ever produced a more extraordinary assemblage of indigenous productions...than Australia." [2]

Captain Blackwood and HMS Fly

As Captain King implied, the combined explorations of Cook, Flinders and himself had achieved a lot but the task was by no means finished as hydrography seemed to be a never ending process and in 1841 the Admiralty decided that the Great Barrier Reef, on which so many ships had been wrecked, needed a more thorough survey. To this end they sent out the corvette, *HMS Fly*, under Captain Francis Blackwood, and her tender, *HMS Bramble*, which was in the charge of Lieutenant Charles Yule. These two vessels left Falmouth in Cornwall in April, 1842, and arrived in Sydney on 15th October.

Although a little short on marine surveying experience Captain Blackwood possessed an enquiring scientific mind, and over the course of the next three years surveyed the Reef for a distance of approximately a thousand miles. He marked the outer line of the many reefs that make up the Great Barrier to a distance of up to five hundred miles from the Australian mainland and he also surveyed and charted Endeavour Strait and the eastern parts of Torres Strait from Cape York to New Guinea.

He began in the Capricorn group of islands near the Tropic of that name. Proceeding north from there "we traversed a space of between forty and fifty miles wide, backwards and forwards, without finding any shoals except a five fathom patch of coral within sight of the Capricorn group". [28]

Mr. Jukes, the naturalist on the *Fly*, was impressed by the coral and the animal life that it contained. "What an inconceivable amount of animal life must here be scattered over the bottom of the sea, to say nothing of that moving through its waters, and this through spaces of hundreds of miles. Every corner and crevice, every point occupied by living beings, which, as they become more minute, increase in tenfold abundance." [29]

However, the antlers and branches of this beautiful coral could be treacherous for ships as cables could get caught under some ledge of coral. This happened to *HMS Fly*, which had its messenger [chain] carried away and its hawser pipes damaged.

At Lizard Island, the 1,200 foot high mound of granite which Captain Cook had visited to look for a way out through the reefs, Captain Blackwood climbed to the summit and stayed the night there in order to get the angles in the morning. The survey party carried two barometers so that they could ascertain the height of the hill, and they took observations while they were both climbing and descending. In the words of the *Fly's* naturalist, Mr. Jukes, "The sunrise was a magnificent one; the morning calm, the sea like one of molten lead, with its horizon quite indistinguishable or melting into the air, which was rather hazy with a low bank of clouds." [30]

The shallow water of the reef appeared green while the deeper water was dark blue, the boundary between them being clear and sharp. It is not surprising that there was such a distinction as the white, sandy patches at the bottom of the sea could be seen clearly among the large, dark masses of coral whereas outside the reef one could not get any bottom at a depth of 280 fathoms.

On 24th June, 1843, the surveyors went ashore to measure a meridian distance (longitude and latitude) between the Barrier Reef and Cape Direction, at the foot of Lloyd Bay, which is a few miles south of Cape York. They took with them a chronometer, sextant, theodolites, etc. and left two armed men to guard the boats on the beach.

After taking the observations Lieutenant Yule and his team packed up their instruments but, while returning to the boat, one of them, Mr. Bayley, who was in the rear with a musket under one arm and the artificial horizon box under the other, was felled by a sharp spear thrown by a native. The attacker paused for a moment to see if the weapon had had its effect and then dived into the gully and disappeared.

Lieutenant Yule broke off the long end of the spear, which was "deeply fixed in the back between the shoulder blades". [31] The victim, "writhing on his hands and knees in great pain" [32] was carried on to the small boat but there was "great difficulty in withdrawing the spear....and, when we did so, we found that the point and barb had remained behind". [33]

Penetrating four and a half inches, it had passed between the heads of two of the ribs and the spine, splintering the bones of both, and through the left lobe of the lung. Its point was a piece of bone three and a half inches long and about a quarter of an inch thick in the middle but coming to a very sharp point at each end like a spindle. This was fastened to a groove in the side of the spear.

They eventually got the rest of the spear out except for the point, which remained in Bayley's chest. He lingered for three days and then passed away. This unhappy survey ended at Cape York where the *Fly's* tender, the *Midge*, was unrigged and hoisted back on the *Fly*.

Part of Captain Blackwood's brief from the Hydrographic Branch of the Admiralty was to choose a suitable site for a beacon that could warn ships of any particularly hazardous area, although one beacon in such a vast area of ocean was not exactly a major step in aiding navigation.

In July, 1843, the *Fly* anchored twelve miles off Raine Island, a remote, uninhabited stretch of coral and sand that formed part of the Outer Reef near the top of Australia. Captain Blackwood and Mr. Jukes were rowed the dozen miles from their ship to the low lying island and camped there for a night among the noise and smell of thousands of sea birds. Captain Blackwood decided that it would be a suitable place for a beacon and he sent his recommendation to the Admiralty. The following year the government vessel, *Prince George*, arrived with twenty convict masons and their guards.

The materials for building the beacon were taken from the island and nearby seas. Forty miles south of Raine Island was the wreck of the merchantman, *Martha Ridgeway*, which had hit a coral reef some four years earlier. Beams were taken from her for the woodwork on the beacon while the stone was quarried and cut by the convicts on the island. Lime was obtained for the mortar by burning coral and clam shells. The wood for the fires had to be brought from nearby islands and so the boat crews were kept busy loading the cut firewood and taking it to Raine.

The stone tower was forty feet high with walls five feet thick. However, it was not possible to adorn it with a light and so the top of the tower was covered with a brightly painted canvas to attract the attention of mariners during the hours of daylight.

It took the convicts three months to build it, for which effort they were each rewarded by having six months taken off their sentences when they got back to Sydney. Goats were released on the island to provide fresh meat for any sailors who might be shipwrecked there - as happened five years later when the *Enchantress* ran ashore there and her stranded passengers lived off the goats and sea eggs until they were rescued.

Captain Stanley and HMS Rattlesnake

In 1847 the work of the *Fly* was continued by *HMS Rattlesnake*, which used the same tender that had serviced the *Fly*. The *Rattlesnake* had been fitted out in England for the purpose of conducting a survey of the coasts of Australia, New Guinea and the Louisiade archipelago (off the south-east tip of New Guinea) – a task that was expected to last five years.

She was under the command of Captain Owen Stanley. This great hydrographer, whom we shall meet surveying the coasts of northern Australia, New Guinea and New Zealand, was born in 1811, the son of Right Reverend Edward Stanley, Bishop of Norwich, and the nephew of Baron Stanley of Alderley. He entered the Royal Naval College in 1824 and six years later – in January, 1830 – he joined the sloop *Adventure*, on which Captain Phillip Parker King was surveying the Straits of Magellan. Stanley gained further surveying experience on the *Mastiff*, charting Greek islands, and on the *Terror* where he had charge of the astronomical and magnetic observations during the Polar (North Pole) expedition of 1836. All this was good training for what awaited him in the South Pacific. He was also a Fellow of the Royal Society and of the Royal Astronomical Society.

The zoologist and assistant surgeon on the *Rattlesnake* was twenty-two year old Thomas Huxley, who later became one of the world's leading zoologists and scientists. His service Down Under proved lucky for Huxley as in 1847 he met a young lady in Sydney, Kate Heathorn, who was to become his wife. The naturalist on board was John McGillivray, who saw enough of Australia during his service on the station to convince him to return and settle there.

The *Rattlesnake* sailed out of Plymouth harbour on 11th December, 1846, and reached Hobart on 8th July the following year. Also on board were Captain Stanley's brother, Charles, and his wife. Charles was also a captain but in the Royal Engineers. He was on his way to Hobart to be Private Secretary to Sir William Denison, the Lieutenant-Governor of Van Diemen's Land (Tasmania), who was a fellow officer of Charles' in the Royal Engineers.

After her long voyage from England the *Rattlesnake* spent two months at Sydney but the men were far from idle as she re-surveyed Sydney harbour, taking soundings and marking channels and shoals that had shifted since the previous survey. "This was a necessary work as it is now above twenty years, we believe, since it was last done," wrote a Sydney newspaper. [34]

This completed, it was time for her to commence the task for which she had been sent out, viz. the survey of the vast area of northern Queensland, Torres Strait and New Guinea.

The *Rattlesnake* and her tender, the *Bramble*, left Sydney on 28th April, 1848, and were away for nine months. The former carried Edmund Kennedy's thirteen man expedition, who were to explore the interior of the Cape York peninsula, as well as their horses, sheep, flour, sugar, tea, scientific instruments, shot and "sufficient ammunition to serve as protection in case of necessity". [35] Only three of the party survived, including Kennedy's faithful aborigine, Jacky Jacky, who hailed from a tribe near the Hunter River in New South Wales.

After dropping off the Kennedy expedition at Tam O Shanter Point in Rockingham Bay on 24th May, the *Rattlesnake* and her tender surveyed and charted the inner passage of Torres Strait, beginning the work at the Palm Islands on a scale of half an inch to the mile, and completing it at Cape York. Where the passages were narrow the survey was on a larger scale. At the head of Lloyd Bay they discovered several islands that had not been marked on any previous charts.

"During the survey every reef, sand patch, and island has been clearly defined, and not a single obstacle can possibly be in the way when once the charts of the *Rattlesnake* are published for the most timid shipmaster to encounter," stated a press report at the time.[36] Altogether eleven charts were made of the north Queensland coast from Rockingham Bay to Jarvis Island for the benefit of mariners using the Inner Route through the Reef. In Torres Strait Captain Stanley re-examined the three previously known channels and discovered the five remaining ones.

The *Rattlesnake* left Cape York on 2nd November, 1848, and sailed around the western and southern coasts of Australia, reaching Sydney on 24th January, 1849. From there she sailed north again to survey the southern coast of New Guinea where Captain Stanley collected a large variety of native handiwork.

The survey completed, the *Rattlesnake* left New Guinea waters in the latter half of September, 1849, arriving at Cape York on 1st October. Whilst lying there the ship's watering party came across a white woman who had come over from Prince of Wales Island to the mainland in a boat manned by blacks.

She was the only survivor of a shipwreck in Torres Strait some four years earlier, her husband being the skipper of the stricken vessel. One of the natives was out catching turtles and he approached the wreck, found her and carried her through the surf, supporting her with one arm and swimming with the other.

She was taken to an island in the Prince of Wales group near Cape York, where she lived for several years with the tribe and was kindly treated by the men but less so by the women. However, they were very careful not to let her have any communication with any of the European vessels that were occasionally passing.

When news came that the "large war canoe of the white men with the small one" (the *Rattlesnake* and its tender) had arrived in the area she prevailed on her friends to take her across to the mainland, which they did, accompanying her in four large canoes. They did not want her to escape from them but she said that, after seeing her white countrymen and shaking hands with them, she would return.

Once on board the *Rattlesnake* Captain Stanley asked her whether of her own free will she wanted to return to Sydney, where her parents were when she left. "I am a Christian and would rather go back to my own people", she replied and then broke down as she had forgotten much of the English language.

In the words of John McGillivray, "Poor woman; she is not more than twenty (nineteen or twenty she says) and, though not pretty, has a soft, feminine and very pleasing expression and, though living with naked savages for several years, she had not lost the natural feelings of womanly modesty, and appeared to feel acutely her situation, dressed only in a shirt in the midst of a crowd of her own countrymen." [37] Naked savages they might have been but, in the words of the same writer, "She states that on only one occasion was any improper liberty attempted by the men; she was fortunately saved by a friend, who soundly thrashed the intending ravisher, an old man". [38]

She told the three blacks who accompanied her to the *Rattlesnake,* including her original rescuer, that she wanted to go back to Sydney on the warship and they were liberally rewarded with axes, knives, etc. and were allowed to stay on board for a few days. This was intended as an inducement for them to behave similarly should another ship be wrecked in similar circumstances.

She had been born Barbara Crawford, the daughter of a Scottish tin worker in Sydney, and at the age of about sixteen had married a chap named Thomson at Moreton Bay, whence they sailed with some other men in a small cutter called the *America* for Bampton Shoal in the Coral Sea with the intention of salvaging oil from a whaler that had been wrecked there. Unable to find the wreck, they headed for Port Essington. But fate deemed otherwise and they were wrecked in the Prince of Wales Islands.

On board the *Rattlesnake* Barbara Thomson improved both her health and her English, much of which latter she had forgotten during her four years living tribally. The warship returned her to Sydney where, after remarrying, she eventually died in 1912 at the age of eighty-four.

The voyage of the *Rattlesnake* to the tropics was a success for Captain Stanley from the professional point of view but not from the physical. "Captain Stanley's health had gradually been giving way under the fatigues and anxieties attendant upon the arduous duty of surveying in a tropical climate. On his passage from the Louisiade Islands....he was very ill." [39]

At Cape York he learned of the death at Hobart of his brother, Charles, and, upon arrival at Sydney he was informed of the death of his father, the late Bishop of Norwich. It was all too much for him and on 13th March, 1850, Captain Owen Stanley committed suicide and passed from this world on board his own ship in Sydney harbour. He was only thirty-nine and at the height of his career.

At the time it was said that he had had an "epileptic fit" and this probably accounted for the great outpouring of grief that followed. His funeral at Saint Leonards, Sydney, "was attended by all the civil and military authorities, the band and colours, together with a firing party of the 11th Regiment, marshalling the corpse to its last resting place." [40]

"His premature death is a severe loss to the naval service," wrote Auckland's *New Zealander* newspaper.[41] Indeed it was for this was a man who had made many additions to hydrography, including his surveys of Simon's Bay in South Africa, of the inner route through Torres Strait, and his work in charting the south-east coast of New Guinea and the Louisiade Archipelago. As a tribute to his work the great mountain chain of New Guinea was named the Owen Stanley Range.

The death of Captain Stanley left the *Rattlesnake* without a commander and what followed was an outbreak of pettiness in high circles that was unworthy of the late officer.

Captain Keppel, the commander of *HMS Maeander* and the son of the Earl of Albemarle, appointed Lieutenant Yule to the vacant position and told him to sail to England. This officer had been surveying in Australasian waters for nine years and was well fitted for promotion. "Mr. Yule is an old and zealous officer," wrote Auckland's *Southern Cross* newspaper.[42]

When news of Stanley's death reached Captain Erskine on *HMS Havannah* in Wellington harbour he raced back across the Tasman and, upon arrival in Sydney, told Acting Commander Yule that he was not to proceed Home but was to remain on the Australia station until the end of the year. Poor Lieutenant Yule was then told by Keppel to hasten to England as originally ordered.

Although Keppel was senior in commission to Erskine, the latter had been specially appointed to command in the seas of the Australia station.

Captain Erskine threatened that he would proceed to sea in pursuit of the *Rattlesnake* in order to prevent it sailing to England as Keppel had ordered. Upon hearing this Keppel threatened to fire his guns on Erskine's *Havannah* should she attempt to put to sea in pursuit of Captain Yule's vessel.

According to the *Naval and Military Gazette* "There can be no doubt but that Captain Keppel, as the *senior* officer, had the right to fill up *temporarily* until the Commander-in-Chief's pleasure was known the vacancy in the *Rattlesnake* and that, if Captain Erskine or any other junior officer had presumed to get under weigh in order to follow that vessel for the purpose, as declared, of superseding his senior officer's appointment, the proper course for Captain Keppel to have pursued would have been simply to have made *Havannah's* signal to "moor" and to "unbend sails" and that, if her captain had dared to disobey this public official command and had afterwards presumed to get under sail, Captain Keppel should at once have placed Captain Erskine under arrest and have appointed the first Lieutenant of the *Maeander* or some other duly qualified officer to have taken the command of the *Havannah* until the pleasure of the Admiralty or that of the Commander-in-Chief should have been known, and at the same time to have applied to the Admiralty for a court-martial on the Captain of the *Havannah* for mutiny."[43]

To this the *Nautical Standard* added, "Such mutinous examples cannot be safely repeated in the service and, if the laxity of the Board, too frequently exercised when the offending parties are men of family or Parliamentary influence, is allowed to conceal the offenders, we augur ill of the future prospects of the Service and should be inclined to exclaim, with many a gallant veteran, that the service is going to a personage supposed to live in a warm place and whose name is not to be mentioned before ears polite." [44]

In the event the cautious heads at the Admiralty approved of Keppel's conduct in appointing Lieutenant Yule to the command of the *Rattlesnake* but disapproved of his having sent the ship to England before she had completed the surveys that she had been sent to Australia to conduct and which would have occupied her for another six months. Captain Erskine was relieved by Captain Stewart, the son-in-law of the Governor of New South Wales, Sir Charles Fitzroy.

It might be thought that this "captains' tiff" couldn't get any more petty but there was more to come as was reported in the *Sydney Morning Herald* on 3rd May, 1850. "We believe it is customary in the navy for all vessels to hoist the same coloured flag as that worn by the ship of the senior officer in port, except in cases where there is a large fleet divided into squadrons, when each division carried the flag of the same colour as its respective admiral.

This has not been observed during the week by the vessels of war in port. Last week the *Rattlesnake* had a white flag; on Friday last, as soon as the *Havannah* made her appearance round Bradleys Head with a red ensign, the *Rattlesnake* shifted her flag to the same colour.

About three hours afterwards the *Meander* entered the port with a white flag, when the *Rattlesnake* again shifted and hoisted the white flag. The *Havannah*, however, took no notice of the *Meander* but continued to hoist the red ensign every day. The whole matter in dispute between Captains Keppel and Erskine has been referred to the Lords of the Admiralty." [45]

New Zealand

The rough chart of the west coast of New Zealand made by the Dutch explorer, Abel Tasman, in 1642 left many questions unanswered and these were largely resolved by Captain Cook's six month circumnavigation of New Zealand in 1769-70. Indeed, Cook was the man who literally put New Zealand on the map and some parts of the charts that he made in the reign of George III were still being used in the reign of Elizabeth II.

70

Cook and his men were entering what were effectively uncharted waters and so, without maps, he had to be very skilful and very careful so as not to lose his vessel on some hidden subterranean reef or on the rocky coast in a storm.

Not surprisingly, Cook made some errors. He had Stewart Island as a peninsula and Banks Peninsula as an island and he put the northern part of the South Island some 40 minutes too far eastwards of its true longitudinal position. He more or less corrected the last mentioned mistake on his second voyage in 1773.

On this second voyage he made a map of Dusky Sound, which is widely regarded as the best map to come out of the voyage.

With the opening up of New Zealand to trade and settlement in the 1830s and 1840s there was a need for more accurate charts of the harbours and coast line and the first survey of Auckland harbour was done by *HMS Herald*, which had brought Captain Hobson to New Zealand from Sydney in 1840 for the purpose of proclaiming British sovereignty. The *Herald* made a survey chart and named some points and bays. Its own name has been given to Herald Island, opposite Hobsonville, in Auckland harbour.

The surveying work that was started by the *Herald* was continued by Captain Owen Stanley, whose hydrographic activities in New Zealand were just as fruitful as they were in Australia and New Guinea. In 1840 he took the twenty year old sloop, *HMS Britomart* from Sydney to New Zealand, arriving in the Bay of Islands on 2nd July. He and his surveyors immediately got to work, sounding and tracing the entrance to the harbour. But that was not to be their only work.

The first Governor of New Zealand, Captain William Hobson R.N., became aware that a shipload of French settlers, accompanied by a French frigate, were headed for the South Island which, it was feared, they might try to annex in the name of Britain's traditional enemy. So he sent Captain Stanley and the *Britomart* racing down to Akaroa on Banks Peninsula, the intended landing place, to thwart any such move.

After a very stormy passage, during which her stern boat was washed away, the *Britomart* arrived at Akaroa on 11th August, 1840, and immediately raised the British flag.

When the French warship, *L'Aube*, arrived, together with a whaler carrying fifty-seven French immigrants, they saw the Union Jack flying over the peninsula and, whatever their original intentions, they accepted the fact of British sovereignty and in due course the immigrants became British subjects and added a Gallic strain to New Zealand's predominantly Anglo-Celtic bloodstock.

From Akaroa Captain Stanley sailed to Pigeon Bay where, in his own words, "....finding no inhabitants, I merely remained long enough to survey the harbour which, though narrow and exposed to the northward, is well sheltered from every other wind, and is much frequented by whalers, who procure great numbers of pigeons.

From Pigeon Bay I went to Port Cooper...Between Port Cooper and Cloudy Bay I could hear of no anchorage whatever from the whalers who frequented the coast." [46]

An obelisk, made of Port Chalmers stone, was later erected on the site at Green Point, Akaroa, where Captain Stanley hoisted the flag. It was unveiled in June, 1898, by the Governor of New Zealand in front of more than 2,000 people, including fifty bluejackets from *HMS Tauranga*, which was anchored in the bay below. There is also a font in Christchurch cathedral, commemorating Captain Stanley's role in securing the South Island for the British Empire; it was given by one of his brothers, who was Dean of Westminster.

When Governor Hobson decided to move New Zealand's centre of government from Russell in the far north to Auckland he got Captain Stanley to carry out a trigonometrical survey of Auckland harbour. Part of Stanley's remit was to make a plan of the harbour with proposed wharves and other facilities.

In Auckland Stanley's name is perpetuated in Point Stanley and Stanley Bay on the North Shore and Stanley Street in the city while his ship gave its name to Britomart Point (to-day Britomart Place) in central Auckland.

The 1840s was the decade in which New Zealand really got going as, under the security of British rule, its fertile acres were taken up by hard working and enterprising settlers from Home and it wasn't long before they, and more particularly the sea captains who provided them with a lifeline to the outside world, were calling for a more exact survey of the coast than that which had been done by Captain Cook some eighty years earlier with somewhat primitive instruments, and had been added to piecemeal by the occasional visiting naval ship such as the *Herald* and the *Britomart*. The mariners wanted to know how to avoid treacherous rocks, sand banks and currents and this led to the voyages of *HMS Acheron* and *HMS Pandora*. As a result of the systematic survey by these two

72

vessels, the first since Cook's, the Admiralty was able to publish fifty-five charts giving detailed drawings of the coast line, harbours and their entrances, and navigable rivers.

Sandy beaches and rocky points were marked and so were the depths in fathoms of both seabeds and rivers. They also marked man made features such as wharves, lighthouses, whaling stations, settlements and wrecks and, later, submarine cables. Information useful to mariners such as "Channel marked by beacons" or "Mud flats dry at low water" were inserted where necessary.

HMS *Acheron* was a wooden, steam, side paddle vessel of 760 tons, 160 hp and a coal capacity of 240 tons. Barque rigged, she had been built in 1838 for the mail route between Marseilles and Malta, taking the letters from England to the Navy's most important base in the Mediterranean. In 1848 she was refitted at Woolwich for her new mission in the South Pacific.

She had a ship's company of approximately a hundred men and was commanded by Captain John Lort Stokes (1812-85), who had entered the Navy in 1824 as a first class volunteer on the *Prince Regent*. He gained his surveying experience as a midshipman on *HMS Beagle* (1825-30) when she was surveying the Straits of Magellan. From 1831 to 1836 he was assistant surveyor on the *Beagle* when she was charting the coast of South America and making a circumnavigation of the globe to complete a meridian distance survey.

As a steamer the *Acheron* could get on with her exacting task without having to worry about the vagaries of wind. The experienced captain of the *Acheron* was supported by his commander, George Richards, and the Sailing Master, Frederick Evans. Both these men later became Hydrographers of the Royal Navy while Richards and Stokes also became admirals.

In 1841 John Stokes had married Fanny Marlay in Sydney and they had one daughter. They had lived mostly in England but Mrs. Stokes sailed with him from England on the *Acheron* as she had relations in Sydney, who were looking forward to seeing her. Unfortunately she died during the *Acheron's* stopover at the Cape of Good Hope and so it was as a grieving widower that John Stokes had to commence his important work in New Zealand.

Arriving in November, 1848, the *Acheron* began surveying and defining Auckland harbour and its approaches through the Hauraki Gulf by taking regular soundings, sending parties ashore in small boats, placing buoys and marking them on the charts. This was

73

already the busiest harbour in New Zealand with an ever increasing number of ships arriving with settlers from Britain and coal and other cargos from Australia and there had been pressure on the Navy to conduct a comprehensive and up-to-date survey. The promontory between Shoal Bay and Little Shoal Bay on the north shore of Auckland harbour is named Stokes Point after the captain who surveyed it.

Captain Stokes' first social engagement in New Zealand was to take part in the ceremony at which the Governor of New Zealand, George Grey, was installed as a Knight of the Bath, the new knight being dubbed by the Chief Justice of New Zealand, Sir William Martin, acting as Commissioner on behalf of the Queen.

From Auckland the *Acheron* steamed down to Wellington to take soundings in and around its harbour. The ship's diary was written up by one of Captain Stokes' subordinates, Mr. Hansard, and his observations of the future capital of New Zealand, which was then in its ninth year of existence, are not without interest. "Enclosures of corn land and meadow mingle with the houses upon every level spot, which give Wellington in early summer a very rural and verdant aspect....Wines and British and foreign spirits sell to an incredible extent....Amongst the higher grades of society the usual routine of English fashionable life has been reproduced at the Antipodes."

Of the Maori pa (village) at Wellington he wrote, "A stroll inside their enclosure is rather an amusing thing. Some bask and smoke in the sunshine, others manufacture nets, repair canoes, scrape flax, one knot of young men chanting the multiplication table."

The original road between Wellington and the Hutt Valley was described as follows: "A smooth, winding road follows the sinuosities of the harbour. Washed on one side by the waves and bounded on the other by steep banks overgrown with trees, lichens and pendant ferns, it leads to the agricultural district of the settlement, called the valley of the Hutt. In the fine days of this healthy, invigorating climate nothing can be pleasanter than a ride or a walk in that direction...the light tilted carts and gigs of the Hutt farmers bowl along, hurrying to and from the town with wife and daughter seated alongside. Herds of cows slowly driven by flaxen-haired cowboys, home to the milking, young and wealthy settlers dashing by on their thoroughbreds, the public caravan or omnibus well-horsed, and loaded with passengers, all so much belong to the details of rural England that by an effort alone one recalls the 16,000 miles of separation. [This was before the opening of the Suez Canal, which reduced the distance to approximately 12,000 sea miles]. The intermixture of a few dark, tattooed faces with flaxen mats and sandaled feet serves occasionally to remind us we are in a distant land." [47] The Maoris called the *Acheron* "H. M. Tema" (steamer).

From Wellington Captain Stokes took his ship down to Akaroa in February, 1849. The Government had recently bought land there from the Maoris and the Commissioner responsible for the transaction, Mr. Mantell, took passage on the warship together with the money (about £1,000). Trouble was expected as different Maori factions were already squabbling over their share of the loot.

Less welcome passengers were half a dozen Maori chiefs who had been in Wellington and for whom the Lieutenant Governor had solicited passages back to Akaroa. In the words of Mr. Hansard, "One, a brutal, burly looking old savage, named Tairoa [Taiaroa], never ceased wrangling with his fellows during the whole passage about his claims on the distribution, coming incessantly aft and endeavouring to intrude into the cabin 'to see the cap'un' in hopes of his interest to secure the lion's share.

No sooner had the vessel anchored in Akaroa than a deputation from the mob of Maoris encamped there came off in a canoe although it was nearly dark. They wished to be allowed on board to bother the Commissioner. Failing in this, a fierce altercation began between old 'Boanerges' as we nicknamed Tairoa and the strangers, who lay a little way off.

They seemed to be of a hostile tribe for the old cannibal – he was a monstrous one in his youth – springing upon the starboard paddle-box, poured out a volley of abuse, vituperation and scorn that forbade the putting in of a word edgeways by his listeners. After about half an hour's furious gesticulation and noise the canoe sheered off and Boanerges descended to the forecastle, seemingly quite elated with his triumph. We wished he had fallen overboard...

The settlements of Akaroa, as seen next morning by sunrise, looked cheerful and pleasant. The concourse of natives awaiting the payment of their claims was camped like a vast gypsy horde along the level beach. All had risen, some being engaged fishing from their canoes, some, particularly the younger people, sporting like mermaids in the waves. Their olders were holding council, either squatted in long lines and huddled in mat or blanket, or standing to gaze wistfully at the steamer in hopes the Commissioner would disembark. Among the trees fires showed that the women were busy preparing the first meal of the day." [48]

On the day of payment for the land a parchment deed was laid out on a table ashore and the Maoris arrived one by one to sign and "marched off with a roleau of gold and the rest in bank notes". No sooner was the general result known among the ladies "than a furious melee began, to which Babel or Billingsgate could afford no parallel".

The French settlers of Akaroa, who had earlier caused such anxiety to Captain Hobson and Captain Stanley, were now settled in, having "won a few clearances from the dense, beautiful forest". In the words of the *Acheron* diary, they were "not rich but probably far better off than their class in any district of their fatherland…Vines and peaches grow luxuriantly in their garden patches for the climate of Akaroa is as genial as the South of France". [49]

From the turmoil of Akaroa the *Acheron* sailed the short distance round to what was then known as Port Cooper to examine and report on its fitness as a harbour for the new settlement of Canterbury, which was being planned in a big way back in England under the auspices of the very aristocratic Canterbury Association and with the blessing of the Archbishop of Canterbury. This was to be the best organised and most successful settlement that the British would make in the whole of their vast empire.

"We are at anchor opposite the spot which the port town of Lyttelton will hereafter occupy, now a solitary hill slope overgrown with fern and ti plant," wrote Mr. Hansard. "The entrance of Port Cooper is very broad and, being exposed to the long swell of the Pacific, the ship maintains an incessant roll night and day – no interval of rest. For many weeks the officers' sleep has been exposed to this horrible oscillation.

The general aspect of the country, too, is far from prepossessing; bare hills of pale russet hue everywhere surround us, and no timber is visible save in the mountain gullies, a remarkable exception to the general character of New Zealand scenery, which generally looks one vast forest from the summit of its mountains to their base. Here are scarcely any Natives and only three white settlers in the neighbourhood." These were the Deans brothers at Riccarton, who lived in the only house on the Canterbury Plains, a Scottish family called Gebbies, and "Rhodes farm, on the opposite side of the harbour, whence we were supplied with excellent bread, cheese, milk and mutton.….In truth, the pasturage is so excellent, so abundant that sheep attain very unusual size, many brought on board for our use weighing upwards of ninety pounds." [50]

The surveying of Banks Peninsula was done from boats that had provisions for several weeks at a stretch as it sometimes took that long for them to carry out their exacting work.

While his men were thus engaged Captain Stokes and a small party travelled inland to Mount Grey, which they climbed, and Kaiapoi. At the latter place they were shown over the site of Te Rauparaha's killing fields by Maori guides and could see several sets of whitened bones – even those of infants – sticking up out of the ground where New Zealand's most notorious cannibal had left them after gorging himself on their flesh.

In the words of the *Acheron* diary, "The demon devoured all his prisoners, himself tearing open the living mother and holding the half-formed embryo upon a pointed stick in the flames to be afterwards devoured." [51]

Their Maori guides laughed as they told the story. "Then Rauparaha 'made a beef'," joked these young men, whom Hansard described as "the merriest rascals possible". It was Te Rauparaha's habit, when more flesh was cooked than could be eaten on the spot, to pack the remains in flax baskets and take them home with him to eat later – a type of "doggy bag" except that it was not for the dog.

On their trek back to the ship by a different route the *Acheron* party stopped at a village and conversed with a native chief called "Charley", who showed them his new wife, a girl of sixteen. This was his second wife. In the words of Mr. Hansard, "The former rib had played him false, so, quoth he, 'I broke her head and her mother's head, and turned them out; and this one, if she deceives me, I'll break her head too." [52]

In April, 1849, the *Acheron* sailed south to make the first authentic survey of Dunedin harbour with its fifteen miles of shore line. So thorough was Stokes' survey that the chart that he issued was still being used in the twentieth century, although with a few amendments as to depths in the ship channels and the waters at Taiaroa Heads "but otherwise it is the Admiralty chart of 1850 that is now in use," wrote the *Otago Witness* newspaper in 1906. [53] Not surprisingly one of the promontories in the harbour is named Acheron Head.

Much the same could have been said by Captain Stokes of Cook's original survey for, in the words of one of the *Acheron's* crew, Arthur Fullarton, "We had the maps of Captain Cook and, though they were necessarily imperfect, our captain often remarked that they showed very good work considering the kind of instruments that were in use in the days of the great navigator." [54]

The Scottish settlement of Dunedin was only a year old when the *Acheron* arrived and the future city contained about 750 settlers living in 130 houses. Despite their small numbers these enterprising Gaels had already formed a Mechanics' Institute and – strange for a Caledonian settlement – a cricket club. In the words of the *Acheron's* diary, "The beach is strewed with the ribs of whales, measuring eleven feet long. Birds numerous; great numbers of small parraquet with green, purple and grey plumage...There are several inns – in fact, too many....Many settlers' houses built close to the water's edge around the harbour." [55]

From Dunedin the *Acheron* returned to Wellington and then spent six weeks examining and surveying the littoral of Cook Strait, which divides the North and South Islands.

In Queen Charlotte Sound she anchored in Captain Cook's old stamping ground of Ship Cove which, with its deep water extending right to the shore line, was a perfect anchorage. "A canoe filled with wild looking natives soon came alongside," recorded the *Acheron's* diary. Then a Maori "as soon as he got on deck, pointed with his arm to a small bay, exclaiming 'You like see Capinny Cook's tree?' This was a tree standing close to the shore to which the Great Navigator had secured his ship by a hawser. It was now about three feet in circumference and various ships' crews had carved their names on it." It seems that wherever one went in the Pacific the ghost of Captain Cook was never far away.

The Maoris came on deck trying to sell their parrots. "Being mostly ill clad, they seemed to feel the cold much, and earnestly begged permission that they might light their pipes and warm themselves at the galley fire. Then all sat down to smoke....Mats and coarse grass mantles are hawked about the deck, their owners rivalling our Jews of Monmouth Street in importunate attempts at extortion." [56]

After investigating the Sound the *Acheron* proceeded to Nelson and the ship's observant diary writer noted its bare hills, like those of Canterbury. "Frequent cottages line the shore and the hillside. One comfortable, English fashioned dwelling, to which was attached a large. well-cultivated garden enclosed by a hedge of the golden blossomed gorse, stood opposite our anchorage, being not indigenous to New Zealand, must have been perpetuated from seed brought out by the proprietor of the clearing, who probably was desirous at once to create a familiar and graceful memento of the land he had quitted." [57] Unbeknown to him, the prickly gorse would spread like wildfire in New Zealand's warmer climate and would become one of that country's most noxious plants.

To the men of the *Acheron* Nelson, a town less than ten years old, resembled "a comfortable English market town....Places of public accommodation hang out their signs of entertainment for man and horse at conspicuous points, as in the Old Country." [58]

Nelson, of course, had been named after Our Greatest Sailor and its main streets bore – and still bear – names like Trafalgar and Hardy. With such familiar nomenclature it is not surprising that this was the *Acheron's* favourite port-of-call. "From many pleasant circumstances not recurring elsewhere Nelson was voted by the *Acheron's* crew – and deservedly – to be the most agreeable, warm-hearted community they had hitherto visited in these islands." [59]

Back in Wellington harbour the *Acheron* ran into one of the heavy storms for which the place is well-known and she took part in rescuing the stricken merchant vessel, *Inconstant*.

During the *Inconstant's* passage from Adelaide some of the crew went on strike and, on beating in to Wellington Heads under the eastern shore, she missed stays and there were not sufficient men to remedy the situation and so she drifted stern on to the rocks. As soon as Captain Stokes heard of her predicament he got the *Acheron* under way and went to the spot to render assistance. During the night by great exertion the *Acheron* towed the *Inconstant* off the beach and the following morning brought her safely into Wellington harbour even though she was taking on water. "The Captain, Officers and Crew of the *Acheron* are deserving of the highest praise for the prompt and energetic manner in which assistance was rendered," wrote Wellington's *Independent* newspaper. [60] Yes, but they got something out of it. In the words of the *Acheron's* diary, "Salvage was demanded and recovered for this service in the Admiralty Court." [61]

The *Acheron's* survey work was very much appreciated by the colonists, who wanted to know where the safe havens and anchorages were and what places to avoid. There had been some ungrounded fears that certain harbour entrances and other places were unsafe and, by soundings and observation, the *Acheron* was able to dispel these doubts in certain cases and so open up such places to safe shipping although the word "safe" in the context of

New Zealand's rough weather and often jagged coast line should be used in a relative sense only.

Furthermore Captain Stokes had a very fine and professional crew who seem to have been well liked wherever they went. He carried a couple of race horses on board, one of which was called the "Lady Eleanor", and on 14th February, 1850, she ran in a race at Burnham Water Race Course on Wellington's Miramar Peninsula during a meet that was held in honour of Captain Stokes by the Wellington Jockey Club.

Of the *Acheron*, Wellington's *Independent* newspaper wrote, "She has been so long a denizen of our harbour that we shall regret to see her taking her departure, and trust before long to see her ploughing her steady course again through the waters of Port Nicholson. Her visit to New Zealand will, we have little doubt, prove of the greatest benefit to the colony. The very high character which her gallant commander has attained as a nautical surveyor and the great length of his distinguished services....will give a weight to the charts...executed under his command". [62] The *Acheron* left the name of its doctor, Doctor Lyall, in Wellington – Lyall Bay.

Wellington has many disadvantages ranging from an excess of wind to a dearth of flat land in its commercial centre but its harbour is one of the best and most secure in the world. "Here all the navies of Europe might ride in perfect security; at the entrance there is 11 and 12 fathoms water," wrote the *New Zealand Journal* on 5th June, 1841. It was not the navies of Europe that gathered there but in the winter of 1942 some hundreds of ships of the United States Navy, which used it as the take-off point for the invasion of Guadalcanal.

After leaving Wellington the *Acheron* steamed up to Auckland and thence back to Australia for repairs and to replenish her dwindling stocks of coal, there being neither docking facilities nor a coal industry in New Zealand at the time.

In early 1850 she was back at Lyttelton where she found not the single Rhodes farm house of the year before but "a small village of wooden houses and barracks for the first settlers, to be inhabited by them until more permanent dwellings can be erected...The first detachment of emigrants expected out about September next." [63]

There was already an unlicensed pub but "So scarce is small change, particularly copper money, among the settlers that clay pipes and cigars were offered and accepted by those from the *Acheron* who visited the 'Port Cooper Hotel'." [64]

After this she was in the freezing waters off southern New Zealand to chart Foveaux Strait, between the South Island and the even more southern Stewart Island. Captain Stokes noted that Bluff would be a suitable site for a port – as indeed turned out to be the case.

In these waters Captain Stokes also examined the Oreti River in a whaleboat for almost thirty miles and marked the site of the future city of Invercargill, which was to become the southernmost city in the British Empire.

On Stewart Island the sailors established a base whence they conducted their survey in small boats. They noticed that the earrings worn by the Maoris of Stewart Island were English coins bearing the image of George IV whereas the Maoris in other areas generally wore earrings of shark's tooth or greenstone. Some had even stuck soldiers' brass buttons through the large apertures in their ears.

With the approach of spring the systematic Captain Stokes resumed the survey by charting Massacre Bay near Nelson and then sailing up the west coast of the North Island to survey Taranaki and advise on the laying down of moorings and the construction of a harbour at New Plymouth.

The *Acheron* then did a virtual circumnavigation of the South Island, spending quite a bit of time in Milford and other Sounds on the south-west coast.

In these deep water inlets beneath the high and steep mountains Captain Stokes noted, "As the *Acheron* steamed slowly to her anchorage beneath these cliffs, towering on either hand several thousand feet perpendicularly, her masts seemed to dwindle into nothing, and from her insignificance we were able to more fully comprehend the vast elevation of their snow capped summits." [65] They found no bottom at more than 200 fathoms.

In Duck Cove, Dusky Sound, the cove having been named by Captain Cook for the quantity of bird seen there, the *Acheron* anchored in 11 fathoms at a point one and a half cable's length from a boulder beach with the mountains on either side rising almost vertically to heights of 3,000 feet – not unlike the Norwegian fjords. In this Sound the ship's name is perpetuated by the Acheron Passage, an arm of the sea connecting Dusky and Breaksea Sounds, through which she steamed.

However, it was only with considerable difficulty that astronomical observations on shore could be made by the *Acheron's* officers as they had to take refuge from the sandflies in the thick foliage a short distance from the beaches where the little blighters did not penetrate. This was at Facile Harbour but sandflies were (and still are) common to all west coast sounds.

While the *Acheron* was lying at Preservation Inlet in the Sounds a slight noise was heard one night in the bay and in the morning it was discovered that Bishop Selwyn had come in and anchored his schooner, the *Undine*, between the *Acheron* and the shore.

The Bishop of New Zealand was on a voyage to the Auckland Islands, far to the south of New Zealand. This product of Saint John's College, Cambridge, who had rowed in the Cambridge Eight in 1829 in the first ever Boat Race, went on board the *Acheron* for breakfast. He then rowed back to his own vessel and, being a Sunday, he returned to the *Acheron* in the afternoon "robed in all his canonicals, and conducted public worship on the quarter-deck." [66]

While off the west coast of the South Island the crew of the *Acheron* were able to look out at the high mountain range running down the west side of the island which Cook had named the "Southern Alps". Eyeing the highest peak, Captain Stokes named it Mount Cook. From the ship he assessed its height at 13,200 feet whereas it is, in fact, 12,349 feet. They also named the famous Mitre Peak in Milford Sound because its shape resembles a bishop's mitre.

The reports made by Captain Stokes on such things as harbours and their hinterland were of value not only to mariners but also to those organisations back in Britain that were in the business of promoting emigration to New Zealand. In particular, Stokes' survey of the hitherto virtually unknown area of Southland and his suggestions that it was a suitable place for settlement led to the purchase of the area from the Natives by the Government, Stokes having already got the local Maoris to mark on his map which areas they would wish to retain as reserves.

John Stokes was a keen observer of the fauna and flora of the land whose coast he was exploring and his reports on these were of benefit to those in the fields of botany and science.

In May, 1851, the *Acheron* returned to Sydney where she remained while Captain Stokes and his officers, together with twenty-nine non-commissioned officers and twelve rank and file marines from the ship, took passage to England via Rio de Janeiro on *HMS Havannah*.

The last known survivor of those who took part in the survey by the *Acheron* was Arthur Fullarton, who joined her as a boy seaman for her voyage to New Zealand. He subsequently served on *HMS Rodney* through the Crimean War, being present at the taking of Sebastopol. He retired from the Navy in 1857 and later settled at Port Chalmers, which he had first seen from the deck of the *Acheron* during her survey of Dunedin harbour in 1849. In 1908 he was still regaling his listeners with tales of the *Acheron's* survey.

The comprehensive nautical survey of New Zealand, begun by the *Acheron*, was continued by *HMS Pandora*, a surveying vessel of six guns under the command of Commander (soon to be promoted to Captain) Byron Drury. This officer acquired his interesting Christian name from the fact that his grandfather, Rev. Doctor Joseph "Harry" Drury, the Headmaster of Harrow, had taught the great poet there.

The first survey that the *Pandora* carried out in New Zealand waters was that of Hokianga harbour, in the far north of the North Island, in September, 1851. They took soundings, marked safe channels and compiled tide tables for the benefit of mariners.

In November, 1852, the vessel spent three weeks surveying in and around the harbour of Tauranga, reporting as follows, "Between Mercury Bay and Wellington, Tauranga in the Bay of Plenty is the only safe anchorage in all winds for vessels of burden. There is room for a fleet.

The approach to it is remarkably distinct. The difficulty of entering this harbour in its deepest channel is the somewhat tortuous course and the liability to eddy winds on rounding Mount Mongonui, and the channel at one place is only half a cable wide, but during those winds which would cause the Bay of Plenty to be a lee shore, Tauranga is most accessible." [67] Needless to say, Tauranga is to-day one of New Zealand's largest exporting ports.

Like Captain Stokes, Byron Drury also made informative reports on more general matters. "Te Papa, the residence of Archdeacon Brown, is a thorough, comfortable English establishment, the site well chosen on elevated ground on the south side of the harbour, three miles from Mongonui.

Two miles to the westward of it is the Village of Otumoiti where there is a Roman Catholic establishment and a very neat church, the interior gorgeously decorated by Native wicker work.

Four or five Englishmen reside here, chiefly engaged in building small craft and, I am informed, three Frenchmen live at the mouth of the Wairoa.

The total Native population of the Tauranga district is estimated at 1,000, and large tracts of land are under cultivation." [68]

As a result of the very thorough surveying work Captain Drury produced a much needed chart of the harbour as well as sailing directions for future users of the port. These future users included a veritable fleet of Royal Navy vessels taking troops, weapons and provisions to Tauranga during the Maori War of the 1860s.

During the lengthy survey of the Bay of Plenty the *Pandora's* officers, in Drury's words, "have walked the whole line of country on the coast" [69] but he noted that "at rivers in the Bay of Plenty, where no European was within reach, the Natives' exorbitant demands for crossing a few yards in their canoes were found a great source of annoyance and delay". [70]

The following year the *Pandora* carried out a survey of the Manukau harbour, to the west of Auckland. "I have the greatest satisfaction in informing His Excellency that there is a straight and direct channel of considerable breadth into this harbour, through which *HMS Pandora* passed to-day at near low water in four and a half fathoms. At spring tides, low water, there is not less than three and a half fathoms, at high water not less than five and a half," wrote Drury to the Governor. [71] This became known as the "Pandora Channel" although some wits referred to it as "Drury Lane".

The survey of this, New Zealand's biggest harbour, and all its many inlets was conducted on a large scale (six inches to a mile) and summer weather of "a most unseasonable" [72] nature prolonged the work. According to Drury, "The open boats, in which they (the officers) and the crews lived and slept, were absent from the ship in the channels for a fortnight at a time but no casualty or sickness of any kind occurred." [73]

The Acting Master, Mr. Kerr, sounded the outer waters. Another officer and Mr. Stanley, the Master's Assistant, walked and surveyed the coast line from Kaipara Heads to Manukau while Mr. Oke, the Second Master, and Mr. Ellis investigated the Papakura and Waiuku channels, and two others surveyed the three channels leading to Onehunga.

Like Stokes before him, Captain Drury qualified his recommendations by saying whether or not the waterways were navigable in all weathers and at night.

He also made a recommendation for placing a signal station and flagstaff "on the Apex 350 feet above the sea" [74] and pointed out that any guiding light would need to be revolving or coloured to distinguish it from the fires of the Maoris. He marked the positions for two outer buoys and a smaller buoy for the spit, off the south head.

The Drury Creek, which flows into the Manukau, is named after the man who conducted the survey of the harbour as also is the adjoining south Auckland township of Drury.

In 1854 the *Pandora* traced the Waimea River, French Pass and the Pelorous Sound at the top of the South Island and made "valuable suggestions for the erection of buoys and beacons". [75]

In January, 1855, the ship was in Wellington harbour when a big earthquake struck. In Captain Drury's words, "At eleven minutes past nine o'clock, the gale still blowing strong, we felt suddenly an uncommon and disagreeable grinding, as if the ship was grating over a rough bottom. It continued with severity for more than a minute; the ship slewed broadside to the wind; we were then in six fathoms so there was little doubt but it was an earthquake. Lights were seen running to and fro in all parts of the town and evidences of consternation, combined with a loud crash.

Lieutenant Jones and myself immediately landed. We found the tide alternatively ebbing and flowing. The first scene before us on landing was the Government Offices entirely destroyed, the upper storey lying on the ground, the staircase, the Council Chamber, the papers and documents in heterogeneous confusion…while the doorway of the public house was a confusion of broken bottles…We have to be thankful to God that, amidst the general wreck of property, but one life has been sacrificed and not more than four persons seriously wounded up to the time of our departure….Recurring to our landing after the first shock, Lieutenant Jones and myself went into several houses. The panic was certainly great and many accepted the offer to go on board; the houses we were in swinging to and fro and the ground in a constant tremulous motion…. We returned to the ship at 2 a.m., the tide having at that time receded about four feet lower than at ordinary spring tides….For eight hours subsequent to the first and great shock the tide approached and receded every twenty minutes, rising from eight to ten feet, and receding four feet lower than at spring tide." [76]

He then made an interesting comparison between the people of Britain and the New Zealand colonists. "What a scene would have occurred in the fatherland! With shops exposed and every temptation to plunder, there seemed to be neither fear nor thought of robbery but a generous and manly feeling to lessen each other's burdens pervaded all classes….nor can I forget to mention the ready asylum afforded by the merchant vessels in the harbour to the houseless and more nervous inhabitants." [77]

Between them, the surveying ships *Acheron* and *Pandora* conducted the first systematic survey of New Zealand since Captain Cook's. Their efforts resulted in the publication of 250 charts which meant that New Zealand now had suitable charts for virtually all its 9,824 miles of coast line, much of it deeply indented.

These charts were published in London by the Admiralty and were sold to the public (and foreign navies) for prices ranging between one and two shillings. They were sold by chart sellers at their establishments near the London Docks and by nautical instrument makers further afield.

According to the nautical advisor to the New Zealand Marine Department, speaking in 1945, "The charts now in use are based mainly on the original surveys made by *Acheron* and *Pandora* between the years 1848 and 1855." [78]

Few countries were in greater need of properly charted coasts than New Zealand since, with its mountainous and thickly forested interior, the sea was the only effective means of getting from one isolated coastal settlement to another. That was why the New Zealand Pilot, the work published by the Admiralty as a result of the surveys of *Acheron* and *Pandora*, was of such value to New Zealand's colonists and mariners.

New Guinea

The discovery, charting and opening up of the eastern half of New Guinea and surrounding islands was done largely by the Royal Navy operating out of Sydney. The reasons for wanting to become better acquainted with this least known part of the planet were many and various – the wish of naturalists to identify the flora and fauna of what is the second largest island in the world, the need for vessels passing through Torres Strait at the top of Australia to have safe passage without any trouble from the New Guinea shore, the usual itch of the missionaries to be first and foremost in any new territory, the naïve belief that New Guinea was a last frontier for Australasian settlement and, later on, the expectation that its mountains and rivers contained large and valuable supplies of gold. In the mid nineteenth century the prospect of gold or, even better, its actual discovery, was the greatest colonising force of all and one which could change whole countries and populations over night. For example, the population of Melbourne rose from 80,000 to 420,000 in the gold rush years of 1851-4, thereby establishing the state of Victoria and virtually getting Australia going.

The western half of New Guinea up to the 141st degree of east longitude had belonged to the Dutch since 1828 but, in the words of Captain Moresby R.N., speaking in 1873, they had done "little to civilise the western races of New Guinea". [79]

In 1845 *HMS Fly* (Captain Blackwood), with her tender *Bramble* (Lieutenant Yule), surveyed part of the Gulf of Papua, on the underside of New Guinea, thereby lifting the veil that had hitherto rested over this little known island.

It was during this voyage that they discovered and named New Guinea's longest river, the Fly, after their ship. Its great mouth was "so full and abounding with fresh water as to influence the sea for miles outside". [80]

In 1848 the work of the *Fly* was continued by *HMS Rattlesnake* (Captain Owen Stanley) and its tender, again the *Bramble*. In the Louisiade archipelago, the string of islands off the south-east tip of New Guinea, they resumed the survey that the *Fly* had terminated at Cape Possession on the New Guinea mainland. It was believed that no certain passage existed off this cape but, after a detailed survey, it was found that a channel, forty miles wide from land to seaward, extended to Cape Possession.

They also found a "good and clear passage inside Sud Est Island, at which was found a spacious harbour with good anchorage. To this Captain Stanley gave the name The Coral Haven." [81]

They then surveyed the inner part of the reef and established relations with the natives of the group "both on board and on shore, who were of a superior description, being well-proportioned and of an amicable disposition, bringing off in their canoes (which were of large dimensions, some measuring 55 feet in length) flax, arrowroot, yams in abundance, tortoise shell and all varieties of tropical fruits, which they eagerly sought to barter with". [82] In exchange "tomahawks, red cloth, etc. were offered but the only article they seemed to prize was hoop iron, and that which was rusty pleased them best". [83]

Relations with the natives during the survey were generally good but not always "as hostile intentions were often shown towards the *Bramble* when in shore among the reefs". [84] The result of

Captain Stanley's work was that in 1850 the Admiralty published a series of charts of the largely unknown coast of New Guinea and these charts were still being used in the Second World War.

Nineteen years after the *Rattlesnake's* voyage *HMS Salamander* sailed up to New Guinea to continue the survey of its south coast and offshore islands. They too found the natives to be "a fine race of men – very good humoured but with a bearing of manly independence which indicates that they would not bear to be trifled with". [85]

There was one unnerving experience, however, when some of the *Salamander's* officers went ashore to visit a native village. They went into one of the houses, that "was well-built of close-plaited cane". [86] It was shaped like a beehive and with a doorway so small that access was on hands and knees only. It was so dark inside that one of the officers struck a match and "their horror may be imagined when they perceived before them a dried woman. Yes, a woman dried with her flesh on her, and standing bolt upright before them, propped up by a spear under the chin. It appears she was the wife of the proprietor of the hut and that, being loth to part with her, he had, instead of burying her, resorted to this, to us, strange device of securing the continuance of so valued a companionship." [87]

The most comprehensive survey of New Guinea was carried out by *HMS Basilisk*, an old-fashioned, three-masted paddle steamer of 1,031 tons and 400 hp., that was specially chosen for the task. She carried five 64 pound guns and a ship's company of 178 officers and men. She was under the command of Captain John Moresby, the son of Admiral Fairfax Moresby who had earlier served in the Pacific.

Something of the young captain's energy can be seen from a quote from Wellington's *Evening Post* during a visit by the *Basilisk* to New Zealand. "Captain Moresby intends to take his ship into every bay, harbour and inlet in the three islands in which there is sufficient water to float her and to visit infrequented harbours." [88]

The *Basilisk's* voyage to New Guinea carried the hopes of the people of Australia and New Zealand who, having more or less exhausted their own gold fields, could not get the "gold bug" out of their systems and were always on the lookout for further discoveries in lesser known areas.

To this end an expedition of seventy-five adventurers sailed out of Sydney harbour on 20th January, 1872, on the brig *Maria*. According to the *Australian Exchange*, "The expedition was not a mere trading expedition, bent on visiting the coast of New Guinea and on collecting pearl shell or other produce there, but its members were mainly bent on discovering gold." [89] The only white people in New Guinea at the time were a handful of missionaries from the London Missionary Society and they had reported that there was gold in those mountains!

In 1873 New Zealand's *Grey River Argus* wrote of New Guinea, "towards which the eyes and hopes of thousands in this colony, and throughout Australia, are turned as the new El Dorado in which new fortunes are to be amassed and fallen fortunes retrieved". [90]

However, the *Maria*, a leaky old brig that should never have been allowed to put to sea, never made it to New Guinea as she was wrecked on 26th February on Bramble Reef, about thirty miles from Cardwell in Rockingham Bay, north Queensland. Some of the crew reached Cardwell in boats; others died from exhaustion after landing in remote spots on rafts and a few were murdered by aborigines. However, others "met with kindly treatment from the blacks, which was the means of saving their lives." [91] *HMS Basilisk*, on a cruise to the pearl fishing stations in Torres Strait at the time, "was instrumental in saving some of the crew of the ill-fated *Maria*". [92] Before leaving Cardwell Captain Moresby left one of the *Basilisk's* boat crews there for the purpose of co-operating with the native police in searching for any further survivors.

After returning from this northern cruise the *Basilisk* anchored in Sydney's Darling harbour where she was caulked throughout and given some new spars. Then, on 8th December, 1872, she sailed out of Sydney harbour for a six month voyage to complete the exploration and charting of the waters and coast of New Guinea, that had been started by the *Fly* and the *Rattlesnake*.

After calling at Brisbane, Bowen, Cardwell, Fitzroy Island and Cape Grafton the *Basilisk* proceeded north to Somerset at Cape York where she stayed for six days. She next visited Brothers Island and then Lewis Island, where she touched on a sand bank, and the islands of Dungeness, Coconut, Dalrymple, Darnley and Bramble Cay. Like all the best Navy surveyors, Captain Moresby had an inquisitive mind and he liked to check out as much as possible. It should be pointed out that, although these islands can be reduced to a sentence or two, we are talking about very great distances. For example, the distance from Sydney to Torres Strait (1,700 miles) is equivalent to that from England to West Africa.

Near Bramble Cay Island "a somewhat exciting scene broke the monotony of the voyage and gave Jack what he always enjoys, a bit of fun" [93] when a giant turtle, weighing 480 pounds, came into close proximity with one of the *Basilisk's* paddle wheels and was hit hard. Limping away, she was pursued by officers and men in boats and, when captured, was the biggest that any of them had ever seen. Its black and white striped shell was surprisingly soft and could be pierced with a pen knife. The soup on board that night "would have made a London aldermanic gourmand's mouth water". [94] At Murray Island, at the top of the Great Barrier Reef, "the natives came on board in great numbers and proved very friendly". [95]

The *Basilisk* left Murray Island on 11th February for the still relatively unknown land of New Guinea. In the very month that she had left Sydney the *Sydney Morning Herald* reported that eighteen people (mainly Europeans), while fishing for pearl in New Guinea waters, had been murdered and eaten by the natives [96] while New Zealand's *Otago Witness* wrote of the New Guinea natives in the same year "Nearly all the accounts agree in describing them as fierce and cruel". [97] Happily the cruise of the *Basilisk* was to prove otherwise.

In what is now known as the Gulf of Papua the *Basilisk* surveyed and charted the coast for a hundred and forty miles between Yule Island (named after Lieutenant Yule of *HMS Bramble*) and Hood Point. When she was about twenty-five miles ENE of Yule Island she found herself off a vast extent of driftwood and uprooted trees of great size. In the pre-dawn light they believed it was a reef, which caused considerable anxiety. They thought that the trees might indicate a great river into the interior but this was not so. They did find the river that was the source of the floating logs but its current was too swift for the ship's boat to ascend very far.

Apart from some bold headlands they found that the mainland was one vast expanse of flat, swampy ground that extended six or eight miles inland to a low range of hills, backed up by a mountain range rising to peaks of 12,000 feet and more.

On this swampy, mangrove fringed, malarial coast the air was thick with mosquitoes "which seemed to like the flavour of Anglo Saxon blood". [98] There were also flying foxes and the brightly coloured birds for which New Guinea would become famous. "At night what we suffered from the mosquitoes can only be described by reference to an unmentionable place," said Captain Moresby. [99]

These painful nights were relieved by humorous "Evening Readings" by Lieutenant Hayter and others, who satirised various events and encounters of the voyage

"The whole of the natives on this line of coast were found to be....of a most friendly and hospitable disposition," wrote the *Rockhampton Bulletin* after the *Basilisk's* return. [100]

At Redscar Bay they made contact with the mission station and, finding the people there to be very sick, Captain Moresby took them on board for medical treatment and later took them to Cape York.

At Redscar Bay Moresby left the *Basilisk* in the charge of Lieutenant Hayter, while he set out with Lieutenant Mourilyan in the ship's galley and cutter to explore the coast that ran down to the east. By the first night they had reached Daugo (Fisherman's) Island where they dined on a meal of Torres Strait pigeons that were there in great numbers.

The next morning they rose early to find out more about the area. While Mourilyan went off in the cutter to explore the big bay that they could see in the distance but which seemed to be obstructed by a reef, which spread across its entrance, Moresby went further down the coast to Pyramid Point and, with a young sailor called Head, climbed to the summit of its hill. From here, at an elevation of 600 feet, they could see through the clear sea a dark blue stretch of water that indicated a deep and safe passage through which big ships like the *Basilisk* would be able to pass to get into the extensive bay.

That night Moresby and his men slept in the boat on shore, having established friendly contact with the natives. The next day they met up with an excited Lieutenant Mourilyan who reported that, at the head of the bay that he had explored, was another harbour – "a harbour within a harbour" – that was calm and sheltered and would accommodate the biggest ships. This, coupled with Moresby's sighting of a channel through the reef, suggested a discovery of particular importance. They took the small boats through the channel, depth sounding as they went, and it proved every bit as good as it had looked from the top of Pyramid Point.

The next morning the galley and the cutter went back up the coast to find the *Basilisk*, which was coming down to look for them, Lieutenant Hayter having become slightly alarmed at their longer than expected absence. They met midway, off the village of Lea Lea, in a bay that, because of the abundance of shoals, Moresby named Caution Bay. From here the surveying ship was taken down the coast, through the opening in the reef, which Moresby named Basilisk Passage, and into the double harbour.

In Captain Moresby's words, "From the foretop, whence every reef could be seen, I conned her through the passage into the still waters of Port Moresby to Jane Island, and past it into the landlocked, many bayed Fairfax Harbour, where we anchored in five fathoms of water." [101] Captain Moresby named both Port Moresby (the outer harbour) and Fairfax Harbour (the inner) after his father, Admiral of the Fleet Sir Fairfax Moresby. This choice of harbour was a good one and it has ever since been the chief port and administrative centre of the eastern half of New Guinea. Lieutenant Mourilyan left his name not in New Guinea but in north Queeensland where the port of Mourilyan was named after him.

"We must have been a surprising sight to the natives," wrote Captain Moresby, "for they flocked on board in hundreds, eager and curious, chattering like monkeys, as they pointed out to each other the marvels that took their fancy." [102]

Around this sheltered harbour the land was not flat and swampy but hilly and well timbered, with fertile valleys between the hills and, not surprisingly, there was a greater number of native villages, "the houses built in Malay fashion on poles, some standing far out on the shore reefs in quiet waters, others clustering among plantations on the hill sides". [103]

The *Basilisk* stayed in these sheltered waters for several days whilst her boats surveyed and examined the surrounding coast, which they found superior to that of Redscar Bay some forty miles away. When the boats went along the coast on an exploration/surveying expedition the natives would run along the shore line to keep pace with them and they delighted in trying to outrun them.

The men of the *Basilisk* found that they were able to move about amongst the natives "with perfect confidence and mutual good feeling on both sides". [104] An added bonus for the crew was the presence of wallabies which made for good shooting. These were the only wild animals they saw although there were some domesticated pigs and dogs.

The *Basilisk* returned to Somerset, Cape York, on 6th March to replenish her coal stocks and provisions. Two weeks later she made a second cruise to New Guinea, this time to explore the south-eastern tip of the island, "a locality never before visited by civilised man". [105]

This tip of the island was believed to end in a wedge but the *Basilisk's* survey showed that this was not the case. They discovered that the south-east cape was in the shape of a fork with an extensive bay, 30 miles long and 10 to 15 miles broad, separating the two prongs of the fork. This they named Sir Alexander Milne Bay after the First Sea Lord at the Admiralty. It later became known as Milne Bay, the scene of some bloody fighting in the Second World War.

The north-eastern fork they named East Cape but, being short of fuel, the ship could not sail around it; instead the ship's boats put to sea to examine the coast line.

At Hayter Island, named after Lieutenant Francis Hayter, the 1st Lieutenant of the *Basilisk*, Captain Moresby did what every captain yearned to do at some point – he raised the British flag and, in the presence of the ship's company, read a proclamation declaring that he "took possession of this and the adjacent islands in the name of Her Most Gracious Majesty the Queen, and by right of discovery". Three volleys were fired, followed by three cheers from the sailors. Unfortunately the British government rejected it.

Here the natives were still friendly and they willingly supplied large quantities of yams, bananas, sugar cane, paw paws and other tropical produce for small pieces of iron hoop. So brisk was the business in the metal that the men of the *Basilisk* even named one place Iron Hoop Bay. Another place was named Yam Bay for the profusion of yams while two of the bigger islands were named Moresby Island and Basilisk Island. Like Captain Cook, John Moresby liked to give names to geographical features but, unlike Cook, he named the best ones for his own family.

Although the natives were eager to barter they were surprised and somewhat in awe at the sight of a mirror. Nor could they be induced to go near a sheep that was on board the *Basilisk*.

At the end of the two cruises Captain Moresby was able to say, "The natives appeared a very harmless, inoffensive race. Only one was seen armed....They seemed almost destitute of weapons, a few wooden spears and stone clubs comprising all. We roamed over their country and visited their villages as freely as if they were English people. If any of our fellows got lost in the bush, the natives took them to their villages, fed them, and offered every hospitality before bringing them back to the ship....

Taking them altogether, they are as genial and pleasant a race of savages as could well be met. At the same time I have no doubt they do a little cannibalism among themselves. They took pains to make us understand as an event they were proud of, that they had eaten the former owners of the skulls hung up in their villages and of the human bones and ornaments they wear, but the skulls were so few and ancient that I am inclined to think it is only on very rare occasions….At one island, before they opened a friendly intercourse, they brought a dog on board and knocked out its brains on the quarter deck, looking upon the rite as a ratification of friendship, at least we so understood it…..

Wandering through their peaceful, luxuriantly planted villages it often made me sad to think that our discoveries must inevitably, sooner or later, bring white men among these contented creatures, with sin, disease and misery in their train". [106]

It was near the south-east tip of New Guinea, between Basilisk Island and the mainland, that Captain Moresby discovered a strait which, believing that it would provide an eventual route between Australia and China, he named the China Strait.

The *Basilisk* arrived back at Cape York on 15th May, 1873 – before the worst of the rainy season – having spent about three months in New Guinea waters and adding considerably to outside knowledge of the place.

Back in Sydney captain and crew were able to show examples of native pottery, cloth made from flax fibre, wooden swords and paddles, head dress feathers, stone axes, and beautiful birds "both alive and prepared as ornithological specimens" [107] but the greatest attention was focused on the ship's blacksmith who was showing pieces of quartz, impregnated with gold, each about twenty-four ounces in weight, which he claimed to have found at a spot a few miles south-east of Port Moresby.

It was a Sunday afternoon not long after the *Basilisk* had left Fairfax harbour and a large number of men were permitted to go ashore. The blacksmith became separated from his friends and, being by himself and about half a mile from shore, he came upon some very peculiar rocks jutting out of the ground. Believing that they must be quartz, he detached a piece from a large rock and, upon examining it, saw specks of what he believed was gold. The detached part of the rock was broken into three parts, which he took back to Australia but he did not tell anybody of his find until the *Basilisk* reached Brisbane.

94

Such was his story – the type of tale that one would hear a hundred times a day on a gold field but such was the electric nature of the word "gold" that within a very short time the Premier of Queensland was being interrogated in Parliament as to the veracity of the blacksmith's story.

In the words of New Zealand's *Grey River Argus*, writing of the prospects of New Guinea, "It only requires the authentic confirmation of the rumoured intelligence that gold has been found in sufficient quantities to pay for working, to draw thither an influx of population, the like of which has seldom taken place, even in the history of new gold countries." [108]

Apart from gold there was widespread interest in the discoveries that the *Basilisk* had made and on 20th September, 1873, Captain Moresby gave a one and a half hour lecture "entirely without notes" [109] at the New Zealand Institute in Wellington, which was also read at a meeting of the Royal Geographical Society in London a couple of months later.

The lecture was laced with "humorous illustrations and droll anecdotes" [110] so that "the lecturer was frequently interrupted by roars of laughter and irrepressible outbursts of applause". [111] Captain Moresby also presented a cassowary to the Wellington Botanical Gardens. [112]

In 1874 the *Basilisk* made a further cruise to New Guinea to continue where she had left off in the waters near the south-east tip of the great island. Here Captain Moresby fixed the position and surveyed the coast line of the islands of the D'Entrecasteaux group, naming the three biggest ones Normanby, Fergusson and Goodenough – the first two after Governors of New Zealand and the last after the murdered and much lamented Commodore Goodenough.

They then came across a passage, north of the Engineer group of islands, that was "a fine, clear one, of three to four miles in width, perfectly clear of all dangers….it is fit for any sailing ships, the original China Straits being quite put out in the cold". [113] This new passage shortened the route from Australia to China by two days although later mariners preferred the Jomard Entrance further east. Others avoided New Guinea altogether, choosing to sail on a semi-circular route, which curved out north-eastwards from Sydney to San Christobal in the Solomons and thence north-west through the vast Caroline group to China and Japan.

The *Basilisk's* next stop was Possession Bay on the north coast where they found the natives to be great thieves. According to one of the ship's officers, "The natives about Possession Bay are on no account to be trusted; they are so different to the natives of Port Moresby." [114]

At the end of this cruise the same scribe wrote, "The little steam pinnace has done wonders since our arrival in New Guinea; it has steamed close on 1,200 miles of soundings. We have done more in six weeks than we could have done in six months had we been without the pinnace, as the schooner was perfectly useless to us on account of the light winds and variable ones". [115]

In 1875 *HMS Basilisk* returned to England after nearly four years of exploration, surveying and charting in the waters of northern Australia and New Guinea. She had achieved what she set out to do by surveying about 1,200 miles of coast line, adding twelve first class harbours, several navigable rivers and more than a hundred islands large and small to the chart, and finding a new route between Australia and China, which shortened the journey by about three hundred miles, while the extremely good relations with the natives and the generally good health of the crew in a tropical, mosquito ridden climate were almost without parallel in the history of South Pacific exploration.

Pearl Harbour

As we have seen, the first survey of Pearl Harbour was done by Vancouver's surveyor, Joseph Whidbey, when they visited Hawaii in 1793 on *HMS Discovery*.

A much more comprehensive survey of this famous anchorage was done in January, 1857, by *HMS Havannah*, which had already carried out a similar survey of the port of Honolulu at the request of the government of the kingdom of Hawaii, which was still independent.

In the words of Captain T. Harvey, the commander of the *Havannah*, "Went with the Master to examine Pearl River or Lagoon. One entire day was spent sounding on the bar without obtaining any satisfactory result. The channel in has only twelve feet water, is intricate, and requires a skilful pilot to take the smallest vessels through it. The harbour is very extensive, with sufficient water for any ship, six or seven fathoms being found alongside small cliffs not more than from ten to twelve feet above the level of the sea, the land behind them being flat.

Fresh water might be conducted from a stream in the neighbourhood, at a trifling expense, to a point where tanks or boats could fill alongside. Well water is brackish: used by the natives with impunity though invariably disagreeing with strangers. The surrounding country is capable of affording supplies in any quantity. It being considered practicable to open a deep channel into this magnificent sheet of water, the extensive and rapidly increasing traffic of Upper California with Australia, India, China, etc., the consequent rising importance of these islands and the inestimable value of such a port, if made available, is my reason for noticing it here." [116] Besides being able to command a ship Captain Harvey was obviously a man who was also blessed with the gifts of judgement and foresight.

Pearl Harbour did develop to its true potential and, after Hawaii became a colony of the United States, the anchorage that Captain Harvey surveyed became the main base for the U.S. Pacific Fleet, thus luring the Japanese bombers on that terrible Sunday morning in 1941. This brought the United States into the Second World War, thereby ensuring ultimate victory for Britain. Thus did Pearl Harbour in the fullness of time serve the interests of the Royal Navy, Britain and the Empire. In surveying this "lagoon" and recognising its potential, Captain Harvey was building better than he could ever have imagined.

Later Surveying

Even after the main harbours, rivers and coastlines had been surveyed there was still plenty of hydrographic work for the Navy. The end of the nineteenth century brought new challenges such as cable laying and submarines, both of which required surveying of great depths that had hitherto remained unknown. In October, 1888, when the survey ship *HMS Egeria* was operating off Tonga, she made one of the deepest soundings that had ever been made. A few miles off Pylstart Island, the southernmost of the Tonga group, her commander, Captain Aldrich, obtained a sounding of 4,228 fathoms.

The old instruments and equipment used by Cook and Vancouver were vastly improved upon and those two captains would have been envious of Admiral Vesey Hamilton, commander-in-chief of the China Squadron in 1887, when he led thirteen ships to Goshkevitch Bay, near Vladivostok.

The waters of this bay had not been surveyed and so the Admiral, in the words of the chaplain on one of the ships, *HMS Calliope*, "formed the fleet in column line abreast with light draught ships leading, and steamboats with leads .... and in this fashion the fleet entered the bay and took up an anchorage, which proved a remarkably good one. Afterwards a survey of the place was started by the navigators and in future the entry will be made without difficulty." [117]

It might be thought that the work of taking measurements and soundings in small, exposed boats, day after day and starting at the crack of dawn, would become tedious and monotonous, not to mention the difficulty of landing on rocky shores to fix the distance of bays and other features but that would depend on the imagination and open-mindedness of each sailor. While rounding a rocky point into yet another pristine and uninhabited bay might be boring to one mind, it would be both exciting and uplifting to another. The camaraderie of a survey ship and the common aim of completing a much needed survey to the highest degree of accuracy would be sources of both solidarity and pride to all those involved – from the captain to the ordinary oarsman, the latter's biceps positively bulging by the end of the mission from all the rowing.

As Captain Moresby wrote during his survey in New Guinea waters, "I would I had the power to tell you of the glorious panorama which greeted us from the top of Glenton Island, the summit of which we had cleared with immense labour from its giant forest trees, that the tiny theodolite might sweep an horizon never before gazed on by our race.

Six hundred feet below us, almost as the plumb drops, the light waves curled on a snowy coral beach. To the west the wooded peaks of Moresby Island closed the view but on every other side island after island floated on the bosom of an intense blue sea, some volcanic, lofty and rugged, others coralline, low, white and covered with graceful trees, with every variety of form and tint, of light and shadow, in the nearest ones whilst those beyond faded out as they distanced into dim shapes, faint clouds – very dreams of islands – giving one a sense of the profusion of creative power that was almost overwhelming". [118]

THE SEARCH FOR SPARS

When Captain Cook sailed from the Sandwich Islands (Hawaii) to Nootka Sound, Vancouver Island, in 1778 he found that the foremast head of the *Resolution* was damaged and so the mast would have to be taken down and repaired ashore.

While the carpenters were working on it there was a terrible storm which damaged the mizzen mast and so that was taken down as well. It was found to be so rotten that the head came off while it was being landed. A new mast was required and the midshipmen cut it from the forest of Vancouver Island and dragged it down to the beach where the carpenters had set up their "shop". This was probably the first mast from the Pacific littoral to grace one of His Majesty's naval vessels. It would not be the last.

The French blockade of Continental ports during the Napoleonic Wars interrupted the traditional supply of spars to the royal dockyards from the Baltic countries. The gap was filled largely by the colonists in Canada who, not for the last time, showed the hand of friendship to Britain in her hour of need. Some logs were taken from New Brunswick and others were floated down the Saint Lawrence from Ontario for onward shipment to Britain. "Canadian timber undoubtedly pulled the Navy through the crisis of the Napoleonic wars," wrote Robert Albion in his book, *Forests and Sea Power.* [1]

However, the quality of the Canadian timber was not as good as the Baltic product that it was replacing and so the perfectionists who were building the sailing vessels in the dockyards cast their eyes further afield.

After the loss of their markets as a result of Napoleon's blockade the big Baltic timber dealers never really recovered and, although some Baltic timber was imported after peace was restored, the area was no longer able to supply the Navy to the extent that it had in the past.

Just as the loss of the American colonies forced the British government to look to Australia to house its convicts so too was its attention drawn to New Zealand to supply spars of kauri, which could be used to fill the convict vessels on their return journey to Britain from the Antipodes.

Captain Cook had been impressed by New Zealand's kauri trees when he saw them up a river that he named the Thames "on account of its bearing some resemblance to that river in England". [2]

The Firth of Thames, where the river flows into the sea, was very shallow and so he refused to take the *Endeavour* any further, opting instead for a trip up the river in the pinnace and long boat. These set off at the crack of dawn on a warm November day in 1769 with Cook and the *Endeavour's* botanists, Joseph Banks and Doctor Solander, being rowed "to see a little of the interior parts of the country and its produce..... After landing we had not gone a hundred yards into the woods before we found a tree that girted 19 feet, 8 inches, six feet above the ground and, having a quadrant with me, I found its length from the root to the first branch to be 89 feet; it was as straight as an arrow and taper'd but very little in proportion to its length, so that I judged that there was 356 solid feet of timber in this tree clear of the branches. We saw many others of the same sort, several of which were taller than the one we measured and all of them very stout." [3]

Aware of Cook's observation, the Navy became interested in New Zealand as a source of supply for its spars. The first known spar from New Zealand to be used on a warship was a kauri one that was collected in December, 1818, at the Bay of Islands by the whale vessel *Catherine* (Captain Graham); it was taken to England where it was used for a fore-topgallant mast for *HMS Dromedary*. It proved to be first rate and was on the *Dromedary* when she visited New Zealand two years later.

The kauri tree was known as "the monarch of the New Zealand forest" and some of the larger trees were up to 1,500 years old. It is one of the strongest and most durable of softwoods and has a large, clean trunk that is almost as smooth, long and straight as Nelson's Column in Trafalgar Square.

The Navy's requirements for their topmasts were that they should be between 74 and 84 feet in length and 21 to 23 inches in diameter and perfectly straight. In London such a mast could fetch the princely sum of £200. For facility in handling the trees needed to be near a harbour, shore line or navigable river, from which they could be floated out to the vessel collecting them.

The earliest naval vessels to become convict/kauri ships (convicts out, spars back) were *HMS Dromedary* and *HMS Coromandel*, both of which visited New Zealand in 1820.

The *Dromedary* took on two hundred convicts at Sheerness and a further hundred and sixty-nine at Spithead. The *Coromandel* carried another three hundred prisoners as well as sixty soldiers as guards and a ship's company of ninety. Plus nine wives of the soldiers and six of their children. The *Coromandel's* convicts were from the prison hulks, *Leviathan* and *Laurel*. The *Leviathan* had formerly been a 74 gun man-of-war that had fought in the line at Trafalgar.

The *Coromandel's* prisoners were divided into three sections – fore, main and aft – and, in clear weather and a smooth sea, two of the sections would be allowed to exercise on deck together. They were also allowed to wash their clothes on deck- one group in the morning, the others in the afternoon.

When one of the convicts, John Brooks, was insolent and uttered mutinous expressions to the *Coromandel's* officers, he was given twenty-four lashes of the "cat". If the purpose of punishment is to redeem the criminal, those lashes were a waste of time as not long afterwards he was sentenced to more lashes for the same offence and for cutting his irons.

After unloading her convicts in Australia the *Dromedary* sailed across the Tasman Sea to New Zealand for the next stage of her mission, having taken on some bullocks at Sydney, which would be used to drag the felled logs down to the ship. In May, 1820, at the Bay of Islands, at the top of New Zealand's North Island, the *Dromedary* met up with the *Coromandel*.

While the former loaded her spars at Wangaroa the *Coromandel* sailed to a harbour on the western side of a peninsula, to which harbour she gave her name. Later this whole area became known as the Coromandel Peninsula. In this harbour three "wooding parties" were landed by the vessel's launch, yawl and jolly boat, together with their tents, axes, etc. At sunset these small boats were hauled up on to the *Coromandel* and were lowered again the next morning. Other parties would catch fish for the wooding parties and take water casks ashore to refill them from the stream. In this still savage land these parties were protected ashore by armed guards.

After being felled, the logs were towed to a bay (named "Timber Bay") on an island in Coromandel harbour so that the carpenters could square them for shipment back to Britain. The work was both hard and slow, and it took almost a year (from 23 June, 1820, to 15 May, 1821) for the *Coromandel* to load a hundred and five spars. Altogether it took the two ships a combined total of twenty-two months to load two hundred and twenty-five spars, exclusive of the voyage time between England and the Antipodes.

Shortly after the *Coromandel* reached Portsmouth at the end of 1821 the spars were unloaded and a party of prisoners assisted

101

with clearing out the shingle ballast, thereby underlining the close connection of convicts and kauri – a relationship that continued when the *Coromandel* was put out to grass as a convict hulk herself at Bermuda.

As a result of all the time spent by the wooding parties to collect so few spars the Admiralty switched to buying its kauri from the small number of European timber dealers who had set themselves up on the New Zealand coast. From 1827 they had a series of contracts with Captain Ranulph Dacre, who sourced them from around his timber station on the Hokianga harbour in northern New Zealand. This was ideal as the timber grew close to the banks of the river, which was wide enough for the logs to be floated down to the waiting vessel to take them to England.

An important enthusiast for New Zealand kauri for the Naval Dockyards was Rear-Admiral Sir William Symonds, who was Surveyor of the Navy from 1832 to 1847. He declared that New Zealand kauri provided the longest spars and he promoted them accordingly. His son, Captain William Symonds R.N., was commissioned by New Zealand's first Governor, Captain William Hobson, to negotiate the acquisition of Auckland and the family's name is remembered in Symonds Street, one of Auckland's main thoroughfares.

When *HMS Vernon* (50 guns, 2,028 tons) was launched from the Woolwich stocks in 1832 she was regarded as the finest frigate ever built. Like all the best ships, she was made of English oak but her topmasts were of New Zealand kauri and lasted fourteen years – a long time for masts exposed to salt and wind. In the words of Captain (later Admiral) Sir Francis Collier, "New Zealand spars for large ships are excellent; I never saw such topmasts and jib boom stand like *Vernon's*." [4]

The year after the *Vernon* was launched the Navy sent *HMS Buffalo* (589 tons) to the Antipodes to collect more spars. The *Buffalo*, made of teak, had been built at Calcutta in 1812 and was acquired by the Navy soon afterwards; the Admiralty always liked to get teak ships where possible. She was given the name Buffalo in memory of the successful raid on Buffalo, New York in the War of 1812-14 when, in retaliation for an American raid on a Canadian settlement, the British sacked and burned the town of Buffalo.

With a gun deck 120 feet in length she was originally a store ship and her gunnery included 6 eighteen pound carronades, known in the Navy as "smashers", that had been made at Carron, near Falkirk, Scotland – hence the guns' name.

For her voyage to the South Seas the *Buffalo* was designated a "Timber Ship on Particular Service", her "particular service" being of a dual nature for, on the outvoyage from Portsmouth, she carried a shipload of female convicts to New South Wales. This suited the Admiralty as the Home Office was paying for the voyage out and the *Buffalo* would more than pay for her journey home with the spars for the Naval Dockyards.

Arriving in Sydney in October, 1833, she unloaded the naughty women, and her skipper, Captain Sadler, engaged a civilian who had had experience of trading on the New Zealand coast, Captain J.R. Kent, as "trading master and interpreter".

Sailing from Sydney in November, 1833, their intention was to find the desired spars at Hokianga but, upon reaching there, they found that the draught of the *Buffalo* would not allow her to cross the bar of the harbour and so she sailed around the top of the North Island to the east coast, calling at Wangaroa and Mahurangi. The former was described as "a favourite place for Admiralty spars". [5]

It took her six months to get what she wanted and the spars were acquired mainly from timber stations on the coast that were run by Europeans. When spars were bought from the Maoris, payment for the wood and their labour was in the form of axes and other European goods that they wanted.

One Maori chief who got his people to cut the trees and float them out through the creeks to the *Buffalo* was Titore, who afforded Captain Sadler every assistance and who gave the captain a letter to give to King William IV. The letter asked the King to examine the spars to see how good they were. "Should you and the French quarrel," stated the letter, "here are some trees for your battleships.....a native canoe is my vessel. The native canoes upset when they are filled with potatoes and other goods for your people." [6] Accompanying the letter was a greenstone *mere* (a war club) and, as a return gift, the King sent Titore a suit of shining armour.

In addition to collecting spars the *Buffalo* also surveyed the Hauraki Gulf, north of what would later become the city of Auckland.

She sailed from Wangaroa harbour, New Zealand, on 26th June, 1834, and reached Portsmouth in November. It took a month to unload her timber.

Two years later the *Buffalo* made a second trip to New Zealand which, like her first voyage, was a multi-tasked one.

With a complement of ninety-three officers and men she took the Governor and founding settlers out to South Australia, arriving off Glenelg on 28th December, 1836. There she disembarked the first Governor of the colony, Captain Hindmarsh R.N., about two hundred settlers, two horses, two mules and a cow.

She stayed off Glenelg for about six months while her sailors built Hindmarsh a house, which was made of mud pushed between laths and supported by uprights of native wood, plus a thatched roof. While it was being built Hindmarsh's "Government House" was on board the *Buffalo*.

When the house was finished the *Buffalo*, under the command of James Wood, described as "a sea dog of the old school", [7] sailed on to New Zealand, arriving at the Bay of Islands on 19th September, 1837. She spent seven months in New Zealand waters as it took that long to find, cut and load the spars. She obtained some of her cargo from the Whangaruru harbour, south of the Bay of Islands, but most of it from Tutukaka, a good kauri district, where she landed a forest party who toiled ashore for several months to cut the trees and prepare them for loading by means of floating and a barge. These she unloaded at Chatham after arriving there via Cape Horn on 28th November, 1838.

Towards the end of the following year the *Buffalo* made her third and last voyage to New Zealand in search of those precious kauri spars. Her commander was again James Wood. This was also a voyage with more than one purpose.

She embarked troops at Chatham and took them to Quebec. The *Buffalo* was anchored in the Saint Lawrence River on 27th September, 1839, when the steamer *British America* came alongside and unloaded fifty-eight convicts from Montreal for transportation to that great prison in the south. At half past four the same afternoon another steamer, the *Saint George*, came alongside with a further eighty-three prisoners from Upper Canada (Ontario). These were mostly political prisoners who had taken part in a rebellion in 1837. Thus loaded the *Buffalo* sailed the next day and reached Hobart on 13th February, 1840. There she unloaded the Ontario prisoners before sailing on to Sydney where she got rid of the Quebec lot.

One can imagine the sighs of relief of captain, officers and crew at the completion of this unpleasant task and within hours of the last convict stepping off the vessel into the arms of the law on

Sydney harbour "the carpenters (were) employed knocking down the lower deck prison and returning it to the Commissariat Department". [8]

At Sydney the ship took on more people - Major Bunbury and a detachment of the 80th Regiment as well as Mrs. Hobson and her children, four servants and five horses. Mrs. Hobson and her entourage were on their way to join New Zealand's first Governor in his new and rather raw colony.

Unlike on her previous voyages to New Zealand the *Buffalo* was now in British waters since New Zealand had become part of Queen Victoria's dominions a few months earlier. Upon her arrival at the Bay of Islands she fired a sixteen gun salute for Governor Hobson.

This time she proceeded down the east coast of the North Island and anchored off Cook's Beach in Mercury Bay in her latest quest for spars. An initial party was landed to prepare tents and tools for the shore party whose task was to cut down the trees. The shore party landed on 20th May but the weather was wet and stormy. On the two earlier voyages they had arrived in New Zealand waters at the beginning of summer and had cut the wood in mostly fine weather but this was the beginning of winter.

On 28th July a terrible storm came up from the east and in the early afternoon a heavy gust parted one of the *Buffalo's* anchors and damaged the other. The storm lasted three days and blew the storeship across the bay where she was wrecked on the beach. Those on board did everything they could to save her, lowering yards and topmasts and letting go of the anchors, but to no avail.

Two of the crew were drowned – a seaman named Charles Moore and a boy, John Cornes. Those who had been on shore set off in an open boat in aid of their shipmates but they met turbulent seas and had to shelter in a creek.

For the next few weeks the officers and crew had to camp on the sand near their beached ship. This is now known as Buffalo Beach, Whitianga.

The old girl was resting in only a few feet of water and could be reached at low tide. They managed to get off some of the provisions, which they ate during the seven weeks that they were camped there. Some of the cannon were brought ashore, one of which stands to-day in the Returned Servicemen's Association Memorial Park at Whitianga.

105

Their plight became known through the means of a passing ship and Governor Hobson sent down the revenue cutter, *Ranger*, with supplies. New Zealand was not yet six months old and yet it already had a revenue cutter – a grim omen of things to come in what would later become one of the most highly taxed nations on earth.

The crew were taken up to the Bay of Islands on the Nova Scotian built trading vessel, *Bolina*, which was hired to take the men back to England. Some of the planking was taken from the wreck of the *Buffalo* to put an extra deck on the *Bolina* and to build racks over her quarter deck for the cutters. They also salvaged some of the spars and gear.

At the Bay of Islands Captain Hobson, in the seventh month of his governorship of the new colony and with his usual far-sightedness, interviewed them and offered discharges from the Navy for those who might like to stay and help him build a British New Zealand.

One who took up the offer was John Kennedy, who settled at a place not far from where the *Buffalo* sank. It became known as Kennedy's Bay, an important source of kauri on the Coromandel peninsula whither ships would come and load the logs for distant markets.

Another was Henry Tucker, known by his messmates as "Honest Ben Tucker". He had been the purser on the *Buffalo* and became the Colonial Storekeeper of New Zealand.

Yet another who remained in New Zealand was the *Buffalo's* boatswain, Thomas Duder, who later commanded the pilot boat cum revenue cutter in Auckland harbour, that boat being one of the longboats from the *Buffalo*, which was raised and decked for the purpose.

This was not the only part of the *Buffalo* to be put to good use; some of the timber from the old ship was taken to South Australia to make the Mayoral Chair for the city of Glenelg, in whose founding the ship had played its part on Day One of South Australia.

The *Buffalo's* captain, James Wood, faced a court of inquiry for the loss of his ship but it was soon found that his navigation and seamanship during that terrible storm were of a high order and he was not only exonerated but also given command of a bigger ship, HM Storeship *Tortoise* (963 tons), for yet another trip to New Zealand to load the spars that the *Buffalo* had failed to collect. This old East Indiaman had been purchased by the Admiralty way back in 1806 and had more carrying capacity than the *Buffalo*.

She too took convicts to Hobart on the outward voyage and these required a guard of 105 men in addition to her normal complement of eighty sailors, quite a few of them ex-crew of the *Buffalo* – those who had not taken up Hobson's offer to swap naval service for a settler's life in New Zealand. The convicts this time were males and some three hundred and ninety-four of them walked on board in their clanking chains at Plymouth. The *Tortoise* also carried a passenger, Mr. Thomas Lasslett, a "purveyor of timber" who would advise on what was wanted for the Dockyards.

The cutting of spars was selective. Mr. Lasslett would choose a tree which seemed to suit the purpose and it would then be felled – rather like the Hawaiian chiefs who would go into the forest and select the right *wiliwili* tree, whose soft balsa like wood was considered the best for making both the hulls of their canoes and the long *olo* boards on which they would surf the waves.

Having made the selection, the Hawaiians would cut it down with a stone adze and then dig a hole in its roots where they would leave a red *kumu* fish as an offering to the gods in return for yielding up the tree – a custom that Mr. Lasslett and the men on the *Tortoise* did not follow.

The *Tortoise* went looking for kauri on the east coast of the North Island, sailing past the wreck of the *Buffalo* in Mercury Bay and down to a place called Timber Station, near the Tairua River, where she arranged with European timber merchants for the supply of the spars.

Here she lost one of her Able Seamen, William Samson, who drowned when the jolly-boat capsized in the big surf. A native of Devonport, England, he had enlisted as a volunteer when the *Tortoise* was in Hobart unloading the convicts and so his naval career was both short and tragic.

Not entirely comfortable on the exposed east coast of the Coromandel Peninsula, where he had so recently lost the *Buffalo*, James Wood sailed the *Tortoise* up to Nagle Harbour on Great Barrier Island, a small but secure anchorage inside the bay known as Port Abercrombie. While there the ship's cutter was sent across to another bay but it sank in a squall, drowning yet another sailor, Thomas Harrison, a boy, second class. The survivors returned to the *Tortoise* in a canoe and the cutter was later raised.

After taking on more kauri at Slipper Island the *Tortoise* was fully laden and she left New Zealand on 19th June, 1843, arriving at Spithead by way of Cape Horn in October. Also on board were the widow, Mrs. Hobson, and her children; poor Captain Hobson had died of his labours in September, 1842, at the age of forty-nine.

In its search for spars in the Pacific the Navy's problem was not in the finding of them, since extensive forests existed in New Zealand, British Columbia and Oregon, but in shipping such a bulky product over such a long distance to the Royal Dockyards in England and landing it there at a price that could compete with logs produced more efficiently closer to home.

New Zealand was fortunate in that the Navy needed a cargo to fill its ships on a return trip after dropping off a load of convicts in Australia – and the sailors definitely preferred having their ship filled with logs rather than lags. British Columbia, although equally endowed with good timber, was not so fortunate as in the mid nineteenth century very few vessels capable of carrying a load of logs sailed from Canada's western coast to Britain, such a voyage being around Cape Horn where the whole shipment might be lost in one of the terrible storms for which that particular area is notorious.

Captain Cook was happy with "the proper stick" that was put on the *Resolution* in Nootka Sound and later naval captains also used the forests of Vancouver Island and thereabouts to repair their masts. For example, when *HMS America* sailed out of the Strait of Juan de Fuca for Hawaii in October, 1845, she was heavily laden with spars that had been cut at Port Discovery, on the southern bank of the Strait, by a timber cutting party of the *America's* sailors.

These spars were used to replace those of the Pacific Squadron's flagship, *HMS Collingwood*, and its other ships, that had seen too much salt, sun and sea. No doubt old Collingwood would have approved of this new timber on the ship that was named after him as in England he always used to carry acorns in his pockets so that, whenever he saw some promising soil, he would throw them down in the hope that they would grow so that England would always produce enough oak for its "wooden walls".

So pleased was the Flag Officer, Rear-Admiral Seymour, with the *Collingwood's* new pieces that he arranged with a British merchant ship, the *Palinurus*, to take a load of Vancouver Island spars of Douglas fir to the naval dockyard at Portsmouth where it was well received.

As we saw with Captain Dacre in New Zealand the Navy preferred to get its masts and spars by letting contracts to particular timber dealers. Captain Dacre's counterpart on Vancouver Island was Captain William Brotchie, who had formerly been a captain of Hudson Bay Company ships on the north-west coast of Canada. In 1852 Brotchie sent a shipment of spars to the Navy in England on board the Company's vessel, *Norman Morison,* but, due to a shortage of suitable vessels, the trade did not develop as it could have although from time to time a visiting warship would purchase what it needed for its own purposes from either Captain Brotchie or some other timber dealer.

By 1876 the export of masts and spars from both New Zealand and British Columbia had died away and the only "sticks" that the Navy was buying were from Oregon but even this was spasmodic. And soon, with the replacement of sail by steam, the hunt for spars would disappear altogether from the Navy's list of tasks.

HMS ALLIGATOR TO THE RESCUE

On 17th August, 1834, there arrived in Sydney harbour the schooner, *Joseph Weller*, from New Zealand, which at the time had not yet been colonised and was notorious for the cannibalism of the Maoris. "There is not a bay, not a cove in New Zealand which has not witnessed one of these horrible dramas," wrote a French whaler of the time, "…. woe to the white man who falls into their hands". [1] On board the *Joseph Weller* was the leader of a shore whaling gang, John Guard, and three Maoris. John Guard had a tale to tell and he told it to the Executive Council of New South Wales on 22nd August.

Four months earlier he had sailed from Sydney to New Zealand with his wife, Betty, son John, daughter Louisa and a gang of whalers. Also on board were two Mates and twenty-three ordinary seamen. Their vessel, the *Harriet*, had been driven ashore near Cape Egmont, on the west coast of the North Island, and had been battered to pieces at a spot that is to-day known as Harriet Beach.

They all reached the shore safely and made tents out of some of the sails that they had taken from their stricken craft. Three of the ship's boats were got off safely and they decided to use one of them to try to get a small party to Cloudy Bay in the South Island where they hoped to find a whaling ship that could come and rescue the others.

Before they had put this plan into effect they were visited by a tribe of about two hundred Maori men, armed with muskets, tomahawks and spears, who plundered their stores and threatened to kill and eat them.

Two days later the Maoris launched a dawn attack and two of the unlucky Europeans were killed, cut up and eaten. Others were taken prisoner, including Mrs. Guard and her children, but John Guard managed to escape with thirteen others and they headed north but on their way they encountered another large group of Maoris and had to surrender.

Guard managed to persuade the Maoris to let him escape in one of the *Harriet's* boats to fetch a ransom of a cask of gunpowder. In a small, leaky whaleboat he and some others sailed to Cloudy Bay whence they took passage to Sydney in the *Joseph Weller*. In short, John Guard asked for naval and military help to retrieve his wife, children and crew.

110

Thus were *HMS Alligator* (Captain Lambert) and the government schooner *Isabella* despatched across the Tasman with three officers and sixty men of the 50th (Queen's Own West Kent) Regiment aboard. Guard and his sailors accompanied the expedition while Sydney waited with bated breath for the rescue of Mrs. Guard and her infant children.

Upon arriving in the area where the captives were held, the *Alligator* dropped off an interpreter and a pilot but the weather then forced the ship to run for shelter at the top of the South Island where the troops landed and did some target practice in preparation for any possible action with the Maoris. They anchored in a beautiful bay on D'Urville Island, which they named Port Hardy in honour of Nelson's famous captain. Other features were given the Nelsonian names of Victory Island, Trafalgar Point, Nile Head, Fleet Rock and Nelson's Monument (a tall pinnacle of rock).

They then proceeded to the Egmont area and managed to secure the release of eight of the *Harriet's* crew who had been in the hands of the Maoris for five months and were, in their own words, "eaten up with vermin, half starved, nearly naked, and our lives in hourly danger". [2] However, Mrs. Guard remained a captive.

The reason why these eight men – plus one other, John Oliver, who had been some time in the area as a flax dealer – were given up was that the Maoris were frightened of the warship with her sailors carrying pistols and "big knives" at their sides.

On the morning of Sunday, 28th September, a party of thirty soldiers and marines landed with the boat's crew of the *Alligator* to attack the well fortified pa where it was believed that Mrs. Guard was being held. However, the Maoris fled, taking Mrs. Guard and her daughter with them. The three year old son, John Guard, was being held by another tribe.

At the deserted pa "only a solitary pig grunted at the troopers". [3] They did, however, find a stash of potatoes and they lit fires to cook them. While all this was going on in the pa a party of natives came out of the bush and plundered the ship's boats, taking away three oars and a rudder.

Two days later the Maoris gave up Mrs. Guard and her daughter in return for a local chief, Oaoiti, who had been captured by the soldiers and incarcerated on the *Alligator*.

Mrs. Guard had been in the hands of the Maoris for five months, during which time she witnessed them killing and eating several of the captives, including her own brother.

The *Alligator* sent a message to the tribe that was holding the Guards' son, demanding his return, and the warship waited off the pa for a reply. The boy was then brought to the shore by his captors and was cheekily displayed to those on the *Alligator*. Lieutenant Thomas approached the shore in a boat but was fired upon by the Maoris. Captain Lambert then brought his ship as close as he could and shelled the two pas that were within striking distance as well as the canoes on the beach. The man-of-war and the *Isabella* were, in fact, so close in that they touched bottom but they were safely out of range of the primitive weapons of the Maoris. During the three hours' bombardment some 306 shots were fired from the *Alligator's* guns since there was nothing that angered the Navy more than an attack on one of its officers or ratings.

After this day's work a westerly gale forced them to return to Port Hardy for three days where Lieutenant Woore occupied himself by completing a survey of the harbour that he had begun on the previous visit.

On 6th October they returned to make a further rescue attempt as Captain Lambert was determined to get the young child safely on board. Six officers and 112 men, including John Guard and his sailors, landed about three miles south of the pa with four days' provisions and 70 rounds per man.

Success seemed possible when the boy arrived, carried on a chief's back and with feathers on his head. The chief demanded a ransom and, when refused, turned to run away. One of the sailors by name of Ruff, the captain of the forecastle on the *Alligator*, grabbed the child and, seeing that he was tied to the chief's back, cut him adrift with a knife and the boy fell on to the beach. Then, in a fit of anger against the murderers of their shipmates, one of Guard's men shot the chief dead.

Next thing firing spread all along the lines. It was started by Guard's men, seeking revenge and being outside military discipline, and in the confusion was taken up by the soldiers until the officers managed to get their order to "cease fire" obeyed.

That evening the troops were visited ashore by Lieutenant Thomas and Midshipman Dayman, who brought a fresh stock of ammunition but their boat was stove and they and their crew had to remain ashore. A fire was lit in the deserted pa to cook food for the men but it soon got out of control and a number of native huts were burnt and "a considerable quantity of powder exploded". [4] Better than Guy Fawkes Night!

Before reboarding the boats to take them back to the *Alligator* Guard's men found a decapitated head, which they identified as being that of Clarke, who had been on the *Harriet*.

Captain Lambert sailed his ship and its rescued captives to Kapiti Island where Te Rauparaha was living. This inveterate cannibal expressed his pleasure when he heard what had been done to his enemies, the Taranaki Maoris, but regretted that the body count was so low. He also asked why none of the bodies had been brought to him to eat. According to William Marshall, the surgeon on the *Alligator*, Te Rauparaha's "appearance, conduct and character were those of a complete savage". [5]

Before leaving Kapiti Captain Lambert issued the following notice to the chiefs of the North Island in the convoluted language of the time: "Two ships of war, belonging to His Majesty King William the Fourth, having arrived on this coast in consequence of the horrid murder of part of the crew of the *Harriet*, the remaining part having been made slaves....and to require the said people to be given up, which has been effected after a most severe punishment inflicted on the said tribes by burning their pas, their property, and killing and wounding many of them; and at the same time to point out to the other tribes that, however much the King of England wishes to cultivate friendship with the New Zealanders, the indignation he will feel at a repetition of such cruelty to his subjects, and how severely he will punish the offenders." [6]

From Kapiti the *Alligator* sailed up to the Bay of Islands where the crew of the *Harriet*, except the carpenter and the Guards, took passage to London on the *Elizabeth*. They had had enough of the wild Antipodes.

The *Alligator* carried out its difficult mission with total success as all the captives who were still alive were rescued. In a letter to the *Sydney Times* the *Harriet's* carpenter wrote, "After being among the natives for about five months, we were happily relieved by the aid of Captain Lambert, to whom I return my most sincere thanks for his humanity towards me and my shipmates. Words can not express the feelings of my heart towards him and his officers, who not only behaved to me but to all my shipmates as gentlemen in every respect; they gave us all in their power to make us comfortable." [7] The *Alligator's* mission was the first encounter between the Royal Navy and the Maoris. There would be several more – mostly of an unpleasant nature.

THE OPIUM WARS

The title that history has given to the mid nineteenth century wars between Britain and China is somewhat misleading as, although opium was the catalyst for conflict, these wars were about more important things such as the opening up of China to foreign trade and shipping and the acquisition of a haven for British vessels on the turbulent and troublesome China coast.

The opium was produced legally in British India from the poppy and was exported to China where, although illegal since 1729, it was allowed into the country upon payment of bribes to local mandarins and customs officials.

At the time opium was widely used in England and elsewhere as a panacea for all sorts of ailments, including influenza, toothache, ulcers, insomnia, cholera and hay fever. George IV used it to help him get over his many hangovers and so did Queen Victoria – but not as a hangover cure. Disraeli smoked it and so did Wordsworth and Coleridge, the latter writing *Kubla Khan* while under its gentle influence. Clive of India used opium for twenty years while William Wilberforce took it daily for forty-five years and still succeeded in ending slavery.

The reason why so much of the product was sent to China was that the Chinese wanted it; it was one of the few things that could give them temporary relief from their lives of hardship, misery and brutality. As with the drug laws to-day, the worst aspect of opium was not its effect on those who took it but the smuggling, piracy and corruption that was caused by its "illegality".

For a long time the Chinese authorities were not concerned about opium as too many of their officials were getting their "squeeze" on it and the imports of the product could be paid for by the export of China's tea and porcelain. However, by 1830 they were importing it at the rate of about 450 tons a year and their exports were no longer able to cover it with the result that silver was being sent abroad in payment. And the Celestial Empire did not like being depleted of its silver.

It was for this reason that China's imperial government decided to "crack down" on a trade to which it had turned a blind eye for more than a century. Thus did they precipitate the First Opium War.

The man who lit the fuse for this Chinese tragedy was Lin Tse-hsu, the Imperial Commissioner whom the Emperor sent to stamp out the opium trade at Canton where foreigners had been allowed to trade for years through their *hongs* or warehouses on the banks of the Canton River. This and the nearby Portuguese colony of Macau were the only points on the whole China coast where any trade was carried on with the West.

Lin arrived at Canton on 10th March, 1839, and his first act was to make an example of a local man accused of dealing in opium by executing him in front of the foreign *hongs* – a draconian and brutal punishment that is still practised in barbaric countries such as Iran, China and Singapore.

When Captain Charles Elliot R.N., the British Trade Superintendent based at Macau, arrived in Canton two weeks later he found the English warehouses there surrounded and held hostage by Lin's soldiers. A man of conciliation, Elliot agreed to Lin's demand that British traders hand over their opium and accordingly some 20,283 chests of the precious product (worth about £2,500,000) were duly delivered.

Not content with this, Lin then threatened to execute any British or other sea captains who might be found with opium in their holds. This bravado killed the trade of Canton, turned Elliot against the Chinese, and served to emphasise the deeply unsatisfactory situation whereby British shippers and traders were subject to the vagaries and brutality of Chinese law. Lin might have killed the opium trade at Canton but, in accordance with the law of supply and demand, it simply moved to other places such as the island of Chusan, near Ningpo, and within nine months a further 8,000 chests had been smuggled in to China where, because of the increased risk, they fetched a higher price, thereby requiring more silver to pay for each chest of opium.

When Lord Palmerston, the Foreign Secretary, heard of these goings-on he decided, with his trademark boldness, that the time had arrived to strike a blow against this obdurate empire which for decades had willingly received the opium, which gave neither liberty nor security to British traders and sea captains, and which had now seized and destroyed property belonging to British traders in the form of the chests of opium. He instructed Captain Elliot accordingly.

When Lin next indulged his hatred of the foreigner by forbidding the Chinese merchants of Canton to provide foreign ships with food, water and other supplies, Captain Elliot led a small fleet of British naval vessels to the island of Hong Kong in the hope, but not necessarily the expectation, of getting what had been denied to them at Canton. Here too Lin's writ seemed to run and the merchants of Kowloon, like those at Canton, also refused to sell victuals to the British warships.

Captain Elliot gave the authorities until 2 p.m. on 4th September, 1839, to allow the local merchants to victual his ships and, upon the expiry of the ultimatum, Captain Smith of the frigate, *HMS Volage*, turned his guns on to the nearest of the Chinese war junks that were obstructing the sea passage between Kowloon and Hong Kong island (to-day the busy harbour of Hong Kong) in order to prevent the victualling of the British warships.

Thus was fired the first shot in the Opium War, which was essentially a naval war. This, the "Battle of Kowloon", was the first ever naval engagement between a Western power and an Asian one in the Pacific. Sadly it would not be the last.

Each war junk had ten guns and the Chinese sailors frantically dragged them all over to the side of their vessels that faced the grape and round shot of the *Volage* and *HMS Louisa*, which latter vessel fired 104 rounds in the course of two and a half hours. The Chinese guns were outdated and missed most of their targets by firing too high over them. The battle eventually petered out when the British ships ran out of ammunition and the wind died down.

The Chinese deluded themselves that they had won a victory. This was their invariable practice no matter how badly they performed as no officer ever wanted to report anything other than total success to the emperor since dismissal, torture and execution were the lot of those who failed. The true result of this battle can be deduced from the fact that a few days later the British warships were given all the supplies that they wanted.

The war became more serious in June, 1840, when sixteen warships, carrying about four thousand British troops and marines, arrived off Macau and then proceeded north to attack the port of Tinh-hai on Chusan, an island that Britain was already eyeing as the haven for her shipping that was so desperately needed on the China coast. But it was to get Hong Kong instead.

When the people of Ting-hai saw all the foreign ships they were delighted since it looked as if the opium trade was at last coming to their doorstep in a big way. They suffered a rude awakening when the broadsides of fifteen British cruisers opened fire and reduced the jerry-built, paper thin buildings of Ting-hai to a pile of rubble. Marines and troops then landed from their hot and stinking ships and occupied the port and adjacent countryside.

Still the Chinese government refused to negotiate and the several approaches made by the British side were all insultingly rebuffed, thereby highlighting one of the reasons for the war, viz. China's refusal to treat other nations on an equal basis, insisting instead that they were mere "vassals" of the Chinese empire and must do as they're told – not unlike the current Chinese attitude to Tibet.

With no sign of a Chinese willingness to negotiate the next step was to attack the Celestial Empire's forts, which "protected" the river approaches to Canton. Accordingly, on 7th January, 1841, some 1,400 British troops and Royal Marines were landed two miles south of the fort of Chuenpi. While they attacked it from the landward side it was simultaneously bombarded from the river by the guns of *HMS Calliope*, *Larne*, *Hyacinth*, *Queen* and *Nemesis*. The last mentioned, a 184 foot long iron gunboat with two large 32 pound cannon, five 6 pounders and a Congreve rocket launcher, was the most powerful vessel in Chinese waters. Needless to say, the fort was taken with heavy Chinese losses but with only thirty-eight wounded on the British side. One of the problems for the Chinese was that their empire was so corrupt from top to bottom that some of the Chinese gunners were diluting their gunpowder with sand (sometimes more than 50%) and were selling the good powder so displaced to British smugglers – just as during the Second World War much of the military equipment that the Allies supplied to Nationalist Chinese forces was onsold by their corrupt officers to their communist enemies.

A little further up the Canton River was the fort of Taikok, which was bombarded for an hour by the combined guns of *HMS Samarang*, *Druid*, *Modeste* and *Columbine*. After this softening up it was assailed and captured by the bayonets and cutlasses of a landing party of Royal Marines and troops.

Taking advantage of her shallow draught, the paddle steamer *HMS Nemesis* went into Ansons Bay and attacked eleven war junks at anchor there. The first rocket from the *Nemesis* set one of the largest junks ablaze with the result that it exploded, killing all on board. With the aid of some small boats from the squadron the *Nemesis* managed to destroy all the rest of the junks of this unsuspecting fleet that thought they were safe from the guns of the big warships in this shallow anchorage.

An attack, led by *HMS Blenheim* (74 guns), on the Bogue forts at the mouth of the Canton River (also known as the Pearl River) was planned for 8th January but a Chinese emissary asked for a ceasefire, promising genuine negotiations, and so for the moment the Bogue forts were spared.

Captain Elliot went in *HMS Nemesis* to a point near Whampoa, down river from Canton, to resume negotiations with more hope than expectation of success. A preliminary agreement was reached but was almost immediately dishonoured by the Chinese and so this dreary war continued.

The new commander-in-chief of the fleet, Commodore James Bremer, a veteran of Trafalgar, led his ships in their successful attack on the battery of Anunghoy and other forts and, by the time that Canton was at the mercy of the British, the Chinese again offered to negotiate and another settlement was reached that in its turn was broken by the Chinese when they placed stakes and stones in the river to obstruct passage. And so Captain Joseph Nias of *HMS Herald* took a force up the Canton River and destroyed the North Wangtung fort, sinking and burning junks as he passed. Among the hazards of this river war was the floating of fire rafts down the river by the Chinese in an attempt to set the wooden walls of England alight but these were usually dealt with successfully by the warships' boats.

In August, 1841, a "northern expedition", consisting of nine warships, four steamers and twenty-one transports, set out from Hong Kong and sailed north to attack Amoy, an island fort and city that was protected to the seaward by six other islands, including Colongaou.

The British fleet slipped through one of the channels between the islands, and the next morning (6th August) they inspected the Chinese defences, which "consisted of a straight face of battery along the beach...in length about 1,100 yards, mounting ninety guns. It was constructed of granite, in thickness about fourteen feet at the base, faced with turf, having merely ports in the wall like the sides of a ship". [1] There were further batteries on Colongaou and another island.

A conference was held on *HMS Phlegethon* to plan the attack, which was begun in the noonday heat when the two frigates, *HMS Druid* and *Blonde*, assisted by *HMS Modeste*, battered the Colongaou fort from the front.

Upon the batteries returning the fire, some other warships joined the fray. *HMS Wellesley* lay broadside on to the Colongaou battery and, in the words of one of her officers, "we opened a very heavy fire, keeping it up wherever an enemy's gun could be seen to maintain its fire. We were only 400 yards from the battery, so were enabled to let them have it, like the coachman's brandy and water – 'hot, sweet and strong' – and, truth to tell, the Chinese did endure the fire right manfully. To the last they kept some of their guns going until shot down by musketry in the rear of them.

The direction of their fire was very good but the elevation too great; their shot passed close over us for the space of an hour, so that on the poop there was an incessant rush of shot, hurtling and hissing rather unpleasantly....They put a shot through our mizen trysail mast, three through our jib, cut away some of our shrouds and running rigging, and put a shot or two in our hull, yet, strange to say, no one was hit or hurt in any way." [2]

At around 4 p.m. the marines and troops landed from *HMS Nemesis* and *Phlegethon*. "They escaladed the wall at the lower or outer extremity of the battery and, a few minutes after we landed, a party of seamen at our end drove the garrison from the guns, killing many of them....The troops advancing along the battery drove all the enemy out and by six o'clock all opposition was over and the *Modeste*, *Pylades* and *Cruizer* were at anchor in the inner harbour and it was ours." [3]

Some of the warships and a small detachment of troops remained at Amoy "for the protection of British ships which might happen to call" [4] while the rest of the expedition went north and occupied Shanghai. They then evacuated it, and a force of 9,000 troops and marines and 3,000 sailors was sent up the Yangtse River, the great waterway that has its source in the snows of the Himalayas and then waters the heartland of China. Further up the river from Shanghai lay Nanking, the southern capital of imperial China.

In the interests of safety *HMS Plover* and *HMS Starling*, together with a steamer, went ahead and made soundings for the main expedition, which began its river voyage on 6th July, 1841, in an effort to bring the war to the heart of China's government in the hope of ending it.

Besides the problems of navigating in this unknown waterway the ships also had to struggle against its powerful current, not to mention the occasional gunfire from the banks, during which

HMS Pluto, Nemesis and *Modeste* were all hit at various times but none seriously.

On 19th July, 1841, this formidable fleet of more than seventy warships and transports anchored abreast of the city of Chin-kiang, the gateway of the Grand Canal, which itself is known as "the very lungs" of China, and only a few miles down from Nanking. A landing was made by Royal Marines, soldiers and a naval brigade and, despite some spirited opposition from the Tartar troops defending it, the city was soon occupied.

Two small boats, belonging to *HMS Blonde*, delivering field-pieces and howitzers to the artillery, were fired upon from the city wall and twenty-eight bluejackets in the boats were wounded. When no more resistance was possible some of the Tartars slew their wives and children and then killed themselves. Their general, Hai-ling, burned himself to death along with all his papers.

The fall of Chin-kiang was the catalyst that at last persuaded the emperor to end the war but, as always, he took his time, during which *HMS Plover* sounded and surveyed the river between Chin-kiang and Nanking in preparation for a further advance.

The expedition actually got to Nanking and anchored off the northern angle of its city walls but the white flag was flying and so the commander of the British force, Sir Henry Pottinger, Bt. (soon to be the first Governor of Hong Kong), suspended operations and on 20th August, 1842, emissaries were received on *HMS Cornwallis* beneath the walls of their capital. Nine days later this long and tortuous war was brought to an end by the Treaty of Nanking, which was signed in the cabin of *HMS Cornwallis* on 29th August.

With so many of China's main cities having been bombarded and/or occupied almost at will – Canton, Ningpo, Amoy, Shanghai, Chin-kiang – the victorious British were able to impose their own terms, and this they did.

China agreed to open five of its ports – Canton, Amoy, Foochow, Ningpo and Shanghai – to British trade. To these ports the Treaty allowed Britain to send consuls to protect the interests of British traders and to communicate directly with Chinese officials.

Under the Treaty the Chinese government had to pay the British six million silver dollars as compensation for the opium that the hot-headed Lin had seized and destroyed at Canton, thereby starting the war. They also had to pay three million dollars in compensation for debts owed to British traders by Chinese merchants at Canton plus another twelve million to compensate

Britain for the cost of the war. Britain agreed to withdraw its troops from Nanking and the Grand Canal upon the emperor confirming the treaty and paying the first instalment of the money but British soldiers would remain in two other places until the final two instalments were paid.

Probably the most important of the Treaty's clauses was the cession of the island of Hong Kong to Britain as a Crown Colony "in perpetuity" – a condition which the British Conservative government later breached when they handed it back to China's oppressive communist regime in 1997 without allowing the people of Hong Kong any say in the matter.

By acquiring a safe haven on the China coast free from the vagaries and threats of China's unstable and unpredictable government as well as extra-territoriality in the five "treaty ports" for its subjects, Britain achieved its major war aims and would henceforth be able to use the commercial supremacy so attained to make itself the dominant Western power in the China trade. The Royal Navy maintained a warship at or near each of the treaty ports.

Humiliated beyond all measure by being dictated to by a country that China had hitherto refused to deal with other than as a vassal, the Celestial Empire withdrew into its traditional isolation and surliness, having learned nothing from this encounter between ancient war junks and modern warships. Not so blind were the Japanese, who took note of what had happened and decided to modernise their country and, more importantly, build a navy based on that which had just defeated the Chinese.

There was no mention of opium in the treaty and the product continued to be smuggled into China, especially through the new treaty ports. It would have been better for China if that ardent crusader against the poppy plant, Lin Tse-hsu, had left well alone.

*****

What is referred to as the "Second Opium War" was also sparked by a rash act on the part of the Chinese authorities although there were deeper, underlying reasons as well.

The *Arrow* was a Chinese lorcha that was registered in Hong Kong. On the morning of 8th October, 1856, she was lying among the shipping anchored below the city of Canton when she was boarded by a large force of Chinese officers and soldiers, who seized twelve of her crew, carried them off and hauled down the British flag that was flying from her mast.

Knowing how ready the Chinese were to take advantage of perceived weakness, the British demanded an apology, redress and an assurance that such action would not happen again. When these were not forthcoming Rear-Admiral Sir Michael Seymour, the commander-in-chief of the East Indies station, which then covered the China seas, sent a large force of British men-of-war to capture and burn the Chinese forts on the Canton River.

By 28th October all the defences of Canton were in British hands. Thus began the Second Opium War which, with intervals, was to last even longer than the first one (nearly four years).

The *USS Portsmouth* was lying nearby at Whampoa and she sent eighty-one marines and seamen in four small boats to protect American lives and property at the American Factory at Canton. These were soon reinforced by another sixty-nine sailors from *USS Levant*, which had joined the *Portsmouth* at Whampoa.

Initially the Americans were neutral and their interest was confined to protecting their own nationals but the Chinese, unable to help themselves when it came to creating enemies, fired on a U.S. navy boat and it wasn't long before the Americans were fighting alongside the British against a common enemy.

With the Chinese continuing to refuse to negotiate over the return of the *Arrow*, Rear-Admiral Seymour ordered the bombardment of the High Commissioner's compound by the 10 inch pivot guns of *HMS Encounter*. The reaction of this xenophobic Chinese official was to offer $50 for the head of every Englishman brought to him. However, he didn't get any as the force against him was overwhelming. In addition to the Americans, in 1857 the French came in as allies as well. The latter had been provoked into action by China's execution of a French missionary priest, August Chapdelaine.

As in the First Opium War, the extensive estuary of the Canton River was the favoured battleground and on 1st June, 1857, a large fleet of Chinese war junks was attacked in the Fatsham Creek, just south of Canton. This was a bloody affair for both sides.

The British fought mainly from the warships' small boats as the creek was narrow and unsuitable for bigger vessels. In the words of Commodore Henry Keppel, "The Chinese fired occasional shots to ascertain exact distance but did not open their heaviest fire until we were within 600 yards...We cheered and were trying to get to the front when a shot struck our boat, killing the bow man. Another was cut in two….a shot passed through both sides of the boat, wounding two more of the crew; in short the boat was sunk under us. The tide rising, boats disabled, our oars shot away, it was necessary to re-form. I was collared and drawn from the water by young Michael Seymour, a Mate of his uncle's flagship, the *Calcutta*. We were all picked up except the dead bow man….As we retired I shook my fist at the junks, promising I would pay them off."

After re-forming, "I hailed Lieutenant Graham to get his boat ready, as I would hoist the broad pennant for the next attack in his boat. I had no sooner spoken than he was down, the same shot killing and wounding four others. Graham was one mass of blood but it was from a marine who stood next to him, part of whose skull was forced three inches into another man's shoulder…Her (the *Hongkong's*) deck was covered with the wounded who had been brought on board from different boats. From the paddle box we saw that the noise of guns was bringing up strong reinforcements. The account of our having been obliged to retire had reached them. They were pulling up like mad….I called out 'Let's try the row-boats once more, boys,' and went over the side into our cutter, in which were Turnour and the faithful coxswain, Spurrier. At this moment there arose from the boats, as if every man took it up at the same instant, one of those British cheers so full of meaning that I knew at once it was all up with John Chinaman. They might sink twenty boats but there were thirty others which would go ahead all the faster. It was indeed an exciting sight. A move among the junks! They were breaking ground and moving off, the outermost first. This the Chinese performed in good order, without slacking fire. Then commenced an exciting chase for seven miles. As our shot told they ran mostly on to the mud banks and their crews forsook them. Seventeen junks were captured. Three only escaped." [5]

Some months later reinforcements arrived and the Canton River was blockaded and then on 28th December, 1857, a fleet of thirty-two British and French warships bombarded Canton. The occupation force that was landed included about 1,500 men of a Naval Brigade.

As in the First Opium War the Chinese government remained obstinate and refused to negotiate even though it was simultaneously having to deal with the Taiping rebellion from among its own people. This was one of the greatest insurrections in history in which an estimated twenty million people were killed. In an attempt to push the Chinese government to seek terms Lord Elgin, who was in command of the Allied forces, decided on a naval demonstration closer to the northern capital of Peking and so the British and French warships sailed north to the Gulf of Pechili where they anchored off the mouth of the Peiho River on 14th April, 1858.

When negotiations broke down with the Chinese emissary, who had been sent down from the emperor in Peking to treat with them, Elgin demanded that the Taku forts, that were within the range of the guns of the British and French warships, be delivered up within two hours. When no reply was forthcoming the signal flag was hoisted to commence the bombardment.

The enemy returned the fire but it lasted for only an hour and a quarter, after which the Allies landed in a morass of mud that was two feet deep and stretched for fifty yards inland. However, they managed to reach the forts, from which the Chinese had fled. At the height of the action the Chinese sent down several junks full of flaming straw. These "fireships" were guided from the shore by means of ropes but the straw all burned before the junks reached their targets. Pretty, but ineffective.

Rear-Admiral Seymour in the *HMS Coromandel* led two other British gunboats and two French warships up the river to Tientsin, all of them towing a number of manned boats. Any stacks of straw or small timber that they passed were destroyed to prevent them being used as combustible fuel for a fire-raft. For the same reason junks were ordered out of the river and those that did not obey were destroyed.

On 26th May this small fleet reached Tientsin, which was promptly occupied by about a thousand British troops and half that number of French. This show of force impressed the crumbling Chinese empire sufficiently for them to agree to a new pact, the Treaty of Tientsin, which allowed Britain to send an ambassador to the Chinese court at Peking, required China to tolerate Christianity and the conversion of Chinese to the Christian religion, enabled foreigners to travel to all parts of China, opened up many new ports to overseas trade, concerted measures for the suppression of piracy, paid an indemnity for the war and, most importantly for the Royal Navy, allowed its warships to go to any port in China (including the big ports up the rivers).

After destroying the Taku forts the allies evacuated them and withdrew their warships from the Gulf of Pechili.

At the time China was racked by civil war with the Taipings, and the emperor's writ did not extend everywhere and this led to breaches of the newly signed treaty and a resumption of hostilities.

When the Chinese blocked the mouth of the Peiho River in June, 1858, *HMS Opossum* was ordered to open a passage through it. The river had been cunningly blocked by three booms. The lowest was made with iron piles and the next one with heavy spars of wood that were lashed with cables. The third and highest boom was made of large pieces of timber, cross lashed to form an obstructive mass that was a hundred and twenty feet wide and three feet deep.

The *Opossum* made fast a hawser to one of the iron piles of the first boom and with difficulty managed to pull it out. Then, supported by *HMS Plover* and followed by two other vessels, *HMS Lee* and *HMS Haughty*, she proceeded to the second boom but was fired on by between thirty and forty guns from the nearby forts.

Commander Rason of the *Plover* was cut in two by a round shot and others were wounded. In these circumstances the ships re-formed below the first boom where they were reinforced before returning to the fray.

After a while *HMS Kestrel* sank, both the *Lee* and the *Haughty* went aground while the *Plover*, almost disabled, was lashed to the starboard side of *HMS Cormorant*. Many of those on the *Plover* had been killed or wounded while the rest were worn out with the fatigue of all the firing in the intense heat of the day.

Into this predicament steamed a vessel of the United States Navy, the *Toey-Whan*. By this stage of this "stop-start" war the United States were officially neutral and the *Toey-Whan* had the Stars and Stripes flying from her stern. On board was Flag Officer Josiah Tatnall, the senior American officer in Chinese waters, who had fought against the British in that unfortunate war of 1812. He got his coxswain to row him up through the gunfire to the starboard gangway of the *Plover*, the coxswain being hit by Chinese gunfire as the bow man was getting out the boat hook.

Tatnall climbed on to the *Plover*, crossed her bloodstained deck and then stepped on to her lashed friend, *HMS Cormorant* where Rear-Admiral Hope was lying wounded in the cabin. While Tatnall was offering to tow the British wounded down river in boats behind his steamer, which he did a short time later, the sailors who had brought him thither were in their boat in the lee of the *Plover*. Seeing the exhausted men of the *Plover* working the bow gun, these "neutrals" climbed on board and relieved the gun's crew until it was manned entirely by Americans.

When Tatnall reappeared he said rather mischievously, "Hulloa there! Don't you know that we are neutrals?"

"Beg pardon, sir," said one of the Americans, "they were very short-handed at the bow gun and so we thought we'd lend them a hand for fellowship's sake." And so they did, with Tatnall justifying this friendly, fraternal help with the words "Blood is thicker than water". [6]

Not long afterwards America's Civil War broke out and Tatnall, like so many other Southern officers, including General Robert E. Lee, chose the Confederate side and became a captain in its navy. Upon their victory the Northerners were no less cruel to the South than the Rebels had been to those who had remained loyal to the Crown in the War of Independence and Josiah Tatnall was forced to flee to Nova Scotia where he lived at Halifax in genteel poverty. Upon hearing of this, British naval officers subscribed a sum of money to enable this true friend of the Royal Navy in its hour of need to live out his life in dignity. The officers probably would have given twice over – once in appreciation for Tatnall's gesture at the Peiho and again to express their disgust at the way he had been treated by the Northerners. Throughout the Civil War Britain – and especially the officer class – both empathised and sympathised with the Confederates, whom they regarded as more gentlemanly than the vulgar and ever troublesome Yankees of the North.

Meanwhile back at the River Peiho the firing from the Chinese forts ceased at the end of the day and a force of about four hundred marines and bluejackets landed but they were soon impeded by stakes in the mud and ditches and had great difficulty getting through. Altogether on this terrible day the British lost three ships and had eighty-nine men killed and a further three hundred and forty-five wounded.

The ships withdrew to Shanghai for the wounded to be taken ashore and to plan another attack. As part of the preparations for an attack with a stronger force a thorough survey of the Gulf of Pechili and the Pehtang and Peiho Rivers was carried out by *HMS Cruizer*. It was dangerous work as the banks were held by the Chinese. Reinforcements of men, horses and guns arrived from Britain, India and France, and by June, 1860, the force consisted of 12,600 British and Indian troops and nearly 8,000 French.

126

This huge force, landed from 173 vessels, captured the Taku forts (again!) and advanced to Tientsin and thence to Peking itself, which was captured and its Summer Palace burned. On 24th October, 1860, the Treaty of Peking was signed. It confirmed the earlier Treaty of Tientsin, thereby giving the British and French the trading rights that they demanded and for which so much blood and money had been expended. For the British the icing on the cake was the cession of the Kowloon Peninsula, south of to-day's Boundary Street, so that the Crown Colony of Hong Kong would now include part of the mainland as well.

By now Chinese, mainly from Canton, were pouring in to Hong Kong where there was more security and prosperity than in the Chinese Empire. They were simply exchanging one foreign sovereign for another since the Manchu dynasty was an alien one of Tartars, who had imposed themselves on the Han Chinese in much the same way as the Moguls imposed themselves on northern India.

As a result of these two naval wars Britain emerged as the pre-eminent power in China, her power being underpinned by the continuing presence of Royal Navy vessels in the ports and up the rivers of China. Britain controlled three quarters of China's trade, mostly through Hong Kong and Shanghai, and from these two ports British sailors in Her Majesty's gunboats policed the rivers while other Britons administered the Chinese Customs Service. The final irony of these two long wars was that, by the Treaty of Peking, the opium trade was legalised and so China had fought the wars for nothing and had gained only humiliation.

There are lessons to be learned from every war and the Opium Wars were no exception. The most persistent constant throughout the seven years of fighting was the Chinese government's inability to keep its word on any matter. There were numerous occasions when each of the wars could have been brought to an end but in every case (except the last) the Chinese broke their word and thereby reignited the fighting.

The same thing happened in the Second World War when Chiang Kai-Shek's Nationalist forces gave numerous undertakings to the Allies, every one of which they broke. And again with the communist regime in China, which signs trade and other agreements with the West and then promptly breaks them. There is a lesson in all this for Westerners in their dealings with any government of China. Not even the Chinese people trust their own government and they never have.

RECRUITMENT

He rose at dawn, and, fired with hope,
Shot o'er the seething harbour bar,
And reached the ship and caught the rope,
And whistled to the morning star....

'Fool', he answered, 'death is sure
To those that stay and those that roam,
But I will never more endure
To sit with empty hands at home.

My mother clings about my neck,
My sisters crying 'Stay for shame';
My father raves of death and wreck –
They are all to blame, they are all to blame.

God help me! save I take my part
Of danger on the roaring sea,
A devil rises in my heart,
Far worse than any death to me."

The Sailor Boy, Tennyson

There were numerous reasons why young men wanted to go to sea. In the eighteenth and nineteenth centuries many people lived their entire lives without ever going more than a few miles from their farm, village or town and the "romance of the sea" was more than just a phrase of the poets.

The effects of the Industrial Revolution were reverberating around the world as distant continents and islands were being brought into the world's trading system and were being made known to the public by means of books and the stories of sailors returning with all sorts of interesting shells, costumes, carvings and curios. Joining the Navy gave a youngster a chance to see the world and expand his mental and geographical horizons beyond the little milieu of his own locality.

It was also a way for boys to escape an unhappy home environment such as a drunken father or a cruel stepmother. Going to sea certainly had its attractions when compared with following one's father into the local factory or mine to work long hours for low wages.

There was, of course, the possibility of shipwreck, disease or being killed in action but young chaps with a whole life ahead of them tended not to dwell too much on those sorts of things. In the days of rope and hemp a sailor in the Pacific was far more likely to die of disease than to be killed in action; typhus was spread by lice, tuberculosis was caused by ships being constantly damp (as many of them were), while yellow fever was also a lurking danger.

There was also the patriotic motive as the Navy has always had a special place in the hearts of the British people – second only to that of the Crown itself. In any military parade through the streets it was the Navy that attracted (and still attracts) the loudest and most genuine applause. With sails flying in the wind, its trademark spit and polish, guns firing a salute, and the white hats, bell-bottoms and shining buttons which the sailors wore with such pride and confidence, the Navy had always had style and from 1805 it also had that indefinable thing called "the Nelson touch". Plus, of course, there was always the prospect of "prize", medals, glory, and all the lovely ladies who would be waiting on the dockside at every port-of-call. All pretty potent stuff to any adventurous young fellow who loved his country and wanted to serve it at the sharp end. And, oh, what a cause! There never has been and never will be anything to match the British Empire in style, power, prestige or the sheer good that it did for mankind, not the least being the unprecedented century of world peace, known as Pax Britannica, that the Royal Navy oversaw and enforced between 1815 and 1914.

In the words of Sir Arthur Bryant in *The Age of Elegance*, "For pacific Britain's Navy made the waters that divided the land-masses of earth corridors of peace. It did more. In retaining a part of the gains won for her by Nelson and his contemporaries, Britain unconsciously signposted the human future." [1]

Britain could never have been such a great sea power without the maritime tradition that had been built up over the centuries. Uniquely in Europe the British Isles were an island nation and any invader would have to come across the water – as Julius Caesar did, and the Saxons and the Danes and the Normans.

The insular nature of Britain stimulated seamanship, shipbuilding and an interest in the sea since any trade or communication with the outside world could be only by ship. With a coast line of 11,072 miles, the British people had over the centuries developed large fishing and shipbuilding industries, and its discoverers and traders had sailed to the farthest ends of the world in pursuit of adventure and profit. Thus the Navy – both Royal and Merchant – had a huge reserve of tradition and manpower to call on – sturdy young men with weatherbeaten faces who had been brought up literally with the sea salt in their veins – people like the fishermen of Yarmouth and Grimsby, those who sailed the colliers between Whitby and the Thames, the boatbuilders of Bideford, and those who had served some challenging seasons on the boats of the herring fleet in the stormy seas off Wick.

The sailors were usually most particular about appearances – in respect of both themselves and their ship. They were proud to wear the Sovereign's uniform and in most cases did it justice. In the early 1800s some sailors sported a pig-tail that fell down their backs. There was a further development on the hair front in 1869 when the Admiralty gave permission to dispense with razors. Many did and this gave the Navy a new "face" as full but trimmed beards became popular.

Until the Continuous Service Act of 1853 a captain of a naval vessel selected his own ship's company. First he would select his officers and then they would usually help him pick the rest of the crew. This could take various forms. When Admiral Lord Cochrane was looking for sailors for *HMS Pallas* in 1805 he had posters printed – "My lads….The Flying Pallas of 36 guns at Plymouth is a new and uncommonly fine frigate. Built on purpose and ready for an expedition as soon as some more good hands are on board…The sooner you are on board the better….None need apply but seamen or stout hands, able to rouse about the field pieces….Cochrane".

The seamen who were recruited for a long voyage to the Pacific (usually three years) were drawn mainly from the merchant service and fishing fleets as it was much easier to take on those with knowledge and experience of the sea than to have to teach a large number of landlubbers on board a cramped and busy ship, battling her way through all the vagaries of weather.

Of course, influence counted and many a captain was leaned on by friends and acquaintances to employ their offspring and connections. When Captain Cook set out on his first voyage to the Pacific, he took on board a sixteen year old seaman, Isaac Smith, who was his wife's cousin. If this was nepotism it was also wise as Isaac turned out to be a good and conscientious sailor and later rose to the rank of Rear-Admiral. Hardly surprising in view of the excellent training that he would have had under his uncle. In those days the training that a seaman received depended very much on the captain.

Sixteen was not all that young for a boy to go to sea; lads as young as nine could enlist as cabin boys, in which capacity they also did sail training high in the rigging, hence the term "learning the ropes". In 1794 the age for these boy seamen was raised to thirteen and then in 1853 it was raised again to fifteen.

A good captain like Cook or Vancouver would often keep the same men from voyage to voyage, which must have made things easier for both captain and crew. A man joined a particular ship and identified with that ship rather than with the Navy itself. Transfers of sailors between ships were rare and each warship was both a world in itself and the home and workplace of those on board. Indeed the ship was the sailor's life. With so many crammed into such a relatively small vessel discipline and efficiency were paramount and these were fortified by the ancient traditions of the Navy.

The selection of seamen could take many forms. When a young seaman, James Smith, dressed in a common sailor's garb, was walking across London Bridge in the 1840s, he politely touched his cap to one of the Queen's naval officers who was striding the other way. He then turned slightly after the officer had passed as if to speak to him and, noticing the young man's hesitation, the officer called him to come forward.

It was Captain Edward Stanley, who was about to take *HMS Calliope* out to New Zealand to assist in quelling the native disturbances. It just so happened that Smith had been placed by his uncle on the immigrant ship, *Lady Nugent*, as a bound apprentice when she took a shipload of colonists out to Wellington, New Zealand, but, because of problems with the captain on the way out, some of the crew had deserted in Wellington and they induced Seaman Smith to do the same. After the *Lady Nugent* had sailed out of Wellington they had taken employment in the growing settlement.

After a while Smith shipped back to England on the barque *Jane* but he returned to Wellington a second time on the *Tyne*. He again remained for some time and, along with three other seamen, he used to go out in a boat to act as pilot for sailing ships coming through the difficult entrance of Wellington Heads. Smith then returned to England and was about to seek out his uncle to explain himself when he crossed London Bridge and encountered Captain Stanley.

He told the captain of his past experiences and said that he would like to join the Queen's navy and wear the uniform if the captain would help him get a place. Stanley immediately agreed to take the young man on his own vessel as he believed that, with his knowledge of the Wellington coast, he might prove useful when the *Calliope* reached those waters, which had barely been surveyed.

Captain Stanley had him enlisted and sufficient money was given him to join the *Calliope*, which was down at Portsmouth getting ready to sail together with *HMS Driver* to this most distant of Her Majesty's colonies which, at the time, was "a much spoken of but little known British possession". [2]

Smith was the only one on the *Calliope* who had previously visited New Zealand and he was appointed to the position of coxswain. Upon reaching the destination he piloted both the *Calliope* and the *Driver* into Wellington Harbour.

After serving on the *Calliope* through the Maori troubles James Smith got the permission of the man he met on London Bridge to stay on and settle in New Zealand rather than returning to England on the warship.

While in New Zealand waters Captain Stanley found that he needed a few more hands, so he inserted several advertisements in the local newspapers: "Wanted for H.M. Service: 6 or 7 boys to serve on board *HMS Calliope*; they must be at least 14 years of age, 95 lb in weight, and 4 feet, 9 inches in height, agreeable to the Regulations of the Service." [3]

In Sydney in the late 1860s colonial boys were trained in the art of sailing by Lieutenant George Woods on the *Loelia*, a recently decommissioned vessel of the Australia Station.

After the Continuous Service Act recruitment and the terms of engagement became more organised. There was paid leave for the bluejackets between commissions and better terms for sick pay but a sailor still had the right to choose the ship on which he would live and work for years.

When Midshipman the Hon. Frederick Walpole decided to go to sea in 1844 he joined *HMS Collingwood* at Portsmouth prior to her sailing to Valparaiso to join the Pacific squadron. Walpole described his arrival on board as follows, "It was a little after noon when, having performed the ceremony of reporting myself on deck, I descended to see my mess and make acquaintance with my new messmates. The gun-room door was open and even a landsman might have known that there dwelt the "mids". Two deal tables....were placed on either side. The space left clear was occupied by two pugilists who were milling like mad. Beer abounded in large jugs; admiring gazers on the fight sat round, drinking the same; in the ports men of milder mood were solacing themselves with pipes and cigars. One or two, fresh from quieter scenes, were perseveringly trying to read or write. Desks, books, the gifts of tender mothers perhaps, or of fathers who hoped for clever sons, were piled in the corners together with boat gear, swordsticks and heaps of other things. From such a beginning you may judge what our life was to be....

The lieutenants have their own cabins (cupboards seven feet long by eight or nine wide) with a hole three inches round to admit light and air. This lets in a gleam big enough to shave by. The mids sleep in two large, low places called the fore and after cockpits, in large bags, hung up at either end....These hammocks are lashed up and taken on deck every morning at half past six. All the mids wash and dress in public and a noisy, skylarking scene it is, till time has cooled the love of practical jokes; then it tires." [4]

In the latter part of the nineteenth century all officer cadets were given a two year training in the two wooden hulks, *Britannia* and *Hindustan*, that were moored at Dartmouth but in 1902 the navy took over Queen Victoria's residence on the Isle of Wight, Osborne House, and cadets were trained there for two years before going on to the newly built Royal Naval College at Dartmouth for two more years of instruction.

Thus were boys prepared for a life at sea. Whether life on board one of the Sovereign's vessels fulfilled one's expectations or not depended on a lot of things but the "romance of the sea" was more likely to be found in the world's largest, most varied and most exotic ocean than anywhere else.

AUSTRALIA'S NORTHERN OUTPOSTS

"It is widely acknowledged that the ever present protection of the Navy enabled the country (Australia) to pursue its erratic development as an entirely British dominion."

- Lt. Cdr. Geoffrey Ingleton R.A.N. in *Charting A Continent* [1]

In the early nineteenth century Australia began to develop a trade with its northern neighbour, the Dutch East Indies. Merchantmen would sail out of Sydney and up the east coast, rounding Cape York and then into the Arafura Sea bound for Kupang in Timor, Batavia (Jakarta) or Surabaya. The most common place for shipwrecks was near Torres Strait where the coral and shoals of the Great Barrier Reef were both treacherous and largely uncharted.

The closest ports were Sydney to the south and Kupang to the north, with a more or less empty coast in between. There was a growing need for a settlement in the Far North to receive the survivors of shipwrecks and to provide a store of provisions and coal for passing vessels.

For naval officers, who had spent much of their careers fighting France, there was a strategic reason as well for having a base on the north coast of Australia. This was a new continent and it was important to keep it as a single entity under the British flag so as to avoid a replication of the North American situation where there was French Quebec, British North America and the assertive and troublesome republic to the south.

There was such a huge distance between the settled southeast corner of Australia and the uninhabited north coast that it was not at all inconceivable that a foreign power would plant its flag there – not so much because it held a lot of promise but to annoy Britain and thwart its growing empire in Australasia – and it was to the eternal benefit of Australia that the Royal Navy kept an eye on the north and did what it could in the difficult circumstances to establish a base on the north coast of this wide open continent.

The selection of a spot for a settlement was not easy as this was an area almost mind boggling in its vastness. There were islands and river mouths and wide bays and coves and what one captain might regard as a suitable site another might regard as a poor choice.

The first attempt at a northern settlement was made in 1824 when *HMS Tamar*, under the command of Captain James Gordon Bremer, whom we last met fighting the Chinese in the Canton River, and two escort vessels sailed up from Sydney to establish a permanent military outpost. The *Tamar* had been specially sent from England for this purpose as the British government was keen to get its hands on some of the trade of the East Indies, in which the Dutch had a monopoly, and there were even a few giddy-headed idealists who talked of creating a second Singapore.

On these three ships were soldiers, marines, convicts, free labourers and even a few wives of the military officers. There were also livestock, plants and seedlings, and preserved food to keep them going during the crucial first few months, which could make or break a new settlement. Also on board were some prefabricated buildings to house the officers and contain the stores so as to keep them dry.

During his survey of this coast in 1818 Captain Phillip Parker King had written enthusiastically of Port Essington, which he had named after one of his friends, Vice-Admiral Sir William Essington, and Captain Bremer's instructions were to go there and establish a settlement. However, upon seeing it and after a brief and fruitless search for water, he decided to move on to Melville Island, the large island to the north of the later city of Darwin. It had been named after Henry Dundas, the first Viscount Melville, who had been Pitt the Younger's great war minister.

The *Tamar* arrived there on 26th September, 1824 and Captain Bremer raised the Union Jack on Luxmore Head, near the northern entrance to Apsley Strait. He claimed both Melville Island and the nearby Bathurst Island in the name of King George IV, that part of Australia being outside the boundaries of the colony of New South Wales and therefore hitherto unclaimed territory.

They immediately began construction of a fort, which they named Fort Dundas after Sir Philip Dundas, the First Lord of the Admiralty. Using the convict labour that they had brought with them, they established a blockhouse, pier, garden, observation posts and an underground magazine for storing gunpowder. There were also cannon to deter any foreign warships that might want to contest the occupation.

One of the *Tamar's* officers, Lieutenant John Septimus Roe, made a survey of the harbour. This was later published by the

Admiralty and it was still being used, almost unaltered, as late as the Second World War.

After Captain Bremer left in the *Tamar* this fortified settlement was run by the Army but after cyclones, tropical fever, white ants eating the wood, various bouts of heat exhaustion and a series of skirmishes with the aborigines, who killed the doctor and storekeeper with their spears, the government in London decided that it formed no useful military purpose and that the price was greater than its value. It was therefore abandoned in 1829, by which time the garrison had moved to Raffles Bay on the Coburg Peninsula, on the mainland, which had been founded a year earlier by Captain James Stirling (later the first Governor of Western Australia) on *HMS Success* and was called Fort Wellington. Here there was even worse trouble with the natives and this too was abandoned so that by the end of 1829 there was no remaining British settlement in northern Australia.

In October, 1838, a third attempt was made when Captain Bremer took another vessel, *HMS Alligator*, and two supply ships to establish a post at Port Essington. This time he was more favourably disposed towards the place than he had been in 1824.

Nevertheless the new settlement was not all that friendly a place – as had been acknowledged by Captain King. When the *Mermaid's* boat got entangled in mangrove roots, its men were attacked by spears and stones thrown from inside the mangroves. In Captain King's words, "Two muskets loaded with ball, and a fowling piece with small shot, were fired over their heads, which had the desired effect, for they gave up their premeditated attack and quickly disappeared among the bushes, where they remained screaming and vociferating loudly in angry, threatening voices." [2]

The *Mermaid* then hoisted sails and steered round the shore of the bay. They saw the natives' canoe secured to the beach by a small rope and, in Captain King's words, it "offered so good an opportunity of punishing these savages for their treacherous attack, that we landed and brought it away. In it we found not only their clubs but also a large quantity of shellfish so that we had not only deprived them of their boat but their supper, and three very formidable clubs....The canoe was nearly new, it measured eighteen feet in length and two feet in breadth and would easily carry eight persons....The canoe was made of one sheet of bark." [3]

Despite this inauspicious introduction Captain King spoke highly of Port Essington. "As a harbour Port Essington is equal, if not superior, to any I ever saw; and from its proximity to the Moluccas and New Guinea and its being in the direct line of communication between Port Jackson (Sydney) and India, as well as from its commanding situation with respect to the passage through Torres Strait, it must, at no very distant period, become a place of great trade and of very considerable importance." [4]

Captain Bremer shared King's enthusiasm for this large, landlocked harbour, which was sixteen miles from its entrance to its head and was surrounded by swamps, mudbanks, mangrove marshes and some lagoons. "The blue gum trees, the finest and stateliest trees of Australia, grow along the river courses," noted Captain Keppel of *HMS Maeander* when he visited the place in 1849. [5]

A town, called Victoria, was built near the head of the harbour, and the settlement was protected by a detachment of Royal Marines. On 25th November, 1839, its buildings were flattened in a cyclone, which killed twelve people and drove *HMS Pelorus* aground.

The place was rebuilt with the help of convict labour; there was a wooden cottage for the commandant, a wooden hospital, a mess room and officers' quarters, and huts made of reeds and thatch for the men. Some had gardens around their huts and there was also a large garden on the edge of the settlement, in which grew melons, pumpkins, yams, sweet potatoes, bananas, chilis, peppers, pineapples and breadfruit. Then in 1846 a Catholic Mission was established.

However, Port Essington also suffered from sickness (mainly fever and digestive problems), the white ant and a climate that was both unhealthy and unbearable – especially in the rainy season from December to May. There was also the occasional crocodile. Oh, and a million flies.

The natives sometimes stole the stores but otherwise did not give much trouble. As a refuge for shipwrecked sailors Port Essington was hardly more successful since most of the wrecks occurred near Torres Strait – six hundred miles away.

When *HMS Fly* visited the port in August, 1843, its naturalist, J. Beete Jukes, wrote, "The aspect of the place was anything but cheerful or inviting, even to us who had been so long at sea." [6] From their ship the men of the *Fly* could see a clearing in which there were a few white buildings and there was also a small, wooden blockhouse with a flagstaff on a projecting cliff. The people "looked very sickly and debilitated and many were still in hospital or had only just come out of it." [7]

When Captain Owen Stanley arrived at Port Essington on *HMS Rattlesnake* in November, 1848, he too found the settlement "in a very sickly state". [8] The buildings were neither windproof nor watertight and the Catholic missionary, Father Angelo, had just died of fever.

Of Port Essington John McGillivray, the naturalist on the *Rattlesnake*, wrote, "When will that useless pesthouse be blotted off the face of the earth? At this anchorage we were baked and roasted as usual without a breath of air for days." [9] These sentiments were endorsed by Thomas Huxley, the *Rattlesnake's* zoologist, who described it as "most wretched, the climate the most unhealthy, the human beings the most uncomfortable and houses in a condition most decayed and rotten." Little wonder then that the following year (1849) Port Essington, after eleven years of struggle, joined the list of abandoned settlements in the north of Australia.

News of its death knell came in November, 1849, when *HMS Maeander* arrived with orders to evacuate it. The Marines were delighted and, with considerable enthusiasm, joined with the sailors in destroying all the buildings. It was considered that these jerry built structures would be of little use to the natives, who were wanderers rather than settlers, and it was feared that, if they were left standing, they might provoke bloodshed between the tribes as jealousy would attach to whoever might take up residence in the Commandant's house. Also, the British government did not want any other Europeans to settle there. What they did leave behind them was a number of cattle and some horses, which quickly went wild. The last day was 1st December, 1849, when, in the words of Captain Keppel of the *Maeander*, "The garrison marched down to embark with the band at their head." [10]

The unfavourable view of Port Essington by the *Rattlesnake* people was coloured by the fact that they sailed there from Cape York where Captain Stanley and his men had been impressed by a bay on the west side of the Albany Islands, four and a half miles from Cape York, which he named Port Albany. He thought that it would be suitable as a coal depot in the event of steamers plying between Sydney and India. There was plenty of depth in the water, a place for a wharf and some coarse sandstone nearby for building. This was also the opinion of the first Governor of Queensland, Sir George Bowen, who had recently visited the area on *HMS Pioneer*.

The Cape York area did replace Port Essington as Australia's northern settlement but not immediately and it was not at Captain Stanley's preferred choice of Port Albany but at Point Somerset (later "Somerset"), a few miles south-east of Cape York. It was named after the then First Lord of the Admiralty.

The advantage of a settlement here was that all vessels passing through Torres Strait had to come within sight of Cape York and Point Somerset. This gave it a strategic importance as in wartime an enemy vessel occupying Cape York would command all the commerce passing between Sydney and Asia.

The climate was better at Cape York than at Port Essington – "The atmosphere (at Port Essington) felt very hot and close after the fresh breeze we had been accustomed to in Torres Strait," wrote J.Beete Jukes of HMS Fly.[11] Also, being near the coral reefs that caused the wrecks, it would be easier to save both crews and cargos from the stricken vessels. It was important to put a stop to the constant murders of shipwrecked crews by the blacks.

The task of establishing this new settlement in the dense, tropical jungle and taking to it pre-fabricated wooden houses was entrusted to HMS Salamander but there were so many stores, building materials and people to convey that her captain, Hon. John Carnegie, chartered the barque Golden Eagle as a storeship.

The two ships arrived at their destination from Sydney at the end of July, 1864. On board the Salamander was a detachment of twenty marines under Lieutenant Pascoe to guard the new colony against any attacks by natives.

The officials included a Government Resident/magistrate, Mr. John Jardine, an ex-Dragoon officer, as well as a Clerk of Petty Sessions, Rev. L. Rumsey, who also conducted church services. There was a surveyor to lay out the town while the medical charge of the settlement was entrusted to Doctor Haran of the Royal Navy. Both Lieutenant Pascoe and Mr. Jardine gave their names to rivers on the Cape York Peninsula.

The marines spent their first days felling trees with the help of the Salamander's carpenters in order to clear a place for them to pitch their tents as convict labour was no longer available.

The Golden Eagle arrived a few days after the Salamander and landed 252 sheep on Albany Island as well as seven horses on the mainland. "Nearly the whole of the crew of the Salamander, with the two paddle-box boats and cutters, were employed from ten to twelve hours a day.....clearing the Golden Eagle and landing the

139

building materials and stores in Somerset Bay....and in coaling the *Salamander* and placing 154 tons of coal in reserve on Albany Island.....as many men as were required were sent daily to remove the framework, etc. for the houses on the beach to the site on Somerset Point. The direct ascent being too steep for the horses and drays, the material was hoisted by means of a large winch, erected near the summit." [12] Hard work in the heat and no doubt some of the older hands yearned for the easier days of convict labour.

During the first few months five of the marines were speared by the blacks; in fact, so hostile were the natives that it was not safe for the marines to move more than half a mile from their wooden barracks. These natives were members of the same tribe that had murdered the botanist of the Leichardt expedition in 1845 and the explorer, Edmund Kennedy, and members of his party in 1848.

HMS Salamander continued to supply the new settlement and survey the surrounding seas. A few months later, on 20th January, 1865, while steering to the south-west through the Blackwood Channel on the recommended route, the *Salamander* struck on an unknown coral patch with only seven feet on its shoalest part at low water. This tricky patch was about 230 yards long and 110 yards wide and had ten to seventeen fathoms all around it. It is now known as the Salamander Bank.

The ship also gave her name to the Salamander River when in 1867 her commander, Captain Nares, sailed her a few miles down the coast from Cape York and anchored off Middle Reef, Weymouth Bay. He led a party up a previously unknown river in the boats, its shallow mouth being marked on the charts as "Kennedy's last camp" – after the explorer, Edmund Kennedy. The boats penetrated about ten miles up the river, which at that distance was about thirty yards across and twelve feet deep. "Each side of the river is clothed with palms and pandanus, and is very picturesque and tropical looking," wrote Australia's *Port Denison Times.* [13]

HMS Salamander's surveying work in the area was of vital importance as there were still some very nasty and treacherous reefs and shoals that were still uncharted, and wrecks were common. On 19th July, 1866, the barque *Cathay*, bound from Sydney to Java, struck a reef that was not marked on any chart. The crew managed to get off in a boat and, after being at sea for five days, each subsisting on a biscuit and a half a pint of water a day, they arrived off Stephen's Island in Torres Strait where the schooner *Melanie* was lying at anchor. She took them on board and delivered them to

140

Somerset where *HMS Salamander* took them to Cleveland Bay, whence they got passage to Sydney.

In the same month the barque *Adelaide*, going from Sydney to Java with a cargo of coal and flour, struck a reef near the Olinda Entrance to the Great Barrier Reef. This crew also got away on a boat but with no provisions or water. After landing on an island and eating some birds' eggs they reached Orford Bay on the mainland whence they sailed up the coast to the new settlement at Somerset.

Yet a third wreck in the same month of July was the *Conqueror*, bound from Newcastle, N.S.W., for Bombay with a cargo of coal. She too hit a reef and the sailors escaped in boats. After eleven days in the boiling sun and limitless sea, they reached Somerset. These three wrecks in the course of a single month provided ample justification for the establishment of the nearby settlement at Cape York rather than having to travel six hundred miles to Port Essington – as had hitherto been the case.

With the establishment of Somerset northern Australia at last had a suitable outpost although in 1877 the official class moved to a new site on Thursday Island. The establishment of these bases had been achieved through much trial and error, the only constant being the presence of the Royal Navy at every stage of the tortuous process. Be it starting a settlement or abandoning it, there were always one or two naval vessels in these waters, and the knowledge that they were there served to dissuade foreign powers from sending a warship or two to start a settlement on the northern coast of this newly discovered continent.

As the mistress of the sea throughout the nineteenth century Britain did not need to have a great fleet in any one place to act as a deterrent to others; one or two ships flying the White Ensign were enough to make the point. That was the whole purpose of sea power whereby the world had one overwhelming navy that called the shots for the good not only of the British Empire but of all mankind.

In the words of Admiral Mahan, the great American authority on sea power, "The peace of the world is assured by the strength of the British Navy". That Australia is to-day a unitary state, the only country in the world to cover an entire continent, is due in no small way to the stop-start outposts on its northern coast which kept the Royal Navy constantly in the area. These scattered outposts might not have seemed a lot in such a large area but, representing as they did the might of the British Empire, they were sufficient.

ISLAND DEPOTS

As the dominant force on the waters of the Pacific in the nineteenth century the Royal Navy assumed an awful lot of responsibilities – not just to British ships and seamen but to those of other nations as well. Among these duties was to search for lost vessels and scour remote islands for castaways from wrecks.

In 1819 Captain Phillip Parker King R.N. in the *Mermaid* surveyed the "Inner Route" up through the Great Barrier Reef. This enters inside the reef at its southern extremity and runs up the coast of Queensland between the land and the reef – or, more exactly, the reefs since the Great Barrier is a series of reefs rather than one long reef. Although often narrow and intricate, the Inner Route was considered safe because there were good anchorages the whole way and the reefs provided an ideal shelter from the turbulence of the ocean beyond.

Ships passing between Sydney and the East Indies/China began to use this route but their captains had to be very careful as, if a vessel was blown on to a sharp coral reef, that was usually the end of it.

In the first half of the nineteenth century there were no white settlements in north Queensland that could give provisions and safety, and from 1838 to 1849 the nearest station to Torres Strait, through which all ships taking the Inner Route passed, was at Port Essington on the Coburg peninsula.

The waters of Torres Strait were always dangerous for navigation as the smallest mistake could put a vessel on a coral reef very quickly. To be so wrecked on a reef was less fatal for the crew and passengers than for the ship since the water around the reef was shallow and one could usually get away in a small boat. However, the survivors of a wreck in Torres Strait were faced with a voyage of six hundred miles to Port Essington in a ship's boat and, even then, there was no guarantee of getting there as, apart from the perils of the sea, the low, featureless land around Port Essington was difficult to make out and it could easily be missed or passed in the night and then could not be regained in the wind. The next stop in these vast seas was the small port of Kupang in Dutch Timor – another five hundred miles further west than Port Essington.

In these circumstances a small depot was established on Booby Island, a rocky islet about fifty feet high and a third of a mile in diameter which forms the western limit of the dangerous part of

Torres Strait. It had first been visited by Captain Cook in 1770 but was given its name by Captain Bligh when he landed there in 1788 during his epic voyage in the longboat from Tonga to Timor after he lost *HMS Bounty* to the mutineers. They named it after all the boobies (gannets) that lived there. These birds, about the size of a duck, had in turn been given their name by British sailors who noticed how these dumb creatures allowed themselves to be caught in the masts and yards of sailing ships.

When the *Mermaid* visited Booby in 1819 Captain King wrote, "Some slight vegetation was perceived upon it but it was so entirely covered with the excrement of birds that it had the appearance of being whitewashed. The number of these birds was almost incredible and they hovered over and about us as we passed, as if to drive us from their haunt." [1]

Booby Island was already being used as a "post office" of the seas; the following year Captain King noted that ships' crews had made piles of stones at the summit as mementos of their visits while on a board was recorded the safe passage through Torres Strait of the merchantman *Sea Flower*, which left Sydney on 21st May, 1820, and took the Outer Route through the Great Barrier Reef, reaching Booby after a voyage of twenty-two days. Captain King was able to check the *Sea Flower* off the list that he had been given in Sydney of ships that had left there and would pass through Torres Strait. The post office on Booby took the form of a cave where a captain could leave a letter, knowing that it would be picked up and delivered by a captain passing the other way.

When the merchant ship, *Louisa Campbell*, passed through Torres Strait in 1842 her captain, W. Darby, reported, "Saw Booby Island from topsail-yard WSW steering for the islands; at 6 p.m. hove to….and sent a boat to the post office for what letters there might be, and left some more for the next ship. By letters we obtained there, found that the ships which came the inshore passage had all lost either anchors or windlass pauls, and made long passages. The ships which came our route were much better off, and I always recommend the outside….The passage is not so dangerous or intricate as I had anticipated. After entering the Barrier every danger is to be seen from the topsail yard and can be easily avoided." [2] Ah yes, whenever sailors from different ships communicated – either by word of mouth on Booby or by letter through its post office – the main topic of conversation was the respective merits of the Inner and Outer Routes up through the Great Barrier Reef.

In 1844 Captain Blackwood of *HMS Fly* decided to add to Booby's facilities by establishing a depot there as well with supplies that could be used by sailors who might be shipwrecked in these tricky seas but managed to reach Booby.

The men of the *Fly* erected a shed on the island and left there a keg of beef and some biscuit. There was also a box containing a blank book, pen and ink for passing captains of merchant vessels to record their presence in the area, the date and their proposed route after leaving Booby so that it would be easier to locate ships that might get into trouble.

To make sure that sea captains were aware of the new facility a "Notice to Masters of Vessels Intending to Pass through Torres Straits" was inserted in the New South Wales Government Gazette, the final sentence being "Directions for finding the provisions will be left at the place called 'The Post Office' on Booby Island." [3] A treasure hunt!

There were some amusing entries in the book, including one from a lady passenger who sent her love to any other lady who might pass; she even left her address, which was Bow Road, London.

A year after setting up the depot and stocking it *HMS Fly* was surveying the coast of New Guinea with her two tenders, the *Prince George* and the *Midge*. Unfortunately, the shoal bank, stretching out from the shore near the mouth of the Fly River, was so shallow that neither the *Fly* nor the *Prince George* could get close enough to the coast to trace its outline and so they sent off parties in the *Midge* and the *Fly's* second gig with five days' provisions to do the work while they ran along the coast further out in deeper water. On these two small boats were three officers and twelve men. all well armed, and the *Midge* had a small boat gun fitted on her forecastle.

The *Prince George*, having a shallower depth than the *Fly*, was ordered to keep as close in as the depth of the water would allow so as to be in signal distance of both the two boats inshore and the *Fly* further out. The sea was a dirty green – not unlike the English Channel – while the river water flowing down the Fly was of a mud brown colour.

The weather turned dirty and, when it cleared, there was no sign of the *Midge* or the second gig. Since neither the *Fly* nor the

Prince George could get closer than eight miles from the shore the cutter and the first gig were sent off to look for the missing boats but they returned without finding them and it started to rain again, limiting visibility. It was feared that the two lost boats had been swamped in heavy seas or had landed and had their men killed by the natives.

By now provisions were running low on the *Fly* and so it was decided to return to Australian waters without the two missing boats. These boats had, in fact, run south for Booby Island so that, when the *Fly* passed Booby, they saw the previously arranged signal for good news flying from the island. And, better still, the crews of the *Midge* and the second gig had used the very provisions that the *Fly* had left on Booby the previous year.

In addition to naval vessels replenishing the stock of provisions whenever they were passing the Governor of New South Wales issued a proclamation asking merchant vessels to do the same, if they stopped there and found that supplies were running low, and many of them did. When Captain D. Welsh of the *Lady Octavia*, bound from Sydney to Calcutta, was passing through the waters of Torres Strait in 1866 he noticed two recent wrecks so he stopped at Booby to leave a letter for the next Royal Navy vessel that called there, giving the location of the stricken vessels. He also landed a bag of bread and some fresh water to replenish the food stocks.

After leaving Sydney for Batavia in 1863 the Dutch warship *Djambi* dropped off fresh supplies at Booby. In the words of its captain, P. A. van Rees, "I brought over an iron tank and provisions. It blew a stiff easterly gale, and there was a very rough sea, so that I was obliged to anchor close to the isle for shelter.

I found in the cave of the isle still left some provisions but some of the casks of salt meat and bacon were burst open, and the insects were devouring the contents, giving a most disgusting smell.....I took the letters out of the box and posted them at Batavia." [4]

From time to time the natives would sail across to Booby and ransack the provisions but on the whole this conception of Captain Blackwood of the *Fly* served its purpose and some of the shipwrecked sailors owed their lives to what they found there. Among these were some of the survivors of the merchantman *Sapphire*, which was wrecked on the Great Barrier Reef in 1859. Eighteen of the men made it to the mainland where they were massacred by the natives while another eleven reached Booby Island "and availed themselves of the provisions stored there for shipwrecked mariners". [5]

The establishment of a permanent post at nearby Point Somerset in 1864 rendered Booby Island somewhat superfluous as a depot but that does not diminish its value as a rendezvous of the seas, in which capacity it served for several decades during which time it was the saviour of many a shipwrecked sailor.

*****

The Auckland Islands and Campbell Island are as far away from Booby Island in distance and climate as one could imagine but, like Booby, they too contained depots with provisions that were maintained by the Royal Navy.

These bleak, remote, storm ridden islands between New Zealand and Antarctica were sometimes visited by whaling vessels but there were often long periods between visits. In January, 1839, four men were found on Campbell Island who stated that they had been left there four years earlier by a vessel called the *New Zealander.* [6]

The Aucklands, three hundred miles south of New Zealand, had been discovered by a whaling ship in 1806 and, like New Zealand's largest city, were named after Lord Auckland, the First Lord of the Admiralty. In 1849 a colonising attempt was made from London but, not surprisingly, it failed and, after 1856, the Aucklands were, like Campbell Island, uninhabited. However, like Tristan da Cunha in the South Atlantic, these rocky islands received the wreckage of ships from time to time. In 1864 there were three shipwrecks: the *Minerva* (only four survivors), the *Invercauld* (nineteen of the crew of twenty-five reached the shore and all but three later starved to death), and the *Grafton*, whose crew lived on fish and seal meat for eighteen months before a party of them set out for Stewart Island at the bottom of New Zealand. After the wreck of the *General Grant* in 1866, the Admiralty ordered that a naval vessel must visit the islands every six months to look for any shipwrecked crews and maintain the food stores that were kept there.

The *General Grant* had left Melbourne in May, 1866, for London via Cape Horn with thirty-four male passengers (mostly men returning from the Victorian gold fields), six women, twenty

146

children, twenty-three crew and a cargo of wool, hides and 2,470 ounces of gold.

Like most vessels sailing from Melbourne to the Horn, the *General Grant* took a very southerly route so as to take advantage of the strong, sub Antarctic gales. She was so far south that in a fog she was wrecked on the Auckland Islands.

Only fourteen men and one woman made it to the shore. Between them they had only one dry match and so they lit a fire that was never allowed to go out during the eighteen months that they were stranded on this cold, bleak, uninhabited island. They killed seals for food and made clothes and shoes from the seal skin. Needles were made from the wing bones of albatrosses and were used to sew a thread made from flax.

With no sign of any help four of them set out in an open boat without a chart, compasses or nautical instruments. They were never seen again.

Eventually, on 21st November, 1867, the others were spotted by a passing brig, the *Amherst*, that was hunting for sea elephant oil and sperm whale oil, and so they were taken on board and then had to put in two months on the ship while it carried out its mission. They were then taken to New Zealand whence they were repatriated to Melbourne and so, after two years, they were back where they started.

Captain P. Gilroy of the *Amherst* then returned to the Auckland Islands to establish depots of supplies for the benefit of anyone who might be shipwrecked there in the future. At the depot on Enderby Island he left a case that contained clothing (no more wearing of seal skins to keep warm!), blankets, compass, matches and tools. He attached a notice to the box, which read: "The curse of the widow and fatherless light upon the man who breaks open this box whilst he has a ship at his back".

The first naval vessel to inspect and replenish the depot after it was set up was *HMS Blanche*, which left Wellington on 11th March, 1869, on a voyage that the Wellington *Independent* described as being "seldom looked upon as a yachting tour". [7]

For the first few days the *Blanche* was under steam but then she met the south-west gales and so she went the rest of the way under sail. One blast of wind was so strong that it carried away the jib-boom. "Instantly and without hesitation numbers of men sprang out to clear the wreck" [8] but one of them lost his hold and fell into the freezing ocean. "At once the sharpest eyes were set to watch the

147

small speck as it got farther and farther. The ship was stopped and a boat lowered in the space of a moment. He had got hold of a lifebuoy and, though it was some time before he could be seen from the boat and longer before he was picked up on account of the heavy sea, still all were thankful that he was saved, so doubtful it was that the man had given up all hope," wrote the Wellington *Independent*. [9] While in the water his greatest danger was not drowning but being killed by albatrosses, which "kept darting at him and compelling him to duck his head under water to avoid them". [10]

After arriving in the Aucklands the *Blanche* anchored in the deep harbour known as Sarah's Bosom at Port Ross and the next day boat parties were sent out to examine the state of the depots. It was found that they had not been touched. Nevertheless the sailors added to them a cask of beef, a cask of bread and one of other condiments, all the casks being water-tight and hermetically sealed.

Some parties went shooting while others spent their days cutting roads "and accomplished the arduous task of making a most useful road through one mile of the densest bush imaginable". [11]

On 16th March the captain and officers of the *Blanche* landed and took formal possession of these god-forsaken islands "in the name of Her Most Gracious Majesty Queen Victoria for the New Zealand government. *Feu de joies* (sic) were fired, and three hearty cheers given for our new possession". [12]

The *Blanche* left Port Ross on 19th March and put in at another part of the main island called Norman's Inlet, "a narrow strip of sea running some six miles into the heart of the island". [13] Here the ship "encountered a heavy gale and, during one of the squalls, she parted her cable and drove ashore but got off again without damage. For seven days after this she had to contend against a fearful westerly gale, hove to under a close reefed maintopsail and forestaysail." [14] When water blew over the ship in the form of spray, it "stung the face like hail". [15]

So bad were conditions that, instead of inspecting further depots at Carnley Harbour, the *Blanche* headed back to New Zealand where it was reported that "Her officers speak of her behaviour during this trying time in the highest terms and think her fit to encounter any weather". [16]

Perhaps that was why she was sent back to the Auckland Islands the following year to look for the *Matatoka,* which had left Lyttelton, New Zealand, for London with forty-five passengers and thirty-two crew and was never heard of again.

The men of the *Blanche* again checked the food stores, which they found had been emptied with the casks left exposed to the weather and having considerable water in them. The sailors dried the casks and left a fresh supply of food, clothes and blankets. They also rethatched the small hut in which these provisions were kept and placed a signboard on the shore, showing the road to Pig Point where a large type of flagstaff had been erected. It was painted white so that it could be seen as far out to sea as possible. In sealed bottles at its base were placed papers for passing mariners to record the dates of their visits and their ships.

In trying to find any survivors of the *Matatoka* as well as six missing men from the schooner *Daphne*, the *Blanche* went around the main island under easy steam, keeping as close to the shore as possible and firing her guns periodically to attract attention but there was no sign of any shipwrecked sailors.

The *Daphne*, a Melbourne registered schooner, had gone to the Auckland Islands to look for the *General Grant* or, more precisely, to try to recover the gold that was said to be on that doomed vessel. During her search she lost six of her own men, who failed to make a rendezvous on one of the islands, and she then returned to Bluff, New Zealand, to recruit replacements. The kind Captain Gilroy went back with them to search for the six lost souls but they were never found.

In 1874 the *Blanche* made another trip to the Aucklands to check the food depots. While on one of the islands, Enderby, the captain and a party, including the ship's doctor, went walking and they "were suddenly brought to a standstill by the sad spectacle of an almost perfect skeleton of a man". [17]

This time they also managed to visit Carnley Harbour, which was described as "a magnificent harbour, abounding in small bays and inlets, which in many places form smaller harbours, almost landlocked. In one or two of the bays the Channel Fleet could find a safe and convenient anchorage. The only drawback is the wind, which blows in great gusts down the gullies, making it difficult for sailing vessels to reach the inner anchorage." [18]

After leaving the Aucklands the *Blanche* went further south to Campbell Island and renewed the stocks at the depot that had been established there. Although no castaways were seen, "A very large number of seals and albatrosses were captured and are now alive on board." [19]

These depots grew and improved with every visit by the Navy as no doubt the sailors put themselves in the place of the shipwrecked men as they tended the stores. When *HMS Emerald* made an inspection of the depots at the Auckland Islands in 1879 the main depot was described as "an extensive one, abundantly supplied with provisions, tools and a Snider rifle. Major Campbell, a guest of Captain Maxwell (of the *Emerald*) left behind a liberal supply of ammunition." [20]

Another communications post was set up in the Magellan Straits but this was more of a "post office" than a depot for supplies. It took the form of a barrel that was chained to the rocks and in it mariners could leave letters that would be picked up by passing vessels.

THE SIEGE OF PETROPAVLOVSK

The big event for the Royal Navy in the mid nineteenth century was the Crimean War, which was essentially a naval war. The only way for Britain to attack Russia was by sea and, besides transporting the troops to the Crimea, the Navy also fought engagements with the Russian ships in the Black Sea, the Baltic, the White Sea and the North Pacific. The Czar's navy was weak and this was an important factor in the war's outcome.

The British and French ships of their respective Pacific squadrons were ordered to engage the Russians as it was feared that Russia and the United States might join together against Britain and France, which would threaten the supremacy of the Royal Navy in the Pacific. In the event this didn't happen in the 1850s but it did a century later at Suez in 1956 when that dirty old adulterer, Dwight Eisenhower, who had relied on superior British generalship to win the War, repaid the debt by sticking the knife into Britain at the first opportunity when, as President, he sided with the Soviet Union to support Nasser's act of international piracy in seizing the Suez Canal by force.

In the Pacific the Czar's three vessels, *Pallada*, *Aurora* and *Dvina*, were outnumbered by the combined British-French fleet comprising the frigates *HMS President* (flagship) of 50 guns, and *HMS Pique* (40 guns), the paddle steamer *HMS Virago* (6 guns), and the French warships *Forte* (60 guns), *Eurydice* (30 guns) and *Obligado* (18 guns). All the ships were painted entirely black to confuse the Russians.

Aware of his opponents' superiority, the Russian commander, Rear-Admiral Putyatin, decided not to risk a sea engagement but to lure the Allies into Avatska Bay, at the top of which is the town of Petropavlovsk (sometimes spelt Petropavlovski and translating as "Peter and Paul"). Although not much more than a small garrison town, this was Russia's main port on the bleak Kamchatka peninsula and it was defended by several shore batteries.

Putyatin sent his biggest ship, the *Pallada* (60 guns), across to the Amur River to reinforce the weak garrisons on its banks while the other two ships took up position in Avatska Bay. Into this reasonably well defended bay the Allied fleet sailed on 29th August, 1854. In the words of one of the British officers, "On making the high land of Kamchatka, our excitement was very great, having little or no idea of the position and strength of the batteries we were about to attack." [1] The approach to the bay was "very grand; high mountains (volcanoes) appearing on either side, covered with snow, and looking magnificent amongst the clouds. On one side of the bay, on a hill about 700 or 800 feet high, we perceived a lighthouse, in front of which and commanding the entrance is a large gun which, as we neared the land, was fired to give the alarm to the batteries and town, situated out of sight of the entrance and about eight miles up the bay. We passed this point in great style, the *President* (with the admiral's flag flying) leading the way. We anchored out of gunshot of the batteries, which were all manned and ready to receive us.....The place is situated at the base of a mountain about 12,000 or 14,000 feet high – a volcano covered entirely with snow. We had the pleasure of witnessing it in action. The town lies in a hollow, and another huge mountain is behind it. The shape of the harbour is something like a horseshoe and at the entrance to the port on one side is a battery of three heavy guns." [2]

Further in towards the town was another battery of eleven guns, situated on an elongated, narrow promontory that projected a long way into the harbour and behind which lay the Russian frigate *Aurora* and corvette *Dvina*, the sole remaining Russian vessels to defend the place, their broadsides facing the entrance to the harbour. Altogether there were eight batteries mounting about fifty guns.

On the previous afternoon the British commander-in-chief, Rear-Admiral David Price, boarded the *Virago* to reconnoitre the enemy positions at Avatska Bay. One glance would have told a wise commander that this was a well-defended bay and that little could be achieved by bombarding its forts.

Unfortunately Price was neither wise nor experienced. In fact, this sixty-four year old admiral was quite unfit to be in command of a ship, let alone a fleet. Although fighting bravely as a young man in both the Napoleonic Wars and the War of 1812 against the Americans he had been put out to grass in 1815 and served only four years at sea in the ensuing thirty-eight years! And the elderly and sick French commander, Rear Admiral Fevrier-Despointes, was not much better. As a result of his reconnaissance Price ordered a direct frontal assault on the powerful forts and batteries for the next day. Thus began the terrible and unnecessary tragedy of Petropavlovsk, an engagement that has been all but buried from sight by subsequent historians.

The 29th was the day chosen for the Allied bombardment of this far western outpost of the Czar's empire. Rear-Admiral Price was on the deck of *HMS President* by 6 a.m. and climbed up the rigging as high as the maintop to obtain a better view of the enemy positions. He next visited the French admiral and then returned to the *President*.

A few minutes after climbing back on to his flagship he went below to a side-cabin and, obviously out of his mind, put a pistol to his left breast and pulled the trigger to shoot himself through the heart. He couldn't even get that right and the bullet went into his lung instead. He lingered for about three hours, crying out, "O God, kill me at once!" and then passed out of this world, leaving behind a leaderless fleet and a hopeless plan of attack.

In the words of Rev. Thomas Holme, chaplain of *HMS President*, Price "was always very weak and vacillating in everything he did". [3] So why was he appointed to command a fleet?

It is not unknown for admirals to crack up under the strain of war, e.g. Prince Louis of Battenberg couldn't face his duties as First Sea Lord when the First World War broke out and suffered a nervous breakdown while his successor, Lord Fisher, went mad under the same stresses and, like Price, deserted his post in time of war. But for a commander-in-chief to desert his post on the eve of battle in such spectacular fashion seems to be unprecedented in the history of the Navy.

The bombardment planned for that day had to be called off while Sir Frederick Nicolson Bt. took over command of the fleet and of Price's flawed battle plan.

At eight o'clock on the following morning the attack was resumed when *HMS President*, *HMS Pique* and the French *Forte* opened fire on three batteries that had a total of nineteen guns.

The smallest battery was captured with the help of a landing party from *HMS Virago* and its pieces were spiked and the gun carriages and platforms destroyed. The other two batteries were silenced before dusk but during the night the Russians repaired them all and they were back in action the following morning.

The *Virago's* next task was to take the body of Rear-Admiral Price across the water to an unfrequented part of Tarienski harbour to be buried beneath a tree, his initials being cut on the tree to mark the spot. During this short voyage she picked up three American seamen who had deserted from whaling vessels.

These three scoundrels – deserters from vessels at the lowest level of the shipping trade – gave certain information that was either treacherous or mistaken, the result of which was a decision by the

British and French commanders to make a landing so as to try to take the batteries from the landward side.

Early on the morning of 4th September the ships sailed across to a low part of the peninsula to land troops. As they approached, *HMS President* suffered serious damage when, in range of one of the Russian batteries, a shot entered a port on her main keel deck, killing two of a gun's crew and wounding all the others.

Several more shots entered her starboard side and one actually passed through a chest belonging to a junior officer. The battery was eventually silenced by the French warship, *Forte*.

With the two nearby projecting batteries out of action, some seven hundred Allied sailors and marines were landed in accordance with the Americans' advice. Above this landing place was a hill covered with thick, tangled brushwood as well as Russian soldiers.

The latter were driven back as the Allies forced their way to the top of the hill but, when they tried to advance along its summit, they were lured by their new American "friends" into a position where they had bullets fired at them by Russian sharpshooters. Many of them were killed and not all by the Russians as in the confusion it was almost impossible to tell friend from foe.

The only course now was to retreat back to the warships but the terrain was difficult and there was great confusion, resulting in more casualties. The whole exercise had lasted only three hours and had cost the lives of 107 British and 101 French. "From the ships our men appeared to be falling down the sides of the hill as if shot; some headlong, some rolling, and all in the greatest confusion," wrote a British officer on board one of the warships. [4]

After the last man was brought on board the warships withdrew out of range so that the medics could attend to the wounded. In the words of the chaplain of *HMS President*, "The scene on board the ships now became terrible. Each minute some new wounded man was handed down, and our attention was continually called from those who had before been handed down wounded to new wounds." [5] Some of the dead were taken ashore and buried fifty yards from the grave of Rear-Admiral Price.

In the words of the historian of the Royal Navy, William Laird Clowes, "In spite of the difficulties in their way, both British and French behaved with great bravery." [6]

Then, on 7th September, the British and French ships sailed away from this wretched Kamchatka coast. During their short visit they had lost officers and men by both gunfire and suicide and had

154

achieved virtually nothing. Most of their woes sprang from Price's suicide as, had that deranged officer not taken his own life, they would not have gone to sea and encountered the American deserters, who were the source of so much trouble.

Some two hours after getting outside Petropavlovsk harbour the warships had their only stroke of good luck when they came across the *Sitka*, a 700 ton vessel belonging to the Russian American Fur Company, which was bound for Petropavlovsk with the winter store of provisions and ammunition for the garrison. She was captured as a prize and her crew of twenty-eight were taken on board the *President*.

Running short of both food and water, the British ships sailed to Vancouver Island to reprovision while the French vessels went on down to San Francisco for the same purpose.

The Navy returned to Petropavlovsk in the spring of 1855 when *HMS Encounter* (14 guns) and *HMS Barracouta* (6 guns) kept watch over the port from a safe distance. The Russians knew that they could not withstand another onslaught and so, on 17th April, Petropavlovsk's garrison was evacuated under the cover of fog and snow. The men-of-war, *Aurora* and *Dvina*, and four merchantmen took them to safety across the Sea of Okhotsk at the River Amur. The civilians of Petropavlovsk moved to the village of Avatcha.

When the Allied squadrons returned in May, 1855, to renew the bombardment they found a virtually empty port and so it was not difficult for them to destroy the arsenals, batteries and magazines. This they did but they spared the town and its buildings.

The British warships *Pique*, *Barracouta* and *Amphitrite* then went west to patrol the waters of the Sea of Okhotsk while the other warships returned to Esquimalt, on Vancouver Island. The Okhotsk patrol had another rare stroke of luck in this otherwise wretched campaign when on 1st August *HMS Barracouta* intercepted the brig *Greta*, which was carrying part of the crew of the Russian frigate *Diana*, which had been wrecked on the coast of Japan a few months earlier. The *Greta* was seized and taken to Hong Kong as a prize.

Although the United States did not enter the Crimean War they probably came out of it the best as the financial problems that the war and its aftermath inflicted on the Czar's government persuaded it to sell Russian Alaska to the American government for a knock-down price of US$7,200,000.

THE WRECK OF HMS ORPHEUS

The saved stood on the steamer's deck,
Straining their eyes to see
Their comrades clinging to the wreck
Upon that surging sea.

And as they gazed into the dark,
Upon their startled ears
There came from that fast sinking bark
A sound of gallant cheers.

Again, and yet again, it grew,
Then silence round them fell –
Silence of death – and each man knew
It was a last farewell.

Sir F. C. Wraxall *The Wreck of the Orpheus*

HMS Orpheus, a 254 foot long steam corvette, was commissioned at Portsmouth in 1861 for the Australia station but instead she was despatched to North America for a short time in the wake of the *Trent* affair which, at the height of America's Civil War, very nearly brought Britain into a war with the Northern states, a war that was averted only by the Federal Government backing down from its impertinent position of claiming the right to board British ships at sea, with Abraham Lincoln wisely declaring that "One war at a time is quite enough."

From Halifax, Nova Scotia, the *Orpheus* sailed down the Atlantic to the Cape of Good Hope and thence to Sydney, where she arrived on 20th March, 1862. Her armament consisted of twenty 8 inch broadside guns and two pivot Armstrong 110 pounders, and her engines were powered by steam from four boilers.

In early 1863 Commodore Burnett, the head of the Australia station, received orders to take the *Orpheus* to New Zealand where she would join *HMS Niger* and *HMS Harrier* in Manukau harbour to assist in the Maori War. At the time Manukau was New Zealand's naval harbour since it was the nearest safe anchorage to the Waikato River where the fighting was taking place, the naval vessels ferrying troops, stores and ammunition to the scene of action.

The *Orpheus* left Sydney at 4 p.m. on 31st January, 1863, having taken on extra midshipmen in Australia for her voyage to the war zone. In the words of the ship's boatswain, James Mason, "The (Sydney) dockside was thronged with people long before we left; they were mostly mothers, wives and friends and there were many scenes of affectionate leave-taking before we finally cast off. Many of the young midshipmen were parting from their loved ones for the first time.....

After clearing Sydney heads very steep seas were met, causing the *Orpheus* to dip and roll for some considerable time. By nightfall, however, when away from land and well out into the Tasman Sea conditions had improved and all hands settled down for the long trip ahead to England's southern colony.

There were many young Australian and English midshipmen on board and making their first voyage across this vast stretch of ocean. Notable among them was Midshipman Barkly, son of Sir Henry Barkly, Governor of Victoria at the time.....

Our ship being a vessel of war, most of the space on the main deck was taken up by guns and gear.

Our leisure time was occupied with reading and discussions; the main topic being the native uprising in New Zealand.

Under steam and sail the *Orpheus* made good progress at about eleven knots across the Tasman Sea. We were told that it was in one of its rare good moods and only the occasional high comber crashed over the ship...

After a calm and uneventful voyage of seven days the west coast of New Zealand was sighted a few minutes before seven o'clock on Saturday morning, 7th February. ...It was a lovely clear morning and it was not long before we could make out the rugged coastline and the seas breaking around the entrance to Manukau Harbour. We were then about nine or ten miles away.

At seven bells (11.30 a.m.) and half an hour earlier than usual the crew were sent to lunch. The reason for this was to allow plenty of time to take in sail and make ready for entering harbour.

After lunch all were in good spirits with the usual shipboard feeling of anticipation as land is neared after days at sea. Officers, midshipmen and sailors alike were looking forward to renewing acquaintances on the other warships at the naval station inside the harbour.

As our warship neared the coast on this fine morning it was possible to see the signal-staff in the distance, high up on the

157

clifftop. The narrow harbour entrance could be seen far below the towering headlands. The whole coastline for miles around looked bleak and desolate from the decks of the *Orpheus*.

We came on, and just after 12.30 we were about five or six miles from the Heads, steering south.

On the bridge at this time I noticed Commodore Burnett, Commander Burton and Sailing Master Strong. They appeared to be studying the chart and alternately inspecting through the glass the signal-staff on the distant headland.

No alteration to the course was made, and our ship continued on. Steam was raised for half-speed.

It was a few moments later that I was surprised to see Frederick Butler being escorted towards the quarter deck. He was a prisoner confined in the ship's brig for alleged desertion of his ship, *HMS Harrier*, in Sydney. We were all curious to learn what was happening, and it was not long before we heard the disturbing news.

Lieutenant Yonge told us that Frederick Butler had called out and in great anxiety had asked to be allowed out of the brig to speak with the Sailing Master. He had seen from his porthole that the ship was heading into danger and (was) not on the correct course to enter the harbour safely. Butler was familiar with the area, having crossed the bar on two previous occasions as Quartermaster on *HMS Harrier*. He knew that treacherous reefs and sandbanks surrounded the entrance to this harbour.

After speaking with Master Strong, Butler was quickly taken to the Commodore and Commander Burton on the bridge. Sensing that something was amiss many of the ship's company centred their attention on what was taking place with some trepidation. It was a dramatic moment for those of us within earshot when we heard Frederick Butler tell the Commodore that the ship was 'going wrong'. Butler pointed to the north on the port bow, indicating the true position of the bar and main channel.

The Commodore had a chart in his hand, which he quickly drew to Butler's attention. This caused Butler to become very agitated and he cried out in a loud and alarmed voice, 'It is not the right chart'. He again pointed out where the main channel was.

Commodore Burnett acted quickly. He immediately ordered the helm to be put a-starboard and the engines reversed. But it was too late. A minute or so later she struck! She ploughed on a short distance, then struck again with a heavy jolt that shook the whole ship.

All was chaos for a few minutes as guns and other objects careered across the decks. The *Orpheus* broached to on the shoal, with her head pointing to the north. A big sea made a complete sweep over the port broadside.

Order was soon restored and all hands were put to lightening ship. Attempts were made to hove overboard most of the heavy guns.

Disaster had come upon us so suddenly it was moments before any of us realised that we were hard aground, held fast, with surf breaking all around us. Several midshipmen and sailors received nasty injuries when the guns broke loose. I was able to get clear of the havoc and confusion caused by the sliding guns and other heavy objects but others, including several of the boys, were not so fortunate....

Attempts were made to get the undamaged boats off but the water was a seething cauldron around the ship. Excellent discipline was maintained despite the desperate position we were in and the peril facing us all, a fine example of calmness and courage shown in particular by the Commodore and all officers.

It was not long before Commodore Burnett ordered all those who wished to save themselves to get the launch overboard and attempt to make the shore. The launch was got away but, when near the bows, it was struck by a roller, swept under the bows and stove, drowning Lieutenant Jekyll and about forty men before our eyes.

A little later the pinnace, with Lieutenant Hill, Paymaster Amphlett, twelve men and the ship's papers, managed to get clear of the ship.....

In the late afternoon the sea's onslaught increased in intensity, breaking over the ship continually, giving all a fearful time. There were some swept overboard, ending quickly their ordeal. Soon all hands were forced into the tops when large rollers began sweeping the decks completely.

During this frightful time on the *Orpheus* there were many instances of chivalry and personal courage in the face of danger, several midshipmen leaving the safety of the rigging and being almost swept overboard while helping the injured into the tops; down again to free a young lad pinned to the rail by sliding gear; supporting shipmates when they became too weak to hold on aloft; many acts of valour which could never be forgotten by those of us so fortunate to survive....From the Commodore down to the youngest boy, all acted up to the highest traditions of the Royal

Navy." [1] By now those still on the *Orpheus* were being forced higher and higher up the rigging in an effort to flee the rising water.

The only other vessel in the vicinity was the inter-provincial mail steamer, *Wonga Wonga*, which passed out of the harbour by the correct channel to go south. Upon spotting the stricken warship, the mail steamer went as close as she safely could (about 200 yards) but, as the afternoon progressed, the waves were becoming wilder and bigger. The *Wonga Wonga* put off her boats to pick up any survivors who might have battled their way through the now raging surf. About twenty were saved thus. The *Wonga Wonga* also collected those who had escaped in the pinnace, the only boat that succeeded in getting away from the *Orpheus*. One lucky sailor, who could not swim, clung on to a spar and floated with it for eight hours until he was picked up inside the Manukau harbour.

To continue with the boatswain's account, "As darkness approached our ship was reeling under the continual battering from the breakers. The wind had increased, making the masts sway alarmingly, adding to our misery as we clung to the yards. It was grimly apparent to all of us that the *Orpheus* would soon break up....The hull was almost under water now. The end seemed very near...It was about this time there came a soul-stirring few moments. Above the noise of wind and sea came the voice of a midshipman from over on the foremast, then joined by others, singing in the face of death the beautiful hymn 'Abide with me, fast falls the eventide; The darkness deepens, Lord with me abide...I feel Thy presence every passing hour...In life, in death O Lord abide with me....'

Soon afterwards we decided to take the only chance for life that seemed left and jumped into the sea. Those who jumped from abaft the foremast were soon drawn down by the eddies and currents around the ship....Other slid down stays until reaching the jib-boom which overhung the deeper water. But few who jumped from there fared any better. We were horrified to see our shipmates drown in their courageous bid for life.

I was among many in the mizzen-mast rigging. We left ourselves in God's hand, trusting that, when our mast went we may be fortunate enough to be thrown clear of the worst breakers and be helped by wreckage in our fight for survival.

Darkness was now closing in fast. Huge waves were crashing viciously over our helpless ship, reaching hungrily up for us in the rigging. Then the masts started to go overboard. The

160

mainmast went first. Despairing cheers rang out from the men on it, as if taking farewell of life; others in the tops shouting encouragement to their comrades as they fell….Soon it would be our turn. I was a fairly strong swimmer with youth on my side but that surf was raging furiously around the ship. Before I went into the sea, I can recall thinking that my only chance for life was to try for a stout bit of the wreckage that was being tossed about in the breakers. I remember thinking that I must fight for my life and not give up easily and that the water would at least not be numbing cold at that time of the year.

A few moments later the foremast went, quickly followed by our mizzen-mast, taking the last of us into the sea." [2] In the words of the *Sydney Morning Herald*, "Imagination refuses to follow this scene to its conclusion and to think of those brave spirits struggling for life and wrestling with the waves in vain…In such times the mind assumes a tremendous activity, and we may be sure that in the battle of life and death in which so many were doomed to fall, a thousand remembrances strayed to the towns and villages of England. Many thought of their pleasant homes – here the image of an aged mother whose tears have yet to flow, there tender recollections of orphans to be or of a wife now in unconscious widowhood." [3]

Boatswain James Mason was one of the lucky ones; he was picked up in a state of semi-consciousness by one of the *Wonga Wonga's* boats. Others were not so lucky. Those "who clung to the fore and mizzen rigging echoed the death cry of their companions and in a few minutes most of them slept, with their fellows, the still sleep of death". [4]

Commodore Burnett was between the top and futtock rigging of the mainmast when the top fell on him, sending him overboard to a watery grave.

Commander Burton was in the foretop when it was washed away with the mainmast and his head was caught between the shrouds as the ship lurched, killing him instantly.

The captain of the foretop, John Davy, was descending from the maintop to the foretop when the stay was carried away and the coil caught him round the neck, strangling him. Like a criminal, he was hanged in the rigging.

Of the 258 men on board the *Orpheus* there were only sixty-nine survivors. About twenty bodies were washed up on remote parts of the sandy coast and were buried by the Maoris, who marked the grave sites, while another eight bodies were picked up by the pilot at Manukau Heads, Thomas Wing, who sailed seven miles up the coast in his pilot boat, pulling in whenever he saw a body and burying it in the sand dunes with a marker.

One of these was that of John Pascoe, the chief boatswain's mate, which was found behind some rocks about half a mile north of the pilot station. A few days later his corpse was exhumed and taken to Auckland as the required sample body for an inquest. He was identified by a mark on his left breast, which he received from a wound in the Crimean War.

Those who survived their ordeal in the sea were taken by the military from Onehunga across to Auckland, where they were accommodated on *HMS Miranda*, which was in Auckland harbour. Two of the survivors were singled out for particular praise by Auckland's *Southern Cross* newspaper for their help in rescuing others. One of these was Frederick Butler, the deserter from *HMS Harrier*, who, had he not been locked up in the brig, might have been able to save the ship by bringing the problem to the notice of the navigating officers earlier.

So, what went wrong? As we saw in the hydrography chapter the Manukau harbour had been surveyed in 1853 by *HMS Pandora* (Captain Drury) and his chart was issued to all shipping, both naval and mercantile. But the shoals around this bar were of a shifting nature and so Drury's chart and instructions were updated in 1859 in the form of Veitch's Sailing Orders, made by Mr. Veitch, the Master of the steamship *HMS Niger,* one of the warships inside Manukau harbour when the *Orpheus* struck. A further notice was issued from the Hydrographic Office on 11th October, 1861, notifying that the outer South Bank had moved north. [5] However, for reasons unknown since all the navigating officers of the *Orpheus* went down with the ship, they were using Captain Drury's chart when they attempted to enter the harbour in 1863.

The shore signalman at the Signal Station on the hill, Edward Wing, saw the man-of-war when she first appeared on the horizon. "The British warship looked a grand sight under all sail, as she gradually came further into view," he wrote. [6]

On this clear morning with a moderate sea (before it got up), a slight south-westerly breeze, and the tide just beginning to ebb, thereby giving sufficient water over the bar, Wing gave the signal by semaphore that it was safe to come across the bar and into the channel leading in to the harbour. The bar lies across the harbour, some four miles out from the two heads, through which vessels passed to get into the Manukau.

The *Orpheus* was approaching under both steam and sail and the signal to proceed was made when she was about two miles out from the bar. However, instead of taking the bar as directed, she proceeded southward towards the dangerous and shallower south channel, causing the signalman to put up a Number 10 signal "Keep Further North". Instead the *Orpheus* continued on her perilous way, heading for the notorious Middle Bank, which was completely covered with water since it was still near full tide.

The next signal from the shore in the still clear air was Number 14 signal "Keep More Off Shore. Danger!" Again, no response from the *Orpheus*, which almost immediately struck the shoal, about two and a half miles from land. The signalman was the only one on the shore to see what had happened but he did not have a boat to go for help up at the more populated Onehunga or to one of the warships further up the harbour.

On 27th April, 1863, the Admiralty held an inquiry on board *HMS Victory* at Portsmouth, which found that "The loss of the *Orpheus* was occasioned by the shifting nature of the Manukau bar, and which rendered navigation particularly difficult". This was both the wrong finding and the right one.

It was wrong on the facts. The *Orpheus* went down because she was trying to enter the Manukau harbour in a dangerous place with her navigating officers using the wrong chart and ignoring the clear semaphore messages from the signal station.

However, in the wider view of things, the finding was right, as what on earth could be gained by publicly pinning the blame for such a terrible catastrophe on those who had lost their lives as a consequence, all the navigating officers being drowned? Sometimes truth has to give way to higher interests and this was certainly one of those occasions.

Where the Admiralty's court of inquiry was correct was its second finding that "The discipline of the ship and the conduct of all showed how British seamen could face death with that gallant, chivalrous fortitude for which they were proverbial and would be held as an example for others in after days".

The *Sydney Morning Herald* took this a bit further, "There is scope for heroism in its highest forms in dangers where there is no human enemy. The thunder of the ocean may equal the roar of artillery, and the crash of masts create a sense of peril as appalling

163

as battle….The number of officers who perished is a glorious commentary upon the character of the British Navy without in the least reflecting on the equal merit of those whom Providence has reserved for other duties…..So long as British seamen are ruled by such officers, no perils of the deep – no rage of the enemy – will snatch the trident from the hands of Great Britain." [7]

To commemorate those who lost their lives in what seems to have been an avoidable disaster, a mural tablet and bas-relief was erected by private subscription in the chapel of the Royal Naval College at Greenwich. A white marble memorial tablet was also erected in the Mariners' Church, Hobart, that being the last port that the *Orpheus* visited before returning to Sydney to prepare for her fateful voyage to New Zealand.

In Auckland an Orpheus Relief Fund was set up by the stunned citizens for the benefit of the widows and orphans of those who were lost and the princely sum of £8,000 was collected. This was passed on to 145 adults and 200 children. The people of Auckland also gave practical help to the survivors, who had lost all their personal possessions when the ship went down.

The funeral of John Pascoe, the chief boatswain's mate who was the subject of the inquest, was held on the afternoon of 17th February and, "by the time announced for the procession to start, a very large gathering of persons had assembled in the barrack square, many of whom were habited in deep mourning and who joined the procession on its formation". [8] The coffin was taken from the military "dead-house" by some of his surviving shipmates and was placed on a Royal Artillery gun carriage, drawn by six fine horses.

Before leaving for England the surviving officers and crew issued a statement. "Exposed to one of the common accidents of a seaman's life but far distant from all known friends and relations, the officers and men have not language adequately to express what they feel at the ready and unlooked for assistance which has been tendered on this occasion by utter strangers…..The Service will never forget the noble generosity of the kind people of Auckland." [9]

HMS Orpheus struck on the western side of the treacherous Middle Bank, which had shifted three quarters of a mile since Captain Drury's report of eleven years earlier. This shows how important was the Navy's continual surveying throughout the Pacific as not only did newly discovered shores have to be mapped but also older charts had to be constantly updated. Upon learning of the disaster, the Lords of the Admiralty ordered that warships above a certain tonnage must not cross the bar of the Manukau harbour, and for many years, until it was resurveyed, the Navy was absent from the waters of New Zealand's largest harbour.

The rigging, spars, blocks, etc. of the *Orpheus* were bought by the Meiklejohns, a shipbuilding family who had their own boat building yard at Omaha, north of Auckland. They salvaged the various parts from the wreck site and used them in their own yard in an early example of "recycling". However, some of the blocks were too large for the small ships that they were building but other pieces were used in the vessels that came out of their busy shipyard. [10]

Other parts of the wreck were found up and down the coast for years to come. A year after the disaster some local Maoris in the Kaipara area, north of Manukau, found a medal belonging to Lieutenant Jekyll, who had drowned when he tried to take the launch, full of men, from the *Orpheus* but it was swamped by a wave. The medal had been earned by him for service in the Baltic during the Crimean War and had Queen Victoria's head on one side and Jekyll's name engraved on the medal's edge. The Maoris gave it to Rev. Gittos, the Wesleyan minister at Kaipara, who forwarded it on to the Navy so that they could pass it on to the next-of-kin.

In 1879 a sub-lieutenant's skeleton was found at Maunkau Heads with trouser buttons bearing the names "Battan and Adams, Devonport" on them. None of the skeleton's bones had been broken.

A year later, while raising the steamer *Hannah Mokau* at the mouth of the Mokau River, some hundred miles south of Manukau, they discovered the thirty-four foot bowsprit of the *Orpheus* embedded in the sand. It was immediately cut up and used to help raise the *Hannah Mokau*.

Ten years later the hull of the *Orpheus* was washed up at Manukau Heads on the morning of 27th May, 1890, while at Easter, 1907, a party of campers saw a piece of wood sticking up out of the sand on the beach some two and a half miles north of Manukau Heads. They dug it up and found that it was the mizzen-topmast of the *Orpheus* – the piece to which many of the officers clung until they were washed off it and drowned.

The *Orpheus* remains New Zealand's worst ever maritime disaster; it was also the worst disaster ever suffered on the Navy's Australia Station. Auckland's *Southern Cross* newspaper wrote at the time, "She was the largest and finest man-of-war we have ever had on this station, and her loss is a public calamity quite apart from the greater one of so many lives being sacrificed." [11]

165

THE RIVER WAR

What will they say in England,
When the story it is told,
Of Rangiriri's bloody fight,
And deeds of brave and bold?

Twas there the rebels made a stand,
Resolved their lives to sell,
Charge after charge our heroes made,
And numbers of them fell.

First dashed the gallant Sixty-fifth,
In vain they fought, though well;
Then, leading the artillery,
The gallant Mercer fell.
And then the rebels had a chance
To fire upon poor Jack,
And, though they fought like lions loosed,
They too were driven back.

On Friday was the fight begun,
Late in the afternoon,
Soon Rangiriri's silent hills
Flung back the cannon's boom;
Right bravely fought our gallant troops,
Each did their duty well,
Before the morrow's sun could rise
Te Rangiriri fell.

Two hundred men for quarter cried,
And soon laid down their arms;
For fighting in the open fields
For Maoris has no charms.
We lost some noble officers,
Likewise some comrades dear,
And thousands followed to their graves,
And dropped a pitying tear.

All honour to the braves, say I,
To those who fought and bled;

Let's join in praise of those who live,
And sorrow for the dead.
Yet, while we join with one accord
To raise the song of joy,
Let's not forget the soldier's wife,
Nor the soldier's orphan boy.

On the Taking of Rangiriri. By "A Soldier" (Air: *Partant pour la Syrie*)

When *HMS Curacoa* arrived on the Australia station from Portsmouth in September, 1863, she was sent almost immediately to take part in the Maori War in New Zealand.

In 1840 New Zealand had become part of the British Empire by virtue of the Treaty of Waitangi, which granted the status of "British subjects" to the Maoris, who had hitherto lived in a state of anarchy and savagery and were actually on the point of wiping themselves out as a result of their inter-tribal wars in which, in the years immediately preceding 1840, they had killed an estimated 80,000 members of their own race.

The Maoris welcomed the Treaty because they knew that it was the only structure under which they could live in peace and establish some sort of land ownership as, under the Maori system, a tribe could be dispossessed of the land they were living on by a larger tribe with better weapons. In the words of the *Sydney Morning Herald*, "Never has a savage people received such benefits from the establishment of a colony, and never was a sovereignty exercised with such consideration for the weaker race than during the dominion of Victoria over the Maori population of New Zealand." [1]

From 1840 the Maoris lived under the Queen's Peace but a minority of them became dissatisfied and reverted to their old ways. They started by committing some savage murders of colonists in the "outsettlements" and this grew into a full scale rebellion that was limited to certain areas and certain tribes and which was put down by the combined forces of the British Army, the Royal Navy, colonial militia and friendly Maoris.

The *Curacoa* sailed from Sydney to Auckland on 22nd September, 1863, with a detachment of the 12th Regiment on board (sixteen officers and 240 rank and file). She also carried six horses –

167

two for the colonel (a grey and a bay), and one each for the Adjutant, Quartermaster, doctor and instructor of musketry.

The horses were hoisted on board in a canvas sling, that was slung under them and banded around them as well. During hoisting they "kicked a good deal". [2] Once on board they were put in horse boxes around the stern but these were only just big enough for them to stand up in.

The *Curacoa* also took on board two 40 pounder Armstrong field pieces and some ammunition wagons. And so, with her own crew as well, the ship had a very crowded passage. It was also a rough one and many of the soldiers were seasick and were chundering over the sides.

After nine days at sea they reached Auckland on the last day of September. "This town seems a thriving one, notwithstanding the war," wrote Midshipman Foljambe on his first sight of this settlement that had not yet been twenty-five years in existence. "Certainly it is a very pretty one, with Mounts Eden and Hobson rising behind it. All the hills round here seem to have their tops cut off." [3] (They were extinct volcanoes).

At 5 a.m. on 17th October four companies from the *Curacoa* and some other naval vessels in the harbour were marched seven miles to Onehunga with baggage on their backs. They were off to war, from which some of them would not return.

From Onehunga two companies were taken across the Manukau harbour to Drury, whence they would march to battle over the newly formed road while the other two companies boarded a recently acquired armoured steamer that bore the appropriate name of "*HMS Pioneer*".

The *Pioneer* crossed the treacherous bar of the Manukau harbour, on which *HMS Orpheus* had been wrecked only a few months earlier, and sailed down to the mouth of New Zealand's longest river, the Waikato, up which she would sail to take the battle to the Maoris' inland forts – just as, two oceans away and at the same time, the Northern forces in the American Civil War were using gunboats on the rivers to supply the armies that were fighting inland.

Hitherto the rebels had felt safe on the banks of the Waikato since warships could not get across its shallow bar. However, all that changed with the introduction of specially adapted vessels with extremely low draught.

The *Pioneer* drew just three feet of water and was one of two paddle steamers that the Navy used on the river during the campaign to tow four smaller gunboats. The other steamer was the *Avon* of 40 tons; each steamer was armed with a 12 pounder Armstrong gun in the bows and their armour plate consisted of iron plates bolted under the bulwarks. They each towed two gunboats, which were really converted barges that could carry many men. Each of the four gunboats was in the charge of a midshipman. The *Pioneer* and *Avon* had to be reasonably small to negotiate the snags and occasional shallows of this wide river.

The first Maori position that they encountered as they steamed up the river was at Meremere, which rose slightly above the river. "This hillside was one rabbit warren of rifle pits," wrote Midshipman Foljambe. [4]

Nevertheless, Meremere was the "key of the Waikato"[5] and, as such, had to be taken, and so the men of the *Pioneer* lugged the two 40 pounders that the *Curacoa* had brought over from Sydney all the way up to the Whangamarino heights, from which they fired down on the Maori stockade.

Next day the flat bottomed fleet went closer to the enemy position and, in the words of Midshipman Foljambe, "The natives opened fire on us with their smooth bores and flint-locks….We returned it with rifles and shells from the two 12 pounder Armstrong guns we had on board, brought from the *Curacoa*. The bullets made no more impression on our iron sides than if I had struck them with my fist….Their shots went over us as, except when pressed, a Maori never puts his gun up to his shoulder, as he is afraid of its kicking, but fires while the gun is in his hands at the 'ready'." [6] One reason for the bad shooting was that it was dusk and the Maoris could not take good aim.

On 31st October the *Pioneer* and *Avon* towed their gunboats up past Meremere shortly after midnight in order to land seven hundred soldiers and bluejackets at a spot where they hoped to cut off the enemy's retreat. However, this was not easy as the river had burst its banks to create a large inland sea a mile wide, across which many Maoris escaped in their canoes. Nevertheless, they did retreat and so Meremere, which the Maoris had spent so much time in building and fortifying, was abandoned and fell to the British without the loss of a single life on either side.

The *Pioneer* approached this abandoned riverside fort and "all the bluejackets jumped out and charged up the hill with the boatswain and one or two other officers. The men first got up to the rifle pits and then to the stockade but not a soul was inside; all had run. So our men quietly pitched their tents at the top and hoisted the English flag".[7]

With the fall of Meremere the *Pioneer* and *Avon* and their four little gunboats were able to penetrate fifteen miles further up the river to the Maoris' next strongpoint, Rangiriri, which was to prove a much bloodier affair.

As they approached Rangiriri those on the boats could see the others, from whom they had parted at Onehunga, coming over the hills, having taken the overland route through the thick bush, making a total of about 1,200 men. Thus Rangiriri was shelled from two sides – from the vessels in line on the river and from the landward side by the *Curacoa's* guns.

At about half past four in the afternoon of 20th November the overland soldiers charged the redoubt across the fern clad hills. Many natives ran away through the fern to the swamp and the bluejackets were sent after them. They shot some of them but were up to their waists in the water of the swamp.

Meanwhile the frontal attack on the fort from the river was not going well and so General Cameron sent a message to Commodore Wiseman, who was in command of the river flotilla, that the natives were caged up and firing from behind the stockade. The attacking soldiers were sustaining heavy casualties and were not getting anywhere in their attempts to storm the pa. So the call went out to the bluejackets. In the words of the war reporter for Auckland's *Southern Cross*, "The question then was not who was to go, but who was to be left behind – all being equally anxious to have a slap at the Maoris; but even for the active tars the works proved too strong, the only results being to compel them to retire after two officers had been wounded and some men killed and others more or less hurt. Hand grenades were then thrown in over the parapets which, from the appearance of some of the dead bodies, must have caused the enemy some loss.

The soldiers and bluejackets could reach the first rifle pit but the second, which enclosed the centre of the fort and was about nineteen feet high from the bottom of the ditch to the top of the wall, remained impregnable." [8] In the words of Midshipman Foljambe, "We had to rush up this hill, open to their fire, for we could not see them as they only showed their heads for a second and then bobbed down and let fly at us without taking much aim…Our first

170

lieutenant, Mr. Alexander, was shot in three places, one in his shoulder and two in his right arm. One of our midshipmen, Watkins, was shot through the head and killed immediately….right in the centre of his forehead. He had nearly got on the parapet when he was shot down. Captain Mayne of the *Eclipse* and Lieutenant Downes of the *Miranda* were shot, Mayne in the leg and Downes in the shoulder….One of the bluejackets was shot in seven places – four in one arm, one in his right leg, one in his left and another in his shoulder – but I think he will recover". [9]

"The bluejackets, with rifle and cutlass, dashed at the works and endeavoured to swarm up the straight-scarped parapet but once more the stormers were thrown back, and dead and dying men strewed the ditch and the ground in front of it. A few reached the top of the parapet," wrote James Cowan in *The New Zealand Wars*. [10]

On the edge of the battle stood a small Anglican church, which was made of timber frames, with thatch on the roof and reeds on the walls. During the fighting its walls were perforated in places with rifle shot. It served as a field hospital for the casualties.

Sporadic fighting continued through the night while nearby a party of sailors captured six canoes in the swamp to the right, "two of them being of great size and capable of holding sixty or seventy men." [11]

All night the *Pioneer* lay alongside the river bank and served as a hospital ship "and the wounded were conveyed on board as fast as they could be brought down from the scene of action. There they were attended by the medical officers and disposed in the cabin below, every attention being paid to their comfort," wrote the *Southern Cross*. [12] "The numbers being so great, it was found necessary to convey some on board the *Avon* and the cabins of both vessels were well filled.….The scene below in the cabin of the *Pioneer* that night defies description. The wounded men were lying in every available place and others, who had received slight injuries, were waiting their turn….Assistant Surgeon Messer of the *Curacoa* was indefatigable in his attentions and during the whole night was engaged in tending and relieving the unfortunate sufferers." [13]

When dawn broke the Maoris put up the white flag of surrender as they had run out of ammunition and so Rangiriri also fell to the forces of the Crown but at the cost of five sailors and forty-two soldiers dead and another twenty injured sailors and eighty wounded soldiers. The Maoris were believed to have lost about fifty men, including six chiefs.

171

One hundred and eighty-three Maori prisoners were taken as well as 175 stand of ammunition. More than half of them were the old army musket flint-lock and there were also some second hand, single-barrelled fowling pieces while some of the chiefs had second hand double-barrelled guns. One of them even had an Enfield rifle and thirty rounds of ammunition which was found to have belonged to a British soldier murdered by them which, in the words of Midshipman Foljambe, was "one of the murders which occasioned the war". [14]

Fifty of the worst prisoners and the most important chiefs were put on board the *Pioneer*, which took them downstream to the camp, known as "The Bluff", just below the confluence of the Maungatawhiri River and the Waikato.

During this short run a volley of shots was fired at them by a small group of Maoris from a slight rise above the river bank but one of the Maori prisoners on board stood up and yelled at them to lay down their arms. No more shots were fired but shortly afterwards one of the prisoners jumped overboard in an attempt to escape. He was immediately shot by a sailor, the ball hitting his leg, and he was picked up and taken back on board.

Also on board were some of the British wounded, who were taken in small boats from the mouth of the Maungatawhiri to the sailors' encampment, which was in the Redoubt up a small hill. At the end of their river journey horse drawn wagons were waiting to convey the wounded up the hill "but their services were dispensed with by the sailors who, with a laudable spirit of sympathy for the sufferers, hoisted them shoulder-high and carried them to the Redoubt – a mode of transport much easier than that of a cart, however cleverly contrived to travel smoothly". [15]

Forty-six of the soldiers and bluejackets were buried in the churchyard at Rangiriri - near the side of the river where they fell. In the words of the *Southern Cross*, "A separate grave was dug for each, alongside the church, arranged in rows but having a distinguishable division between those belonging to each corps. The bodies were all carefully washed in the morning and sewn up in blankets and at twelve o'clock the men of each regiment marched down to pay the last tribute to their departed comrades. Archdeacon Maunsell read the burial service, after which three volleys were fired over the graves and the sad ceremony was concluded.

On visiting the spot this morning I found that a mound had been raised over each, and green sods laid down; also shrubs planted

172

at the head and feet so that, if allowed to remain undisturbed, a marked spot will remain to commemorate the scene of one of the sharpest engagements that has ever taken place in this country." [16] Whenever sailors die in battle their shipmates are always very particular that they receive a decent and dignified burial and this was certainly the case at Rangiriri.

To-day they lie in this small cemetery, together with some of the district's early settlers and also some of the Maoris who fell in the battle, the natives having been buried in a mass grave on the edge of the burial ground. Unfortunately in death they do not enjoy the peace that they deserve as the main highway between Auckland and Wellington passes within only a few yards of this otherwise peaceful place; in fact, this noisy road actually crosses the centre of the Maori position during the battle.

The victory at Rangiriri, to which the bluejackets had contributed in no small way, was the turning point in the River War. There would still be a few exchanges of fire with isolated groups of Maoris and the naval vessels would continue to patrol the waters of the Waikato but Rangiriri had broken the back of the Maoris' resistance.

The British sailors and soldiers, whose bones lie in the rich soil of the Waikato valley, did not die in vain; the result of their sacrifice can be seen to-day in a peaceful and prosperous New Zealand, and a pre-condition for this happy state was the defeat of those natives who chose to rebel against the Crown, thereby igniting the Maori War which resulted in their defeat.

In the words of James Cowan, the leading authority on the Maori Wars, "Without this flotilla General Cameron could not have carried on the Waikato campaign. The gunboats and the troops they carried enabled him to outflank the Maori positions at Meremere and Rangiriri, to capture Ngaruawahia unopposed, and to keep his army fed and equipped on the Waipa Plain. It was the great water road into the heart of the country, Waikato's noble canoe highway, that gave the British troops command of the Kingite territory and prepared the way for permanent European occupation." [17]

THE BATTLE OF GATE PA

The capture of the forts on the Waikato River did not end the Maori War as there was also the need to deal with the tribes in the Bay of Plenty to prevent them joining up with the remaining hotheads in the Waikato, to whom they had been sending supplies. To prevent the traffic of both arms and men the small port of Tauranga was blockaded by *HMS Miranda*.

Meanwhile the Maoris had built – in only two weeks – a new fortification at Gate Pa, which General Cameron decided to capture – just as he had taken Rangiriri at such considerable cost.

He sailed from Auckland to Tauranga on *HMS Esk*, which was also full of troops as the only way that the soldiers could reach Tauranga was to be carried there by the Navy. Auckland's "Queen Street Wharf was crowded yesterday with troops, embarking for Tauranga," wrote the *Southern Cross* on 25th April, 1864. "The embarkation commenced at an early hour in the morning, *HMS Falcon* having come up to the end of the wharf to receive them."

The night of 28th April was wet and cold as the British took up their positions to attack the new fortification of Gate Pa, which was so called because it was built across the line of road to the interior where the gate on the boundary fence of the mission property stood. Unlike the classic Maori pa, it was not high on an eminence. The natives had cleared and deepened an old ditch, that had been thrown around the mission house as a boundary, and formed it into rifle pits, which were roofed with tree branches and thatched with fern. These were complemented with fences and intervening stakes to form the outer defences.

Among the attacking troops was a Naval Brigade made up of about four hundred and twenty bluejackets from *HMS Esk*, *HMS Falcon* and *HMS Miranda*. They were under the command of Lieutenant Charles Hotham, who later became an admiral. Their first task was to drag the 110 pound Armstrong gun from *HMS Esk* up to its position in readiness for the bombardment. It weighed 83 cwt and by the end of the journey they were "begrimed with sweat and dust". [1] It was placed on a breastwork at a range of 800 yards from the pa and was operated by the naval gunners under the direction of Captain Hamilton, the commander of *HMS Esk*. Other sailors were then despatched to the rear of the pa in order to cut off the Maoris' escape route.

The attack on the front of the pa began shortly after dawn on 29th April "and a salvo from the large guns and mortars awoke the echoes, and began in earnest the tragedy of war", wrote the *Southern Cross'* correspondent. "From 6.45 a.m. until four in the afternoon almost without cessation a fire was kept up from the four batteries on the pa, and during that time the rebels did not show themselves in front." [2]

Besides the *Esk's* 110 pounder there were eight mortars, varying from four to eight inches, two 24 pound howitzers, and two 6 pound Armstrongs. The last mentioned, together with the mortars, were placed closer to the objective at distances of 500 to 600 yards.

All this firepower was concentrated at one point with the intention of making a breach for an assault party. Unfortunately several of the hundred shells that were fired by the *Esk's* 110 pounder overshot the mark and burst where the other bluejackets were at the rear of the pa. In the words of the *Southern Cross* correspondent, "The practice, however, was beautiful, and the fault lay with the guns and not with the gunnery." [3] When these shells, called "Whistling Dicks", did hit the front of the pa their noise was described as "identical to the snorting of an express engine starting from a railway station." [4]

By 4 p.m. the result of all this firing was a hole in the ramparts no more than thirty yards wide but it was considered big enough for a storming party. To ease their way "the fire was quickened, and the earth almost shook with the concussion and explosion of shells for several minutes." [5] The storming party consisted of 150 seamen and marines under Commander Edward Hay of *HMS Harrier* and an almost equal number of troops from the 43rd Regiment.

Led by their officers, they advanced four abreast in skirmishing order. As soon as they saw them approach, the Maoris, who had been lying low all day in underground hideouts while the shells burst above them, suddenly appeared with a vengeance and opened fire. In the face of this, as well as all the thick smoke of the action, they continued their advance at the double "and with a cheer that was re-echoed by the spectators in the camp and batteries, dashed through the smoke and bullets and carried the breach". [6]

Once inside the pa, some fierce hand to hand fighting took place. "Nothing could be seen but the flash of the pieces and the smoke; nothing heard but the cheers of the stormers and the counter cheer of the defenders, mingled with the sharp roll of musketry." [7]

In the words of James Cowan, "Navy cutlass met long-handled tomahawk....Skulls were cloven – Maoris were bayoneted – tomahawks bit into *pakeha* (white men's) limbs." [8] During the fighting the gunner of *HMS Miranda*, Mr. Watts, was killed when one of the enemy sliced half of his head off with a tomahawk. The cut went from the crown down to the lower jaw – straight through the centre of his nose.

With the storming party inside the pa a second force, consisting of bluejackets and troops of the 43rd Regiment under the command of Captain John Fane Hamilton of *HMS Esk*, advanced through the breach "with a ringing cheer" [9] Captain Hamilton sprang upon the parapet and shouted, "Follow me, men!" He then dashed into the fight – only to be shot dead by a bullet through his brain.

Captain Hamilton had been through several stormings of strongpoints during the Opium War of 1841-2 when he was on *HMS Blonde*. He was also part of the Naval Brigade at the siege of Sebastopol in the Crimean War. His name is remembered in New Zealand by its fifth largest city, Hamilton, which was named after him.

Hamilton was not the only officer to fall. Lieutenant Charles Hill, the most senior officer to have survived the wreck of *HMS Orpheus*, was shot through both cheeks and the centre of the neck as he tried to get through to the centre of the pa. He retired to the parapet and tried to stanch the flow of blood by tying a handkerchief round his head. In this state he rushed again to the centre of the pa with the second storming party under Captain Hamilton. He did reach the objective but then fell down dead.

There was something poignant about his death for, as the senior surviving officer of the *Orpheus* when she went down, he had faced the routine court-martial back in England, which was always held whenever a ship was lost. At the close of the case each member of the court-martial shook his hand and the president returned his sword with the following words, "Lieutenant Hill, I have great pleasure in returning this sword to so resolute and brave an officer as yourself for, I feel assured that, whenever your country may call upon you to use it, it will be found that it could not have been placed in better hands." [10] Indeed.

Under intense fire and deprived of their officers, the bluejackets and soldiers began to retreat through the breach and it was in this withdrawal that many of them were killed or seriously wounded. "The natives were, as usual, exultant at their success," wrote the *Southern Cross* correspondent. [11] "They howled and shouted fearfully, and challenged the forces to advance." Apart from the gunfire, this seems to have been a noisy battle of yelling warriors on both sides.

The Maoris' counter-attack was of little use to them as it caused them to run out of ammunition around 9 p.m. and so they had to abandon the pa as they had done at Rangiriri only a few months earlier – also after a bloody battle. Under cover of darkness they escaped across a swamp, scattering in all directions to elude capture.

The next morning at daylight the British entered the pa to retrieve the bodies of their dead comrades who had fallen within its confines. "On entering the pa a harrowing spectacle presented itself," wrote the *Southern Cross* correspondent. "Within a space of a few yards the bodies of four captains of the 43rd were lying; and further on, in line with the others, Colonel Booth of the same regiment was leaning mortally wounded against the rear paling of the pa.

Officers of the ships of war were lying stark dead in the same lines of trenches. As they lay alone they must have been in advance of their men, and fell nobly in the execution of their duty....In the centre rifle pit of the pa lay the body of Lieutenant Hill of *HMS Curacoa*." [12]

The wounded Maoris, deserted by their own people, were taken out of the pa, put on stretchers and taken to the British camp where they received medical attention while their dead were laid out in front of the pa and covered with blankets.

"One Maori had been cut in two by a shell, and the head, trunk and extremities were carefully gathered and placed in line with the remaining dead in front of the pa", wrote the *Southern Cross*. "....Another rebel had had his skull cloven by a blow of a cutlass, given by the black sailor of the *Miranda*, who has already figured conspicuously during the war. Poor fellow, he fell dead in turn in the pa." [13]

So the British captured Gate Pa but at a cost of thirty-one dead on our side and about twenty-five on the Maori side. Amongst those of the Naval Brigade who fell, apart from those already mentioned, were Ordinary Seaman James Harris (*HMS Curacoa*), Stoker William Leigh, Ordinary Seaman R. Fuller and William Dalton (all of *HMS Esk*), Stoker Andrew Greenbow, Able Seaman George Young and a boy seaman, Henry Clarke (all of *HMS Harrier*) and a Royal Marine, Sergeant Harding of *HMS Eclipse*.

Despite their overwhelming firepower the British did not succeed in their storming of Gate Pa, which the Maoris held in the face of a nine hour bombardment of atrocious fury.

Two months after the battle the Maoris were seen to be constructing another pa at Te Ranga, some three miles inland from Gate Pa, and so Colonel Greer attacked it at once and took it. This was the final battle of the Tauranga campaign and about a hundred and twenty Maoris were killed while the British lost thirteen. This was followed by the surrender of the tribes around Tauranga and the end of hostilities in the area.

In spite of the problems there were acts of heroism on the part of the sailors at Gate Pa that were in the highest traditions of the Navy, and the Victoria Cross that was awarded to Samuel Mitchell, the captain of the foretop of *HMS Harrier*, for carrying Commander Hay out of the pa under heavy fire was well deserved.

The medal itself, brought out from England and, like all Victoria Crosses, made out of the metal from the two cannon that were captured at Sebastopol in 1855, was presented to Mitchell later in the year by Sir John Young, the Governor of New South Wales, in the Sydney Domain. In the words of Midshipman Foljambe of *HMS Curacoa*, "The Volunteers and Militia and what few regulars that are here were all present......and every seaman and marine that could be spared to go there, officers in full dress, and the men in white frocks, blue trousers and white cap covers". [14]

The young ladies were all kissing Mitchell and "after that they chaired him all round the place and then in the evening they got a horse for him, and he rode in triumph round the town, when they presented him with a purse." [15] Lucky Mitchell!

Nor was this the only good thing to come out of Gate Pa. As a result of that battle and the later one at Te Ranga a peace was brought to Tauranga and the Bay of Plenty which has prevailed ever since. To-day the site of the battle is a green park and nearby is the Gate Pa shopping centre, thus demonstrating the changed nature of things.

The Navy's role at Gate Pa and in other actions in the Maori War won the praise, gratitude and respect of New Zealanders. In the words of Grant Howard in his book, *The Navy in New Zealand*, "Such praise was not won easily. It was gained in various actions from Kororareka to Gate Pa, and won for the Navy a respect which has lasted down the years." [16]

On Marsland Hill, overlooking the city of New Plymouth in New Zealand, is a monument to the British and colonial forces killed in the Maori Wars of the 1840s and 1860s and a list of those ships of the Royal Navy that took part – *HMS Blanche, Brisk, Calliope, Castor, Cordelia, Curacoa, Driver, Eclipse, Elk, Esk, Falcon, Fawn, Harrier, Hazard, Iris, Miranda, Niger, North Star, Orpheus, Pelorus* and *Racehorse*. This gives some idea of the debt that New Zealand owes to the Royal Navy, which came to its aid in troubled times just as the United States Navy was to do in 1942, both of which are cogent reminders of how a small country needs powerful allies for its own good.

179

GUNNERY

The guns on a warship were what gave it its power – indeed, its *raison d'être* - and in a battle situation the gunners came into their own when the order was given to clear the decks for action – an exercise that would be completed in only a few minutes. "When the bugle blew to quarters, it was a sight to see the men fly to their stations," wrote a reporter after visiting the cruiser, *HMS Orlando*, in Lyttelton harbour, New Zealand, in 1893. "Every gun was manned, the marine artillery at the two biggest, the bluejackets at the others, and behind the gun crews were the men serving ammunition. Small arms men stood ready for musketry work, armourers were everywhere ready for the call for 'repairs', men stood at pumps and hose reels to cope with fire, others were stationed to pass orders. It was a scene of great bustle and great order. Every weapon was in action and every man in his place a few seconds after the first bugle call." [1]

Whether in twentieth century battles with the Germans and Japanese or in nineteenth century bombardments of Chinese forts or recalcitrant native villages the overriding requirement for gunners was accuracy, and an awful lot of time and effort was devoted to training the artillery up to the high standard that was required.

The Gunnery School was set up on *HMS Excellent* at Portsmouth in 1830 since newer weapons like explosive shells required more skill, while greater accuracy was required for weapons of longer range. Those who graduated would be rewarded with higher pay and better prospects of promotion.

At firing practice the guns of the Navy could be heard all over the Pacific. "Last Wednesday morning we were seduced from our studies by the thunder of cannon, which boomed pleasantly in our ears. Hastening to Smales' Point, we perceived that a rival exhibition between the Royal Artillerists at Fort Britomart and the seamen of *HMS Havannah* was then in full play. The target of the Artillery was a floating one…that of the *Havannah* a fixed object in the shape of a sailor delineated on canvas and posted in a bight on the north shore, and on a level with the frigate's broadside….One of the shots from the *Havannah* knocked him on the head and another ploughed the ground on which but a moment before he stood. To us, to whom sights like these are treats, the day's amusement was one of equal satisfaction and delight. Long may every British man-of-war carry a stock of such shots in her locker – and long may every

British battery point its guns with the same precision that directed those of Fort Britomart," wrote Auckland's *New Zealander* newspaper in 1848. [2]

When *HMS Challenger*, a second class armoured cruiser, was in New Zealand waters in 1909, she had a week's big gun practice in the Hauraki Gulf, north of Auckland, "and also continued the practice on mornings while coming down the coast (to Wellington)". [3]

In the Islands an exhibition of naval gunnery made an indelible impression on the native mind and could even be instrumental in avoiding conflict. When *HMS Havannah* was in Fiji in August, 1849, a target was put on the face of a rock on the island of Ovalau for Cakobau, the de facto ruler of Fiji, to see.

The target was about eight hundred yards from the *Havannah*. After the gunners got to work on the rock it was completely shattered, with some pieces "being thrown with force some distance into the sea. The firing was very good indeed – being precise and quick, and no random shots. After dinner 130 went on shore with muskets, 30 of them being marines. Two field pieces with the carriages were also taken on shore....The bush was ranged, the way being cleared by the two cannon. On the following morning a 24 pound rocket was fired from a rocket gun fixed on shore. The rocket passed over two high mountains and then fell and burst." [4] This so impressed Cakobau that he exclaimed, "This makes me tremble. I feel that we are no longer secure. If we offend these people, they would bring their ship to Mbau where, having found us with their spy-glasses, they would destroy us and our town at once." [5] Cakobau and his chiefs mended their ways without the British having to force them to do so in an actual engagement.

Evidence of their reformation came with the cancelling of a big cannibal feast that was to be held the next day. Cakobau later gave up cannibalism altogether. He also gave up all his wives except for one, and was baptised a Christian.

In the 1880s there was an annual Admiralty prize firing, which each warship had to do at sea while steaming at a rate of eight knots round the target. *HMS Cormorant* carried out this exercise on 20th January, 1880, when she sailed outside Wellington Heads into the open sea. "The weather was fine but there was a good deal of swell on, causing the vessel to roll considerably. This, together with the rate of speed, made it difficult to hit the target, which was of pyramidal form, about ten feet on the base and generally between

1,200 and 1,400 yards distant. Notwithstanding these disadvantages some of the shot went very close nearly all were excellent in line of direction," wrote the *Evening Post.* [6]

Just as well they went out of the harbour as two years earlier when *HMS Wolverine* engaged in some gun and shell practice at Wellington the plastering in the roof of what was – and still is – the "largest wooden building in the world" was cracked to such an extent that it was considered "dangerous" by the army of fragile government clerks who worked there.

HMS Powerful, the flagship of the Australia station, *HMS Challenger* and *HMS Encounter* carried out their prize firing competitions with heavy guns at Norfolk Bay, Tasmania, in 1907. The target measured 14 feet by 21.5 feet, with the size of the bulls eye being ten feet by eight. Out of 117 shots from her six inch guns the *Powerful* made 113 hits while steaming at a speed of twelve knots. The range varied constantly but the average was 1,650 yards and the *Powerful* scored a very high average of 96.5%, with over 60% of the hits being bulls eyes. With her 9.2 inch guns nine shots were fired, of which six were hits.

In those years leading up to the First World War the Admiralty published the annual results of these battle practices in *The Times*. In 1909 the China Squadron performed best in the whole world, followed by the 3rd Division of the Home Fleet.

Two years later the Australia Squadron came first and the China Squadron second, and so the Pacific fared well against the rest of the world. In these firing exercises, as in sail drill and rowing races, there was always a keen and healthy rivalry between ships and this made for higher standards and a better navy.

Rifle shooting – especially for the marines who were on almost every ship – was also important and most port visits included a competition between the bluejackets and the local Volunteers, often with ten or twelve men a side, using such weapons as Martini-Henrys and Snider carbines.

In a match at Wellington in 1869 between twelve of the officers and crew of *HMS Blanche* and twelve from No. 1 Company, Wellington Rifle Volunteers the latter won by 158 points. It was five shots each at 300, 400 and 500 yards, no sighting shots, and any position.

Shooting competitions were not always free of accidents. In 1861 a gunner on *HMS Cossack* accidentally shot William Ward of

HMS Pelorous in the leg at Auckland. Sometimes injuries were sustained not by what came out of a gun but by the gun itself.

When *HMS Cordelia* was sailing between Fiji and New Caledonia on 27th June, 1891, it was the regulation date for the quarterly shot and shell practice, which lasted all day, with several guns' crews taking their turn as required. The seventh shot of a six inch breech-loading Armstrong gun, with a full charge made up of common shell, was about to be fired when it exploded, filling the air with fragments of metal. Some pieces of the shattered gun flew as high as the foretop-gallant lift and the royal sheet, both of which were shot away.

The explosion burst through the upper deck and the breech block of the gun was carried right across the deck, crashing through the fixtures in its tack. Two officers and four men were blown to pieces and many others were wounded. The latter were taken to hospital in Sydney. "The appearance of the *Cordelia's* upper deck is almost as it would be after a sharp engagement," wrote a press report after the damaged vessel arrived in Sydney. [7]

The gun had been used for only about 200 rounds and yet it was guaranteed for 2,000. It was properly loaded and the accident was believed to have been caused by the gun's defective steel. The First Lord of the Admiralty, Lord George Hamilton, told Parliament that all guns of the type that had exploded would be replaced by others of a later and improved type.

This was not the only black mark against the Armstrongs. In 1862 the samurai of the Prince of Satsuma in Japan killed a British merchant, Charles Richardson, and, when the indemnity that was demanded was not paid, the commander-in-chief of the China station, Rear-Admiral Augustus Kuper, took a squadron consisting of *HMS Argus, Coquette, Euryalus, Havock, Pearl, Perseus* and *Racehorse* to bombard the port of Kagoshima so as to let the Japanese know that the killing of British subjects would not go unpunished. It was during this bombardment that the new Armstrong breech loading guns were fired in action for the first time and they did not live up to expectations; there were twenty-eight accidents to twenty-one guns out of the 365 rounds that were fired and so the Navy went back to the old muzzle loader.

An explosion also occurred on *HMS Otter* on 16th August, 1909, when she was at Wei Hai Wei. This torpedo boat destroyer was about to leave her moorings about 6 p.m. to go outside for a night firing when a tube burst below, followed by a huge volume of steam rushing from the hold. Two of the men were killed and several others injured.

A terrible accident occurred on 5th January, 1909, when *HMS Encounter's* longboat was taking sixty bluejackets fully armed ashore for practice at Sydney's Randwick rifle ranges. She left the naval depot at Garden Island in the tow of a small launch but, when they were about two hundred yards off the promontory known as Mrs. Macquarie's Point, the harbour steamer, *Dunmore*, came along and struck the longboat on the starboard side, turning her over and throwing all the heavily armed bluejackets into the water.

Fifteen of them, laden with rifles and heavy cartridge belts, were drowned. They were all single men, aged from nineteen to twenty-one, except for a twenty-eight year old artisan called Gregory, who left a wife and young daughter in Liverpool.

The towing launch, despite being crowded with marines, did excellent rescue work and others were saved by small boats that arrived on the scene from the warships *HMS Encounter*, *Prometheus*, *Fantome* and *Pegasus* at Garden Island within four minutes.

"There were many enquiries made of the naval men at Man-o-War Steps as to the names of those who had been drowned," stated a press report. "And there were some pathetic incidents. Two young ladies came to the doorway. One of them, after a moment's hesitation, advanced towards the sergeant in charge and enquired if a certain person was one of the dead. The sergeant didn't know but procured for her a list of the missing. She read the paper until she came to a name. The sheet dropped from her hand to the floor, and she wheeled and walked away without saying a word. When asked what was clearly a superfluous question whether any of her friends or relatives were among the missing, she said, 'Yes'. 'The name?' 'Bristowe!' And her lips quivered as she spoke but she was too full of sorrow to shed a tear." [8] Like five of the other drowned men, Bristowe was a Londoner who had gone into barracks at Shotley in Essex for preliminary training before being drafted to *HMS Encounter*.

The fifteen unlucky ones were buried the next day with full naval honours. "Between four and five hundred men, dressed in white, first assembled in a temporary chapel which had been erected at Garden Island, where the coffins of their comrades lay, and a brief service was held....After prayer, the assembled men sang in unison the hymn *Brief Life is Here our Portion*. Strong men brushed aside tears as the thrilling service for the dead proceeded, concluding with the hymn *For Those in Peril on the Sea*, and the white robed sailors stood as the Dead March in Saul was played. Then they filed past the row of coffins out into the sunlight to take part in the landing and burial of their dead.

The bodies were landed at the Man-Of-War Stairs where marines with fixed bayonets formed a guard. As the coffins, each covered with a Union Jack, passed, the marines stood to attention and a bugle call sounded. It was the last solemn salute to the dead as the cortege started on the journey to the men's final resting place.....A hushed stillness pervaded the great throng, and flags everywhere were at half mast." [9] Among the mourners would have been Bristowe's lady love.

Torpedoes were fired from ordinary warships as well as from special torpedo boats. In the 1880s a motor torpedo boat was small but fast, with rapid acceleration and an ability to turn tight circles. "The little boat has been whipping through the water fast enough before but now, on a sudden, seems endowed with life and, almost with a leap, goes off vibrating and pulsing all over like a sentient being, at a racing pace which almost takes your breath away....you seem to be rushing 'through' instead of over the sea, which dashes and roars all around you.....It's like a ride on the back of a dolphin," wrote a reporter [10] after a dash across Wellington harbour on one of them, that was armed with a Nordenfeldt gun and could fire mines under the water.

After the Russian war scare of 1885 the ports in Australasia depended for their defence on the combination of fixed guns in fortifications at harbour entrances and torpedo boats, which from a hidden position "would dart out to within five hundred yards of a (hostile) cruiser, and discharge Whiteheads with seventy pounds of gun cotton, nine or ten feet below the surface". [11]

Speed and manoeuvrability remained the essential features of motor torpedo boats, which had to get close to their target to fire their weaponry while being nifty enough to escape and evade the gunfire of the bigger warships. In the battle for Hong Kong in December, 1941, the small fleet of motor torpedo boats more or less fought the naval battle on their own; over a vital period they managed to deny the invading Japanese the freedom of the seas around Hong Kong that the enemy had so arrogantly expected.

Ships' weaponry was always of interest to foreign navies, especially in the lead-up to war. In 1905 a number of sailors of the

185

German cruiser *Falke* were discovered examining the guns at Esquimalt Naval Yard and were summarily ejected.

Three years later, when President Theodore Roosevelt sent America's Great White Fleet around the Pacific on a "friendship mission", its officers were instructed to spy on naval bases in every port they visited. In fact, it was more of an espionage mission than a friendship mission. Among the targets of their spying were bases in Australia and New Zealand; the Americans feared that, in the event of war between the United States and Japan, the British Empire would support Japan – all part of the terrible consequences that flowed from Britain's foolish naval treaty with Japan.

The most impressive feature of the Royal Navy in the two and a quarter centuries covered by this book was the development of armaments. The reader will recall that, a few moments before he was murdered, Captain Cook fired his gun at a Hawaiian but the man was barely touched since the thick cloak that he was wearing protected him – a far cry from the nuclear armed submarines of to-day's Navy.

The tremendous advances in killing power have been largely the result of the wars of the twentieth century. In 1898 Winston Churchill took part in the cavalry charge at Omdurman when, as an officer attached to the 21st Lancers, he galloped into the Dervish mass, which was cut to pieces by the British horsemen with their swords, lances and Mauser pistols. The same man, with the same rugged patriotism and courage, oversaw the development of the atomic bombs in the Second World War. From the horse to Hiroshima in one man's adulthood.

Similar advances have been made in naval weaponry as the cutlasses and boarding axes of the mid nineteenth century have given way to far more effective methods of fighting our enemies.

POMP AND CIRCUMSTANCE

"The royal navy of England hath ever been its greatest defence and ornament."

- Sir William Blackstone [1]

There is no sight more grand or spectacular than a Royal Navy vessel entering or leaving port. In the days of sail there was the added attraction of colourful pennants flying from the masts and the sailors in their smart uniforms spread throughout the rigging.

Nobody could do an "occasion" better than the Navy. The most important day of the year was, of course, Trafalgar Day, which was celebrated every 21st October in the respective messes with loyal and eager toasts.

In London Nelson's Column in Trafalgar Square would be bedecked with flowers and wreaths and this set the tone for the ships in the distant Pacific. On the big day in 1896 Nelson's famous flag signal was exhibited over his Column, great crowds gathered below, and newspapers reported the tale of Trafalgar to readers who had not even been born when the great event took place.

As the nineteenth century drew to its close and the naval race with Germany got under way Navy Leagues sprang up all over the Empire to urge ever greater expenditure on the Fleet and to use Trafalgar Day to spread the legend of Nelson to the young.

In 1896 some two hundred towns in Britain celebrated the day and the teachers in Board schools acquainted the pupils with its meaning. Flags were flown from London's public buildings and clubs, Montreal in French Quebec was decorated and in Auckland, New Zealand "shipowners and private individuals recognised the anniversary….by a fine display of bunting on the shipping, wharves, mercantile houses, etc." [2] And, of course, the city of Nelson, New Zealand, celebrated with a half-holiday and athletic sports.

After the turn of the twentieth century the celebrations got so out of hand in the face of the growing naval rivalry with Germany that France, our new ally, lodged a protest at the excess of it all. As a sop to French opinion the Navy League in London included the French and Spanish colours in the wreaths which they laid at the foot of Nelson's Column while at Portsmouth the French flag was saluted along with our own.

187

By the time of the centenary of the battle in 1905 the Entente Cordiale between Britain and France was one of the lynchpins of our security and so the officers on *HMS Victory* at Portsmouth drank the toast in silence "to those who fell in 1805 – friend or foe" while in Canada "two hundred and fifty towns celebrated the Nelson centenary regardless of race". [3]

The centenary was celebrated in Sydney by a great-grandson of Pasco, the signal lieutenant who had hoisted the famous signal on *HMS Victory*, unfurling the signal at a naval concert at the Sydney Town Hall while down in Hobart there was "a profuse display of bunting", [4] and "the entente cordiale was in evidence by a general intertwining of the Union Jack with the Tricolour'. [5]

On the same day Nelson's last signal was hoisted on the flagstaff at Auckland with the sailors of *HMS Prometheus* forming a square around it. There was a seventeen gun salute followed by a procession through Auckland's streets "and patriotic demonstrations in the Drill Hall in the afternoon and evening". [6]

In Wellington "The children will assemble at their respective schools in the morning, and speeches of a patriotic nature will be made by the headmasters...The school flags will be hoisted and patriotic songs sung, after which the children will be dismissed for the day" [7] while in the small town of Lawrence in New Zealand's Scottish province of Otago "Mr. Donald McDonald played some patriotic tunes on the bagpipes and three cheers were given for the King." [8]

Trafalgar Day was not the only day that the Navy celebrated. The gunners were also busy on Queen Victoria's birthday (24th May) and on the anniversary of her accession to the Throne (20th June). On this latter anniversary in 1846 in Wellington harbour "a royal salute was fired by *HMS Calliope* and colours were displayed from each mast head". [9]

Eleven years later Commodore Keppel on the China station noted in his diary, "Anniversary of H.M's accession. Dressed ships. At noon fired Royal salutes the whole length of the Canton River." [10] Wherever the Royal Navy happened to be on the day, its guns made sure that the locals knew of this royal occasion.

When our present Queen acceded to the Throne on 6th February, 1952, her warships around the world fired a twenty-one gun salute and took part in other celebrations. However, *HMS Ceylon* was busy engaging the enemy in Korean waters and so could not take part. Instead Rear-Admiral Scott-Moncrieff sent her a signal, "On this historic occasion I trust you will arrange to salute by firing twenty-one live shells at Her Majesty's enemies".

There were more sombre occasions as on the death of Prince Albert when *HMS Fawn* in Auckland harbour fired forty-two minute guns in his memory with the ensign at half mast. "All the ships in the harbour, among which were the American whalers, showed the same mark of respect," wrote the *Southern Cross*. [11] The late Prince Consort's name is still remembered in Auckland by Albert Street, one of the city's main thoroughfares, Albert Park, the largest green space in central Auckland, and the suburb of Mount Albert.

The Americans' respect towards our Prince Consort was reciprocated during the Battle of Okinawa in April, 1945, when, upon hearing of the death of President Roosevelt, Admiral Rawlings R.N. ordered the ships of the British Pacific Fleet to fly the colours at half mast for the last hour before sunset even though at sea during a battle the custom is to fly the colours at half mast only when burying or conveying the dead.

This respect shown towards Roosevelt was not so evident on the American warships where their officers for the most part abhorred their late commander-in-chief for his politics and his questionable methods of government – a situation that could never occur on a British or Commonwealth ship because the monarch is above politics and, as such, is able to command the respect of all.

The saddest occasions were when one had to farewell a dead shipmate – either to the deep or in a cemetery on shore. When in 1871 Captain Marcus, a Royal Marine on board *HMS Rosario*, died from tetanus after being hit with a poisonous arrow that the natives of Nukapu in the New Hebrides fired into his left arm, the ship was hove to, the colours hoisted to half mast, the captain – in the absence of a chaplain – read the funeral service and poor old Marcus was committed to the waters of the Pacific in front of all the ship's company as three volleys were fired as a mark of respect.

Christmas was usually celebrated in a traditional but relaxed manner. "This day we kept as Christmas Day," wrote a sailor named Martin of the Christmas of 1777 on Captain Cook's third voyage, "the people were served fresh pork, fish and double allowance of liquor, which enabled them to spend this evening with mirth and jollity". [12]

On Christmas Day, 1871, *HMS Rosario* was cruising in the New Hebrides and, in the words of her captain, Albert Markham, "In the forenoon Divine Service was performed and the ship's

189

company had the remainder of the day to themselves which, to judge from the incessant shouts of laughter which came aft from the forecastle and lower deck, was enjoyed in the manner this festive day usually is on board a man-of-war." [13]

In war time Christmas could not always be celebrated on the exact day. During the first Christmas of the Korean War (1950) the aircraft carrier, *HMS Theseus*, had to postpone the celebration of Christ's birthday for six days until it was out of the combat zone and back in the Japanese port of Kure.

When, during the nineteenth century, a warship visited a South Pacific island with a "king", then the traditional twenty-one gun salute was fired for a head of state. I have deliberately put inverted commas around the word "king" since a king was usually a warlord who, learning of the Europeans' fascination with the concept of national sovereignty, would finish up on top by killing off the other warlords and claiming kingship over the islands – as in Tonga and also in Fiji before it became a British colony. Thus did the King of Tonga and Cakobau of Fiji merit a twenty-one gun salute.

When *HMS Calliope* and *HMS Lizard* arrived in Tonga, carrying the admiral of the Australia station, Admiral Fairfax, not only was the Tonga flag saluted with twenty-one guns but also the admiral visited the king in state and was saluted with fifteen guns upon his departure "so, as far as flags, bands and gunpowder are concerned, we have been having lively times here in Tonga," wrote a press correspondent. [14]

The same when *HMS Cossack* visited Fiji in September, 1872 and Captain Douglas gave Cakobau a twenty-one gun salute and "received His Majesty on board the *Cossack* with the customary honours ever accorded to influential royal personages". [15] In this case the guest, who was received on board in such high old style, had been an inveterate cannibal who had killed and eaten hundreds of his enemies; one of his party tricks was to cut a man's tongue out and then eat it raw in front of the victim before moving on to the next stage. He even ate the crew of a Scottish trading vessel, later claiming that his descendants would be Scottish "by absorption".

When *HMS Calliope* visited Samoa in September, 1852, the British Consul, Mr. Pritchard, visited the ship but, as a consul, he was given only a seven gun salute.

People could get very particular about salutes. When the commander of a small gunboat in Labuan was ordered to fire a salute in honour of Disraeli becoming Prime Minister, he declined to do so on the grounds that, owing to the possibility of accidents, no man-of-war mounting fewer than ten guns was allowed to fire a salute. No doubt he was a Whig! The Governor then dug up some old buried guns and fired them himself – but not to regular time. This farce seems particularly appropriate as in a constitutional monarchy no politician should ever be given a gun salute – not even one as glittering as Disraeli.

If they were reluctant to fire guns for British politicians, there was certainly no lack of enthusiasm to honour foreign navies with salutes. If there was an American warship in harbour on the Fourth of July the British ships would dress themselves with flags and fire the guns in salute to the Stars and Stripes. When the French naval vessel, *Caledonienne*, left Sydney for New Caledonia early one morning in 1865 *HMS Curacoa* "had our band up to play *Partant pour la Syrie*, whereupon the Frenchmen all took off their hats and commenced bowing most politely as they passed our stern," wrote Cecil Foljambe, the signal midshipman on the *Curacoa*. [16]

Even the arrival of the English mail on the China station was marked with ceremony – the firing of a gun accompanied by a couple of rockets to announce the good news to the sailors that their letters from home had arrived.

There was always the ceremony – as there still is – when a commander-in-chief left his station as on 2nd November, 1869, when Rear-Admiral Henry Keppel handed over command of the China station to Vice-Admiral Sir Henry Kellett. Not only were their names almost the same but also both officers left their names in the East – Keppel Harbour in Singapore and Mount Kellett in Hong Kong and Kellett Island, the site of the Royal Hong Kong Yacht Club, off Hong Kong's Causeway Bay.

The Duke of Edinburgh, son of Queen Victoria, happened to be visiting Hong Kong at the time on *HMS Galatea* and so the royal standard was hoisted on that vessel at 8 a.m. "and a general royal salute, with ships dressed, took place". [17] The *Galatea's* barge, manned by the royal visitor and the wardroom officers and steered by the Commodore, took the departing admiral (Keppel) out from the wharf to the P and O liner that was to take him home to England by way of Singapore.

In 1874 a twenty-seven foot high obelisk in honour of Captain Cook was erected on a small piece of land that had been given to Britain by Princess Likelike, the sister of King Kalakau, the

191

last king of Hawaii, to commemorate Cook's discovery of the Hawaiian islands on 18th January, 1778. It was at Kawaaloa Beach and only a few yards from where the Great Navigator was killed, the twenty-five square feet around the monument being sovereign British territory. Twelve old 32 pounder guns were taken there from Esquimalt, Vancouver Island, to form a fence around the memorial.

Then in 1928 three cruisers, *HMS Cornwall*, *HMAS Brisbane* and *HMS Dunedin*, joined *USS Pennsylvania* to commemorate the 150th anniversary of Cook's discovery of the islands. On this occasion the sailors formed a guard of honour to the Cook memorial where a wreath was laid. The action then moved fifty yards away to the exact spot where the great man fell in the shallow water and passed out of this world. Here a bronze plaque, embedded in the seabed and covered by water except at the lowest tide, was unveiled, the ceremony being rounded off by a gun salute from the warships and the playing of the Last Post by four naval buglers.

From here the official party went across to Napoopoo on the other side of the bay to unveil yet another tablet, this one to William Whatman, a member of the ship's company of the *Resolution*, who died here and was given the first ever Christian burial in Hawaii – a service that was performed by Captain Cook.

This day of ceremonies ended with a big feast in a field for 4,300 locals, to which "Kona ranchers, plantation men and business men contributed five bullocks, 4,000 pounds of poi, 3,500 pounds of rice balls, 300 pounds of fish, 20 pigs and 2,500 cases of soda water." [18] The soda water is a reminder that this feast took place during America's foolish experiment with Prohibition. No doubt the British sailors left the eating to the heavy Hawaiians and returned to their vessels for a glass of something more fortifying in the hot, thirsty atmosphere.

The white, gleaming obelisk to Captain Cook, erected in 1874, is arguably the most meaningful naval memorial in the Pacific and for many years after it was constructed the site was maintained by bluejackets from visiting warships, who would trim and keep the area tidy but to-day this impressive memorial is virtually impossible to reach through the overgrown jungle. Hawaii's state government declared it a "conservation area" with restricted access – not to conserve the coral and bush as they claim but to try to keep this shameful deed committed by their ancestors out of public consciousness.

Of all the Navy's ceremonial displays there was probably none more spectacular than Sydney harbour on the evening of 1st February, 1888, when there was a fireworks display, with all the warships illuminated, as part of the celebrations of the centenary of Australia – the first time in history that a gaol had become a nation. This was the culmination of a week of festivities that began on the anniversary itself, 26th January.

The fireworks were let off from Fort Denison, Fort Macquarie, the Domain and the north shore. "The spectacle itself was of surpassing magnificence," wrote the *Sydney Morning Herald*. "The whole of the vessels forming the Australian Squadron now in Farm Cove (*HMS Nelson, Calliope, Rapid, Diamond, Undine, Harrier* and *Dart*) and the Russian corvette, *Rynda*, were outlined with prismatic fires, which had a picturesque effect.....The first illuminations of the ships took place about 8.40 p.m. when, by a pre-concerted signal given by Captain Hammill of the *Nelson*, the whole of the vessels joined in a simultaneous display of light. At the same time Fort Denison and the grounds surrounding the residence of Admiral Fairfax at Kirribilli Point....were turned as if by magic into a brilliant mass of fire.....lighting up the dark space of the harbour waters....Each mast and yard was almost simultaneously outlined by a means of white lights at the yardarms, afterwards changing to red, and then a number of rockets were sent up by the men-of-war....To see such ships brought out in such bold relief against a dark sky, when almost every rope was discernible, was a picture in itself....The fleet came in for quite its full share of admiration for, at such times as the yards were not manned, some of the very best rockets...were fired from the decks of the Squadron."
19

Ah yes, nobody could do these things like the Navy and there could never be a more wonderful setting for a show than Sydney harbour on a summer's night.

WIVES AND SWEETHEARTS

When a seaman went to the Pacific in the days of sail it would usually be a matter of years before he returned to home, hearth and loved ones. For those waving good-bye on the wharf the prospect of never seeing a beloved husband, son, father, brother or beau was very real in view of the triple risks of shipwreck, disease and action.

Mrs. Elizabeth Cook, the wife of the Great Navigator, farewelled her husband on numerous occasions during his naval career, each time wondering if she would ever see him again. During Captain Cook's long absences in the Pacific – and earlier when he went to Canada – Elizabeth had the sole responsibility of bringing up their young ones in their leased house in Assembly Row, off Mile End Road, near the London docks.

The Cooks had six children but three of them died in infancy, leaving three sons, James (jun), Nathaniel and Hugh. The last mentioned was born in 1776, the year that Captain Cook set off on his last voyage, and so he never knew his illustrious father.

When the terrible news of Captain Cook's murder reached England George III ordered that a pension of £200 be paid to his thirty-eight year old widow.

In the same year in which her husband was killed Mrs. Cook lost her second son, Nathaniel, a midshipman on *HMS Thunderer*, when his ship went down in a hurricane off Jamaica, which sank thirteen ships of the Royal Navy.

Her two remaining children, the eldest son, James, and the youngest, Hugh, died within five weeks of each other in 1793-4, James at Poole, Dorset, while embarking in an open boat to reach his sloop of war, *HMS Spitfire*, and Hugh from fever which he caught at Christ's College, Cambridge, where he was studying for the ministry. Thus Captain Cook's line came to an end. On receiving news of the death of the last of her children Mrs. Cook collapsed and did not recover for several months.

However, unlike the deaths of her husband and Nathaniel, at least she had the bodies of James (jun) and Hugh and these were buried in the church of Saint Andrew the Great, across the road from Hugh's Christ's College at Cambridge. She would join them there after her own death on 15th May, 1835, having been a widow for fifty-six years and knowing that some of the lands that her husband discovered were already thriving British colonies.

The Cooks are buried under the central aisle while high up on the wall to the left of the altar is an impressive marble monument recording their deaths and also those of the other members of this unfortunate family.

On the monument is a mourning figure and there are naval objects at the top. Beneath the inscription is the coat-of-arms that was granted to the Cook family (or what was left of it) in 1785. On the shield are two polar stars and between them a map of the Pacific with every tenth degree of latitude marked and every fifteenth degree of longitude, the voyages of Captain Cook being traced in red. The motto – *Nil intentatum reliquit* – translates as "He leaves nothing untried".

Those at sea realised how hard it was for their wives and so in their letters home they often tried to make light of difficulties and dangers. After losing the *Bounty* to mutineers and sailing in a small longboat from Tonga to Timor, in which he almost starved in the process, Captain Bligh wrote to his wife from Timor to inform her of his whereabouts, "I know how shocked you will be at this affair but I request of you, my dear Betsy, to think nothing of it; all is now past and we will again look forward to future happiness." In other words, "I've been through Hell, but don't worry." At least Bligh showed consideration towards his wife even if he didn't show it to his men.

Some officers' wives accompanied their husbands on board the warships but these were not always welcomed by the sailors who believed that the wife of the captain became the real captain when she stepped on board.

During his time on the China station in 1868 Rear-Admiral Henry Keppel took his wife on board *HMS Salamis* as well as their two young children, Colin and May. From Malaya the happy family sailed to Labuan, off Borneo, and then to Manila but just out from Manila Bay they struck the north-east monsoon. "All my party were prostrate," wrote Rear-Admiral Keppel. "*Salamis* was so sudden in her movements that cots were given up and beds spread on the deck. My boy was in a burning fever – caught, we suppose, at Labuan – patient and good, calling only for drink, but unable to bear clothing....On service, wives and children ought to remain at home!" [1] When they reached Hong Kong young Colin soon recovered after being tended by Doctor Hill from the hospital ship, *Melville*.

When Keppel took his family up the Yangtse River the children became distressed one day when, out walking with one of the sailors, they came across a string of rats secured by wire to a six inch stick.

The luckiest ladies were the wives of those officers who served as Admiral of the Australia Squadron between 1885 and 1913 as they got to live in Admiralty House on Kirribilli Point on the north shore of Sydney harbour, just opposite Farm Cove where the fleet used to anchor. With sweeping and unobstructed views of the harbour, this is arguably the best site in Australia and one of the finest in the world.

This elegant two storey sandstone mansion, with ten bedrooms, countless servants, a colonnaded verandah and a covered Admiral's Walk leading down to the jetty where his barge was moored, is to-day the Sydney residence of Australia's Governor-General but still retains the name "Admiralty House" as a reminder of its former use and also of the pivotal role of the Royal Navy in Australia's founding and development.

In the social scene of Sydney during these years the Admiral and his wife were second only to the Governor of New South Wales and his wife and it was a world of balls, yachting, horse riding and endless entertaining.

Before Admiralty House was bought the Commodore of the Australia station lived in another very nice house that was provided by the New South Wales government. When Commodore Goodenough was appointed to command the station in 1873 he sailed out there on *HMS Pearl*, and his wife and two young sons followed shortly afterwards and lived with him in the Commodore's house in Sydney.

Goodenough and his wife had been married in 1864 and this was the first and only time when the commodore lived a settled life with his family in a house as he had been at sea almost continuously throughout his career. In view of what was to happen to him it was nice that he had this brief and ever so satisfying spell of family life before meeting his untimely death, which is dealt with in the next chapter but one.

Not all the wives were back in Britain as some officers took their spouses from the colonial society in which they mixed during their time on the Australia station. The wedding of a naval officer was a major social event in the colonies.

In April, 1886, Captain Marx of *HMS Swinger* married the daughter of Captain Heath, the chief postmaster of Queensland. Bishop Webber performed the service, which was attended by "the Governor and Lady Musgrave, the Premier, the Colonial Treasurer, and other prominent citizens, also the officers of *HMS Opal* and *Raven*....and the principal officers of the defence force. The bride and bridegroom were drawn in a carriage from the church to Captain Heath's house by forty bluejackets of the *Swinger*." [2]

When another of the *Swinger's* officers, Lieutenant G.W. Cornish, was married in Sydney five years later to Miss Nathan the lively bluejackets of that small gunboat rose to the occasion again. While the bride and groom were inside Saint James' church exchanging their vows a party of sailors approached the driver of the horses and carriage that were waiting outside the church and asked him to unyoke the horses as they wanted to pull the carriage themselves – as they had done for Captain Marx in Brisbane.

The carriage driver "did not relish the idea of being deposed but, finding that the sailors were determined to oust him, he whipped up the horses and dashed off at a great pace followed by the tars who expressed their determination not to be outdone. After some time the driver hove in sight again and was immediately pounced on by the men-of-warsmen, who succeeded without much ceremony in ousting him and unhitching the horses. They then installed two of their number on the box seat and, the remainder falling in at the pole with drag-ropes, they drew the brougham up to the church door to await the bridal party.

On the newly married couple making their appearance they were lustily cheered and escorted to the carriage, which was then started on its way by the gallant tars amid the applause of a great crowd of onlookers." [3]

RAISING THE FLAG

New Zealand

When Captain Cook raised the flag of England on the beach at Botany Bay in 1770 he was setting a precedent that would later be followed on hundreds of islands, both great and small, throughout the Pacific.

As the colony of New South Wales grew, its shippers and traders extended their activities to other places, including the islands of New Zealand some 1,200 miles across the Tasman Sea. By the beginning of 1840 there were about two thousand white people living in New Zealand, most of them in and around the whaling port of Kororareka in the far north of the North Island; this was a favoured anchorage as it was well sheltered from the prevailing winds. They were mainly whalers, sealers, sawyers and flax traders and they were living in an uncolonised and uncivilised land where there was no law and order and no native institutions that could be developed to provide them. However, despite several requests, the British government had steadfastly refused to accept these anarchic islands as a colony.

By the end of 1839 the organised settlement of British people in what would soon become the "Britain of the South" was about to get under way under private auspices and there were already ships, organised by the energetic New Zealand Company, on the high seas with their first batches of colonists.

Faced with this sort of pressure, the British government could procrastinate no longer and so it commissioned a captain of the Royal Navy, William Hobson, as Consul and Lieutenant-Governor designate with the brief to negotiate with the Maori chiefs for a transfer of sovereignty. The British government's aim was to acquire sovereignty, establish British law and regulate the coming colonisation – all at the least possible cost to the Exchequer.

Hobson had been born at Waterford, Ireland, in 1793 and had entered the Navy at the tender age of ten. He served on the West Indies station where he met his wife, Eliza, but after their marriage he came ashore for a few years before being given command of the frigate *HMS Rattlesnake* in 1836. He took this vessel to Australia and surveyed Port Phillip Bay, on which was later built the city of Melbourne. The northern portion of this great natural harbour was named Hobson's Bay.

In May, 1837 he took the *Rattlesnake* to New Zealand for the dual purposes of doing some much needed coastal surveying and protecting British subjects who were being threatened by the Maoris. After assessing the unruly scene he made some useful recommendations to the Colonial Office on the future governance of New Zealand and so was an ideal choice for the tricky mission of bringing New Zealand under British rule by peaceful means. He was especially concerned with protecting the interests of the natives and of preventing New Zealand becoming a convict colony like those on the other side of the Tasman Sea.

Hobson arrived in Sydney on *HMS Druid* on Christmas Eve, 1839, and made the final arrangements with Governor Gipps of New South Wales. After taking the oath of office as Lieutenant-Governor designate of New Zealand at Government House, Sydney, on 14th January, 1840, and meeting several Sydney merchants with a knowledge of New Zealand, he crossed the Tasman Sea on *HMS Herald*, which was commanded by Captain Nias, whom we last met destroying the North Wangtung fort in the Canton River during the First Opium War.

Unfortunately, the two captains did not get along with each other and it does not seem to have been the fault of Hobson, who was capable, kindly, patient, diplomatic and broadminded. "By the urbanity of his manners he has gained the goodwill of everybody," wrote the *New Zealand Gazette and Wellington Spectator,* [1] which then added, "As a lieutenant, Captain Nias was undistinguished for anything but his ill temper and litigious disposition." [2] It seems that this "captains' tiff" arose from jealousy on the part of Nias.

Also on board the *Herald* as she sailed across the Tasman was the putative government of what would soon be Britain's newest colony – Felton Mathews (Surveyor-General), Lieutenant H. D. Smart of the 28th Regiment (Resident Magistrate of the Interior), Charles Logie (Colonial Storekeeper), Doctor John Johnson (Colonial Surgeon), Lieutenant Willoughby Shortland R.N. (Acting Colonial Secretary), two clerks, and a sergeant and four troopers of the Mounted Police of New South Wales. With this small party Captain Hobson was expected to govern a land larger than Great Britain in area.

The *Herald* arrived off Kororareka, the only real European settlement in the whole of New Zealand, on 30th January, 1840, and Captain Hobson got to work on board the man-of-war to draw up the proposed treaty with the chiefs. For this he had the assistance of

James Busby, who had been the British Resident in New Zealand for some time but this was an empty title as he had no meaningful authority.

On 4th February the sailmakers and some other sailors from *HMS Herald* were busy erecting a marquee on the big lawn in front of Busby's house at Waitangi, which overlooked the tranquil waters of the Bay of Islands. Other large tents were put up by the seamen for the accommodation of those Maoris who had to travel from afar to take part in this historic occasion and the missionaries were conscripted to round them up.

On the following morning (5th February) crowds began to pack into the marquee, which was bedecked with colourful flags and had a raised platform at one end on which were a table and chairs.

At noon Captain Hobson arrived in his full dress naval uniform and sat at the centre of the table. He had walked the short distance across the lawn from Busby's house, accompanied by Captain Nias and the other officers of *HMS Herald* (all in full dress).

When he got inside the crowded, sweaty marquee Captain Hobson took his place at the table and faced the audience, many of whom had sailed there by canoe. On Hobson's right were several Anglican clergymen from the Church Missionary Society while on his left were Bishop Pompallier and one of his priests as well as some of Hobson's aides.

Some writers have described the Treaty of Waitangi as "New Zealand's Magna Carta" but this is an exaggeration and anyway, by signing the treaty, the rights under Magna Carta would be one of the benefits that the people of New Zealand would now enjoy. Where there is a similarity to Magna Carta is the preponderance of churchmen at the ceremony.

On that historic Monday in 1215 when King John set out from Windsor to ride the four miles down to Runnymede he was surrounded by a small and dusty cavalcade of galloping horses that carried an abundance of clerics – the Papal Legate, the Archbishop of Canterbury and several bishops. When they reached Runnymede there was a tent set up – as at Waitangi - with a little throne for the king. John put his seal on the Great Charter and then got back on his horse and rode back to Windsor with all his churchmen. It is hard to believe that the similarity of the two scenes did not escape the imaginations of Captain Hobson or the brace of missionaries who surrounded him.

As Hobson looked out from his chair in this big tent – a hundred feet by thirty – he could see in front of him, sitting on the ground, a mass of feathered and tattooed chiefs. Behind them were more natives, also sitting on the ground, while at the back were about a hundred Europeans, who were standing. Altogether there were about three hundred people inside the tent on this hot summer's day.

Hobson opened proceedings by telling the gathering that England was, thank God, a free country and that its people were free to come and settle in New Zealand if they wanted to. The Queen would not only protect her people but restrain them as well. He then offered the Maoris the same protection – both of themselves and of their lands – as well as all the rights of British subjects, including living under the Queen's Peace. For a people who had almost wiped themselves out in recent years in their endless inter-tribal wars this could only be an improvement.

The proposed treaty between the chiefs and the Crown was translated for them in their own language by Busby and Rev. Henry Williams. Some of the residents of Kororareka challenged the accuracy of the translation that was being given by Williams since he was widely distrusted – a typical "missionary on the make". However, Hobson let him continue.

Some of the chiefs addressed questions to Hobson, which he answered directly and truthfully. They knew that he had come from the Queen of England, who in New Zealand was regarded as some sort of semi-divine of supreme authority whose warships brought her power and prestige right to the shores of every native village.

To those who expressed reservations, one of their fellow chiefs, Tamati Waka Nene, explained how impossible it was for them to govern themselves without frequent wars and bloodshed.

At 4 p.m. Captain Hobson left the tent so that the natives could continue on their own the discussion of this very important step that they were being asked to take. Hobson and Captain Nias were rowed out to *HMS Herald* and they spent the night on board while a few hundred yards away on shore the Maoris smoked their pipes and continued their arguments long into the night..

The next day the big tent was even more crowded – about five hundred natives altogether which must have made the atmosphere very stuffy. Again there was a short discussion, and some more questions were asked of Captain Hobson by those who had newly arrived. It was during this discussion that the Pope's man,

201

Bishop Pompallier, asked that it be explained to the natives that all religions would be tolerated and protected, and this was done, with Hobson complimenting the bishop for his helpful intervention.

Then, convinced that this was the only real way forward, the chiefs began to put their signatures on the document. About forty-six of them did so that day. The literate wrote their names, others put their tattoo mark while Bishop Pompallier instructed the Catholics to put a cross (as in crucifix) beside their name "as an emblem of their new hope". This historic day was rounded off by the raising of the Union Jack and the firing of a royal salute by the guns of *HMS Herald*.

If Captain Hobson was the hero of the Treaty of Waitangi, then Mrs. Busby was certainly the heroine. This poor woman had some five hundred Maoris camping on her front lawn. Apart from the noise of their chanting and arguing through the night and the smells from their cooking there was also the aspect of their relieving themselves. Ah yes, Mrs. Agnes Busby did her bit for her country and she deserves as much respect and appreciation on the domestic front as Hobson does on the wider front.

Over the next few weeks Captain Hobson travelled around Northland, getting other chiefs to sign, but a month after his big moment at Waitangi he suffered a paralytic stroke and so it was left to Major Bunbury to take the treaty to distant parts of New Zealand, *HMS Herald* conveying him to these places.

For those Europeans already living in New Zealand the Treaty of Waitangi gave them protection and security for their lands, although some of the more spurious purchases were to be investigated and, in some cases, overturned. In order to prevent unjust land deals in the future the Treaty provided that Maoris could sell their lands only to the Crown, which would then sell them on to the settlers.

For the Maoris the Treaty gave them a security and peace that they had never known before. They were confirmed in the ownership of their lands and no longer could they be dispossessed of these by a stronger tribe with better weapons. They would now have a government with the power to protect them as henceforth they would have the same rights as other British subjects. The assumption of British rule brought to an end such unsavoury Maori customs as cannibalism, slavery and infanticide.

For the British Empire the islands of New Zealand were a valuable addition that in the fullness of time would provide a home for many British people while the farms that would be created would help feed the people of Britain for the best part of a century – until the British government turned its back on them by joining the wretched European Common Market.

Thus did the distant, fertile and beautiful islands of New Zealand become part of the British Empire, the whole event being conducted under the auspices of the Royal Navy – as had been the case at Sydney Cove fifty-one years earlier when another naval captain, Arthur Phillip, had become the founding father of Australia, just as Hobson now was of New Zealand.

The anniversary of the Treaty of Waitangi (6th February) is still celebrated each year on the same site, with the Royal New Zealand Navy taking the lead part – just as the officers and sailors of *HMS Herald* did in 1840. And the Christian crosses of the Union Jack continue to fly from the flagstaff at Waitangi, although now as part of the New Zealand flag, thereby symbolising the close and continuing links between Great Britain and New Zealand, which are of people and history rather than politics.

Fiji

Ill equipped to deal with the rapid intrusion of European missionaries, traders and planters into its traditional and primitive society, Fiji was in danger of sinking into a civil war between the 1,786 European settlers, who had bought 863,937 acres of land for plantations of sugar, cotton and coconut, and the native king, Cakobau, who, under the influence of his European advisor, the hated George Woods, ran the islands like a tyrant. Taxes were high and yet the Treasury was always empty and the islands in debt.

Obviously something had to be done. Britain had already refused an earlier request by the Fijian chiefs to put their islands under the Union Jack with the pusillanimous Gladstone declaring in the House of Commons that "England did not require any extension of territory" but then, with his usual convoluted thinking and trademark hypocrisy, he admitted the necessity "of some forward step for Fiji". [3]

His idea of a step forward was to send out Commodore Goodenough R.N. as head of the Australian Station with a further brief to be an Imperial Commissioner in Fiji in company with Mr. Layard, the British Consul for Fiji and Tonga. They were to travel around the islands of Fiji to ascertain the wishes of the people – both native and European – on the prospect of annexation. In the words of Wellington's *Evening Post*, "From the terms in which Mr. Gladstone spoke of Commodore Goodenough in the House of Commons it is evident that the Home Government relies greatly on his intelligence, ability and judgement." [4]

Like so many naval officers, James Goodenough was the son of a clergyman, his father, Edmund, being the Dean of Wells. After leaving Westminster School, he joined the Navy at the age of fourteen. A gunnery specialist, he worked his way up the ranks, taking part in the capture of Canton in 1857 and being sent to America as an observer to its civil war.

Commodore Goodenough sailed to the islands in his flagship, *HMS Pearl*, which carried seventeen guns and had a ship's company of 320 officers and men. He and his fellow commissioner spent five months in Fiji, "including the whole of the worst season. During that period he took his 1,600 ton ship, the *Pearl*, into almost every part of the group, steering her under canvas through intricate reef passages and over coral-studded seas, on many parts of which the most experienced settlers will not trust their little schooners." [5]

Commodore Goodenough "interviewed planters and others on almost every island on which there are white settlers; he ascended the principal rivers to the highest point at which they are navigable, thus piercing to the centre of the large island of Viti Levu, and he performed many toilsome journeys on foot in order to judge from personal observation the condition and prospects of the country." [6] He addressed meetings of settlers at places like Levuka and Messrs. Reece Brothers' sugar plantation at the Upper Rewa, Fiji's largest river. Not surprisingly, the settlers urged annexation as they would have greater security and increased property values under the British flag. In the words of the *Evening Post*, annexation would "relieve the whites from the miserable position of holding both life and property at the caprice of an ignorant savage, over whose mind some unscrupulous European adventurers have gained complete ascendancy." [7]

At Rewa the two Commissioners went up the palm fringed river as far as Nibutautau, where the missionary, Rev. Mr. Baker, had been murdered and eaten a few years earlier by the Kai Colo – the "people of the hills" who "have always resisted the progress of Christianity and maintained a savage independence. With it they have preserved cannibalism and a habit of constant raids on their neighbours of the coast below them." [8]

204

Goodenough's peregrinations around the islands were not without a certain element of adventure. On one occasion the *Pearl* encountered a hurricane in which her stern ports were stove in and the Commodore had five feet of water in his cabin but "she rode it out successfully, and the ship finally left the group without carrying away any lasting reminiscences of treacherous rock or coral." [9]

In a communication to Cakobau, the Fijian "king", the two commissioners stated: "Commodore Goodenough and Consul Layard are the two chiefs sent out by Her Britannic Majesty the Queen of England to visit Fiji, to inquire and consult with the King of Fiji and the chiefs respecting the Government of Fiji...Should it be their true minds (the King and chiefs of Fiji) to give Fiji to England, that it shall become the Queen of England's to govern, there is but one object and design sought, Fiji's peace and welfare in all time. That the King and chiefs, with all their people, and all the inhabitants of the land, may live in peace and prosper. This and this only is the desire and object.

It is no new thing for England to govern islands like Fiji. She owns and governs in several parts of the world a great number of similar islands to Fiji, and it will be very easy for her to govern Fiji also and preserve its peace and promote the welfare and prosperity of its people.

But England will never take Fiji by force or stealth if the King and chiefs do not wish to give it – if they think they can and are able to govern the land themselves.

If the King of Fiji retains the government for himself, that is well and England will only require of him...that he shall govern wisely and righteously with equal justice to native and British subjects resident in Fiji at all times.

But there is one matter to be considered by the King and chiefs of Fiji. They must know that the numbers of foreigners in Fiji will greatly increase from year to year, as well as their property, and their residence in Fiji will cause or create great intricacies" [10]

In view of Fiji's proven and continuing difficulties in meeting the fast encroaching modern world there could be but one outcome and the closing act of the drama took place on board the *Pearl* when a letter was presented to the Commodore, whom they called *Komotoa Kutanofi*, offering to cede Fiji to the Great White Queen (*Marama na Tui Piritani* – "the Lady, the Queen of Britain").

The occasion was reported in the *Fiji Gazette* as follows: "The poor old King surrendering his royal dignity to the Queen of

Great Britain, not at the point of the sword or the bayonet, but voluntarily, must have been a spectacle that would deeply impress itself upon the minds of those who witnessed it. But for white men settling in the Fijis he might have lived and died 'monarch of all he surveyed'. But in his own large canoe he was rowed to Her Majesty's ship, the *Pearl*, where he was received with a royal salute of twenty-one guns. On board he signed the letter in which he offered to cede the kingdom of Fiji to Her Majesty and this was received by Commodore Goodenough and Consul Layard." [11] The document was forwarded to London where the government agreed somewhat reluctantly to add these beautiful islands to an already considerable empire.

On 10th October, 1874, the formal ceremony took place at Nasova, near Levuka, with *HMS Pearl* and *HMS Dido* near the shore. In the words of the *Fiji Argus*, "At a little after two o'clock, there being then at Nasova a very large assemblage of the inhabitants of Fiji, Sir Hercules Robinson (Governor of New South Wales), accompanied by Commodore Goodenough, left the *Pearl* and received the Governor's salute of seventeen guns. On landing, His Excellency, accompanied by his suite, immediately proceeded to the reception room of the building wherein already were assembled Cakobau and the leading chiefs....As His Excellency passed between the two lines of troops they presented arms as the band played the National Anthem." [12]

After the Governor and the chiefs had signed the instrument of cession the now ex-king sprang something of a surprise when he passed to Sir Hercules an ornamental casket containing his old war club. He wanted to present this to Queen Victoria as a "mark of his submission and of his love, in offering his allegiance and in conforming to a new and better state of things in the history of his country. It had occurred to him that his own war club, which before Christianity and civilisation prevailed, was the only law the country was ruled by...would not be unacceptable to Her Majesty." [13] This skull cracker was kept at Windsor Castle until 1932 when it was returned by King George V to be used as the mace of Fiji's Legislative Council.

"The signing being over, His Excellency and suite, etc. proceeded to the verandah of the building and took up a front position in view of the assembled multitude....His Excellency then, in a clear and most distinct voice, said, '...It now, therefore, only remains for me to declare Fiji to be from this time forth a possession and dependency of the British Crown....I hope too that past differences and disagreements will henceforth be forgotten and that all local animosities will this day be buried at the foot of the staff on which we are now about to hoist the British flag' (Loud cheers)." [14]

Then "at a given signal from the Governor a stalwart bluejacket, one of the signalmen of *HMS Pearl*, lowered the Fijian flag" [15] to the sad mutterings of some of the chiefs of *Sa mate! Sa mate!* (Dead! Dead!) Then the British flag was hoisted by Lieutenant Elwyn of the *Pearl*, and it "waved for the first time over the isles of Fiji." [16] Stentorian cheers burst forth, the troops presented arms, the band played God Save the Queen and the flag was saluted by the booming of twenty-one guns from the *Pearl*. "It was a glorious sight and one that can never be forgotten by those who witnessed it," wrote the Fiji *Argus*. [17]

The events were rounded off by Sir Hercules Robinson calling for three cheers for the Queen, which were heartily given. Then he said, "I now ask you to give three cheers for the Vanivalu (Cakobau). He has shown himself to be a great Prince in what he has done, consulting only the interests of his people." [18] A hearty response was given to this call.

The Governor and the Commodore then proceeded through the lines back to their boat, "the troops presenting arms and the people cheering heartily" [19] as they passed. Thus did Fiji, roughly as large in area as Wales, become part of the British Empire with the Royal Navy playing the key role at the ceremony just as it had done on the earlier occasions in Australia and New Zealand.

Before leaving to go back to New South Wales, Sir Hercules Robinson had a final interview with the Fijian chiefs and told them that "whilst British rule is mild, it is at the same time firm and all-powerful" [20] – words that probably sum up the essence – and success - of British rule throughout the empire.

When the first Governor of the new Crown Colony arrived to take up his appointment it was the Navy that waved him ashore. Sir Arthur Gordon, the son of the Earl of Aberdeen (Prime Minister from 1852 to 1855), arrived on the *Pearl* towards noon on 24th June, 1875. The warship, "with all steam up and a favourable breeze into the bargain loomed in sight of Levuka" [21] just as the humid fog, that had for weeks shrouded the hills of Ovalau, cleared away.

Large numbers of people – both officials and others – gathered on the landing to "accord him a truly British welcome...In the square at Nasova a detachment of marines was drawn up, and opposite to them the native force under Lieutenant Oliver presented a very creditable appearance...The buildings, recently renovated, backed with a mass of luxuriant tropical foliage stood out in bold relief whilst the military array of men in their various costumes and the diversified toilettes of the ladies who honoured the scene with their presence, rendered the tableau pleasing and attractive.

At half past eleven the distant strains of the band of the *Pearl* rendering *God Save The Queen* gave the intimation that His Excellency was prepared to debark, and shortly after a Vice-Regal salute of seventeen guns was given and, as each report echoed and reverberated among the surrounding hills, he neared the shore, accompanied by his staff and the several officers of the men-of-war, conspicuous amongst others was the well-known and esteemed Commodore Goodenough." [22]

The new Governor lived on board the warship *HMS Barracouta* for four months while a Government House was being built. The irascible Gordon soon fell out with the captain of the *Barracouta* and sent him off to Samoa on a mission that forms another chapter in our story. (See: *Skullduggery in Samoa*)

New Guinea

The parsimonious and unimaginative British government was as reluctant to annex New Guinea as it had been to accept New Zealand and Fiji and, once again, put off the moment until it became absolutely necessary to take the action that had been urged on it for years by people on the spot. London had not recognised Captain Moresby's flag raising annexations just as it had rejected a later attempt by the colonial government of Queensland when it sent a party to annex the eastern half of the island that lay so close to Queensland's northern coast and which the Premier of Queensland, Ayrshire born Sir Thomas McIlwraith, referred to rather dramatically as "Queensland's Isle of Wight".

By 1884, with the Germans moving in to the top half of the uncolonised eastern part of New Guinea, the British government at last stopped struggling against its destiny and instructed the Commodore of the Australia station, James Elphinstone Erskine, to sail north and do the honours on his flagship, *HMS Nelson*.

Born at Cardross, Scotland, 1n 1838, Erskine had joined the Navy at fourteen. He retired in 1908 as an Admiral of the Fleet, having been an ADC to both Queen Victoria and King Edward VII.

For this proclamation of a British protectorate over south-eastern New Guinea, known as Papua, Commodore Erskine took with him four other men-of-war, *HMS Espiegle*, *Raven*, *Swinger* and *Harrier*.

As had been the case with Hobson in New Zealand, Commodore Erskine wanted the coming proclamation to be known by as many tribes as could conveniently be summoned and, also like Hobson, he enlisted the help of the missionaries to bring it about. For this reason he sent the *Raven* and the *Espiegle* up and down the coast with missionaries on board to collect as many as possible – both chiefs and others.

Altogether about fifty chiefs were brought to Port Moresby either on the warships or from inland, whither another missionary had been sent. Most of the chiefs were from the local Motu tribe.

One warship brought two chiefs who only the day before had been at war with each other, the quarrel having arisen from a dispute over payment for a girl who had been stolen, and had ended with the killing and wounding of several natives and the burning of a village. After they reached Port Moresby Commodore Erskine took them aside and told them that, in the event of a future dispute, they were not to embark on a killing spree but should seek redress through the Queen's government. They both thought that this was a jolly good idea.

When all the chiefs reached Port Moresby Commodore Erskine invited them on to his flagship for a feast and a speech, the ship's band playing stirring tunes and the flags flying in the gentle breeze. It was a study in contrasts, the officers decked out in their full dress uniforms while "most of the chiefs were destitute of clothing". [23] Perhaps they thought that the officers were wearing enough clothes for them all.

"Then a great tub of boiled rice, sweetened with brown sugar, was brought on deck and basins of this mixture were handed round to the chiefs, who devoured the rice with evident satisfaction," wrote the *Sydney Morning Herald*. [24] "Ship biscuits were also served out and the scene presented by the feasting savages and by the grouping of the *Nelson's* officers and the parading of the bluejackets on the opposite side of the deck....was interesting and picturesque." [25]

As Hobson had done at Waitangi and Goodenough at Nasova, Commodore Erskine explained to the native Papuans what life under the British flag would mean in the new and fast changing world, the speech being translated in to the Motu language by one of the missionaries, Rev. Mr. Lawes. "The Queen guards and watches over you, looks upon you as her children, and will not allow anyone to harm you, and will send her trusted officers to carry out her gracious intentions in the establishment of the Protectorate," said Commodore Erskine.

This was pretty heady stuff for Stone Age people who still believed in sorcery but they, like the Maoris and Fijians, were unable to resist the warm embrace of this mystical being – the Great White Queen across the water. To convince any doubting Thomases, the natives were then marched through the captain's cabin – in one door and out the other – where Commodore Erskine shook hands with each of them and gave gifts from a collection of tomahawks, butcher's knives, coloured shirts, figs and tobacco.

The last piece in this effort to impress the natives with the wonders of British rule was the firing of the ship's guns at distant targets, including one at 4,000 yards. The astonished natives were then rowed back to shore in the ships' boats for a good night's sleep in preparation for their change of status on the morrow.

That night *HMS Nelson* was illuminated with blue lights at the yardarms and at the ports that were facing the shore. Rockets were fired from both the *Nelson* and the *Espiegle* while the *Nelson's* foghorn was sounded – "a most unearthly noise". [26] Well, it was Guy Fawkes Night.

The next morning, 6th November, 1884, there was much activity on the water as the ships' boats, each one flying the White Ensign, rowed backwards and forwards from men-of-war to shore, carrying smartly dressed officers and men for the big ceremony, which was to take place at the mission house, the headquarters of the London Missionary Society which overlooked the harbour, thereby underlining yet again the omnipresence and influence of the missionaries in the South Pacific.

For such primitive people it must have appeared a grand affair, with the naval officers in their cocked hats and undress coat and epaulettes, the sailors in their whites and straw boater hats, and the marines with their helmets and white tunics. It was an early morning ceremony to avoid the noonday heat.

The last one to sail ashore was Commodore Erskine and, upon landing, the band struck up a martial tune. The sailors, their white uniforms sparkling in the early morning sunshine, had formed themselves in a hollow square around the flagstaff in front of the mission house while the senior naval officers and missionaries arrayed themselves on the wide verandah of the single storey, weatherboard house.

When everything was ready the Commodore was marched from the beach to the mission house, accompanied by the marines with bayonets fixed and the band. From the verandah he proclaimed the Protectorate of British New Guinea to the chiefs, who were sitting on the ground in front of him. Behind them were lesser natives and at the back, standing, were some interested white spectators – exactly the same array as in the marquee at Waitangi. After the Proclamation the Flag Lieutenant of *HMS Nelson*, Sub-Lieutenant Gaunt, raised the flag on the pole while the band played *God Save The Queen*.

This was followed by the marines firing a *feu de joie* and three ringing cheers for the Queen who, asleep in England, had just acquired another territory, one that was larger in area than England, Scotland and Wales combined. Then it was back to the men-of-war for a big breakfast.

The proceedings over, the warships sailed away, the administrators moved in, and the natives went back to their timeless and primitive villages where, under the light touch of British rule, their lives would continue more or less as before.

Suwarrow Island

Planting the Union Jack on a coral atoll to bring yet another island into the British Empire was every naval captain's dream and the ceremonies at Waitangi, Nasova and Port Moresby were the mirror of other such ceremonies throughout the Pacific.

Twelve hundred miles north-east of Fiji is the Suwarrow group of remote islands that were an occasional stopping off place for ships travelling between North America and the South Pacific. Suwarrow itself has one of the best harbours in the Pacific and was described by Robert Louis Stevenson as "the most romantic island in the world". This speck in the ocean became part of the Queen's dominions in April, 1889, the now traditional ceremony of raising the flag being described by a sailor who witnessed it as follows.

"Having arrived in view of the Group early on 22nd April, *HMS Rapid* proceeded slowly and cautiously up to the island of Suwarrow and on a near approach we could see the flag of the British Mercantile Navy floating over the lighthouse. An early constructed dwelling hut of very small size was situated on the western side of the island.

As the eastern side of the island gradually emerged to our view we steamed in that direction. In close proximity to the lighthouse was a large shed. There was no sign of life, with the exception of a few domestic fowls and an immense flock of sea birds. The group of islands is connected by means of large coral reefs, which stretch along the horizon as far as the eye can see, and are very numerous; hence our caution in approaching the place.

When we arrived nearly opposite the pier we were boarded by an aged and feeble looking man, who was evidently a native of Great Britain and who told us he had been on the island for about two years. I believe he was in the service of the San Francisco mail steamers. He readily placed his knowledge at our disposal by showing the dangerous parts and pointing out a reef here and there which was not visible to the eye and offering suggestions as to the best place to anchor.

At last we dropped anchor in 17 fathoms in what proved to be the channel. At 2 p.m. a party of seamen, under the command of Lieutenant C.C. Dacosta R.N., landed from the ship to act as a guard of honour, followed by a party of carpenters and excavators to erect a flag-staff on which to hoist the flag. A photographer also landed to take a picture of the group while in the act of performing the ceremony. The usual proclamation, signed by Captain Castle, was fixed to a board and, when the flag was hoisted, the men presented arms, the bugle sounded a royal salute and at the same time the ship thundered forth a royal salute of twenty-one guns." [27]

The one, unchanging constant in all these flag raising ceremonies, that extended British rule throughout the South Pacific, was the presence of the Royal Navy, which conducted the proceedings with efficiency, dignity and style. Their fireworks, rockets and faultless drill might have been the visible and most memorable aspect of the establishment of British rule in primitive places but, when the gaily dressed warships sailed away, it was over to the administrators to bring some much needed order and peace to these new colonies. And, if things got difficult, they knew that the Navy would never be far away.

MISSIONARIES, CANNIBALS AND BLACKBIRDERS

In the thousands of islands that litter the South Pacific from New Guinea to Tahiti it was usually the missionaries who were first in the field, followed closely by the traders in their schooners. The different denominations had their own missionary vessels – the *John Knox* and *Dayspring* for the Presbyterians, the *John Wesley* for the Methodists, and the *John Williams* (London Missionary Society) and *Southern Cross* (Church Missionary Society) for the Anglicans. However, these small vessels could not be everywhere at once in such a vast ocean and so the missionaries were also dependent on the Navy for moving them around and, more importantly, for their own protection on these islands of savages.

The Navy in its turn was dependent on the missionaries; when a warship visited an island inhabited only by natives and a missionary, it would seek the missionary's advice on such things as where to go next and which villages and islands were friendly and which were not. Missionaries were also taken on board to act as interpreters since they usually knew the native language. The missionaries would extend hospitality to the captain and officers of a visiting naval vessel and vice versa.

After being entertained on the New Hebrides island of Erromanga by missionaries called McNair, Captain George Palmer of *HMS Rosario* wrote, "Mr and Mrs. McNair came off in my gig to take a look at the *Rosario* and expressed much delight with all they saw. They left about sunset, landing just as the officers' boat was leaving the shore, and they (the officers) told me afterwards that it was quite melancholy to see the two standing arm-in-arm all alone watching the boat pull off to the ship." [1]

Furthermore, quite a few of the naval officers were the sons of clergymen while the bigger vessels carried a chaplain and so the link between Navy and missionaries was usually both natural and comfortable. All this gave the missionaries an influence which they were never reluctant to use for their own purposes and a naval captain had to be very careful not to be used as an instrument of the missionaries' power games as they were constantly at loggerheads with both ministers of other denominations and other white people in the Islands – merchant sea captains and plantation owners. The missionaries wanted to be king-pins and to keep the natives in a state of dependency, and their hatred of white traders and plantation owners was as extreme as it was unchristian.

213

Some of the missionaries, especially those of the Church Missionary Society, were exploiting the natives by taking their land, making them work for them for nothing ("your reward will be in the next life") and sleeping with the native women and they did not want other people like traders and growers around to queer their pitch or see what they were up to.

Before the Treaty of Waitangi brought New Zealand under British rule in 1840 the missionaries were even involved in gun running; they sold muskets to the Maoris, who used them to kill their enemies in the inter tribal wars, in which, as we have seen, an estimated 80,000 Maoris were killed. Had New Zealand not then come under British rule the missionaries would have continued in this trade of death and the Maori race would have been exterminated.

Too many of the missionaries were land grabbers. They were recruited in England from the educated class and sent out to distant lands "to convert the heathen". If they were genuinely concerned with taking the Word of God into dark corners, they would have stayed at home and given their services to the benighted workers in the factory towns of England who, having been driven off their traditional lands by enclosure and other methods, were forced into the cities to work long hours in appalling conditions and whose desperate spiritual needs were all but ignored by the Church Of England (although not by the Methodists). Of course, the factory workers didn't have land whereas the chiefs in the distant Pacific did and that was what determined the priorities of the Church Missionary Society and the London Missionary Society.

Missionaries were not always welcome in the islands and, when they were murdered, the Navy became involved in the recriminations. In describing the cruise of *HMS Curacoa* in the New Hebrides in 1865 Auckland's *Southern Cross* newspaper wrote, "She...shelled a native village at the request of the missionaries, during which engagement an able seaman of the vessel, named George Holland, was shot by the natives in the side and killed." [2]

When *HMS Falcon* visited the same village two years later as part of a 9,000 mile cruise among the islands it was reported by the *Sydney Morning Herald* that "The natives here were most amicably disposed, and seemed to bear no malice in consequence of the castigation they received from the *Curacoa* two years ago. The unexpected bursting of a shell, which that vessel had left behind as a souvenir, and which catastrophe cost several of them their lives, was related rather as a good joke than otherwise." [3]

In seeking to punish the natives for the murders of missionaries the Navy was sometimes frustrated by the missionaries themselves. When Bishop Patterson of the Anglican Melanesian Mission was murdered in 1871 on the island of Nukapu in the Swallow group, north of the main islands of the New Hebrides, *HMS Rosario* was sent to punish his killers as it was believed that, if they thought they could get away with killing a bishop, they would feel less compunction in murdering lesser missionaries.

On her way there from Sydney the warship put in at Norfolk Island where the Melanesian Mission had a thousand acre estate, which had been given to them by the authorities free of charge – much to the disgust of the locals who, on that small island, were rather pressed for land.

While there the Melanesian Mission told the captain of the *Rosario* that he must not use force to punish the natives for the murder of their bishop. The missionaries regarded themselves as the lords of the Islands and they were always trying to dictate naval policy but Captain Markham took no notice of these armchair "do gooders" and proceeded to Nukapu as ordered. Upon arrival he was met by a hail of arrows and so he ordered his ship to fire some shells at the natives, who were among the most unfriendly and violent in the whole of the South Pacific.

Sometimes the Navy and the missionaries were drawn together by a common horror of native practices. As we saw in the Gunnery chapter, when *HMS Havannah* visited Fiji in August, 1849, her demonstration of firepower had a salutary effect on Cakobau and helped persuade him to defer to the white man's standards and give up cannibalism. This was a combined missionary/Navy exercise, with the guns of the warship reinforcing the arguments of the missionaries.

For years the missionaries, and the Wesleyan, Rev. James Calvert, in particular, had been trying to convince Cakobau and his chiefs to give up cannibalism, but without success. After the missionaries took Captain Erskine of the *Havannah* on a guided tour of the stone ovens at Mbau and the sacred killing stone "all bloody with recent use, where the heads of multitudes of victims had been dashed" [4] prior to being cooked and eaten, the horrified naval captain arranged an interview with Cakobau, at which Rev. Calvert interpreted.

215

Captain Erskine denounced the practice of cannibalism and urged the "King of Fiji" to listen to the missionaries and change his ways, and he intimated that, in the event of doing so, Fiji might, like Samoa, be favoured with the presence of a British Consul. To which Cakobau replied, "Yes – you Englishmen have cattle. You salt them down and eat them. We have not – and human beings are consequently our cattle." [5]

A month after the *Havannah* left Fijian waters another of Her Majesty's warships, the *Daphne*, arrived and her commander, Captain E.G. Fanshawe, not only tried to bring the civil war with the Rewa tribes to an end but also continued Erskine's efforts to dissuade Cakobau from cannibalism.

Before leaving the islands Captain Fanshawe sat down at the table in his cabin and wrote a letter to Cakobau to reiterate what he had said verbally. "Being now about to leave the Fiji Islands, I am led by an earnest desire for their welfare and also by a sincere esteem for yourself to address a few words to you in the language of friendship. These beautiful islands have been until now the scene of the grossest impostures and the most degrading superstitions that have ever disgraced mankind, leading in their results to practices in which treachery and murder are stepping-stones to the gratification of the vilest passions and appetites.

No people ever did, or ever will, become great or honourable whilst sunk in so profound depth of ignorance and crime; and it is because I know you to be far too intelligent to be deceived by the flimsy superstitions which surround you, that I would entreat you, for the good of your country, to use your powerful influence in stopping those abominable cruelties which disgrace it, and which can not be thought of without disgust by any enlightened man. I am confident that you can not contemplate the kidnapping of unoffending women and children to supply a cannibal feast nor the murder of a wife on the death of her husband without shame for the cowardice of the former and the folly of the latter, as well as for the cruelty of both.....That Fiji may be blessed and that you may be truly great is the sincere wish of your true friend. E.G. Fanshawe." [6]

The Navy's efforts to rid the Pacific's most beautiful islands of their ugly practices were continued by Captain Sir Everard Home Bt., the commander of *HMS North Star*, when that warship visited Fiji in 1851. He too met Cakobau, who was still at war with the chief of the Rewa people. Among the practices from which Home sought to dissuade the "King of the Cannibal Isles" was the custom of killing a man every time the mast was struck upon a large canoe coming into port.

In the words of Rev. Calvert, "The visits of these ships of war, the commanders of which so greatly helped the missionaries in their work, were of incalculable advantage." [7] In 1854 Cakobau renounced cannibalism and became a Christian. Perhaps the most striking manifestation of the new order was that the old killing stone at Mbau, against which heads had been bashed prior to cooking them and which had so horrified Captain Erskine, became the baptismal font of the Methodist church that was built on the site. And when Queen Victoria's son, the Duke of Edinburgh, was to visit Fiji, Cakobau expressed his intention to cover the entire island with native mats "so that the Queen of England's son should not dirty his foot with the bloodstained soil of Mbau." [8]

With the development of European owned plantations came the need for local labour and in Fiji the people were not prepared to do such work. They grew their own food and sold what they didn't need to visiting European ships. Nor were they overly fond of hard work. Therefore, to get the men who were required on the labour hungry sugar, coconut and cotton plantations, the owners began to import workers from the New Hebrides, paying the ships' captains who brought them a fee of between £15 and £25 and that is where the business became a bit murky as some captains engaged in sharp practices to entice the prospective labourers on to their vessels.

However, the transporting of strong island labourers to work on plantations was an accepted tier of the shipping industry and on many voyages there was a government agent to guard against abuses. The abuses included not only the captains of the labour recruiting vessels "gilding the lily" in order to fill their ships but also the chiefs providing unwilling recruits in return for some of the fee. And not all the labourers returned as some of them died during their service – especially those who were sent to the nickel mines in New Caledonia.

There were also positive aspects of the system as reported by a despatch from Fiji to New Zealand's *Otago Witness* of 3rd January, 1874. "The thousands (of imported labourers) who come to Fiji return after two or three years work with what to them is great wealth, with a knowledge of what to them is a great world, and above all to be able to speak English intelligibly. They come from towns of which the inhabitants have for centuries held no

217

communication with each other, except to fight whenever they meet and to eat whomsoever they can catch. On a plantation they are forced to associate together, and cook with the same pot, and to sleep under the same roof. They go back new people....There are a few – very few indeed – who, living in Levuka, may take to drink but the great majority live on plantations and never touch or see drink....No one would dare to kidnap men whom they knew could and would report the crime at the first consulate they found."

The bad behaviour by some of these labour recruiters, known as "blackbirders", gave the missionaries another stick with which to beat the white mercantile class. It also gave the natives a pretext for taking revenge on Europeans in the form of murder and other atrocities. Except where a missionary was the victim the missionaries invariably tried to excuse the natives' murdering of Europeans on the grounds that the blackbirders' misbehaviour justified such killings – just as some of the missionaries in Rhodesia in the 1960s and 1970s went out of their way to condone the atrocities of the terrorists and even to aid them in their crimes.

As a result of such pieces of legislation as the Pacific Islanders Protection Act ("the Kidnapping Act") 1872, and Queensland's Polynesian Labourers Act 1868 the Navy was sent into the waters of uncolonised islands to enforce these complicated laws against the so-called "blackbirders" by boarding and searching European owned vessels. This was a two edged sword for a naval captain as a wrongful seizure – possibly inspired by the tittle tattle of the missionaries – could lead to a legal action against the officer.

In 1869 the topsail schooner *Daphne* was seized by Captain George Palmer of *HMS Rosario* on suspicion of "piracy and man-stealing (slaving)". She had licences from the Queensland government to recruit fifty labourers in the New Hebrides for Queensland plantations but instead carried double that number of labourers to Levuka in Fiji where Captain Palmer seized her because some of her paperwork was deemed to be "irregular".

Palmer had the labourers taken ashore in the *Rosario's* boats but, because they were "stark naked", they had to be landed beyond the houses of the town and out of sight of the European ladies of Levuka. Upon landing "some cloth was given them to cover their nakedness". [9]

Nor was this the only problem for, as Captain Palmer wrote, "The poor creatures, seeing the officer on duty with a sword on, imagined they were going to be killed and eaten; the landing took some little time". [10]

In the charge of Hon. Richard Bingham, the senior sub-lieutenant on the *Rosario*, and a prize crew and with her former captain and crew as passengers the *Daphne* was taken to Sydney where she was moored alongside the big man-of-war that had captured her.

Unfortunately for Captain Palmer the *Daphne's* Master, Captain Daggett, and her supercargo, Mr. Pritchard, were acquitted of all charges by the Sydney Water Police magistrates as it was considered on the evidence that the natives who were on board had been fairly induced to leave their island and were not intended to be used or dealt with as slaves.

Then in the Vice-Admiralty Court the *Daphne* was released to its owners and Captain Palmer was ordered to pay the expenses of the trial amounting to £179-5-5 although the Admiralty later reimbursed him. The only thing on which Palmer based his extreme action was that there was a slight discrepancy as to some dates in the *Daphne's* papers. From there on he let his imagination take over, for which he had to pay a heavy price. In the words of the judge of the Vice-Admiralty Court, Sir Alfred Stephen, "These men were not slaves in any sense of the word, or intended to be dealt with as slaves." [11]

Captain Palmer's problem was that he had swallowed the missionary line to the exclusion of all others. After being entertained by missionaries on the island of Erromanga in the New Hebrides he wrote, "See these noble men and women, who have in every age gone forth from their country and friends, often bearing their lives in their hands to do their Master's bidding, and preach the glorious gospel of Christ to the heathen; living alone to all intents and purposes in a strange land – often in an unhealthy climate and frequently surrounded by savages who may have murdered their predecessors, and may perhaps kill them…Whether in the Sandwich Islands or New Zealand, amongst the Society, Fiji or New Hebrides groups, I have ever found them the same earnest, God fearing men, striving to their utmost to win souls who, but for them, would never hear of the 'glad tidings of great joy'…men and women whose lives adorn some of the brightest pages of British history." [12] Contrast these laudatory words with his view of the European planters in Fiji – "the majority are the biggest scoundrels unhung". [13]

219

A man with such extreme and pre-conceived ideas about the missionaries who were, in fact, one of the most manipulative and disruptive factors in the South Pacific, was not the best person to exercise a considered judgement as to whether a trading vessel carrying island labourers was a "slaver" or not and the costs that he was ordered to pay by the Vice-Admiralty Court were the result of his poor judgement.

Two years later Captain Montgomery of *HMS Blanche* seized the schooner *Challenge* at Levuka on suspicion of bringing natives there without their consent. She too was sent to Sydney in the charge of a naval prize crew and her commander, Captain Longmore was charged with "slavery" – an absurd and emotive word that was far removed from the reality of the situation. The court decided that the facts did not justify such a charge although Longmore was sentenced to imprisonment on another charge of assault. A bill of £900 was sent to Captain Montgomery by the owners for damages for the loss they had sustained from the illegal seizure and detention of their vessel.

To complicate matters further, there were some labour recruiters who were licensed by the government to bring workers from the New Hebrides and elsewhere to work on Fijian plantations and then return them to their villages two years later. Therefore, the crime was not in the act itself but in not having the right pieces of paper to do it.

Although a captain ran the risk of being sued if a schooner was wrongfully seized there were also rewards in that a vessel that was legally confiscated could be taken as "prize" even though that concept originated in capturing enemy ships in war. Some captains became very heavy handed and greedy in enforcing the laws against blackbirding in order to benefit themselves and their ships' companies.

On 15th January, 1872, *HMS Basilisk* left Sydney for Cape York. Twenty-one days later, while off Cardwell in north Queensland, the ship's company were assembled on deck for morning prayers when the lookout reported a sail ahead. Captain Moresby, who was always on the lookout for prize money, steered the *Basilisk* towards the stranger. Two boats were lowered from the man-of-war and a party under Lieutenant Hayter boarded the schooner, which they found was completely gutted and waterlogged with five feet of water in her hold. There were fourteen Solomon Islanders on board in various stages of starvation – "perfect skeletons in appearance from want of food" – as well as three dead ones in a state of decomposition but there was no food or fresh water. [14] Upon boarding her, the sailors were threatened with some rusty muskets but the would-be attackers were so weak that they were easily disarmed.

The corpses which, in the words of Captain Moresby, were "fast losing the shape of humanity on a deck foul with blood" [15] had some weighty shot attached to their feet by the men of the *Basilisk* and were committed to the deep.

This coffin ship turned out to be the *Peri*, a vessel that had been carrying eighty Solomon Island labourers around the islands of Fiji to drop them off at their respective plantations for work. While she was at sea off the coast of Fiji five weeks earlier these prospective labourers rose up, killed the white crew and took over the ship with the intention of sailing her back to the Solomons. Unfortunately they were better mutineers than navigators – which was why they drifted almost 1,800 miles, ran out of food, and finished up off the coast of Queensland with only a handful of survivors.

Captain Moresby had her towed into Cardwell and put her in the charge of a navigating midshipman and a prize crew while he continued on his way to Cape York. "It is said that the stench on board the schooner when brought into Cardwell was frightfully sickening," wrote the *Sydney Morning Herald*. [16] The survivors refused to answer any questions, believing they would be shot.

The following year Moresby seized the barque *Woodbine* for alleged breaches of Queensland's Polynesian Labourers Act, which prohibited the importation of any Polynesian labourer without a document signed by a missionary or a British Consul stating that the labourer had left his village of his own free will.

The *Woodbine*, with twenty-eight tons of pearl shell on board, had left Somerset at Cape York on 28th December, 1873, for Sydney and, while anchored between Cape Grafton and Double Island Point, was boarded at midnight on 8th January by a lieutenant of *HMS Basilisk*. Because there were three islanders on board with no proper documentation to show how they came to be there, Moresby, with more prize money glittering before his eyes, seized the vessel and had her taken south. By this action plus his seizure of two other vessels belonging to the same owner, Moresby wrecked the pearl fishing business of Mr. Mayor. Not surprisingly, New Zealand's *Grey River Argus* wrote, "The seizure has caused a strong feeling against the captain of the *Basilisk*." [17] When the case was heard the Queensland Vice-Admiralty Court decided that Moresby's seizure of the *Woodbine*, like Palmer's seizure of the *Daphne*, was illegal.

In the same month Moresby also grabbed the *Christina*, which was engaged in the *beche-de-mer* (sea cucumber) trade in the Coral Sea. Upon arrival at Coconut Island the *Christina's* commander, Captain William Walton, had been approached by Captain Delargy, whose schooner *Active* had been wrecked on nearby Campbell's reef twelve months earlier. He asked Captain Walton to convey himself and his hands to Sydney. Captain Walton agreed to take them on at £3 per person, and the *Christina* headed for Sydney, having fulfilled one of the traditional obligations of the "brotherhood of the sea".

They sailed for Sydney on 11th January, 1873, but four days out were accosted by Moresby, who seized the vessel on the grounds that there were no proper papers for the members of the *Active's* crew. After all, she had been shipwrecked! The *Christina* was condemned in Brisbane and was sold for £900 and her cargo was sold as well. So that was another business that someone had built up, only to have it destroyed by Moresby.

Moresby's excess of zeal brought the Royal Navy into disrepute among the merchantmen as it seems that he only had to see the distant sails of a trading vessel and he couldn't get there fast enough to board her and check her papers and, if possible, grab her as a prize. Responsible and honest trading captains did not like to be accosted on the high seas by "prize seekers on the make" and in their eyes Moresby was fast becoming a public menace.

Another captain who liked to throw his weight around was Gordon Douglas of *HMS Cossack* who, upon arrival in Fijian waters, announced his intention of seizing all vessels without the proper paperwork. If they were trading under the British flag, then their papers must be from the British Consul and, if Fijian and above the size of a whaleboat, from the government of Fiji, which at the time was a barely recognisable entity.

In his zeal against the blackbirders Captain Douglas captured the 100 ton brig *Carl* on suspicion of taking natives against their will for the labour trade. He also seized the *Nukulau* when she came into Levuka on 12th September, 1872, after a "labour cruise" with 116 people on board. It was believed that they had been lured on to the vessel and brought to Fiji against their will to be sold to the plantations.

It was five in the evening when the *Nukulau* sailed into the busy harbour of Levuka. "Large numbers of seamen were drawn up on the forecastle (of the *Cossack*), officers were seen rushing to and fro, the bugle was sounded frequently, and the launch was manned. Preparations were thus made in order to meet any emergency which might arise and, upon the *Nukulau's* attempting to cross the bows of the *Cossack*, with all sail set, she was hailed and ordered to tack about and anchor under the stern of that British man-of-war," wrote the *Southern Cross*. "Simultaneously a lieutenant from the *Cossack* jumped on board the *Nukulau* and courteously requested McLiver to accompany him in order that Captain Douglas might be afforded an interview. This McLiver was compelled to do and, as soon as he reached the *Cossack*, he learned to his dismay that he was a prisoner." [18]

A naval court was held on board the *Cossack* on 18th September with Captain Douglas as President and it was decided to remand McLiver and his two accomplices to Sydney for trial on charges of kidnapping. In the event McLiver went free as there were no interpreters to take the evidence of the islanders. In the words of the *Southern Cross*, "In Levuka the event is spoken of in whispers, and even then only in a spirit of sympathy and commiseration for the prisoners (McLiver and his mates)." [19] The campaign against the labour trade was missionary led and, by some of their captains entering into it with such an excess of zeal, the Navy alienated not only the skippers of the trading vessels but also much of the wider merchant opinion.

In nosing around the islands for the suppression of the blackbirding trade the warships sometimes came under fire from the very natives whose interests they were allegedly protecting. When *HMS Sandfly* went up to the New Hebrides on an anti-blackbirding expedition in September, 1874, she was met by a fleet of fully manned canoes on her approach to the island of Santa Cruz. The largest canoe pulled astern and made signs for a rope to tow with the *Sandfly* and, at not being given one, the islanders became very annoyed.

At 10.30 a.m. the *Sandfly* anchored in fourteen fathoms about two hundred yards out from the island but inside Carlisle reef. Natives came off in great numbers in their canoes, many of them bringing pigs and coconuts, which they passed up to the ship in exchange for articles of trade. When they were detected in uncovering bows and arrows the marines got their rifles ready on the after deck, taking care to keep them out of sight.

After the islanders began to gather around the gunwales in a noisy and insolent manner a blank shot was fired from the ship's gun but to little effect. Shortly afterwards the natives let fly with poisoned arrows and Lieutenant Howell, the commander of the *Sandfly*, discharged his revolver at the nearest native and gave the order to his men to commence firing. This frightened the natives and those who were clinging to the gunwales either fell or jumped into the sea, many of them dead and others wounded and struggling in the briny. Altogether about thirty natives were killed and the others escaped into the bush.

The *Sandfly* lowered her boats and their crews spent the afternoon in destroying all the abandoned canoes, some of which were very large, and they also set fire to two of the native villages.

Some time later (October, 1880), when the *Sandfly* anchored at Te Zembokali to survey the east coast of Florida Island in the Solomons, her commander, Lieutenant Bower, and five sailors set off in the whaleboat to take soundings. They pulled into Lavinia Bay, so named after the trading vessel *Lavinia* whose crew had been murdered there. They then went to Naginsland where they pulled their boat on to the beach and some of them went off to bathe, leaving a sailor, Venton, to look after the boat. After a short time the boat was attacked and Lieutenant Bower escaped by running into the bush and climbing a tree in the fading light.

The next morning the natives found him and shot him with the rifles that they had stolen from the whaleboat. He dropped to the ground and "then a series of nameless horrors ensued....the body (when found by the sailors) naked, headless, and divested of the right arm and great pieces of flesh stripped from the back." [20] Of the six sailors in the whaleboat, only one, Savage, eluded the natives to survive. He had shaken off his pursuers by running into the scrub near the beach, and he planned to swim back to the *Sandfly*.

It was not an easy mission as the naval vessel was around the other side of Florida Island and so he hoped to reach another island unnoticed, but the strong current swept him back and he finished up opposite the fires where the cannibals were dancing and yelling as they roasted some of the other bluejackets and Lieutenant Bower. The clouds parted and a chorus of yells showed that the moonbeams had revealed him to the enemy.

Two or three canoes set out to capture him so as to increase the amount of food at the feast and they got to within fifty yards of him when a black cloud swept across the moon. When the moon next appeared Savage saw the canoes going back as they obviously thought that he had gone to the bottom.

He landed on a small island where he sheltered from a heavy storm and then, despairing of rescue, he made a small raft and paddled to the mainland. When half way across a dozen canoes swept down on him. He was taken to the chief of another village, who decided not to dare the vengeance of naval guns and so spared his life. Then, when the *Sandfly* passed the island, her look-out saw Savage signalling and they took him off.

They then sailed into the bay where the murders had been committed and a boat's crew of one officer and eight men was sent ashore to burn the canoes. There were no natives in sight until the boat was pushing off to return to the *Sandfly* and "then droves of savages sallied from the bush and opened fire on the boat, shooting a seaman named Buckle through the left forearm." [21]

After the *Sandfly* returned to Sydney the Commodore of the Australia station sent a bigger vessel, *HMS Emerald*, to Florida Island with an interpreter to demand the murderers of Lieutenant Bower and his men and to deal with two other massacres in the area, viz. the murders of the crews of the merchantmen *Zephyr* and *Borealis*. The crew on the *Borealis* had also been chopped up, roasted in earthen ovens and eaten. At the site of the *Sandfly* massacre the *Emerald's* men set fire to the native huts and all their coconut trees.

Even the missionaries were outraged at these *Sandfly* killings – probably because the victims were naval personnel and not the hated crews of trading vessels. In a letter from Norfolk Island Rev. A. Penny of the Church Missionary Society wrote that, after talking to native students from the area who were at the Norfolk Island mission school, he suspected that the man behind the murders was Linkolilia. "He is a brutal fellow," wrote Rev. Penny, "and it is notorious that he wanted to cut out a ship's or boat's crew for some time….As to the motive for the outrage I believe it to have been a desire for plunder perhaps but chiefly the pleasures of destroying human life – killing for killing's sake." [22]

Rev. Penny rendered good services the following year when *HMS Diamond* went to Florida Island in a further attempt to arrest Lieutenant Bower's murderers. This time they were after a chief called Puka, who had taken a prominent part in the killings. Although they could not find him "his villages and coconut plantation were razed to the ground and his canoes were blown to atoms." [23] It was nearly two years since the outrage and the natives were learning that the Navy has a long memory – especially where its own personnel were the victims.

When news of this reached London there were questions asked in the House of Commons by Messrs. Henry Richard, the M.P. for Merthyr Tydvil, and J.E. Gorst, the M.P. for Chatham, about the punishment meted out by the *Emerald*. To these Mr. G.O. Trevelyan, the Secretary to the Admiralty, replied by justifying their actions and declaring that repeated massacres committed by the "savage natives of those islands rendered some punitive measures absolutely necessary". [24]

He added that more warships should visit the islands more frequently but steered clear of the only real solution, which was for Britain to extend her jurisdiction over the still uncolonised islands of the Solomons and New Hebrides. There have always been apologists in Parliament for those who murder British servicemen abroad and Richard and Gorst appear to have been early examples of that particular species.

Mr. Trevelyan in the House of Commons was not exaggerating when he referred to the "repeated massacres" of ships' crews in the islands as from 1880 to 1882 there were five instances of crews being killed and eaten (those of *HMS Sandfly* and the traders *Annie Brooks*, *Borealis*, *Isabella* and *Favioni*) while another was wrecked on Bougainville Island where the captain was eaten and the crew poisoned. Crews who were murdered (but not eaten) included those of the *Zephyr*, *Hong Kong*, *Prosperity*, *May Queen* and *Atlantic* and there were other vessels where the captains were killed.

To prevent these islands from falling into complete anarchy the Commodore in Sydney in 1886 despatched *HMS Diamond* to sail up there and punish individual villages for the murders of several British subjects, viz. Captain Miller, George Adams, Mr. Reid, Captain Howie, Captain Fryar and his carpenter, Captain and Mrs. Webb and crew, and a seventy-three year old man, Mr. Childe, who had been tomahawked to death. Where the villagers refused to hand over the murderers their huts, canoes and coconut trees were destroyed.

226

Once again, when news of the *Diamond's* cruise reached England there was the usual outcry from the "humanitarian" brigade who, at a distance of 16,000 miles, got very agitated at the burning of native huts and canoes while maintaining a deafening silence in respect of all the British captains and their crews who were being killed and eaten by the cannibals.

Some much needed perspective was brought to bear by Captain Cyprian Bridge, formerly of the Australia station, who compared the British method of punishing the particular village that had committed the crime with the French Navy's method of delivering punishment by steaming round the coast for miles and firing shells at intervals and machine guns at every native who came into sight. The *Times* also chipped in, commending the cruise of the *Diamond* for its discretion and humanity towards the natives. [25]

When a plantation owner, Peter Greig, and his two daughters, Ada (aged eighteen) and Elizabeth (sixteen), were murdered on the island of Espiritu Santo in 1908 *HMS Prometheus* went up from Sydney to punish the killers.

Upon reaching the island they were joined by the French warship, *Kersaint*, and the native police. They managed to surprise the villagers, who all took to the hills. The native police were sent after them under the guidance of a native named Avamasanga, who had been delivered up by his tribe as a murderer of the Greigs and was so incensed at the treachery of his people that he offered to lead the expedition to the village where the ringleader of the murder lived. This chap was shot dead and Avamasanga was later transported to Fiji.

During this confrontation the native police opened fire and among the dead were six women and one boy. In the House of Commons Sir Charles Dilke, the Liberal Member for the Forest of Dean, made a big noise but the First Lord of the Admiralty, Reginald McKenna, replied that the "clothes" that the women were wearing did not distinguish them from the men. Perhaps they should have worn a different coloured fig leaf!

Commodore Wiseman lived up to his interesting name in 1865 when he visited the island of Erromanga in the New Hebrides on *HMS Curacoa*. The islanders had recently murdered a missionary but Wiseman decided not to punish them; instead he warned them that he would return to their island on his way back from the Solomons to see if they had been behaving. Upon his return he learned that they had killed another white man and so he attacked

227

their village, killing several of them, and then steamed out of the bay the next day.

Whether the Navy's tactics towards both blackbirders and recalcitrant natives had the desired effect is difficult to assess but at least one missionary in the New Hebrides, John Inglis, declared that it did. In a letter to the *New Zealander* in September, 1853, he wrote, "All the missionaries who have visited these islands....speak distinctly of the good effects that have been produced upon the minds of the natives, especially at Vate, one of the worst of the islands, by the visits of Captain Erskine of *HMS Havannah* and Captain Oliver of *HMS Fly*. Their firm, prudent and humane conduct inspired the natives with both fear and confidence; at the same time their visits proved a terror to the evildoers that frequent these seas." [26]

THE DEATH OF COMMODORE GOODENOUGH

Slowly the long procession moves, with solemn muffled sound,
Ere one of England's noblest men is laid in new-world ground.
Yea, bear him to the sailor's grave with every mourning rite, -
Perished he yet more bravely than hero in the fight!
For, when the utmost yet is done that public grief can show,
Not half expressed the deep respect that in each heart must flow.
Ah, truly by such holy dead our virgin earth is blest.
We pray our sons may worthy be one day by him to rest.

After taking the first Governor to Fiji and seeing him safely installed in office, Commodore Goodenough sailed out of Levuka harbour on *HMS Pearl* on 13th July, 1875, for a cruise among the islands of the New Hebrides.

On12[th] August the *Pearl* was off Carlisle Island in the Santa Cruz group. These islands lie at the northern extremity of the New Hebrides and are only a short distance from Nukapu island in the Swallow group where Bishop Patterson of the Church Missionary Society had been murdered four years earlier. The inhabitants have been described as "the most ferocious of savages". [1]

Accompanied by some of his officers and men, Commodore Goodenough left the *Pearl* and landed on Santa Cruz island "in hopes of conciliating the natives and opening friendly intercourse with them." [2] A large number of islanders gathered on the beach and accepted presents in an apparently friendly spirit. They were also willing to barter.

The Commodore and others entered the village and for some time mixed freely with the natives, who showed no signs of hostility until preparations were being made to embark.

While the Commodore and one or two others remained near the village a native fired a poisoned arrow which struck the Commodore in the side. The sailors' weapons were all in the boat and, before they could be reached, more flights of poisoned arrows were fired at the party, wounding five men and the Commodore, this time in the head. The sailors then fired some rifles and revolvers to stop this unprovoked attack but only one of the natives fell.

After returning to the *Pearl* the commodore's wound was sucked by the Fleet Paymaster, W.W. Perry and he was tended by Doctor Messer, whom we last met on New Zealand's Waikato River treating the wounded during the Battle of Rangiriri. The natives of

229

the Santa Cruz group poisoned their arrows by plunging them into rotting human corpses and leaving them there for several weeks.

The commodore decided to give the normal punishment of burning the houses of the village near where the attack was made but he gave explicit orders that no life should be taken. Blank cartridges were fired to warn the natives prior to the men landing. The reason for giving the natives a lesser punishment than what they probably deserved was that the commodore believed that their hostility had probably been provoked by some previous outrage committed by white men.

In addition to the commodore five other sailors had been wounded and so the ship sailed south to take them into what would hopefully be cooler weather. The *Pearl* pulled into Mota in the Banks group to leave directions for *HMS Nymph* and then proceeded to Sydney.

For the first few days the wounded seemed to be doing well and great hopes were entertained that they would recover but after five days symptoms of tetanus appeared in three of them and they deteriorated rapidly.

On the night of Thursday, 19th August (seven nights after the attack) one of the wounded seamen, eighteen year old Edward Rayner, who had received an arrow wound in the shoulder, passed away.

The commodore knew that he too was dying and on this same day said good-bye to all the officers in his cabin. He then asked to be taken on to the quarter-deck to speak to the men. He was carried out of his cabin and laid on a mattress on the deck.

From this position he gave his dying speech. "My men, my reason for wishing to come on the quarter-deck is to say good-bye to you and to speak to you of the love of God.

Doctor Messer, good, dear, kind Doctor Messer, has told me that I must die and Doctor Corrie thinks so too, so I come to say good-bye to you. Let me see all your faces.

I wish to tell you to love God; God has been so good to me and I love him. He has been very good to me in giving me the blessing of a great love – you all know my sweet wife, at least most of you do, and my sweet boys; they are such dear fellows. God has been good to me in giving me the love of my sweet wife, and my heart is full of love to Him. I want to tell you all to love God.

From the moment I was wounded I felt that there was a great probability of the wound turning fatal and from that moment I set my thoughts on death and on God's love to me, and now that I know that I am dying I am glad and thankful to be able to say a few words to you. I want to tell you that I love you all. I always did love my Ship's Companies – even those I have punished I have loved, for there was always goodness even in the greatest offender.

We all make mistakes in this life, and I have made many like everyone else but, if I have, I know you do not think of it now, but if any of you have perhaps felt it, I ask you to forgive, wipe it all out of your memory as if it had never happened.

I now wish to say a word to you young fellows, you good looking young fellows, not to yield to temptations which make you break your leave and desert. When you feel tempted, think of the love of God. And you older men, think of the good you may do by a word of advice to your younger shipmates when you see them inclined to fall.

The love which God will Himself give you, if you trust in Him, is very great. It will guide all your goings and doings, and all the words of preachers are nothing to it.

As for those poor natives, it is not worth while thinking about them and what they have done. Don't think about it, they could not know the right or wrong of the matter; probably it was through some mistake, or some offence given by some ship before; perhaps they did not like strangers visiting them. In some twenty years hence, when good men have taught them that we wish them no harm, they may speak of this attack, and then something may be learnt about it.

Before I go back to die I should like you all to bless me, say 'God bless you'." [3] This they did and the dying man uttered three more sentences. "May God Almighty bless you with His exceeding great love, and give you happiness such as He has given me. I should like to shake hands with all of the petty officers, to say good-bye to them for the rest of the ship's company. Good-bye to you, good-bye all of you, good-bye." [4] Thus ended this Nelsonian farewell for, like the victor of Trafalgar, Commodore Goodenough had always taken a compassionate interest in his men and was loved and respected by them in return.

The Commodore was then carried exhausted "but in perfect contentment of spirit" [5] to his cabin, saying, "I suppose there is nothing now to be done but to die quietly" [6] – and that is what he did at 5.30 p.m. the next evening. He was forty-four. The Roman Emperor and Stoic philosopher, Marcus Aurelius, once said that there is nothing more important in life than the way we leave it and, by his dying speech, Commodore Goodenough showed the true greatness of his character. Indeed his death touches on the sublime.

Early the following morning a third member of the ship's company, an eighteen year old seaman named Frederick Small, also died from an arrow wound in the head. The other injured men recovered.

So as not to alarm his wife by having the *Pearl* return without him, the Commodore, in one of his last instructions, directed that it put in to a port first so that a telegraph could be sent ahead of the ship's arrival. Accordingly the warship stopped off Port Stephens, about ninety miles north of Sydney, and a boat was sent ashore to pass on the terrible news.

The funeral of the three men was held in Sydney on 24th August when they were buried with naval honours. The gun carriage, draped with a Union Jack and with the commodore's sword, hat, epaulettes and medals on it, was drawn by his galley's crew. The ceremony was conducted by the chaplain of the *Pearl*. "It was one of the most numerously attended funerals which have been witnessed for many years in the colony. All the public offices were closed at noon....Steamers commenced to ply across the water at an early hour and before long a dense concourse of people, numbering several thousands, had assembled on Milson's Point....The Commodore's body was brought across in his own gig towed by a little steam launch and followed by the state barge of His Excellency the Governor, who was accompanied by Mrs. Goodenough and the Commodore's two little boys." [7] These two youngsters, aged ten and eight, were dressed as men-of-war sailors. According to Auckland's *Southern Cross* newspaper, "fifteen thousand people followed the biers to the cemetery". [8] They included the ships' companies of *HMS Pearl*, *Sappho* and *Renard*.

The late commodore was both well liked and highly respected. He had recently been made a Companion of the Order of Saint Michael and Saint George for his sterling work in connection with the addition of Fiji to the Empire.

In accordance with the commodore's own request the three graves were side by side in the cemetery of Saint Thomas' Church of England, North Sydney, the commodore in the middle, Rayner lying on his right and Small on his left. Thus the commodore was still in the midst of his men. The graves had been dug earlier in the day by marines from the *Pearl*. They were later surrounded by a dwarf wall with pillars supporting a chain-cable with emblematic anchors to show that this was a naval grave. There is a further memorial to him at the scene of the attack on the north shore of Santa Cruz island and his bust was placed in the painted hall at Greenwich Hospital.

There was one last act for the *Pearl*, which had been so closely associated with the late commodore during his Pacific posting, and that was to farewell his widow and children when they sailed for England on the steamship *Durham* a month after the funeral.

The gig, which conveyed Mrs. Goodenough, who was the god-daughter of Queen Victoria, to the *Durham*, was manned by the officers of the *Pearl*, its captain, Hastings, himself acting as coxswain. Upon arriving alongside the steamer, Mrs. Goodenough was received by Captain Anderson and then welcomed by the lady passengers.

As the *Durham* passed the *Pearl*, the crew of the latter, of their own accord, spread themselves over the rigging, yards and masts and cheered heartily. At the same time the signal was run up "Farewell and a pleasant voyage". This was acknowledged by the dipping of the *Durham's* ensign, and the band of the *Pearl* played *Home Sweet Home* and *Auld Lang Syne*.

Ironically the last public act that Commodore Gooodenough performed in Sydney before embarking on his fatal cruise was to unveil the statue of Captain Cook at Randwick where he made a wonderful speech. This eight foot high statue, made of locally quarried Pyrmont freestone and showing Cook in the dress of a post-captain and with his eyes turned towards Botany Bay, still looks out at Sydney's fast moving traffic on the corner of Avoca and High Streets. In the words of New Zealand's *Waikato Times*, "There are some strong points of resemblance between the death of Commodore Goodenough and Captain Cook. Both were on a mission of peace, to each the savages had manifested a friendly disposition, and both were killed when they were about to re-embark, Captain Cook being set upon with clubs and spears while the Commodore was fired upon with poisonous arrows." [9]

Another point of resemblance between the late Commodore and the Great Navigator was that both had a fondness for New Zealand. Cook had made Ship Cove at the top of the South Island his South Pacific base and, wherever he went in the Pacific, he invariably returned to New Zealand, while the Commodore got

233

himself elected to the New Zealand Parliament and spent so much time in Auckland that he became unpopular in Sydney as they suspected that he was going to move the headquarters of the Australia station from Sydney to Auckland.

Commodore Goodenough was widely mourned. During an address at the Guildhall in London Mr. Ward Hunt called it "the death of a Christian hero whose loss at this moment creates so much interest throughout the country" [10] while in Wellington and other cities of Australasia the ships in port dropped their flags to half mast in his honour on the day of the funeral. Both Goodenough Bay and Goodenough Island, just north of the south-east tip of New Guinea, were named after him while the waterway between them is the Ward Hunt Strait. Probably the greatest tribute came to him from Levuka in Fiji; upon hearing the news every bar in the town closed for the day and the citizens gathered for a public meeting with the Governor to express their condolences. This closure of the bars in the hardest drinking town of the South Pacific was without precedent. For the loss of her husband in the service of his country Mrs. Victoria Goodenough was awarded a pension of £300 and she also became a lady-in-waiting to her godmother, the Queen, after whom she was named.

The return of the family to England was not the end of the story as the Commodore's son, William, joined the Navy in 1882, fought at Jutland, was promoted to Admiral and knighted, and retired in 1930 after forty-eight years' service. Cape Goodenough at the entrance to Porpoise Bay, Antarctica, is named after him, thereby adding to the family's nomenclature in the seas of the world.

In Sydney the Goodenough Royal Naval House was established by public subscription to continue the Commodore's welfare work among the sailors.

SKULLDUGGERY IN SAMOA

HMS Cordelia and the Fox Incident

The problem for a naval captain in getting natives to respect British persons and property and in maintaining a semblance of order and security in uncolonised territories was that too lenient a penalty for the murder of British subjects would be regarded as an encouragement to further attacks while one at the other end of the scale would attract the criticism of the loud and well-organised Exeter Hall "humanitarians" who, like their "human rights" successors in the twenty-first century, invariably took the side of the natives - right or wrong.

After the destruction of property belonging to various Europeans during one of Samoa's many civil wars Captain Sir Everard Home Bt. took *HMS North Star* to the islands in 1845 and imposed a fine on the natives for what had been destroyed. However, only part of the fine was paid and so, at the request of the British Consul in Samoa, William Pritchard, *HMS Juno* (Captain Blake) was sent there in 1847 to collect the remainder.

Captain Blake seems to have been a weak and indecisive sort of fellow as, in the words of Auckland's *New Zealander* newspaper, the *Juno's* stay "exceeded six weeks, detained partly by a hurricane, but principally by the vacillating, undetermined movements of her commander. Instead of inspiring the natives with some degree of respect, his public conduct laid him completely open to their ridicule, and pity from the white residents." [1]

Instead of collecting the rest of the fine, which was the purpose of his visit, Blake remitted it, "thus tacitly acknowledging his approval of their conduct….. The natives are not slow to form their opinion of such men…..Captain Blake had scarcely cleared the reef when their depredations were renewed and destruction of property commenced – better had it been had he never visited Samoa." [2]

This sort of dilatoriness and perceived weakness was exasperating for those Europeans who lived in the Islands and had to bear the consequences of such behaviour. The Royal Navy was the most powerful fighting force in the world and yet in Samoa it appeared ineffectual to the natives and downright useless to the European missionaries and traders.

At Salailua on the Samoan island of Savai'i there lived an Englishman, William Fox, and his wife. He was said to be of good character and was in the business of trading tobacco to the natives in return for coconut oil. One day in December, 1856, he noticed that he was missing a small amount of tobacco and his wife told him that she had seen a young man, Sailusi, who was a petty chief of the neighbouring village of Sagone, steal it.

Fox sent the man a message that he was a thief and that he was not to visit the house again. On the morning of 15th December the thieving chief arrived at Fox's house and denied stealing the tobacco but, after a few questions, he admitted it and begged forgiveness. Fox said that he was happy to say no more about it but that the man was not to come to the house again.

William Fox then went and smoked a pipe in the doorway of the partition inside the house with his face downwards. The young chief pulled out a musket and fired it at almost point blank range. The ball entered Fox's heart and he died almost immediately, uttering one last, low groan. There was another European in the house and he chased the murderer, who lost himself in the jungle.

When Mr. Pritchard, the British Consul, heard about it he went to Sagone and demanded that they give up the murderer but they refused.

The people in the village where Fox lived regarded the killing as a slur on their community and so they captured an old man from the murderer's village and chopped off his head, offering it to Pritchard as an exchange for Fox's life!

Now there were two murders and Sailusi was going around boasting that he was going to kill another European as the British could do nothing about it. No doubt remembering the remittance of the earlier fine by Captain Blake, the natives of Sailusi's village cheekily said that they would pay a small fine with some old, worn out cloth.

Mr. Pritchard then wrote to the Commodore of the Australia station, asking him to address the issue. The result was that *HMS Cordelia*, under Captain Vernon, sailed to Samoa with a brief to deal with the matter once and for all. It was now more than two years since the murder of Mr. Fox, during which time "the attitude of some of the younger chiefs towards the *Papalagi* (foreigners) became more insolent and aggressive". [3]

With Jonas Coe, an American and the leading trader in Samoa, on board as interpreter, advisor and pilot, the *Cordelia* sailed to Savai'i and at the offending village demanded the surrender of the man who had so cruelly killed William Fox.

The villagers said that he was not there, whereupon parties of bluejackets from the *Cordelia* were sent ashore where they began destroying houses, plantations and canoes. With the progressive destruction of their huts and gardens the villagers eventually got the message that this was no Captain Blake and the young chief was brought down to the beach as arrogant and defiant as ever.

He was taken to Apia, given a prompt trial, found guilty and sentenced to death. That afternoon the captain of the *Cordelia* was approached by a missionary, Rev. A.W. Murray, who begged that the sentence not be carried out on the grounds that "these poor savages" did not understand our laws.

Resentful of the interference, the *Cordelia's* captain told Murray to return to the ship the next morning for his answer. Murray did – and saw Fox's murderer strung up by the neck and swinging at the yardarm in the gentle breeze – in full view of all of Apia. In the words of the Australian historian, R.W. Robson, "It was cruel and ruthless justice but its significance was not lost on the Samoans. After that there was a new note of respect in their contacts with the *Papalagi.*" [4] Maybe if Captain Blake had kept out of Samoa's affairs, William Fox might not have been killed.

Captain Stevens and HMS Barracouta

The difficulty for a naval captain on the spot to decide whether or not to interfere in a messy situation on shore is exemplified by the Steinberger incident – also in Samoa.

Fiji became a British colony in 1874 but the Samoans was not so lucky and spent four years fighting a bloody civil war. Shortly after the cessation of hostilities there appeared from across the water an intelligent and charming American of German-Jewish descent called Colonel Steinberger, his colonelcy being in the Northern army during the American Civil War.

Having ingratiated himself with the native chiefs and eyeing the possibilities for himself in this uncolonised land, this designing scoundrel returned to the United States where, with money provided by Godeffroys, a German firm that traded in the Islands, he purchased a 45 ton schooner-yacht, the *Peerless*, which had accommodation for six passengers. She was described as "one of the handsomest yachts ever built in San Francisco".

237

The *Peerless* sailed to Samoa although not with Steinberger on board; he arrived a little earlier on a U.S. naval vessel. The *Peerless* made the leg from San Francisco to Honolulu in only eleven days, thereby gaining a reputation for speed.

Back in the islands Steinberger held himself out to the Samoan chiefs as having some sort of vague authority from the United States government. He was, in fact, in cahoots with the current President, Ulysses S. Grant, who talked of "caring for the Samoans" as a mask for feathering his own nest.

Grant had a lot of his personal money invested in the Central Polynesian Land and Commercial Company, which had made extensive land purchases (both outright and in the form of options at dirt cheap prices), and Grant wanted to get the Company's land titles in Samoa formally recognised so as to get plantations established to enrich him and his fellow shareholders. However, the secret collusion between Steinberger and Grant was not known to Mr. Samuel S. Foster, the U.S. Commercial Agent who, in the absence of a consul, was Washington's "man on the spot", and Foster took a great dislike to Steinberger.

Upon arrival in Samoa Steinberger had his own designs on the land of the Central Polynesian Company and so the corrupt Grant was ill served by his unofficial emissary.

Never one to let the legalities get in the way, Steinberger conned the Samoans into letting him set up a government in which he would be Premier for life while the two rival chiefs would serve alternatively as "king" for four year terms only. In other words he would be the perpetual Premier to a puppet king.

Unfortunately, like every budding dictator, Steinberger was not prepared to stop there. Next came a burdensome tax regime and a Customs house backed up by a hundred and fifty armed and drilled natives under the command of Steinberger's drunken friend, Major Latrobe, late of the Confederate Army and the brother-in-law of the Governor of Maryland. Latrobe had loaned Steinberger money and followed him to Samoa to keep an eye on him.

Then came the arming of the *Peerless* with a 12 pounder, stacks of rifles, revolvers, cutlasses, boarding pikes and other weapons as well as a crew of twenty-six toughs. Thus armed she was sent to neighbouring islands – especially to the far eastern Samoan island of Tutuila - to demand taxes literally through the barrel of a gun.

As well as the natives there were some European traders, missionaries and others living in Samoa and soon it was barely possible to move without being confronted by some of Steinberger's armed troops and being forced to pay a toll in order to continue one's journey. Even visiting ships were subjected to his extortion. To give his thieving activities a veneer of respectability the colonel flew the American flag on his mini man-of-war.

The row between Foster, the U.S. representative, and Steinberger escalated and, when *HMS Barracouta* arrived in the bay of Apia in December, 1875, it heralded the end of Steinberger's dictatorship.

Rigged like a barque, the *Barracouta* was a paddle steamer but the side wheels were so well disguised that they could scarcely be noticed at a distance. Weighing 1,053 tons, her engines were of 300 hp nominal but could be worked up to 800 hp. She carried four 60 pound, muzzle loading broadside guns, three 12 pounder breech loading Armstrongs and two more guns of smaller calibre. There was also a good supply of small arms consisting of long and short Enfield rifles, converted into breech loaders. The long rifles were fitted for the ordinary bayonet while the short ones had cutlass bayonets which, from being protected at the hilt by a broad metal shield for the hand, formed capital cutlasses when detached.

The *Barracouta* also carried several small boats, including a steam launch that "did good service when she was employed off the Gold Coast of Africa during the Ashanti War". [5]

The warship's deck was described as "flush and roomy. The after portion of the main deck is occupied by a large and handsomely fitted up saloon for the captain, with smaller sleeping cabins opening off it. The cabins of the various officers and the wardroom are situated further forward, off the gunroom, and they are roomy and comfortable. The seamen and marines are accommodated, the former under the fore and the latter under the after part of the main deck". [6]

Altogether she carried a total of 177 officers, bluejackets and marines. Before arriving in Samoan waters she had carried the first Governor of Fiji, Sir Arthur Gordon, to his new fiefdom.

As we have seen, the *Barracouta* was used as Gordon's official residence pending the building of a Government House. Unfortunately, differences arose between the commander of the *Barracouta*, Captain Charles E. Stevens, and the Governor. Gordon,

239

who had earlier requested the *Baracouta* for his temporary abode, now asked for a replacement vessel under a different captain.

Stevens' orders before he left Sydney had been to remain in Fiji and not to visit Samoa but Sir Arthur Gordon, in order to get rid of him, gave him approval to go to Samoa on a flag waving voyage. This mischievous act of Gordon's was part of his power struggle with the Admiralty over British policing procedures in the South Pacific.

Upon arriving in Apia the captain of the *Barracouta* was acquainted with the situation by both the British and U.S. representatives, and the *Peerless* was seized on the grounds that she was in breach of the U.S. neutrality laws by carrying arms while flying the Stars and Stripes.

Steinberger claimed that the 12 pounder on the bow of the *Peerless* was only for firing salutes but this was at variance with its role as an armed revenue collector.

The *Peerless* was sold as a lawful prize for US$2,200 to Captain Murdoch McKenzie of Auckland, who was visiting Apia at the time on a trading voyage. Steinberger challenged the new owner's legal right to the vessel, calling the transfer "an atrocious, illegal act". Captain McKenzie then sailed her out of Samoa's waters forever and she sank a few months later off Suwarrow Island.

With more than a little prompting from the British and U.S. representatives, the Samoan king, Malietoa, then dismissed Steinberger from his position as "Premier for life" and asked Captain Stevens to remove him from Samoa. The captain hesitated as Steinberger had some influential friends on the island, including his band of armed toughs.

Nevertheless, the deed was done on the morning of 8th February, 1876, when Steinberger was duly arrested by a party of marines from the *Barracouta* and escorted to his house with "forty men before and forty behind". There he was allowed to collect a few items of clothing before being marched a mile along the beach to the warship where this erstwhile master of Samoa was placed under guard for deportation. This was vehemently opposed by some of the other chiefs who forced Malietoa to abdicate as king.

A messy situation ensued and on 13th March a large public meeting was held on the Mulinu'u peninsula to resolve the issue of kingship. It was attended by chiefs, missionaries, Consuls and citizens as well as a guard of honour from the *Barracouta* under the command of Captain Stevens, who had been asked to attend by some Samoan chiefs. The bluejackets marched to the site along the road, which had tropical bush on one side and the sea on the other.

With proceedings hardly begun, "it was reported to the officers by one of the bluejackets that a lot of armed natives (Steinberger's 'toughs') had been seen stealing along in the bush" [7] and that they commanded the road along which the sailors had to return to their ship.

The *Barracouta* men were ordered to penetrate the bush but were not instructed to load their rifles or even fix their bayonets because no resistance was expected. Their orders were not to fire unless fired upon but within two minutes "bang! went the first shot from the natives and very quickly firing became pretty general." [8]

For fifteen to twenty minutes bullets were flying in all directions and, not surprisingly, the meeting broke up in disorder with panic stricken people fleeing into the trees. At the end of the skirmish eight Samoans lay dead and thirty-five were wounded while seven marines and four bluejackets were wounded, of whom three died.

Able seaman William Morrison died half an hour after the action from a wound in his chest. Private W. Watson of the light infantry passed away the following day from a wound in the abdomen while Ben Kelsey died after being shot through the spine.

Six of the British wounded were put on a German barque, the *Etienne*, and were taken to Levuka in Fiji. They were later taken to Auckland for medical treatment on the *Barracouta*, which followed the *Etienne* to Levuka.

In the words of a report to the *Southern Cross* newspaper in Auckland, "Hitherto it has always been considered a safe indication that no fighting was intended whilst women and children were present at any meeting but in this case there was a complete departure from their usual custom for several women and children were present whilst the fight was going on. It is a singular custom with the Samoans that they do not count a man dead unless they get his head in their possession, and they entirely failed in this respect with the *papalangis*, as they term Europeans....If they had attempted anything of the sort, it would have gone very hard with them, for our men would have stood no nonsense of that kind, as they were all pretty close together and a head could not have been cut off without it being instantly known to all." [9]

After the fight five of the principal insurgents were taken on to the *Barracouta* as hostages for the good behaviour of the natives

241

in the future and, when the shaken sailors were marched back to their ship, several chiefs were marched with them to ensure against any treachery *en route*.

Two days of meetings between the chiefs and the consuls resulted in an agreement that, if Steinberger's armed supporters would return home, the guns and men of the *Barracouta* would be withdrawn. Then, on 29th March, *HMS Sapphire* relieved the *Barracouta* and took over the hostages.

After being incarcerated on the warship for sixty-three days Steinberger was dumped ashore at Levuka, whence he made his way to Auckland on a mail steamer, the *City of San Francisco*, arriving there around the same time as the *Barracouta*.

During his time on the warship Steinberger used his considerable charm to impress the crew just as he had taken in the Samoans. While walking along Auckland's Queen Street the colonel was spotted by a bunch of about forty jolly tars from the *Barracouta* who were on shore leave. "Here's Colonel Steinberger,' says one, and immediately the whole of the tars started in pursuit and brought the colonel up with a round turn. 'How are you, Mr. Steinberger?' they all shouted and forty or fifty hands were held to the bewildered American to shake. 'Well, you must drink to our health', a few chimed in and the colonel was dragged back until the Cosmopolitan Hotel was reached, into which they good-humouredly forced their charge, for Colonel Steinberger was without doubt again in custody. Drinks were called for and the late Premier of Samoa was toasted with three times three." [10]

In the words of one of the sailors, "We found the colonel a right good sort and not one of the ship's crew has a word to say about him." [11] But many others did – especially after the discovery of papers at his house in Samoa which showed that he had made corrupt agreements with the German firm, J.C. Godeffroy and Sons.

In Auckland Captain Stevens had to answer for his actions to Commodore Hoskins as to why he disobeyed the instruction not to go to Samoa. In his wisdom Hoskins decided to go to Samoa himself on *HMS Pearl* to find out more about the circumstances that led to the deaths of some of the sailors on his station and, while he sailed north-east, he ordered Captain Stevens to go to the north-west and inquire into a recent attack on a British merchant vessel in the Solomon Islands. This suggests that Hoskins still had trust in Captain Stevens' judgement.

Captain Stevens' role in the arrest and deportation of Steinberger, an American citizen, from a place where Britain did not exercise jurisdiction remained controversial. In the words of the *Pall Mall Gazette*, "The endeavour to restore King Malietoa at a time of such excitement certainly appears injudicious, and we have already far too many responsibilities in connection with our tropical dependencies to render the acquisition of others desirable. It is nevertheless essential, in view of our increasing interests in the Pacific, to take good care that other powers should not obtain any dangerous advantage through our neglect, and the presence of such an adventurer as Steinberger at Samoa – a point from which, with an armed vessel or two, he might have preyed upon our commerce in war-time – could not have been passed over unnoticed." [12]

The aftermath of the affair was messy on all sides. The British Consul and American Commercial Agent in Samoa were both replaced while Captain Stevens and the *Barracouta* were ordered home where he was court-martialled and dismissed from the Navy – not for his decision to intervene in Samoa's internal affairs, which led to the deaths of three of his sailors, but for treating Mr. Gain, the paymaster of his ship, harshly and forcing him to make an advance of £30 out of the ship's chest in an irregular and illegal fashion. Stevens had requested the paymaster not to enter it in the cash account and the money had been used to meet the expenses of entertaining the Governor of Fiji on the *Barracouta*.

Messy too for the Samoans. For their part in the killing of the British sailors they were fined $10,000 plus a further $10,000 for threatening the British Consul and another $10,000 for insulting Queen Victoria on her birthday. They were never able to pay and so had their gunboat, *Elizabeth* (successor to the *Peerless*), seized and towed by *HMS Sapphire* to Fiji where it was sold. [13]

In 1899 it was agreed by Britain, Germany and the United States for each to take different parts of Samoa but Britain backed out of the agreement, prompting New Zealand's Premier, the staunch and loyal Richard Seddon, who for security purposes always wanted British islands around his small and vulnerable country, to accuse the Mother Country of a "great betrayal" – the same words that were so aptly chosen a century later by Ian Smith, the Prime Minister of Rhodesia, for the title of his autobiography in which he too, like Seddon, had seen his loyal little country shafted by Britain's Foreign Office.

243

THE APIA HURRICANE

By the far Samoan shore,
Where the league-long rollers pour
All the wash of the Pacific on the coral-guarded bay,
Riding lightly at their ease,
In the calm of tropic seas,
The three great nations' warships at their anchors proudly lay.

Riding lightly, head to wind,
With the coral reefs behind,
Three German and three Yankee ships were mirrored in the blue;
And on one ship unfurled
Was the flag that rules the world –
For on the old Calliope the flag of England flew....

Then at last spoke Captain Kane,
"All our anchors are in vain,
And the Germans and the Yankees they have drifted to the lee!
Cut the cables at the bow!
We must trust the engines now!
Give her steam, and let her have it, lads! we'll fight her out to sea!"

And the answer came with cheers
From the stalwart engineers,
From the grim and grimy firemen at the furnaces below;
And above the sullen roar
Of the breakers on the shore
Came the throbbing of the engines as they laboured to and fro.

If the strain should find a flaw,
Should a bolt or rivet draw,
Then God help them! for the vessel were a plaything in the tide!
With a face of honest cheer
Quoth an English engineer,
"I will answer for the engines that were built on old Thames-side!"

"For the stays and stanchions taut,
For the rivets truly wrought,
For the valves that fit their faces as a glove should fit the hand.
Give her every ounce of power;

244

If we make a knot an hour
Then it's way enough to steer her, and we'll drive her from the
land."

Like a foam-flake tossed and thrown,
She could barely hold her own,
While the other ships all helplessly were drifting to the lee.
Through the smother and the rout
The Calliope steamed out
And they cheered her from the Trenton that was foundering in the
sea.

Ay! drifting shoreward there,
All helpless as they were,
Their vessel hurled upon the reefs as weed ashore is hurled,
Without a thought of fear
The Yankees raised a cheer-
A cheer that English speaking folk should echo round the world.

- Ballad of the Calliope, Andrew Barton "Banjo" Patterson.

After the *Barracouta* incident the situation in Samoa
remained unstable and potentially troublesome, as seemed to be the
case in virtually every uncolonised territory. The Royal Navy had to
maintain a more or less constant presence in Samoan waters and this
became something of a drain on the resources of the Australia
station. There was always the potential for conflict as the navies of
Britain, America and Germany sought to protect the interests of their
respective countrymen, who were busily pursuing their own interests
with vigour and greed.

In January, 1889, *HMS Calliope* was ordered to replace
HMS Royalist as Britain's shop window in Apia. Her remit was to
watch over British interests "during the present trouble". [1]

Martial law had been declared and the Germans were
blockading the port of Apia and searching British vessels for what
they termed "arms and contraband". The Germans were engaged in
a power struggle with a truculent faction of Samoans and they
claimed that foreign merchant ships were bringing weapons to these
"rebels", who had already killed eighteen German seamen and two
of the Kaiser's officers.

"Affairs are still very unsettled at the group, and the effect of the present disturbance is to completely paralyse all trade in Samoa," stated a press report at the time. [2]

After arriving in Apia, it was reported that Captain Henry Kane of the *Calliope* and the British Consul "have been making strenuous efforts to promote a good feeling between the Germans and Britishers here but their efforts have been entirely unavailing." [3]

The American Navy was there in the shape of the U.S. warships *Nipsic*, *Vandalia* and *Trenton* (flagship) while the Germans relied on their men-of-war *Eber*, *Adler* and *Olga*, whose boat crews were boarding merchant ships to enforce the blockade. In all, Apia was quite a crowded harbour and it all amounted to a very good recipe for a bust-up among the three powers, each one wary of the other two. But the hurricane that came was from something far more powerful than mere warships.

On Friday, 15th March, 1889, the barometer fell alarmingly and the *Calliope's* lower yards and topmasts were sent down and steam was raised in three boilers. By dawn the next morning the gale had become a hurricane and the wind moved from NE to north, which meant that it was blowing directly in through the harbour entrance.

During the night some merchantmen had been wrecked and at 5 a.m. on this fateful day the German gunship *Eber* was thrown on to the inside of the reef where she heeled over into deep water and was smashed to pieces. Only a small part of her bow remained above the water. About a dozen of her men jumped on to the reef and battled the waves to get ashore but the rest of her crew – about seventy-five men, including the captain and officers – drowned.

By now all the warships were dragging their anchors and the *Adler* collided with the *Olga*, knocking a great hole in her quarter.

The *Olga* then hit the *Nipsic*, taking away her funnel. Not being able to steam without a funnel, the *Nipsic* ran ashore but fortunately on a soft patch of sand and so most of her crew managed to get off although six were drowned.

Around 8 a.m. the 900 ton *Adler* was thrown on to the coral reef on her beam ends, keel to seaward, with her decks vertical. Most of her men got back under the lee of the ship and remained there for more than twenty-four hours although fourteen of them drowned.

The out-of-control *Olga* collided again, this time with *HMS Calliope*, damaging the latter's foreyard, carrying away her lashings and leaving her swinging about.

Next it was the turn of the *Calliope* and *Vandalia* to hit each other – twice. In the first round the *Calliope* lost her jib boom, and in the second all the securings of her bowsprit.

In this dance of the drunken warships Captain Kane had the choice of trying to go ashore on a fairly safe spot – as the *Olga* succeeded in doing – or of steaming out of the harbour in the teeth of the hurricane and, being a brave Irishman, he decided on the latter. Steam was raised in all six boilers, the remaining cables were slipped, and the *Calliope* embarked upon her all but impossible mission.

Almost immediately she rose clear on end and then made a terrific plunge down. The captain later wondered how the vessel's machinery, rudder and engine stood the shock.

He called to the engineer, Mr. Bourke, "for every pound of steam he could give us". In the words of Mr. Bourke, speaking after the event, "I was about calling upon some extra men who were off duty to go below when every man of them volunteered and all through the hurricane, though we were boxed up there in the engine room and the stoke hold and could hardly hear each other's voices for the howling of the storm, yet every man did his duty without a murmur. It takes a time like this to show what a Britisher is." [4]

A few minutes after the shock the *Calliope* gathered steam, her engines going at a rate capable of driving her fifteen knots in ordinary weather but on this terrible day making only three quarters of a knot. In the words of Captain Kane, "The engines worked admirably and little by little we gathered way and went out, flooding the upper deck with green seas, which came in over the bows, and which would have sunk many a ship". [5]

While steaming at sixty revolutions she struck the *Vandalia* full on the quarter and the engines were stopped to prevent further damage.

The *Calliope* then drifted astern within five feet of the reef on which the other vessels had been wrecked, and for self-preservation she had to press on even though she again struck the *Vandalia*, this time without doing any injury.

To get out of the harbour she had sixty men at the wheel – ten on the gun deck, ten on the lower deck and the rest on the relieving tackle on the lower deck.

"The American officers and Captain Kane's own officers are unanimous and emphatic in their expressions of admiration at the magnificent way in which he handled his ship. The *Calliope* had to pass between the *Trenton* and the reef with only a few yards to spare but the thing was accomplished in the most skilful manner," wrote Wellington's *Evening Post*. [6]

As the *Calliope* steamed past, the *Trenton's* officers took off their caps to Captain Kane and the American sailors cheered him heartily. Kane later said that this spontaneous encouragement was the handsomest compliment he had ever received. A minute later neither ship could see each other in the mist and driving rain.

"Once outside her (the *Trenton*) it was nothing but hard steaming; if the engines held out, we were safe; if anything went wrong with them, we were done for," said the captain. "Thanks to the admirable order in which the engines and boilers had been kept, all went well....I can not speak too highly of the conduct of every officer and man on board the ship. During the hours we passed, when any moment might have been our last, every order was obeyed with alacrity and without confusion." [7] Indeed, Kipling could have been thinking of the *Calliope* when he penned the lines in his poem *Together*:

"When crew and captain understand each other to the core,
It takes a gale and more than a gale to put their ship ashore;
For the one will do what the other commands, although they are chilled to the bone,
And both together can live through weather that neither could face alone."

As a result of her various collisions the *Calliope* had lost her cutter, dinghy, skiff and copper-punt and, on her way out through the harbour entrance, the jolly boat went too – washed away from astern.

While the *Calliope* was getting further and further away from the harbour the chaos inside continued with the *Vandalia* sinking within about a hundred feet of where the *Nipsic* was grounded. Some of her crew clung to the rigging while others tried to make it to shore "but the current took many of the poor fellows away". [8] Forty-two from the *Vandalia*, including the captain, were drowned.

248

The *Trenton* took on water, her rudder was carried away, the propeller rendered useless and she sank next to the *Vandalia*.

With hardly any more warships left for her to bump into the *Olga*, was beached by her crew, none of whom lost their lives.

Towards noon on Sunday the wind and the sea moderated slightly and at 5.30 p.m. a short "stand-up" thanksgiving service was conducted by the *Calliope's* chaplain, Rev. Arthur Evans.

Then next morning, with the worst of the storm appearing to be over, the *Calliope* changed her course and steamed back to Apia harbour, which was by now a ship's graveyard. With sunken craft littering the harbour the British warship was afraid to enter and so at the entrance she fired a gun and hoisted her signal for a pilot. The eyes of the *Calliope's* sailors were looking out to see which ships had gone under since they left.

With the uncertain state of the weather and reduced to one anchor and no boats, starboard jib-stays or bowsprit, Captain Kane decided to head for Sydney immediately. She loaned some of her diving gear to help in the rescue operation as the horribly mutilated corpses of the men of two navies were still being washed up on the beach. As a return gesture the *Trenton* very kindly loaned the *Calliope* a cutter for her voyage to Sydney while the *Olga* also gave her steam pinnace. Coaling began immediately and by Wednesday night 150 tons had been taken on board.

At quarter past seven the next morning the *Calliope* weighed anchor (her last one!), saluted Admiral Kimberley on *USS Trenton* with thirteen guns and headed out of Samoan waters and into legend where her epic feat of seamanship was to be remembered long into the future, her story being the inspiration for poems, paintings and plays.

In the words of her chaplain, "All on board were heartily glad to see the last of Apia". [9] Of her ship's company of around three hundred there was only one casualty throughout the terrible drama and that was Thomas John, a carpenter's mate, who was washed against the coaming of a hatchway just before the *Calliope* headed out of the harbour. In Sydney he spent some months in Saint Vincent's Hospital and had to be invalided out of the Navy.

The ship headed under easy steam to Sydney where she showed her battle scars – such as they were. "The hull forward shows evidence of the havoc played by her anchor and chains," stated a press report. [10]

In Sydney the officers and men "were fairly astonished at the enthusiasm which our recent experiences had aroused, and by the warmth of the reception we received." [11]

The day of her departure for England was described as follows by the *Sydney Morning Herald*, "Just to give her a cheer took thousands of well-dressed people out yesterday afternoon, and down to where the famous *Calliope* was lying, with her homeward-bound streamer flying at the main, and ready to cast off from her moorings in Farm Cove. Standing ashore immediately opposite to where she was lying, and looking way out along the foreshore to the extreme point of Fort Macquarie on the one side and as far as Lady Macquarie's chair to the right, might be seen an almost unbroken line of spectators, all testifying their appreciation of the good ship by waving hats and handkerchiefs, or cheering to the echo the gallant bluejackets who hung in clusters to the ratlines or waved their hats and lustily cheered from the *Calliope's* shrouds....

The scene amongst the bluejackets on board was an animated one. The *Calliope's* sixteen 'dogs of war' had been run in and snugly housed, ready for the homeward cruise. All the gear usually seen about the decks was clewed up, and everything clear for a fair start for Old England. Every sailor's face wore a broad smile, and some hearty shaking of hands went round as boat-load after boat-load of shore folk came and went. Such a collection of parrots, cockatoos, and birds of all kinds, presents from friends ashore, were to be seen stowed temporarily away in the first place to hand. There were shells from Samoa, native ornaments and curios from Fiji and the New Hebrides, and spears and poisoned arrows, dogs' teeth and sharks' teeth from the Solomons; in short a veritable museum of South Sea Island novelties.

There was no lack of enthusiasm on board the *Calliope* an hour before she left but it is not unworthy of notice that a steadier body of men never left this or any other port. To whatever good influence or cause it may be attributed, it was remarked, not by one but many visitors to the vessel, that intemperance in no single instance could be detected....As four o'clock drew near, the time fixed for getting under way, a flotilla of watermen's boats ablaze with bunting put off from Fort Macquarie Point.

Much credit is due to the licensed watermen....Their house at the Point was covered with strings of flags stretched from point to point in such a way as to give a pretty appearance to the boat-landing. Each waterman also ran a line of small flags from stem to stern of his boat....Leaving the steps as mentioned, this flotilla fell into two lines and, passing *HMS Lizard*, made a circuit of the outgoing warship *Calliope*.

Forming into processional order and headed by a capital band carried on board a large cutter saved from the wreck of one of the American warships at Apia in the very storm in which the *Calliope* so distinguished herself, the watermen took a turn round the flagship *HMS Orlando* and then fell into two lines out in mid-channel, one line towards Fort Denison and the other towards Garden Island.

In this position they formed a guard of honour as the *Calliope*, under very easy steam, moved down the harbour. Precisely at 4 p.m. the bugle sounded on board the *Calliope* and, as quick as thought, her yards were manned. This was the signal for immense cheering. From the bows of the *Lizard* close handy there was hearty cheering, and Farm Cove resounded again and again with the ringing echoes from the crews afloat, from the crowded pleasure steamers and the thousands who stretched from the shaded sloping point at Lady Macquarie's Chair to the extreme of Fort Macquarie....

Directly the ship was under way the yards of the other ships were manned. The *Orlando* 'manned ship', and continuous cheering followed the vessel down the harbour. Some fine music came from the band on the *Orlando*, and a boat afloat, sent down to do honour to their departing comrades by *HMS Opal*, at present at Fitzroy Dock, took an active part in the 'send-off'. A number of harbour steamers....took part in the procession....When the vessel was out in mid-channel, the fine band on board the Orient liner *RMS Orizaba* struck up and continued to play until the vessel rounded Bradleys Head where the whistling of the steamers' 'Cock-a-doodle-doo' and the hurrahs of the people afloat expended themselves and Captain Kane signalled 'Farewell to the port'. [12]

While the bluejackets were being feted in Sydney their American counterparts were faring less happily in Samoa. "Mr. Blacklock, the U.S. Vice-Consul at Samoa, has issued instructions to the hotelkeepers at Apia that they must not furnish liquor to any sailor from any American man-of-war, and warning any person disobedient of this order that his saloon will be broken into and the liquor emptied out," reported Wellington's *Evening Post*. [13] (2 April, 1889). It was quite all right to be shipwrecked in the service of Uncle Sam but woe betide anyone who might want to have a drink afterwards. And what right did the U.S. Navy have to smash up pubs in someone else's country?

Back in Britain the achievement of Captain Kane and his crew became the toast of the hour and there were calls for him to be given some sort of honour, to which the official response was given by Lord George Hamilton, the First Lord of the Admiralty, who declared rather grandly that no honour would be conferred on the captain because the courage and skill displayed by him, his officers and men "was not rare in the British navy and did not deserve any special recognition". [14]

However, Queen Victoria made him a Companion of the Bath in 1891 and he was promoted to Rear-Admiral while Mr. Bourke, the *Calliope's* engineer at Apia, was promoted to fleet engineer.

Of the eight midshipmen on the *Calliope* as she battled her way out of Apia harbour on that fateful morning six would serve with distinction in the First World War against the very navy whose ships they saw wrecked on the Apia reef. They were Captains Glossop, Fox, Nicholson, Brandt, Drury-Lowe and Admiral the Hon. A. Hood.

When *HMS Calliope* ended her active service in 1907 she became the headquarters for the Tyne Division of the Royal Naval Volunteer Reserve. She served in this capacity until 1952 but her exploit in Apia harbour on that terrible day is not forgotten; each year on the anniversary of the hurricane a mess dinner is held in the wardroom of the Newcastle-upon-Tyne Naval Reserve headquarters on Gateshead's Quayside, that particular division of the R.N.R. bearing the name, *HMS Calliope*.

252

GETTING THERE AND BACK

Where lies the land to which the ship would go?
Far, far ahead is all her seamen know.
And where the land she travels from? Away,
Far, far behind, is all that they can say."

Arthur Hugh Clough

"On the 25th May, 1863, at 5 p.m. we sailed out of Spithead and bade adieu to dear old England....The *Pigmy*, a small Government steamer, came out about a mile with us, with Lady Wiseman (wife of the captain) on board, but we soon left her far behind. We all remained upon the taffrail, watching the last of the houses of Portsmouth and the white chalk-pits on Portsdown Hill," wrote Cecil Foljambe, the signal midshipman on *HMS Curacoa* as she left England to take up her position as flagship on the Australia station in 1863. [1]

For this midshipman and for the vast majority of those who served in the Pacific in the nineteenth century, the absence from "dear old England" would be for three years and most of them no doubt shared his sentiments as their wooden (later iron) walls pulled out from Chatham, Portsmouth or Plymouth to make their way down the Channel. They were like the Roman legions who marched to the furthest extremities of the empire and stayed there for years on end to secure its borders against hostile tribes.

"It is curious how sailors take partings," wrote Lieutenant Hon. Fred Walpole in the 1840s. "Many who have been tossed about all their lives care not at all; many have no homes, their families are dispersed, the whole world is their home." [2]

In the years before the opening of the Suez and Panama Canals (and even for a time thereafter), the most common route for naval vessels was via the Cape of Good Hope on the way out to Australia and Cape Horn on the way home so as to take advantage of the prevailing westerly winds. However, if they were going to the Pacific station, based at Valparaiso, they would go around Cape Horn, usually stopping at Madeira and Rio de Janeiro.

When the infant colony of New South Wales was running short of food in October, 1788, Captain Phillip sent Captain John Hunter on *HMS Sirius* to Cape Town to buy supplies. Instead of taking the shorter route through the southern Indian Ocean Hunter sailed east from Sydney all the way across the Pacific, around Cape Horn and across the south Atlantic – a voyage that took three months but was still quicker than battling the strong westerly gales of the Roaring Forties.

With a new crew that had to learn to work together as a team, drills and exercises would take place as soon as a warship left the Channel. In the words of Chaplain Evans of *HMS Calliope*, which sailed for the China station early in 1887, "During the cruise (to Madeira) sail was used whenever possible without getting off the course…..A considerable amount of drill was got through, making and shortening sail, up and down top-gallant masts….The ship's company were exercised on most evenings." [3] They were worked hard and there was always a lot of activity just before dawn – getting ready for yet another day at sea.

The ships sometimes stopped at Madeira, anchoring in the Funchal roads, before trying to catch the Trade Winds and avoid the Doldrums of the mid Atlantic. When Captain Cook set out on his second voyage to the Pacific he anchored the *Resolution* in the Funchal Roads on 29th July, 1772, to take on wine (cheaper than in England), water, fresh beef, fruit and a thousand bunches of onions for the men, "a custom I observed last voyage and had reason to think that they received great benefit therefrom", he wrote. [4]

Cook's next stop was Porto Praya in the Cape Verde Islands where he took on live pigs, goats and fowls. There were also monkeys ashore and some of his crew took them on the *Resolution* as pets for the voyage. After a short time Captain Cook found that they were making the ship dirty and so they all had to be thrown overboard into the Atlantic. Although the *Resolution* was filled with livestock Captain Cook decided that monkeys were just one species too far.

It is important to remember that one of the constants in the history of the Royal Navy is that its warships have always been welcome at Portuguese ports – be it Lisbon, Madeira, the Cape Verde Islands, Luanda in Angola, Beira in Mozambique, Goa, Timor, Macau or Rio de Janeiro (in the days before Brazil became independent). The reason for this is that Portugal is England's oldest ally, the friendship dating from 1373 when our King Edward III signed a treaty with King Ferdinand and Queen Eleanor of Portugal. This treaty is the basis of more than six centuries of amity and good feeling between the two countries. Unfortunately, this means more to the Portuguese than to the English, who all too often in their history have shown themselves to be indifferent towards their friends while being over-accommodating to their enemies, e.g. Rhodesia and Northern Ireland, not to mention the spurning of the loyal Commonwealth in order to join the German dominated European Common Market.

The next step after these Atlantic islands was the Equator and some horseplay and ducking for those who were "crossing the line" for the first time. When the British Pacific Fleet was sailing out to fight the Japanese in February, 1945, a nicely inscribed certificate – "Neptune's Warrant" – was given to those sailors who were entering the Southern Hemisphere for the first time.

At the bottom of Africa most warships to the Pacific would sail around the Cape of Good Hope, dominated by its high lighthouse, and in to Simon's Bay (also known as Simon's Town), on the eastern side of South Africa's Cape Peninsula. In the mid nineteenth century the voyage from England to the Cape usually took between six and eight weeks.

The merits of Simon's Bay were perceived by Captain Arthur Phillip before the Cape had even become a British colony. Arriving at Cape Town with the First Fleet to Australia in 1787, he noted, "It is exposed to all the violence of the winds, which set into it from the sea, and is far from sufficiently secured from those which blow from the land. The gusts which descend from the summit of Table Mountain are strong enough to force ships from their anchors, and even violently to annoy persons on the shore by destroying tents or other temporary edifices…and by raising clouds of fine dust….The storms from the sea are still more formidable, so much so that ships have frequently been driven by them from their anchorage and wrecked at the head of the bay….False Bay is more secure than Table Bay during the prevalence of the north-west winds…The most sheltered part of False Bay is a recess on the west side called Simon's Bay." [5]

Simon's Bay became the largest Royal Navy base in the southern hemisphere and remained so until 1975 when Britain's Labour Prime Minister, Harold Wilson, terminated the arrangement unilaterally – ostensibly on the grounds that he opposed South Africa's apartheid policy but in reality to oblige his Soviet masters, who had a hold over him and who had big plans for southern Africa that included the need to get the Royal Navy out of the way. When the Falklands war broke out in 1981 there were more British casualties because of the longer lines of supply necessitated by Wilson's act of treason.

In the mid nineteenth century Simon's Town was a pleasant base – good climate, naval environment and plenty of cheap fruit, including peaches, pears, oranges, apples and quinces. In the words of that most descriptive historian of the British Empire, James Morris in *Heaven's Command*, Simon's Bay "was one of the snuggest and prettiest places imaginable, and unchangingly British. Trimly around a sheltered inlet clustered its demure villas, its cottages, its sailors' barracks, its steepled church and its esplanade of shops, the whole nicely washed and painted, and built to a happily domestic scale....and everything in the place was comfortably Navy." [6] In front of Admiralty House was a jetty where the senior naval officer would anchor his vessel. Tied to the piles of the jetty were live turtles that he could select for his soup. When a Royal Navy vessel called there en route to the Pacific the Admiral in command at the Cape would pay a visit on board.

In 1847, on his way out to the Australia station in *HMS Rattlesnake*, Captain Owen Stanley, carried out a much needed survey of Simon's Bay, taking soundings of the depths, and charting the channels, shoals and currents for the benefit of other mariners.

After leaving Simon's Bay to continue the journey eastwards a ship would be accompanied by flocks of Cape pigeons, albatrosses and other birds, that would remain aloft for several days, making a great noise.

On a long voyage to the Pacific – maybe for a three year commission – a naval vessel would be packed to the gunwales with people, cargo and provisions. HM's ships were used to take British troops out to Australia and to the Maori Wars and some were used to transport convicts to Tasmania and New South Wales.

They also carried large amounts of specie that were needed in the various colonies as an armed warship was considered the best courier for that particular cargo.

The *Rattlesnake* travelled to Australia by way of Madeira, Rio de Janeiro, Simon's Bay and Mauritius. She landed £50,000 of specie at the Cape, £15,000 at Mauritius, £4,000 at Hobart and £4,000 at Sydney for the respective Commissariats.

When HM Steamer Sloop *Inflexible* sailed from Plymouth on 9th August, 1846, she carried 2,000 stand of arms, 800 barrels of gunpowder and £55,000 of specie. Some of this was given to the Commander of the Forces at the Cape (£20,000 and 106,000 rounds

The officers and men of HMS Basilisk raising the flag on Hayter Island, off the coast of New Guinea, in 1873.

The survey vessel HMS Acheron at anchor in Port Chalmers, Dunedin, New Zealand.
(Photo : Alexander Turnbull Library, Wellington, New Zealand. Ref. No. G-3300-1/1)

the Gunboat Pioneer shelling the maori position
at moremere, Waikato River, 1863.

From a sketch
by an officer
H.M.S. Curacoa

The low draught vessel, HMS Pioneer, on New Zealand's Waikato River
during the Maori War of 1863.
(Photo : Alexander Turnbull Library, Wellington, New Zealand. Ref. No PUB-0033-1864-093)

The memorial to those of the Naval Brigade who were killed in the Battle of Rangiriri,
New Zealand, in 1863.

Captain Kane and his officers on HMS Calliope.

The escape of HMS Calliope from the Apia hurricane of 1889.

HMS Calliope at the newly opened Calliope Dock at Devonport, Auckland. Named after an earlier HMS Calliope, the dock received the later Calliope as its first customer in 1888.

Some "bluejackets" on HMS Calliope.

of ammunition) while another £35,000, 293.500 rounds of ball cartridge and 2,000 stand of arms were landed at Algoa Bay (Port Elizabeth). Thus lightened, she reached Sydney on a voyage from England of only seventy-three days, having steamed the whole way.

When Captain (soon to be Commodore) Goodenough took his flagship, *HMS Pearl*, from Portsmouth to Wellington, New Zealand, in 1873, he did the journey in ninety days at sea, exclusive of stoppages. To keep everybody informed of what was going on a manuscript newspaper called the "Diver" was published on board.

The *Pearl* spent four days at Simon's Bay, during which time Goodenough heard a rumour of a ship being wrecked at Amsterdam Island which, like its neighbour, Saint Paul Island, was an isolated and uninhabited French owned outpost about midway between the Cape and the south-west tip of Australia. He decided to go there to have a look for any survivors.

A boat's crew from the *Pearl* landed and they found a deserted hut, an overgrown cabbage garden and some animal footprints but no people. The hut, obviously built by some hermit who had since departed, was made of earth and stone and had a "well thatched roof of rafters of rough wood from the trees in the neighbourhood". [7]

Convinced that there were no people on the island, the *Pearl* proceeded to Perth where her 320 officers and men spent four days ashore. "The officers speak in warm terms of the kind reception given them by the people of Perth, who feted them and gave a grand ball in their honour," reported Wellington's *Evening Post*. [8]

An important reason for Goodenough going to so much trouble on the basis of a mere rumour was that the Navy at this time was rather sensitive about these remote islands as two years earlier some 350 of its sailors had been stranded there for eighty days when the naval transport, *HMS Megaera*, sprang a leak and was wrecked off Saint Paul Island.

These were officers and men who were being sent out to Australia as relief crews for *HMS Blanche* and *HMS Rosario*. Sometimes relief crews were taken between England and Australia if a ship was being recommissioned in the Pacific or for other reasons.

The *Megaera* was a leaky old tub that should never have been allowed to sail – especially with such a precious cargo as 350 of Her Majesty's sailors.

Before leaving British waters she had to put into the Irish port of Queenstown (to-day Cork) as water was coming through the leaky ports and she was overladen. So they patched her up, took off 100 tons of cargo and sent her on her way.

Twelve days into the Indian Ocean from the Cape of Good Hope a leak was discovered and pumps and buckets were manned. Water continued to seep in and so Captain Thrupp headed her towards Saint Paul Island where she anchored on its south-east side on 17th June, 1871

A diver found a hole near her keel and so she could not go any further and the captain ran her on to the bar, which ran across the bay.

Using the ship's boats, they unloaded stores and provisions – a task which took ten days. Ashore in the freezing and damp air they made tents out of sails and built huts of canvas, turf and stone.

They constructed a flagstaff out of a stunsail boom and erected it on the cliff behind their camp at a height of 845 feet above sea level and, whenever a sail was spotted in the distance, a fire was lit and boats were sent out to try to attract its attention but, at a distance of eight to ten miles, such efforts were in vain.

Not knowing when they would be rescued, they went from short provisions to half rations and then quarter, which was about one biscuit and a bit of pork/beef a day. Fish was their staple food and fishing and boating expeditions their chief occupations as well as chasing penguins whenever they were washed ashore.

They had a fife and drum band, which was a source of entertainment, while Captain Thrupp, who was a keen golfer, got the ship's carpenter to make him some golf gear so that he could practise his swing.

After a month Captain Visser, the Dutch skipper of the *Aurora,* bound from Holland to Surabaya in Java, sighted the island on his proper course and was surprised to see what he thought was a tree on its highest point. On his regular voyages he had never seen a tree before and he wondered how it could grow so quickly. Sailing closer, he distinguished the ship's ensign showing a sign of distress and so he shortened sail and came in view of the stranded ship. He gave them some bread and eight barrels of flour and took on board Lieutenant Jones, who went on to Surabaya where he alerted the Navy.

The Admiral in Hong Kong chartered the P and O vessel, *Malacca,* which went to the island and took the stranded sailors to

Melbourne, which they reached on 27th September after a longer and more eventful trip than most sailors took to Australia.

After the opening of the Suez Canal in 1869 the voyage to Australasia was shortened. A typical route was that followed by *HMS Diadem* when she sailed out to the Australia station in 1903, stopping at Malta, Suez, Aden and Colombo. Some 730 miles east of Aden she fell in with a derelict yacht, the *Vajairo* (8 tons), which was on her way to Bombay from Mombasa in Kenya.

Owned by a Parsee in Bombay, she was manned by a crew of three natives and was flying a sign of distress as she had been at sea for forty-eight days from Aden. Her rudder had broken loose and they were out of provisions and water and so the *Diadem* hoisted her up on the davits and took the crew on board. Both yacht and men were put down at Colombo, from where they no doubt made their way to India.

When the battleship *Prince of Wales* was sent east for her fateful tryst with the Japanese Air Force in 1941 she took the old route around the Cape of Good Hope because the Mediterranean was considered too risky at the time for the Suez route.

With three destroyers as escorts – *Electra*, *Express* and *Hesperus* – the *Prince of Wales* sailed from Greenock, at the mouth of the Clyde, on 25th October, 1941, and passed round the top of Ireland so as to get as far out into the Atlantic as possible and away from enemy U-boats and long range Luftwaffe planes operating from Occupied France.

Travelling at around 20 knots and zig-zagging in an effort to avoid U-boats, the ships put into Freetown, Sierra Leone, on Guy Fawkes Day – eleven days after leaving Scotland.

After refuelling in this British colony she headed back out to sea and, until the range became too great, had the protection of Sunderland flying boats, based in Sierra Leone, which did anti-submarine patrols.

With the Equator approaching the weather became unbearably hot and the men sweated terribly as they stood watch, performed "action station" exercises and gunnery drills. The heat was so intense in the engine room and boiler room that spells of duty were reduced to two hours. Shortly before arriving at Cape Town they struck a terrible storm and a sailor was lost overboard from the *Express*.

The *Prince of Wales* put into Cape Town on 16th November while the *Electra* and *Express* went round the Cape to Simon's Bay.

They were only two days at the Cape but in that time the sailors were entertained royally by the South Africans – both British and Boer – whose reputation for hospitality is as legendary as it is justified.

On the day when the ship arrived at Cape Town docks there were hundreds of cars on the quays waiting to take them to private homes or on sightseeing trips. For many of these doomed sailors this was their last party before they met their watery grave.

While in South Africa Admiral Tom Phillips, the commander of the force, had a meeting with General Smuts, the wise and far-sighted Prime Minister of South Africa. After the meeting Smuts sent a telegram to Churchill, stressing his fear that this British fleet for Singapore was not being joined with the American fleet at Pearl Harbour, "each separately inferior to the Japanese Navy, which thus will have an opportunity to defeat them in turn….If the Japanese are really nippy, there is here an opening for a first class disaster". [9]

The ships then sailed for Colombo, with stops at the beautiful island of Mauritius and then Addu Atoll (Gan) for refuelling. In Ceylon the *Prince of Wales* joined the *Repulse* and they and their escort vessels reached Singapore on 2nd December.

The sight of these big and powerful looking ships steaming through the Straits of Johore to the "impregnable" naval base was as impressive as it was reassuring. This was the type of thing that the Singapore base had been built for.

*****

When a ship on the Australia station reached the end of her commission she often returned home via Cape Horn to take advantage of the westerly winds. This meant that New Zealand was most likely to be her departing point from the station. Because of its more southerly position Wellington tended to be the last port they saw rather than Auckland and the people of New Zealand's capital would turn out in force to wave farewell to what was called a "Homeward Bounder".

The feelings of sailors approaching the end of their Pacific service was probably best summed up by the chaplain of *HMS Calliope*, just before she set out from Sydney for Home in October, 1889. "Although the prospect of a speedy return to England was a very pleasant one, yet much regret was felt at leaving a pleasant station and many kind friends." [10]

In similar vein Lieutenant Hon. Fred Walpole wrote after four years on the Pacific station, based at Valparaiso, (1844-8) "The news that our relief was telegraphed was not so well received as our friends at home might have wished. Many of us liked Chile, more the Chileans. Many were in debt, more in love. Many had not forgotten that half-pay was but five shillings a day, paid quarterly, and ill-adapted to maintain the horses and other luxuries to which they had become accustomed....more than one mother will have to welcome as a man the son she wept over at parting from as a boy." [11]

When *HMS Clio* left Wellington for Portsmouth via Cape Horn on the morning of 16th October, 1873, the *Evening Post* wrote, "The sight was an extremely striking one as the noble ship, with royal yards, steamed grandly out of the bay, the waters of which were as smooth as glass, whilst masts, yards and rigging of all three men-of-war – the *Clio*, *Pearl* and *Basilisk* – were crowded by officers and men, who exchanged three enthusiastic cheers, good wishes and farewells, amidst which the *Clio* glided out of sight." [12] In England the *Clio* was given to the Marine Society in London to be used as a training ship.

The spectacle was even more striking nine years later when *HMS Emerald* left Wellington for Home in May, 1882. She had been on duty in the South Pacific longer than most vessels – a total of three and a half years and, as such, was entitled to a longer pennant streaming from the main-royal masthead. In the words of the *Evening Post*, "The ordinary length of a pennant of a man-of-war when first commissioned is from the mainmast to the mizzen. On the expiry of her commission – which is meant to last three years – the length of the pennant may be doubled and for any term exceeding three years the whip-line, as it is called, may be increased to almost any length, so that the extraordinary length of the whip-line displayed by the *Emerald* signified a long cruise." [13]

Not all the ships made New Zealand their last port-of-call. *HMS Esk* took her departure from Sydney. "The harbour of Port Jackson has seldom seen a prettier sight than that which was exhibited when *HMS Esk* took her departure on Saturday from the smooth waters of Farm Cove on her homeward voyage. For some time previous to the hour appointed the decks of the ship were crowded with friends from the shore and brother officers from the other ships of war, and there was a large display of that open-hearted, joyous friendship which seems to be the peculiar characteristic of those whose business is on the great waters.

At half past ten the *Esk* tripped her anchor and, as the screw began to move, her yards and masts became suddenly thronged with men, with a sailor on each truck and on each yard-arm, with flags of all colours, and the farewell signal at the main-royal-masthead.

As the ship moved slowly up to the starboard quarter of *HMS Challenger*, three hearty cheers from each ship rent the air while the waving of the flags produced a most affecting and effective display. This singular custom was also observed: the man at the main truck threw a live cock into the air, which fluttered from the dizzy height till it fell into the water, when a boat from the *Challenger* dashed up and picked the bird up to be reserved for similar distinction on some future occasion.

The *Esk* passed next across the port bow of *HMS Charybdis*, when equally hearty cheers were exchanged, ensigns dipped, and all the vociferous expressions of farewell indulged in amidst waving of white handkerchiefs from the shore and from the numerous shore boats by which the ship was surrounded.

On rounding the *Charybdis*, the *Esk's* head was turned down the harbour and, as she steamed slowly past the Italian frigate *Magenta*, the same farewell civilities were exchanged and, these being ended, the crowd of shore boats dropping off, away the good ship went, a long, parting look at the girls they left behind them being all that both officers and men could then indulge in.

God speed the *Esk* and the gallant crew, for seldom have we seen a more gallant or more amiable commander, a more gentlemanly set of officers, or a more well-behaved ship's company. Well may the hearts of Englishmen burn within them in these distant parts of the British Empire when they see such types of the national character as have just departed from these shores." [14]

Ships in the North Pacific also sailed around Cape Horn to and from their station at Esquimalt. When HM Steam frigate *Zealous* was sent out as the flagship to relieve *HMS Sutlej* she sailed around the Horn and stopped at Callao in Peru and then San Francisco, which she reached on 25th June, 1867, some 199 days after leaving England. She was the first British ironclad to visit the North Pacific and for that reason was an object of interest. "This fine vessel attracted much attention at San Francisco and her commander courteously invited the public to inspect her during her short stay of one week," stated a press report of the time. [15] After handing over the station to her successor the *Sutlej* returned to England via the Horn, stopping at Valparaiso. On the way down the west coast of America she "saluted the Vanderbilt and other forts, and the United States commanders returned the compliment." [16]

The voyage around the Horn from either New Zealand or the North Pacific was a long one and ships would often put into Rio de Janeiro for water and provisions. As they proceeded north "Our heavens changed, the Southern Cross rose less and less till this fond emblem of our faith sank down far, far away behind us." [17]

For some on board this would be the last port before Blighty and, with every passing day, the prospect of seeing loved ones after an absence of about three years would be that much closer. Some would be relieved to get home and show off their curios, shells and pets collected from exotic islands. For others it would be somewhat unsettling and, of these, some would, after a decent period of leave, sign up for another Pacific commission while others would return to the Antipodes as settlers. After all, three years of one's life spent on a Pacific station could not help but leave a mark on a man in one way or another. What they had seen was a new world – not only geographically but in their minds and imaginations as well. It was not always easy to settle back in a country cottage or tenement in an industrial town after all the space, light and exotic sights and experiences of the Pacific station. In some respects one's shipmates had become one's family. In the words of Lieutenant Hon, Fred Walpole, returning to England after four years on the Pacific station, "The tired friends, the brother-voyagers, whose names were associated with all our frolics, all our funs; who had roared at our mishaps, grieved over our misfortunes, and befriended us in many curious scenes, would soon be scattered….after a sad day spent in irksome duties and leave-takings, it was with a heavy heart I stepped into a shore-boat, master of myself. As I pulled away the sunset gun fired and the pennant was hauled down. That pennant I had followed through weal and woe eighty-three thousand miles." [18]

CARPENTERS AND SAILMAKERS

The Carpenters

When a warship left England for the distant and somewhat uncivilised Pacific in the days of sail every man on board had a useful and vital role, none more so that the carpenters and sailmakers, who were largely responsible for keeping the vessel in "life and limb".

In the days of wooden vessels the crafts of shipbuilding and carpentry were synonymous; a man who served his apprenticeship building ships could also build houses as well as wooden wharves and bridges. Boys began their apprenticeship (usually seven years) in their early teens so that by the time they were twenty or twenty-one they were skilled tradesmen with a wealth of practical knowledge and experience. These apprenticeships were done on shore but some of the apprentices, especially those who worked in the royal dockyards, chose to go to sea – either at the end of their time or after a few more years' more experience on land. Depending on their experience they would be taken on as either a carpenter or a carpenter's mate.

The position of carpenter on a man-of-war was a most responsible one as he was in charge of the tools, loose pieces of timber, bolts, nails, copper and lead sheeting, and pitch and tar. If a mast split in a storm, he would have to attach a splint to strengthen it and, when a ship went into action, the carpenter and his team would be stationed deep in the heart of the ship and below the water line so as to be on hand to plug any holes from gunfire with oakum, wooden plugs or sheet lead. Because he was always "on call" a carpenter was excused watch duty.

They would do work on the ship as she sailed but their busy times were when a vessel had to be repaired in some bay or harbour. At the end of a long journey from England there was usually a lot of work to get a vessel "ship-shape and Bristol fashion" so that she could begin her Pacific service.

When Captain Cook's *Endeavour* arrived at Ship Cove in New Zealand for some much needed repairs, he wrote, "This day (Saturday, 27th January, 1770) we got the tiller properly secured which hath been the employment of the armourers and part of the carpenters since we anchored at this place, the former in repairing and making new iron work and the latter in fixing a transom, for the

264

want of which the tiller has often been in danger of being broke (sic), the iron braces that supplied the want of a transom have broke (sic) every time they have been repaired. Coopers still employed by repairing the casks, some hands with the long-boat, getting on board stones to put into the bottom of the bread room to bring the ship more by the stern, while others were employed cutting wood, repairing the rigging and fishing." [1] Three days later he noted, "The carpenter went into the woods with part of his crew to cut and square some timber to saw into boards for the use of the ship." [2]

If a leak or other problem occurred at sea the carpenters would be let down in a boat to do the necessary repairs to the outside of the hull – as happened on Cook's last voyage when the *Resolution* sprang a leak off the north-west coast of America. To fix it, she was pulled over on her port keel and the carpenters were dropped over the side. They found that the oakum in the seams had rotted.

When they reached Kealakekua Bay in Hawaii the carpenters lived in a house at one end of the beach while they repaired the mast. However, the work had not been completed by the time they had to make their hurried departure in the aftermath of Cook's murder, and so they dismantled their erstwhile shore establishment and took everything back on to the *Resolution*; the mast was laid on the forecastle and quarter deck where they finished their work.

Thirteen years later the Navy's carpenters were also busy at Kealakekua Bay when Captain Vancouver set them to work to build a vessel for the powerful chief, Kamehameha, whom Vancouver was trying to oblige so that he might cede his islands to Great Britain. Kamehameha had started to build a thirty-six foot schooner, which would be the biggest native owned vessel in the islands and which he thought would provide him with protection against his enemies. Unfortunately the Hawaiians' shipbuilding skills did not extend beyond canoes and so the construction of this important vessel had come to a dead stop when Vancouver arrived on the scene and put the *Discovery's* carpenters to work to finish it. Vancouver also provided cordage and canvas for it and the chief was very happy with the finished product.

The carpenters' skills were really put to the test when a ship was found to be rotting when she was thousands of miles away from her base. This happened to Flinders' *HMS Investigator* when she was surveying in the Gulf of Carpenteria in 1802.

While at an anchorage there her carpenter and his mates embarked upon some caulking to replace any worn oakum. As they proceeded they found more and more rotten places – in the planks, bends, timbers, tree-nails (wooden pegs that swell when wet), etc. and so Flinders got the master and the carpenter to carry out a full investigation (of the *Investigator*!).

Their report stated that "Out of ten top timbers on the larboard side, near the fore channel, four are sound, one pretty rotten, and five entirely rotten…..On the starboard bow, close to the stem, we have seen three timbers which are all rotten…..The stem appears to be good, but the stemson is mostly decayed….The ends of the beams we find to be universally in a decaying state. The tree-nails are in general rotten…" [3] Upon hearing this, Flinders terminated his survey in these distant waters and returned to Sydney. He was concerned that, if anything happened to the ship, he could lose not only his men but also his charts that he had spent so many months compiling. In Sydney Thomas Moore, the master builder to the colony of New South Wales, carried out an inspection and found that the ship was so rotten that it was not worth repairing. And it wasn't.

When *HMS Fly* was at her rendezvous at Cape Upstart in northern Queensland in 1843 awaiting the storeship with its fresh supplies, the time was utilised by landing the pinnace and getting the carpenters to fit her with a false keel and shifting-deck to make her more useful for her role of taking small parties along the coast and up rivers and inlets during the survey months to follow. When working ashore like this a sail was usually tied to some trees so as to protect the carpenters from the hot tropical sun. When the *Fly's* woodworkers finished their task the old pinnace was cutter-rigged "and a much more seaworthy craft than before, though still sufficiently wet and uneasy". [4] She was named the "Midge" and performed sterling service for the rest of the voyage.

Sometimes the carpenters would build an entire new boat for the ship – as happened when *HMS Dido* was at Borneo in 1844. She was anchored at the main settlement in Sarawak and, in the words of her commander, Captain Keppel, "Within a few yards of the ship was a Chinese workshop. Our boats were hauled up to repair under sheds….Mr. Jago, the carpenter, built a very beautiful thirty foot gig, having cut the plank up in the Chinaman's sawpit." [5]

The carpenters had an extra role on those ships that were sent out to the Pacific to collect spars for the royal dockyards; they

266

not only helped to select the trees that were to be felled but they often had to square and trim the spars before putting them on board for the long voyage back to Britain. No wonder they didn't have time for watch duty!

The Sailmakers

The main task of the sailmakers was to sew and patch torn sails and make new ones when necessary. In gale, typhoon, storm or battle the sails received a battering if they weren't got down in time and in parts of the Pacific the wind can come up very quickly. Each ship did have a spare set of sails but there was still plenty for the sailmakers to do on board - repairing the jacks, pennants, tents, bread bags and deck buckets and even the canvas bath of the captain. Like the carpenters, they were spared watch duty and so they got a good night's sleep.

The busy times for the sailmakers were when a ship was ashore as, needing a large space to lay out the sails, they generally did their work on land as the deck of a wooden ship was not large enough.

It was skilled work as the 24 inch wide sail cloth had to be spread out and then made into the correct pattern. The sailmaker's tools included a tape measure, a stretching hook (sometimes called a "third hand"), a stretching palm (a type of thimble but for the palm of the hand), knives for cutting the canvas and making holes, and the all important chalk, needles and linen thread. Each sailmaker worked while sitting on a bench with his tools beside him.

The craft of sailmaking was passed on from master to apprentice; nothing was really written down and working methods differed – a situation that would no longer be tolerated in our new age of enforced uniformity.

The sailmakers of *HMS Sirius* were really put to the test at the beginning of Australia when 1,030 people had to be landed from thirteen ships at Sydney Cove at the end of January, 1788. There were tents for the male convicts, tents for the female ones, tents for the sick, tents for the guards and a large, portable "canvas house" for Captain Phillip.

The sailmakers also had a key role to play in the founding of New Zealand in 1840. Under the superintendence of the first lieutenant of *HMS Herald* they erected a marquee on the lawn at Waitangi in which Captain Hobson R.N. and the Maori chiefs signed the treaty, which ceded New Zealand to the British Crown. This "large tent" [6] measured a hundred feet by thirty and at one end was a platform with a table and seats arranged for the historic occasion. As already stated, they also had to erect other tents to accommodate the Maoris who had come to Waitangi from distant places.

It was important that the sailmakers keep the sails and tents well aired as there was nothing worse for sailors than to be sent ashore for a few nights only to find that their tents were rotten and leaking. Some of the wooden sailing ships were perpetually damp, which must have made the sailmakers' job more difficult.

In this chapter we must also give a nod to the armourers. Not only did they attend to the small arms – muskets, pistols, cutlasses, pikes, and boarding axes (tomahawks) but they were also skilled ironworkers who were often called upon to repair the anchors and make bolts, nails, hinges and locks. Like the blacksmiths on land, they were the engineers of their time. When *HMS Fly* was surveying off the coast of central Queensland in 1843, she struck a storm and her cable got caught in some coral and began to cut through the wood work of the ship's bows. They cut down some pine trees on Entrance Island, near Shoalwater Bay, for the carpenters to repair the bows while the broken hawse pipes were replaced by iron bars that were crafted by the armourers out of a small anchor. These were placed at the lower part of the hawse holes.

Broken anchors were always a problem. When Captain Phillip Parker King took *HMS Mermaid* up the coast of eastern Australia in 1819 he lost two of his three anchors. He believed that they broke because they had been poorly made in Sydney and did not compare with English made anchors.

FROM SAIL TO STEAM

When asked in Parliament in 1816 why the Admiralty was so indifferent to the development of steam the First Lord replied that the benefits of steam power didn't really go any further than towing men-of-war out of their ports when adverse winds prevented them sailing out. This was neither heresy nor undue conservatism since the big engines of existing steamers consumed an awful lot of power in pushing their way through the ocean and they frequently ran out of fuel. For example, when the sailing paddle steamer *Savannah* became the first steamship to make the Atlantic crossing, she had to finish the voyage under sail because she had run out of fuel.

However, with improvements in the design of ships, boilers and engines, the establishment of more and more coal depots, the growing need for certainty and regularity in the delivery of trade goods, and the increasing speed of steamers, steam vessels started to come into their own and the Navy, whose officers had become extremely comfortable with ships resembling the wooden walls of Nelson's fleet, were forced to confront this revolutionary new phenomenon that was transforming the shipping world.

By the 1840s steam was starting to be used as an adjunct to sail on Her Majesty's vessels, with ships proceeding under sail in favourable winds to conserve fuel and under steam through the Doldrums or in adverse winds. After all, fuel cost money whereas wind was free. When *HMS Rodney* was ordered from Hong Kong to Singapore in October, 1869, the Admiralty instructed her commander not to use steam unless in actual danger; not surprisingly the voyage took longer than usual.

Similarly, when *HMS Basilisk* was surveying in Pacific waters in 1873 Captain Moresby frequently took the floats off the paddles so that she could proceed under sail alone. Under his command the *Basilisk* covered a total of 73,915 nautical miles, of which 46,106 were solely under canvas, the remainder being by a combination of sail and steam.

One reason why a captain would use sail as much as possible was the vast distances in the Pacific coupled with the small reserves of coal that they carried when they left Sydney. A voyage around the islands of the South Pacific would be several thousand miles and, on those islands like Fiji where there was coal, it was sometimes offered only at exorbitant prices by the dealers.

From 1845 onwards the Navy's larger vessels were steam driven but all were rigged until 1869. There was a deeply held and largely justified belief that a sailor could best learn his craft by training under sail – a practice that is still followed in the Chilean Navy. On a sailing vessel, ploughing silently through the ocean, one has a keener sense of sight, hearing and smell without the distraction of such things as the noise and vibration of machinery, the haze of steam or the smell of coal and, later, oil.

By the end of the nineteenth century steam was displacing sail entirely, thereby creating a whole new culture on board. For the captains and navigating officers it required new thinking and new attitudes while for the men it meant no more climbing up the rigging or mending sails.

From the health and safety point of view the change was both good and bad – good because there would no longer be sailors falling from the high rigging and dying or injuring themselves horribly, and bad as, deprived of the exercise of going aloft, the seamen started to become flabby and unfit, necessitating the Admiralty to introduce a new Physical Training Branch in 1900.

It required considerable deftness to work the heavy canvas sails at a height of up to 120 feet above the deck – especially if the ship was rolling in a turbulent sea not long after one had taken the daily tot of rum. In working the ropes and pulling in the sails a sailor had to use both hands at once and his concentration could never be allowed to wander. Of course, there were accidents.

When *HMS Calliope* was approaching Tonga on 8th August, 1852, one of her sailors fell from the mainyard and was devoured by sharks before any assistance could be rendered by the ship, which was travelling at nine knots.

When the same ship had been in New Zealand waters in 1846 Thomas Low, described as a "promising lad", [1] was aloft when he missed his footing, fell headlong on the deck and was killed instantly. The next day his fellow messmates and some of the officers buried him in the Wellington cemetery.

A similar accident happened on *HMS Esk* in Auckland harbour in 1866 when one of her sailors, nineteen year old William Matthews, fell forty-five feet from the mizzenmast in the morning and died later in the evening. He was on his way down after the order had been given to "clear the tops" and he missed his footing.

In December, 1843, the men of *HMS Agincourt* in Hong Kong were exercising aloft when one of them lost his hold and fell from the mainyard-arm. He hit the rigging and then "bounded with frightful force from the spare-topsail yard and fell insensible into the sea." [2] Lieutenant Vansittart jumped overboard after him and "with almost superhuman exertions (being burdened with the whole of his uniform) saved the poor fellow's life, supporting him a considerable time until a boat could be lowered." [3]

During his Pacific service on *HMS Curacoa* in the early 1860s Midshipman Hudson fell from aloft as they were furling sails. They were short handed as nine of the usual twenty-four men were away and so the midshipman "went on to the main topsail yard himself and stood on it, hauling up the sail, when the line he was hauling on snapped and he went backwards, struck the top with his head, turned over and over three or four times down the rigging, hit the muzzle of an Armstrong gun and went overboard – a fall of about ninety feet." [4] Another midshipman and two sailors jumped overboard to save him. He survived but his arms and legs were badly cut and bruised.

One can feel less sympathy for Walter Hill, one of the maintop-gallant yard men on *HMS Rosario*, which was cruising off the island of Santa Cruz, to the north of the main islands of the New Hebrides. All around were natives in their canoes, marvelling at the wonders of the big ship, and Hill was showing off by running very smartly down the rigging. He then fell into the sea and, instead of going to his assistance, all the canoes sailed away. He was rescued by the *Rosario's* cutter and, in the words of her captain (Markham), "He was picked up and brought on board none the worse for his immersion." [5]

One of the biggest effects of the move from sail to steam was the need to build coal depots at strategic points to supply the warships – either directly or by large colliers, of which the Navy ran several. In the event of hostilities at sea the outcome could be determined by a navy's coal supply. Without coal – or arriving at the scene of action with only a little in the bunkers – a ship had to take the weaker position, viz. the defensive.

In the Pacific there were supplies of good steaming coal at Vancouver Island, Labuan (an island off the coast of Borneo and one of the Straits Settlements), Townsville and Newcastle in Australia, and Westport in New Zealand. Welsh coal also fuelled the Pacific fleet – not just of Britain but of Japan too. During the Russo-Japanese war of 1905 Japan bought two and a half million tons of coal from the valleys of South Wales to power her fighting fleet.

271

Loading the coal on to a warship was hard work. When *HMS Rodney* was steaming off Russia's Sakhalin Island in July, 1868, "Coaling was performed by our own people filling bags and then loading alternately our pinnace and a boat belonging to the settlement, which was towed backwards and forwards by the steam launch; by these means we managed to get about forty tons per day," wrote Rear-Admiral Henry Keppel. [6]

Things were not so good the following year when *HMS Salamis* had to take on coal in the Peiho River in China. "The coaling of the *Salamis* painfully slow; lazy coolies passing the coal on board in small baskets holding less than a shovelful each," wrote the same officer. [7]

When the cruiser *HMS Grafton* took on coal at Esquimalt on Vancouver Island in 1904 her crew, using shallow baskets only, put on board 600 tons of coal at an average of nearly 195 tons an hour – up from their best performance of two years earlier of 80 tons an hour. Soot covered, tired and aching, these sailors no doubt yearned for the less onerous activity of running up the rigging in the clean air.

They were not the only ones who might have had reservations about steam. In China, where most people still lived in mud huts and tilled the fields literally with their bare hands, there was a deep suspicion of all forms of steam. They tried to resist the construction of the British financed Kowloon-Canton Railway on the grounds that the smoking steam engines would set fire to their fields and huts while the local Chinese authorities opposed steam boats on their inland waters, believing that the turbulence from these faster vessels would damage the houseboats. However, by treaty British warships were allowed to go to any part of China – coast, rivers and inland lakes – and that is exactly what they did.

When *HMS Curacoa* visited Vavau, Tonga, in 1865 she was the first steam driven vessel to do so. Upon seeing her the natives ran to the local missionary in a state of fright, crying, "A ship is coming in without sails and is on fire."

ROWING

The Navy's important work of surveying the Pacific could not have been done without the muscled oarsmen, who pulled the small boats up and down the bays and rivers so that the surveyors could do their sounding, observing and charting. Sometimes the skills of the oarsmen could be lifesaving. Rowing was in the blood; after all, had not our Saxon and Viking forebears arrived in England by rowing their long-boats all the way across the North Sea?

During Captain Vancouver's survey of the north-west coast of America in July, 1794, Joseph Whidbey and his surveyors were in a boat that was tracing the northern end of Stephens Passage, between Admiralty Island and the mainland (near Juneau, the present capital of Alaska), when they were threatened by a group of Indians.

In Captain Vancouver's words, "As the day declined with every prospect of a dismal, boisterous night, the party anxiously looked out for some place of shelter and endeavoured to get rid of the Indians by firing some muskets over their heads; but, instead of this measure having the desired effect, it seemed only to make them more daring and encouraged them to advance nearer to the boats. Thus unpleasantly circumstanced, they (the surveyors) continued at their oars until ten at night, without having gained more than four miles from the place where they had dined and without the most distant probability of the Indians taking their leave.

Although this branch had every appearance of being closed not far ahead, yet as Mr. Whidbey wished to ascertain that fact positively, the party steered for the shore with an intent of there passing the night. This the Indians perceived, made the best of their way thither and got possession of the beach before them, where they drew up in battle array with their spears couched ready to receive our people on landing.

There was now no alternative but either to force a landing by firing upon them, or to remain at their oars all night. The latter Mr. Whidbey considered to be not only the most humane but the most prudent measure to adopt." [1] The oarsmen rowed all night and at dawn the next day (19th July) they reached the northern tip of Admiralty Island where, according to Vancouver's laconic statement, "they stopped to take some rest". [2] They named this place Point Retreat. This raised some eyebrows as in naval parlance the word "retreat" was not a good word. This was but one example of sailors reaching safety through the energy and co-ordination of the rowers.

During the Second Opium War in 1858 the storming of the Taku forts was preceded by some reconnaissance that was carried out by a couple of naval officers, Lieutenant Bullock and one other. During the night of 19th August, 1858, these two officers rowed a short distance up the Peiho River from their warship "to have a nearer look at the barrier, and got well up between the forts before we were discovered....suddenly we found ourselves alongside an armed junk, their guard boat. She had been lying by the bank and, as it was low water, she was quite screened from observation until we heard them moving on deck. They saw us and immediately commenced blowing up their matches in a great state of excitement...We had the ebb tide, a fast-pulling boat, and darkness all in our favour. The junk fired a rocket at us but by some great good luck it became detached from its arrow and, turning right back, struck the man who fired it in the face!....A few minutes hard pulling removed us from any risk of being struck, and we could then enjoy a very pretty pyrotechnic exhibition, improvised on our account...until we got on board at 3 a.m." [3]

Sometimes a confusion of oars in a dangerous sea could lead to disaster – as happened in 1850 when *HMS Acheron* was surveying off the coast of Wanganui, New Zealand.

"The cutter, with six men and two officers, Mr. Paget and Mr. Burnett, went away on detached duty for three days," stated the *Acheron's* diary. [4] As they were returning to the ship at night in a heavy sea the oars got seriously out of sync at the same time that two seas came over the stern. The cutter capsized and four of them were drowned – Mr. Burnett, two seamen (Waters and Beale) and a Maori boy known as "Boy Newton", whom they had taken on board in Foveaux Strait, at the bottom of New Zealand. The sad irony was that the boy's father had opposed him going to sea and, exasperated at his son's disobedience, had said in a fit of rage that he wished the boy to drown on his first cruise. All four were buried at sea, wrapped in the ship's ensigns.

Even after the advent of steam, rowing would remain of paramount importance and boats' crew's would be kept up to the mark by training in bays and harbours and rowing competitively against other man-of-wars' boat crews in regattas.

The first regatta on Sydney harbour took place in April, 1827, to mark the fortieth anniversary of the founding of the colony.

274

It was arranged by Captain Henry Rous, whose frigate *HMS Rainbow* had arrived in Sydney three months earlier. The races were primarily between the oarsmen of his ship and those of *HMS Success*, the only other warship in port at the time. Local teams also took part.

There were three races – two for rowing boats and one for sailing boats. The first race for rowing boats was from Sydney Cove to Pinchgut and back and was won by Captain Rous in his gig, *Mercury*. The other two races were also won by the *Rainbow's* men, the purse for the day being donated by the two captains of the warships. Large crowds watched the races from Dawes Point (site of the later Harbour Bridge) and Bennelong Point. There were also many small craft on the water, all of them crowded with cheering spectators. At the end of the races many were invited on board the men-of-war and quadrilles were danced on the decks.

In the Auckland anniversary regatta of 1862 a race between the rowing boats of *HMS Miranda* and *HMS Fawn* was won by the former in one hour, five minutes. "The crews of both ships cheered loudly as the victors pulled alongside." [5]

In 1872 a race took place on Sydney harbour between the cutters of *HMS Blanche* and *HMS Cossack*. They rowed from the *Blanche* around Garden Island and then to a boat in Neutral Bay and on to the *Cossack*. The men in the *Cossack's* boat won by ten lengths.

Several Antipodean settlements celebrated their anniversaries with a sailing regatta and the Patron of the Regatta was invariably the Commodore of the Australia station while the vice-presidents were the captains of the various warships in port at the time. And there was nothing like a regatta to lure the men-of-war to a port for some competitive rowing.

In 1866 there were six entries for the naval boats' race at the Auckland regatta – crews from *HMS Brisk*, *HMS Esk*, *HMS Falcon*, *HMS Eclipse* and two from the Commodore's flagship, *HMS Curacoa* (the first cutter and the second cutter).

There were ten in each crew with a coxswain but the boats differed in size and weight. The *Curacoa's* boats looked the best and were the favourites. "The evenness and regularity of the strokes was very generally admired," wrote the *Southern Cross* of this four mile race. [6]

They sailed round the *Curacoa*, which was at half distance and, sure enough, the flagship's men came through. "Towards the end *Curacoa* Number 1 gradually gained ground by a fine, steady stroke until the finish", wrote the *Southern Cross.* [7]

The same enthusiasm was manifested at other regattas. "The Jack tars appear to take an extraordinary interest in this affair, and it may be anticipated that the races allotted to the Squadron will be some of the most interesting of the Regatta," wrote Wellington's *Evening Post* of the coming Anniversary Day Regatta on Wellington harbour in 1889. [8]

In addition to the competitive aspect the regattas were also highly social affairs. After the Wellington Autumn Regatta in 1883 "various crews dined together at the Occidental Hotel....The repast was of the most *recherché* description. The usual loyal toasts having been given, that of "The Army and the Navy" was proposed. Lieutenant Ommaney of *HMS Espiegle*, in responding, thanked the Wellington people for the opportunity that had been afforded the crews of both war vessels (*HMS Espiegle* and *HMS Diamond*) of taking part in the various sport," wrote the *Evening Post.* [9]

Nothing inspired the competitive instincts of the oarsmen more than a race against a foreign navy. When the German warship *Bismarck* was in Sydney in October, 1879, a cutter race was arranged between the men of the *Bismarck* and those of *HMS Wolverine.* "The Germans started with twelve pulling and the British with ten. Immediately after the start Tuffnel, one of the *Wolverine* men, snapped an oar and thereupon jumped overboard to avoid being deadweight in the race. The remaining nine continued and won by a dozen lengths. Tuffnel was rescued by a waterman's skiff." [10] Good old Tuffnel! He did his bit for his country – exactly what was expected of a British sailor when up against the Kaiser's seamen. Or the Americans.

In 1903 Sydney witnessed a thrilling race between the bluejackets of the flagship of the Australia station, *HMS Royal Arthur*, and the American sailors on the U.S. Navy's transport vessel *Glacier*. According to the *Australia Star* it was "one of the most interesting and exciting sights ever witnessed in Sydney harbour". [11]

At 5 p.m. on 16th February the picket launch from the *Royal Arthur* took the two crews, consisting of six men each, in tow down to Shark Island (off Rose Bay). "Vice-Admiral Fanshawe and party followed in his launch, and then came such a flotilla of steam launches crowded with sightseers as has seldom been seen....The two crews stripped to singlets and pants and made for the starting point – the Pile light. The Yankees took the inside running, and went between the light and the Island, but the *Royal Arthur's* men kept outside. They were level almost immediately when – bang! – went the starting gun and they were off.

With powerful strokes the Yankees immediately jumped to the front, getting the best of the start....The *Royal Arthur's* men jumped their boat away with short strokes and then settled down to a long, sweeping stroke. Both crews battled against a moderate westerly wind and just two minutes after the start the Britishers, going splendidly, had overhauled the Yankees and got their boat in front....The bluejackets began to forge ahead and, after five minutes had elapsed, were four lengths to the good. The Manly steamer *Brighton*, packed with people, stopped off Bradleys (Head) to view the race and cheer after cheer rent the air as it was seen by those on board that our men were ahead. 'Cock-a-doodle-doo' went her whistle as the crews shot by her.

The steamer *Woy Woy* was next met, filled with Yankee supporters, many of them waving the Stars and Stripes. Her occupants cheered the Yankees on and waved American flags but all to no purpose.

The northern end of Garden Island was black and white with British sailors, some in navy blue and some in white, who went frantic with excitement as it was seen that 'the boys in navy blue' were leading...Passing Garden Island, the *Royal Arthur's* crew were ten lengths ahead.

As the crews neared the *Glacier* the American sailors lined her side and cheered the Yankees on but it was too late. Then followed a most soul stirring sight as the flagship's crew rowed past her to the finish. Hundreds of Jack Tars swarmed the rigging and lined her side and went almost mad with excitement. The cheering was vociferous. Jack Tars shook hands, threw their caps into the air, pushed and slapped each other good-naturedly on the backs and cheered and clapped again.

The winning gun, as the *Royal Arthur's* crew shot across the winning line, was the signal for a renewed outburst of cheering from the flagship, and the occupants of dozens of steamers, sailing and rowing boats, and other craft which swarmed in the vicinity, while the blowing and shrieking of steamers' whistles, which was taken up by vessels all over the harbour, heralded the news to those far off that the British Jack Tars had won. 'Uncle Sam's' crew finished just 35 seconds, which represents about a dozen lengths, their final effort being a treat to watch.

No sooner had the race been won than a boat occupied by several of the fair sex – evidently the bluejackets' sweethearts – was alongside of them, and bunches of flowers, Union Jacks, handshakes and a heap of congratulations – in fact, everything but huggings – were showered upon the winners by Jack's proud feminine admirers." [12]

The race was completed by the winners in just over twenty minutes and, although the *Royal Arthur's* gig was a little longer and heavier than the *Glacier's*, it gave them little advantage against the wind. The Americans had very light pine scull-oars while the Brits had the usual ash-oars.

Sometimes, when pulling ashore on a mission, the oars had to be muffled to prevent the enemy from being alerted to a raid – as happened during the capture of Te Rauparaha in New Zealand.

This chief, the perpetrator of numerous acts of murder, terrorism and cannibalism against both Europeans and other Maoris, was holed up in his pa in the sand dunes above Plimmerton beach, north of Wellington, with his wives, tribesfolk and slaves.

After defeating the rebel chiefs, Hone Heke and Kawiti, in the north Governor Grey moved his naval and military forces south to deal with the threat to Wellington where the settlers were living in fear of their lives due to periodic raids by Te Rauparaha and his nephew, Te Rangihaeta.

Te Rauparaha's pa covered quite a large area of flat ground above the beach (between the present railway station and the stream to the south) but was undefended on the night. The steamer, *HMS Driver*, had sailed north from Wellington with both Governor Grey and members of the 58th and 99th Regiments on board as well as whatever bluejackets from *HMS Calliope* in Wellington harbour that could be spared. When in sight of Te Rauparaha's pa during the afternoon of 23rd July, 1946, the *Driver* made a feint of sailing out of the bay towards the South Island. By dusk they were – to any watching eyes - mere disappearing specks in the distance. However, come darkness they turned around and sneaked back into the bay.

By 2 a.m. they were near the shore and they anchored around the point and just out of sight of Te Rauparaha's pa. From there a party of bluejackets and soldiers were rowed ashore by boats with muffled oars. To preserve the silence of the night on the tranquil waters of this quiet bay they were forbidden to speak.

In the words of Sub-Lieutenant Henry McKillop, who had been specially entrusted with Te Rauparaha's arrest by Governor

Grey on the *Driver,* "When we reached the pa not a soul was stirring but our heavy steps soon brought some of the sleepers to the doors of their huts, knowing we were not of the bare-footed tribe. Upon informing him that he was my prisoner, he immediately threw himself (being in a sitting position) back into the hut and seized a tomahawk, with which he made a blow at his wife's head, thinking she had betrayed him. I warded the blow with my pistol and seized him by the throat, my four men immediately rushing in on him, securing him by his arms and legs." [13] The old man struggled and called out to his people to rescue him "but the troops and bluejackets coming up at the same time and surrounding the pa, prevented any attempt at a rescue." [14]

Still livid at being taken, Te Rauparaha made one bid for freedom by snapping his dirty fangs – those teeth that had chomped their way through so much human flesh – through the arm of one of the tars, an old salt called Bob Brenchley, who was holding him. The bite went right through, "making his teeth meet". [15]

"Why, ye damned old cannibal, d'ye want to eat a fellow up alive?" exclaimed the stunned sailor. [16]

Some of Rauparaha's men "stood to their arms, but were taken so suddenly that they were unable to do any mischief". [17] About fifty of the Maoris fled into the bush but the four whom Grey wanted arrested (Te Rauparaha and three others) were all captured.

The arrests were made without a shot being fired, which was just as well as a later search of the pa by the soldiers and bluejackets turned up a stash of thirty-two muskets, eight double-barrelled guns, five full and three half casks of powder and "a great number of tomahawks and other weapons". [18]

By now the boat, that had rowed Sub-Lieutenant McKillop ashore around the point, had arrived in front of the pa, concealment no longer being necessary as a new day shone its light on the busy scene.

Captain Stanley, the commander of *HMS Calliope* who was on board the *Driver* for the occasion, now came ashore and, upon being told what had happened, addressed himself to the interpreter, Mr. Deighton, who had laid much of the ground for the arrest. "Here you, Mr. Deighton," he called out, "it was you who discovered the old devil's treachery; you shall, if you like, have the honour of taking him off." [19]

Te Rauparaha and his fellow captives were taken by boat out to the *Driver*, and they were told that, if they attempted to escape, they would be shot.

HMS Driver steamed around the bottom of the North Island to Wellington. The prisoners were confined below in the workshop, which was next to the engine room and just above the boilers. During the night the sailors heard loud screams from the room and, fearing that these cannibals might be about to murder each other, they went to have a look. Their tiny enclosure was full of steam, caused by a leak in one of the boilers. Perhaps Rauparaha, who had roasted so many others, thought that he was about to be steamed to death. They were taken out of their steam bath and put elsewhere.

In Wellington they were transferred to *HMS Calliope*, which took them to Auckland, the then capital of New Zealand, where Governor Grey could keep a close eye on them. There they were incarcerated for eighteen months and were then released – much to the disgust of both the settlers and all those Maori tribes who over the years had suffered so grievously from Rauparaha's bloodthirsty actions. But his power and prestige had been broken forever and settlements like Wellington were able to develop and prosper free of Te Rauparaha's threats.

This early "combined operation" had been executed to perfection and reaffirmed the New Zealand settlers' continuing faith in the Royal Navy as the guardian of their safety.

FEEDING THE FLEET

Before leaving England a captain would fill his ship with preserved food for the long voyage out to the Pacific and often some livestock as well. When Commodore Wiseman took *HMS Curacoa* out to be the flagship on the Australia station in 1863 he took not only his wife, two brown spaniels and one setter but also some twenty sheep with the result that those on board were "treated to a variety of noises at times". [1]

Food could be replenished at the Cape of Good Hope but feeding the crew of a big ship like the *Curacoa*, with around three hundred hungry sailors on board, was quite a challenge and, by the time she was nearing her destination in eastern Australia, one of her midshipmen wrote, "We have only hard salt meat left, and harder biscuit, and a little wine of our own store but all our stock of beer and porter (though we renewed it at the Cape) is gone". [2]

Commodore Wiseman later replaced his livestock in Sydney; when he left on a Pacific cruise in 1865 he took on board a cow, a calf, a sheep and some poultry. [3]

These were supplemented at Norfolk Island when the *Curacoa's* officers bought several sheep at fourteen shillings a head. "They are really the finest I have seen since leaving England, being very fat off the rich pasturage of Norfolk Island," wrote an impressed midshipman, Cecil Foljambe. [4]

During the China Squadron's summer exercise of 1887 *HMS Linnet* and *HMS Calliope* broke off from the other eleven warships to go into Vladivostok harbour for fresh provisions as the Russians would let in only two British warships at a time. They took on live bullocks and vegetables for the other vessels, which were further out at sea. In the words of the *Calliope's* chaplain, Rev. A.C. Evans, "The upper deck, for the time, became quite a farmyard, as bullocks were tethered between the guns, and fodder and vegetables stowed in all possible places." [5] Things improved when the fleet anchored in Saint Vladimir Bay and the provisions were unloaded on to the other vessels.

When *HMS Fly* went surveying in the Torres Strait area they had the prescience to take a sow and a boar on board, which they released on one of the Sir Charles Hardy Islands so that, when they returned the next year, nature had taken its course and there was a litter of young pigs.

It was not unusual for a captain to take one or two hunting dogs on board and these came in useful on a long cruise when hunting game. And every wooden ship carried one or more cats to catch the rats.

The most important victualling item was the casks of rum, from which the "tot" was doled out each day. In 1834 the rum ration was halved from half a pint per person per day to a quarter of a pint and in 1850 it was halved again and one could then opt for tea and sugar instead of rum. By 1932 only a third of sailors were taking the rum ration, the others receiving cash in lieu thereof and spending it on extra tea.

Rum – especially the quantity of the tot before 1834 – might not have been all that conducive to one's health and well-being but lime juice certainly was and in 1795 it was issued every day in an effort to prevent scurvy. It was known as "service lime juice" while the sailors themselves became known as "limeys" – a word that some Americans still apply to the British. It was stored on board in old rum casks.

In earlier times bread had to last a long time and it sometimes deteriorated but by the early twentieth century it was being baked daily on the larger ships. Bread was stored in casks but Captain King of the surveying vessel *Mermaid* complained in 1818 that these, like the water casks, had been manufactured cheaply in Sydney from the staves of salt-provision casks and the water stored therein "was perfectly useless". [6]

For a long voyage a captain would have to take a lot of preserved food on board. When *HMS Investigator* set out from Sydney in 1802 for a cruise up to Torres Strait and the Gulf of Carpentaria she was stocked with 30,000 pounds of biscuit, 8,000 pounds of flour, 156 bushels of kiln dried wheat, and 1,483 gallons of rum. The rum was purchased for six shillings and sixpence per gallon from two American vessels that had recently arrived in Sydney. On the meat front Captain Flinders purchased some sheep, weighing between 30 and 40 pounds when dressed, as well as some live pigs, geese and fowls.

When *HMS Investigator* returned to Sydney in the winter of 1803 after a long circumnavigation of Australia some of the ship's company were in such poor health that Captain Flinders put them on a diet of fresh meat – pork one day, mutton the next. He also took on a large supply of port wine "and a pint was given daily to all those on board whose debilitated health was judged by the surgeon to require it". [7]

Trips to the Islands were a different story. When *HMS Blanche* made a 189 day cruise around the islands of the South Pacific in 1872 the ship's company had eight days' fresh meat and 181 days of salt meat. Whether cruising among the Islands or surveying the Australian coast, they could shoot, fish, buy from the natives or pick out of the ground. When Captain Cook took *HMS Endeavour* into Mercury Bay, New Zealand, in 1769, his men collected wild celery, which was boiled for breakfast with soup and oatmeal. Another delicacy of Mercury Bay was rock oysters.

Birds were frequently shot for the pot. On their second Christmas on Cook's first voyage the men of the *Endeavour* were at sea off the northern tip of New Zealand but that didn't stop Joseph Banks shooting some gannets, which were used to make a goose pie for Christmas Day. In Banks' words, "Our goose pie was eat with great approbation and in the evening all hands were as drunk as our forefathers used to be upon the like occasion." [8] No wonder the *Endeavour* had so much difficulty getting round this northern point.

A century later when *HMS Rosario* was chasing blackbirders around the New Hebrides in 1872 its captain, Albert Markham, wrote, "We shot several pigeons of the bronze-wing kind, which proved capital eating." [9]

While *HMS Chatham*, one of the two vessels that Captain Vancouver had for his exploration of the coast of North America, was waiting to re-cross the bar of the great Columbia River (to-day the border between Oregon and Washington state) in 1792, the sportsmen on board got out their guns and, on the marshes surrounding the bar, they shot numerous geese, ducks and snipe while one midshipman, Thomas Manby, managed to kill a fallow deer "so that what with venison, wild fowl and salmon, which the natives brought us in abundance, we contrived to live tolerably well" wrote Edward Bell, the clerk on the *Chatham*. [10]

However, shooting on the Sabbath was not considered the "done thing" – rather surprising really since in Tudor times people in England would go to church on Sunday morning and then take off to the butts to practise their shooting. Of *HMS Salamis'* voyage up the Yangtse River in March, 1869, Rear-Admiral Keppel wrote, "On the Sabbath afternoon I invited Risk, my secretary, to accompany me in a stroll. My feelings were shocked to see him, on landing, produce a gun and well-stocked bag of cartridges, while Ponto, a pointer, but still a better retriever, soon came on the scent of game. Snipe and teal got up in twos and threes, a fair proportion falling to Risk's gun. The temptation was too great for me. Borrowing the gun, while Risk looked on, in the course of a few moments I returned him an empty cartridge bag. Fortunately he had a few cartridges left, and was rewarded by a brace or two of pheasant on the homeward journey. The spring snipe afford splendid shooting…The birds are nearly double the ordinary size, the result, I presume, of good feeding in the paddy fields." [11]

When Captain Cook was at Dusky Sound, New Zealand, on his second voyage he came across some seals, which were killed and made into steaks while their oil was used to fuel lanterns on the ship.

During the surveying voyage of the *Acheron* in New Zealand in 1850 they, like Cook's men, were always on the lookout for fresh food and in Milford Sound, near Dusky Sound, they managed to shoot twenty wild ducks, two wood hens and a small hawk. The same crew had earlier shot what they claimed was a wild pig at Port Hardy, at the top of the South Island. They hauled it on to the cutter and took it back to the *Acheron* – to the delight of the ship's cook, who started on his work. Next thing a Maori arrived in his canoe, demanding to see "Capinny Toke" (Captain Stokes). He claimed ownership of the pig, saying that he had bought it from a white man, and demanded £3 for it.

"No," said the tars, who were every bit as cunning as the Maori, "it was definitely a wild pig." After considerable wrangling the price was reduced to thirty shillings, the Maori went off in a huff and the sailors sat down to their pork dinner. [12]

As every hunter knows the thrill is in the chase as much as in the capture and in this respect a rabbit shoot on Phillip's Island, off Norfolk Island, was not so satisfying as the rabbits were so tame that the men of the *Curacoa* "could knock them over with our sticks easier than we could shoot them, so we did not get any sport but, after taking what we intended for our messes, we returned to the main island, taking a look at Nepean Island, which is a small rocky island between the two larger ones, with only three pines on it. It is where they used to hang the convicts, who had mutinied or murdered any of the guards." [13]

Fresh food was necessary to keep seamen healthy and, when it ran low on a long voyage, it could be a godsend to come across another vessel and either take or buy some extra food. When *HMS Actaeon* came across an American whaler that had recently been wrecked and left abandoned at Monterey, California, in 1836, they took from her stores enough beef, pork, flour, bread and spirits to last them for three months.

When *HMS Fly* was surveying in Torres Strait in 1843 the tins of preserved meat, provided by the New South Wales government, were found to be of bad quality, "the contents being in a filthy, putrid state". [14] She had been eight months away without touching at a port where fresh vegetables or meat could be procured and they were getting tired of eating limpets and oysters off the rocks. "Our crews (of the *Fly* and its tenders) had now been so long on salt provisions that the scurvy was beginning to show itself with rather alarming force," wrote Mr. Jukes, the naturalist on board. [15]

By now scurvy had been more or less eradicated from the Navy and this was the first time that the *Fly's* doctor, Dr. Muirhead, had seen it. There were twelve men on the sick list, one or two of whom could hardly stand. It was more than time for some fresh food when the *Fly* fell in with three merchant ships that were making their entrance within the reefs to Torres Strait. The *Fly* was able to purchase "though at rather a heavy price...sheep, Hobart potatoes and some excellent ale." [16] These were issued to all hands and the change produced by the new diet was most beneficial.

Things improved when they reached Port Essington where they were able to kill a buffalo every day during their six day stay but it was so hot that they had to eat it immediately as it would not keep. Here they were also able to buy yams and sweet potatoes. These two products were also purchased from the natives in the Islands in return for iron, clothing and other items.

In the New Hebrides the men of *HMS Rosario* bought from the natives a pig, which weighed two hundredweight. And the price? One empty bottle. Before forming a judgement on what might appear to be a one-sided transaction it is important to remember that the natives on remote islands placed a lot of importance on glass as they used it for sharpening their weapons and shaving. For fresh yams and vegetables at the same place the sailors traded beads and red paint, which latter the natives liked to smear on their faces.

Not all the provisions they obtained in the Islands were by way of trade. When *HMS Havannah* arrived at the island of Aitutaki in the Cook Islands in February, 1857, it was met by the natives in a whale-boat who presented them with oranges and pineapples. The islanders insisted that they come ashore and one of them, who was called Jim, undertook to pilot the *Havannah's* cutter through the reef. The entrance to the lagoon was no more than ten yards across although five fathoms deep and it was marked by a flag on a pole.

The 1,200 people of Aitutaki were Christians and most of them could speak English in varying degrees. In the words of the *Havannah's* commander, Captain Harvey, "On returning to our boat after our agreeable visit, the chief men had assembled in the market to express the gratification which our presence had afforded them, and requested our acceptance of a large quantity of everything the island produced – all this having been collected and placed in front of the building.

It was explained that the Queen's ships had nothing in the way of trade to offer in exchange – that even our boat could not carry the tenth part of it. But it was immediately replied they did not want anything in exchange, they were too happy to see an English man-of-war at their island and that their boats would embark all of it for us. This was irresistible and we invited them to come and see the ship. The oldest man accordingly came in our boat while their whale-boats, four in number, heavily laden, accompanied us, three of them taking our laden cutter in tow.

When on board they refused any refreshment excepting tea, and were astonished and highly pleased with everything they saw and, with delight in his eyes, the old man's son told me it would cause a big talk of many days." [17]

Fish, of course, was a mainstay of the diet and every ship in the Navy was issued with a seine – a large fishing net with floats at the top and weights at the bottom. It required quite a few men – the "seining party" - to operate it.

When *HMS Salamis* was cruising off Russia's Pacific coast in the summer of 1868 "The ship's seine was brought and cast outside the mouth of the river when, in a few hauls, some five hundred salmon were taken – more than enough for the ship's company and some to salt besides." [18] Captain Cook's *HMS Resolution* even had a "fish room" near the stern, in which casks of fish were kept. Lovely smell!

While *HMS Investigator* was surveying in the Gulf of Carpentaria in 1802 Captain Flinders wrote, "The sea afforded a variety of fish and in such abundance that it was not rare to give a meal to all the ship's company from one or two hauls of the seine." [19] Thus began the Gulf fishing industry.

When *HMS Rosario* was in the New Hebrides in 1872 "We took every opportunity of hauling the seine at the different places where we anchored, and usually with success, which afforded a pleasing variety to the everlasting chicken and preserved meats. The takes generally consisted of mullet and bream," wrote Captain Markham. [20] The mullet had to be cooked immediately because of the heat "but this was no drawback to Jack, who as a rule is always ready to 'pick a bit'." [21]

Two years earlier the *Rosario's* previous commander, Captain Palmer, described seining in Vila harbour in the New Hebrides as follows, "During our stay here a large party was sent to the bottom of the harbour inside the reef to haul the seine, and caught grey and red mullet enough for all hands. It was a pretty sight watching the officers and bluejackets up to their necks in the water clearing the net from the coral in which it often became entangled, and then hauling in on both ends with a rattling good sea song...

There was a delightful little spot about a quarter of a cable from the stream, which ran up a little creek with beautiful clear, deep water, cut off from the rest by a sand spit. It was here the fires were lit for cooking the fish, the men bringing their hook pots filled with tea from the ship.

The trees overshadowing the place formed a shelter from the showers that frequently fell, rendering it dry and snug and, after several good hauls, all hands would congregate round the fires and eat their supper, keeping the mosquitos away with many a well-filled pipe; but there was no getting rid of the sandflies, which stung and tormented us unceasingly. Many of the men would prefer taking to the water, where they might be seen enjoying their smokes in peace, until the boatswain's pipe would summon them to one more haul before going off to the ship.

My dog, Punch, on these occasions would be quite in his element, rushing about in a state of the greatest excitement, barking at the fish as the seine came to the beach, splashing about in the water with the men, and firmly believing he was rendering the most valuable assistance to the party. It was only on these occasions he was allowed to land at the island, as a small dog belonging to the Commodore had fallen a victim to the gross appetites of the Erromangans." [22]

There were always a lot of keen fishermen on every ship and the biggest challenge was to hook a shark and, the more the brute struggled, the greater the thrill. Of a shark being hooked Captain Palmer of *HMS Rosario* wrote, "There is always great excitement when this happens although, of course, of frequent

287

occurrence in the tropics." [23] These sentiments were echoed by Lieutenant Hon. Fred Walpole of *HMS Collingwood*, "Catching a shark is, of course, a grand event; it is a fact even the most most uninterested must become acquainted with for....he leaves a smell, when fried, by no means pleasant." [24]

When *HMS Fly* was surveying near the Capricorn group, off central Queensland, there were numerous sharks "and of great size and strength". [25] One was hooked under the bows of the ship and, while still in the water, "was harpooned, pierced with a whale lance, and another very strong hook and line fastened in his jaws but, before a sufficiently large rope could be passed round his body to hoist him in by, he bent both the harpoon and the lance, disengaged himself from them and, breaking both lines, got away". [26] The ones that they did catch in these islands "were remarkable for their girth round the shoulders and capacity of mouth". [27] Sometimes, to speed things up, they would fire one or two rifle bullets into the shark.

When *HMS Curacoa* was at Niue Island in 1865 "The Commodore shot six sharks, of which there were a great many round the ship, some very large ones; two were caught with the hook but the natives did not appear afraid of them." [28]

When Captain Phillip King was surveying the north coast of Australia on the *Mermaid* in May, 1818, he and some others went ashore one evening to have a fire on the beach as there was plenty of wood nearby. They also fraternised with some aborigines, who were attracted by the fire. After returning to the *Mermaid* the sailors put a line over the side and hooked a shark "which, from the extraordinary capacity of its mouth and maw, could have swallowed one of them (the natives) with the greatest ease. On opening the animal we fully expected to discover the limbs of some of the natives....but we only found a crab, that had been so recently swallowed that some of our people made no hesitation in eating it for their supper". [29]

The actual method of catching a shark was described by Captain Palmer of the *Rosario*, who was writing of a successful hooking of one off the Fijian island of Viti Levu in April, 1869. "When one (a shark) is observed the boatswain's yeoman and the ship's steward are in instant request, the former for the shark-hook, which is supplied to every man-of-war, and the latter for a four pound piece of pork to bait it with. One of the small ropes is bent to the three feet piece of chain that is connected with the hook, and then thrown well out on the weather quarter. Soon we see the cautious monster smelling at it, together with one or two little blue pilot-fish which generally accompany him.

If he is hungry, it is not long before the white of his belly is seen as he turns over to swallow it; in another moment he is hooked, and then all hands are up to see him played and got on board.

Darting about from side to side, he is now and then allowed to dash away as far as the rope will let him, and then gradually hauled in till he is brought close under the counter exhausted. A running bow-line is then made round the line with a stouter rope, which is dexterously slipped down over his head....he is thus soon roused in over the taffrail with the caution of "Stand from under"; lashing out with his huge tail right and left, everybody keeping clear of him until a handspike from the after pivot-gun partially disables him, much to the wrath of the gunner who says the boatswain's handspikes are supplied for that sort of work, at which the latter grins. The place of execution is generally the lee-gaugway, when a sharp pointed knife inserted about a foot from his head penetrates his heart, severing also the vertebra and instantly paralysing him." [30]

When Captain Cook was exploring and charting the icy coast at the top of the Gulf of Alaska shortly before his death he came across some huge walruses. The boat's crew that he sent out managed to kill about twelve of them and they provided excellent fresh meat for the ship's company. As with the seals in New Zealand, their oil was used for the lamps. Another northern delicacy on this voyage was salmon and halibut, which the *Resolution's* parties caught in abundance off the island of Unalashka.

Thirteen years later, on Captain Vancouver's second voyage to North America, one of the officers, Thomas Manby, wrote of their celebrating George III's birthday on 4th June, "(We) partook of bear steaks, stew'd eagle and roasted mussels with as much glee as a City Alderman attacks his venison". [31] With all these new and exotic foods the job of cook on one of these vessels must have been every bit as challenging as that of captain.

In the Islands some of the fish that were caught were poisonous – as Captain Cook found out on his second voyage on *HMS Resolution* when he was in the New Hebrides and all the wardroom officers, several midshipmen and the carpenter became very ill from eating the fish that had been caught. They had acute headaches, spasms in the bowels, and diarrhoea and were vomiting over the gunwales into the calm blue sea. They couldn't do any duty for a week and so the watches had to be kept by the gunner and the boatswain. Mercifully, neither Captain Cook nor the doctor was affected as on the night in question the doctor had dined at the captain's table and they had been served different food.

In the tropics the officers often dined on the deck under the stars as it was too hot to be indoors. It was also only a short trip to the side in case of being served a helping of poisoned fish.

Not everybody recovered from poisoned seafood. When Vancouver's *HMS Discovery* was surveying in southern Alaska in 1793 one of the ship's boats was sent out to trace Mathieson's Inlet northwards. They were near the head of this deep bay when they stopped for breakfast, their day having begun at 4 a.m.

The normal rations were taken ashore from the small cutter and, as on several previous occasions, they prised some mussels off the rocks to supplement the meal. Unfortunately, Midshipman Barrie, who was in command of the cutter, and three of the men were stricken with acute food poisoning and one of the men, Carter, died within a matter of hours. Interestingly, this was the only death on the three voyages that Vancouver made to the north-west coast – not a bad record.

When he heard of what had happened Captain Vancouver forbade the eating of mussels for the rest of the voyage. And he made sure that nobody would ever forget it by naming nearby places Mussel Inlet, Carter Bay and Poison Cove.

Sometimes the sailors' fears of poisoned food were groundless. When *HMS Havannah* visited Fiji in August, 1849, her commander, Captain Erskine, visited Ngavinde, the Chief of the Fishermen and the second most powerful person in those beautiful islands. In Erskine's words, "As we approached his door, a party of men were engaged in taking out of a hot stone oven, constructed on one side of the pathway, a whole pig, intended for our entertainment....The pig was then brought in and presented to me and, having been, by my desire, cut up in Fijian fashion, portions were handed round, together with excellent yams, on banana leaves and flat pieces of wood. Being asked how the rest was to be disposed of, I begged those present to accept of a quarter, and desired the remainder to be sent down to the barge's crew. I heard afterwards that our men, having some suspicion that all was not right, had thrown it overboard, but we, who had had ocular proof of its identity, had found it tender, juicy and well-flavoured." [32]

There was no delicacy that the seamen savoured more than turtle. When Captain Cook arrived on Christmas Eve, 1777, at the group that he so aptly named Christmas Island he found an opening in the reef and sailed into the lagoon where he anchored in twenty fathoms of water. Parties were sent ashore to catch fish and turtles and, after a week's effort, they had 215 turtles that weighed from about 45 pounds up to 132 pounds. In Cook's words, "They were all of the green kind and perhaps as good as any in the world". [33]

When Captain Matthew Flinders was surveying the Gulf of Carpenteria at the top of Australia in December, 1802, he anchored his ship, *HMS Investigator*, at the bottom of the gulf to go ashore on one of the islands. Seeing evidence of turtles, he despatched Lieutenant Fowler and a landing party to spend the night ashore to see what they could catch. In the words of Captain Flinders, "Next morning (4th December) two boats went to bring off the officer and people with what had been caught but their success had been so great that it was necessary to hoist out the launch and it took nearly the whole day to get on board what the decks and holds could contain without impediment to the working of the ship...We contrived to stow away forty-six, the least of them weighing 250 pounds and the average about 300, besides which many were returned on shore and suffered to go away." [34] They were similar to but not the same as the green turtle and the ship's naturalist, Mr. Brown, thought that they were a hitherto undescribed species.

There were also bustards that seemed to live off the turtles and, when a turtle came out of its hole and ran down the beach to the sea, it seemed to be in a hurry to escape the bustards.

Yet another predator was the shark and one of the turtles that was hauled on to the *Investigator* had had a large, semi-circular piece taken out of it by a shark, which amounted to about one tenth of the turtle's size. While waiting for the turtles Flinders' men caught seven tiger sharks from the ship, each of them being between five and nine feet long.

Of the forty-six turtles that were taken on board, most were females and each had between four hundred and seven hundred eggs in them so that, if there were no predators like bustards, sharks, sailors and natives, one would probably have been able to walk across the Gulf of Carpenteria on their backs.

In the following season the same ship's company caught one that weighed 459 pounds and had 1,940 eggs. Not surprisingly Captain Flinders named this three mile island, on which they were caught, "Bountiful Island".

Considering the logistics of feeding a full ship's company in lands that were still being discovered the men did not fare too badly while the thrill of catching sharks, shooting pigs and trading for yams added an extra dimension to shopping for food which sounds a lot more exciting than buying your food in a supermarket.

Seamen from poor families in Britain were better fed in the Navy – and especially on the Australia station - than they would have been at home. When the *Curacoa* was in New Zealand's Manukau Harbour in 1863 to take its part in the Maori War the sailors were able to take oysters and other shellfish from the rocks as well as snapper and the odd shark from the deep. "We were fed very well on the whole," wrote Cecil Foljambe. [35] And he was the head of a noble house.

Every bit as important as food was the need to keep the casks of fresh water adequately supplied. When they ran low all sorts of means were employed to find the precious fluid. When the *Rosario* was off the island of Santa Cruz, above the New Hebrides, in 1872 "We experienced some very heavy rain squalls, which enabled us to collect a large amount of water, that commodity being very precious. It was rather amusing, on the approach of a shower, to witness the rush by all hands for baths and tubs, awnings being sloped, and every available means resorted to for the purpose of obtaining a large supply." [36]

Watering parties would be sent ashore to look for fresh supplies but they were not always successful. Even if they found a stream flowing into the sea they sometimes had to go up it a mile or so to find drinkable water. When they did find water they would frequently wash their clothes there as well.

When *HMS Fly* and her tenders were off central Queensland in 1843 they were down to only two or three weeks' supply so they sent a watering party in their pinnace to the Percy Islands but to no avail. They also tried sign language with the aborigines on the mainland, showing a cup and making a drinking gesture but this too was unsuccessful. As a last resort they struck into the bush a little and "came upon a watercourse, in which were several holes full of excellent water...The next day we went ashore to fill our breakers [casks] at the water holes and met three natives....By means of a force pump and hoses the casks could be filled on the beach, not far from where the boats were anchored, but, as the ship could not approach within much less than three miles of that spot, it was, of course, a rather protracted business." [37]

It could also be a dangerous business as Captain Cook, Captain King and others found out. On his second voyage to the Pacific Captain Cook sent a party ashore to get water on one of the Tongan islands. They found some and filled their casks but then, just as they were about to roll them down to the waiting launch, they were jostled by the natives, who stole one of the officer's guns and some tools. Through all this they managed to get the casks on to the launch but then Captain Cook arrived on the scene and decided that this, on top of an earlier theft of another gun, was the last straw and so he sent for the marines and ordered that the ship's guns be fired. He seized two of the natives' canoes and shot and wounded an islander who wouldn't let go of them. Upon this show of force the Tongans returned one of the stolen guns and an adze and so Cook restored their canoes while the *Resolution's* doctor treated the wounded Tongan.

Similarly, in August, 1891, when Captain Phillip Parker King was surveying the coast of northern Australia on the *Mermaid*, a watering party went ashore at Goulburn Island, near Port Essington. They were drawing water from a well when a shower of large stones were thrown at them by some natives from the top of a cliff. The ship's boat was moored just off shore and the sailors who were guarding it went for their muskets and fired a volley over the heads of the stone throwers. They scattered but after a time went to make another approach. Upon seeing them move in the direction of the watering party, the men back on the *Mermaid* raised her flag in warning so that the boatmen would be ready again with the muskets. Watering parties knew that they would be watched by men who were often hidden and they usually took the precaution of having an armed party at the ready.

Sources of water were particularly important for survey ships as they would mark them on the charts that they were creating for the convenience of mariners and these would be published by the Admiralty. On Lizard Island, off north Queensland, the diarist of *HMS Fly* noted, "On this plain (on Lizard Island) is a freshwater swamp, from which a small brook runs out to the beach, on the north-west side of the island, where there is a cove with a very good anchorage and where vessels may get an abundance of wood and water for their use and great convenience." [38] Just the type of information that a mariner in the vast spaces of the Barrier Reef and 1,500 miles from Sydney would value.

COLLECTING CURIOS

Upon returning to Sydney on 13th October, 1865, after a 9,284 mile cruise around the Pacific Islands Sub-Lieutenant Cecil Foljambe of *HMS Curacoa* wrote in his diary, "The Commodore (Wiseman) has got all his curiosities on shore and is going to exhibit them for the benefit of Bishop Patterson's Melanesian Mission". [1] Sub-Lieutenant Foljambe did not elaborate on what these "curiosities" were – presumably because he did not have enough ink in his pen to do so since Wiseman brought back not mere "curiosities" but a whole museum.

During this voyage, that included visits to Norfolk Island, the Solomons, New Hebrides, Fiji, Tonga, Samoa and Niue, Commodore Wiseman managed to collect no fewer than 1,246 items of artefacts, native clothing and native heads.

The collection included feathers, spears, stone adzes, war clubs, bows and arrows, fans, model canoes, fishing nets and hooks, bamboo baskets, kava bowls, combs, a battle axe made from the back-bone of a turtle, a chief's sunshade made out of the leaf of a fan palm, mother-of-pearl spoons, sponges, carved canoe paddles made from mother-of-pearl and even a full canoe.

On the hair front he managed to score the "hair of a Fijian chief", which would have been rather impressive in view of their fuzzy tops, and "a woman's back hair" (presumably she was allowed to keep her front hair).

From the island of San Cristobal in the Solomons came, in Wiseman's words, "the skull of a bushman who was speared, clubbed and eaten". [2] There were also twenty-five skulls that had been hanging together in a canoe house "like so many coconuts". The teeth had been taken out to be used as ornaments.

"The natives of the Solomon Islands are supposed to be the most treacherous and bloodthirsty of any known savages," wrote the *Sydney Morning Herald*. "They are the most inveterate cannibals and apparently their sole object in life is to get each other's heads. They are not, however, a courageous race, rarely, if ever, fighting openly but attacking suddenly and from the rear." [3]

From Rewa in Fiji had come the skull of a chief's wife, who had been strangled nine years earlier at the time of her husband's death. Like suttee in India, the custom for a dutiful wife was to find a kind relation to strangle her so that she could accompany her husband into the next life. It had to be done on the same day as the husband's death and, if there were no "kind relations" on hand, she would strangle herself.

At this time the Pacific was a whole new frontier and it is little wonder that there was so much interest in its fauna, flora and other products. Among those on board the *Curacoa* during this long cruise to the islands were a botanist (Mr. Veitch), a naturalist, a birdstuffer, a photographer and a conchologist. The last mentioned was a specialist in shells – the ones you pick up on the beach and not the ones that warships fire at the enemy.

This conchologist dredged for shells at various places during the cruise while Mr. Veitch collected orchids from a mountain in Samoa and on one occasion walked twenty-eight miles in the tropical heat to get some other flowers. [4] When Veitch got back to Sydney he exhibited what he had collected at a Flower Show in Sydney's Royal Botanic Gardens and "notwithstanding their voyage, they looked very fresh and healthy". [5]

What was collected was often given to public institutions. In 1850 Hon. Captain Keppel of *HMS Maeander* gave about fifty species of rare shells – marine, freshwater and terrestrial – to the Royal Society of Van Diemen's Land in Hobart. He had collected them over the years on the Chinese coast, at Borneo, New Ireland and in the adjacent seas. Another collection of dried and preserved Pacific shells was presented by Lieutenant Ferguson of *HMS Blanche* to Wellington's Colonial Museum in 1873 while the same institution received the skulls of some seals that were brought by the officers of the *Blanche* from the Auckland Islands in 1871.

When *HMS Fly* was surveying the southern coast of New Guinea in 1845 its officers shot some colourful and interesting looking birds which they donated to the British Museum.

Ironically, in view of his own death from a poisoned arrow, Commodore Goodenough took a keen interest in the poisonous and stinging fish of the Pacific and he preserved in spirits a specimen of the dreaded and ugly n'ou fish of the Hervey group of islands and then submitted it to an analyst.

It was not difficult to obtain curios as the natives were usually willing to trade and often brought their wares out in canoes and then took them on board, the man-of-war's deck becoming a veritable market place. When *HMS Fawn* was at Niue (then called Savage Island) in 1862 the natives rowed out in their canoes to the ship, climbed up ropes that were lowered down to them and set up little stalls all along the deck, offering "pigs, bananas, Malay apples, coconuts, spears and other articles of commerce". [6]

In the words of Mr. T.H. Hood, an Australian settler who was travelling as a guest on the *Fawn*, "We soon found they had a 'pretty smart idea' of the value of a 'tanna', as they had learned to call a shilling, and of doing business – gained, no doubt, by their intercourse with whalers sailing under the Stars and Stripes, which we found were now constantly in the habit of coming here for supplies.

Instead of the uncouth, ferocious savages we had expected, we found them pleasant, good looking fellows, of a light olive complexion, with well shaped features, quite sufficiently attired for the climate, very merry and happy but quiet and well-behaved. The younger men were ready for any lark and, after being decorated in fantastic style in the forecastle with red and green paint, some of them danced with great glee, and in good time, to the jigs and hornpipes played by the ship's musician." [7]

From time to time naval vessels carried live creatures and plants from one place to another. When Captain Phillip arrived with the First Fleet to start Australia in 1788 he had a breeding stock on board that consisted of one bull, four cows, one bull-calf, one stallion, three mares and three colts. While travelling to Australia on *HMS Sirius* he had put in at Rio de Janeiro and the Cape of Good Hope, collecting at both places fruit trees for the orchard that he was to create near his house on the east side of Sydney Cove. These included grapes, figs, oranges, apples and pears.

In 1792, when the storeship *Daedalus* was returning from North America to Sydney after taking provisions to Captain Vancouver and his two ships, she took back to the convict colony cattle and sheep that had been given by the Spanish commandant in California, Senor Quada, at the behest of Captain Vancouver, who knew that New South Wales was in dire need of livestock to feed its fairly unproductive population.

Not all the creatures on these modern "Noah's Arks" were for eating or breeding as most vessels had a "ship's pet" – a dog, cat, parrot, goat, etc. – which brought some welcome domesticity into life on board a man-of-war. Dogs and cats were the most useful as they killed rats and mice and served as an outlet for the affections of the sailors in the sometimes grim environment of a warship. Jack was known for his kindness to animals – a very British trait. In the words of Captain Henry Keppel of *HMS Salamis*, "There are few ships without a favourite dog – in *Salamis* Suttie has one Carlo, an intelligent mongrel and great favourite. On shore he can take his own part, although not too big. He is besides a good pointer as well as a retriever." [8]

Unfortunately, when the *Salamis* left Singapore on 15th April, 1858, "there was consternation on board on its being discovered that Carlo was nowhere to be found. His description was written out and a reward offered on shore for his recovery." [9] They feared for his life since it was the season in Singapore when the police had been ordered to destroy all stray dogs.

Anyway a lost dog could not be allowed to interrupt the smooth running of a vessel under way and so everyone got on with their tasks and, upon passing the small Nipa Palm islands, Captain Keppel decided to give the gunners some firing practice.

Upon the first cartridge being fired Carlo sprang forth to everyone's delight. He had somehow got himself locked in the magazine, which had not been opened since the previous Sunday. "How he existed or what his feelings were in that atmosphere he knows best," wrote Captain Keppel. "If I had not fancied the Nipa Palm for a target, poor Carlo might have been smothered or starved to death." [10]

Of course, in places like Singapore and Hong Kong one had to be particularly watchful of a dog to make sure that it didn't finish up on the plate at a Chinese banquet. When the wife of Governor Patten of Hong Kong was taking her two dogs, Whisky and Soda, for a walk in Mid Levels, Hong Kong, in the 1990s one of them was lured away, never to be seen again. "Probably finished up on Deng Xiaoping's plate," opined the Australian Foreign Minister, Gareth Evans, at a press conference.

There were so many ship's pets, in fact, that in a little corner next to the Fitzroy Dock on Cockatoo Island in Sydney harbour there was a small cemetery for them. Many little stones over the graves were adorned with memorial verses in honour of departed favourites. For example, the epitaph for Bill the Goat of *HMS Lizard* was as follows:

Here lays the remains of Bill the goat,
Who had no rum to oil his throat.
He joined the teetotallers for a change,
And died that night on the ship's cook's range.

Bill the Goat was not the only pet to come to grief in the galley. In the words of Captain George Palmer of *HMS Rosario*, writing as his ship was heading from Sydney to New Caledonia in March, 1869, "The pets of the *Rosario* were at one time very numerous and consisted of a bear, four cats, a kangaroo, a sea gull, a bittern, four dogs, a canary, together with a black rabbit – a truly happy family. Time had however thinned their numbers, accelerated by turpentine....it appears bluejackets regard a good dose of turpentine, accompanied with a rubbing down before the galley-fire, as the grand cure for all complaints which animals are heir to. The kangaroo had a dose, not feeling well, and gave up the ghost in front of the range.

This was the first victim of the sick-bay man's skill. The Australian bear, belonging to the first-lieutenant, was a tailless animal but made up for it by a pair of enormous ears, like an elephant. This little beast was always wanting to go aloft, and had to be put under restraint in his explorations after gum leaves in the main-top....This morning he was discovered by the captain of the mizen-top on the after-gratings, as flat as a pancake, under a possum rug which some person had been sleeping on....

Two of the cats, Jack and Ginger, were of opposite dispositions....Jack went aloft every morning with the captain of the main-top, who was his particular chum, and there was a general howl of lamentation throughout the ship when he disappeared mysteriously one morning, it is supposed in the coal-hulk, which had been alongside the ship at Auckland, into the holds of which he had been foraging for rats.

When in harbour both these cats frequently fell overboard, when they would immediately swim to the screw-well, get on the banjo, and mew loudly until the quartermaster of the watch came to their assistance. Ginger ultimately vanished one night while chasing a rat overboard but, as we were at sea, her fate was not known with certainty until the next day.

There was a certain wild cat who lived on rats down below and was never seen. In the dead of night scuffles and squeaks would be heard in the neighbourhood of the screw alley, and sundry unearthly noises would come from behind the boilers." [11]

In the early 1890s when the British squadron was steaming out of the Chinese port of Chefoo "a little black cat fell overboard from *HMS Wanderer*. At once the ship stopped and signalled to the rest of the fleet 'Cat overboard', and the entire squadron came to a standstill. A boat put off from the *Wanderer* and rescued puss who was swimming for dear life after the ship. The sailors would have been furious if the cat had not been saved for, not only was she a great pet, but they firmly believed that disaster would follow if a black cat was allowed to drown." [12]

All this ended in 1975 when the Navy fell prey to the "health and safety" killjoys who banned all animals on Her Majesty's vessels for reasons of "hygiene". So now, without the ship's cat, the rats are able to run riot – especially in Asian ports. Hardly a promotion of "hygiene"!

In 1862 *HMS Miranda* sailed from Hummock's Island, off the north-west tip of Tasmania, to Auckland with some rabbits, that were released in New Zealand. On the return voyage she took back some pheasants that were set free on Hummock's Island. [13] These birds had been introduced to New Zealand from England.

In October, 1864, *HMS Curacoa* (Commodore Wiseman) took a virtual menagerie from Sydney to New Zealand for the Governor of New Zealand, Sir George Grey. There were sixteen kangaroos and wallabies, fourteen black swans, two emus, some wonga-wongas (Australian pigeons) and an Australian magpie "which can whistle several times and talk a little". [14]

One of the kangaroos broke loose at sea and ran around the deck whereupon one of Commodore Wiseman's dogs started barking. This so frightened the roo that he jumped right off the ship into the Tasman Sea.

When a vessel was "homeward bound" the number of pets – especially exotic ones – tended to increase as bluejackets liked to take some living specimen home to their families. One could imagine a sailor leaving a wife and young children for a three year spell in the Pacific and asking the little ones what they would like him to bring them back since, in the matter of pets, there seemed to be no limits.

When *HMS Rodney* was ordered home from the China station in 1869 she had been cruising off the Russian Pacific coast. In the words of Rear-Admiral Henry Keppel, "She being ordered home, had all sorts of live animals. Among them were two bears, who had the run of the ship. In the summer months hammocks were little used; the bears lay where they liked, the men using them as pillows. Each bear would accommodate ten or a dozen at a time. By day they were all over the place, generally aloft, in the tops or along the yards, from which they could see every arrival on board." [15]

Keppel's four year old daughter, May, was on board at the time. "While on the poop she found herself rolling around the deck in the embrace of a bear she had not before seen. Of course, she was immediately released. She knew not what fear was. The next moment she had seized one of the mizzen-topmast broomsticks, and the bear made the best of its way aloft. He was a young Siberian given (to) me," wrote Rear-Admiral Keppel. [16]

If a homeward bound sailor couldn't get his hands on a bear, there were usually plenty of exotic birds to impress the folks back in Britain. When the same ship (*HMS Rodney*) was in Castries Bay, on Russia's Pacific coast, in the same year, the sailors went ashore on picnics and, in the words of Rear-Admiral Keppel, "I had much difficulty in preventing the men from taking numerous young birds that were found in the holes and crevices of rocks, Jack always fancying that because the small things opened their mouths and he could feed and rear them. The greatest number were a species of diver about the size of a widgeon, with the brightest orange-coloured legs and beak, with ornamental horns and plumes on each side of the head; the plumage black; eye, light green with small black spot in the centre; narrow red edge to eyelid." [17] By the time the ship reached Singapore Keppel was given "a pair of cassowaries to add to the museum on board *Rodney*." [18]

However, it should be remembered that these were men-of-war and there could be risks for the pets. When *HMS Glasgow*, operating in South American waters, was "homeward bound" for Britain in 1914 her sailors collected about fifty amazing looking parrots to take home as pets. They were placed in cages on board and were fed by their owners. The *Glasgow* was suddenly ordered to join Admiral Cradock's squadron to hunt the German cruisers, *Scharnhorst* and *Gneisnau*, and, when battle was about to be commenced off Coronel, the parrots were released in the hope that they would fly to the Chilean shore, which was not far away.

They flew up from the deck in a blaze of colour – green, orange, blue – but, instead of heading to the safety of land, they perched on the upper works of the ship and were deaf to all entreaties to shoo them away.

As soon as the German shells started to arrive on or near the *Glasgow* – about six hundred of them altogether – the poor birds clung in terror to the yards and arms of the ship's two tall masts, screeching and squawking as the battle raged all around them.

300

Obviously not intended by nature for this weird human activity, they began to fall on to the deck where they were either swept overboard or trampled on by running feet. Two of them settled on a six inch gun barrel and stayed there until they fell off unconscious. Only ten of these beautiful birds survived the battle.

Plants, especially fruit and vegetables, were transported around the Pacific by the Navy. We have already seen how Captain Bligh took the *Bounty* to Tahiti for the purpose of collecting young breadfruit saplings to grow in the Caribbean and, although he didn't accomplish the task on the *Bounty*, the Admiralty later gave him the command of another vessel, *HMS Providence*, which, with its escort ship, the appropriately named *HMS Assistance*, he took to Tahiti and the West Indies to accomplish what he had been unable to do on the *Bounty*.

Sweet potatoes were introduced to Hawaii in 1849 when Captain Courtenay brought them from Peru in *HMS Constance*. Many plants were taken to the islands of the South Pacific from Sydney's Royal Botanic Gardens in order to help feed the people and get their economies going "and rare indeed were the occasions that a British warship, bound for the Islands, went away without a case or two (of seeds or plants) from Sydney". [19]

This was a two way trade as the men-of-war brought back many exotic plants from the South Seas to the Royal Botanic Gardens in Sydney; some were even taken all the way back to England on a returning Navy vessel and given to the Royal Botanical Gardens at Kew. The first of these were the hundreds of new and exotic plants that the naturalists, Joseph Banks and Daniel Solander, brought back from Tahiti, New Zealand and Australia on the *Endeavour*.

The *Endeavour's* botanists tried to keep the plants fresh with wet cloths and, if they wilted and died, then at least the ship's artists would have done a coloured drawing of them. In a two week period one draughtsman on the *Endeavour* made ninety-four sketches of different plants. [20]

When Captain Matthew Flinders took the *Investigator* to Australia in 1801 she carried not only a botanist, Robert Brown, and two botanical artists but also a pre-fabricated greenhouse that was taken on board at Sheerness and stowed in pieces. When the vessel reached Australia the greenhouse was put together on the quarter deck and planks were sawn up to make boxes to put the plants in. When the ship got back to Sydney after circumnavigating Australia the plants that had been collected were put in the gardens of Government House until such time as they could be taken to Kew.

When the *Mermaid* was carrying out its survey at the Endeavour River, north Queensland, in 1819, the botanist, Mr. Cunningham, "in return for the plants he collected, sowed peach and apricot stones in many parts near the banks". [21]

Salmon were introduced to Tasmania in 1864 when *HMS Victoria* took the first living ova from Melbourne to Hobart. They arrived on 20th April, 1864, and two days later were deposited in the gravel beds, which had been prepared at the River Plenty. On 5th May Tasmania's first salmon was hatched and the process continued until 15th June, by which time it was estimated that there were about 3,000 of the wee fry.

DIVERSE TASKS

As the primary force in British colonies in the Pacific in their formative years the Royal Navy played so many diverse roles that life on board the warships was never dull. The Navy laid cables, transported missionaries, shipped gold, designed harbours, fought fires, rescued merchant seamen, erected observatories, conducted a census on Pitcairn, and took Governors and royal personages to their destinations amidst much splendour and pageantry.

In the mid nineteenth century Britain's Pacific colonies were being connected not only by steamer routes but also by telegraph cables, many of which had to be laid under the sea.

In 1861 there arrived in Canterbury, New Zealand, a telegraph engineer of energy and ability. He was Birmingham born Alfred Sheath, who had had ten years of practical experience with Britain's Electric Telegraph Company and the Red Sea and Indian Telegraph Company. He immediately set to work and created New Zealand's first telegraph between Christchurch and its port of Lyttelton. He then supervised the construction of lines from Christchurch to Invercargill and Christchurch to Picton and Nelson. It was now time for Mr. Sheath, who was by now the Government's Telegraph Engineer, to carry the line under Cook Strait and to build a telegraph system in the North island which, because of the more rugged terrain and native wars, lagged behind the South Island in this and other respects.

Cook Strait was quite a challenge for cable layers as, besides being very deep, it is also one of the roughest channels in the world; one may leave Wellington harbour when it is as calm as a millpond but, upon entering the strait, there is invariably a heavy swell for a vessel to plough through. So, it is hardly surprising that the first effort to lay a submarine telegraph across this turbulent stretch of water on 7th August, 1866, ended in failure.

Lieutenant Wiseman and twenty-five sailors from *HMS Esk* were assigned to the expedition and they were given a gratuity of £1 a head by the government for their services. Their job was to assist in the uncoiling of the cable from the tank on the barge, that was towed across the route by a steamer.

The *Esk* herself provided back-up support for the expedition, which left Wellington at 10 p.m. on 6th August and worked through the night. They began by securing the cable to the station house at Lyall Bay beach, just outside Wellington Heads, and then unrolling it across the thirty-three miles of strait to the other side. The cable was one and three quarters of an inch in diameter and contained three conductors, around which was wrapped a coating of hemp.

Unfortunately, when they were half way across, one coil adhered to the adjoining one so tightly that it could not be freed in time to prevent its dragging the layer out of position with the result that the fouled cable came tearing through the machinery on deck "and the damaged cable was flying through the conducting gear astern, stripped of its covering and gradually becoming wrenched and torn like pack thread until it parted". [1] Some of the *Esk's* sailors brought up buckets of sea water to throw over parts of the machinery that were overheating in the wreckage.

The expedition was forced to return to Wellington, their hopes dashed. A month later, on 4th September, a second attempt was made to link New Zealand's two islands by submarine cable, this time successfully.

Meanwhile *HMS Salamander* was busy taking soundings for a submarine telegraph from Australia's Cape York to Java and ten years later in 1871 *HMS Basilisk* (Captain John Moresby) took soundings for the proposed cable between Australia and New Zealand. With a line and apparatus supplied by the Sydney Postal Telegraphic Company he began by laying out 1,700 fathoms of line north-west of Sydney Heads but without obtaining any bottom. Unfortunately the line broke by its own weight and both line and apparatus were lost to the deep. The laying of cables under the sea was never an easy task.

The biggest cable challenge in the Pacific was the laying of the cable from Vancouver Island down to the Antipodes. The first choice of a relay station was Necker Island, an uninhabited rock north-west of Hawaii, as it was in the direct line of the cable. Accordingly, in the early 1890s *HMS Champion* took soundings in depths of up to 12,000 fathoms (about 13 miles) and prepared charts of the area.

Unfortunately the United States government made a claim on Necker on the most spurious of grounds. The Senate, still with a chip on its shoulder from the Revolutionary War and determined to do Britain down at every opportunity, gave an adverse vote and it soon became obvious that Necker was not worth a row with America's tetchy government.

304

The next choice was Fanning Island (nine miles by four) and, to avoid complications with Washington, Britain very sensibly annexed it in 1888 along with Suwarrow, Christmas and Penrhyn Islands.

In 1899 the 940 ton screw surveying vessel, *HMS Egeria*, took a line of soundings from Vancouver Island almost as far as Fanning Island and the following year the cable laying began. It went from Port San Juan on Vancouver Island to Fanning and then on to Fiji and Norfolk Island, from where one line went to Brisbane and the other to New Zealand. Thus was created the Pacific Cable.

No less tricky than the Americans were the missionaries who sometimes got the publicly funded Navy to give them protection as they swanned around the islands in their classy schooners. "*HMS Havannah* may shortly be expected with the Lord Bishop of New Zealand (Selwyn) from New Caledonia, it having been arranged that that vessel, after visiting the Navigator Islands (Samoa), should meet His Lordship in his schooner, *Undine*, at the Isle of Pines," wrote Auckland's *Southern Cross* in 1849. [2]

The following year Bishop Selwyn still had the Navy at his beck and call when he got *HMS Fly* to accompany him on yet another voyage of the *Undine* around the Islands. It seems that Selwyn, who had rowed for Cambridge in the first ever Boat Race, had the Navy round his little finger. He managed to get the New South Wales government to grant his Melanesian Mission free of charge a thousand of the best acres on Norfolk Island and then, when it was time to put up the buildings, he got *HMS Falcon* to carry all the materials up from Auckland. [3] If the Navy would not dance to the tune of the Anglican missionaries in the South Pacific, then the bishops in the House of Lords would make a noise and that was usually more than the Admiralty, with all its power and might, was prepared to face.

The Navy even carried judges around their circuits. In December, 1818, Captain Phillip Parker King took *HMS Mermaid* from Sydney to Hobart and back again with Mr. Justice Field, a judge of the Supreme Court, on board both ways – presumably so that the old geezer could go down to Tasmania and hang a few more convicts.

A more appropriate passenger was a Governor and these exalted personages usually travelled around their fiefdoms on a warship, with the guns on board firing a nineteen gun salute whenever they entered a harbour.

When Lord Hopetoun, the first Governor-General of the Commonwealth of Australia, sailed to Sydney at the beginning of his term in December, 1900, on board *HMS Royal Arthur*, the ocean liners and intercolonial steamers followed *HMS Porpoise* and *HMS Archer* out of Sydney harbour to meet him.

After clearing the Heads they saw the *Royal Arthur* appear on the horizon about 9 a.m. under a full head of steam. "The sight was impressive as the fleet manoeuvred to allow the *Royal Arthur* to pass between the lines. When the incoming vessel was abreast of the first two warships she turned outward and fired a salute, the succeeding vessels performing the same manoeuvre." stated a press report of the occasion. [4]

Inside the harbour "With the noble panorama of the Botanical Gardens and Government House grounds, the bright flowers and foliage as the foreground, and the wooded hills on the opposite side of the harbour as the background, countless thousands of people lined the wide sweep of the foreshore and a crowded flotilla dotted the waters of the bay.

The flagship followed by the escort vessels put the finale to a magnificent spectacle as she swept between the long lines of steamers and sailing vessels, gaily decorated with bunting and moored on each side of the harbour, to her anchorage at Farm Cove. The Governor-General was transferred to a pinnace and landed amid a booming salute of nineteen guns fired from the forts, and the cheers of a great concourse of people." [5]

A lot of the problems in the Pacific were created by the crusading and manipulative missionaries and there were times when the Navy was called in to clean up the mess. When *HMS Actaeon* arrived in Honolulu in 1836, her captain, Hon. Lord Edward Russell, was asked by the local residents to rectify some of their many grievances. The twenty-one year old native king was a greedy drunkard, whom the missionaries encouraged in his vices so that he would do their bidding. Nobody's property was safe and, when one died, the estate went to the king, with the most valuable pieces of land usually finishing up in the hands of the missionaries.

Russell and his officers spent much time and effort settling new regulations, giving the people greater rights and security. The young king was definitely impressed by a British warship. At this time in the Pacific the only force that could trump the power of the missionaries was the Royal Navy. And the Navy was a far more positive factor in the Pacific in the nineteenth century than the missionaries, whose main attribute was to seize power and land behind the cloak of a very superficial form of Christianity.

The situation between Catholic and Wesleyan missionaries on Wallis Island, north-east of Fiji, became so explosive that, when *HMS North Star* visited the island in 1844, it found the natives divided into two hostile parties, one led by mischievous Catholic priests and the other by equally mischievous Wesleyan missionaries.

It was like Belfast on a Saturday night after a Rangers-Celtic match and the *North Star's* captain, Sir Everard Home Bt., and his officers had to spend several days on the island trying to restore peace between the two sides. In the words of Auckland's *Southern Cross*, "What a pity that the propagators of the Christian religion should so much neglect its spirit while they dwell so much upon its empty forms. It is a sad delusion to suppose that Christianity consists in a knowledge of the forms and ceremonies of the Church of Rome, of England, or any other country; and how absurd in Missionaries to perplex the simple minds of the natives with the formal and ceremonial part of religion while its great truths and general principles, on which all might be agreed, are considered as minor things." [6]

The Navy sometimes had to settle disputes between whalers. In September, 1838, *HMS Pelorus* arrived at Cloudy Bay, near the top of the South Island of New Zealand, to find a row taking place between the crew of an American whaling ship and one of the shore whaling gangs over their respective rights to a whale which the shore gang had in its possession and refused to give up. The American vessel had cleared for action and was about to fire on the shore men when the white sails and ensign of the *Pelorus* were seen approaching from the north. The captain of the *Pelorus*, Lieutenant Chetwode, managed to settle the argument by a combination of tact and the threat of superior fire power. During this voyage to New Zealand waters some two years before those anarchic islands became a British colony the *Pelorus* left her name in the Pelorus Sound and Pelorus River while Lieutenant Chetwode is remembered by the name of the nearby Chetwode Islands.

Lieutenant Chetwode's tact at Cloudy Bay was typical of naval captains throughout the Pacific. When Captain Elliot of *HMS Fly* visited Pitcairn Island in 1838 he had to deal with complaints from the islanders about the lack of organised authority. Not only did he raise the Union Jack to bring the island under British jurisdiction but he also arranged for the election of a magistrate (or elder), which would be held on the first day of each year with all the residents over the age of eighteen – both male and female – having a vote; this was probably the first experiment of female suffrage in the Pacific. The magistrate was to be assisted by a council of two, one elected and the other nominated by the elected magistrate. The magistrate was to report to the captains of H.M. ships on their visits and to keep a register of proceedings and of general events on the island. Captain Elliot drew up these regulations and had them signed on board the *Fly* on 30th November, 1838.

In the words of Sir Charles Lucas in his Introduction to *The Pitcairn Island Register Book*, "The visit of the *Fly* brought a more organised life among these primitive citizens and it was initiated by one of the captains of Her Majesty's ships. All the world over, from generation to generation, those in command of the ships of the Royal Navy have added to protection of outlying bits of the British Empire, the functions of advisors, arbitrators, and friends in need of their inhabitants, applying kindly good sense and the proverbial handiness of the sailor to patient solution of endless petty problems, such as cause discord and discontent in small communities cut off from the outside world."[7]

Not all problems were as easy to solve as those of Pitcairn. When in August, 1891, the forces of the Congressional Party in Chile ousted the Balmacedists in a bloody battle, the victors occupied Valparaiso. A series of outrages followed which became so bad that the British and other foreign warships in the harbour had to send parties ashore to protect the consulates and properties of their nationals. About a hundred and fifty men from *HMS Champion* and the sloop *HMS Daphne* landed to guard the British consulate and to perform some much needed police duties. When the desperate Balmacedist leader tried to fire on civilians from two machine guns Captain St. Clair of *HMS Champion* joined the American and French commanders and stood in front of the guns, thereby dissuading the hot-headed Balmacedist leader from firing, and so preventing a massacre.

A more profitable "assistance to the civil power" was undertaken by the officers and ratings of *HMS Herald* during her long survey voyage in the late 1850s. Various Chinese had been smuggling gold into Sydney without paying duty on it and, since they put up spirited resistance to the customs officers, the Navy was called in. Not only was the gold confiscated but much of it was given to the ship's company of the *Herald* as "prize".

308

During the Victoria gold rush Her Majesty's vessels, with their guns for protection, were sometimes given the task of taking the gold to England. For example, in March, 1852, at the height of the Mount Alexander rush in Victoria, *HMS Havannah* took on board 1,298 ounces of the precious metal and delivered it safely to England.

When, during the First Opium War in 1841, the Chinese government paid an indemnity of six million silver dollars in compensation for damage to British property at Canton, the money was packed on to *HMS Conway* and *HMS Calliope*, which immediately took the precious cargo to British territory, one warship sailing to England and the other to Calcutta.

Sometimes the Navy assisted the development of a gold field. When a prospecting party went to Sud Est Island, off the south-east coast of New Guinea, in 1888, they were returned to the Queensland port of Cooktown (a distance of 400 miles) by *HMS Swinger*, which also carried a portion of quartz that was taken back to Australia for assay. While at Sud Est the *Swinger* towed another vessel, the *Hygeia*, carrying twenty prospectors, across to Wolla Island, which was found to contain veins of quartz.

When a fire broke out late at night in Wellington in April, 1882, and swept through several buildings of the inner city, "a crew of thirty men with an engine were sent ashore from *HMS Miranda* and rendered excellent service in extinguishing the flames. At one time these seamen were heartily cheered by the crowd for their plucky efforts to get the fire under (control)." [8] At this time not every town had a fire brigade and the disciplined service of the Navy would often fill the breach.

On 16th May, 1891, a whole block of commercial buildings went up in flames in Suva, Fiji, and "the business portion of the town seemed doomed to destruction. The efforts of the townspeople, with the miserable plant at their disposal, were utterly useless to check the spread of the fire, and despair was seizing upon all when, with a ringing cheer, a band of about eighty bluejackets from *HMS Cordelia* dashed the spectators aside and in a moment had their engine under way and a brisk stream of water playing on the burning buildings. The bluejackets, under the command of Captain Grenfell, Lieutenant Spearman, Mr. Broughton and several midshipmen, took charge of affairs and, aided by another detachment of a hundred men from the ship, brought fire buckets and all the fire paraphernalia of the vessel into use. The bluejackets were the means of saving the buildings at the Pier Street corner of the block; indeed, but for their efforts it is almost beyond the shadow of a doubt that the town would have gone….the fire was got under (control) about 9.30." [9]

No less valuable than the firefighting crews were the divers. When the mail steamer *Macgregor* ran aground on a reef near Kandavu, Fiji, in 1874, her captain tried everything to refloat her but without success. In the words of the *Sydney Morning Herald*, "The whole of the cargo and coal were thrown overboard, but this had no effect in floating her….*HMS Pearl* then came to his assistance, Commodore Goodenough being most kind in placing at Captain Grainger's disposal his gear and crew. The successful method used by which the *Macgregor* was floated was as follows: - The *Pearl* laid out 160 fathoms of her bower chain, and from her stern passed on board of the *Macgregor* 115 fathoms of the second bower, which was then hove taut. The result was that the weight of the chain connecting the sterns of the two ships, together with the swell of the ocean setting into the harbour and acting on the heavy hull of the *Pearl*, drew the *Macgregor* off without the assistance of steam." [10]

When the merchantman *Eli Whitney* sank in Wellington harbour it was "a dangerous obstruction to the navigation of the harbour" [11] and so in July, 1879, *HMS Emerald* sent a diver down to examine it. He found that the hulk was completely broken up, with the stem lying near the stern. He fastened some gear to the stem and it was hauled up and brought ashore. A few days later the men of the *Emerald* let off some explosives in order to clear this unwanted obstruction.

The Navy also picked up shipwrecked sailors. For example, in 1844 the *Prince George*, the tender of *HMS Fly* during her survey of northern Australia, picked up the crew of the *Lady Grey*, which had been wrecked on the Alert reefs in Torres Strait, and took them to Singapore, and the following year the *Fly* herself took fifty-five of the shipwrecked crews of the merchantmen *Coringa Packet* and *Hyderabad*, which had been wrecked near Torres Strait, to Singapore. It seems that half the wrecks in the Pacific were in Torres Strait.

In 1888 *HMS Hyacinth* brought two shipwrecked crews into Honolulu, fifteen from the German ship *Hermann* and eight from a Swedish barque, *Virgo*. These two vessels had been at Malden Island, south of Christmas Island, loading guano (the excrement of birds that was used as manure) and on 27th November, 1888, a heavy westerly gale set in and drove both ships on to the reef even though they were strongly moored. They were both total wrecks but sufficient provisions were got from the *Hermann* to feed the survivors until *HMS Hyacinth* arrived on the scene on 14th December.

Not all searches for shipwrecked sailors were as successful as this one. There was, in fact, a black hole in the Pacific and that was the east coast of the island of Formosa (Taiwan) and those who were unlucky enough to be wrecked there did not survive to tell the tale. By 1858 the situation of these lost merchant seamen was so bad that the Navy sent *HMS Inflexible* on a visit to the island to find out what was happening – rather like the attempts of the United States government to find out the fate of those unfortunate American pilots who were shot down over North Vietnam and never heard of again.

The captain of the *Inflexible*, Commander Brooker, had about four hundred proclamations printed, offering monetary rewards for any Europeans who may be found or any clue as to their whereabouts, and these he distributed wherever he went on the island. At the time the Chinese controlled the western part of the island while the mountainous east coast was inhabited by the native aborigines, whom the Chinese regarded as savages.

Commander Brooker cruised around the island, occasionally going ashore with an armed party to distribute his proclamations – but to no avail. Upon encountering the "wild aborigines" who had been described to him in such lurid detail by the Chinese, he wrote, "Having now seen these savages and the determined manner they would have attacked us even under the fire of the ship, I can not think that any foreigners, if wrecked on the East side, could escape from the clutches of these barbarians." [12]

Although *HMS Inflexible* did a complete circuit of the island, surveying much of it at the same time, they did not find any shipwrecked sailors, leading Commander Brooker to conclude, "either there are no Europeans on the island or, if there are, they are secreted away amongst the aborigines, which I can scarcely believe, for I think they are too bloodthirsty and savage a race to spare the life of a white man five minutes after one fell into their hands." [13]

When the merchant barque *Rover* was wrecked at Formosa in 1867 the locals captured and later murdered the captain and his wife (newly married), and the crew. Only one Chinaman managed to escape and he it was who told the tale to Captain Broad of *HMS Cormorant* at Amoy, one of the treaty ports in China. The *Cormorant* set out immediately to the bay where the captured crew were reported to be, and its whaleboat and cutter went ashore with armed men. They were immediately fired upon and so Captain Broad ordered them back to the ship.

Assuming - correctly – that the *Rover's* crew had been murdered, the captain ordered the firing of shells on to the thickly wooded foreshore. These people were headhunters who had recently fired into the boats of *HMS Swallow*. The fate of the *Rover's* crew simply reaffirmed Formosa's reputation as the most savage island in the whole Pacific. And that's saying something!

Another search that failed was that for Sir John Franklin, who was lost in the Arctic wastes while making one last search for that elusive North-West Passage. The Navy stationed *HMS Rattlesnake* at Port Clarence on the Bering Strait as a supply base for the expedition that was looking for Franklin. This task went on for years, mainly as a result of pressure from his persevering wife.

Another occasional task of the sailors was construction. When Captain Edward Stanley sailed *HMS Calliope* into Auckland harbour at the beginning of the 1840s he was so inconvenienced at finding that there was no wharf to tie up at that he offered to put his men to work to build one if the government would pay them "the trifling consideration of ten pence per diem" [14] but "the generous offer was disdained". [15]

The bluejackets were able to build more than wharves; 1n 1847 Captain Owen Stanley of *HMS Rattlesnake* erected an astronomical observatory near Sydney pursuant to instructions from England and a month later he went down to Twofold Bay in southern New South Wales "for the purpose of fixing a site there for the erection of a Customs house." [16]

When, in 1912, it was decided to put adequate lighthouses on the Queensland coast from Cape Moreton to Torres Strait the government engaged Commander Brewis of the Royal Navy to carry out an investigation and make the appropriate recommendations. These were acted upon with the result that an extra thirty-four lights were added to the existing thirty.

There was no more enjoyable task for the Navy than to escort members of the Royal Family on their visits to the Pacific. The most famous vessel so employed was the 32,000 ton battle cruiser, *HMS Renown,* which, after the First World War, took the Prince of Wales (later King Edward VIII and then H.R.H. the Duke of Windsor) on two landmark tours, one to New Zealand and

Australia in 1920, and the other to India, Hong Kong and Japan in 1921-2.

On the first tour the *Renown* entered the Pacific through the Panama Canal, which had opened six years earlier, and the first stop was at San Diego in California where they were escorted into the port by six American destroyers. All the functions that the Prince and the naval officers attended in San Diego were "dry" affairs for this was in the dark days of Prohibition.

From the North Pacific *HMS Renown* took the Heir to the Throne down to New Zealand and Australia where he was greeted with enthusiasm and loyalty wherever he went. It was a gruelling time for the Prince, less so for the *Renown's* sailors who at least enjoyed a bit of leave while their distinguished passenger was being sent by rail across the country in order to be seen by as many people as possible. It seems that every ex-serviceman from the World War wanted to shake his hand and that every one of them did.

One of the more interesting engagements (but maybe not for the Prince) was when they carted him hundreds of miles inland to some God forsaken spot near the New South Wales/Victoria border to lay the foundation stone for Canberra, the proposed national capital that had been dreamt up by empire building bureaucrats.

As the Prince looked around at the bleak, featureless landscape, with only a few corrugated iron sheds to represent "civilisation", he might have wondered at the folly of building a brand new and very expensive capital in the middle of nowhere to service a country with a population smaller than that of London.

Canberra had its genesis in the inability of Sydney and Melbourne to agree on anything, least of all which of them should be the capital of Australia. For the first few decades of the existence of the Commonwealth of Australia Melbourne was the capital but Sydney could never allow such an intolerable situation on a permanent basis. Hence, the compromise of Canberra, which would be the largest drain on public funds in Australia's history and would become a word synonymous with high taxes, wastage of public funds and government arrogance.

It would have been more economical to have spent one hundredth of the funds required to create Canberra in the purchase of a large luxury liner with two big saloons (one for each House of Parliament to sit in) while the cabins could be used as the offices for the ministers and Members (and boudoirs for their wives and mistresses). This, the *ss Canberra*, could have sailed between

313

Sydney and Melbourne, spending six months of the year in each place to satisfy the peculiar wants of the people of those cities.

It could have had a permanent (well, for six months anyway) berth in each city and, in the event of legislative deadlock, the Speaker could have ordered the ship to sea and not return the Members to the delights of King's Cross or Saint Kilda until they reached some sort of agreement.

In any event, the Prince laid the foundation stone for the new capital and it is only fair to point out that this was the limit of his responsibility for this new monstrosity. He then hied back to urban Australia to continue shaking the hands of the ex-servicemen.

On the second tour the Prince and his aide-de-camp, Louis Mountbatten, were entertained in Japan by the Crown Prince Hirohito, who stood in for his father who was confined to a secret part of the palace because he was insane. Neither the Prince nor Mountbatten took a liking to their host. Before long Hirohito would unleash war against the country of the Prince, whom he was entertaining, and would be responsible for cruelty and savagery unknown since the time of Genghis Khan. It is little wonder that both the Prince and Mountbatten were pleased to get back on the *Renown* and sail for home.

JACK ASHORE

When Captain Cook sent turtling parties ashore on Christmas Island in December, 1777, two of the men got lost – one for twenty-four hours and the other for two days. This was on a small, flat island with hardly any vegetation to obscure the view and the tall masts of Cook's ships, *Resolution* and *Discovery*, dominating the skyline. And they really were lost as, when found by searching parties, they were both thirsty and starving; there was no fresh water on the island and one of them had resorted to drinking turtle's blood. In his journal Cook wrote laconically, "Considering what a strange set of beings the generality of seamen are when on shore, instead of being surprised at these men losing themselves, we ought rather to have been surprised there were no(t) more of them." [1] These sentiments were echoed more than sixty years later by Lieutenant Hon. Fred Walpole, who served on the Pacific station in *HMS Collingwood*, "Seamen are fine fellows, open-hearted, generous....They are the very personifications of simplicity and require the most unremitting attention to induce them to take care of themselves." [2]

A long spell at sea, where there was routine, discipline and order and little need for a man to think for himself, was not always the best way to prepare Jack for a run ashore and that was why, when the Navy was in town, everybody was aware of it.

The tall masts of the men-of-war entering a harbour set the girls' hearts a-flutter while the publicans would lick their lips, the cops wipe their brows and all sorts of committees – church, social, sporting and charitable – would get into gear to entertain the lively and responsive sailors whose interests were as diverse as could be imagined.

As we shall see in this chapter the Jolly Jack Tar on leave could be quite a phenomenon for the staid burghers of Hobart or Wellington but there were many sailors who looked forward to a spell of leave after a long cruise among the Islands for reasons other than wine, women and song.

We shall start this interesting chapter with a description of "pay day" on board *HMS Clio*, which happily occurred while she was berthed at Hobart in May, 1873.

About a dozen lively and imaginative tars used their pay to hire a horse omnibus, "which had been decorated in a decidedly novel fashion. A piece of quartering had been nailed on the roof

315

lengthways, and 'astern' the projection served as a sort of davit, to which a wheelbarrow had been slung. On the piece of quartering that projected over the front of the bus a large doll had been fixed as a figurehead, and there was a barrel of beer on the box.

There were various other decorations, including some sheets of painted canvas bearing mottoes, and three or four large flags.

The costumes of some of the occupants of the vehicle were most extraordinary. One had his trousers ornamented with rope ends, which hung like scalp locks from the leggings of a Red Indian, another was dressed in parti-coloured trousers of blue and white, two were dressed in women's costume with flowers in their hair while others wore battered white hats of the bell-topper order. A cab that was driven behind the bus also contained some strangely dressed individuals.

As the vehicles were driven through the town one of the men in the omnibus took soundings with a bunch of carrots tied to a long string and the same operation was carried on in the cab behind, a sheep's head serving for the lead in this instance.

The sailors all seemed bent on fun and they drove through the streets singing merrily. Whenever the omnibus and the cab stopped and it was time to start again, the order 'All aboard' was shouted out and the driver was commanded to 'shove off' without delay.

Coming up Elizabeth Street at half past three in the afternoon a marine fell from the box of the bus. The cry of 'Man overboard' was raised, the vehicle was 'brought to', the wheelbarrow lowered and the marine placed in it and restored to his former seat on the box. Subsequently several members of the police force were severely handled by the sailors in an attempt to apprehend several of the men by order of the Commodore." [3]

Later in the same year it was Wellington's turn when *HMS Pearl* paid a visit. "During the past week the streets have been greatly enlivened, if somewhat incommoded, by the presence and eccentric performances of numerous specimens of the British Tar, ashore on leave from the newly arrived *HMS Pearl*.

Gratuitous exhibitions of naval hornpipes, wrestling matches, illustrations of the 'noble art of self-defence', forecastle songs and other nautical amusements have been supplied at brief intervals during the last few days and nights to numbers of admiring spectators.

Occasionally the performances have been varied by experiments on the cohesive power of glass and the exact percussive force required to cause fracture.

Unfortunately, the windows experimented on proved so ridiculously brittle that the mere impact of a mass of stone or iron simply propelled against its surface by the unaided force of the human arm proved sufficient to cause commuted fractures….Some of the experimental philosophers failed to recollect the termination of their leave and were accordingly chased by a picket of their comrades and, being ingloriously captured, were conveyed *vi et armis* on board." [4] However, if a few broken windows was the price that Wellington had to pay for the Navy surveying its coasts and protecting it from Maori raids within and Russian threats without, then it was a very small price indeed.

The men of the *Pearl* seemed to be a particularly lively lot as, three years after their "Wellington window leave", they, together with their compatriots on *HMS Sappho*, "created a great rumpus in Queen Street (Auckland). There were nearly a dozen of them on horseback quite drunk, riding on the paths and shouting like mad. No accident occurred." [5]

Skylarking was one way for young men, who had been cooped up on their ships for a lengthy period, to let off some steam and have a bit of fun. At a sports day at Newtown, Wellington, in 1882 "every tramcar was packed, large numbers having to walk the whole way…..This little difficulty was to some extent coped with by some half dozen bluejackets belonging to *HMS Cormorant* and *Miranda*, who were seen stretched at full length on the top of one of the cars and looking the very picture of jollity and content." [6]

When the British tar was ashore with his pay in his pocket, the temptations were almost limitless and he was preyed upon by prostitutes and publicans. Of these two species the latter was probably the worse as they plied the young and gullible sailors with alcohol – even when they had had more than their fill – and then screamed the loudest if, in a state of inebriation, Jack might break a glass or give the bar staff some "lip".

After a combined shore leave in Australia of the men of *HMS Cormorant* and *HMS Wolverine* in 1880 the licensed victuallers held a meeting to protest against both the conduct of the men and that of Commodore Wilson for "incivility" towards the publican involved, a Mr. O'Shannassy. [7]

317

The combination of beer and women proved almost too much for Petty Officer William Levette of *HMS Pearl*, who in Christmas week 1875 wandered into the Star of Peace Hotel on the corner of King and Kent Streets, Sydney. There were already quite a number of tars in there from both the *Pearl* and *HMS Sandfly*.

When he walked into the bar a woman named Flora Evans, whom he knew, rushed towards him with open arms but he pushed her away. Unfortunately, she fell down and became insensible. The publican, Mr. Ryan (a large number of publicans were Irish) got some water and tried to make her drink it but, finding that she could not swallow, had her put in a horse cab and taken to the hospital where she died.

The police arrested Levette on suspicion of having caused her death but the inquest decided that he had merely pushed her and so the verdict did not go against him. [8]

Another who had a "woman problem" in Sydney was twenty-five year old John Payne, an able seaman on board *HMS Orlando*. When that ship was in Sydney in December, 1890, Payne and one of his shipmates, James Bear, took two sisters, the Miss Lambs, to the Theatre Royal to see a performance of "Hero and Leander".

Payne had been drinking during the day and, before going into the theatre, had a quarrel with his Miss Lamb in consequence of her showing him a letter that she had received from some other beau.

Able Seaman Payne sat gloomily in the stalls through the first act and then, jumping up from his seat and shouting "Good-bye", he rushed on to the stage in his naval uniform and, standing between the curtain and the footlights, drew a revolver and shot himself in the abdomen. "He fell forward heavily, breaking one of the electric footlamps. The wildest excitement prevailed. Women screamed and some had to be carried out in a fainting condition....As soon as the excitement had subsided, the performance was continued as usual." [9] Payne was taken to hospital by the police with the bullet penetrating his liver.

Auckland could be just as exciting as Sydney. When some sailors from *HMS Clio* were "a trifle disorderly" [10] in one of Auckland's streets they were remonstrated with by Constable Cummings. A scuffle ensued with about fifteen bluejackets and several civilians joining in the attack on the cop, who "sustained a painful injury to his right eye." [11]

Some of the sailors appeared in court the next morning but, since the magistrate believed that they would be punished by their captain, they were ordered only to "come up for sentence if called upon". [12] The joining together by sailors and civilians suggests that Constable Cummings was looking for trouble and he certainly found it.

Things got really out of hand when *HMS Zealous*, the flagship of the North Pacific, arrived at Panama from San Francisco on 19th October, 1870. On the Sunday after her arrival some sailors were given leave and they got into a fight in which six men were injured, two of them with serious wounds to the head. The Alcalde of Tobago, a local official, arrived on the scene and tried to quell the disturbance but he was struck on the head by some of the missiles that were flying about. The surgeon of the *Zealous* landed immediately and tried to help the Alcalde but to no avail and he died a few hours later. The flagship's police were then despatched to bring the men back before they caused any more trouble and the captain expressed his condolences and assured the local authorities that the miscreants would be punished. At the time (pre Canal) Panama was part of Colombia and the President of that state demanded $5,000 damages, a demand that the captain of the *Zealous* passed on to the British government.

It would be wrong to regard the aforementioned instances as the full story of sailors on shore leave or even a major part of it. Far more common was the report in Wellington's *Evening Post* in January, 1889, "A number of liberty men were allowed to go ashore last evening and remained on leave until this morning. The jack tars were exceedingly well-behaved and we have not heard a single complaint of misbehaviour." [13]

This is not surprising in view of the wide range of positive and self-improving activities that were laid on for the sailors at the different ports. Unlike the French and German navies, the Royal Navy had – and still has - a strong Christian ethic and has been well served by its excellent corps of chaplains. "The (Royal) Navy, as a service, retains much of the old religious sense," wrote Sir Shane Leslie. "Admiral Beresford notes truly that the men swear but do not blaspheme. In Germany the Navy is the secondary service, and the calibre of the middle-class atheists who pace her decks cannot compare with the Christian gentlemen under the white ensign." [14]

Church parades were well attended – especially on the eve of battle. When the Fleet was in Wellington in 1888 the *Evening*

Post reported, "About 200 men from the squadron attended service at Saint Mary's Roman Catholic Cathedral yesterday morning, mass being sung by a strong choir and the sermon being preached by Archbishop Redwood. The Garrison Band, under Bandmaster Cimino, headed the procession from the landing stage...to the cathedral." [15]

On the evening of Christmas Day, 1905, the Sailors' Mission in Dunedin, New Zealand, held a Christmas tea for the men of *HMS Prometheus*, which was in port. A "ditty" bag containing Bible, writing material and many articles useful at sea was given to each man. [16]

In 1909 a Missions to Seamen bazaar was held in Wellington to raise money for the sailors. In the words of the *Evening Post*, "There is no finer patriot than the sailor; his service is always 'active'. The walls of the fine Mission hall were buttressed round with the bows of ships carrying names familiar to every Briton, and under the represented vessels stalls were thickly arranged. It is impossible to imagine stalls so generously laden. Red, white and blue were, of course, the colours, and the stallholders were dressed for their parts. ....Evidence was abundant of the means employed by the son of the sea in beguiling his monotonous life. It is extraordinary how many useful things can be fashioned out of hemp." [17]

Probably the largest Mission to Seamen was in Sydney where it had been founded by an energetic and benevolent gentleman called John Shearston, who had been born on Trafalgar Day, 1853. He visited virtually every ship that arrived in Sydney harbour – Royal Navy, foreign navies and merchantmen. He was taken out to them in a skiff rowed by a young aborigine.

Mr. Shearston and his wife also attended to their wants ashore. For example, when *HMS Calliope* arrived in Sydney for the first time in 1887 Mr. Shearston was the first man aboard and he arranged an excursion to the Blue Mountains for those on general leave, visiting Wentworth Falls and other sights.

In 1889 he opened a Royal Naval House for bluejackets on shore leave. Situated in Grosvenor Street, between George and York Streets, it had overnight sleeping accommodation for three hundred tars plus a library, gymnasium, dining rooms and billiard rooms. His aim was to keep the young sailors away from the publicans and prostitutes, whose only interest in Jack was to fleece him of all his pay. The captains of the ships on the Australia station gave the

320

Royal Naval House their full support and it was eventually affiliated with the Mission to Seamen.

The officers were no less fortunate; when a man-of-war arrived in Sydney harbour the gentlemen's clubs of the city would send cards on board extending honorary membership to the officers during their stay.

Ashore in Hong Kong the sailors frequented the Royal Naval Canteen, a blue coloured, three storeyed building that was on the foreshore of Hong Kong island, near Arsenal Street before subsequent reclamation. In the 1920s this building was demolished as part of one of Hong Kong's many reclamation schemes and it was replaced by the China Fleet Club which, with its billiard rooms, reading rooms, dining rooms, theatre, dormitories and bars dispensing beer, wine and spirits, was a "home away from home" for those on the China station.

In the late nineteenth century there was a Temperance Lodge on nearly every one of Her Majesty's vessels and many sailors were members of the Royal Naval Temperance Society, which had been started by Miss Weston in Devonport, England. The lodge would hold meetings ("sessions") both on board and ashore and the members would be entertained by local Temperance lodges when they were on leave. The members took the pledge to abstain from alcohol.

The cause of Temperance should not be confused with that of Prohibition. The Temperance people chose not to drink themselves whereas the wretched Prohibitionists tried to inflict their views on all mankind by means of laws outlawing alcohol – as happened in that most intolerant of societies, the United States, in the 1920s.

The lodge sessions provided an environment for mutual support but again they should not be confused with the Alcoholics Anonymous movement of later times as for the most part the men in the Temperance lodges had never had a drink problem; they just chose not to imbibe it.

By 1889 there was only one vessel on the Australia station that did not have a temperance lodge. In 1880 Wellington's *Evening Post* wrote, "It appears that considerable interest is being evinced by the temperance people of this city on behalf of the seamen on board *HMS Cormorant* for a large party went off to the vessel on Sunday afternoon when, after some devotional exercises, a number of addresses were given and several hymns sung." [18]

The Temperance lodge on *HMS Cormorant* was named "Light of the Ocean Lodge". That was also the name of the lodges on *HMS Espiegle* and *HMS Goldfinch*. In 1892 the *Goldfinch* abstainers had a session in Wellington's Primitive Methodist School-room with the Star of Wellington Lodge and "the bluejackets brought the fraternal greetings of lodges that they had visited." [19]

Wherever the ships went in Australasia there would be a Temperance lodge to provide fellowship and entertainment. At a session in Wellington's temperance hall in 1888 the members of the Red Cross Lodge of *HMS Nelson* read the minutes of the two preceding sessions, one held in Auckland and the other on board their ship. Then, at 8.30 p.m., "by which time an immense crowd of the general public had collected in the ante-rooms and in the hall, the large folding doors were thrown open and all who could find room inside were admitted.

So great, however, was the concourse that large numbers were obliged to content themselves with standing outside on the footpath.

Harmony was entered into with spirit and the jolly tars and gallant marines kept the ball rolling to the delight of the large audience until 10.15 when the evening's amusement was brought to a close by the singing of the National Anthem." [20]

Songs and recitations were given at these sessions. A sailor from *HMS Basilisk* "made a very good speech on the subject (temperance) and gave a recitation for which he was much applauded," wrote Auckland's *Southern Cross* in 1873. [21]

Other lodges were The Gem of the Sea Lodge on *HMS Diamond*, the Sea Nymphs' Lodge on *HMS Rapid*, the Pearl of Peace Lodge on *HMS Pearl*, the Union Jack Lodge on *HMS Calliope*, and the Naval Star Lodge on *HMS Encounter*. In fact, the *Calliope* had two lodges – one for the officers and one for the men.

Of the *Calliope's* total complement of 300 officers and men, some 175 were members of one of the two Temperance lodges. The *Calliope's* skipper, Captain Kane, was a believer in total abstinence and no doubt encouraged the lodges. Whether or not more people joined if the captain was so inclined I am unable to say but it could be that membership of a Temperance lodge on a ship like the *Calliope* would improve one's chances of promotion.

In the words of Lieutenant Risk of *HMS Orlando*, the flagship of the Australia station in 1890, "Abstainers are generally more to be trusted....By a man becoming an abstainer he gains many small privileges. For instance, a man is to be sent on shore on an errand; it is customary to send a petty officer in charge of him but, if he is an abstainer, he is often trusted to go alone. He has more shore liberty granted for, the officers knowing him to be an abstainer, know well enough that he will not miss his boat through being drunk and that he will conduct himself when on shore in a better manner than his 'moderate drinking' shipmates." [22]

There would, of course, be some subtle distinctions between the drinkers and the abstainers – a bit like those of more modern times between non-smokers and smokers when the latter gather outside bars or offices to enjoy a pipe or a fag. On *HMS Ringdove*, which was on the Australia station in the 1890s, there was a special dramatic group called the "Temperance Crew", which put on concerts in the ports they visited and whose membership was confined to non-drinkers.

The sailors were generous with their time, and the maintenance of the graves of their fallen comrades was always a priority. Of course, they maintained the graves of Commodore Goodenough and his fellow victims in Sydney while in New Zealand there were many naval graves of those who had fallen in the Maori Wars. When *HMS Wolverine* was at Tauranga in 1878 her men trimmed the area around the graves of those who had fallen in the battles of Gate Pa and Te Ranga in 1864 and they also repaired and painted the surrounding fence. [23] A letter to the *New Zealand Herald* in 1873 noted, "On visiting the Church of England cemetery we observed with much pleasure a sailor from *HMS Blanche* busily occupied in painting the head stones of several of the officers of the navy who fell in action during the Maori War." [24]

For those in need the sailors were always ready to apply their amateur dramatic skills in the form of a benefit concert. Every ship had its drama or singing troupe and they liked to give themselves zany names like the "Snowdrop Minstrels" of *HMS Pearl* and the "Nigger Troupe" of *HMS Cormorant*.

The *Calliope's* dramatists stole a march on the others when they took advantage of their stay in Hong Kong to purchase colourful Chinese costumes and stage fittings for the shows that they would put on when they reached the Australia station.

In July, 1876, the officers of *HMS Barracouta*, assisted by gentleman amateurs, gave a performance in the Queen's Theatre, Sydney, in aid of the newly formed Goodenough Royal Naval

Home, named after the late Commodore. They performed in the burlesque "Kenilworth" and the farce "Browne, the Martyr". [25]

In 1873 more than nine hundred people crowded into Wellington's Theatre Royal – "one of the largest houses ever assembled in the city" [26] – to hear the Snowdrop Minstrels of the *Pearl* perform in aid of the Royal Seamen and Marines' Orphan Schools and the Female Orphan Home back in England.

In the presence of the Governor and his suite, the two Commodores, Captain Moresby of the *Basilisk*, dozens of naval officers and all the "youth, beauty and fashion of the metropolis" [27] the Minstrels did "a scene from 'Still Waters Run Deep', an amusing farce, 'A Manager in a Fix', and a droll negro farce, 'The Darkie Photographer'." [28] During the intervals the audience was entertained by the band of the *Pearl*.

The sailors formed the staff of the theatre for the night and the proceeds were sent to England where they were used to provide a "heavy tea" for the orphans and a performance by a conjuror, with the balance being applied to a building fund for a school house.

When a local Volunteer, Francis Donald, was accidentally shot at Wellington's rifle range the men of the *Cormorant* put on a benefit concert for his widow and five young children. It concluded with a dance. "The gallant bluejackets deserve great credit for coming forward so generously in aid of such an object," wrote the *Evening Post*. [29]

The amateur players practised their pieces on their ships and sometimes gave concerts on board. When *HMS Rosario* was off the island of Nguna in the New Hebrides on her 1871-2 cruise her captain wrote, "We lost the wind directly we got outside, and lay becalmed nearly all night. During the evening a little entertainment to relieve the tedium of the voyage, consisting of singing and dancing, produced a good audience. The stage was rigged up on the after part of the quarter deck, which was housed in and well lighted. The parts were well sustained and on the whole the performance went off with great éclat." [30]

Sometimes the entertainment on deck under a tropical sky was performed not by the sailors but by the natives. When *HMS Curacoa* was on a cruise round the islands of the South Pacific in 1865 she stopped at Pago Pago in Samoa. "In the evening the natives, to the number of about two hundred, danced and sang on the main deck," wrote Sub-Lieutenant Foljambe. "They looked very grim, covered with coconut oil and nothing but their kilts on (composed of red leaves), after which we fired some rockets and burnt some blue lights for their edification, which delighted them all very much. They said they thought they were in heaven." [31]

The entertaining skills of the sailors went far beyond singing and dancing. In 1882 at Wellington's Theatre Royal the bluejackets of *HMS Cormorant* demonstrated sword feats, boxing and fencing. They also did a cutlass and glove exercise and one of their number danced a hornpipe while another sang "Empress of the Seas". [32]

Boxing was always popular – especially in the early nineteenth century, of which Sir Shane Leslie has written, "Prize-fighting was the national sport and the 'champion of England' was, after the Archbishop of Canterbury, unofficially the second person in the realm." [33]

Different ships had their "champion" and, when *HMS Nelson* visited Wellington in January, 1888, one of her sailors, Jerry Ford, was matched against William Murphy, a lightweight champion. The fight was staged at the Princess Theatre, "a great number of those present being men belonging to the war vessels now in port". [34]

Ford was smaller than his opponent and at the end of the eleventh round he announced that he was winded and could not continue and so the stakes of £10 a side were awarded to Murphy.

Previous to this Ford had been knocked down several times but he "displayed considerable science, and the general opinion was that Murphy would have had a very lively time if the bluejacket had been in better condition." [35] The proceedings were described by the *Evening Post* as "very orderly". [36]

Not so orderly or noble was a fight that took place in Auckland in 1873 when, according to an "eye witness", a number of seamen belonging to *HMS Blanche* and *Rosario* were carousing in a hotel in Shortland Street. "Amongst the number present were two lads aged about sixteen. One of them belonged to the *Rosario*, the other to the *Blanche*. After they had been made nearly drunk by the men it was suggested that the unfortunate lads should have a fight. They were soon stripped and, being urged on by the men, they commenced.

For about half an hour the two boys, covered with blood flowing from the wounds inflicted on each other, continue to fight until at last one of them did not answer to the call of 'time'. The boy was too weak to move but after about five minutes the men placed him upon his legs and again called 'time'.

The other lad rushed at him and, with a violent blow in the face, felled him to the floor amidst the cheers of the seamen. The poor boy was picked up and placed on a chair, completely exhausted. The seamen then, with apparent reluctance, allowed the fighting to cease." [37] Ah yes, Temperance had its merits.

It would be wrong to deduce from the above incident that there was ill will between different ship's companies as the reverse was more likely to be true. When more than one warship was in town the bluejackets on leave mixed easily and happily with their brother sailors with different cap bands. Some vessels had a "chummy ship" where those on board one vessel had close and friendly links with those on another. When *HMS Calliope* arrived in Sydney harbour in 1887 after a long voyage from Hong Kong, *HMS Diamond* extended a hand of welcome and gave her some most welcome fresh meat. The ship's companies of these two vessels struck up an immediate rapport as "chummy ships" and, whenever they were in the same place, there was much to-ing and fro-ing between the two vessels.

The British love of sport was never far away when the sailors were ashore, the officers inclining towards field sports while the men played cricket and football.

With the officers it was largely hunting, fishing and horse racing. When four men-of-war were at Auckland in 1876 it was reported that, "The naval men enjoy the shooting while those lucky enough to get a mount have had one or two pleasant days with the Pakuranga hounds." [38]

When the *Pearl* visited Portland, Victoria, in February, 1875, the officers joined local hunters for "a capital day's sport near Cape Nelson, in a kangaroo hunt that numbered from thirty to forty horsemen. Thirty kangaroos were killed." [39] The officers seem to have been particularly keen on hunting kangaroos and wallabies since a taste of kangaroo meat, preferably shot by one's own hand, was a "must" for British sailors in Australia. Unfortunately, not all "roo shoots" finished as happily as the one at Portland.

When the flagship *Curacoa* returned to Sydney in October, 1865, after a 132 day cruise among the Pacific Islands some of the young officers asked Commodore Wiseman if they could borrow the Commodore's yacht *Enid* to sail her up the coast to Brisbane Water, just north of Sydney (and not to be confused with Brisbane in Queensland), whence they would walk the fifteen miles overland to

Tuggerah Lake where the shooting of kangaroos and wallabies was said to be good.

Since Wiseman was still busy counting the thousand plus curios that he had brought back from the Islands he gave his permission and so the four young blades set off full of enthusiasm. They were Lieutenants Broughton and Meade from *HMS Brisk* and Sub-Lieutenants Foljambe and Hunt from the *Curacoa*. Hunt was a survivor from the wreck of the *Orpheus* in New Zealand.

Since they had only two days' leave they got going about nine o'clock on Sunday night (12th November) with a two man crew – Petty Officer Clarke and Able Seaman Tilly. The latter had also been on the *Orpheus* when she sank.

They "sailed down the harbour under reefed sails and stormy jib with a fair wind" [40] and called at Manly Beach to pick up some hounds, which a friend of Lieutenant Meade's had offered to loan them.

Three of them went ashore to collect the dogs – "two of the finest kangaroo hounds in the colonies, belonging to a Mr. George Smith, and a fine bloodhound with a touch of mastiff in him, belonging to a Mr. Bagnell". [41]

It was after midnight when they passed through Sydney Heads and the barometer was falling and the weather deteriorating. It was cold and, over their jackets, they wore oilskins to protect them from the sea spray.

When Petty Officer Clarke relieved Lieutenant Meade at about 1 a.m. Meade told him not to lose sight of the light behind North Head because, if he did, there would be the possibility of hitting Long Reef.

By 2 a.m. the waves were starting to wash over the deck of the little craft and were flooding the cabin. Next thing she capsized and they all finished up in the sea. The shore was a few hundred yards off but not all of them made it as both Clarke and Tilly drowned. The former was a good swimmer but the latter, despite being saved from the *Orpheus*, could not swim a stroke. The hunting dogs were all washed up dead.

The surviving officers, shaken and exhausted, reached the coast near the Deewhy Lagoon. Two of them went looking for help while the others remained on the beach, hollering for Clarke and Tilly.

The yacht was washed up high and dry "with part of her port side gone and the deck and everything washed clean out of her". [42]

The officers then had to tell the Commodore the fate of his precious yacht but that was not all. The *Curacoa's* carpenter and a team of ten men set off overland from Manly to the site of the wrecked yacht and hauled her on to the beach on rollers. Then the *Curacoa's* launch went to retrieve her but the launch was thrown ashore and had all her copper stripped off and a big hole in her bottom. So the steam tug had to go up from Sydney and tow them both back to the harbour. The result of this kangaroo hunt was no kangaroos but two dead seamen, three dead dogs and two wrecked boats. If that didn't put Commodore Wiseman in a bad mood, then nothing would.

Fishing was no less popular than hunting. In 1904 Mr. Guthrie, the engineer on *HMS Clio*, won the prize (a valuable pipe) for landing the first hapuka fish during the Taniwha Fishing Club's outing on *ss Gael* off Kawau Island in Auckland's Hauraki Gulf. [43]

Sightseeing was also on the agenda. When *HMS Basilisk* was at Tauranga, New Zealand, in November, 1873, it was reported that "Several of the officers....are visiting the lakes (Rotorua) at present." [44]

Many captains found a reason to take their warships into Port Phillip Bay for the Melbourne Cup in November. "The whole world and his wife are off to the race course for Cup Day....by a curious coincidence the *HMS Diamond* just managed to arrive in Hobson's Bay (the port of Melbourne) last night." [45]

When HRH the Duke of Edinburgh, the son of Queen Victoria, was in Christchurch, New Zealand, in 1869 the Canterbury Jockey Club put on a race meeting, to which the Duke drove himself "four-in-hand, accompanied by the Governor and the captain of *HMS Blanche* and the principal officers of HM's ships *Galatea* and *Blanche*, some of whom were seated in the drag driven by the Duke while others were accommodated in carriages." [46]

The Duke, who mixed freely with everyone, was described by the *Christchurch Press* as "the true type of the real English sportsman". [47] Just after the second race "a nasty sea fog drifted over the plains, accompanied by a bleak north-easterly wind" [48] – not untypical Canterbury weather.

Cricket was always popular and, if a ship couldn't quite get a team together, the locals would lend a hand – as happened in

Auckland in 1873 when the Auckland Cricket Club played against a team consisting of nine officers and men from *HMS Basilisk*, assisted by two members of the Club. [49]

A very early match was played in Auckland in 1849 between *HMS Havannah* and the 65th Regiment, each side fielding only five players in a single wicket game.

It did not take long for a ship's company to organise a cricket team. When *HMS Calliope* sailed from England in 1887 for the China station it already had a cricket team up and running by the time it reached Saint Vincent in the Cape Verde Islands. In the words of the ship's chaplain, Rev. A.C. Evans, "The Calliope Cricket Club here played their first match, which resulted in a victory for the Saint Vincent eleven." [50] No doubt the sailors were still finding their form.

When the aircraft carrier, *HMS Illustrious*, was at Gibraltar on her way to the Pacific at the beginning of 1945 there was an American warship in port as well and so a tennis court was marked out on the flight deck of the *Illustrious*, on which a Royal Navy team played the Americans. The British won.

Robust sport and games were not every sailor's cup of tea. When Lord Salisbury, the future Prime Minister, was serving on *HMS Havannah* in Auckland in the 1840s he used to walk out to Onehunga, a distance of seven miles, and spend a night in learned discussion with Doctor Purchas, a clergyman of the Church of England who often officiated at naval marriages, and then walk back to his ship the next morning.

Another who enjoyed a more mind testing activity than cricket or football was Captain Byrne of *HMS Hyacinth*, who was a keen chess player. When his vessel was in Yokohama in 1890 he took part in the Yokohama Chess Club's first tournament, in which he came fourth with nine wins and four losses. He was described as "a most genial companion and a bold and brilliant player....a great favourite with members of the club." [51]

When *HMS Calliope* visited New Zealand in 1888 one of its bluejackets wrote in his journal of the locals as follows: "Like all our people out here in the southern hemisphere, they seem to think they can never do enough for a bluejacket. They will feed you, lodge you, walk you out, and show you all the places of interest. 'You don't see this in the old country' they say....The old country lingers in all their ideas and thoughts." [52]

This royal entertainment by the locals was reciprocated in the usual style of the Navy. The first return of hospitality took place on *HMS Endeavour* shortly after she arrived in Tahiti in 1769. It was the birthday of King George III, that famous Glorious Fourth of June, which is still commemorated by the Eton-Harrow cricket match, and Captain Cook noted in his journal, "Yesterday being His Majesty's Birthday we kept it to-day and had several of the chiefs to dine with us." [53]

In 1871 Commodore Stirling of *HMS Clio* gave a picnic on Auckland's North Shore, to which he invited about two hundred citizens, including the Governor and the visiting Duke of Edinburgh. "The large naval depot had been gaily dressed with flags and evergreens for the occasion....after doing ample justice to a most sumptuous luncheon dancing to the music of the bands of *HMS Galatea* and *Clio* was indulged in and kept up throughout the day with unflagging energy." [54] At the end of the day the boats of the men-of-war took the guests back across the harbour to the town of Auckland.

On the night of 24th June, 1868, Captain Lyons and the officers of *HMS Charybdis* gave a "splendid ball" on board their warship in Sydney harbour. The guests were ferried out to the floating dance venue by the *Charybdis'* boats. "Over the after part of the deck was stretched an awning, lined with the flags of all nations, very tastefully arranged," wrote the *Sydney Morning Herald*. "This impromptu ballroom was brilliantly lighted by splendid chandeliers, a large number of coloured lamps, and candles. The gangways to the wardroom, gunroom and cabin were beautifully arched with roses and camellias, interspersed with ferns and other native evergreens.

Numerous lounges, draped with flags, were ranged along the after part of the deck. The dancing took place between the main and mizzen masts, and commenced on the arrival on board of His Excellency the Governor and the Countess of Belmore at about half past nine. Shortly after eleven the guests retired to the cabin where a sumptuously appointed supper was served." [55] Among the guests were the Consuls of France and Spain, who by now were probably starting to get over the pain of Trafalgar.

Admiral Tryon chose an afternoon "at home" when he entertained about two hundred guests, including the Governor, on board *HMS Nelson* in Wellington harbour on 19th January, 1886. "The *Nelson* was beautifully decorated and the spacious deck afforded ample accommodation for an afternoon dance to the capital music of the ship's band," wrote the *Evening Post*. [56]

There is no need to stress the attraction of some of the young naval officers at these dances. "A ball will be held at Greytown to-night," wrote New Zealand's *Wairarapa Mercury* in 1869, "and will be attended by Captain Montgomery of *HMS Blanche* and the spicy aide-de-camp who made such havoc among the ladies' hearts on the occasion of his last visit to the valley." [57]

"The Australian squadron could not be considered a social institution to steam from port to port," said Admiral Bridge, who had formerly commanded *HMS Espiegle* on the station. [58] Not everyone would have agreed.

These shipboard balls and parties provided an opportunity for the dashing young officers to meet the local ladies, and in some cases romances blossomed which led to marriages. When *HMS Herald*, under Captain (later Admiral) Henry Denham, was in Sydney during her long surveying cruise in the late 1850s, a dance was held on board at which Lieutenant Arthur Onslow met Elizabeth MacArthur, the daughter of James MacArthur of Camden, south of Sydney, who was one of Australia's greatest landowners. A love affair resulted and they were married in 1867. There is to-day a gentlemen's club in Sydney which is so exclusive that its membership is confined to the members of the MacArthur-Onslow family.

Another way of repaying the locals for their hospitality to "Jack ashore" was to open the warships to the public on certain days – usually at week-ends. When *HMS Curacoa* visited Melbourne in August, 1864, they had as many as 4,000 on board each afternoon. In the words of Midshipman Foljambe, later the Earl of Liverpool, "They seemed an orderly and respectable lot on the whole". [59]

Sometimes there was an impressive display. "A very large number of Wellington citizens took advantage of the fine day yesterday to pay a visit to *HMS Emerald* where they were courteously received," wrote the *Evening Post* in 1879. "While the visitors were on board the order was given to send down topgallant masts and yards, the order being executed with a promptness, celerity and speed which seemed little short of marvellous to the landsmen and amateur sailors." [60] What better way to 'show the flag' and impress potential teenage recruits of the fun and adventure of a life at sea?

Sometimes exercises were replaced by "the real thing" as when *HMS Swinger*, a small vessel of four guns and a ship's company of sixty-five men, was open to the public at the Rattray Street Wharf, Dunedin, in March, 1888, and a passing yacht overturned, which gave the *Swinger's* men an opportunity for rescue in full view of their visitors.

In 1869 Captain Montgomery of HM steam corvette *Blanche* threw his vessel open to the public when she was at Port Chalmers, the port of Dunedin, New Zealand, "and a very large number of persons availed themselves of the opportunity of seeing this fine specimen of the 'wooden walls of Old England'." [61]

They were ferried out to the ship by a steamer, which had a brass band aboard and they approached the warship with the band playing "Rule Britannia". The visitors inspected all the fittings, recesses and armament of the ship, that had been launched at Chatham two years previously and had a couple of six and a half ton shunt guns placed between the fore and main masts "and running on brass slides in the deck so as to bear on objects at any point of the compass". [62] She also had a 24 pound howitzer and two 24 pound Hales rockets that could be used for storming batteries beyond the range of the ship's guns and shelling stockades and villages.

The part of the vessel "between decks" was the quarters for the officers and men, the fore part being used as a hospital. In the words of a reporter visitor, "This part of the ship is thoroughly and most efficiently ventilated…. a stream of cold air being kept continually flowing through this long range of deck, without which, crowded as it is by so many men, it would be in warm climates insufferably hot and close.

Along the beams supporting the upper deck are ranged water breakers for the use of the men when on land service. Abaft the galley are the marines' quarters, similarly fitted to those of the seamen, and here are ranged the small arms consisting of breech loading Snider rifles, with cutlasses, which can be used as bayonets, and carbines with sword bayonets….The boarding pikes are kept further forward…With the small arms are kept the boarding axes….

The berths for the officers and engineers are ranged along both sides of this portion of the ship, and are roomy and well lighted by large square ports. Descending at this point down an iron companion, the adventurous explorer finds himself in the engine-room, the vessel being fitted with two surface condensing engines, having an aggregate of 350 horse power although they can be worked up to a much higher power. To drive these engines at the top of the ship's speed it is necessary to consume about 84 tons of coal per diem but at an average speed of eight and a half knots a consumption of 12 tons per day only is necessary....The coal bunkers have a capacity for 280 tons....The captain's cabin is neatly but plainly furnished and consists of sitting, bed and bath rooms." [63]

The thrill of looking over a shining warship full of spunky sailors was only part of the attraction. In the words of Mr. T.D. Taylor in his book, *New Zealand's Naval Story,* "The 'Old Country' was actually home to the great majority of the residents, and the arrival of a number of warships from British ports brought to them the realisation that, though they had journeyed thousands of miles from their homeland, they were still members of the family, and that the strong arms of the Navy could reach out to the uttermost ends of the world and offer protection if needed." [64]

When the ships of the Navy's Australia Squadron visited Wellington nineteen years later "Some thousands of visitors went on board the warships yesterday afternoon and from two o'clock until nearly dusk the steamers *Mana, Aorere, Dispatch* and *Colleen* were engaged in plying between the vessels and the wharf. The influx of excursionists to the *Nelson* was so great that at about five o'clock the officers were obliged to prevent any more persons from going on board. On each vessel the rushes of returning passengers to the gangways whenever their steamers came alongside were very exciting and it is a matter for surprise that no serious accident occurred." [65]

An accident did occur at Brisbane in 1876 when the river steamer *Emu* was returning from a visit to *HMS Pearl* at Moreton Bay after dark. There were about two hundred excursionists and Volunteers on board when the *Emu* ran into the river bank near Brisbane, smashing her paddle-box against an overhanging tree. Six people were thrown into the water but all were saved except a cadet, J.S. Mort, who was drowned. [66]

In 1903 the Royal Navy's Australia Squadron visited Lyttelton, the port of Christchurch and the ships *(Royal Arthur, Ringarooma, Archer, Phoebe* and *Karrakatta)* were thrown open to the children of some twenty Canterbury schools. In the words of one of their adult chaperones, "I soon made friends with a pleasant looking tar, who seemed to think that nothing was of too much trouble in the way of answering my frequent inquiries. He was delighted beyond measure with the treatment the sailors had received during their stay in Lyttelton…..By this time the children had been let loose on the warships and they and the sailors were thoroughly enjoying themselves. With all the confidence of young colonials, the youngsters set to work to examine the cannons and everything else they came across. They raised and depressed the guns, worked all the handles they could find, and even had an impromptu performance with the big drum and most of the band's instruments. Never a word of remonstrance from any of the crew; they seemed to enjoy it as much as anyone and I saw one sailor hurry off to get permission to take out five little girls for a row on the harbour." [67]

Then it was afternoon tea time. "The tea was served out in great basins about as big as four teacups but it tasted none the worse for that. Lollies and cakes were there in great abundance and the men made excellent hosts, the ladies especially receiving a great deal of attention. Few of them were allowed to leave the ship without at least one keepsake." [68]

Back on the wharf the children gave three cheers for the sailors, their cheers being "returned in hearty British fashion by the sailors, who acknowledged that this was the best time they had spent for many a long day". [69]

All these onshore activities forged friendships and links between the sailors and the colonists and there was genuine regret when a familiar ship and her crew ended their commission and had to return to England.

When *HMS Calliope* ended her stay in Australasian waters in 1848 the citizens of Wellington presented its commander, Captain Edward Stanley, with an Address acknowledging the important services he had rendered the southern settlements of the North Island during his command and expressing their regret at his departure. Of the same ship Auckland's *Southern Cross* wrote, "Captain Stanley has won golden opinions from all parties, and the exertions he made in defence of the Colony in times of danger have secured for him universal gratitude." [70]

"*HMS Cossack*, after lying at Levuka for more than two months and being of incalculable benefit in aiding the formation of settled institutions, has left amidst the hearty regret of all classes, from whom Captain Douglas and his officers have won golden opinions in trying times," wrote a press report of the time. [71] Of the same ship Auckland's *Southern Cross* newspaper had earlier written that "the ship's company have been distinguished for their harmless good humour". [72]

When *HMS Emerald* left Wellington to return Home in 1882 "A large number of spectators assembled on the wharf to witness her departure," wrote the *Evening Post*. "Captain Maxwell and the officers of the *Emerald* have always been deservedly popular in this colony while the crew have been noted for their good and orderly behaviour ashore." [73]

And that "good and orderly behaviour ashore" seems to have been the norm rather than the exception of the British men-of-war in the Pacific as the Navy developed a place in the hearts of the Australasian colonists that was second to none. Writing in 1967, Rear-Admiral John Ross of the Royal New Zealand Navy declared that "the feats of the Royal Navy and the Naval Volunteers had firmly established the Navy in the regard of the people of New Zealand". [74] And that sentiment seems to have been universal throughout the Pacific.

RUNAWAY SAILORS

With the end of press gangs at the conclusion of the Napoleonic Wars the rate of desertion dropped and more leave was able to be given to sailors since men who were not impressed were less likely to desert. Nevertheless, desertion for whatever reasons was a problem that would continue. In 1875 it was estimated that just over 1,200 sailors and marines deserted from the Navy throughout the world [1] but, relative to the size of the Navy at the time, this was not an excessive figure.

When the Australia Squadron, consisting of four screw frigates (*HMS Liverpool, Liffy, Phoebe* and *Endymion*) and two screw corvettes (*HMS Barossa* and *Scylla*) did a tour of eastern Australia and New Zealand in 1870 there were 223 desertions out of a total complement of officers and men of 2,488. Some 150 deserted at Melbourne, 27 at Sydney, 1 at Lyttelton (Christchurch), 4 at Wellington and 41 at Auckland. [2]

Between 13th January and 19th December, 1882, *HMS Nelson* lost 187 men through desertion – 95 at Sydney, 4 at Hobart, 6 at Wellington, 21 at Auckland, 35 at Melbourne, 24 at Adelaide and the rest elsewhere. In Sydney the Water Police were kept busy trying to catch them.

Desertion on the Australia station had become such a problem by 1883 that the Admiralty informed Commodore Erskine in Sydney that in future as few young sailors as possible would be sent to the station. The Commodore was asked to make a strenuous effort to recapture them and to use not only the Sydney Water Police but also plain clothed cops to make visits to inland areas in an effort to find them. He was further instructed that every deserter had to go before a court-martial.

In commenting on a rumoured mutiny on *HMS Orlando* a press report stated, "There seems something in the air of the Australia station which is injurious to discipline. *All* the trouble cannot be wholly due to severity on the part of the officers. It appears more probable that the sailors when ashore imbibe notions anent the 'rights of man', etc. which are not consistent with man-o'-war life." [3]

To desert was a serious crime and, if caught, one was subject to a range of punishments depending on the circumstances. To a certain extent the rate of desertion from a ship depended on a captain and how he selected his crew in the first place and then treated them on board. A harsh and unreasonable captain – and not many of them were – could expect a higher rate of desertion than one who took better care of the needs and welfare of the men.

The two most popular places for desertion in the Pacific seem to have been Tahiti (for the women) and Victoria during the gold rush of the 1850s when Her Majesty's vessels in Australian waters found it harder and harder to retain their men.

The pleasures of Tahiti definitely had a seductive effect on the sailors and Captain Cook had more problems with desertion at Tahiti than anywhere else. As he was leaving Matavai Bay on his second voyage one of the gunner's mates, John Marra, dived overboard and started swimming towards a waiting canoe; instead he was recaptured by the *Resolution's* cutter. He was put in irons for a few days but was released on 4th June in honour of George III's birthday. Captain Cook decided not to punish him further on this occasion but, when he deserted again a few months later at Ship Cove, New Zealand, Cook gave him twelve lashes.

When the Great Navigator stopped at Tahiti on his third voyage he summoned all his men on deck and gave them a lecture on the evils and perils of desertion that was laced with both threats and entreaties. When one of the marines, John Harrison, deserted, Cook set out with two armed boats to the other side of the island, found him and brought him back on board.

A few days later Alexander Mouat, a sixteen year old midshipman and the son of a naval captain, deserted with a gunner's mate, Thomas Shaw. They both wanted to be with their Tahitian lady loves. To get them back Captain Cook invited some young offspring of the local chief, Orio, on board and then held them hostage until such time as the chief would return the naval deserters. A general manhunt ensued which resulted in the natives handing over Mouat and Shaw and receiving their own people back in return. Both men were put in irons and Shaw was given twenty-four lashings.

Sometimes there were mass desertions from a particular ship and not always without reason. For example, when the cruiser *HMS Encounter* was assigned to the Australia station in 1905 she found it difficult to find a crew for the voyage out to the Antipodes. The problem was that she was deemed an unlucky ship and was not thought capable of reaching her destination safely. In the event these fears proved groundless.

It had taken four years to build her at Devonport and her construction "was marked by a strange series of blunders and misfortunes". [4] On her sea trial she sagged considerably, indicating a lack of adequate rigidity, and she developed such alarming structural weakness that she was returned to the dockyard where for six months they strengthened her hull with additional girders. At a normal speed of 120 revolutions a minute her decks "literally buckled and the entire hull quivered in a manner that was ominously suggestive of transverse weakness". [5] It was believed by some naval engineers that, unless a smooth passage to the Antipodes could be guaranteed, "it is courting a grave risk to despatch her to the other end of the world". [6]

Not surprisingly, word of all these problems got around. She left Devonport on 16th December, 1905, with a nucleus crew for Chatham where a full complement was made up by a draft from the Chatham Naval Barracks. Then the first watch was granted forty-eight hours leave before departing for Australia but very few of them returned.

A sick ship was not the only spur to mass desertion as sickness on board was also a disincentive for men to return from leave. When *HMS Acorn* arrived in San Francisco from Acapulco in August, 1889, she had suffered two deaths during the voyage and there were six men down with fever in the sick bay. And this on top of allegedly harsh treatment where the able seamen were said to have been treated like schoolboys.

The *Acorn* was meant to stay at the Golden Gate for a week but there were twelve desertions and so, to prevent any more, the captain weighed anchor and headed up the coast to Esquimalt. On one night in San Francisco seven men took French leave. In the words of the *San Francisco Chronicle*, "The first two escaped by means of a small boat. Soon after this the steam launch was lying at the gangway waiting orders to go ashore for Lieutenant Valentine, executive officer of the *Acorn*. Charles Matthews, an able seaman, was in the stern sheets of the launch and the engineer was also in his place and, when she left the gangway, Matthews ran the little launch under the boom and immediately three men named Connor, Thomas and Hubert dropped into the boat. The action was seen from the *Acorn's* deck, and the engineer was commanded to stop the boat. He did as ordered, but the three men sprang upon him and overpowered him. Matthews took charge of the engine while one of the others took the tiller, and the cutter started for the shore at a lively rate.

338

Meanwhile those on board the *Acorn* had not been idle and, before the steam cutter was well under way, the second whaler had been launched and was after the runaways in hot pursuit. The whaler was easily distanced, however, and the deserters reached the new float several lengths ahead of her. They sprang upstairs and disappeared in the darkness just as Lieutenant Valentine drove up the landing.

The whaler grazed the float and a sailor named Williams, who was in the bow, jumped out under the pretence of going after the runaways. He was met...by Lieutenant Valentine, who sternly ordered him back. Williams struck out with his fist and hit his commanding officer between the eyes. Then he ran up the steps and soon found his shipmates in a neighbouring hostelry on the waterfront where he delighted them with the narration of his escape and his treatment of Lieutenant Valentine. [7]

If a deserter was caught, he was kept in custody until it was convenient to pass him back to his own ship or, failing that, another one. Thus, how long one spent in civilian custody depended on whether there was a warship currently in port. If it was in a remote place, with no vessel due for a while, he could be in civil detention for quite a long time before facing the music in front of his captain. But not all deserters were caught and some of them were given considerable help by others – sometimes their own shipmates – to avoid recapture.

When a deserter from *HMS Pearl* was arrested by a constable in Auckland in April, 1876, some thirty other sailors rescued him "severely maltreating the constable and a Mr. Hendry, who went to his assistance". [8]

Cops who arrested deserters were not always popular. In 1891 after a Sergeant Donovan arrested a "Mongolian deserter from *HMS Cordelia*, the Chinese in Auckland have boycotted the police", reported Auckland's *Observer*. [9] At the time Chinese were often referred to as "Mongolians" or even "Celestials".

Despite their occasional unpopularity for arresting a deserter the police got well paid for their efforts. For example, in 1880 the going rate was £3 for the capture of every deserter within a month, £2 within six months, and £1 before the expiration of a year. When Detective Brown was walking along Wellington's Lambton Quay in July, 1880, he spotted a man who answered to the description of a tar by name of Craven who had deserted from *HMS Emerald* almost a year earlier. The detective opened a conversation with him and managed to extract an admission that, yes, he had been connected with the *Emerald* and so Craven was arrested, brought before the Magistrates Court and returned to the Navy to face a court-martial. In addition to the normal capture fee Detective Brown was given a further subsidy by the New Zealand colonial government of £5. A very profitable afternoon's work. [10]

In Australia and New Zealand deserters often tried to make their way inland but this was not always successful as a new face in a small country town might appear to suspicious locals to be a deserter.

To employ a person, knowing him to be a deserter, was an offence punishable by a fine of not less than £30 (a lot of money in the mid nineteenth century when this rate applied). Alternatively he could be sentenced to six months imprisonment with or without hard labour. [11]

However, if a deserter arrived in an inland town and took honest employment and kept his nose clean there was little incentive for anyone to report him to the authorities.

This was the case with Albert Needham, a boy seaman who deserted from *HMS Cormorant* in 1881 when she was in Auckland harbour. He made his way inland and eventually arrived at Rotorua where he met a nice girl, married her, settled down and had a family. He was "earning his living by the sweat of his brow, a respected member of the community with whom he had cast in his lot, when, unfortunately for him, fate threw him in contact with Doctor Hope Lewis, ex medical officer of the *Cormorant*." [12]

For more than two years Doctor Lewis lived in the same small town as the runaway sailor but he made no sign of recognition. Then Lewis moved to Auckland and the first thing he did upon arrival was to report Needham to the authorities, who arrested him and put him in irons on *HMS Nelson*.

In dobbing this man in after knowingly ignoring the situation for so long Doctor Lewis did little more than demonstrate his own nastiness and perverted sense of duty. If the Navy had had the same exalted sense of duty as Doctor Lewis, they would have arrested him for not reporting the presence of Needham earlier. But they didn't and, with their characteristic humanity, they discharged Albert Needham and returned him to his wife and children. In the words of Auckland's *Observer*, "I am quite sure that there is not a man, woman or child in the province (unless it is Doctor Hope Lewis) who will not rejoice to hear the news." [13]

Another case where the deserter had the sympathy of the public was that of William Willcox, who was arrested in Tauranga, New Zealand, in 1872 and was put on board the schooner *Dauntless* to be taken to the naval authorities in Auckland. There was also a lunatic on board who was being taken to the Auckland Asylum and during the voyage and in a furious gale this fellow jumped overboard. Without hesitation William Willcox dived into the sea and saved the man's life.

The saloon passengers on board all signed a letter to the Captain and officers of *HMS Blanche*, to which Willcox was being sent, begging that "you will, in the carrying out of your duty to your country, show such leniency to the prisoner as is consistent with the public service and the feelings of a brave man". [14] In the words of the *Auckland Star*, "We mistake the spirit that animates British naval officers if such a manifestation of characteristic spirit will not condone for a breach of discipline. Willcox may have been temporarily seduced from the paths of duty by the delights of life ashore but we venture to say that, if an enemy was in front, it would be in such as him that British honour would find its security." [15] Ah yes, it was not always easy to find the right punishment for a runaway sailor.

Deserters who were taken on to other vessels were often given a fresh start but in some cases this could turn out to be a double edged sword. When the battleship *Prince of Wales* put into Cape Town on her way to Singapore in 1941 she took on a number of sailors who had deserted from earlier Royal Navy ships visiting South Africa. The captain of the *Prince of Wales* told them that their desertions would not be held against them and neither they were but less than a month later the poor fellows finished up either dead or in the South China Sea when the *Prince of Wales* was sunk by the Japanese.

For some men, who had decided that a life at sea was not for them, it was not always easy to bring it to an end and there were several instances of men deserting and being recaptured several times.

Adolphus Letter, a member of the sailmakers' crew on *HMS Blanche*, was obviously not a happy chappy on the ocean wave as he deserted with another man, William Darby, when their ship was in Auckland in October, 1869. Ten months later they were caught at Wanganui, New Zealand, and were returned to their ship.

When the *Blanche* was at Melbourne a year later Adolphus ran away again, this time with the acting master-at-arms, Joseph Bryant, and a reward was offered for their recapture but the reward for Bryant was three times the amount that was offered for Adolphus. Maybe the Navy didn't really want him back.

William Barlow deserted from *HMS Pioneer* when she was in Sydney and served forty-two days in gaol. When the *Pioneer* reached Auckland in March, 1910, he deserted again and made his way inland where he worked on a farm but he was discovered by a sharp-eyed detective, who returned him to the Navy. He told a reporter that he would never go to sea again. If he did, he would commit such an offence as would compel his dismissal from the Navy.

But for every William Barlow there were a hundred others who, for all its ups and downs, enjoyed a life at sea and, under a good captain, found a security, good order and companionship that were not always easy to find on land.

THE PURSUIT OF PIRATES

China

Among the provisions of the Treaty of Tientsin between Britain and China, later ratified by the Convention of Peking of 1860, was one that required China to work with the Royal Navy for the suppression of piracy off its coasts. The whole reason why the Navy was in the Pacific was to make it safe for British shipping and trade and this brought it into conflict with the gangs of Chinese pirates who had been operating in the China seas for centuries, often with the active connivance of the Chinese government.

Under section 52 of the Treaty of Tientsin British warships could, when chasing pirates on the high seas, enter any Chinese port but, no matter how many pirates' boats they chased and sank or how many pirates they killed, there always seemed to be another fleet of pirates' junks not very far away. After all, piracy was an old Asian custom and a horrible one too as there was always a victim – usually an innocent junk owner who lost what was probably his only asset (sometimes his home) and who might be beaten up or killed in the process.

For the British sailors there was nothing more exciting than a pirate chase; in fact, it made up for all the heat and other discomforts on the China station. And the pirates often gave as good as they got.

When the steamship, *HMS Medea*, was in Mirs Bay, north-east of Hong Kong, on 4th and 5th February, 1850, her sailors managed to kill two hundred and twenty pirates and take another twenty as prisoners. This was not as satisfying as it may seem as another six hundred and sixty of them escaped. However, during the operation four honest trading vessels were rescued and restored to their rightful owners.

This was the first occasion when the Chinese authorities had specifically asked the Royal Navy to "co-operate" with them in suppressing a fleet of pirates although "co-operation" is probably not the right word since virtually all the work was done by the *Medea*, which was better equipped for it than the primitive war junks of imperial China. Where the Chinese government could help was with intelligence; sometimes they were co-operative, other times not – depending on which Chinese officials were "in" with the pirates and which were not.

343

In the month following this expedition another of the Navy's steamers, *HMS Renard*, captured three junks within sight of the western point of Hong Kong island. Fourteen of the pirates were arrested and taken to Hong Kong for trial. They were part of a gang that captured the informants' fishing boats and murdered parts of their crews off Macau the week before.

Five years later two lorchas and five junks, that were travelling in convoy with the steamer, *Eaglet*, were cut off by pirates in the bay of Kulan. The *Eaglet* was not in a position to confront the attackers, "who displayed such a formidable battery and determined front" [1] and so her captain sought the assistance of *HMS Rattler*, which was commanded by Captain Caldwell.

Upon sighting the pirates the *Rattler* chased them into the bay and as far as her draught would permit, the pirate vessels drawing less water. The *Rattler* then returned to Hong Kong and sought the aid of the officers and men of the *USS Powhatan*, a steam frigate which was being repaired at Hong Kong and which was named after the father of Pocahontas.

The *Rattler* returned to Kulan bay, towing the *Eaglet* and, behind her, the boats of the *Powhatan*. A hundred of the Americans were put on board the *Rattler* while many of the *Rattler's* bluejackets transferred to the *Eaglet*. The Anglo-Saxons were off to engage the pirates.

On the morning of 4th August, 1855, they encountered the pirate fleet with their prizes, numbering in all some thirty-six vessels. Their boats were at anchor in a narrow and shallow passage of the bay.

The engagement was opened by some Congreve rockets being fired from the quarter deck of the *Eaglet* by Mr. Pine, the *Rattler's* gunner, and two marine artillerymen while the *Rattler* herself fired "two or three well-directed shots from her thirty-two pounder". [2] This startled the pirates from their imagined security for, up to that time, they had either not observed the British and American boats or thought that they would not have the temerity to attack them.

The pirate fleet then bore up and rounded a small point and "then from the deck of the steamer was witnessed as bold an attack as was ever made in these waters," wrote the *China Mail*. [3] "The pirate fleet formed a dense mass, the larger and heavier armed junks bringing up the rear, every now and then firing their broadsides at the boats, from which, in reply, tiny puffs of smoke arose as the howitzers in their bows discharged their more deadly contents, the shrapnel bursting over the junks and making frightful havoc among their crews.

The boats soon neared the pirates. Lieutenants Pegram and Rolando, with the launches of the *Powhattan*, first by volleys of musketry cleared the decks of the two largest, then boarded and drove the pirates overboard at the point of the bayonet. This, however, was not done without a hard struggle for the miscreants fought with the fury of despair but they had, of course, no chance against the marines and bluejackets.....

The pirate chief's junk, after being shelled by the first launch, was boarded almost simultaneously by her crew and that of the *Rattler's* gig, and Captain Fellowes was fortunate enough to secure the chief's flag. The chief himself, Lee Afyee, a principal leader of the Whampoa 'patriots', was shot by an English marine who had jumped on deck from the *Powhattan's* launch, and four women threw themselves overboard and were drowned. The ammunition on board the pirate fleet may be judged of from the fact that this junk alone is believed to have had nearly a hundred kegs of English gunpowder besides stink-pots, cartridges and loose powder.

Up to this time only one serious casualty had happened to the attacking force, a young American marine named Adamson having been shot with a musket ball in the groin, but two other fatal accidents followed in quick succession. The *Rattler's* first cutter, in charge of paymaster Brownsdon, ran alongside of a large junk. Several stink-pots thrown at them missed but at last one, hove from the raised poop of the pirate (boat) by a woman with a child slung to her back, fell into the boat and, being followed by others, the crew were compelled to jump overboard where two were speared and a third was wounded and drowned. One of these, a marine, who had been wounded by a spear thrust, called to his comrade to save him and, the other being an excellent swimmer, got hold of him for that purpose.

The Chinese then threw a mat over them and the marine, still holding on to his wounded friend, dived below and came up clear of the mat but, as soon as he was observed, several stink-pots were pitched at him, one of which struck him on the head and, though not much hurt, he was stunned for a second or two and lost sight of the man he had displayed such a determination to save...

The other fatal accident was the blowing up of a junk which, for a time, had offered the most determined resistance to the gig….She blew up with a tremendous explosion and both officers and men were hurled into the water. Three of the men were killed, and several others frightfully scorched….In this junk was an immense quantity of treasure, said to amount to 200,000 dollars and the desperation with which her crew fought may be judged from the fact that, even after the Americans gained the deck, they were encountered hand to hand." [4]

Altogether ten junks were destroyed. Five of them were substantially built, "evidently for war purposes, as they differ in many respects from the common trading junks," wrote the *China Mail.* [5] On these were mounted serious guns – 32, 24 and 12 pounders and on one was found a sixty-eight pounder. One junk had no fewer than twenty-one guns mounted. Fighting a fleet of pirate junks was like fighting a whole navy. Two lorchas and seven junks that were being detained by the pirates were released but, since two of these could not be brought away because of lack of time and an adverse wind, they were burnt since it was feared that they might be recaptured by the pirates who had escaped. The result of this combined British-American operation was approximately two hundred guns destroyed and about five hundred pirates killed.

The Royal Navy lost four of its men in this engagement while the Americans lost five. They were all buried together in the cemetery at Happy Valley, Hong Kong, where a granite monument was erected "by the officers and crews of the U.S. Steam Frigate *Powhatan* and H. B. M. Steam Sloop *Rattler* in memory of their shipmates who fell in a combined attack on a fleet of piratical junks off Kuhlan, August 4th, 1855. Killed in the action: *Rattler* – George Mitchell, A.B., James Silvers, Carpenter's crew, John Massey, Gunner, R.M.A., M. Oliff, Private, R.A. *Powhatan* – John Pepper, Seaman, James A. Halsey, Landsman, Isaac Coe, Landsman, S. Mullard, Marine, B.F. Addamson, Marine." To-day they lie together in this crowded graveyard between Stubbs Road and the Royal Hong Kong Jockey Club's Happy Valley racetrack, their peace disturbed on Wednesdays by the distant shaking of the ground as the galloping hooves of the horses race towards the finishing line.

A somewhat different tack was taken in the war against piracy by Lieutenant Wildman, the commander of H.M. Steam Gunboat *Staunch*, when he attacked three pirate vessels which the *Staunch* came across as she was sailing from Shanghai to Hong Kong. In the lieutenant's words, "I went ahead at full speed on to the largest junk, giving orders to lash her alongside us; but the instant

346

we touched, such a shower of stink-pots and other combustible matter was thrown on board us, it was impossible for any person to remain forward or to see through the dense smoke they occasioned.

It was at this moment…that Able Seaman Edward George, who was actually engaged in lashing the junk alongside, having gallantly jumped on board her for that purpose, was cut to pieces and his remains thrown overboard.

The strong breeze favouring the junk and a heavy swell making it difficult to lash her, she sheered off, and the Chinese in the meantime, having cut our boats adrift, and being close to the rocks, I backed astern and, having picked them up, I remounted the howitzers which had been dismounted from the rapidity of my fire, and renewed the engagement, running alongside one and boarding, killing a great number of her crew, many of whom endeavoured to escape by jumping overboard, but only a small number reached the shore.

Leaving this vessel in charge of Mr. Morice, the second master, and a party of men, I gave chase to a second in my gig and, having come up with her, I boarded and took possession, making prisoners of the only two living men on board, many having been killed and a few escaping by jumping overboard.

The third junk in the meanwhile having gone some distance away and not having more than five effective men left after the engagement, I deemed it prudent not to follow her among the numerous rocks and intricate passages she had taken and, being unable to spare any officers and men for the captured junks, I gave directions for them to be burnt." [6]

The impetus for an attack on pirates was usually complaints from those whose boats had been seized by these heavily armed thieves. When four Hong Kong passage boats were detained in a notorious pirates' nest in Macau, that was known as "Pirate Creek", *HMS Fury* and HM Gunboats *Firm* and *Bustard* set out with the four Chinese on board, whose boats had been stolen, as well as the Registrar-General for the Chinese in Hong Kong, Mr. Caldwell, who could speak Cantonese.

When one of the Chinese on board identified a large boat as being a pirate junk, it was immediately burned. Before it was set alight five of the captured Chinese, who were being detained on it, were released.

Piracy continued into the twentieth century despite the efforts to suppress it, although without the guns of the Royal Navy it would have been much more rife than it was. On 22nd March, 1927, the Indo Steam Navigation Company's vessel, *ss Hop Sang*, en route from Swatow to Hong Kong, was boarded by pirates at midnight near Bias Bay, sixty-five miles north of Hong Kong. As was their custom they robbed the officers and crew and then, still in the night, disembarked at Bias Bay with their loot.

Bias Bay, like the earlier Pirate Creek in Macau, was a well-known pirates' haunt and the response of the Navy was swift and sure. The cruisers, *Frobisher* and *Delhi*, the minesweeper *HMS Marazion*, the sloop *Foxglove* and, best of all, the aircraft carrier *HMS Hermes*, all sailed out of Hong Kong harbour at 6.30 p.m. the next night and anchored off Bias Bay at 1.30 a.m. the following morning. Also on board were detectives, constables and interpreters.

The landing force was divided into three parties. They were either rowed ashore or towed there by motor boats. The water off shore was very shallow and the three hundred sailors and police involved had to wade for distances of between forty and four hundred yards.

They were under orders to destroy the two villages, which were known to be the pirates' haunts, but, if possible, to spare human life. They were also told to destroy the junks in the bay.

The first village was deserted but they found the inhabitants hiding in the trees nearby and so they were told to collect their belongings out of their houses prior to having them burnt. When this was done about twenty matshed houses were set alight as well as twenty junks and sampans.

At the next village, Hoichau, thirty houses were destroyed by fire and eight others by explosives. "It is noteworthy that explosions, obviously of ammunition, were heard coming from the burning structures," wrote the *Manchester Guardian*. [7]

At the Fan-Lokong inlet more junks were burned, on one of which was found a quantity of rifles. The sailors and police on the ground were assisted by planes from the *Hermes*, which were observing, reporting and covering the landing parties as they went about their work. "The neighbouring hillocks were covered with Chinese watching the operations. Smoke from the burning matsheds rose high into the sky and was visible for miles around," wrote the *Guardian*. [8]

On 10th October of the same year the pirates struck again. They boarded the China Merchants Steam Navigation Company's steamer, *Irene*, which was packed with passengers as it made its way from Shanghai to Amoy. The attack came at breakfast time and the pirates quickly overpowered the officers and robbed the passengers. They then ordered the ship to slow down as they did not want to reach their lair in Bias Bay until it was dark. After collecting the loot they spent the rest of the day on board gambling and feeding their faces. The *Irene* did not reach Bias Bay until 8 p.m.

It just so happened that HM Submarine *L4* had been exercising off Bias Bay and was under the lee of the land for the night. When her commander, Lieutenant Halahan, observed the big steamer with no lights on entering the bay, he suspected piracy and flashed the sign to "Stop Immediately".

When the *Irene* did not stop, the sub switched its lights on her and fired a blank round. Still no response and so she fired shots across the steamer's bow.

The *Irene* kept on her course and so *L4* fired on her in an attempt to disable her. A shell burst in the engine room, completely disabling the engine and killing one of the pirates. Soon the *Irene* was on fire from another of the sub's shells. People were leaping in to the sea and so Lieutenant Halahan took *L4* alongside and began to pick up those who were struggling in the water. All the passengers and crew were got off the vessel, which by 10 p.m. was blazing from stem to stern. On several occasions the submariners dived into the sea, which was running a heavy swell, to rescue survivors.

With 222 of the *Irene's* passengers and crew on board, the *L4* headed for Hong Kong harbour. Her place was taken at the scene of action by the cruiser, *HMS Delhi*, which picked up another twelve passengers out of the sea. Upon arrival in Hong Kong the police processed the passengers, among whom they identified three of the pirates. A few days later seven others were arrested and all ten were hanged after being found guilty.

Pirates often disguised themselves as fishermen (as many of them were) to mask their evil intent. When *ss Hsinchi* left Shanghai for Foochow on 6th November, 1928, with a general cargo, 632 bags of mail and five hundred passengers, she ran into a thick fog at the mouth of the river, during which she grazed an uncharted rock and began to take on water. The passengers were taken off and the ship beached. "For some time previously a number of supposed fishermen had been hovering around but the moment the *Hsinchi* was aground they revealed their true character, swarming aboard and, despite a vigorous resistance by the crew, making off with a considerable amount of loot. The next day they returned and repeated their tactics, and on the day after came back with reinforcements and helped themselves afresh.....Captain Tollefsen and his officers (his second mate was a Chinese and proved himself a gallant man) did their utmost....to save their ship and her cargo but the odds were too strong and, after putting up a stout defence, they were compelled to abandon the *Hsinchi*....They were lucky enough to find one boat whose crew were willing to be bribed to take them ashore, by the offer of the contents of the captain's cabin and a letter of indemnity, and the next day....they were rescued by *HMS Serapis* whence they were transferred to a coastal vessel and landed in Shanghai. The *Serapis* captured two large junks loaded with plunder but the remainder escaped with their booty. Such cases....are serious matters to shipowners who have almost despaired of inducing the authorities, whoever they may be, to pursue an active campaign against the pirates and those who are behind them." [9]

In 1932 the Admiralty sent a gunboat to the Yellow Sea for the specific purpose of acting against pirates. She managed to sink about a dozen of their junks as well as numerous sampans, "blowing them out of the water and taking no prisoners". [10]

The same year saw one of the most audacious acts of piracy when they captured and looted the British steamer *Helikon* (2,323 tons) with three hundred passengers on board. She was two days out of Hong Kong when, at a given signal, a score of pirates, who had been disguised as peaceful passengers, drew revolvers and invaded the bridge, engine room and cabins. A few officers tried to resist but they were bashed with the butts of the revolvers. The pirates put the wireless out of action to prevent them calling for help and then forced the vessel to put into Honghai Bay, near Bias Bay.

There she was held for forty-five hours while the pirates ransacked it before making off with their booty and she was then allowed to proceed to Hong Kong, where she gave the alarm. Two of the wealthy Chinese passengers, preferring death to the horrors and tortures which normally follow kidnapping, committed suicide by leaping overboard and drowning.

Anti-piracy patrols were an important part of the Navy's work on the China station and the icing on the cake for the sailors was that the captured pirate vessels could be claimed as "prizes", with all the ship's company sharing in the proceeds but with the officers receiving a bigger proportion than the ratings.

Borneo

In the southern part of the South China Sea it was the Malays and Dyaks who manned the pirate fleets. "The piratical character of the Malays in general has never been disputed," wrote Captain Keppel R.N., who spent part of the 1840s chasing them. [11] In the words of a Dutch writer, "It is in the Malay's nature to rove on the sea in his *prau*, as it is in that of the Arab to wander with his steed on the sands of the desert. It is as impossible to limit the adventurous life of a Malay to fishing and trading as to retain an Arab in a village or a habitation." [12]

The north-west coast of Borneo was shared by the Malays and the headhunting Dyaks. It was the Malays who introduced piracy to Borneo but by the mid eighteenth century the Dyaks were helping to pull the oars of the *praus* in return for receiving the severed heads of the victims. It was Dyak custom that every prospective bridegroom must present a human head as the price of his bride. If any squeamishness was shown on the part of the young man, he would be taunted as a coward by the women of the village.

The Dyaks soon became excellent seamen and built their own vessels, known as *bangkongs*, which drew only a few inches of water. A *bangkong* had sixty to eighty paddles and was lighter and faster than the *praus*. Each of these Dyak vessels could be turned at full speed in its own length. "They are equally efficient for pursuit and for flight, and their stealthy and noiseless approach gives no warning to their victims, who have been too often surprised and overwhelmed with a shower of spears in the dead of the night," wrote Captain Keppel. [13]

The *praus* of the Malays were up to ninety feet long and most of them had a gun in the bow and four to six swivel guns on each broadside. There were also about twenty to thirty rifles or muskets per boat and of course, *krises*, the dagger that every Malay man carried. Above the rowers, who were sitting cross-legged, was a bamboo roof, covered with matting, to protect the ammunition and other supplies from the sudden tropical downpours.

The most deadly occasions were when the Malay and Dyak pirates joined forces for a raiding voyage that might consist of a hundred or more vessels. Thus was "extensive and systematic depredation carried out by these pirates", [14] who devastated the coast of Borneo for eight hundred miles, killed most of the honest trade and murdered people by the hundreds.

In the early 1840s *HMS Samarang* and *HMS Dido* combined surveying duties with pirate chasing in this land of jungle, swamp, rivers and mosquitos. In May, 1843, when the *Dido* was doing marine surveying off the coast of Sarawak, her boats were despatched to the small islands of Murrundum (also known as Low Island) and South Natunas with instructions to rejoin the *Dido* at Sarawak. Among those on board one of these small boats was James Brooke, the first "White Rajah" of Sarawak, who had a knowledge of the Malay language.

When the boats arrived at Murrundum they were suddenly attacked by a fleet of five large *praus* and several smaller ones, belonging to "an enterprising tribe of pirates" [15] from the Illanums, a small cluster of islands off the north-east coast of Borneo, who made their living by forming large pirate fleets to attack *praus* carrying cargo from Borneo to Singapore. Each of the large *praus* was rowed with about forty paddles and contained between sixty and seventy natives, armed with guns and other weapons. They shot at the *Dido's* boats, which fired back but "through their extraordinary swiftness in rowing, they (the pirates) made their escape in the direction of the Natunas." [16]

On the following night the *Dido's* boats arrived off the south coast of Palo Serbassu where they anchored. The next day they were approached by six *praus*, their rowers beating tom toms and obviously in the mood for a fight. However, these were not the *praus* of the Illanum people but of another tribe.

The British boats, of which there were three, formed abreast but the *praus* kept advancing and, when they were a hundred and fifty yards away, they opened fire, "their shot cutting through the rigging and splashing in the water all round.....It was an anxious moment for *Dido's* little party. Not a word was spoken. The only gun of the pinnace was loaded with grape and canister, and kept pointed on the largest *prau*. The men waited, with their muskets in hand for permission to fire but it was not until within pistol range that Lieutenant Horton poured into the enemy with his well-prepared dose. It instantly brought them to a halt." [17]

"The pirates on this ceased to advance but continued firing for some minutes afterwards, when one of the *praus* gave in and asked quarter, and the other five, chased by two cutters, made for the shore, keeping up a fire to the last." [18]

All of the pirates' boats were taken possession of and it was found that each one mounted three brass guns and had a crew of about thirty. The largest of the *praus*, belonging to the Rajah of Rhio, was taken by the *Dido* as a prize. During the skirmish ten of the pirates were killed and several others were wounded. Now that the game was up for them they claimed that it had all been a mistake as nothing would have induced them to fire on the British flag had they been able to identify it but the rising sun was in their eyes and they did not discover their error until they had opened fire. Since their story seemed plausible and they had suffered so severely Lieutenant Horton, who was in charge of the *Dido's* boats, decided to let them off with a caution.

The Borneo pirates seemed to be more determined than their Chinese colleagues. On 21st May, 1843, Lieutenant Hunt of the *Dido*, with twelve seamen and four marines, was in a small boat off Cape Datu with instructions to give protection to any vessels that might arrive. It was three in the morning when they saw three *praus* rounding the point within thirty yards of them. The *praus* assailed them with shot, musketry and a shower of stones and the British boats replied by firing a ten pounder, which was in the boat. It was not until a round of grape swept off the men from the paddles on one side of the nearest *prau* that the attack ceased. Its crew jumped overboard and most of them were shot in the water by the bluejackets. During this brief engagement twenty-three of the pirates were killed.

The readiness of these and other pirates to fire on boats flying the British flag persuaded Captain Keppel of the *Dido* to make a study of piracy in these parts. He ascertained that the worst pirates were those from the Seribas River, about fifty miles north-east of Sarawak. They were the "scourge and dread of the coast" [19] and a law unto themselves. They lived up three different branches of that river and were a mixture of Dyak head hunters and Malays. Altogether they had a fleet of a hundred and twenty war *praus*, each one carrying from forty to a hundred men. Sometimes they put to sea in a fleet carrying three to four thousand men. Other pirates, like the Saloos and Lanoons, preserved the lives of their captives and sold them as slaves but those of the Seribas River gave no quarter, the Dyaks taking the heads and the Malays the loot.

Upon learning all this Captain Keppel acted with his usual boldness and mounted an expedition to sail up the three branches of this notorious river and destroy the fortified villages of these pirates. The neighbouring chiefs asked if they could add their boats to the expedition and Captain Keppel agreed, believing that they would be useful in destroying crops and fruit trees and molesting the pirates in the jungle.

Accordingly on 6th June, 1843, Lieutenant Horton, whom Keppel appointed leader of the raiding force, entered the Serebas River with ninety-five officers and men of the *Dido* and about three hundred friendly natives to teach these predators a lesson once and for all. The *Dido's* men were in the ship's pinnace, two cutters and another boat that had been loaned to the expedition by James Brooke. The *Dido* herself remained at sea off the river mouth because the Serebas was very shallow.

The principal and the most distant of the fortified villages was Paddie, which was about a hundred miles up the river. It took them five days to reach this village as there were navigational hazards such as rapid tides, floating logs and dangerous sandbanks in this unknown river and they had to go slowly. At the approach to Paddie the boats were fired on from the first fort as soon the pirates spotted them. In front of the fort was a strong barrier of large trees, tied together by plaits of rattan, that extended across the river to prevent any boat getting through. While they were negotiating this the fire from the first fort continued and three of the *Dido's* men were wounded. The barrier was soon cut through and a landing party took control of Paddie's three forts. Then the friendly natives, who had followed the *Dido's* boats up the river, got to work, pillaging and burning, until the whole countryside for miles around was one huge blaze.

The village had received intelligence of the British boats coming up the river and so had removed valuables, women and children before the engagement. This made it easier for the sailors and the next day they and the friendly natives cut down any coconut and fruit trees that had survived the fire, as well as burning all the *praus* and grain. This was a good effort as for years these people had preyed on and terrified their neighbours and nobody had been able to do anything about it. Now they had learned that there was a new force in their waters with a flag that commanded respect.

However, Paddie was a Malay village and their Dyak colleagues lived twelve miles further up the left hand branch of the river in the village of Lyai. Leaving a strong guard at Paddie, Lieutenant Horton proceeded up the river but after dark the Dyaks, yelling their war cries, attacked his boats from both banks with spears, stones and the occasional musket as well as throwing trees

354

across the river to hinder progress. The *Dido* men replied by pouring grape shot on to them and several pirates were killed.

At daylight the next day the Dyaks realised that the game was up and they approached with a flag of truce, offering to come to any terms. This was accepted and their chiefs agreed to abstain for ever more from piracy.

They explained that they did not have control over the other tribes and so Lieutenant Horton took his men up the other branches of the river and inflicted on the other pirate settlements of Pekoo and Rembas the same punishment that he had given to Paddie. At Rembas four hostages were taken and held until the chiefs fulfilled their promise to meet the Sultan of Brunei "and there entering into solemn compact, after their own fashion, to abstain from piracy". [20] It had taken only seven days to destroy the haunts of the most dreaded pirates on the north-west coast of Borneo – something that the Sultan of Brunei had not been able to do in three recent attempts.

Although this was a check on piracy on the north-west coast of Borneo it did not eradicate it, and further attacks on their lairs and fleets would be carried out by the Royal Navy. The *coup de grace* came in July and August, 1849, when Captain Farquhar took *HMS Albatross* down from the China station to join with Rajah Brooke and his friendly Malays and Dyaks in a massive attack on the pirates of the Serabas River, who had recently captured several trading vessels and rampaged up two rivers where they burned three villages, killed at least four hundred people, including many women and children, and took more than a hundred heads. This combined and well-planned attack by the Navy was to spell the end of piracy on Borneo's north-west coast.

This force, consisting of the *Royalist* (Lieutenant Everest), the East India Company's steamer, *Nemesis* (Commander J. Wallage), the gig, pinnace and cutter of *HMS Albatross*, the *Royalist's* cutter, *HMS Maeander's* steam tender, *Ranee*, Rajah Brooke's new *prau*, *Singh Rajah* (Lion King), and eighteen "friendly" Malay *praus*, left Sarawak on 24th July, 1849. As they made their way to the Serabas River they were joined by the Orang Kaya of Lundu's *praus* with about three hundred men, by eight hundred of the Linga Dyaks in their boats as well as smaller units from other tribes, all of whom had scores to settle with the pirates. The *Albatross* herself remained at Sarawak, her doughty captain, Farquhar, swapping command of his warship for command of her gig. The native *praus* had colourful streamers flying from their slender masts and, with the gongs being beaten, it was a very lively affair. Rajah Brooke sailed at the rear of the column. The white sails of the fleet stood in contrast with the deep green of the jungle that they passed.

Two days later, on the 26th, they anchored off the mouth of the Serebas at 3 p.m. to await the return of a great pirate fleet that they were told had slipped out of the river only a few hours previously.

On the night of 28th Captain Farquhar went on board Rajah Brooke's new *prau* for a council of war that was held on the deck and was attended by all the chiefs. It was decided that Brooke and about twelve of his Sarawak *praus* as well as two of the Navy's cutters should take up position across the mouth of the Kaluka River, to the north-east, which was linked with the Serebas, and so prevent the pirates using this as an alternative route to get their loot back to their up-river fortified settlements. Here Brooke's craft were concealed by a bend near the river's mouth.

A similar formation blocked the mouth of the Serebas, others of the Navy's small boats, as well as forty *praus*, extending from the *Nemesis* in an oblique line towards the river mouth. Fifteen other *praus* were hiding on the further bank of the river. Fast pulling scout boats out at sea were the lookouts and a signal system had been worked out during the council of war on Rajah Brooke's boat.

For three days they waited in great suspense until the pirate fleet of some one hundred and fifty *praus* came into sight towards dusk on 31st July, virtually every boat being armed with brass guns, muskets, spears and swords. In the fleet were nearly all the Malay chiefs of the Serebas and Sakarran rivers, the two most infamous pirate haunts in these waters.

When the pirate fleet set out they had headed for Siriki but this fortified settlement was too well-defended and so they moved on to Palo where they levied a large contribution of salt and rice. From there they paddled their way to the bay of Lassa, capturing a trading *prau* that was laden with sago. They then attacked the town of Mato and captured two other trading vessels, which they burned after stealing their cargoes. Their boats were now so full that it was time to get their loot home.

Two divisions came paddling towards the entrance of the Kaluka River but, upon seeing the *praus* of Rajah Brooke, they headed instead for the mouth of the Serebas, the two man-of-war cutters at the Kaluka giving chase.

At the Serabas Captain Farquhar was waiting for them and it didn't take them long to realise that they were hemmed in on all sides. In the gathering darkness there was a rambling exchange of shots but the pirates, in a state of panic, did not use their guns well. Eighty of their *bangkongs* were run ashore and others tried to get back to the open sea in isolated units. Seventeen of their larger *praus*, in trying to avoid the shoal, passed close to the *Nemesis* and were destroyed.

From the mouth of the Kaluka to the mouth of the Serebas the battle raged for ten miles, with darkness favouring the British and their friendly natives. The warships' boats had blue lights so as to distinguish friend from foe. The night sky was further lit up by the glare of rockets and flashes from the guns while the battle cries of both sides rent the tropical air.

When dawn came it revealed the wrecks of the pirate boats and some 2,500 of them had fled into the jungle in the mistaken belief that it would hide them from the terrible might of Rajah Brooke and his naval friends, especially the wretched *Nemesis*, which they named the "fire ship", never having seen a steamer before.

Altogether more than five hundred pirates were killed and more than eighty *praus* and *bangkongs* were captured; those boats that could not be utilised to carry the expedition up the river were destroyed. It took two days to burn the boats and secure those pirates who had been taken prisoner.

It was now time to move up the river in order to show them that the tentacles of the Navy stretched far and wide. On this expedition orders were given to show mercy to any pirates wishing to give themselves up but this failed to take account of the nature of the pirates as these were desperate people, who were as reckless with their own lives as with those of others. They had swords with them in the water and, even if the British sailors tried to save them from drowning, they would lash out with their swords with murder as their aim.

On 2nd August the expedition set off up the Serebas, using some of the captured *bangkongs* as they drew so little water. Thus, by a twist of cruel irony, the pirates were being chased by their own boats.

On the first afternoon they anchored near the confluence of the Paku, and the Serebas and the next day the *Ranee* and the man-of-war boats led the fleet further up the Serebas, the *Nemesis* remaining at the entrance of the Paku tributary. Behind these boats came a dense mass of the hundreds of *praus* of the friendly natives, numbering about two thousand, who were delighted to be part of this great force against those who had terrorised them for years.

The pirates had placed large trees across the river, and landing parties were put ashore to cut passages through these obstructions. It took five days to raid the pirate villages, capture their weapons and recover some of their loot, after which they returned to the *Nemesis*, which, together with the small boats, went up the Rejang branch for the same purpose. The aim was to punish the guilty and to spare all unresisting men and the ploy worked as, on the evening of 18th August, the pirate chiefs asked if they could come on board Rajah Brooke's *prau*. They arrived about 9 p.m. and were given brandy to drink on the deck.

In the face of this massive show of force - something that they had never seen before or even imagined in their worst nightmares - these chiefs had decided to throw in the towel, as the thrill and rewards of piracy were not what they used to be. The last, formal step in this ending of piracy on the north-west Borneo coast was on 24th August when the pirate chiefs arrived at Brooke's headquarters in Sarawak and offered their submission.

Six months later the *Singapore Free Press* wrote, "A very few years ago no European merchant vessels ventured on the north-west coast of Borneo; now they are numerous and safe. Formerly shipwrecked crews were attacked, robbed and enslaved; now they are protected, fed and forwarded to a place of safety. The native trade now passes with careless indifference over the very same track....where but a little while ago it was liable to the peril of capture. The crews of *praus* are no longer exposed to the loss of life or liberty, and a degree of security now reigns, so remarkably contrasted with the insecurity of past time...The recent successful proceedings on the coast of Borneo have been followed by the submission of the pirate hordes of Serebas and Sakarran." [21]

The eradication of piracy in Borneo was one of the Royal Navy's proudest achievements in East Asia. It was more successful than their efforts off the China coast because in Borneo they were able to co-ordinate their action with that of Rajah James Brooke, who knew that his fiefdom of Sarawak would never prosper until its seas could be cleansed of this age old scourge. This staunch and consistent co-operation was never the case in China where the government was never more than half-hearted in its opposition to piracy and so many government officials were in league with the pirates.

One would have thought that the praise and gratitude that was so eloquently expressed by the *Singapore Free Press* would have been universally shared back in Britain but that was not the case. The "humanitarians", led by both the mischief makers of Exeter Hall and the Liberal Party in the House of Commons, vilified James Brooke and Captain Farquhar for "killing the poor pirates" in much the same way that the "human rights" mob of the twenty-first century criticise the armed forces of Britain and the United States whenever they do anything effective to combat terrorism. In ridding north-west Borneo of piracy, thereby letting the ordinary people live in peace and security, James Brooke and Captain Farquhar did far more for mankind than those loud mouths in London who were simply indulging their bigotries, not to mention their envy, under the mask of "humanitarianism".

When Captain Keppel arrived back in Singapore on *HMS Dido* in 1843 he was able to claim "head money" under an Act of George IV (6 c.49) for the twenty-three pirates who had been killed during the skirmish off Cape Datu. The *Dido's* officers and men were awarded £20 for each of the dead pirates and £5 for the other pirates who had attacked them on that occasion, making a total of £795. A nice amount for a good shore leave in Singapore.

It might be thought strange that the law allowed the sailors to be paid "per pirate killed" but no less strange are the modern methods of chasing pirates. In June, 2009, ten pirates, armed with rocket-propelled grenades, machine guns and grappling hooks were seized on two skiffs in the Gulf of Aden by the frigate, *HMS Portland*. After disarming them the Navy let them go because, under the "rules of engagement", they could arrest them only if they actually caught them in the act of piracy – a virtual impossibility. Had the Navy been under similar restraint in the nineteenth century the coasts of Borneo would never have been cleared of pirates in the way that they were. The indulging of violent criminals so as not to upset their "dignity" or "human rights", thereby letting them get on with their theft and murder, is far less moral than paying sailors a bounty per head of pirates killed.

ESQUIMALT

In the world there may be nations, and there gathers round every throne
The strength of earth-born armies; but the sea is England's own;
As she ruled, she shall rule it, from Plymouth to Esquimalt
As long as the winds are tameless – as long as the waves are salt.

- *The Sea Queen Awakes*, Clive Phillips-Wolley

At the south-eastern end of Vancouver Island is the harbour of Esquimalt which, with its narrow entrance and deep harbour, was said to be the best anchorage on the whole west coast of America, apart from San Francisco. It was also, according to a climate report, the cloudiest place in the British Empire apart from London. [1]

Esquimalt's first real connection with the Royal Navy was in 1846 when the survey vessel, *HMS Pandora*, under the command of Lieutenant-Commander James Wood, sailed up from Valparaiso, Chile, the then headquarters of the Royal Navy's Pacific station, to survey and chart its harbour.

The first of Her Majesty's ships to be stationed there was *HMS Constance*, under the command of Captain George Courtenay, which did some excellent survey work in the Strait of Georgia, between Vancouver Island and the mainland.

The presence of this vessel and subsequent ones was a gentle warning to the expansionists in both Russia and America that this area, discovered by Captain Cook and surveyed by Captain Vancouver and within the domain of the Hudson's Bay Company, was and would be British territory.

The shore base at Esquimalt had its origins in the Crimean War when warships set out from here for the ill-fated Battle of Petropavlovsk. Accordingly a hospital consisting of three wooden huts were built to receive expected battle casualties. However, it was too far away from Russia to be of much use and the real importance of those three crude huts on Duntze Head was that they formed the foundation of what would become an ever growing shore facility.

From Esquimalt the Navy's survey ships went forth to sound and chart the heavily indented west coast of Canada. The surveying season was in the summer months when the bays and inlets were ice free.

360

In 1859 *HMS Plumper*, a screw sloop of eleven guns, spent several months on surveying operations in the Strait of Georgia, during which she discovered several new anchorages between Nanaimo and Cape Lazo. The most important of these was the Courtenay River, which they named after Rear-Admiral Courtenay, who had formerly commanded *HMS Constance* in these waters.

They ascertained that small boats and stern-wheel steamers could travel a fair way up this "considerable river" [2] and noted that on its banks were "extensive tracts of excellent land, varying from 20 to 100 feet in elevation and clothed with a rich, luxuriant grass. This land is ready for the plough, is entirely clear of pine tree, and studded here and there with a better kind of oak than is usually found on the cleared lands of Vancouver's Island. This river....empties itself into a good and spacious harbour, Port Augusta....scarcely fifty miles from Nanaimo." [3] Upon finishing its survey, *HMS Plumper* returned to Esquimalt for the winter.

Some tribes of Indians on the coast of British Columbia were friendly while others were not and, when crews of trading vessels were murdered, punishment had to be meted out by Her Majesty's ships from Esquimalt.

In 1864 a small schooner, the *Kingfisher*, with a crew of two white men and an Indian, went to trade with the natives at Clayoquot Sound, on the west coast of Vancouver Island. They took with them a considerable quantity of blankets but also some whisky, which they gave to some of the Ahooset Indians who boarded the vessel for the purpose of bartering. In the words of an officer of *HMS Sutlej*, stationed at Esquimalt at the time, "Whisky, when given to an Indian, almost makes him mad." [4]

After drinking the good Scotch these Indians turned round and murdered the crew. They then made off with the cargo, which they distributed among the different villages (ranches).

HMS Devastation was sent from Esquimalt to seize the murderers but the whole tribe turned out with the intention of fighting and so the vessel, not living up to her deadly name, returned to Esquimalt.

Then *HMS Sutlej*, the flagship of the Pacific station, set out with a party of marines. This 3,000 ton vessel had a crew of 510 and carried on her main deck four 110 pound Armstrong guns and twenty-two 68 pounders while on her upper deck were eight 40 pound Armstrongs and one of 110 pounds. [5]

She left Esquimalt on 1ˢᵗ October, 1864, and steamed up the north arm of Clayoquot Sound where they stopped at a deserted village. In the words of a young officer of the *Sutlej*, "Mr. Hanbin, the Governor's secretary, who speaks the language well, and his man Friday, were sent on shore for the purpose of having a 'whawha' talk with the Indians. We beat to quarters and loaded all the guns. Mr. Hanbin and his man returned without having met any of the Indians.

In the evening a boat was again sent on shore with some men and the Indian (Friday), who captured one of the murderers who is now at Victoria and will soon be hanged.

We then steamed back to the mouth of the Sound and anchored for the night. October 3ʳᵈ, 4 a.m. Up anchor. We proceeded up Herbert Arm and at one o'clock came to the end of it and in sight of an Indian ranche with lots of Indians in it.

Our Indian was sent on shore to demand the surrender of the murderers. The demand was received very coolly. The Indian was kept on shore until the natives had removed all their gear, when he was sent on board to say it was not their intention to give up the murderers who were, all of them, their friends and relations.

Fire was immediately opened on the ranche and the surrounding neighbourhood with shot, shell and rockets. Boats were then sent on shore with crews to burn the ranche and bring away the canoes.

The boats were fired on and did not succeed in capturing all the canoes. The ranche, however, was burnt together with most of the winter stores of the Indians. A splendid blaze was produced as there was much oil on the spot.

We did not do much the next two or three days. On the 5ᵗʰ, however, fifty marines and forty seamen were sent on shore to attack the natives, who were surprised, ran into the bush and began to fire on the party, none of whom were injured in consequence of the Indians having bad firearms. Eight Indians were killed.....The men were sent on shore on a succeeding day but only one more murderer was captured. We then took our departure, leaving the gunboat *Forward* to watch the Indians." [6]

It was in 1865 that Esquimalt was designated as an alternative base to Valparaiso, which had been the headquarters of the Pacific station since 1837. In the aftermath of both the Crimean War and the United States' aggression in the San Juan Islands,

Britain wanted to have a naval base in the North Pacific to keep an eye on these two expansionist and sometimes threatening powers.

With the advance of steam Esquimalt became an important coal depot. Then in 1887 a graving dock, 450 feet long and wide enough to admit a ship of 65 feet breadth, was opened.

Next came the fortifying of the harbour in order to make it, in the words of that tired old phrase, the "Gibraltar of the Pacific". The harbour's narrow entrance was protected by an intricate system of submarine mines, making it impossible for any hostile ship to pass through. The mines were controlled by the fort in such a way that one or any number of them could be exploded as desired.

Esquimalt was fortified more strongly than any other base in the Pacific and great secrecy surrounded the excavation works in the bowels of the rock that formed the fortifications. "Never has a military undertaking in time of profoundest peace been prosecuted with stricter secrecy than the construction of these fortifications....The new forts are designed for stern work and not for display," stated a press report at the time. [7] The magazines were stocked for siege and so secret was the construction work that the workers were changed about so that it would have been impossible for any of them to disclose the full layout of the defences to a hostile power. And who was the "hostile power"?

Lord Salisbury tried to deflect attention from the real target by waffling on about the need to fortify Esquimalt "in view of the Russian fortifications and naval movements at Vladivostok". [8] This was always good stuff for the British electorate since dislike and fear of the Russian despotism ran deep. However, he was really serving up a "blind" as Vladivostok was inoperable during the winter because of ice, it was thousands of miles from Esquimalt, and, if the Russian fortifications at Vladivostok were such a problem, why did the British government voluntarily cede the strategically sited and easily defended island base of Port Hamilton, off the bottom of the Korean peninsula, only two years earlier? Port Hamilton had been acquired for the very purpose of keeping an eye on Russia's Pacific fleet and, overlooking the entrance to the Sea of Japan through which the Czar's ships had to pass, was much better suited for that purpose than distant Esquimalt.

No, the reason for fortifying Esquimalt more strongly than any other Pacific base was to protect the emerging and very promising nation of Canada from attack by the United States and, on that basis, the fortifications were both justified and sensible since, until the 1930s, the United States Army and Navy were still updating plans for the invasion of Canada and, when America's Great White Fleet made its much vaunted Pacific cruise in 1908 in pursuit of "peace", its officers spied on naval bases and gathered intelligence and maps of the harbours that they visited in the British Empire, including Australia and New Zealand. From such information they plotted attack strategies to be implemented in the event of the Americans starting yet another war with Britain.

Even after the settling of the United States-Canada border in 1846 relations between the greatest monarchy and the loudest republic were anything but harmonious and trusting. The Americans were both touchy and arrogant, and, during the American Civil War, Great Britain very nearly went to war with the northern states after two commissioners from the South were forcibly removed from a British ship, the *Trent*, on the high seas. President Lincoln's government had to climb down from its haughty stance and release the men but this was not the end of what Britain referred to throughout the nineteenth century as "the American Difficulty". Without the Royal Navy at Esquimalt the people of western Canada would have had a much harder time from the aggressive and bullying Americans – just as the Mexicans did when the United States engineered endless wars in order to grab more and more territory off its weak neighbour to the south.

In the early flushes of a nationhood that had been forged in a violent and unnecessary revolt against lawful authority and was sustained by the institution of slavery, the typical American of the nineteenth century was regarded as brash, barbaric and brutal – be it to buffaloes, Indians, Mexicans or anyone else who got in his way. The arrogant Monroe Doctrine and America's economic imperialism and restrictive trade laws were designed to keep Latin America poor and forever dependent on the United States. Hence the importance of the Royal Navy at its bases at Esquimalt and Halifax, Nova Scotia, in keeping Canada safe and free to pursue her own course according to the wishes of her people.

The small islands of San Juan, near Vancouver Island, were considered British territory and were inhabited by British subjects but in 1859 they suffered a rude shock when their main island was invaded by a heavily armed American force under Captain George Pickett. These invaders, waving their Stars and Stripes, then set about grabbing choice plots of land and building on them.

364

The Governor of the colony of British Columbia, James Douglas, despatched *HMS Tribune*, an auxiliary screw frigate of 31 guns, *HMS Satellite*, a 21 gun screw corvette, and *HMS Plumper* which, although primarily a survey vessel, mounted 21 guns and had on board a company of Royal Marines. This was a show of British force but not a use of it as Douglas did not want to start a third war with these immature and hot-headed ex-colonists.

To try to defuse the situation Captain Hornby of *HMS Tribune* invited Pickett on board his warship for a discussion. Captain Hornby described him as "more quiet than most of his countrymen but he seems to have just the notion they all have of getting a name by some audacious act" [9] – a typical but not unjustified British view of Americans at that time. However, the constant gun drills of the British warships forced the Americans to move their camp to another part of the island – which must have been humiliating for these cowboys in uniform.

Douglas' was not the only cool head as, when President James Buchanan in Washington heard of what Pickett and his soldiers were doing, he sent the U.S. Army commander, Lieutenant-General Winfield Scott, to mediate. The outcome was that the forces of both sides withdrew, Pickett was ordered off the island, and his immediate superior, the equally hot-headed General Harney, was forced to resign.

For the next twelve years the San Juan Islands were under the joint control of Britain and the United States until the matter went to arbitration in 1872 when the arbitrator, Kaiser Wilhelm I of Germany, awarded them to the United States.

This was a Pyrrhic victory for a self-assertive republic that wanted to encompass the entire North American continent since the behaviour of Pickett and his Yankee soldiers on these small islands was a big factor in convincing the British people of Vancouver and thereabouts that they should join the confederation of Canada even though most of that nascent nation was on the other side of the continent with not much more than trackless prairie and forest between Toronto and the Pacific coast. Thus it was that around the same time that the United States assumed sovereignty of the tiny islands of San Juan, British Columbia joined the dominion of Canada, thereby putting a stop once and for all to further American expansion on the west coast.

Despite the settlement of the San Juan Islands dispute the Americans were still difficult neighbours. In 1889 an American revenue cutter, the *Richard Rush*, illegally seized some Canadian sealing vessels in the Bering Sea, between Alaska and Russia. In violation of both international law and the Fisheries Treaty between Britain and the United States the Americans claimed that they now had sole rights to the fisheries in the Bering Sea.

When the captain of one of the sealing schooners, the *Black Diamond*, refused to hand over the ship's papers the Americans broke into the cabin, forced the hinges off the captain's chest and grabbed the documents. Another schooner, the *Triumph*, was also stopped and searched but was allowed to proceed since no seal skins were found. The captain had very sensibly hidden them under a large quantity of salt.

Then, in a show of ignorance to match their arrogance, the Americans put *one* seaman on the *Black Diamond* and ordered it to proceed to Sitka in Alaska. Instead, the *Black Diamond's* skipper sailed it to Unalaska in the Aleutians in the hope of finding a British warship there but, there being none, he sailed on to Victoria on Vancouver Island – still with the American seaman on board. The Yank was at all times treated with courtesy but nobody took any notice of his orders. Apparently the U.S. Customs had not yet learned that, if you purport to capture a vessel, you should at least man her with a crew sufficient to see that its orders were carried out.

In response to this cheeky provocation the Royal Navy gathered its ships at Esquimalt and headed north "to protect British and Canadian sailors in case of any future attempts at capture by United States war vessels". [10] There was the flagship *HMS Swiftsure*, the cruiser *Amphion*, the men-of-war *Icarus* and *Champion* and two torpedo boats. The *Amphion* was a twin-screw war steamer with an armament of ten 6 inch breechloaders, four 3 pound quick firing guns, thirteen assorted machine guns, four torpedo tubes above water and two 17 knot torpedo boats.

Faced with this sort of power and resolution, the Americans backed down. A joint British-American Commission was set up to look into the dispute and the U.S. government was accordingly fined $464,000.[11] Much of the adventurism that the young and immature American republic engaged in was motivated by the nature of its "mob politics". When the next presidential election came round a desperate President Harrison tried to reignite the fisheries dispute in his bellicose speeches but it didn't do him any good as he was defeated by Grover Cleveland.

It was not until the Spanish-American War of 1898 that the "American Difficulty" began to ease as Britain was the only European power to sympathise with the United States in this conflict, in which the "Great Republic" was again the aggressor. This laid the foundations for better relations between the two Anglo-Saxon powers, which was more than timely in view of the challenges that they were to face together in the world wars of the twentieth century – wars which, but for the wretched American War of Independence, would never have taken place since Germany would never have dared to take on a Britain that was permanently linked with the entire North American continent.

In 1905 Esquimalt, together with the base at Halifax, Nova Scotia, was handed over to the government of Canada free of charge and ever since Esquimalt has been the Pacific headquarters of the Royal Canadian Navy.

The Royal Navy left behind the graves of fifty-five of its sailors who had died from accident, disease or natural causes. To-day they lie in the south-west corner (the "Naval Corner") of the Old Burying Ground in Pioneer Square, Victoria, the capital of British Columbia, which is not far from Esquimalt.

If one or more men from a ship died while she was based at Esquimalt, the ship's company would erect a memorial in the cemetery before sailing off. Thus the four sailors from *HMS Thetis*, who drowned in 1852 between Victoria and Esquimalt harbour – John Miller (22 years old), James Smith (31), Charles Parsons (35) and W.R. Plummer (23) – are buried together beneath the *HMS Thetis* memorial.

Another drowning occurred on 6th June, 1860, when five men from *HMS Satellite* were lost. They are buried at the *HMS Satellite* memorial together with another six from that ship who died during her visits to Esquimalt between 1856 and 1860.

In 1993 the Victoria branch of the Royal Canadian Naval Association erected a large granite memorial, containing the names of all known Royal Navy personnel who died while at Esquimalt. This is a memorial not only to these fifty-five men but also to the Royal Navy itself for protecting these western seas and shores for the future nation of Canada at a time when there were avaricious eyes on them from both the Russians in the east and the Americans in the south.

PORT HAMILTON

Throughout the nineteenth century Russia was perceived as a threat to India, an impression that Russia's vigorous railway building programme to the east and its military movements in and near Afghanistan did little to dispel.

In 1884 the Russians captured Merv in Turkmenistan, which was too close for comfort for the British rulers of India – especially after 1886 when the Russians linked Merv with their railway network.

In 1885 they seized another town, Pandjeh, killing more than three hundred of its defenders. Although there was no formal border between Turkmenistan and Afghanistan Pandjeh was regarded as an Afghan town and its capture by Russian troops breached the neutrality of Afghanistan, which was meant to be a buffer country between the Czar's empire and British India.

Upon receipt of the news of Pandjeh in Saint Petersburg there was an outbreak of jingoism. When the Czar visited the theatre on 10th April, 1885, the audience, believing that this latest Russian military success had his full approval, "rose...and shook the building with an ovation of applause." [1] The following evening the Russian Minister of War told an assembly of officers that he had "the assurance of the Czar that Russian troops might advance but they would never retire". [2]

These and other bellicose actions led to a "war scare" throughout the British Empire with ports in places as far away as Australia and New Zealand strengthening existing harbour defences and building new ones.

It was in this atmosphere that Britain decided to keep a closer watch on the Russian fleet in the Pacific by ordering the Royal Navy to occupy Port Hamilton, a harbour that is formed of three islands called the Nankow group and which is situated off the southern tip of the Korean peninsula and to the north-east of the large island of Quelpart. Port Hamilton, commanding the strait leading from the Yellow Sea to the Sea of Japan, had been surveyed in 1845 by Captain Sir Edward Belcher on *HMS Samarang* and was named by him after the then Secretary of the Admiralty, Captain W. Hamilton. "Secret" orders were sent to various vessels in Far Eastern waters to prepare for the mission.

In the words of an officer on *HMS Flying Fish*, "We returned to Manila for coals, etc. about 2nd April and found two urgent telegrams from the Commander-in-chief, ordering us up to Hong Kong at full speed......On arrival at Hong Kong....we got telegraphic orders....to hoist our chart-house, cook-house, steam launch, etc. and replace our two 7 inch guns, which we accordingly did, working day and night and making life unbearable. As soon as the job was over and we expected to get a rub of paint and settle down as part of the Hong Kong defence, we suddenly got orders to be ready for sea next day. They filled us up below and on deck with mines, electric cables and torpedo stores....The ship was provided with a tender in the shape of a big steam launch, purchased from the Hong Kong government.

Of course, our orders were sealed but it was an open secret that we were bound for Port Hamilton, which we eventually fetched, having only encountered one gale of wind en route, which compelled us inshore to rescue our tender.

At Port Hamilton we found three or four small craft and a lot of timber sent over from Nagasaki for the defence of the port....We at once set to work to lay down the mines and build the booms wherewith to block the smaller entrance.

I was told off with the captain of the *Merlin* and an ex-gunner to fit and lay the mines and, thanks to the first rate gunner and amateur torpedist, we got on first rate..." [3]

At around 9 p.m. on 10th May, 1885, a Russian transport steamer arrived with allegedly leaky boilers and was boarded by British sailors. The orders had been not to run up the British flag unless the occupation was directly or indirectly challenged and the arrival of the mysterious transport steamer was seen to fulfil that condition.

In the words of our officer on the *Flying Fish*, "In the dead of the night three parties were landed to hoist Union Jacks so that in the morning the summits of the three islands were decorated with our glorious flag, and a sentry looking after each of them....The Ruskie came on board on the morning and congratulated our captain on the latest British possession and, not getting much out of him, he and a Japanese man-of-war cleared out to inform their respective governments and we were left to continue our operations in peace."[4]

The acquisition of this strategically important harbour was acclaimed throughout the Empire. In the words of a sailor on board the *Merionethshire* at Port Hamilton, "This is a lovely harbour, quite landlocked and sheltered. It is a second Hong Kong and, in fact, far better." [5] Yes, and it was 1,100 miles nearer to Vladivostok than

369

Hong Kong, thereby making it easier to prevent aggression in the area by the ever creeping Russian empire.

"Port Hamilton completed the system by which the British fleet could effectively protect the commerce of the Empire in these seas and an immense advantage has been gained," stated a press report of the time. [6] Yes, but not for long.

"Wood is scarce, fresh water is plentiful and good, and easily embarked. Fish may be caught by the seine," wrote the *China Pilot* [7] of the new base.

The island, formerly a Korean penal colony, contained about two thousand inhabitants who were described by an officer of the occupying squadron as "dirty and lazy, the women and children doing all the work and the men sauntering about in soiled white clothes". [8] The islanders were mainly fisher folk "who had distinguished themselves by a habit of murdering such unfortunate sailors as from time to time were shipwrecked near their shores." [9]

The purpose of the annexation was twofold: to provide a much needed coaling station in the north-west Pacific and to keep a watch on the ships of Russia's Pacific Squadron as they passed in and out of Vladivostok and other ports on Russia's east coast.

According to the *Times*, "The fact is simply that we have acquired a coaling station for our ships in the north Pacific similar to that already existing at Labuan. The want of such a station has long been felt, and no better place could have been selected than Port Hamilton, the only advantageous anchorage and shelter for ships around the stormy coasts of Quelpart....By obtaining this advantageous coaling station there can be no doubt that the Government have taken a wise step towards the further security of our naval position in the seas of China and Japan." [10]

The second purpose of acquiring Port Hamilton was immediately grasped in Russia where, according to the Saint Petersburg correspondent of London's *Daily News*, "It is urged here that the British occupation of Port Hamilton and British influence in Korea constitute a continual menace to the Russian possessions in Eastern Siberia and that they can not be tolerated." [11]

Britain wasted no time in making something of its new acquisition and immediately began erecting barracks for troops and storehouses for war materials. In a letter from a sailor at Port Hamilton dated 17th May, 1885, "The port is all laid with mines and torpedoes and we are full up with coals and stores and have provisions for a month for a thousand men. Sometimes the British men-of-war come and take an anchor or five tons of coal away. Two Chinese gunboats came in this morning. I don't know what they want unless they are wind bound for it has been blowing a gale for these few days past." [12]

By 3rd June, less than a month after the annexation, Hong Kong's *China Mail* was reporting, "There are now half a dozen British men-of-war in Port Hamilton and the tender of *Thales* makes frequent trips between that port and Nagasaki with coal, rough spars and stores. The telegraph steamer *Agnes* has just laid a submarine cable between Port Hamilton and the North Saddle, which is the extreme north end of the Chusan archipelago." [13]

The cable steamer *Sherard Osborne* also laid a secret cable between Shanghai and Port Hamilton so that the British naval authorities in Shanghai could be informed by Port Hamilton of the movements of Russian ships in and out of its eastern ports.

By the summer of 1886 some seventy marines, fresh from the Sudan campaign, and about a hundred of the local islanders were working hard at constructing roads and piers.

At the time of its annexation Port Hamilton was nominally owned by the Korean government which itself was under the suzerainty of the weak Chinese empire. Not surprisingly, China made a formal protest against Britain's annexation but the *North China Daily News* got it right when it wrote, "You may safely rely upon it that the protest is formal and nothing more." [14] The report went on to say, "A good story is current that last year Li Hung Chang (the Governor of China's Chihli province) mentioned to a foreign Minister Plenipotentiary that Great Britain should never have Port Hamilton for she already possessed enough smuggling stations in Hong Kong without getting another on the coast of China."

It would be fair to say that Port Hamilton was not the bluejackets' favourite port. "Britain's latest acquisition does not seem to be a particularly pleasant place at times. A heavy typhoon not long ago …. blew down a building covering forty men, who had taken refuge there owing to their tents having been carried away at the commencement of the storm. Three men were badly injured, the others being all more or less bruised. *HMS Champion* dragged her anchor and was drifting about the harbour. The *Agamemnon* also dragged 500 yards from her anchorage. The gunboats *Cockchafer* and *Zephyr* were drifting round the lower end of the harbour and narrowly escaped getting on shore. As it was, the *Cockchafer* got her

371

anchor chain foul of the telegraph cable and it took the best part of two days to get her clear.

The *Zephyr* lost her cutter and the *Agamemnon* her steam pinnace but the *Glenogle* weathered the storm splendidly and did not budge an inch." [15]

There was more trouble on 18th March, 1886 – this time with one of the Nordenfeldt guns on *HMS Albatross*. Some time after firing had ceased the boat's crew was sent to pick up a target. While there, someone on board removed the lever of the firing mechanism of the gun with the result that three of the boat's crew were hit by the discharge which followed. Two of them were killed and the other was seriously injured. [16]

All this was a heavy price to pay for a bleak coaling port in the freezing north Pacific which the British government did not have the stomach to hold. At the end of 1886, after an eighteen month occupation, London agreed to cede Port Hamilton to China upon China agreeing not to allow any other power to annex it even though Chinese guarantees were not exactly gilt edged. Indeed, Russia had the power to take it off China any time it liked.

Simultaneously Russia agreed not to occupy any territory in Korea. This was important from Britain's point of view as the safety of British ships in the north Pacific would be jeopardised if any European power gained a foothold on the Korean peninsula.

Russia was probably making a bigger sacrifice than Britain as she had no Pacific port that was not icebound for several months each year. In revenge for Britain's occupation of Port Hamilton Russia had annexed Port Lazaroff in Korea and her withdrawal from it was part of the agreement.

At the time of ceding it to China the British government claimed that its occupation of Port Hamilton was only ever meant to be temporary and that, in view of China's "guarantee" that it should not pass into the hands of Russia, there was no point in keeping it.

Nevertheless, her action in withdrawing from it so soon after spending so much money in fortifying and developing it was seen for what it was – an act of weakness – and "in accordance with the yielding disposition of modern statesmanship". [17]

Britain's kow towing to China over Port Hamilton was particularly resented in the Australasian colonies where they feared that, as a further act of kow towing, Westminster would try to coerce the southern colonies to repeal the laws that they had all enacted to limit the entry of Chinese immigrants to their shores – a policy that was strongly supported by majority opinion throughout Australia and New Zealand.

The formal act of cession to China took place on Sunday, 23rd January, 1887. As with the handover of Hong Kong a hundred and ten years later, China received a territory that had had a lot of value added to it during the time that it was under the British flag.

With the abandonment of Port Hamilton the Royal Navy no longer had a base for shadowing ships sailing in and out of Vladivostok and Britain's nearest coaling port to Vladivostok was now Hong Kong, some two thousand miles away.

Although the handing over of Port Hamilton to China might have suited the governments of Britain, China and Russia, it was regarded in Japan as a breach of the treaty between Japan and China that neither should occupy any territory in Korea.

WEI HAI WEI

During the Japan-China war of 1895 Wei Hai Wei had been the chief Chinese naval station but, upon the defeat of China, it had been temporarily occupied by Japan pending the payment of an indemnity by China of 200 million taels to the Japanese.

Russia loaned China the money to pay off the Japanese and, in return for the loan, China ceded Port Arthur to the Czar for a naval base. So, the real winner of the Chinese-Japanese war seems to have been Russia which acquired its long desired ice free port in the Pacific as well as command of the entrance to the Gulf of Pechili and consequently of the entrance to Tientsin, the port of the Chinese capital, Peking.

Now into this ruthless game of chess came the British who, in response to Russia's occupation of Port Arthur, obtained from the crumbling Chinese empire the lease of Wei Hai Wei, on the opposite headland to Port Arthur. The result of all this was that China lost her two main naval stations – one to Russia and the other to Britain.

Russia's lease of Port Arthur was for twenty-five years whereas Britain's lease of Wei Hai Wei was to last for as long as Russia continued to occupy Port Arthur. When, however, Japan took over the lease of Port Arthur in 1905 after its victory in the Russo-Japanese war, the British lease of Wei Hai Wei was amended so that it would last as long as the Japanese kept Port Arthur. China, defeated, corrupt and chaotic, was in no position other than to agree to these or any other terms that were demanded by other powers.

Also known as Port Edward (the name of its capital), this new territory of 285 square miles included the island of Li-Kung Tao and a hinterland ten miles deep and it had a population of around a hundred thousand. It was leased to Britain under the Convention of Peking of 1898, the same agreement that leased to Britain 355 square miles of the New Territories and Lamma Island at Hong Kong for ninety-nine years. Wei Hai Wei was situated on a promontory near the tip of the Shantung peninsula, from where the Royal Navy could keep watch on the Russians across the water at Port Arthur and on the Germans, who had established a naval base at Tsingtao. And so, what Russia thought would be a free passage for her ships between the Gulf of Pechili and the Pacific was now subject to the eyes – and guns – of the Royal Navy.

Britain had larger investments in Chinese railways, mines and trade than any other nation and the British government, while having neither respect for nor trust in the Chinese empire, did not want it to suffer a total collapse simply for the reason that the devil you know is better than the one you don't. It was in this spirit that Lord Salisbury, the Prime Minister, hoped that the occupation of Wei Hai Wei by the world's greatest and most civilised power "would inspire China with courage to withstand her enemies, and avert the despairing feeling that Russian domination was her inexorable destiny". [1]

Part of the lease agreement was that Britain would allow Chinese warships to use its new base and a number of Chinese officers would be trained in the Royal Navy. Of course, there would not have been any need to take a lease of Wei Hai Wei if the British government had not ceded Port Hamilton a few years earlier after spending so much money on it.

Port Hamilton was superior to Wei Hai Wei in several respects. For one thing, it could never be attacked from the land. Like Hong Kong, Wei Hai Wei consisted of a small island and a hinterland on the mainland. There was no fear of a landward attack by China as that would be beyond her capability but Russia was another matter as her expansion in Asia was always by land and not by sea. It was not beyond the realms of possibility that, in the event of a total dismemberment of the Chinese empire (not all that unlikely), Russia, with her railway now reaching Port Arthur, would expand through northern China and so threaten Wei Hai Wei from the land.

Britain undertook a survey of the little known harbour and a certain amount of coal and ammunition was taken to Wei Hai Wei from Hong Kong but, beyond that, there was little done in the way of construction or improving the fortifications – especially of the island of Li-Kung-Tao – which, like Hong Kong island, was the key to the base. Even after a year's occupation Wei Hai Wei was rather bare and lacked most of the facilities that the British had spent so much time, money and energy building at Port Hamilton.

In the words of Sir Cyprian Bridge, speaking in 1905 as the recently retired commander of the Royal Navy in the north Pacific, "I have always held the view that to fortify Wei Hai Wei or to establish great coal or other supplies there is worse than useless. It is positively mischievous. There is very little deep water in the inner harbour, which can only hold four battleships, while the cruisers have to anchor outside." [2] He did, however, realise that it had some advantages. "On the other hand, there are advantages worth considering at Wei Hai Wei, if that place be treated as a sanatorium and recreation ground for the six or seven thousand men of the fleet in Eastern waters. We have a naval hospital at Yokohama, and a big hospital at Wei Hai Wei would, in my opinion, be very welcome. Another advantage possessed by the place is that long-range firing at sea, rifle practice on land, exercises and drills can be indulged in without being spied upon by other nations and without danger". [3]

These sentiments were echoed six months later by both Sir Charles Dilke and that great spokesman for the Navy in Parliament, Lord Charles Beresford. In Dilke's words, "It (Wei Hai Wei) is really of very little account. When the lease was effected Lord Charles Beresford and myself pointed out that the place was such a short distance from Port Arthur and had such a very wide entrance that it could not be defended. In fact, it is an impossible place to defend unless a fleet is constantly there. Torpedo boats can get in and out of it easily….It really consists only of a naval hospital and a cricket ground……It is of no account strategically." [4]

Britain raised a regiment of Chinese soldiers under British officers to garrison the new base. When their first payday came due, they were amazed that they got the full amount of what was due to them with nothing mulcted by the officers. This was unheard of in Chinese navies and armies.

In their off hours the bluejackets taught the new soldiers how to play football and their enthusiasm soon produced results. Some of the Chinese showed such promise that, when Mr. T. R. Dewar, an ex-Sheriff of London, was visiting the East, he arranged for them to make a football tour of England but "no players are to be included who do not make up their minds to get rid of the sacred 'pig-tail'." [5] The men of the Shantung province were taller than other Chinese so it was not as ridiculous for them to play football as it is for the Cantonese, who are among the shortest people in China, to play basketball – as they do at almost every school in Hong Kong.

In June, 1900, two hundred of these Chinese soldiers and their officers were sent to nearby Taku to capture the forts that were held by the Boxers, who had already ransacked the foreign quarter at the port of Tientsin – just as their successors, the xenophobic Red Guards of Mao's communist regime, would do to foreigners seventy years later, thereby demonstrating an aspect of the Chinese character that should put Westerners on their guard.

The Wei Hai Wei regiment joined with other forces to repel the Boxers' flank attack but with heavy losses. In the attack on the arsenal to the north-east of Tientsin four bluejackets were killed and another fifteen wounded.

After the end of the Boxer rebellion the importance of Wei Hai Wei declined and the fortifying of the base was abandoned, the garrison withdrawn, and it was handed over to the Colonial Office to administer. Needless to say, the place flourished under the freedom and security of British rule and came to be called "The Peach Garden" by its inhabitants to contrast it with the rest of the Shantung peninsula where disorder, brigandage, rapacious taxation and endemic corruption drove many refugees to seek asylum in Wei Hai Wei. So superior was it to what lay over the border that regular inspections of the boundary stones had to be made to prevent their being moved inland so as to bring outside villages within British rule. For a population of about 180,000 people by 1930 there was a police force of fewer than two hundred men, including three European inspectors.

Wei Hai Wei acquired new significance when the Russo-Japanese war broke out in 1904 when it found itself in the middle of the action. Although Britain was neutral in this conflict, that did not mean that she was immune from what was going on.

The Japanese Navy was stopping British merchant ships in the Gulf of Pechili to make sure that they were not taking any provisions to the Russians at Port Arthur, which was under siege and afflicted by typhoid with thousands of sick and wounded and a scarcity of water and ammunition.

In the interests of humanity the cruiser *HMS Andromeda* sailed from Wei Hai Wei and took to Port Arthur two surgeons, a hospital staff, £100,000 worth of provisions, 350 beds, medical appliances and comforts for the Russian sick and wounded. [6] However, the Japanese refused to allow her to enter Port Arthur and they declined all offers to get life saving drugs and other provisions to those who were dying there – an early and ominous sign of that streak of cruelty in the Japanese character which would reach its full "flowering" in the horrors of their prisoner-of-war camps in the Second World War. It is worth noting that this unfriendly – indeed inhumane – action by Japan towards *HMS Andromeda* took place during the tenure of the Anglo-Japanese naval agreement of 1902.

Wei Hai Wei also attained an importance in the First World War when it became the port from which many of the nearly 200,000 men of the Chinese Labour Corps departed for France where they performed non-combatant duties behind the lines, maintaining railways, roads, dockyards, etc. In France they earned four times as much money as they could in Shantung.

After the end of the First World War the importance of Wei Hai Wei waned again and it never amounted to much more than a coaling station and sanatorium. It was a "free port", the locals were friendly and in summer the climate was ideal. For these reasons it was a more popular base than Port Hamilton had been – especially for those who were escaping the mid-summer humidity of Hong Kong. The sailors called it "Way High". For them it was more of a summer "hill station" than a strategic naval base.

"With its exquisite climate, russet mountains, blue sea and lovely bays, Wei as a summer resort could not be surpassed," wrote *The Times* in 1930. "Every year hundreds of foreigners journey from the fierce heat of Shanghai and Tientsin. There are boating, fishing, golf, lawn tennis, riding, the best swimming in the world, snipe, hares and woodcock to shoot in season, and enchanting walks." [7]

The China squadron would sail north during the hot months from May to August and would put in to Wei Hai Wei to give the sailors some shore leave. At the height of summer in the era before air conditioning Wei was definitely superior to sticky Hong Kong, of which an officer of *HMS Flying Fish* wrote in 1885, "We are at present in Kowloon Dock undergoing a spell of purgatory. The smell, heat, mosquitoes and the hammering of a thousand Chinamen combined is enough to drive one to drink or a lunatic asylum". [8]

While in port at Wei the sailors would throw overboard old clothes and other items that they no longer wanted and these would be fished out of the sea immediately by the boathooks of the Chinese in their sampans. "The British were very kind to the Chinese," remembered one of the locals, Lu Zhenlian, many years later. [9]

On 30th September, 1930, after thirty-two years of British rule, the last Commissioner of Wei Hai Wei, Reginald Johnston, handed the place back to China pursuant to the Washington naval agreement of 1922. There was a parade down to the foreshore where a salute of twenty-one guns was fired by two warships, *HMS Kent* and *HMS Petersfield*. There were twelve other British warships in the anchorage at the time.

That was the official ceremony but a more touching one had taken place a few days earlier when the headmen of the villages throughout the territory presented Johnston with a porcelain bowl full of pure wtaer in recognition of the purity and honesty of the

British administration. In the words of *The Times*, "The improvement in the condition of the population of the Wei Hai Wei territory during the thirty-two years of British occupation has been remarkable. The numbers and the wealth of the Chinese population have increased; anti-foreigner feeling is unknown, and the fishermen, farmers and small traders of the territory have enjoyed a comfort and security unknown in other parts of the distressful province of Shantung." [10]

The locals were amazed that the British did not take any of their property with them – as Chinese would have if they were vacating a territory. All the buildings, government stores, the civil hospital and the cable from Chefoo to Wei Hai Wei were left for the incoming Chinese government.

The local people, fearing the unbridled greed of China's provincial tax collectors and the anarchy that prevailed throughout Shantung province, did not want to be handed back to China and so they sent a petition to London, asking to remain under British rule. This was rejected by the British government with the same callousness that they would later show to the people of Hong Kong when they handed them over to the world's most odious and oppressive regime without consulting their wishes by referendum or otherwise.

So fearful were the traders of Wei Hai Wei of being delivered up, together with their property, into the hands of the grasping Chinese government that in the weeks immediately prior to the handover several of the merchants moved their money away and others sent their stocks of salt to Japan – just as, prior to the handover of Hong Kong in 1997, its Chinese businessmen moved their assets offshore and scrambled for British passports. The fact is that the Chinese do not trust their own government – a problem that they never had with a British colonial administration.

The fears of the people of Wei Hai Wei were realised when the new regime, delighted at finding some part of China that was prospering, imposed heavy taxes, which provoked street riots. The increases in taxes were accompanied by a fourfold increase in government officials, a collapse in land prices and the ending of Wei Hai Wei's status as a free port. As was the case with Hong Kong, these people did not like the hauling down of the Union Jack, the symbol of the British rule that had made their little enclave on the China coast both free and prosperous but, again like Hong Kong, they had no say in the matter.

THE BATTLE OF CORONEL

When the First World War broke out on 4th August, 1914, the main menace in the Pacific was the presence of Germany's East Asiatic Cruiser Squadron, which operated out of Tsing-Tao, the German colony and naval base in the north of China. On the declaration of war the commander-in-chief, Vice-Admiral Maximilian Graf von Spee, had his flagship, the *Scharnhorst*, and her sister ship, the armoured cruiser *Gneisnau*, far away – at Ponape in the German colony of the Caroline Islands, north-east of New Guinea – where they were taking on coal from the chartered Japanese vessel, *Fukoku Maru*. The other ships of this cruiser squadron were scattered – the *Leipzig* was on the coast of Mexico, the *Nurnberg* was on her way there to relieve the *Leipzig*, and the *Emden* slipped out of Tsing-Tao to avoid being trapped there by the ships of Britain's China station.

Fearing that the *Fukoku Maru* would disclose the German ships' position when she returned to Japan, von Spee decided to head north to Pagan in the Marianas, another group of German owned islands which, like the Carolines, spread over a large area of the mid Pacific. Here the *Scharnhorst* and *Gneisnau* met up with the *Emden* and the *Nurnberg* as well as a couple of armed merchant vessels.

That a collier should be the reason for the move to Pagan was telling since the German ships' need for coal was not matched by the availability of coal depots. In other words, coal was the limiting factor for the squadron's activities in the world's largest ocean where distances were so great. Coal determined how long the ships could stay at sea and no move was made without a consideration of the coal supply.

In 1914 the ships of the British Empire carried 43% of the world's trade while Germany, the second nation, transported 12% on its merchantmen. This omnipresence of British merchant vessels on the oceans of the world meant that a squadron such as von Spee's could do quite a bit of damage since it would not be difficult to find a British merchant ship; they were everywhere. However, for the same reason any damage inflicted on British shipping would be no more than a pin prick in view of its preponderance of vessels.

Nevertheless the presence of this enemy squadron in the Pacific was a very real problem as, until it could be found and destroyed, extra precautions would have to be taken by those ships flying the Red Duster and there would be higher insurance premiums on voyages.

From Pagan the *Emden* was sent to the Indian Ocean where she wreaked havoc on British commerce until she went to the Cocos Islands where she was sunk by the Australian light cruiser, *HMAS Sydney*, in November, 1914.

The rest of von Spee's squadron proceeded east through the Marshall Islands and at Fanning Island the *Nurnberg* cut the important telegraph cable between Honolulu and Fiji.

Upon hearing that a New Zealand force had landed and captured the German colony of Samoa and was holding its German governor a prisoner, von Spee steamed down there in the expectation that there would be some British men-of-war in Apia harbour that he could destroy. However, there were no such vessels and, realising that the garrison was probably stronger than any landing parties that he could muster from his three ships (*Scharnhorst*, *Gneisnau* and *Nurnberg*), he sailed away without doing anything other than disclosing his whereabouts. The reason why he did not bombard the island was that most of the Europeans there were Germans.

From Samoa he took his ships to Tahiti, which he did bombard. He then met up with the *Dresden* and *Leipzig* and all five ships sailed towards the coast of South America, taking on more coal at Mas A Fuera in the remote Chilean owned islands of Juan Fernandez, west of Valparaiso. Von Spee's was now a powerful and troublesome fleet.

Coaled up, they steamed towards Chile and landed at the small port of Coronel where von Spee learned of the presence of *HMS Glasgow*, which in turn had been sent to the area to look for the East Asiatic Cruiser Squadron. At last von Spee had found something that was worth chasing.

HMS Glasgow had been sent to the area as part of a hastily put together squadron to find von Spee's ships and destroy them. Not only would this clear an unlikely but nevertheless omnipresent threat to British merchant shipping in the Pacific but also it would free up British warships for other wartime duties.

Upon learning that von Spee was heading towards South America the Admiralty was particularly alarmed as it was thought that he might bring his wretched squadron around Cape Horn and start making havoc among merchant ships in the vital sea lanes of the Atlantic. And so, some warships that were operating in the South

Atlantic were ordered to form a battle squadron and try to engage him so as to put an end to his threat. This British squadron consisted of two heavy cruisers, *HMS Good Hope* and *Monmouth*, the light cruiser, *HMS Glasgow*, an armed merchantman, the *Otranto*, and an old and slow battleship, *HMS Canopus*. The last mentioned had been added to provide superior gun power, her 12 inch guns being superior to those on the German warships.

Command of the squadron was given to Rear-Admiral Sir Christopher Cradock, who was ordered to take the ships around Cape Horn into the Pacific and engage the East Asiatic Cruiser Squadron *as a unit*. This was important as, without the *Canopus*, Cradock's ships would be well and truly outgunned. Unfortunately, due to the lack of clarity of the orders or for some other reason Cradock did not follow them and allowed the *Canopus* to fall a long way behind with the squadron's colliers.

HMS Glasgow was the fastest ship and so she went ahead and by 31st October, when she put into Coronel Bay, she was already picking up wireless signals from the *Leipzig*.

After she rejoined the *Good Hope*, *Monmouth* and *Otranto* at sea and they were in the process of forming into a line abreast for what they believed was a single ship, the *Leipzig*, the *Glasgow* saw some smoke to the north-east, from the direction of the Chilean coast. The smoke then became two large ships with a smaller one slightly astern of them. Suddenly the two opposing commanders realised that their fleets were approaching each other in what would be World War One's supreme trial of naval strength in the Pacific. There was a strong wind blowing from the south-east and the Pacific was not living up to its calm name.

Spee's ships, the *Scharnhorst, Gneisnau* and *Leipzig*, altered course towards the British, the *Dresden* being about twelve miles to the rear and the *Nurnberg* even further back.

On the British side the number was four – *Good Hope*, *Monmouth*, *Glasgow* and *Otranto*, as the *Canopus* was now some two hundred miles behind. Although ordered not to go into battle without the guns of the *Canopus*, Cradock chose to do so. He formed his line in an attempt to bring the German ships to action with the setting sun in their eyes but von Spee countered it by altering course and increasing speed, which latter he had more of than the British ships.

Without the *Canopus*, the *Good Hope* and *Monmouth* were outgunned by the *Scharnhorst* and *Gneisnau*, whose guns were more

382

suitable in a rough sea – as was the case on this day of destiny. Spee had a well-trained and experienced crew of regulars whereas the British fleet contained a lot of reservists. However, in wartime reservists, with their myriad backgrounds and experiences and multiplicity of skills, have shown themselves to be every bit as valuable as the regulars and that is why after the Second World War King George VI made the uniforms of the R.N.V.R. the same as those of the Royal Navy (apart from the letter "R" on the Reserve uniforms).

As the sun was going down the two squadrons were steaming down the coast at an ever decreasing range between them. The waves were now so big that they were breaking over the bows of the heavily rolling warships.

By the time the sun sank below the western horizon the British ships were silhouetted against it whereas the Germans had the advantage of being less visible in the gathering darkness off the land. With the advantage now of both light and guns von Spee opened fire at a range of almost seven miles and was replied to by a thunder from the British guns.

The larger guns of the *Good Hope* did not last long and one of them was knocked out before it had even fired a single shell. It took only a few minutes for the *Monmouth's* fore turret to be hit by a high explosive shell from the *Gneisnau* and it wasn't long before she was burning aft with her ammunition exploding. She began to list heavily to port and then limped out of the battle line.

The *Good Hope*, from which Cradock tried to direct the battle, was targeted by the guns of the *Scharnhorst*. She too caught on fire within a very short time but her guns kept firing even as her decks and bulkheads were being torn away by the explosions. Her guns only began to slow down because those firing them were being consumed by the flames. When darkness came, the red glow of this burning cruiser made her an even easier target for the *Scharnhorst's* superior guns.

She made one final dash towards the enemy, blazing away with whatever guns were still operating, but the two German cruisers concentrated their fire on her with full broadsides and finished her off. A few minutes before 8 p.m. her ever worsening fires blew up a magazine and the flames rose two hundred feet in the air. The noise of this almighty explosion was heard up and down the Chilean coast and it was the end of the *Good Hope*. Those of her ship's company who had not been burned to death were drowned in the dark and freezing sea.

The *Dresden*, having now joined the others in the battle line, and the *Leipzig* concentrated their fire on the *Glasgow* but, despite having about six hundred shells fired at her, she managed to survive. She was hit by only five of them but the damage was minimal.

As the battle raged Cradock ordered the *Otranto* to retire since she was outgunned and could be of little use, and so she drew away to starboard and so survived the battle.

The *Monmouth* limped away in the darkness to the north but, in the light of the moon, was seen by the *Nurnberg,* which fired a salvo into her. The stricken British cruiser could not reply and so the Germans paused in their firing, expecting her to surrender. But surrender is not part of the Royal Navy's battle code and so a further salvo was fired, which sent the *Monmouth* to the bottom of the ocean where her entire ship's company joined those of the *Good Hope* in their watery grave. Altogether some 1,600 British sailors lost their lives during this short battle.

The *Glasgow* and the *Otranto* managed to get away to fight another day while the German ships were barely scratched. Coronel was the first defeat suffered by the Royal Navy in an action at sea for 109 years and it hurt.

At the Admiralty there was both astonishment and grief that Cradock had not kept his ships together as he had been ordered to do and which might have changed the course and outcome of the battle. Without the *Canopus* he faced superior fire power and it is very difficult to avoid defeat under those conditions. In taking on this superior German squadron Rear-Admiral Cradock showed that his courage was greater than his wisdom and for that he and his sailors paid the supreme price.

The reaction at the Admiralty was swift and sure. Two battle cruisers, *HMS Invincible* and *Inflexible*, were despatched to the South Atlantic to form the core of a new force to catch and dispose of von Spee's fleet once and for all. Command was given to Vice-Admiral Sturdee, who sailed south without delay.

They reached the Falkland Islands on 7th December and began coaling. Besides the two battle cruisers the squadron now comprised *HMS Kent, Carnarvon* and *Cornwall* as well as the doughty *Glasgow*, fresh from her encounter at Coronel.

After their victory in the Pacific von Spee's ships had visited Valparaiso where, under international law, they were allowed to stay for twenty-four hours to take on coal and provisions. This was not enough time for all the coal that was needed to get to the Atlantic and then home to Germany and so they returned to the remote Juan Fernandez islands to take on more of that vital fuel, which determined how far they could go.

The East Asiatic Cruiser Squadron then steamed around Cape Horn and into the Atlantic. Cocky after his bloodless victory at Coronel and believing that there would be no British ships in the area, von Spee decided to go to the Falklands and destroy the British wireless station there.

Thus it was that at eight o'clock on the morning of 8th December, while Sturdee's ships at the Falklands were still coaling, the German vessels were spotted and a great battle took place.

All four German cruisers – *Scharnhorst, Gneisnau, Leipzig* and *Nurnberg* – were sunk and out of the total ships' companies of 2,200, only 215 survived. Von Spee went down with his ship as did two of his sons. Two German colliers, the *Baden* and *Santa Isabel,* were also sunk a bit further north from the main action. The British lost only ten men – either killed in action or died later from their wounds.

Thus was Coronel avenged, the Pacific was clear of German raiders for the rest of the world war and the British warships hunting von Spee and his menacing squadron were now free for other tasks. The action in the Falklands was more of a victory than Coronel was a defeat for, without taking into account the terrible loss of life, the cost to the Royal Navy of the latter action was only two rather old cruisers whereas the fruits of the Falklands were much greater than that.

ACCIDENTS AT SEA

We must feed our sea for a thousand years,
For that is our doom and pride,
As it was when they sailed with the *Golden Hind*,
Or the wreck that struck last tide –
Or the wreck that lies on the spouting reef
Where the ghastly blue-lights flare.
If blood be the price of admiralty,
If blood be the price of admiralty,
If blood be the price of admiralty,
Lord God, we ha' bought it fair!

Rudyard Kipling, *The Song of the Dead*

Falling overboard was an occupational hazard and most sailors seem to have finished up in the briny at some point in their careers – be it falling from the rigging or from the wharf while returning from shore leave, or just getting from ship to shore.

When, in May, 1871, *HMS Virago's* whaleboat was bringing ashore under sail the ship's surgeon, Doctor Crosbie, two midshipmen, six seamen and a boy, a sudden gust of Wellington wind turned the boat completely over about two hundred yards from shore. Boats from the Wellington wharves quickly put off to rescue the men but two of them drowned – the warrant officers' steward, Taylor, and the boy seaman named Smith. Taylor's last words before going under were "Oh, my God, save me!" One of the midshipmen, Mr. Forster, was weighed down by his Inverness cape, which was buttoned on; he was saved by having an oar pushed to him by Doctor Crosbie.

When a party of bluejackets were returning to *HMS Calliope* from their leave in September, 1853, one of them dropped his bundle over the side of the liberty boat that was returning them to their ship in Auckland harbour. He leant over the gunwale to recover it, causing the boat to capsize and he was drowned.

On a voyage to Auckland in 1878 one of the sailmakers on *HMS Sapphire* called Hawkes jumped into the sea to rescue another sailor, Begley, who had fallen overboard. Begley was insensible and Hawkes held him up for thirty-seven minutes until a boat arrived from the ship. This was the seventh life that Hawkes had saved in this way and, not surprisingly, he held a Humane Society medal.

Another bluejacket worthy of a medal was the boatswain on *HMS Blanche*, Mr. Williams. During the *Blanche's* commission he managed to save four lives. He was less successful on 27th October, 1870, when he jumped into Auckland harbour to try to save twenty-four year old Albert Smith from Canterbury, Kent, who, while on the foretopmast rigging, had placed his hand above him thinking that the ratlines were there, but they weren't and so he fell off the shrouds, striking the lower rigging and then down to the lower boom, about three feet out from the vessel, where a small piece of his skull was found forced into the wood.

Upon seeing him fall, Williams dived overboard but already the body had sunk. Williams made several unsuccessful dives in search of the corpse but the tide was running out very strongly and the body reappeared some distance below the vessel for a few seconds before finally disappearing – presumably washed out to sea. At the point where Smith hit the sea the water was tinged with blood from his smashed skull. On the voyage out from England another sailor had fallen from the same portion of the rigging on to the deck and had died.

The wind could be just as strong in Fiji as in Wellington. In January, 1874, "a gale raged with great severity", [1] causing havoc among the shipping at Levuka. *HMS Pearl* was off Kandavu and "it came on with such suddenness and violence that they had not time to clew up the topsails, some of which were torn to shreds." [2] A heavy sea broke through the ports, "flooding the Commodore's cabin and destroying many papers of importance". [3] One way to get rid of unwanted paperwork!

In 1851 *HMS Calliope* was travelling from Hobart to Sydney when she was struck by lightning. Her captain, Sir Everard Home Bt., was below when he saw what appeared to be a mass of fire in the forepart of the cabin. This was accompanied by an explosion so loud that it sounded as if the nearest gun had been fired. The electric discharge had struck the mainmast and passed by the conductors through both sides of the ship. Nobody was injured but there was a strong smell of fire on the quarter deck beneath the hood that was spread to keep off the rain.

Shipwreck was another occupational hazard of a life at sea as the men on *HMS Rattler* found out when they were off Cape Soya, Japan, on 24th September, 1868. It was six in the morning and she was under an easy pressure of steam on a calm day when suddenly she struck a reef of submerged rocks.

The *Rattler* had run into a groove in the rocks and was fixed rigidly until she was broken up by the waves. She began to fill with water and the whole crew was got off safely, some with their kits and some without. They sent a messenger to the nearest city, Hakodate, and two weeks later, during which time they had been on reduced rations, the Japanese steam corvette *Dupleix* hove in sight and took them on board.

Another ship to hit a rock was *HMS Clio*, which was taking the Governor of New Zealand, Sir George Bowen, around the South Island in February, 1871, when her port bow struck a sunken rock in Bligh Sound, on the south-west coast of the South Island. This rock was not marked on any charts and so obviously wanted to make its presence known in some way or another.

The *Clio* tried to go on into deep water, the rock grazing along its port side. She had to turn round and steer for the head of the inlet where the leak was attended to and trees from the nearby forest were used to effect repairs. The Governor did manage to shoot several seals, which were sent to the British Museum where they were held to belong to a hitherto undescribed species and were given the name Arctocephalus cinereus.

On 31st August, 1894, it was the turn of *HMS Ringarooma*, which got stuck on a coral reef off the island of Mallicolo in the New Hebrides. "She is now standing almost on end and is dry up to the forward funnel at low water," wrote the *Otago Witness*. "The outer bottom is gone but the inner is still intact. She has been lightened by jettisoning 300 tons of coals and her projectiles on to the reef. The officers succeeded in shifting the ship six feet by wedging." [4]

First on the scene were two French warships, *Duchaffaut* and *Scorff* while *HMS Lizard* rushed there from Brisbane and *HMS Orlando*, in the middle of a refit, got under way from Sydney with the dockyard "working night and day in order to get her away to the scene of the wreck." [5]

After thirteen days and with the help of the *Duchaffaut* and the steamer, *Croydon*, the *Ringarooma* came off the reef. "The men appear to have behaved splendidly, the water tight doors being all closed and the collision mat fixed in an incredibly short space of time and in perfect silence," wrote Wellington's *Evening Post*. "During the first three or four days, while the spring tides were flowing, the ship bumped heavily and, had she not been strongly built, she must have become something very near a complete wreck.

Constant attention to the cables, hawsers and anchors ....greatly relieved the strain on the ship and, coupled with iron shoes which the crew built under the forefoot, not only prevented the vessel moving further up the reef, but helped her off at high water. This was undoubtedly the reason she was saved.

At every tide the hawsers and cables were hove taut. After several unsuccessful attempts to tow the ship off, it was found that, owing to the strain on the cables, she was gradually wriggling off the reef. At noon on 12th September she had slipped aft 13 feet and the same afternoon, by continual heaving on the cables, she got free.....there is no doubt the safety of the vessel was entirely due to the unwearied exertions of all hands night and day for thirteen days without relaxation and to the fact that, by continual rolling, the ship had worn for herself a bed in the coral reef. " [6] She made it to Port Sandwich in the New Hebrides whence she was escorted first to Noumea and then to Sydney by *HMS Orlando*.

The reefs of the South Pacific could be very tricky for wooden sailing vessels. "The dull roar of the sea breaking on these reefs will generally warn a ship of their existence at night but in the day time the surf always leaves a haze which, with the sun right ahead, is very dangerous," wrote Captain George Palmer of *HMS Rosario* in 1869. "No sooner are you inside (the reef) than the water changes from the deep ocean blue to a pale green, and the constant motion caused by the ocean swell is exchanged for smooth water, allowing the lower deck scuttles to be opened, and causing an increased quantity of fresh air to circulate below." [7]

When the 1,475 ton submarine *HMS Poseidon*, was launched in 1929 she was one of only four of the F class subs. She had one 4 inch gun, two machine guns, eight 21 inch torpedo tubes, a ship's company of fifty-three, and a speed of 17.5 knots on the surface and 9 knots when submerged. She joined the fourth submarine flotilla on the China station in February, 1931, and three months later, on 9th June, while exercising on the surface some twenty-one miles north of Wei Hai Wei, she was accidentally rammed by a Chinese steamer, the *Yuta*.

The *Poseidon* lurched to starboard and sank by the bow in about four minutes to a depth of about 130 feet. About thirty of the ship's company managed to scramble into the sea before she went down but twenty-two were killed, eighteen of them inside the sub.

Some survivors were picked up by the *Yuta* and others by the warships, *HMS Medway*, the *Poseidon's* parent (depot) ship, the destroyer *HMS Stormcloud*, and the submarine tender *HMS Marazion*, which all rushed to the scene of the disaster.

As soon as she was rammed the order "Close Watertight Doors" was given and Petty Officer Willis, the torpedo gunner's mate, took charge of the forepart, telling its occupants to close the door of the compartment with themselves inside as that might mean saving the ship. All electric leads had been cut and the frightening darkness in the compartment was illuminated only by the occasional hand held torch.

Petty Officer Willis said a prayer and told the imprisoned sailors to put on their Davis Submerged Escape Apparatus. This underwater breathing system, which gave the wearer a supply of pure oxygen, had been invented the previous year by a Londoner, Mr. R.J. Davis. It resembled a life jacket with a gas mask attached and had been distributed to submarine crews. The breathing bag, to which a small cylinder of compressed oxygen was attached, was strapped to the chest and acted as a lifebuoy.

This petty officer with initiative then started flooding the compartment in order to equalise the pressure with that outside. After two hours and ten minutes the water was up to the men's knees and Willis thought that by now the pressure might be sufficient to open the hatch.

With considerable difficulty the hatch was opened sufficiently for two men to shoot up but the pressure then reclosed the hatch and they had to wait for further flooding to make the pressure more equal before a second attempt could be made. The two men who escaped were Able Seamen Lovock and Holt. The former came to the surface unconscious and died immediately but his body was supported by Holt, himself in a state of great exhaustion, until both were picked up by boats waiting on the scene.

After a further hour, by which time the men in the compartment were nearly up to their necks in water, a second attempt was made. The hatch opened again and four other men rose to the surface, including Petty Officer Willis. They were all plucked out of the sea by the waiting boats. So the Davis apparatus saved five of them.

The *Poseidon* lay on the seabed for several decades and, like all warships, was regarded as a war grave since there were twenty-one dead bodies inside her. There is a general consensus of humanity – both friend and foe – that ships that are war graves are left alone – but not in China where the communist regime sent its naval divers down to raise the *Poseidon* in order to sell her for scrap metal. What they did with the bones of the sailors inside is anybody's guess. In China the authorities shoot healthy prisoners so as to sell their body parts to rich patients in need of a heart or a kidney so why should they have any respect for bodily remains?

These accidents are a small selection of the many mishaps that were suffered by men and ships during the Royal Navy's long service in the Pacific. It was part of the price that had to be paid for keeping the world's largest ocean safe for trade and free of slavers and pirates. Well might Kipling write, "If blood be the price of admiralty, Lord God, we ha' bought it fair!"

THE FALL OF HONG KONG

In 1932 there were fifty-four ships of the Royal Navy on the China Station – the aircraft carrier *HMS Hermes* (with three flights), the Fifth Cruiser Squadron consisting of *HMS Kent, Berwick, Cumberland, Cornwall, Caradoc, Devonshire* and *Suffolk*, the Eighth Destroyer Flotilla consisting of *HMS Keppel, Verity, Veteran, Whitehall, Whitshed, Wildswan, Wishart, Witch* and *Wren*, the Sloops *HMS Bridgewater, Cornflower, Folkestone* and *Sandwich*, the Survey Ship *HMS Herald*, the Submarine Flotilla Four – *HMS Medway* (Depot Ship), *Olympus, Orpheus, Otus, Oswald* and *Pandora,* the Receiving Ship in Hong Kong *HMS Tamar*, the Yangtse Flotilla Gunboats *HMS Bee, Scarab, Gnat, Aphis, Ladybird, Cockchafer, Petrel, Tern, Gannet, Falcon, Cricket* and *Mantis*, the West River Flotilla Gunboats *HMS Tarantula, Cicala, Moorhen, Moth* and *Seamew*, the destroyer *HMS Bruce*, the minesweeper *HMS Marazion*, as well as *HMS Odin, Osiris, Parthian, Perseus, Phoenix* and *Proteus.*

By the time that war came to Hong Kong in December, 1941, "the garrison's naval power had been sadly diminished," wrote Major Oliver Lindsay in his book *Lasting Honour.* [1] Indeed it had been. The cruiser squadron and submarine flotilla had been withdrawn, and the force to defend Hong Kong consisted of one destroyer (*HMS Thracian*), four gunboats, eight motor torpedo boats (MTBs), seven auxiliary patrol vessels and an auxiliary craft with a minefield capacity.

Since the Victoria dockyard on Hong Kong island was only a few hundred yards across the water from the Kowloon mainland a second base was established at Aberdeen on the south side of the island, which was protected by the high rock of the Peak.

With this small fleet of very small boats the Navy was entrusted with the tasks of laying mines in the sea approaches to Hong Kong, of patrolling the unmined sea lane of the five hundred yard wide Lei Yue Mun Channel, preventing the landing of enemy troops in the small boats which the Japanese liked to use in their various invasions throughout the Pacific, assisting in any withdrawal from Kowloon to Hong Kong Island, and supporting the infantry by opening up a second front of firing from the sea.

In the doomed battle for Hong Kong, which lasted from 8th – 25th December, 1941, it was the versatile MTBs that made the major naval contribution since the only destroyer, *HMS Thracian,* after doing some useful minelaying activity, was so damaged by enemy fire on the 15th that the following day she had to be beached by her ship's company on Round Island, out from Repulse Bay, her sailors then fighting with a detachment of Canadian troops and many of them losing their lives. Each of the MTBs was armed with two torpedo tubes, machine guns and depth charges. They were manned mainly by the R.N.V.R. as the officers of the regular Navy had been sent home to Britain to fight the war against Germany. "The crews were a jolly and enthusiastic crowd from all walks of life and various parts of the Far East," wrote Major Lindsay. [2] "Prior to the Japanese attacks all of them had waited patiently to be drafted to fight in the Atlantic or Mediterranean instead of kicking their heels waiting for a war in Hong Kong, which many felt would never come." [3] Now they would see what it was like.

With the breach in the Gindrinkers Line (Hong Kong's Maginot and every bit as useless) up in the New Territories General Maltby ordered that the mainland be evacuated in order to save his troops.

All through the day of 11th December the Navy's small vessels helped carry the troops across to Hong Kong island while MTB 08 evacuated the wounded from the heavily shelled Stonecutters Island.

The last soldiers to cross the narrow stretch of water to Hong Kong Island were two companies of the Rajputs, who had been intended to hold the tip of Devil's Peak peninsula, which overlooks the narrow waters of the Lei Yue Mun Channel. At 4.30 on the morning of 13th December they were suddenly ordered to complete their evacuation of the peninsula and cross to the island under cover of darkness, which would last for only another two hours. The problem was that some of the crews on the Chinese boats, that had been earmarked for the crossing, had deserted and so *HMS Thracian* and four MTBs stepped into the breach and got everyone across safely by 8.30 a.m.

Although they were few in number the MTBs were a thorn in the side of the Japanese, denying the invader freedom of the sea. In the early hours of 19th December the enemy had begun landing near North Point on Hong Kong island and several MTBs engaged them, the attack being led by MTBs 07 and 09. They managed to sink one landing craft and inflicted heavy casualties on some others. It was a bloody affair and MTB 07 was hit twice in the engine room.

The first time a stoker was killed and the next time it was a telegrapher who had taken his place.

After 07 and 09 returned to base their place was taken by MTBs 11 and 12. The latter was struck in the conning tower, which killed the C.O., Lieutenant Colls, and the First Lieutenant, McGill, both of the Royal Hong Kong Naval Volunteer Reserve. MTB 26 was also in the thick of the fight and became a total loss with all her ship's company killed. Neither before nor since in history has a single Naval Reserve borne the entire brunt of the battle on the waves. The R.H.K.N.V.R.'s drill ship was *HMS Cornflower*, and the plaque of this ship can be seen in the Remembrance Chapel of Saint Michael and All Angels in Saint John's Cathedral, Hong Kong, as a memorial of their pluck and valour.

Unfortunately two of these precious MTBs were sunk during the action and two more were damaged, one seriously. Another, MTB 08, was lost on the slip at Aberdeen after being hit by a bomb splinter during an enemy raid on 16th December.

The remaining boats were then engaged in ferrying supplies and ammunition around the island to the pier at Stanley Bay, on the south coast, where a British brigade was cut off by the Japanese land force.

As the enemy advanced over the hill to the south side of the island the MTBs fired at their positions from the sea. When the gunboat *HMS Cicala* was strafed and sunk by enemy aircraft in the Lamma Channel on 21st December, MTB 10, under the command of Lieutenant R. Godwin, R.N.Z.N.V.R., went alongside to take off her crew, one of whom had been killed and two wounded.

The other gunboats, *Moth*, *Robin* and *Tern*, were also scuttled to prevent them falling into the hands of the enemy. The base ship, *HMS Tamar*, had been scuttled on 12th December and five days later the minelayer, *HMS Redstart*, and the small auxiliary vessels, *Aldgate*, *Barlight*, *Cornflower*, *Watergate*, *Ebenol*, *Alliance* and *Port Chaucer* were all scuttled in Deepwater Bay.

By Christmas Day – the day of the surrender – there were only five MTBs left and they played a valuable role in getting important personnel out from under the noses of the Japanese.

Early on that fateful morning MTBs 07 and 09 were ordered to a secluded anchorage at Telegraph Bay, on the west coast not far from Aberdeen, where they lay alongside the Dairy Company's jetty. Their orders were to wait there until just before the surrender, when they would receive further orders to take various important persons out of the enemy's clutches. To conceal their boats from the eyes of Japanese bomber pilots they covered them with straw and tree branches and then hid themselves. They managed to get some cream from the Dairy Farm and that was about the limit of their Christmas dinner. The other three remaining MTBs – Nos. 10, 11 and 27 – were keeping a similar low profile in a lagoon on the south-west end of Aberdeen Island.

The problem for the V.I.P. evacuees was to find their way to the MTBs since these last five small vessels could not be allowed to show themselves for fear of being blown to pieces by the enemy.

At Aberdeen some naval officers found a twenty-five foot motor cutter from the scuttled *HMS Cornflower* but it lacked both fuel and a battery. They managed to lift a battery from a nearby Buick while sixteen gallons of petrol were obtained from a store at the nearby temporary naval base.

They packed sixteen people into the cutter and got her under weigh at 4.45 p.m. Among those on board were Admiral Chan Chak, the one-legged liaison officer of the Chinese government in Hong Kong, and his coxswain. He had lost his leg during an action on the Yangtse. It was important to get the admiral away as, if he had fallen into the hands of the Japanese, he would have been tortured and killed. That was why he was carrying a gun – so that he could shoot himself first. Inside his wooden leg was $40,000 Hong Kong dollars to pay whatever bribes might be necessary to get back to that part of China that was still held by Chiang Kai Shek.

It was a bright sunny afternoon and they took the south channel out of the Aberdeen typhoon shelter but they had not proceeded six hundred yards when they were simultaneously seen by a pill-box below Brick Hill (Nam Long Shan) that was now occupied by the Japanese and an AA battery above. Both went to town with all they had – rifles, machine guns and shells. Two of those in the cutter were killed and another was shot through both legs. Chan Chak was shot in the wrist and bled profusely. The survivors of the shelling swam the short distance to Aberdeen island, the admiral having removed his wooden leg for the journey. They continued to be fired upon in the water but the geysers of spray from the bullets created confusion among those doing the shooting.

Upon reaching Aberdeen island they climbed the hill and saw in the bay below MTBs 10,11 and 27. However, their problems were not over as the first man to reach MTB 11 said, "There are ten chaps following," which Sub-Lieutenant Legge, tired after an all night patrol and currently on aircraft watch, understood as "There are ten Japs following" and so he opened fire with the stripped down Lewis gun and gave the others a hot reception. Fortunately no one was killed by this "friendly fire".

MTB 11 then went to set off to look for Numbers 07 and 09, which were still sheltering in Telegraph Bay awaiting orders. Unfortunately her engine starters had packed up and so Lieutenant Commander Gandy lashed MTB 10 alongside her and towed her while Chan Chak and his party were being lifted on to MTB 27.

On their way to Telegraph Bay both 10 and 11 came under heavy artillery fire, which they avoided by both speed and clever manoeuvring.

All was ready by 21.40 when the little fleet put to sea. The engines made a loud noise as they started up and nerves were on edge. The sea was calm, there was a light wind and they got their speed uo to 22 knots. In the few hours after a ceasefire there is always something of a hiatus while the new occupier is getting ready to take over a shattered society and they were counting on getting away without any trouble. However, they did encounter some Japanese warships that fired at them unsuccessfully in the poor light.

Not long after midnight they pulled in to Nan O, a village on the coast of China that was not yet occupied by the Japanese. This was a friendly village where Chan Chak had contacts and from here they would make their way overland to Rangoon in Burma.

Before starting on their trek they had one more task to perform. While it was still dark it was necessary to destroy the boats so that they would not fall into the hands of the enemy. The sea cocks were opened to let water in and the wooden hulls chopped with axes. The excited villagers even piled rocks on board to hasten their sinking. The first officer of MTB 09 – a sentimental sort of chap – tore the bronze crest off his beloved boat and then lugged it across China and home to England.

The water was only two fathoms deep and so the top few inches of the bridge and about twelve feet of mast were still visible above the water when dawn came and it was time to set off on foot on their long march to Rangoon.

With the sinking of these five small but very useful boats the Royal Navy, which had dominated the North Pacific in 1932 with its fifty-four shining vessels, no longer had a single ship anywhere in the top half of the world's largest ocean. What had once been a British lake was now a Japanese one. But not for long.

THE PRINCE OF WALES AND THE REPULSE

The *Prince of Wales*, the Navy's latest battleship, had taken Winston Churchill across the Atlantic in August, 1941, for his historic meeting with President Roosevelt, the first time that the two statesmen had met since they were introduced to each other in 1918 when they were both guests at dinner at the Benchers' Table in Gray's Inn Hall, London.

The battle cruiser *Repulse* was much older (1915) but it was intended that they be escorted by four destroyers – *Electra, Express, Jupiter* and *Encounter* – and an aircraft carrier, *HMS Indomitable*. Unfortunately, before the convoy set out from England, the *Indomitable* ran aground in Jamaica and so had to be counted out.

To send out such a force of valuable ships without air cover might be thought a risk too far but the stated purpose of this fleet, known as 'Z Force', was to deter further Japanese aggression by "showing the flag". This sort of thing had usually worked among the primitive natives of the South Pacific but the Japanese were a different kettle of fish and were not the sort to cower in the face of a token show of force by a Navy which they knew was inferior to their own in the Pacific.

Until Alamein at the end of 1942 Britain's victories were conspicuous by their scarcity and, with the entry of Russia as an ally after it was invaded by Germany, the Russian convoys had to be supplied, thus putting even more pressure on Britain's military resources. In other words, we were desperately short of both ships and planes for what had to be done in the war against Japan which, from the British and American perspective, was essentially a naval war.

With the Japanese moving south through China and Indochina like a poisonous snake the governments of Australia and New Zealand were crying out for the Royal Navy to do something from the Singapore base which, after all, had been built for this very type of purpose. The Anzac troops were now trained in desert fighting in North Africa and it was undesirable to pull them out for the purpose of defending their home countries. Better to stop the Japanese in Asia.

With all these pressures it is hardly surprising that Force Z was sent East even though its complement fell somewhat short of what was required.

The vessels arrived at Singapore on 2nd December, 1941, and they steamed through the narrow Strait of Johore to the great naval base, known as *HMS Sultan*, where the *Prince of Wales* berthed alongside the West Wall. Singapore rejoiced at this "show of force" and the dancing went on with renewed vigour at Raffles and the Seaview while the sailors went out exploring Change Alley and the shops of the Indian quarter with their exotic and colourful merchandise.

Six days later the Japanese, without warning or justification, launched simultaneous attacks within twenty-four hours on no fewer than eight countries and colonies – Hawaii, Hong Kong, Thailand, Malaya, Singapore, the Philippines, Guam and Wake Island. In these terrible hours, when Japanese treachery turned the hitherto peaceful Pacific into a raging inferno, Singapore was bombed and sixty-one civilians were killed in Chinatown.

Not wanting his ships to be caught like sitting ducks at their anchorage – as had happened at Pearl Harbour – Admiral Sir Tom Phillips, the commander of Z Force, decided to take the ships out into the South China Sea – but without air cover.

Like many naval officers of his generation, Phillips did not fully appreciate the new power of the air to cripple battleships while the faith that he had in the ability of well-armed and heavily armoured battleships to withstand air attacks was both unjustified and tragic.

Phillips' appointment as fleet commander was yet another unsatisfactory feature of Z Force as, like General Percival, the army commander in Singapore, he was a senior staff officer appointed to a fighting command in time of war. It was many years since Phillips had commanded a ship and that was a destroyer in peace time. He had never commanded a battle fleet or even a battleship. His appointment was not as bad as that of Vice-Admiral Sir David Price at Petropavlovsk in the Crimean War but it was not good either. Nevertheless, he assumed command and, in his own doom-laden words, he took the fleet out to sea "to look for some trouble".

Believing that he could hamper any Japanese reinforcements that they might land at their new bridgeheads of Singora in Thailand and Kota Bharu in northern Malaya, Phillips sailed his fleet out of Singapore at dusk on 8th December and they steamed east towards the Anamba Islands, the *Prince of Wales* steaming four cables ahead of the *Repulse* while the escorting destroyers, *Vampire, Tenedos, Electra* and *Express*, screened ahead and on the beam of each of the big ships. They went around the Anamba Islands and then headed north towards the area of intended action, their crews looking forward to an engagement with what they supposed to be an inferior navy, manned by little yellow men with funny teeth.

On their first morning at sea (the 9th) they had the good fortune of having a thick cloud cover, which concealed them from the air, but then the weather began to clear, making it more likely that they would be sighted. And they were – not by a spotter plane but by a wretched submarine (I65), which reported their position to the Japanese headquarters at Saigon. The Nippon pilots then went looking for this prize – the great British Eastern fleet. Their planes were detected by the *Prince of Wales* and so, with the element of surprise forfeited, Phillips decided to return to Singapore.

On the way he received a report – false as it turned out – of a Japanese landing at Kuantan, on the east coast of Malaya, and so he decided to change course to see if he could do anything to disrupt it. Preserving radio silence, he *assumed* that the naval authorities in Singapore would know his intentions and would arrange air cover.

Finding nothing at Kuantan, he decided to go on to Singapore but in mid morning on the 10th a single engined Japanese monoplane – one of about a hundred that were on the hunt for the British ships - caught sight of the prey below through a gap in the clouds – two of the Royal Navy's finest plus three destroyers, the *Tenedos* having been ordered back to Singapore. "Sighted two enemy battleships seventy nautical miles south-east Kuantan, course south-east," was the message that he sent on his radio. The Royal Navy was about to meet the Japanese Air Force for the first time just as the Americans had at Pearl Harbour only sixty hours earlier.

As a wave of eight Nell bombers came into sight at 11.10 a.m. the ships' anti-aircraft guns went into action, their gunners sweating beneath their thick flash protection hoods. The guns of the *Prince of Wales* had a range of 16,500 yards, those of the *Repulse* 11,000 yards. However, because of the turn of the ships, the guns missed their targets and it was with both amazement and horror that those on the deck of the *Repulse* could see the bombs leaving the bomb-bays of the planes and then falling through the clear air.

While eight of the nine bombs missed and sent up great geysers of water the ninth went through the hangar and marines' mess of the *Repulse* and then exploded on the armoured deck. It started a small fire, which was rapidly put out.

Next came a force of sixteen torpedo bombers. Captain Tennant of the *Repulse* succeeded in turning his ship round sharply through 45 degrees but the *Prince of Wales* was not so lucky as she took a hit, the vibration of which seemed to lift her, and she listed heavily to port. Her stern sank until that part of her deck was only a few feet above the sea. Worse still, she lost most of her power supply, which put many of her anti-aircraft guns out of action. Her rudder was smashed and her port propeller shafts jammed. The three black balls, signifying that the ship was not under control, were run up her masthead. While sailors were manning the pumps and medics were attending to the dying and wounded there was a growing feeling that this great battleship might not, after all, make it back to Singapore.

Fifteen minutes later a co-ordinated attack by two squadrons of torpedo planes and another of bombers was made on the *Repulse* but Captain Tennant and the ship managed to evade every torpedo of this mass attack.

Twenty minutes later his luck ran out as the third wave of air monsters – twenty-six Mitsubishi Bettys – attacked from several directions. This time the *Repulse* was hit square amidships by a torpedo while the *Prince of Wales* copped four of them and the ocean started to come in through the jagged holes in her hull.

Then came the fourth attack – again from more than one direction and Captain Tennant could dodge no longer as his ship was holed in five places by torpedos in the course of only four minutes. Water started to pour in and he called the ship's company to the deck. "All hands on deck. Prepare to abandon ship. God be with you," he told them in this moment of crisis. This well-timed order undoubtedly saved many lives.

The sailors scurried up hatches and off ladders in an orderly fashion and, in Captain Tennant's own words, "I never saw the slightest sign of panic or ill discipline". The list of the ship prevented the lifeboats from being launched.

The first thing was to inflate the rubber life belts and put them round their waists. With a 30 degree list to port it was dangerous to go *down* the deck, from where there would be only a short distance to jump in to the briny, as it would be too easy to get caught up by the suction when the old girl actually sank and so they scampered *up* the deck and slid on their bottoms down the much longer starboard side into the sea, which was fast filling with oil. During their slides down the side of the vessel many of the sailors

400

HMS Rosario.

A sketch of the Rosario in full sail overhauling the alleged blackbirding vessel "Carl".

Britain's China Fleet off Wei Hai Wei in the 1930s.

Sea Belle II, the official steam "yacht" of the Governor of the Straits Settlements. This was the first vessel to enter the new King George the Sixth graving dock at the Singapore Naval Base on 14th February, 1938, her razor sharp bow cutting the ceremonial ribbon across the dock's entrance.

HMS Prince of Wales on fire and listing badly shortly before she sank in the South China Sea on 10th December, 1941.

The bow of the Prince of Wales high in the air immediately before she sank.

A group of officers on board the aircraft carrier, HMS Illustrious, on the way to Okinawa. The author's uncle, John Cope, is second from the left, standing.

A near miss on the aircraft carrier, HMS Victorious, by a kamikaze during the Battle of Okinawa.

tore their flesh on the sharp barnacles. It was all over in only a few minutes and those who were trapped in deeper compartments and many of the wounded did not make it and went to the bottom of the sea with their ship. Of the *Repulse's* complement of 1,309 officers and men, some 534 did not make it but the rest, including Captain Tennant, were picked up by the destroyers, *Vampire* and *Electra*.

The *Prince of Wales*, the great battleship on which Churchill and Roosevelt had conferred only a few months earlier, was not long in following. Since she had a bit longer to prepare for her doom her wounded were launched into the sea from the stern in Carley floats.

Her list was not so great and men were able to jump over the starboard side into the sea or swing down on ropes. Then, as the list increased, they too had to slide down on their bottoms. Of her ship's company of 1,612, some 327 went down with their vessel, including Admiral Phillips. Altogether the action had lasted ninety minutes with fifty-eight Japanese planes taking part in the attacks.

It was the destroyer *Express* that picked up most of the *Prince of Wales* survivors as, by the time of the closing action, the *Prince of Wales* and the *Repulse* had been about four miles from each other and so the destroyers picking up the *Repulse* men were that far way.

Lines were thrown to the men in the water and nets were also used for them to scramble up on to the rescuing vessels. Most were coated with dirty, black oil, which they had to scrape off as soon as they were out of the water. Those who had swallowed oil were vomiting it up.

All those who were alive were plucked out of the sea and taken back to Singapore on the destroyers, a voyage that took about eight hours and was made easier by the issue of a generous tot of rum.

The three destroyers pulled into the Singapore Naval Base about midnight, the wounded being carried off on stretchers while the others, some clad in only their underpants, staggered ashore as best they could.

They were now sailors without a ship and, while some were returned to England on the transport *Erinpura*, others were redeployed to other naval vessels in Singapore, *HMS Mauritius* and *HMS Exeter*.

Fifty sailors were sent to Penang to operate the ferries between Penang island and the mainland because, in the face of the deteriorating situation, the native crews had fled.

Other survivors were allocated to operating hospital trains that were bringing the wounded from the fighting in Malaya down to Singapore while 150 Royal Marines joined the 2nd Argyll and Sutherland Highlanders, the regiment becoming known as the "Plymouth Argylls" in a takeoff of Plymouth's football team.

The Argyll and Sutherlands (the "Jocks") had been severely depleted during the fighting in Malaya and so the Marines, after some basic training in soldiering, were most welcome additions to the regiment. Some of them were killed during the battle for Singapore. The Admiralty ordered all its officers and men to get away from Singapore before the surrender but not all of them did, in particular the Plymouth Argylls and those seamen who were wounded.

Eighteen of those who were killed on the *Prince of Wales* and *Repulse* are buried in the Kranji war cemetery, in the north of Singapore island, and the others are commemorated in the Memorial to the Missing on Plymouth Hoe, from where Drake went out to face down the Spanish Armada.

Throughout the battle Captain Tennant of the *Repulse* acted with outstanding skill and judgement. As a result of his manoeuvring the *Repulse* had dodged sixteen torpedos before she was hit.

Unfortunately the same can not be said of Admiral Phillips who, after a series of misjudgements, seemed to lose his nerve as the battle proceeded. What is, however, beyond dispute is the orderly and heroic conduct of the sailors in the water amidst so much death, destruction, debris and oil. That they were all rescued before the end of this terrible day was a great credit to the three rescuing destroyers. Describing the survivors in the sea, Flight Lieutenant Vigors, one of the R.A.F. pilots of the aged Brewster Buffaloes that flew belatedly over the scene after the ships went down, said, "During that hour I witnessed a show of that indomitable spirit for which the Royal Navy is so famous… I had seen many men in dire danger, waving and cheering and joking as if they were on holiday at Brighton, waving at low flying aircraft. It shook me, for here was something above human nature." [1]

With the *Prince of Wales* and the *Repulse* at the bottom of the South China Sea and the U. S. fleet crippled at Pearl Harbour, the war in the Pacific had started very badly for the Allies – just as it would end very badly for the Japanese.

402

THE RISE AND FALL OF THE SINGAPORE NAVAL BASE

With the destruction of the German Fleet at the end of the First World War the three largest naval powers in the world were Great Britain, the United States and Japan. Britain's navy exceeded those of all other nations combined but, as after Waterloo, many vessels were decommissioned upon the close of hostilities.

The demise of German naval power meant that naval rivalry moved to the Pacific and, although comrades-in-arms in World War One, the three remaining naval powers were busy making plans to cover the possibility of war with the other two.

As we have seen, the United States were suspicious of Britain joining her "ally", Japan in the event of trouble between America and Japan, and Britain was equally suspicious of America, which was building sixteen new capital ships, the purpose of which seemed to be to undermine, if not destroy, the Royal Navy's age old supremacy at sea. And the Japanese, having quietly built up their navy while Britain and America were busy fighting the First World War, were already making plans to strike at both the United States and Britain at an opportune moment.

It was in these circumstances that, in 1921, the U.S. Secretary of State, Charles Hughes, called Britain and Japan to a "naval disarmament conference" in Washington that resulted in a limitation of battleships on the part of these three powers, the ratio being 5 (Britain): 5 (United States): 3 (Japan). This translated to 525,000 tons each for Britain and America and 315,000 for Japan or, in capital ships, fifteen each for the two former and nine for Japan. Although this would appear to favour the two Anglo-Saxon countries it should be remembered that they had more than one ocean to defend and so Japan would have a superiority in the north-west Pacific.

It was further agreed that Japan should withdraw from her concessions on China's Shantung Peninsula while Britain would make a similar withdrawal from Wei Hai Wei and would also give up her concessions at certain Chinese ports and cede her supervisory control over the Chinese Customs service.

Part of the deal, insisted on by the United States government, was that Britain must end the naval alliance that she had had with Japan since 1902. Some writers have suggested that this was an important factor in making an enemy of Japan but the wider picture would imply that from an early stage – and certainly

403

before 1921 – the Japanese were on an aggressive course and sooner or later would have come into conflict with the British and American interests in the Far East.

The naval alliance of 1902 meant that, for the duration of the treaty, the Japanese were our "paper friends" but not much more. Despite the hiccups along the road destiny dictated that the United States was Britain's natural ally in the Pacific and not a "new chum" like Japan, whose slavish and absolute imitation of Western techniques and materialism was a disturbing sign of both immaturity and insecurity.

According to Charles Hughes, who was the "godfather" of the Washington treaties and, like most American politicians, a slick and unprincipled crowd pleaser, they were "the greatest step in history to secure the reign of peace" [1] and would "usher in an era of good feeling in the Far East" [2]

The problem was that the agreements were based on mere promises with no means of enforcement and, as events would prove, the word of the Japanese was not worth the paper it was written on.

Even though they had no intention of respecting the agreements the Japanese played "hardball" and, as a sweetener to get Japan to sign on the dotted line, the United States and Britain agreed not to build any major bases between two longitudinal lines of an area that included Guam, the Philippines and Hong Kong. But bases beyond these lines were permitted, i.e. Hawaii (further east) and Singapore (further west). For the British this was not too big a concession to make since Japan, with its encroaching interests in China, was now seen as a long term threat and there was no way that Hong Kong could be defended from a landward attack from a Japanese controlled China. Singapore seemed a much more suitable place for a base and that is why Admiral Jellicoe made a report advocating the establishment of a major naval base there with dockyard facilities for an entire fleet. This was accepted by the Committee of Imperial Defence in London in 1921.

Being strategically sited at the junction of important shipping lanes, Singapore was already a coaling depot for the Royal Navy. Furthermore, it had more and better infrastructure than anywhere else in Asia apart from Japan and possibly Hong Kong, including existing naval docking facilities at Keppel Harbour where there were five graving docks, the largest being King's Dock, which was 873 feet long and 93 feet wide. Singapore also had a labour force of hard working natives to build the new base – men who were already experienced in all types of construction work from erecting bamboo scaffolding to carrying baskets of rubble on their bony but sturdy shoulders.

The chosen site was on the north side of Singapore Island. It was on the southern bank of the narrow Strait of Johore, which separates Singapore from the thick jungle of Malaya across the water.

The 2,250 acres that the base would cover were given by the colonial government of the Straits Settlements, which also gave another 597 acres for an aerodrome. The base would take sixteen years to complete and would cost £63 million, making it the (then) most expensive construction job in the history of the British Empire. However, not all of it was paid for by London. The rulers of the four Federated Malay States (Perak, Selangor, Negri Sembilan and Pahang) gave £2 million, New Zealand £1 million and Hong Kong another £250,000.

It was said that this mighty project would make Singapore "the Gibraltar of the East" as, when completed, the dockyards would be capable of servicing as large a fleet as would ever be needed in the Pacific. Hitherto the Navy had been reluctant to send its largest vessels – battleships of the Royal Sovereign and Queen Elizabeth class, and aircraft-carriers – outside the Atlantic or the Mediterranean as, in the event of battle or other damage, they would be too far away from the docking facilities of Britain and Malta. There was no dry dock east of Malta that could accommodate a battleship.

When war came at the end of 1941 this mighty behemoth of a base was damned by some as a "white elephant", whose protecting guns were all facing out to sea and so could not protect it from land attack.

That does not seem entirely fair. When it was conceived in 1921 no one could have predicted how much air power and the range and capability of aircraft would develop in the next twenty years – especially under the stimulus of war after 1939. And anyway the protecting 18 inch guns were on swivels and could be turned 360°. The problem was not the guns themselves but the lack of foresight by providing them with mainly armour piercing ammunition suitable for use against the iron hulls of warships rather than with high explosives.

405

The real problem was that this massive project took so long to complete (sixteen years) that in 1941 it was a little bit difficult to justify it on the same grounds as when it was planned in 1921.

By 1938 the Japanese forces were barnstorming their way south through China and building up a huge air force at home and so the British assumption that no enemy could reach Singapore through the "impenetrable" jungle of the British controlled Malay peninsula was becoming less realistic by the day. It had always been said that any hostile attempt to land on the coast of Malaya would be stopped by the Royal Navy. And so it would have been if the Navy and the Royal Air Force had been given the tools to do the job but, with air battles raging over Europe, land battles in North Africa and U-boat warfare in the Atlantic, there were just not enough ships and planes to furnish adequately a further front in the Far East. But we are getting ahead of the story.

Work began on the base in 1923 and proceeded as fast as the irregular flow of funds would allow. Jungle was cleared, the sea bottom dredged, a river diverted, millions of tons of earth removed, piles laid for the piers and breastworks, and cranes rigged up that could lift an entire gun-turret out of a battleship. They built repair shops, boiler sheds, rope shops, storage sheds, railways, power stations, galleys, barracks accommodation for crews on shore leave, runways from the sea for sea planes, a powerful Admiralty transmitting station, and wharves for revictualling and refuelling ships. There were also huge underground storage facilities for water, fuel and ammunition, and an on-base "town" to accommodate the 12,000 Asian workers complete with hospital, churches, cinemas and seventeen football fields. Huge oil tanks were put up and a complementary air base, R.A.F. Selatar, was built nearby. In June, 1928, a great floating dock was towed the 8,500 miles from the Tyne to its new home in the Johore Strait. The sections were divided into two convoys and the latter convoy arrived safely in November.

The assembly of all the different parts into a unit was completed by March, 1929, and the finished dock had a lifting capacity of 50,000 tons, which was considerably greater than the full load of *HMS Hood*, at the time the heaviest warship in existence. Inside the walls of this great floating structure were workshops and other service areas.

However, in a battle situation more than one big warship might have to be repaired at the same time and, to complement this floating dock, a great graving dock, capable of taking a vessel of

50,000 tons, was dug into the foreshore. In other words, two ships as big as super Dreadnoughts could be repaired simultaneously. There was also a smaller floating dock for the repair of destroyers and submarines. All this made Singapore the largest dockyard in the world and increased the strategic mobility of any British battle fleet that might be sent to the Pacific.

The official opening of the graving dock took place on 14th February, 1938, when the Governor of the Straits Settlements, Sir Shenton Thomas, and his wife sailed up the Strait of Johore in their official yacht, *Sea Belle II*, just as the clouds were clearing after a tropical downpour. Lady Thomas was a first cousin of Field-Marshal Viscount Montgomery of Alamein.

The little *Sea Belle II* reached the dock at 5.30 p.m., her sharp bow cutting the ribbon as she entered. She was then secured to the wall of the great structure. Her escorting warships, *HMS Duncan* and *HMS Diamond,* made fast at the opposite end. There were also some small escorting vessels of the local RNVR.

In his welcoming speech the Civil Lord of the Admiralty, Colonel Llewellin, declared, "The British Empire has been and is an immense force for peace and good government. Its world-wide mission in these respects is by no means finished in the East and elsewhere, and let none imagine that it is. The Singapore base forms no threat or menace to anyone, and no warlike desire has prompted its building....We wish friendship with all and seek enmity with no one." [3]

These sentiments were reinforced by Sir Shenton Thomas, who said, "The base is no challenge to war but an insurance against war....Other countries have watched the development of the base with sympathy and satisfaction, for the British Empire is one of the most potent influences on civilisation that history has ever known...It must be strong." [4] Then it was time for the Governor to name the new facility the "King George the Sixth Dock" after the newly crowned sailor-king. The night was rounded off by a flypast of two squadrons of the Fleet Air Arm from *HMS Eagle* and then the illuminated warships gave a rocket display.

The next fireworks at the base were of an altogether different order. We are now in the last week of January, 1942, and the jungle across the strait in Johore is alive with the flash and thunder of gunfire as the last battles are being fought on the mainland. Most of His Majesty's ships have left the base but several hundred men are still in the barracks. Skilled civilian personnel have

407

been evacuated to Ceylon and the civilian labour force of 12,000 workers disbanded in preparation for blowing up this marvellous facility which British and New Zealand taxpayers, Malayan sultans and others had contributed so much to build.

Once it came within range of Japanese guns across the Strait of Johore the base had no further use as it could not repair ships while under fire or potential fire from the enemy. The great floating dock was flooded and sunk just off from the shore with the result that there was now no dock where the Allies could dock a modern battleship between Durban and Pearl Harbour.

As the Navy sailed out the Sappers moved in with their explosives and other demolition equipment and for a while much of Singapore was blacked out by smoke from the burning base and oil storage tanks. This obscene sight was especially disheartening for those troops who were still fighting in Johore as troops never like to see demolitions taking place *behind* them as it tends to make them think that they are fighting a pointless battle. If the authorities had so little confidence that they believed it necessary to destroy the most important base on Singapore island, then why were the soldiers risking their lives in Johore?

In the words of a special correspondent of *The Times*, who visited the base a few days after its destruction, "A visit to the famed Singapore naval base a few days after it had been evacuated by the Navy was a most moving experience….A few Indian sentries were on duty at the gate. Hardly anyone was to be seen where formerly there had been scenes of such tremendous activity. The Japanese were lobbing mortar shells into the base from across the Strait in a desultory fashion. An occasional lorry, going down to bring away supplies, sped to the warehouses. On the waterfront British troops were in position, seeking what protection they could from the mortar shells.

We crept along, keeping behind buildings as far as possible. Even so the Japanese must have spotted us as we crossed one rather exposed stretch, for one mortar shell landed with a resounding crack only fifty yards in our rear." [5]

The upper works of the sunken floating dock could be seen above the water line while shells had fallen through the roofs of the boiler shop, the light machine shop, the foundry and the administration building. The room of the Commander-in-Chief in the last mentioned building "was empty save for a large Admiralty chart of the world on the wall and some old books of reference. Two dartboards and some billiard tables and the remains of a hastily eaten meal were all that remained in one of the petty officers' messes. One of the oil tanks was on fire. Flames were leaping up and gusty clouds of black smoke were blowing over the Straits of Johore. Two or three Japanese reconnaissance aeroplanes were wheeling round in clouds like kites. The purr of their engines, now swelling, now dying away, went on all the afternoon." [6]

It was, of course, imperative that the enemy should not be allowed to capture such a mighty base intact but the action of blowing up this icon of empire was the surest sign yet that the end was near – the end of the battle for Malaya and Singapore and, more distantly, the end of the British Empire in the East since the loss of this great bastion was as traumatic for the ruled as it was for the rulers. Of course, the Navy got the base back in 1945 but things would never be the same again.

THE BATTLE OF THE JAVA SEA

After the fall of Singapore on that terrible 15th February, 1942, what was left of the Royal Navy in the surrounding seas gathered at Tanjong Priok, the port of Batavia (now Jakarta) on the island of Java, to help the hard pressed Dutch protect their great colony from invasion by the apparently unstoppable Japanese.

The warships were now under the ABDA Command (American, British, Dutch and Australian), which had hastily been set up under the command of General Wavell, who seems to be the one who was always landed with hopeless tasks during the War. Thus did the heavy cruiser, *HMS Exeter*, a veteran of the Battle of the River Plate, and the light cruisers, *HMS Danae* and *Dragon*, and the destroyers, *HMS Electra*, *Jupiter*, *Encounter*, *Scout* and *Tenedos*, carry out escort duty for ships on the west coast of Java.

On 25th February *Exeter*, *Electra*, *Encounter* and *Jupiter*, together with *HMAS Perth*, left the burning port of Tanjong Priok, their flags flying in the black, smoky air, and headed to Surabaya, Java's second largest city, which was twenty-four hours' sailing time from Tanjong. They got there the next day and were piloted through the minefield that spread across the entrance to Surabaya's river port, which was alive with raging fires and air raid sirens.

A Japanese invasion force, heading for Java, had been spotted by reconnaissance planes and so the British warships were allowed to spend only two hours at Surabaya before joining the Dutch ships for an encounter with these enemy transports and their powerful escort vessels. There was no time to refuel the cruisers while the destroyers managed to take on only a fraction of the fuel that they wanted.

Surabaya was in a state of chaos with periodic Japanese bombing raids. On the Queen Olga Rock was a burning freighter of the Rotterdam Lloyd line which had grounded there and was on fire, adding to the pall of black smoke that was thickening over the port.

The two hours were up for the British ships at 10 p.m. on the night of 26th February and they sailed out of Surabaya with some Dutch warships, the whole of this "Combined Striking Force" being under the command of the Dutchman, Admiral Doorman. They were off to do battle with the advancing Japanese transports on the grounds that it was better to sink invaders at sea rather than have to deal with them after they had landed.

410

They sailed north into the Java Sea and early the next morning were attacked by Japanese bombers but came through more or less unscathed. Later in the day they returned to Surabaya as, having been out to sea in such a hurry, they needed to replenish their fuel, stores and ammunition.

However, as they were entering Surabaya Admiral Doorman received an order to proceed to sea immediately to engage the 2nd and 4th Destroyer Flotillas of the Japanese Navy. These included the heavy cruisers *Nachi* and *Haguro*, the light cruisers *Jintsu* and *Naka*, thirteen modern destroyers, several smaller minesweepers and patrol boats and forty-one transports that were carrying a fully fledged invasion force to take over the rich and important island of Java. They had been spotted near the tiny island of Bawean - only ninety miles away. The sailors on the allied ships were hot and exhausted from their forays of the last forty-eight hours and it was in this state that they put to sea yet again in an attempt to come to terms with the ever advancing enemy.

The fleet that sailed out of Surabaya for its meeting with destiny was under the command of Admiral Doorman and consisted of his flagship, the cruisers *RNA De Ruyter*, *HMS Exeter*, *HMAS Perth*, *USS Houston* and *RNA Java* These were screened by the British destroyers *HMS Electra*, *Encounter*, and *Jupiter*, the American destroyers *USS John D. Edwards*, *John D. Ford*, *Paul Jones* and *Alden*, and the Dutch destroyers *RNA Witte de With*, *Eversten* and *Kortenaer*. The *de Ruyter* and the *Kortenaer* were named after Dutch admirals who had fought against the English navy in the time of Charles II.

While they were travelling north at a speed of 26 knots Captain Oliver, the commanding officer of *HMS Exeter*, told his men to go and have some tea while they had the chance as the ship was ready for action, with decks cleared, etc. The tea was interrupted by the thunder of the ship's guns, which opened fire on a Japanese plane that had been spotted.

Around 4 p.m. on 27th, with the visibility clear and the sea as calm as The Serpentine on a summer's day, the look-out on *HMS Electra* detected the vague, dark figures of the Japanese ships on the north-east horizon. They were at a point that was only thirty miles north-west of Surabaya.

A few minutes later the Japanese heavy cruisers, *Nachi* and *Haguro*, opened proceedings by firing all twenty of their 8 inch guns at our heavy cruisers, *HMS Exeter* and *USS Houston*, at a range of

28,000 yards. The allied cruisers retaliated but with only twelve 8 inch guns, the others being either damaged or unworkable. The allied ships would have preferred a closer range so as to bring in the guns of their light cruisers.

Japanese float planes were spotting for the *Nachi* and *Haguro* whereas the allied fleet was without any form of aerial protection or even reconnaissance.

The atmosphere became thick with the smoke of battle and the sea was no longer calm as great fountains of water soared up into the air from the exploding shells. Doorman moved his ships further to starboard in an attempt to close the range and this caused the Japanese commander to fear for his transports and so he decided to launch a torpedo attack while he still had the daylight. Altogether some sixty-four torpedoes were fired from the enemy's 2nd (Destroyer) Flotilla.

As the torpedoes were speeding through the water *HMS Exeter* was hit by a shell, which landed on one of its 4 inch guns and then continued into the boiler room, causing an almighty explosion. With the escape of steam from the boiler room and six of the vessel's eight boilers out of action, she suffered a reduction of both power and steam. Unable to keep up with the rest of the fleet, the *Exeter* turned to port and limped out of the battle.

One result of the hasty putting together of a fleet comprising warships from four nations was that no coherent or efficient system of signalling had been worked out and, seeing the *Exeter* turn, the captain of *USS Houston* thought that it must be as a result of a signal that he had not seen and so he turned his ship to port as well.

The sight of two ships turning convinced Captain Waller of *HMAS Perth* that this must definitely have been ordered and so he too made a sharp turn to port. In these circumstances it is hardly surprising to record that the captain of the rear cruiser, *RNA Java*, decided that the majority could not be wrong and so he turned his vessel in conformity with the others.

The fifth cruiser, the *De Ruyter*, was now ploughing on alone but Doorman soon realised that he too would have to make the same unauthorised turn in order to re-form the line of battle.

As this unintended manoeuvre was reaching its completion the Dutch destroyer, *Kortenaer*, was hit amidships by a torpedo and she broke in two and sank. One hundred and thirteen of her survivors were picked up by *HMS Encounter* and, once on board, were given a change of clothing and a glass of rum – one of the advantages of being picked up by a British warship rather than a "dry" American one. The *Encounter*, having done her duty, sailed back to Surabaya with all these survivors.

Upon realising the plight of the *Exeter* the commander of *HMAS Perth*, the dashing Captain Waller, sailed over to provide her with a smoke screen as she was still attracting the enemy's fire.

At 5.20 p.m. Admiral Doorman tried to regroup his ships by leading them to the north of the damaged *Exeter*. As he passed between the enemy and the *Exeter* he signalled the British cruiser to withdraw to Surabaya.

Then, fearing another salvo of torpedoes against the *Exeter*, which might well finish her off, Doorman ordered the British destroyers to counter-attack but only *HMS Electra* was in a position to do so immediately. Her brave commander, Captain May, mounted the attack alone and the *Electra* ploughed through the smoke zone and straight into a barrage of five and a half inch shells, which broke the mains in the boiler room. This brought her almost to a halt and the Japanese gunners had a field day. Even in this state the *Electra's* gunners were not idle and they fired several torpedoes but to no avail.

In the midst of shells coming at her in all directions the *Electra* began to list to port and so Commander May gave the order, "Prepare to abandon ship". Her bows were sinking as the concentration of enemy fire showed no abatement. While her sailors were jumping into the warm sea Commander May remained on the bridge, waving farewell to them. He went down with his ship when she sank in this brave act of trying to protect the *Exeter*.

Doorman now ordered *RNA Witte de With* to escort the seriously damaged *Exeter* back to Surabaya while he again re-formed his line, his own ship leading its fellow cruisers, *HMAS Perth*, *USS Houston* and *RNA Java,* and the destroyers. With the *Exeter* out of the fight the hard pressed Dutch admiral now had only six 8 inch guns (the *Houston's*) against the enemy's twenty. And the *Houston*, not having had the time to re-arm at Surabaya, was running out of ammunition.

It was now pitch dark and Doorman ordered his ships back to Java for the night. The American destroyers had now run out of torpedoes and so they quit the action.

As the fleet was sailing along the north coast of Java at around 9.15 p.m. *HMS Jupiter* struck a floating Dutch mine, which made a huge hole in her starboard side and through this part of the

Java Sea started to flow. This veteran of the action which sank the *Prince of Wales* and *Repulse* managed to stay afloat for another four hours, during which time most of the crew were got off in Carley floats. In all, seventy-eight of her ship's company made it to Java, where they would shortly be captured and put into Japanese prisoner-of-war camps.

With the loss of the *Jupiter* Admiral Doorman decided to change course since, if the *Jupiter* could be hit on this heavily mined coast, so could others. He took his cruisers away on a northern course but without the escorting destroyers.

Around 11 p.m. – just as this momentous day was coming to its end – Doorman's cruisers and those of the enemy came within sight of each other and fire was opened by the exhausted gunners on both sides.

The shelling duel in the dark was not getting anywhere and so the Japanese admiral, Takagi, ordered a torpedo attack and twelve of them came tearing through the sea towards the allied cruisers.

The *De Ruyter* was hit aft and she caught on fire with everything seeming to go up at once. The sailors rushed forehead in an attempt to escape the raging inferno while those on the Japanese ships, able to see everything in the bright lights of the flames, danced a jig of joy on their decks while screaming out that repulsive word "Banzai". Three hundred and forty-five sailors, including Admiral Doorman, were killed on the *De Ruyter* – a terrible loss for the brave Dutch Navy.

Almost immediately the *Java* was struck by a torpedo and she too went up in a blaze of flames. Her bows rose high into the air and the only thing that could quench her fires was the sea itself, into which she sank within minutes of being hit. But in those few minutes five hundred of her sailors managed to jump into the oily ocean, giving three cheers for their beloved Queen as they did so.

Doorman's last order to the remaining cruisers, *HMAS Perth* and *USS Houston*, was not to risk almost certain destruction by hanging around to pick up the Dutch sailors out of the sea but to make for Batavia and that is exactly what they did.

As midnight struck the allied fleet was no longer a fighting unit and the island of Java, the core and heartland of the Dutch East Indies, was wide open to invasion by the barbarians from the north. There were, of course, some allied ships that got away – the *Exeter*, which reached Surabaya at 11 p.m. with her faithful friend, the *Witte de With*, and also the *Perth* and the *Houston*, which were on their way to Batavia, the American destroyers that had run out of ammunition, and the *Encounter*. It is now necessary to record what became of them.

On the morning after the battle the stricken *Exeter* was tied up alongside the quay at Surabaya, her utterly exhausted sailors getting her ready to leave that night as, to remain in this exposed port, about to fall to the Japanese, would be a recipe for disaster.

The American destroyers were also getting ready to leave Surabaya to make a dash to Australia but they left *USS Pope* to help the *Exeter*. As the three American vessels sailed out of the bomb ravaged harbour they passed *HMS Exeter* at her berth. The crews of the American ships lined the decks and gave three hearty cheers to the *Exeter* – just as the ship's company of *USS Trenton* had cheered *HMS Calliope* as she made her dash out of Apia harbour in the teeth of the hurricane in 1889. And, just as the *Trenton* had kindly lent a boat to the *Calliope* to enable her to get away, so too had *USS Pope* stayed to help the *Exeter* – typical examples of the good will that has been the trademark of relations between our two navies in the Pacific over the years. The three American destroyers then sailed to the east and then down through the Bali Strait on their way to Australia, which they reached without any further dramas.

Also on this day (28th) the British buried their dead – fourteen from the *Exeter* – in Surabaya's European cemetery of Kembang Koening. In the words of Lieutenant Commander A. Kroese in his book, *The Dutch Navy at War*, "Notwithstanding the near approaching end of the Allied cause on Java the commander of the *Exeter* wished to give his dead a funeral with full naval honours. A large detachment of British Marines went through the ceremonial drill. Two chaplains in full dress conducted the service. Buglers sounded the Last Post. Salvos were fired over the communal grave. The red rays of the setting sun shone through the murmuring trees and over the graves. It was all very tragic, this impressive ceremony, the beautiful uniforms, the immobile faces, and as background the lost cause of the Allies in the Indies." [1]

The *Perth* and the *Houston* managed to reach Tanjong Priok, the port of Batavia, whence they planned to make a dash through the Sunda Strait, between Java and Sumatra, and get to Colombo in Ceylon.

They left on the night of 28th but, unbeknown to them, they were being shadowed by a Japanese destroyer, the *Fubuki*. When these two battle damaged cruisers came across some Japanese

415

transports they opened fire on them but were then torpedoed by the watching *Fubuki*. The *Perth* and the *Houston* turned hard to starboard and returned the fire. All nine of the *Fubuki's* torpedoes missed but ironically some of them went on and hit the Japanese transports.

The *Perth* and the *Houston* then turned north where they ran into a veritable armada of Japanese warships. From ranges varying from 5,000 to 500 yards a deadly fire was opened on both sides. The two allied cruisers must have known that they were doomed but they resolved to take as many of the enemy with them as possible. They didn't but they did manage to inflict quite a lot of damage on the other side.

A few minutes after midnight *HMAS Perth* sank at the entrance to the Sunda Strait. All the enemy fire could now be concentrated on the *Houston* and she sank forty minutes later. Of the *Houston's* ship's company of 1,008, some 370 survived – only to be captured and put in the Japanese prison camps for the rest of the War – if they survived.

The *Perth* had lost 353 out of a total ship's company of 682. Of the survivors, more than a hundred died during their captivity – a telling example of the brutal way that the Japanese treated their prisoners-of-war. Of those who survived the ordeal of incarceration many were scarred for life.

Back at Surabaya the task of getting the badly damaged *Exeter* out with the help of the two destroyers, *HMS Encounter* and *USS Pope*, was about to get under way. Unlike the American destroyers that went to Australia, they could not pass through the narrow Bali Strait because it was too shallow for the heavy cruiser. So they too sailed along the north coast of Java towards the Sunda Strait where they suffered the same fate as the *Perth* and the *Houston* by coming upon a large group of enemy ships and, as with the *Perth* and *Houston*, both sides opened fire on each other.

The *Exeter* was hit in numerous places and the old girl went down shortly after Captain Gordon gave the order to abandon ship.

HMS Encounter also took several hits and she too was abandoned and then sank, leaving *USS Pope* to face the enemy alone. But not for long as this old veteran of the First World War was not equipped to take on what seemed like the entire Japanese Navy and she too sank to the bottom of the sea. About fifty officers and seven hundred and fifty ratings from *HMS Exeter* and *HMS Encounter* were picked up by the Japanese and incarcerated in prisoner-of-war camps. Their war was over, their horror was about to begin.

Many things went wrong for the ABDA ships in this terrible and destructive battle – lack of air cover, a destruction of radio communication, the lack of a coherent signals system and *HMS Jupiter* striking a "friendly" mine but nothing could have prevented what happened for it was a doomed battle from the start. As a result of the fall of Malaya and Singapore the Japanese forces – land, sea and air – were now supreme in the area.

Four warships of the Royal Navy went into the Battle of the Java Sea and none survived. Proportionally the loss for our brave Dutch ally in both ships and men was even greater. Those who were killed in action might have been the lucky ones as they had short and relatively clean deaths – unlike the hundreds of their shipmates who would die in the prisoner-of-war camps after being starved, beaten and tortured by the most cruel and barbaric enemy that British sailors have ever fought against.

The Battle of the Java Sea was the largest sea battle since Jutland. There would soon be bigger naval engagements at sea in the Pacific and for the most part they would not go the enemy's way.

KAMIKAZES AT OKINAWA

In view of the disasters suffered by the Navy at the hands of the Japanese in 1941-2 it was only natural that honour should be redeemed by a return in force to the ocean which had been largely a British lake for so much of its known history.

Since the terrible events of Hong Kong, Singapore and the Java Sea the Royal Navy had confined its warfare to the Mediterranean, the Atlantic and the Indian Ocean, leaving the vast expanses of the Pacific to the Americans, whose late entry to the War was welcomed by those in the British Empire who had been fighting the cause of freedom on their own for so long.

With the end of the war in Europe approaching – although not as fast as it would have if we had had a more competent and courageous Supreme Allied Commander than Eisenhower, a man so ignorant that he did not even understand his own battle plan for Normandy in 1944 – the Royal Navy was at last able to muster a task force for the Pacific which, although only a fraction the size of the American fleet in that ocean, would nevertheless be the most powerful naval force that Britain had ever sent there.

Its immediate task was to co-operate with the U.S. Navy in the battles which still had to be fought as the Allies, under the brilliant leadership of General MacArthur, moved relentlessly towards Japan but there was a wider purpose as well; Britain had been evicted by the Japanese from several of her Pacific colonies and protectorates – Hong Kong, Singapore, Malaya, Sarawak, North Borneo, Brunei and the Solomon Islands – and it was time to get them back.

These places had been built with British capital, British laws, British organisation and British engineering skills and, in spite of uninformed and self-interested American criticism, were Britain's to take back.

When Britain acquired Singapore from the Sultan of Johore in 1819 the island's population consisted of only about three hundred fishermen, most of whom lived on their boats, while Hong Kong, at the time that British sovereignty was proclaimed in 1842, had about two thousand people and was aptly described by the Foreign Secretary, Lord Palmerston, as "a barren rock with hardly a house upon it". From such unpromising beginnings did Britain create the two richest and greatest trading ports in Asia, which stood

418

in strong contrast to the poverty, disorder and civil war that were the hallmarks of the United States' colony of the Philippines.

A British return to the colonies from which she had been so violently ejected would be welcomed by the locals of those places but not by the American government which, with the end of the war against Germany and Japan in sight, was already starting to direct its attention and resources to destroying the British Empire in order to break once and for all Britain's unique power in world affairs – a process that reached its fulfilment at Suez in 1956.

Franklin Roosevelt never lost an opportunity to lambast "British colonialism" and yet at Yalta he was quite happy to collude secretly with Stalin, probably the most bloodthirsty dictator in all of history, to hand over to that monster, without any reference to the wishes of the local inhabitants, all of eastern Europe as well as southern Sakhalin and the Kuril Islands off Japan.

The British government were well aware of the chicanery and hypocrisy of their American "ally" and this provided much of the impulse to send to the East what was, in fact, the largest and most powerful fleet that Britain floated in the entire War. With these ships (and the carriers' planes) Britain would have the wherewithal to take back her lost colonies without having to rely on the Americans, whose only interest in the matter was to try to prevent the return of Britain, Holland and France to their colonies so that the greedy business interests that have always controlled Congress and the White House could move in to unsophisticated territories and grab their resources at a cheaper price than would be the case if they had to negotiate with colonial officials.

And so it was that the Royal Navy re-entered the Pacific war in March, 1945, when the warships gathered in the huge anchorage of Seeadler Harbour in Manus, the largest of the Admiralty Islands, approximately two hundred miles north of New Guinea.

Hot, humid, wet and jungly, the Admiralty Islands, only two degrees south of the Equator, had been named in 1767 by Captain Philip Carteret R.N., and were under Australian rule until they were invaded by the Japanese in 1942. The Americans dislodged the Japanese in February and March, 1945, and erected a large base, that was centred around the excellent anchorage of Seeadler Harbour, fifteen miles by four in extent and twelve to fifteen fathoms in depth.

Here the Americans built airstrips, wharves, bridges, barracks, a church, hospital and cinema and laid about a hundred and fifty miles of roads that were paved with broken coral that they dredged from the sea. They also put in two floating docks, each of which could accommodate a battleship. It took the British sixteen years to build two docks at Singapore for battleships and yet the Americans managed to get two floating docks of similar size up and running on Manus in less than three weeks. Admittedly they were acting under the impetus of war but, in spite of this, the comparison does credit to American working methods at the expense of those of the British.

The Royal Navy sailed to Manus on 7th March, 1945, from Sydney where they had taken up their old berths of the nineteenth century at Garden Island. As they made their way up through the sparkling sea the pilots did plenty of flying from the carriers in preparation for what lay ahead. At Manus they took on stores, ammunition, water and fuel in readiness for their coming combat role in the Battle of Okinawa. For the Allies this was "Operation Iceberg" – a perverse name in view of the heat and humidity of the central Pacific where the sailors often slept on deck to escape the worse heat below. This was slightly more difficult on the British aircraft carriers where the men had to wait until almost midnight for the steel plated, armoured deck to cool sufficiently. The decks of the American carriers were made of wood and so they were better for sleeping but not when kamikazes landed on the flight deck. It was then that the Americans looked on the British carriers with envy.

This British fleet, named Task Force 57, left Manus during the 17th and 18th March. It consisted of four aircraft carriers, *HMS Indomitable, Illustrious, Victorious* and *Indefatigable*, the cruisers *HMS Swiftsure, Black Prince, Argonaut* and *HMNZS Gambia*, the destroyers *HMS Euryalus, Grenville, Ulster, Undine, Urania, Undaunted, Quickmatch, Quiberon, Queenborough, Quality, Whelp* and *Wager* as well as *HMS King George V* and *HMS Howe*. On the carriers were 218 planes – Hellcats, Avengers, Corsairs, Seafires, Walruses and Fireflies, the last mentioned being a most effective fighter-bomber that could fire rockets.

For the first time in the Navy's history in the Pacific the coming actions would be more about planes than ships. Most of the action and excitement would be in the air, with the pilots living life on the edge and the sailors doing the routine tasks of working the ships, and loading and servicing the planes. It was the pilots of the Fleet Air Arm who were the new gods of naval warfare.

This fleet of grey leviathans must have looked most impressive as it ploughed its way north through the blue Pacific to Ulithi island in the Caroline group to join the American navy. However, some perspective was brought to bear at the sight of the American fleet – 385 warships and 828 assault craft for the attack on Okinawa, a small, mountainous island south of Japan in the Ryukyu archipelago.

The role of the British Pacific Fleet in the coming battle was to station itself south of the main operations and prevent the Japanese from reinforcing Okinawa with aircraft from the south, which would have made it harder for the American landing forces, whose job was already difficult enough since the enemy had about 10,000 planes on Okinawa, including kamikazes.

The actual position of the British fleet was about a hundred miles south of the islands of the Sakishuma Gunto group, also part of the Ryukyus and roughly midway between Formosa and Okinawa.

There were six enemy airfields in the Sakishuma Gunto group which had to be cratered and put out of operation. The planes from the British carriers got on with the job and destroyed runways, installations and Japanese planes on the ground but, no matter how many times they bombed the runways during the day (and these were always daytime operations) the Japanese would repair the damage during the night so that they all had to be re-bombed the next day. However, eventually, through attrition, they were rendered useless to the enemy. This bombing of the same targets day after day became exceedingly monotonous for the pilots. There were, of course, other targets as well, including wireless stations and small vessels in the harbours.

The Japanese anti-aircraft fire was a real problem and on the first two days of air strikes (26th and 27th March) there were nine airmen killed and seventeen planes lost out of a total of more than 500 sorties. The first day of April was the day set for the landings on Okinawa and so, as the date approached, so did the air attacks on enemy positions intensify.

At dawn on 1st April, as our American ally was landing its forces on the island, a Japanese Zero came zooming down on to the flight deck of *HMS Indefatigable* with a 500 pound bomb that went off, wrecking the flight deck barriers, sick bay and briefing room. It made a three inch dent in the armoured deck but did not penetrate it. A fire broke out in the hangar below but was soon extinguished.

Altogether fourteen of the ship's company were killed and another sixteen wounded. The fleet had had its first introduction to the mad and dangerous world of kamikazes, whose trademark trick was to speed along the length of the deck rather than across it in an attempt to destroy as many planes on the deck as possible.

Also on this fatal morning another 500 pound bomb detonated near the destroyer, *HMS Ulster*, penetrating its hull, wrecking the boiler room and killing two sailors. Since she could no longer get up power she was towed by *HMNZS Gambia* to the repair base at Leyte in the Philippines.

Two days later it was the turn of *HMS Illustrious* when a kamikaze dive bomber burst out of the cloud and on to the deck, destroying a couple of Corsairs. The ship's guns fired away at this uninvited guest and so successful was their aim that the plane skidded into the sea where its bomb detonated. However, that wasn't the end of the visitor as part of his skull and his little brown eyeballs were blown on to the flight deck where they were picked up by curious sailors.

As if the bombing of the airfields in the Sakishuma Gunto group were not enough the British Pacific Fleet also assumed the extra responsibility of bombing enemy airfields on Formosa. This was meant to have been done by General MacArthur's forces. However, that great but rather prickly man was having one of his many "demarcation disputes" with Admiral Nimitz, one result of which was that the Brits had to go in and do the job in addition to their own. Thus were the Formosan airfields of Schinchiku and Matsuyama bombed by planes off British carriers in exceptionally bad weather.

After twelve days of air strikes the British task force had lost nineteen planes to enemy fire and another twenty-eight during operations. Needless to say both ships and planes were in dire need of repairs and so retired to Leyte. So too were the men – especially the pilots – whose nerves were on edge. They had dropped 412 tons of bombs during 2,444 sorties and had denied the enemy the use of the Sakishuma Gunto airfields in the vital days in the approach to and the aftermath of the American landings on Okinawa.

At Leyte there was a shortage of small boats to carry sailors between ship and shore and so they were compelled to stay on board in the blazing heat. However, some cold beer was brought on to the warships and the sailors sat on the deck under awnings to sip them – just as earlier sailors had dined on the deck at night in the South

Seas in the same type of heat and with the palm trees waving their fronds in the breeze on the hazy shore. During the fighting off Sakishuma Gunto the tot of rum had still been served but not until the evening as there was too much activity and too much danger during the day.

From Leyte *HMS Illustrious* sailed to Sydney for a much needed refit and was replaced by the carrier *HMS Formidable* when the fleet sailed back to give some more punishment to Sakishima Gunto.

On 4th May the *King George V* led a large force to bombard the island of Miyako Shima in the Sakishima Gunto group, including its airfields of Hirara, Nobara and Sukhama, but this left the carriers less guarded and it was while the bombarding force was away that twenty-six enemy planes made an attack on the British carriers.

HMS Formidable, the "new chum" in the group, got her baptism of fire when she was hit by a crazy kamikaze, whose 500 pound bomb exploded on the flight deck, wrecking ten Avengers and a Corsair, killing eight men and wounding another fifty-one. Fires broke out in the torpedo shop and hangar below and a cloud of black smoke settled over the carrier. The bomb had blown a hole in the flight deck but it was repaired by means of steel plates and quick setting cement.

Shortly afterwards another kamikaze in a Zero flew right along the flight deck on the starboard side of *HMS Indomitable* and then fell into the sea where its bomb exploded. There was very little damage but, as with the *Illustrious*, the pilot wanted to leave something of himself on board and so his right hand flew on to the carrier's deck.

King George V and her bombarding force got back from their mission in the early afternoon and the rest of this memorable day was spent fixing up things on the two carriers that had received kamikazes.

The next big day was 9th May when a kamikaze took aim at *HMS Victorious* and wrecked four Corsairs on her flight deck. Three of her men were killed in this attack.

The *Formidable* got a second dose on this same day when a kamikaze dropped a bomb on her flight deck, destroying six Corsairs and an Avenger. Fires broke out but they were extinguished within a quarter of an hour and the only fatality was one poor chap who was decapitated by a flying wheel from a plane.

Altogether some eighty-five members of the British Pacific Fleet were killed or missing during the task force's service off Sakishuma Gunto but it achieved its purpose of rendering the airfields on these vital and strategic islands all but useless to the enemy. To lose eighty-five sailors and pilots in action is tragic but in the same battle the United States Navy lost 4,907 of its men.

There were two aspects of this batle which would have been both novel and challenging for the sailors and which made action in the British Pacific Fleet very different from pre-war service in the same ocean. As already stated, the first was the new priority of aerial combat, which had advanced by enormous strides since 1939 under the impetus of war.

The second was having to play second fiddle to the Americans in an ocean where Britain had been predominant since the time of Captain Cook. This too arose out of the changing forces of war. Unlike the Great Republic, the British Empire had gone to war in 1939 for the sake of Poland and of all the peoples of the world – especially those in small countries – who want to live their lives free from the threat of external aggression. The drain on Britain and the Empire was crippling in those first two and a quarter years of war when we stood alone, with France defeated and the United States engrossed in its material pursuits and apparently unmoved by either honour or the tremendous forces of history which were being played out on the wider world stage.

The American government screwed Britain until she was literally down to her last ounce of gold and it was only then that, in a blaze of propaganda and self-congratulation, Washington introduced Lend-Lease but even that was a matter of self-interest as, having revved up their production of armaments, the Americans needed buyers and, if Britain could no longer pay in cash, then they would jolly well grab bases in British colonies on very favourable terms.

However, by 1945 all this was a matter of record only. There had been such a great shift of power and wealth as a result of the War that the Royal Navy was no longer capable of resuming its dominant role in the Pacific and the United States Navy was the best placed to take over the important function of keeping the world's largest ocean free from the aggression of great powers – a task that it has performed with the same big-heartedness, competence and courage as the Royal Navy did but not with the same style, fun or sense of tradition. It was a case of the Roundheads taking over from the Cavaliers.

A DARING SUBMARINE RAID

The 15,781 ton Japanese heavy cruiser, *Takao*, was damaged by torpedoes from the *USS Darter* on 23rd October, 1944, and so she proceeded to the Singapore naval base for repairs – the very same base that had so painstakingly been built by the British throughout the 1920s and 1930s.

It was soon obvious that, in view of Japan's deteriorating situation, the *Takao* could not be put back into fighting order and so, anchored in the shallow Strait of Johore, she was used as a floating anti-aircraft battery. Nevertheless she was a Japanese warship and the British had a few scores to settle, dating back to the first hours of the Pacific War with the sinking of the *Prince of Wales* and the *Repulse*. Although late in the day, "Operation Struggle", the underwater attack on the *Takao*, would help to even the scales.

The *Takao's* eight inch guns would be a threat to any British forces trying to get across the Strait of Johore to recapture Singapore and they would also be a problem for any allied shipping entering the Strait since at this stage the atomic bomb had not been dropped and the plans for Operation Zipper, the amphibious landings to retake Malaya and Singapore, were well advanced. For security reasons the planners of Zipper had not been told of the imminent dropping of the big bomb.

On 26th July, 1945, the fifty-seven foot long British midget submarine *XE3* was towed by the bigger sub, *HMS Stygian*, from Labuan, Borneo, towards Singapore - across the very stretch of ocean, under which lay the *Prince of Wales* and *Repulse* together with their drowned sailors. Her target was the *Takao*. Attached to her sides were two detachable tanks that held two tons of high explosives.

XE3 was commanded by Lieutenant Ian "Titch" Fraser from High Wycombe in Buckinghamshire and, like all the X-craft, she had a crew of four. Her diver was Leading Seaman James Magennis, a twenty-five year old Catholic from the Falls Road area of Belfast who, two years earlier, had volunteered for "special and hazardous duties". He would soon be put to the test.

HMS Stygian and *XE3* parted company at 2300 on 30th July at a point some forty miles from the target. From there the midget would have to make her way to the Strait of Johore through minefields, enemy listening posts, sunken craft and other hazards.

425

Lieutenant Fraser had been briefed by intelligence that the buoys marking the channel would be lit but, apart from the Horsburgh Light, this was not the case and he had to navigate blind, sometimes sitting astride the midget's outer casing with binoculars to scan the course ahead.

Shortly after 0200 on 31st July the main engine was stopped as they went past a known hydrophone post and the electric motor was used instead. Once safely past this obstacle, the main engine was turned back on and the sub, deep in the heart of enemy waters, chugged along at four and a half knots. By now they had passed all the known hydrophone posts and, not knowing where the others were, Fraser opted to avoid them by leaving the safe channel and passing through a known minefield.

At around 0400 a big tanker, escorted by a motor launch, was spotted approaching at high speed and so *XE3* did a dive. When she resurfaced about twenty minutes later the two enemy vessels were still there and so down she went again to the ocean depths.

A potentially serious obstacle was the anti-submarine boom that stretched across the Strait of Johore and which had been built by the British, but by some miracle the gate was open and so *XE3* passed through it, her echo sounder recording a depth of about thirty feet inside the Strait.

XE3 continued to approach the target, travelling at periscope depth. The *Takao* was sighted at 1250 and so was a wretched liberty boat with about forty Japanese sailors on board. By another miracle *XE3* went undetected. Contact was well and truly made when the midget hit the cruiser's hull with a loud bang. Fortunately the Japanese had only a skeleton crew on her and the collision was not noticed.

The *Takao* was in such shallow water that she was nearly aground. It took Lieutenant Fraser about forty minutes to wedge his vessel into a fifteen foot depression in the seabed under the cruiser's midship section and, even then, there was only a foot of water between *XE3* and the *Takao's* keel.

In this confined space James Magennis donned his diving gear and then went to pass through the sub's wet-and-dry compartment. However, after unlocking the diver's hatch, he found that it was too close to the *Takao* to open fully and so he drew in a deep diver's breath and took off his breathing apparatus so that he could squeeze through the gap, putting it back on again as soon as he was in the water.

Attached to his body were the six magnetic limpet mines that he was to put on the cruiser's hull. But, in order to attach them, he had to spend about thirty minutes scraping away the thick weed and barnacles on the *Takao's* bottom even though there was a leakage of oxygen from his breathing apparatus and it was ascending in bubbles to the surface.

He eventually managed to place the mines across some forty-five feet of the vessel and then squeezed his way back into the *XE3*, using the same method as before. Mission accomplished? Not quite. There were also the two detachable tanks – port and starboard – which were to be released from inside before leaving the target area. When Lieutenant Fraser operated the mechanism to release them, only the port one became detached. The other one refused to budge. The only way was for someone to go back outside into the water and release it manually.

Noticing that Magennis was exhausted after his dive, Fraser began to don his frogman's gear. However, Magennis insisted that he was the best one to do it. "I'll be all right as soon as I've got my wind, Sir," he said. And so once again the boy from Belfast went through the hatch and, with a large and heavy spanner, managed to release that clinging starboard charge. This time he was out of the sub for only seven minutes.

The next problem was to get the sub out from underneath the target as the tide was falling and it seemed that the big Japanese brute was starting to settle more and more firmly on the poor little sub. In Lieutenant Fraser's words, "For half an hour we went full speed astern and full ahead, with no success. I made a mental plan to abandon ship before the charges went off. But just as I was despairing we felt a movement and *XE3* climbed out from under the ship. We were all exhausted. After that it was 'Home, James, and don't spare the horses'." [1]

At 2130 on 31st a hole, twenty-three feet by ten feet, was blasted in the starboard side of the *Takao's* hull by Magennis' mines. Although the big blast buckled her keel, disabled her turrets and flooded her compartments she didn't sink. But she was out of the War for good.

XE3 retraced her passage of the night before but, being daylight, she travelled at periscope depth at a slow rate. She made her rendezvous with *HMS Stygian*, which towed her back to Labuan, arriving on 4th August. Two days later the atomic bomb was dropped on Hiroshima.

There were few feats of the War more daring or more dangerous than this raid deep into enemy waters and, of the four man crew of *XE3*, two of them, Lieutenant Fraser and Leading Seaman Magennis, had Victoria Crosses pinned on their uniforms by the King at Buckingham Palace. Of the other two, Sub-Lieutenant William Smith R.N.Z.N.V.R., who was at the controls of *XE3*, was awarded the Distinguished Service Cross while Engine Room Artificer Charles Reed received the Conspicuous Gallantry Medal.

THE NAVY IS BACK

Hong Kong

The naval fleet that reclaimed the lost colony of Hong Kong set out from Sydney on 15th August, 1945, within hours of hearing the good news that Japan had surrendered. It was commanded by Rear-Admiral Sir Cecil Harcourt, who had entered the Navy in 1904 as a midshipman at the age of twelve. The Admiralty could not have made a better choice.

The ships sailed first to Subic Bay, the great American base in the Philippines, arriving there on 25th August to take on as much fresh food, medical supplies and other provisions as they could for the starving ex-prisoners-of-war whom they would find upon arrival in Hong Kong. They also took on some extra firepower in the form of the submarine depot vessel, *HMS Maidstone*, her eight submarines and six Australian minesweepers. After only two days in port they sailed through the heavily mined sea lanes between the Philippines and China, and were off Hong Kong around noon on 29th.

Besides the aforementioned vessels the fleet also included the aircraft carrier, *HMS Indomitable* (Harcourt's flagship), *HMS Venerable*, *Swiftsure*, *Euryalus*, *Kempenfelt*, *Ursa*, *Whirlwind*, and *Quadrant* and *HMCS Prince Robert*. Off Hong Kong they were joined by the battleship, *HMS Anson*, the destroyer, *HMS Pyrias* and the hospital ship *Oxfordshire*. Further additions to this mighty fleet were the Australian corvettes *HMAS Castlemaine*, *Stawell*, *Bathurst*, *Broome*, *Fremantle*, *Strahan* and *Wagga*. Having been entrusted with the important and symbolic task of re-taking this jewel of the East, the Navy decided to do it in strength and style.

There was, of course, a more important reason for returning in such force and that was a fear that the Japanese, who had set the Pacific on fire and who had so many weird customs such as hara kiri and kamikaze, might do something both silly and dangerous after the official cessation of hostilities. After all, they had not been the most rational of enemies.

The warships sighted the storm clouded islands of Hong Kong at a distance of three to four miles off the Stanley peninsula, on the south side of Hong Kong island. There they paused until the sea lanes into Victoria harbour were swept by the Australian minesweepers. It was a cloudy and humid day with sporadic rain –

not uncommon at that time of the year. However, the visibility was good enough for those on the warships to see through their binoculars the barracks of the Stanley prisoner-of-war camp. And, even better, the inmates of the camp could detect the profiles of the high, grey ships on the horizon.

Before they came in sight of Hong Kong and while still several miles out at sea a flight of Hellcats had taken off from *HMS Indomitable* on a reconnaissance flight over the soon-to-be-restored colony. In order to demonstrate the new situation as plainly as possible they flew very low over the harbour as well as roaring up the length of Nathan Road and then at near rooftop level over the tenements of Kowloon. No enemy war planes rose from the ground and there was no sign of hostility.

Then an Avenger, with a flight escort of Hellcats, took off from the *Indomitable* for Kai Tak airport in order to bring a Japanese envoy, Mr. Makamura, out to the aircraft carrier to receive instructions from its commander, Captain Eccles. Makamura brought a chart with him, showing the minefields that had been laid by the Japanese and also the "searched channels" that the enemy had cleared but these could not be relied on as, judging from the number of sunken craft sticking up out of the harbour and elsewhere, it seemed that there were mines – recorded or not – all over the place.

The next day, Tuesday 30th August, the sky cleared, the sun came out and there was no wind – as if God Himself had lent a hand. The minesweepers, with their red floats, led the column of warships up the east side of Hong Kong island and then turned to port to pass through the Lei Yue Mun channel, across which the last of our troops on the mainland, the brave Rajputs, had been ferried to Hong Kong island by the MTBs on 13th December, 1941.

The leading ship was the minesweeper, *HMAS Mildura*, and she was followed by the destroyer *HMS Kempenfelt* and then *HMS Swiftsure*, to which Rear-Admiral Harcourt had transferred his flag since she drew less water than the aircraft carrier. Then came the Canadian vessel, *HMCS Prince Robert*, with the *Maidstone* bringing up the rear. There were also two submarines. The rest of the ships stayed at sea in the meantime with a constant protective air cover.

The sea sparkled in the morning sunshine as this impressive array of British and Commonwealth sea power passed slowly through the three hundred yard wide Lei Yue Mun channel, on the banks of which could be seen Japanese gun positions with their soldiers standing alongside. At some points the steeply rising hills seemed extremely close and there was apprehension on board as, in the event of any last minute Japanese trickery, these waters were too narrow to turn in. In other words, each warship was a sitting target. But the air cover was both tight and continuous, the planes swooping down low as if in a protective embrace.

Nevertheless on every ship there was both tension and silence as the ships' companies concentrated on the tasks of the moment. Those who were not at their work stations were leaning over the rails, watching the slowly passing panorama. When three Japanese suicide boats tried to leave their moorings they were attacked from the air; one was sunk, another beached while the third returned to shore. [1]

HMAS Mildura became the first of His Majesty's ships to enter Victoria harbour since December, 1941, as she led the others past all the sunken craft and other obstructions and then berthed at the Kowloon dock about noon. On the quay were about fifty local Chinese who were clapping and cheering. Russell Clark, an Australian war correspondent from Sydney, who was on board *HMCS Prince Robert*, has recorded his first impressions upon stepping ashore at Kowloon. "An American civilian came running on to the jetty. He threw out his arms, and tears were streaming down his face, and he was crying. 'Thank God you've come at last! We've had four years of hell! I tell you, the bastards have given us hell.'

Then the planks were down and we went ashore. People began to arrive on the dock – just a dribble. A couple of Indian Army officers were first. Their uniforms were very clean, very neatly pressed, painstakingly patched. You did not have to be told that they had been hoarding them for this day….There is a degree of happiness that hurts. I never knew it until that day. Nor until that day did I realise how proud I am to have sprung from this British stock.

An English major walked up to me with his hand outstretched. We shook hands and introduced ourselves. He said, 'Did you have a pleasant trip up?'

That rocked me. It could have been straight out of *Punch*. I couldn't have answered even if it had been possible to get the words past the lump in my throat.

I had come ashore armed with a pistol and a haversack crammed full of cigarettes. I pushed a packet at him and he stared at them in an uncomprehending sort of way and said, 'Are you sure you have enough?' Then took *one*. And they had not seen real

431

cigarettes in almost four years....I pushed the packet back at him. I said, 'There's beer and food on board ready for you people.' Then I wandered off towards the dockyard gates." [2]

On this first day ashore Rear-Admiral Harcourt did the decent thing and drove out to Stanley to reassure the internees that what they were seeing and hearing was not a dream. He told them that they should stay in the camp for a week or two as, should they be transported to their home countries in their present weak state, they would be likely to suffer from seasickness and other ailments. But they were invited on to the warships for food, drink and some much needed social contact with the outside world. He was impressed by their spirit. "I received a most tumultuous reception and it was magnificent to see the high state of morale in spite of the obvious effects of malnutrition," he said. [3] His most important task was to hoist the Union Jack in their presence.

In the words of Russell Clark, "It was a short, simple ceremony – quiet and deeply touching. About five o'clock a truck loaded with Marines drew into Stanley Camp. After it came three cars – 'liberated from the Japs'...They (the internees) sang the National Anthem. Then slowly in the fading light the Union Jack crept up on its staff and hung there stirred by an evening breeze.

After that came the flags of every nationality represented in the camp. One by one they swept up to take their places. The first strong bugle notes of the Last Post rang out over the stark, hushed peninsula. It was like a man walking and looking up to the promise of a new day.

There were few eyes that were dry in those overflowing minutes. And in those moments no one tried to hide what he felt. It was all too mixed up – a world that had been suddenly stood on its end...a world of free, happy men. And, above all, it was a world full of the tragic memories of those who did not live to see this day – the men who were shot, bayoneted, tortured, beheaded.

Hong Kong that day was something to remember. It was a time and a place to remember, because of its living and because of its dead." [4]

Back on the warships that night skeletal ex-internees were being entertained in the wardrooms and ratings' messes, which were jam packed and full of life and laughter. The ships' cooks and stewards were the heroes of the hour as they worked and sweated in relays all night, all the next day and all that night. Of these first two days Russell Clark wrote, "It was one of the happiest bedlams I shall ever see. Also they were the two most irregular days any naval ship could ever hope to experience." [5]

Among those on board the Canadian ship were soldiers of the Royal Rifles of Canada and the Winnipeg Grenadiers, who had arrived in Hong Kong not long before the outbreak of war, had fought bravely with the small amount of equipment they had, and were treated with particular brutality in the prisoner-of-war camps by the enemy – although not as bad as the poor Indians, who received the worst treatment.

As the bottled beer was opened and downed in the summer humidity the universal sentiment was "Thank God we've been liberated by the British and not the Americans with their wretched 'dry' ships."

Parties of armed marines went ashore and one of their first duties was to rescue some Japanese right outside the dockyard gates who were being attacked by a crowd of Chinese – but not before one of the Japanese was killed. In view of the millions of Chinese whom the enemy had been butchering since the early 1930s the attackers at least had a motive. So frightened were the Japs of scores being settled that two thousand of them locked themselves in a prisoner-of-war camp as protectioin against the Chinese.

Air patrols operated continuously over both Kowloon and Hong Kong island and within two days all the enemy had been rounded up on the island and sent across the harbour to Kowloon.

With 20,000 Japanese in the colony and only 350 Marines in the landing parties there was a great fear that something would go wrong. Ratings were not allowed to go ashore except on sentry duty and no officers were permitted to go beyond the dockyard area except for good reason, and they had to be armed.

With such a preponderance of numbers – although not firepower – the Japanese could have made things very tricky but they didn't – probably because of the old adage that the greatest bullies always become the most craven cowards when the tables are turned on them. In the words of Russell Clark, describing the beaten enemy "A few of them hated your guts with their burning little piglike eyes. Nearly all of them were just plain scared – scared as hell of what was going to happen to them....They were badly beaten and badly scared – scared of us and scared of the Chinese." [6]

Within an hour of landing the marines made contact with those in the internment camps and, in the words of Russell Clark,

"The re-occupation went ahead with a smoothness, efficiency and complete orderliness that was a credit to Harcourt and his staff." [7]

This was of great importance as the British had lost a lot of face with the local Chinese when they had been bundled out of the colony so ignominiously in 1941 and it was necessary to impress them that the British were again the best ones to rule this key enclave on the China coast.

Chiang Kai-Shek had some troops not far from the Hong Kong border but his interest in Hong Kong seems to have been confined to being in a position to deny it to his communists enemies should they make a grab for it. But they didn't and Chiang agreed to the British returning and accepting the Japanese surrender. No, the real threat was the United States government as Roosevelt had told his "new friend", Stalin, at the Yalta conference that he hoped that the British would never get Hong Kong back despite the fact that this was a British creation that had benefited the whole world – not least the people who lived there and prospered under the freedom and security that only Britain could provide in that part of the world.

Hong Kong was not Roosevelt's to give away and it was a good thing that he died when he did (April, 1945) as his successor, President Truman, was a man superior to Roosevelt in honesty, morals, patriotism and courage. He had all the character that Roosevelt lacked and, thankfully for mankind, he also had a more realistic view of the communists.

And so it was that the Navy, with its smartly dressed patrols, courtesy in the face of an extremely complicated situation, and efficiency insofar as the lack of coal, electricity and food would allow, created a very favourable impression as it went about its work on the streets of Hong Kong.

The Kowloon-Canton railway got back under way when a couple of naval officers found a diesel engine and ran it along the rail lines for a lark. [8]

After a force of commandos arrived from Ceylon to help keep order the pipe band of the 3rd Commando Brigade paraded through the streets as soon as it was ashore.

The crowning moment came on 16th September when Admiral Harcourt received the surrender of Major-General Okada, in charge of Japanese forces in Hong Kong, and Vice-Admiral Fujita, the commander of the South China naval forces. The ceremony took place at Government House, Hong Kong, and not on

434

board a warship "where blood would get all over the carpet if the little bastards decided to cut their throats afterwards." [9]

To avoid any hara kiri or other funny business the Japanese officers were strip-searched before entering the lovely white hall at Government House and they protested strongly, arguing that the word of a senior Japanese officer should be trusted. To this preposterous claim Captain Eccles of *HMS Indomitable* replied with considerable understatement, "We think that your behaviour at Pearl Harbour does not perhaps support such a claim." The two Japanese then entered the hall, "bowing low on their entry and departure". [10] The two officers had to surrender their swords, which they didn't like at all, but they and their colleagues should have thought of that before unleashing bloody war on the whole of the western Pacific.

In the words of our inimitable scribe, Russell Clark, "That ceremony increased my admiration for and my understanding of that almost incomprehensible race of people who call themselves British. For example, Fujita, in signing the surrender document, took an unconscionable time to do it. If you watched him closely, you could see he was doing it deliberately in an effort to discomfort his victors. He might have saved himself the trouble. His victors, being British, were completely at ease. He could have taken a month to sign his name and it would not have worried them unduly." [11]

It was only a short ceremony but impressive nevertheless. At the end of it the Japanese were marched out and, still in the words of Russell Clark, "Out front, on the lawn and driveway, were units of every service in Hong Kong – British Commandos, Navy, Hong Kong Volunteer Defence, Indian…this day belonged to them.

Then the band was playing – one brisk chorus of *Rule Britannia*. That was all. Just one chorus – and briskly. No more, no less. Somehow it was so sharp, and appropriate, and unexpected that it left you breathless.

I think that is the most completely British act I have ever known. It is impossible to imagine anything more representative – no fuss, no sentimentality. It was so completely *correct* that it left you with a throat that was tight with pride.

They ran the flag up and the band swept into the slow majesty of the National Anthem. On the last note of that, with perfect timing, there came the first rumbling salute from every armed ship in the harbour – and the harbour was full of ships." [12] Ah yes, nobody could do these things like the Royal Navy with its centuries of experience and tradition.

435

While all this was going on in Hong Kong the Navy was not exactly inactive in other areas of the Pacific that were just getting over what had been the greatest convulsion that the world's largest ocean had ever known.

The British cruisers *HMS Bermuda*, *Belfast* and *Argonaut*, the light fleet carrier *HMS Colossus*, and the destroyers *HMS Tyrian*, *Tumult*, *Tuscan* and *Quiberon* evacuated all known prisoners-of-war from Formosa. Those who were the most dangerously ill were put on the New Zealand hospital ship, *Maunganui*. The prisoners on Formosa had been worked as slaves in the copper mines at Dincasi, which was the scene of some of the worst atrocities of the War.

For the next eight months Rear-Admiral Harcourt governed Hong Kong as the British Military Administrator and it was administered by the Navy, whose role was challenging to say the least. "Looting was at one time very bad but marines and bluejackets have been landed to patrol the city, and general security now prevails," wrote the London *Observer* in November, 1945. [13]

In the prisoner-of-war camps that they liberated and on board the warships taking the emaciated ex-internees back to Britain the bluejackets and their officers saw with their own eyes and heard the stories with their own ears of the true horrors that had been perpetrated by the Japanese on those who were their prisoners – British, Canadian, Dutch, Chinese, Indian, etc. Over the course of two centuries in the Pacific the Royal Navy has fought many enemies – the Russians, Chinese, Maoris, South Sea Islanders, Germans, pirates, blackbirders – but Jack has always been a fairly easygoing creature and, apart from in the heat of action, has borne little malice to those at the other end of a gun. But the Japanese were different. At every level – from their emperor right down to the lowest prison guard – these people had put themselves outside the realms of humanity. The behaviour of Japanese sailors, soldiers and airmen was beneath contempt and for the first time ever the Royal Navy had fought an enemy that it hated.

Singapore

With the defeat of the Japanese forces in Burma by the British Fourteeenth Army under its outstanding commander, General Slim, it was time to undertake the long awaited amphibious re-occupation of the Malayan peninsula, which was to be assailed on

436

its west coast by the forces of Mountbatten's South East Asia Command (SEAC). However, with the merciful news that the dropping of the atomic bombs on Japan had ended the Second World War the operation changed from landing on a hostile coast to the retaking of it without – hopefully – any resistance, a hope that was realised.

After the landings at Port Swettenham and Port Dickson the sea lanes to Singapore, through the Strait of Malacca, were swept by the 6th, 7th and 37th Minesweeping Flotillas, and on 2nd and 3rd September the vessels of the 6th and 7th Flotillas, together with *HMS Cleopatra* and *HMIS Bengal*, reached Singapore, their White Ensigns – "that flag that has braved the battle and the breeze" – flying in the warm, tropical wind.

They were the trailblazers and the following day they were joined by convoys bringing the 5th Indian Division as well as *HMS Sussex*, the flagship of Rear-Admiral Holland. That same evening (4th September) the surrender of 77,000 Japanese in Singapore and Johore was signed on board the *Sussex* by Lieutenant-General Itagaki and Vice-Admiral Fukudome. Lieutenant-General Christison signed for the allies. The next morning at 11 a.m. the Indian troops started disembarking to begin the re-occupation of Singapore.

Members of the Japanese Navy, who were holed up at the Singapore Naval Base, were averse to surrendering to the Army and so the destroyer, *HMS Rotherham*, steamed up to the Strait of Johore, its men at action stations to guard against any last minute Japanese trickery from this Navy that had so sneakily attacked Pearl Harbour.

The surrender was duly taken and Captain Biggs of the *Rotherham* made an inspection tour of the huge base, which was deserted apart from a small group of Japanese naval personnel.

Captain Biggs immediately took over the dockyard and posted his sailors as sentries on its main gate while others patrolled its perimeter. Specialist officers of the *Rotherham* were put in charge of those parts of the base that matched their skills.

By 8th September most of the ship's company were being accommodated ashore in the barracks. The sports field was overgrown so they got about five hundred Japanese to cut it for them with scissors so that they could play football. This was done less for sadistic reasons than because more effective tools could not be found, it being a trademark trick of the Japanese to strip their conquered territories of useful things and take them to Japan.

However, it wasn't long before all the Japanese on Singapore island were packed off to Malaya and so the British footballers lost their "ground staff".

Within a week of taking over the base Captain Biggs and his men had it back in working order, which was of vital importance considering the huge number of British warships that were pouring into Singapore with troops, supplies and food; some of these vessels would need to be repaired.

Singapore's surrender ceremony took place on 12th September when Mountbatten rode in an open car to the stately Singapore Municipal Building, where the formalities were held. The streets were lined with sailors and Royal Marines, who all looked clean and sparkling in their white, tropical uniforms, and the local people, who seemed very happy to see their torturers being humiliated in such public fashion.

When Mountbatten stepped out of his car at the foot of the steps leading up to the Municipal Building, overlooking the great green sward of the *padang*, he was greeted by the three service heads in Singapore, Admiral Sir Arthur Power, General Slim and Air Marshal Keith Park, the last two mentioned being among the greatest leaders of the War – Slim in Burma and Park in the Battle of Britain.

Mountbatten then inspected four guards of honour, mounted by the Royal Navy, the Royal Air Force, the Indian Army and Australian paratroopers. Then the massed bands of the many warships that were in port struck up *Rule Britannia*, after which there was a seventeen gun salute.

The foyer of the Municipal Building was decorated with the flags of the Allies and a picture of King George VI. Inside the main chamber were the Royal Arms, which had been hidden throughout the War in the Singapore Museum in the sure knowledge that one day they would be needed for a ceremony such as this. At each of the eight main pillars stood an armed sentry, one from each of the Allied nations.

The focal point of this momentous occasion was in the middle of the chamber where two long tables, six feet apart, stood, with a raised dais at the Allied table for the Supreme Allied Commander. Behind the table for the Japanese were about four hundred onlookers – Army, Navy and Air Force officers, photographers and, most important of all, some recently released prisoners-of-war.

438

The Japanese (Lieutenant-General Itagaki and seven others) did not have such a happy arrival at the entrance of the Municipal Building as they were greeted by loud and deeply felt catcalls from the Chinese spectators. So much for Japan's much touted "Greater East Asian Co-Prosperity Sphere"!

The Japanese entered the chamber in silence – as they did in Hong Kong. But there was no Field Marshal Count Terauchi, the senior commander who was meant to sign this surrender of all Japanese forces in South East Asia – just a telegram saying that he was too ill to attend. Mountbatten had prior notice of this non-attendance and, not really believing him, had sent his own doctor, Surgeon Captain Birt, R.N. to examine him. He confirmed that Terauchi really was sick (he had had a stroke upon hearing of the loss of Mandalay in Burma) and so he was excused on condition that he later made a personal surrender to Mountbatten, which he eventually did at Saigon, handing over his priceless swords; one, a short sword that had been forged in the sixteenth century, was later presented to King George VI while Mountbatten held on to the other, which was even older.

In Terauchi's place was Lieutenant General Itagaki, who must have been getting quite experienced at this sort of thing as he it was who had earlier signed the surrender of the Japanese forces in Singapore and Johore on board *HMS Sussex*.

Having to sign two surrenders must have been particularly galling to Itagaki as he was one of Japan's most unrepentant warriors. Even after the Japanese emperor announced the end of the war in Tokyo Itagaki expressed his determination to continue the fight on the ludicrous grounds that the Japanese armies had not been defeated on the battlefield. He was snapped out of his delusions by his superior, Field Marshal Terauchi, who said that further resistance would disgrace the "honour" of the Japanese army, which was a bit of a long shot since it is arguable whether Japan's army has ever had any honour.

Mountbatten was very particular to impress on the Japanese that they had been beaten in the war that they had started as no one wanted a repeat of 1918 when the Germans got the impression that they had negotiated an armistice, thereby encouraging them to re-arm and start another war. In case Hiroshima and Nagasaki had not sufficiently conveyed to them the new reality of utter defeat Mountbatten, in his speech, said, "I wish to make this plain; the surrender to-day is no negotiated surrender. The Japanese are submitting to superior force, now massed here." Indeed they were.

In his Order of the Day to his troops Mountbatten left them under no illusions as to what he thought of the vanquished. "They are finding it very hard to accept defeat, and have not been too proud to try to wriggle out of the terms of their surrender. You may all rest assured that I shall put up with no evasion or trickery on the part of any defeated Japanese, however important he may consider himself. You may well find that those Japanese, who have a fanatical belief in their divine superiority and who feel we are too soft to put them in their place, will try to behave arrogantly. You are to stand no nonsense from these people. You will have my support in taking the firmest measures against any attempt at obstinacy, impudence or non-co-operation."

Mountbatten and Itagaki signed a total of eleven copies of the Instrument of Surrender, after which the Supreme Allied Commander went back outside into the bright sunlight and stood on top of the great flight of stone steps, that lead up to the main entrance of the Municipal Building. From here he watched the hoisting of the Union Jack at the saluting base. The flag itself had been kept hidden all through the War inside Changi Gaol. In the words of Sir Shenton Thomas, the Governor of Singapore at the time of its fall in 1942, speaking a few days earlier, "When our flag came down I knew we should want it again so I hid it. The Japanese never found it and it will be used again when they surrender Singapore." [14]

As the flag made its way up the white pole all the massed bands of the naval vessels in the harbour played *God Save The King*. The British were back in Singapore.

New Guinea and the Solomons

The formal surrender of 130,000 Japanese servicemen in New Guinea and the Solomon Islands took place at 11.15 a.m. on 6th September aboard a brand new, light aircraft carrier, *HMS Glory*, which was stationed twenty-eight miles south-east of Rabaul, the main port on New Britain, which itself is an island off the north-east coast of New Guinea.

The *Glory* had been built in Northern Ireland during the War and had arrived in Sydney on the day of the Japanese surrender.

The enemy commanders were Vice-Admiral Jin-ichi Kusaka, the commander-in-chief of Japan's south-eastern fleet (or, at least, what was left of it), and General Hitoshi Imamura. Originally it was to have been only Imamura to sign but he requested that Kusaka sign too and this was accepted. No doubt Imamura wanted to share the shame.

The two men and fourteen other Japanese were taken out first to *HMS Hart* and then on to the *Glory* by launch but, by the time they reached the aircraft carrier, they were wet through by the waves breaking over the boat. No doubt the captain of the launch drove her in such a way as to ensure a good drenching. In the words of the *Sydney Morning Herald*, "The Japanese were sociable on the *Hart* but Imamura did not like the trip. He was seasick." [15] Oh dear!

When these "drowned rats" appeared on the flight deck there were a thousand officers, ratings and marines lined up to watch the signing ceremony. The Japanese were marched along the deck to the red clothed table by a guard of four marines with carbines.

Imamura, short, middle aged, jack booted and spurred, was wearing khaki with an open necked white shirt and a cloth forage cap. He must have looked like one of those Japanese in the comic books.

The two enemy officers signed the document, using their own brushes and ink. Both signed with large Japanese characters but Imamura then added his signature in English. For the allies the deed was done by Lieutenant-General V.A.H. Sturdee, the G.O.C. of the 1st Australian Army.

After the signing was over Imamura, with the usual obsequiousness of defeated Japanese, thanked General Sturdee for the consideration shown to the Japanese during the pre-surrender negotiations and he promised to implement Sturdee's surrender directive immediately – a challenging task in view of the fact that Japanese soldiers were scattered over thousands of square miles of thick jungle and countless islands.

Like the Hong Kong surrender, this was a short ceremony that lasted only forty minutes. All through the ceremony the *Glory* was manoeuvring slowly in case of a last minute attack by these maniacal desperadoes. An unidentified plane was spotted and was chased by the *Glory's* Corsairs but it turned out to be an innocent unarmed American Dakota transport aircraft.

General Sturdee warned his visitors that any Japanese, other than authorised police and guards, found in possession of arms or explosives was liable to be shot on sight. He also assured Imamura that all Japanese would be treated with "firmness, justice and humanity", [16] the last two of which were more than any of their conquered peoples in Asia ever got from the Japanese.

According to the *Sydney Morning Herald*, "The happiest man aboard the *Glory* yesterday was Leading Steward Shufong Tsung, the thirty-two year old Chinese valet to Captain Buzzard. He had lived for the day when the Japanese would grovel in the dust. Tsun last heard of his parents at Wei Hai Wei in May, 1940." [17]

After the ceremony the *Hart* returned the Japanese to their base at Kabanga Bay, and Australian minesweepers began sweeping the waters of Simpson harbour, Rabaul, with air cover provided by the Royal New Zealand Air Force.

The Japanese also furnished lists of allied prisoners whom they were holding – planters, traders and others who had been nabbed when the enemy sprang their surprise attacks back in 1942 and who were just as emaciated as their fellow prisoners in Hong Kong, Singapore and elsewhere. Even more so as, because of the growing allied superiority at sea, no supplies had come from Japan – not even for the Japanese military – since April, 1944, and they were all living off sago and potatoes.

Rabaul, a huge Japanese sea and air base, showed General MacArthur's "island hopping" strategy at its finest. Instead of trying to capture it, which would have been a very bloody affair, he simply bypassed it, contained it, occasionally bombed it and let it wither on the vine. Now it was free again and the Australian and British administrators of these islands had a lot of work to do to get them up and running.

HMS AMETHYST ON THE YANGTSE

"The fact that everyone on board the frigate, from the oldest to the youngest, faced the situation with poise and equanimity was indeed salutary and our greatest asset. The spirit of leadership and devotion to duty was fully exemplified by officers and senior ratings, and this, after all, is the fundamental basis of naval training and the essence of everything that the Royal Navy has stood for in the past, stands for at the present time, and will stand for in the future. One and all, *Amethyst's* ship's company has shown that courage and fearlessness in adversity are still the finest attributes of the British peoples."

- Lieutenant-Commander John Kerans of *HMS Amethyst*

Section 52 of the Treaty of Tientsin, which was signed at the end of the Second Opium War, gave the Royal Navy the right to sail to any port in China, including its big river ports. The rivers of China are its arteries and the penetration of British warships up these busy but dirty waterways took them into the very heart of the world's most populous country and ensured the pre-eminence of Britain in the China trade.

How far a warship could steam up these rivers depended on how much water she drew, and gunboats with shallow draughts were specially designed and constructed for the China station. On the Yangtse and the West River the Royal Navy maintained permanent patrols, with a senior naval officer in charge of each of the two river squadrons. "The conduct of the Chinese when the gunboat on the station is at her post is very different from what it is when she is absent," stated a press report of 1862.[1]

The first chart of the Yangtse was made not by a naval captain but by a captain of the Royal Artillery, Thomas W. Blakiston, who had commanded a detachment of his regiment during the fighting around Canton in the Second Opium War. Article 9 of the Treaty of Tientsin of 1858, as ratified in 1860, stated: "British subjects are hereby authorised to travel for their pleasure or for purposes of trade to all parts of the Interior under passports which will be issued by their Consuls and counter-signed by the local authorities." Having fought in the war that resulted in this treaty, Captain Blakiston decided to take advantage of the rights that it conferred on British people and he joined an exploring party that was conveyed up the Yangtse as far as Yo-chow by British warships, fresh from the fighting that had just ended.

Blakiston and his party eventually reached a point some 1,800 miles from the Yangtse's mouth, which was twice as far as any other Europeans had ever ventured apart from some crafty Jesuits who had disguised themselves in Chinese costume. From this trip Captain Blakiston produced a fairly accurate chart of China's great river from Hankow to Pingshan. It was published in 1861 and was of particular use to the trailblazing British warships that worked their way up the river since the Yangtse was (and is) one of the trickiest rivers in the world for navigation, with numerous hazards that were liable to move. Even with the chart, the men-of-war usually travelled only in daylight and would find a safe place to anchor for the night.

The navigable channel along the river was often narrow and tortuous, allowing ships to pass but not giving them enough room to turn, especially when the river was low. It was a tricky river to navigate since "the sandbanks are liable to change rapidly in the strong current, and the navigable channel one day might be in a position quite different from the day before. Such rapid changes are difficult to detect except by the Chinese river pilots who have a lifetime's experience of the river and its vagaries." [2] Penetrating into the heart of such a strange and little known land as China could be challenging – as Rear-Admiral Keppel found when he took *HMS Salamis* up the Yangtse in 1869 "with Blakiston's geographical flying survey of the river as our only guide." [3]

Keppel was up river from the treaty port of Hankow and more than five hundred miles inland from the sea when he decided to investigate the branch that leads to the Tung-ting Lake. The *Salamis* came to off a large port called Yo-chow. "A high wall hid from our view the city, which appears to have been built on a bluff," he wrote. [4] "...There was a good assortment of trading junks; two Customs boats were showily decorated, the Captain was entertaining a tea party. Our surveying officers landed to take sights for chronometers and soon collected a crowd, some of whom, when the officers had picked up their instruments and turned their backs to go down to the boat, began hooting and throwing stones, a number of specimens of which were brought on board, some of them quite big enough to have knocked a man off his thwart.

Observing what was going on I ordered a blank gun to be fired to remind them that we were a vessel-of-war and might pitch something into them that would hit harder than stones." [5] He then told one of his officers to go and demand an explanation from the Captain of the Customs, "who was at that moment sitting down to entertain his guests." [6] The Captain sent a message to the Prefect, telling him of the outrage and recommending that he send down a force to keep the peace.

Keppel had the Captain of Customs brought on board by means of one of the boats of the *Salamis*. "I informed him," wrote Keppel, "that it was a very serious offence; that by treaty a man-of-war was allowed to go to any part of China and have protection; that the affair at Swatow commenced in the same way by some roughs, over whom the authorities professed to have no control, throwing stones, which ended in my having to destroy three large towns with great loss of life to the inhabitants." [7]

Nothing further happened and, by the time the *Salamis* left Hankow, Keppel was able to write, "The ill feeling by a few roughs was anything but the prevailing one among the natives, who swarmed alongside to see the ship, bringing vegetables and sweetmeats for sale." [8]

Nearly eighty years later, in another outburst of Chinese xenophobia, *HMS Amethyst* was viciously attacked further down the same river near Nanking.

In 1949 the destroyer, *HMS Consort*, was off Nanking, the capital of Nationalist China, standing by in case it became necessary to evacuate the British diplomatic staff in the event of them being endangered by China's civil war. The communists were already on the north bank of the river while the Nationalist army continued to hold the south bank.

When the *Consort* ran short on fuel and supplies it was decided to replace her with the 1,495 ton frigate *HMS Amethyst*, which left Shanghai on 19th April, 1949, and proceeded up the Yangtse at eleven knots. There is an old Chinese saying, "May you live in interesting times" and it certainly came true for the 183 members of the ship's company of *HMS Amethyst* as they headed for the war zone. Included among them were fifteen boy seamen who were new not only to the ship but also to the Far East station.

At 8.30 the next morning (20th April), as the *Amethyst* was still about seventy-five miles short of Nanking, she came under shell fire from the communist held north bank of the river even though she was flying the White Ensign and had a large Union Jack painted on her hull.

445

The bridge, wheeelhouse and low power room were all hit. The damage to the brige and wheelhouse meant loss of control and so the ship steered to port and ran aground in the mud off Rose Island, a small, flat piece of ground that rose out of the muddy river.

The bridge was in chaos with dead and wounded all over the place, including the ship's captain, Lieutenant-Commander Bernard Skinner, whose wounds were such as to prevent him from exercising command and so he told the First Lieutenant, Geoffrey Weston, to order the gunners to return the fire although, with the disabling of the low power room, the guns were unable to fire in Director control. Weston, who was also the gunnery officer, gave the order and a minute later he was hit by a hot piece of flying steel which penetrated through to his ribs. It was in this dazed state that he had to take over command of the *Amethyst* from the even more seriously injured Skinner.

When they saw that she was stuck in the mud the communists continued to fire shells at her at almost point blank range. The sick bay was hit by a shell, which killed Boy Seaman Maurice Barnbrook.

The unwounded were ducking and crawling in order to avoid flying splinters of hot metal. Also hit were some storage batteries, which sprayed their acid over one of the men. The *Amethyst's* last message was "Under heavy fire. Am aground. Large number of casualties". A few minutes later the ship's radio was silenced when shellfire brought down the aerials but not before this desperate message had been received by the *Consort*. To restore communications a jury aerial was rigged.

The Electrical Artificer, L. Chase of Pittenweem in Fife "refused to take any rest until he had established emergency electric light and, when he had conquered the darkness between decks, he immediately devoted his energies to the tending of the sick".[9] Seeing the sailors on deck trying to get their wounded below, Mao's men, with their trademark brutality, aimed their fire on the busy and blood spattered deck.

By midday there were already seventeen British dead and another twenty-five who were seriously wounded, including one of the two Chinese pilots who had come on board to help direct the warship up the river.

In their helpless position the surviving officers of the *Amethyst* destroyed the ship's codes and they also tried to get the men ashore apart from a skeleton crew who would be needed to get

446

up steam. The *Amethyst's* motor boat had been cut in half by shellfire and was never used. There was only one serviceable boat – a whaler that could be rowed. This was lowered and, in an attempt to save as many lives as possible, was filled with the walking wounded and those who could be spared from the ship. Some of the men jumped overboard while others shinned their way down a rope and swam to Rose Island, a distance of about 150 yards. Unfortunately two of them drowned. The enemy turned their guns on the men in the water and this put a stop to the attempt to land men on the island. Rose Island had been mined by the Nationalists but they very considerately pointed out where the mines were. Altogether about sixty men reached the island where Chiang Kai-Shek's men gave them fresh clothes to replace their torn and bloodstained white tropical uniforms as well as cigarettes to calm their nerves.

The Assistant Nnaval Attaché at the British Embassy in Nanking, Lieutenant-Commander John Kerans, and an American naval doctor called Packard arrived to assess the situation on shore and during the nights of 21st and 22nd they managed to locate most of the men who had been landed – both the wounded and the fit. These were all taken to Chin-kiang, from where they were put on a train for Shanghai where they arrived "ill clad and tired. Some were bandaged".[10] On the way to Chin-kiang both Lieutenant-Commander Skinner and an Able Seaman died of their wounds.

At Shanghai the wounded were looked after on an American hospital ship, the *Repose*. This was simply the latest instance of co-operation in Chinese waters between the British and American navies that dated back to Josiah Tatnall and his men helping the gunners on *HMS Plover* during the Second Opium War.

Two of the sailors who could not walk (Bannister and Martin) were not found and so were left on Rose Island. They were later taken to the south bank of the river and carried on bamboo stretchers along narrow lanes between the paddy fields to a point thirty miles down stream in a journey that lasted thirty-four hours. The peasants who carried them were both gentle and kind.

Meanwhile for those who were still on the stranded warship the communists ceased their shelling – presumably because there was not much more that shells could accomplish, and so they would preserve them for their battles with the Nationalists.

Shortly after 1 a.m. on the morning of 21st the *Amethyst's* crew got the ship off the mud bank after jettisoning the kedge anchor, derricks, awning stanchions and any other heavy items that could be moved, and pouring oil over the side from the forward tanks. The frigate then proceeded two miles up the river until she was beyond the range of the worst of the communist guns.

Lieutenant Stewart Hett was alone on the bridge when the *Amethyst* came off the mud. He was then joined by Lieutenants Weston and Berger. However, because of their wounds these two officers could not stay on the bridge for long and they would not let Lieutenant Hett steam up the river any further on his own.

Both the *Amethyst's* doctor and the medical rating were dead and so on the afternoon of 21st a Nationalist medical team went on board to treat the injured. Then, after dark, they arranged for the seriously wounded to be taken ashore in sampans – except for Weston who, in his injured state, was still in command of the vessel.

Hope of a kind came in the early afternoon when the Nationalist air force began firing tracer bullets at the communist batteries from five hundred feet and then, through the clouds of smoke from the gunfire, could be seen *HMS Consort* coming down the river at a rapid rate. The communists poured a concentrated fire on her too but she gave a good account of herself, silencing three of the enemy's shore batteries. However, to take the *Amethyst* in tow would have jeopardised the *Consort* and so, with her bridge, wheelhouse and wireless office all hit and nine of her own men dead and several more wounded, her commander, Captain Robertson, himself wounded, proceeded down the river to the Nationalists' naval anchorage at Kiang-yin, on the south bank of the river, where her wounded were treated.

The *Amethyst* was now alone, helpless and stranded hundreds of miles up a treacherous river and in the sights of the communist guns that were hidden among the reeds on the nearby bank of this wretched waterway.

The Yangtse is infested with rats and mice and so every warship that frequented it had a resident cat on board. The *Amethyst's* was a black and white tomcat called "Simon". He had joined the ship the previous year when he was found in the dockyard at Stonecutters Island, Hong Kong, by seventeen year old Ordinary Seaman George Hickinbottom. The strays of Stonecutters Island often provided ship's cats to the warships. No doubt the sailor thought that he would have more of a life as a petted creature on the ship than in Hong Kong where he would very likely finish up as part of a Chinese banquet.

INSTRUMENT OF SURRENDER.

We, Major General Umekichi Okada and Vice Admiral Ruitaro Fujita, in virtue of the unconditional surrender to the Allied Powers of all Japanese Armed Forces and all forces under Japanese control wherever situated, as proclaimed in Article Two of the Instrument of Surrender signed in Tokio Bay on 2nd September, 1945, on behalf of the Emperor of Japan and the Japanese Imperial Headquarters, do hereby unconditionally surrender ourselves and all forces under our control to Rear Admiral Cecil Halliday Jepson Harcourt, C.B., C.B.E., and undertake to carry out all such instructions as may be given by him or under his authority, and to issue all necessary orders for the purpose of giving effect to all his instructions.

Given under our hands this 16th day of September, 1945, at Government House, Hong Kong.

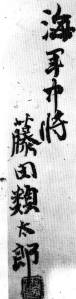

In the presence of *Cecil Harcourt*

On behalf of the Government
of the United Kingdom.

Cecil Harcourt

On behalf of the Commander-in-Chief,
China Theatre.

The Instrument of Surrender of the Japanese at Hong Kong, 1945.

The Master of H.M. Hospital Ship Oxfordshire, Captain A. Beharrel, M.N., chatting with some ex-captives of the Japanese who were among the first to be taken out of Hong Kong after the re-occupation of the colony by British sailors.

The surrender ceremony of Japanese forces in New Guinea and the Solomon Islands on board HMS Glory, 1945.

Some of the damage to HMS Amethyst in the Yangtse Incident of 1949.
(Photo : Maritime Quest)

Some of the ship's company of HMS Amethyst during the time they were
stranded up the Yangtse. Also in the photograph are "Able Seacat" Simon
and the ship's dog, Peggy (Photo : Lt-Cdr. Stewart Hett)

The lowering of the flag for the last time at Hong Kong by
Nick Tarrant of HMS Chatham, 30th June, 1997.

On board Simon proved his usefulness by catching rats and he quicly became a favourite of both captain and crew. He even followed the captain when he did his evening rounds and he slept in the captain's cabin, sometimes curling up inside the officer's cap.

Simon was in the captain's cabin when a shell struck it, throwing him into the air. He survived the shock but not without injury; his whiskers were burned off, his fur singed and his back and legs covered with blood from the cuts caused by shell splinters. These wounds were later cleaned and stitched. The *Amethyst* also carried a pet dog called Peggy who, like Simon, survived all the shelling and other weird manifestations of human beings fighting each other.

The dead were collected from various parts of the ship, which was by now afflicted with the stench of burnt flesh and powder not to mention the decks that were slippery with blood. The badly mutilated corpses were wrapped in hammocks and all were spread out on the quarter deck. For the burial service each body was wrapped in a hammock and weighted with two 4 inch shells. They were then piped over the side where they fell with a splash into the muddy Yangtse.

When the stricken vessel's desperate signal was received at Shanghai, Vice-Admiral Madden, second-in-command of the China station, took the cruiser, *HMS London* and the frigate, *HMS Black Swan*, up the river but they too were attacked. When the *London* was within a few miles of the *Amethyst* she was suddenly fired on by five artillery batteries. She hesitated before returning the fire and was then swept by a second round from the gun emplacements that the communists had so sneakily placed in the reeds and rice fields on the northern bank. This time the *London* opened up with a massive broadside. During the engagement her captain and fourteen others were killed. Those on the *Amethyst* heard the gunfire and knew that it was their fellow warships even though they never saw them.

The *London* had no option but to return to Shanghai and Vice-Admiral Madden sent a signal to the *Amethyst*, "Am sorry we can not help you to-day. We shall keep on trying". When the *London* went alongside Holt's Wharf at Shanghai her battle scars were very visible – twelve shell holes in the port hull and numerous splinter holes in her superstructure.

A Sunderland flying boat flew up from Hong Kong and landed on the river some seventy-five yards from the *Amethyst*. She brought some urgently needed supplies and an R.A.F. medical officer, Flight Lieutenant Michael Fearnley, but it too came under fire from a field battery about two thousand yards away and so the pilot had to take off in a hurry but not before Fearnley had climbed into a sampan with his bag of medical supplies. This took him to the frigate and, together with another doctor provided by the Nationalists, he was able to attend to the wounded.

By the 22nd Geoffrey Weston was in a state of utter exhaustion from both the stress of battle and his wounds and so Lieutenant-Commander Kerans, the Attaché from Nanking, boarded the *Amethyst* and took over command. He brought with him morphia and a booklet of Yangtse charts in case the *Amethyst* had lost them. In fact, the passage on the Yangtse from Nanking to the sea involved some eight Admiralty charts and the only one that had been lost was the one that was being used on the bridge at the time it was hit.

By now there were only eighty-one members of the ship's company left on board. On the morning of 23rd April, Saint George's Day, the Nationalists retired from their positions on the south bank and Mao's troops poured across the river but without firing any more ammunition on the poor old *Amethyst*.

Three days later, on 26th, the local political commissar, Colonel Kang Nao-Chao, began negotiations for giving the *Amethyst* a "safe conduct" back down the river. With their trademark dishonesty the communists insisted that the British admit that they had fired the first shot, which was not true. They then tried to extract an admission that the *Amethyst* had "wrongly and criminally invaded Chinese waters", which was also a lie since, under the Treaty of Tientsin, British warships had the right to navigate Chinese rivers. Kerans was told that, if he tried to move the ship, she would be blasted out of the water.

Of these interminable and pointless "negotiations" Lieutenant-Commander Kerans said, "I was treated with the utmost discourtesy. Everything was thrown at me. I was treated with personal vilification for weeks on end....We once argued for three hours about one sentence." [11] This was yet another example of Chinese perfidy and insincerity – something with which the British negotiators became familiar during the talks leading up the handover of Hong Kong to China in 1997 when they, like Lieutenant Commander Kerans, were subjected to the rudeness and deceit of Chinese negotiators with the traditional "chip on the shoulder" that emanates from their inferiority complex when dealing with countries that, unlike their own, have been able to build worthwhile

450

institutions that rest on a more solid foundation than corruption and the brute force of the government.

In the three months that they were held hostage the men of the *Amethyst* were allowed only one consignment of mail and stores from Shanghai but they arrived badly pilfered.

As the weeks wore on the sailors occupied themselves by repairing the battle damage to their ship, keeping her clean and serviceable and trying to deal with the summer heat and humidity, not to mention the rats and mosquitoes. To conserve fuel they shut down all power on board – no light, no ventilation, no water supply (although they could hand pump header tanks) and no refrigeration - and so they had to suffer the stifling heat of a Yangtse summer with no better equipment than Captain Keppel's *Salamis* had back in the 1860s – except that he avoided the river in summer, spending those months in northern waters and Japan.

Adversity seemed to bring out the best in the men. Of their more than three months imprisonment in the most trying of conditions Lieutenant-Commander Kerans signalled, "I can not speak too highly of the conduct, bearing and fortitude of my remaining ship's company. They have endured a long period of hardships under almost intolerable conditions with a cheerfulness and courage which can have few equals in time of peace. Many of them are new arrivals at the station, and nearly all are extremely young. The British spirit in adversity has once again shown itself to be unassailable." [12]

The main problem was that the *Amethyst* did not have enough fuel to make it to Shanghai, 140 miles down river, but then after a plea by Lieutenant-Commander Kerans for oil to fuel the ship's ventilators and refrigerators, the communists allowed the delivery of fifty-four tons of oil on 11th July in the belief that it was to help the ventilation on board, their "line" being that their quarrel was not with those on the *Amethyst* but with the British Government and its naval command.

With this extra fuel Kerans, showing the trademark initiative and courage of the naval officer, decided to run the gauntlet of the riverside batteries and make a dash for freedom. He sent a coded signal to the naval authorities that he intended to break out at 2200.

He was motivated by two considerations, viz. the worsening physical and nervous condition of his remaining men (they were down to half rations) and his belief that the communists would never agree to a safe passage down the river. He revealed his plan to only one other officer, and the ship's company were told only on the day of the projected escape, 30th July. Kerans believed that, the less time they had to think (or worry) about this venture, that he himself put at no better odds than 50/50, the better for their morale. Of the two Chinese pilots who had brought the frigate up the river one had been wounded beyond repair while the other had deserted and so Kerans was on his own.

At 10.12 p.m. on this last Saturday night of July – one hundred days after she was first fired on - the *Amethyst* slipped her cable as silently as possible and, since she was facing up river, she had to make a 180 degree turn. This was, as Kerans later said, the trickiest part of the whole operation since the guns of the communists were trained on her to prevent any getaway.

The cable had been packed with sacking and bedding to minimise noise when it was slipped. Dark canvas had also been erected along parts of the superstructure in an effort to alter the warship's appearance in the dark.

Fifteen minutes after the *Amethyst* slipped her cable the communists, who now occupied both banks of the river, noticed that, after a hundred days, the warship was no longer there, and one of the batteries fired flares to light up the night. Some of Mao's gun batteries then opened fire on the *Amethyst* but without inflicting any serious damage. In self-defence the warship fired back with her only remaining four inch gun. Kerans signalled "I am under heavy fire and hit". In these circumstances and with more than a hundred miles to go, the plucky skipper considered adopting Plan B, which was to beach his warship and blow her up.

However, in the darkness the enemy gunners did not manage to strike her again and Kerans had taken advantage of a merchant vessel, the *Kiang Ling Liberation*, that was going down the river, treating her as a pilot boat to lead the *Amethyst* through these little known waters on which British naval captains had traditionally not ventured during the hours of darkness. But the *Amethyst* needed the darkness to mask her daring escape.

The *Kiang Ling Liberation*, in whose wake the *Amethyst* was following, went aground on a mudbank and, thinking that this was the warship, the communists aimed their fire at her, thereby letting the *Amethyst* slip away in the night. But the night was yet young and shortly after midnight she had to pass the shore batteries at the Kiang Yin forts, recently captured by the communists, as well as the boom that formed a barrier across the river. This boom, made of sunken ships, had originally been laid by the Chinese at the beginning of the Sino-Japanese War.

There was a channel through the booms but only one of the two expected lights could be seen. Kerans took a punt, choosing to go to port of this only light on the boom and, like so many decisions he was to take on this memorable night, it was the right one.

The *Amethyst* continued her way down the "tortuous, pitch-dark channels of the Yangtse". [13] Below Kiang Yin were the biggest navigational challenges of the night as the river "debouches into an expanse of dangerous – and constantly shifting – sandbanks". [14] Even without the enemy fire "the *Amethyst's* night passage without a pilot would have been a notable feat of seamanship", wrote *The Times*. [15]

The next obstacle was the heavily armed forts at Woosung, which she reached at 5.30 a.m. Here the searchlights poured their glare on her as she sped past at her full speed of nineteen knots but she was not fired on. Her engines, like those of the *Calliope* in the teeth of the Apia hurricane, were being driven for all they were worth and the heat in the engine room rose to 150° - so stifling that two of the men in there fainted.

The receipt of Kerans' coded message was followed by *HMS Concord* proceeding a short distance up the Yangtse and standing by below the Woosung forts with orders to cover the *Amethyst's* passage by firing back at the forts in the event of them opening fire – which they didn't.

The two warships came in sight of each other shortly before dawn – a meeting that was not unlike that of Livingstone and Stanley. "Fancy meeting you again", was the signal that *Concord* sent to *Amethyst*, to which Kerans replied, "Never, repeat never, has a ship been more welcome".

Escorted by the *Concord*, the *Amethyst* made her way down to the wide estuary of the Yangtse. Her long ordeal was over. "Have rejoined the fleet south of Woosung. No damage or casualties. God Save the King." was the joyful and loyal signal that Lieutenant-Commander Kerans sent. To this the Commander-in-Chief of the China station replied, "Welcome back to the fleet. We are all extremely proud of your most gallant and skilful escape…Your bearing in adversity and your daring passage to-night will be an epic in the history of the Navy." The refusal of the *Amethyst's* captain to admit that the ship had "wrongfully and criminally invaded Chinese waters", as demanded by the communists on numerous occasions, and her daring escape had lifted British prestige in the East and captured the imagination of the world.

The men on the *Amethyst* later received a message from the King, congratulating them on their "daring exploit" and ending with the words that warm the hearts of all sailors "Splice the mainbrace!"

"It is a story in the highest tradition, bearing comparison with anything in the stirring annals of the little ships of the Royal Navy in the Far East." wrote *The Times* of this great escape. [16]

"The outstanding features of this operation were the skill with which it was planned and the determination with which it was conducted," declared the Admiralty. [17] Timing was everything as, to make the dash to freedom, the ship had to slip her moorings after dark and yet pass the Woosung forts, a hundred miles down river, before dawn. The whole journey took seven and a quarter hours at an average speed of twenty-two knots on a river that was high at the time in the aftermath of Typhoon Gloria, not to mention the simultaneous melting of the snows in the Himalayas. This fullness of the river was both a help and a hindrance, the latter because it concealed certain well-known sandbanks and other landmarks.

The escape of the *Amethyst* caused the Chinese communists to suffer a serious loss of face – not only for letting her escape under their very noses but also for their unprovoked attack on her in the first place. Britain's relations with this brutal regime got off to a bad start; this attack on several of His Majesty's ships was the first in a long list of outrages that would give the British people reason to regard the government of China with mistrust and contempt.

The *Amethyst* reached Hong Kong on 3rd August to a hero's welcome. It was a grey and rainy morning as she passed through the Lei Yue Mun channel, preceded by the cruiser, *HMS Jamaica*, and the destroyer, *HMS Cossack*. These escorting vessels anchored in the stream, allowing the *Amethyst* to circle the harbour alone, followed by many small craft with R.A.F. Spitfires flying overhead. "All the ships in the harbour blew their sirens, and the air was loud with the crackle of Chinese crackers exploding along the waterfront," wrote *The Times*. [18]

As she drew alongside the naval dockyard to the cheers of a large crowd the band of the Middlesex Regiment struck up Heart of Oak "and there was indeed something deeply moving in the spectacle of this little grey ship, bearing many jagged scars of battle, at last reaching her haven after so many toils and dangers". [19]

All the ship's company were given local leave. When the fleet recreation officer invited local residents to accommodate men in their homes for a few days, the response was so immediate that within a few hours places had been found for all of them.

The *Amethyst* was patched up in the dockyard and, when she left for England on 9ᵗʰ September – again in grey, showery weather – she looked "a very different ship form the dirty, scarred warship that several weeks ago steamed slowly into Hong Kong harbour. She has been freshly painted and, as a result of repairs carried out in the dockyard here, there is little evidence of her clashes with the Communists," wrote the *Times*. [20]

It was only right that Lieutenant-Commander Kerans should command her on her voyage home. The first stop was Singapore where she was greeted by sirens from all the ships in Keppel Harbour, that were dressed for the occasion. "The only ships that were not dressed were four Soviet vessels," wrote *The Times*. [21] "Thousands lined the water front and cheered as the *Amethyst* passed on her way to the naval base. She received a special cheer from the men of *HMS Laburnum*, depot ship of the Royal Malayan Naval Volunteer Reserve while R.A.F. Dakotas and Mosquitoes flew overhead in greeting." [22]

From Asia's "Lion City" Lieutenant-Commander Kerans took his plucky little vessel through the Suez Canal and on to Malta G.C. where she entered the Grand Harbour. "A rousing cheer greeted the ship from the Saint Elmo breakwater, which was manned by soldiers and the Royal Malta Artillery band, while the U.S. cruiser *Des Moines*...paraded a guard and band which played the British national anthem as the ship came in," wrote *The Times*. [23]

At Gibraltar "a tumultuous welcome greeted *HMS Amethyst* this morning as she steamed into the harbour in perfect weather," wrote *The Times*. [24] "She was met off Europa Point by fifty small craft which, formed in two lanes, escorted her to Admiralty Harbour while R.A.F. aircraft circled and dipped low in salute. The band of the Royal Northumberland Fusiliers, drawn up on the quayside, played *Heart of Oak*, *Rule Britannia* and *All The Nice Girls Love A Sailor*."

The next welcome was at Plymouth and this was followed by London where the ship's company were received by the King and Queen at Buckingham Palace. They also marched through the capital of the Empire from Horse Guards Parade to the City. When "they marched off the parade ground, strode through Admiralty

Arch and wheeled twice to make the half circuit of Nelson's Monument, the act caught the imagination of thousands waiting there," wrote *The Times*. [25] "The cheers broke out with happy spontaneity and the bells of Saint Martins-in-the-Fields in Trafalgar Square, where the men broke their march for half an hour to attend a thanksgiving service, added to the joyousness of the occasion." [26] Nelson, looking down on the scene from atop his Column with his one good eye, would have been proud of them.

Among those who returned to England on the *Amethyst* was Simon, the ship's cat, who was still catching vermin but not as many as on the rat infested Yangtse. But his days were numbered and he died four weeks later while in quarantine. A coffin was made for him and it was draped with the Union Jack as he too had been wounded while in the service of his King and country. He was buried with full naval honours in a small plot in the pets' cemetery at Ilford in Essex, having been awarded the Dickin Medal (the animals' Victoria Cross). This was the first time it had been awarded to a cat, the previous recipients having been homing pigeons, dogs and horses.

This was not the only award as a total of three D.S.O.s, one M.B.E., four D.S.C.s and seven D.S.M.s were made to members of the ship's company as well as many Mentions in Despatches.

Altogether this "Incident on the Yangtse" cost the lives of forty-six members of the Royal Navy, with another sixty-eight wounded. It is believed that about two hundred and fifty of the enemy were killed by the guns of either the *Amethyst* or the other ships that tried to rescue her.

In contrast to the callousness of the communists was the humanity of the Nationalists, who did what they could to succour the dying and the wounded in a difficult situation. And among those who went through the long and unpleasant ordeal on the *Amethyst* were eight Chinese mess boys who "displayed never failing cheerfulness". [27] Thus did China redeem some honour out of this bloody and unnecessary incident.

THE KOREAN WAR

"My heartfelt congratulations on the splendid conduct of the Fleet units under your command. They have added another glorious page to the long and brilliant history of the navies of the British Commonwealth."

- General Douglas MacArthur to Admiral Andrewes.

On Sunday, 25th June, 1950, the army of communist North Korea invaded South Korea, that ancient kingdom having been divided by the disastrous Yalta conference of 1945 with that part of the Korean peninsula that lies north of a line running roughly along the 38th Parallel being in the Russian camp and the Americans looking after the south.

In sending his troops into South Korea, where elections had recently taken place resulting in an independent Korean government, the North's leader, the irrational and brutal Kim Il Sung, was acting as a surrogate of both Stalin and China, which latter had recently fallen to the communists – partly due to the incompetence of the U.S. Secretary of State, General Marshall, who turned out to be a far worse diplomat than he had been a soldier.

Within three days of the invasion Seoul, the capital of the South, fell to the communists, whose blitzkrieg continued until only a small perimeter around the southern port of Pusan remained in South Korean hands.

To their credit the Western nations, under the leadership of the United States and its stalwart President, Harry Truman, went to the aid of South Korea as in later times they would rally to the support of Kuwait when it was invaded by Iraq.

The major Western contribution was made by America, with Britain being the second largest contributor. During the three years of fighting the Royal Navy had a total of five aircraft carriers, six cruisers, twenty-one destroyers and frigates, and eighteen Royal Auxiliary Fleet ships in Korean waters and they played an important and honourable role in preventing the southern part of the Korean peninsula from falling permanently to the communists.

At the time of this sudden and unexpected invasion there were twenty-two British warships in the Far East and, by a stroke of good fortune, a Royal Navy task force of the 5th Cruiser Squadron was cruising in the nearby waters of Japan, including the 18,000 ton light aircraft carrier, *HMS Triumph*, the cruisers, *Belfast* and *Jamaica* (known as "The Fighting J"), as well as five escort ships. The *Jamaica* was a Colony class cruiser – hence its name. She had been sent to the Far East to replace *HMS London* after that vessel had been damaged while trying to help the *Amethyst*. The *Triumph's* aircraft included twelve Seafires (the naval version of the Spitfire) and nine Fireflies, which we last met in the Okinawa chapter, as well as the amphibious Sea Otters, used mainly for rescues and transporting mail. In winter the rescues had to be fast as in the freezing temperatures a downed pilot was unlikely to survive in the sea for more than a few minutes.

These ships were sent immediately to the east coast of Korea to bombard the coastal roads that were being used by the enemy's troops in their push south. Their targets included railways, bridges, wharves, roads and power stations. The trick was to aim high so as to bring down cliffs, rocks and other debris which would block the convoys of troops who travelled only at night. They would then have to clear away the obstructions under lights, thereby making themselves easy targets for the guns of the warships.

On 2nd July, 1950, the *Jamaica* and the frigate *HMS Black Swan*, a veteran of the Yangtse incident, took part in the first naval action of the war when, cruising close to Korea's east coast, they were attacked by six E boats. The British gun crews opened fire with a mighty salvo that was followed by others at regular intervals. So deadly was the ships' fire that five of the enemy craft were sunk while the remaining one was grounded and deserted by its crew. It was a good lesson for the British and their accompanying vessel, *USS Juneau*, and after that they stayed further out from the coast. But not far enough as, six days later, these same two ships (*Jamaica* and *Black Swan*) were attacked by a mobile battery on shore. One of its shells exploded on the *Jamaica's* mainmast, killing Able Seaman J.D. Mawdsley and five soldiers, three from the Royal Artillery and two from the 1st Middlesex Regiment, who had come on board in Hong Kong and were helping the naval gunners in their hot and dangerous work. All six were buried at sea.

On 5th August *HMS Kenya* (also a Colony class cruiser), together with HM ships *Belfast* (in later times moored on the Thames at London), *Charity* and *Cossack*, all of them protected by planes from *HMS Triumph*, bombarded oil storage tanks and North Korean positions at Inchon, the Yellow Sea port some eighteen miles from Seoul in preparation for the landings, which were to change the course of the war in the Allies' favour.

On 13th September, two days before the actual landings, the "softening up" of the enemy positions began. Elderly Firefly planes from *HMS Triumph* were used to spot targets such as the artificial harbour at Inchon and several gun emplacements; these were bombarded by *HMS Kenya* at a distance of seven and a half miles.

On the following day the *Kenya's* target was the guns on the island of Wolmi-do, which protected the inner harbour of Inchon. In the words of Brian Crabb, in his book *In Harm's Way*, "By 13.30 the Corsair pilot reported that *Kenya* had blown one gun off its emplacement, two were on their sides, a fourth was distorted and chipped while an ammunition store was burning furiously." [1] Not a bad day's work!

15th September was the day of the landings. This masterpiece of General MacArthur's planning, which turned the North Koreans' flank, comprised 260 transport ships and escorts, 500 landing craft and more than 70,000 men – mostly U.S. Marines. It was not exactly Okinawa but it was a big show all the same.

HMS Kenya and *Jamaica*, together with the heavy cruisers, *USS Rochester* and *Toledo*, delivered a thunderous bombardment of Wolmi-do in the early hours of the morning. Each of the British cruisers was served by a spotting Firefly from the *Triumph* and the high point of this day long bombardment was when the *Jamaica* hit an ammunition dump with great effect – both visual and aural. Although a considerable distance from the target, the force of the explosion shook the cruiser from stem to stern.

On this first day of the landings a total of about 13,000 Marines managed to get ashore. By midnight they controlled the port area and by dawn on 16th most of Inchon was in Allied hands.

Just before dawn on Day 3 of these historic landings the *Jamaica* was attacked by an Il-2 (kown as a "Yak"). This Russian built plane, manned by North Koreans, fired from close range – about a hundred feet altitude and only about fifty feet off the ship's port side. In the words of Boy Seaman Michael Stephens on the *Jamaica*, "Our four inch guns were unable to engage but our pom poms and bofors opened up almost instantly. Sitting in my tractor style seat in the director, I could plainly see him as he flashed down the opposite side, white/blue flames squirting from his wings; then he was out of my line of vision behind the superstructure. The next I saw he was tumbling into a flaming dive with bits spraying from him. He hit the water just forward of our bow and the only recognisable part remaining, bobbing down our starboard side, was his right landing wheel and leg. Some bits went right through our foc'sle into the Royal Marines' mess deck and paint locker below – which caused a tad of consternation.

Unhappily he had hit F2 pom pom and my messmate, Boy Seaman Ron Godsall, suffered fatal wounds. Ironically it was his F2 pom pom that was credited with the shoot down." [2] After transfer to the U.S. hospital ship, appropriately named the *Compassion*, Ron Godsall died of his wounds and he was buried at sea.

The wheel of the downed plane was later presented to the *Jamaica's* commander, Captain F. A. Balance, as a souvenir, General MacArthur having put his signature on the tyre.

Although the turning point in this nasty little war, the Inchon landings did not end it and it dragged on until 27th July, 1953. Like Okinawa, it became very much a "carriers' war" and in one three day period the *Triumph's* Seafires and Fireflies destroyed almost thirty enemy craft.

HMS Theseus, another light carrier, carried out as many as sixty-six sorties in a single day and, by the time her deployment ended, she had delivered to the enemy 6,617 rockets, more than 1,400 bombs and half a million rounds of cannon shells, resulting in the destruction of 93 junks, 166 railway engines and carriages, 73 lorries, 36 bridges, 66 store dumps, 6 railway tunnels, 5 power stations, 8 tanks, 10 command posts, 2 wharves, 19 factories and a tug. Little wonder that her air group was awarded the Fleet Air Arm's Boyd trophy when they returned home.

"Train busting" turned out to be a particularly exciting activity – especially for *HMS Cossack*, which seems to have specialised in such operations. In a single night she managed to destroy two trains on the line running down the east coast, which was one of the communists' main supply routes – just as the Ho Chi Minh Trail would be in the Vietnam War.

From the point of view of weather there is probably no less pleasant place on the planet to fight a war than in Korea – stifling hot in summer and unbearably cold in winter. The summer closeness was not helped by the smell emanating from the land as one of the more unpleasant customs of the Koreans was to fertilise their cultivated areas with human excrement.

The winters were terrible with the snow blowing down from the great land mass of Manchuria. During the particularly cold

460

winter of 1950-1 the ocean sometimes froze over with ice – shades of the Russian convoys of World War Two! The first task of the shivering sailors each morning was to chop away the ice so as to restore the balance of the ship. In addition to the temperature extremes there was the added thrill of typhoons, the worst of which, Typhoon Marge, struck in August, 1951, smashing some of the ships' small boats.

At the end of 1951 there began the hundred days' "Battle of the Islands" when the enemy tried to occupy several small offshore islands, using flat bottomed junks. The guns of the destroyer, *HMS Cockade*, sank several of them while planes from *HMS Glory*, *HMAS Sydney* and two American carriers also did their bit.

In freezing temperatures, sometimes below 20 degrees Fahrenheit, bluejackets and Royal Marines used small boats to carry out patrols and intercept suspicious looking junks that were in the vicinity of the islands – just as their predecessors had done in the Opium Wars. By March, 1952, they were able to claim victory as the enemy had been cleared from these offshore islands.

In August, 1951, the *Kenya* sailed to Singapore for a re-fit. During her time in the combat zone she was credited with killing hundreds of communist troops with the almost 20,000 shells that she fired from her powerful guns while the *Jamaica* fired 1,290 rounds of 6 inch ammunition and 393 rounds of 4 inch. Communist propaganda claimed to have sunk the *Jamaica* three times and so she became known as "The Galloping Ghost of the Korean Coast".

The role of ships like the *Kenya*, the *Jamaica* and the *Triumph* in the Korean War was in the long tradition of the Navy's mission of bringing peace and order to the lands of the Pacific. An independent country with an elected government had been invaded by a proxy of the Soviet Union, which at the time was ruled by Stalin, who had already gobbled up all of Eastern Europe. Had the communists succeeded in taking South Korea as well, then Japan would have been the next item on their menu.

The Korean War was the last occasion on which the Royal Navy fired shots in anger in the Pacific and those shots were fired in as honourable and worthwhile a cause as any that the Navy has undertaken in that great ocean. Indeed, the naval aid that we gave the Americans, who were running the show, could be regarded as a "return gift" for the help that their warships gave to Britain from time to time during the Opium Wars and other actions in the Yellow Sea in the mid-nineteenth century.

461

THE HANDOVER OF HONG KONG, 1997

"I began to wonder how it was ….that Englishmen could do such things as they had done….with the barren rock of Hong Kong within seventy or eighty years, while in four thousand years China had achieved nothing like it".

- Sun Yat Sen, founder of the Chinese Republic, speaking in 1923.

Ever since Commodore Bremer raised the British flag at Possession Point on 26th January, 1841, Hong Kong island – and later the bustling area of Kowloon on the mainland – were familiar places to the officers and ratings on the China station.

In 1897 the iron screw troopship, *HMS Tamar*, named after the river dividing Devon from Cornwall, became the base ship at Hong Kong. She remained in this capacity until a shore station was built and that too was named HMS Tamar. The old ship herself was scuttled in Victoria harbour on 12th December, 1941, to prevent her falling into the hands of the Japanese. Thus was HMS Tamar the heart and soul of naval activity in Hong Kong from 1897 until 1997, with only a three and a half year gap during the Second World War.

It would be no exaggeration to say that, in spite of the summer humidity, the overcrowded streets, the strange cooking smells and the rip-off bars on Lockhart Road, Jack grew very fond of Hong Kong, which was a haven of order, prosperity and good government on the otherwise turbulent and largely unfriendly coast of China. Hong Kong worked, it was fun, it was unique. Most of its people were refugees or the descendants of refugees, who had fled famine, poverty, tyranny and communism across the border in China.

Hong Kong was freehold, having been granted to Britain by the Chinese emperor "in perpetuity", and so was Kowloon on the mainland up as far as Boundary Street; beyond that was the area known as the New Territories that Britain acquired by a ninety-nine year lease from China in 1898. However, the rulers of China – imperialist, Nationalist and communist – recognised that their large, poor and basically ungovernable country depended very heavily on the trading, shipping and governing skills of Hong Kong's talented businessmen and administrators. At any time – especially since 1949 – Chinese soldiers could have marched across the border and taken the place by sheer weight of numbers, but they never did. Nor did they even threaten it during the Korean War. A British ruled Hong Kong was too useful and too valuable to upset.

When negotiations began with China for the return of the New Territories the British Conservative government, having lost the will to govern any colonies, decided to throw Hong Kong island and Kowloon in as well, all the while propagating the lie, "We must hand *all* of Hong Kong over to China in 1997 because the lease expires". And so, what should have been by international law the mere termination of the lease of the New Territories became the shameful and shabby "handover" of all of Hong Kong in violation of the United Nation's resolution on colonies, which states that the interests of the inhabitants must be paramount.

Interestingly the British government at no time consulted the people of Hong Kong by referendum or otherwise as to how they felt about being handed over to Asia's most brutal regime. This was the same Conservative government that literally went to war with Rhodesia, demanding "one man, one vote" for primitive tribespeople, many of whom were not far removed from the Stone Age, and then rigged the ensuing election to ensure that the Foreign Office's favourite terrorist, Robert Mugabe, should win.

While acknowledging its achievements in breaking the destructive power of militant trade unionism, helping end the Cold War and driving the Argentine invaders out of the Falkland Islands, it should be pointed out that the Thatcher government's treatment of the people of Hong Kong was every bit as shameful as its treachery in Rhodesia.

Many of the problems stemmed from Margaret Thatcher's poor choice of Foreign Secretaries. Lord Carrington, grossly overpromoted in view of his limited ability, poor judgement and questionable character – "that duplicitous bastard" (General Alexander Haig, U.S. Secretary of State) and "the most two-faced of them all" (Mr. Ian Smith, ex-Prime Minister of Rhodesia), turned out to be the worst Foreign Secretary in British history, while Geoffey Howe was not much better. It was not until Mrs. Thatcher was deposed that her successor, John Major, decided to redeem some honour for Britain by making the inspired appointment of Christopher Patten as the last governor of Hong Kong.

Although a man of strong principles and with a faith in the ability of the talented and enterprising people of Hong Kong to govern themselves, Patten could work within only very narrow parameters since the transfer of sovereignty to the Chinese dictatorship had been decided before he and his wife and two of their three lovely daughters arrived in the colony on 9th July, 1992.

They landed at Kai Tak Airport and were ferried across the narrow stretch of harbour to the island in a convoy led by a Royal Navy warship. The Patten vice-royalty was to last for five tremendous, tumultuous and prosperous years, during which the "Last Governor" also became the most popular governor. Popular with the ordinary people, whose rights he fearlessly upheld, but less so with the amoral, kowtowing business elite who, like their counterparts in Singapore, did not mind dictatorship so long as it didn't interfere with their profits. These people, egged on by their cheerleader, the treacherous Sir Percy Cradock, began a whispering campaign against Patten that was more of a reflection on their own characters than on his.

If a man is best judged by his enemies, then Patten comes up trumps as he was absolutely reviled by the Chinese communist leaders, who believe that government can rest only on brute force and not on such a flighty thing as the will of the people through genuinely elected representatives. They feared the freedom and democracy that he preached and in their nasty, childish way damned him as "The Triple Violator" (1992 version) and "The Criminal of a Thousand Generations" (1995 version). Coming from such types, this is probably the greatest compliment that Christopher Patten ever received. But for his long, courageous and difficult struggle to entrench basic rights before the handover, the people of Hong Kong would to-day enjoy far fewer freedoms than they actually have.

Despite doing such a wonderful job – and doing it with such spunk and style – the last governor was anything but happy with the result, and the tears in his eyes as he sailed out of Hong Kong harbour on *HMY Britannia* on that last, sad day in June, 1997, bespoke his sorrow at leaving a place that he both loved and cared about as well as his fears for the future. Needless to say, the officers and ratings of the Navy, who were sent there to participate in the ceremonial parting, approached their task out of a sense of duty, but without any enthusiasm. Walking away from Asia's greatest success story and forcing its six million locals to exchange the freedom of British rule for communist China's tyranny was not something to celebrate. But the job had to be done and the Navy would do it.

HMY Britannia steamed into Hong Kong's busy harbour on 23rd June, 1997, on a typically wet, humid summer's day. She tied alongside the wharf, with the high rise buildings of the district appropriately known as "Admiralty" staring down at her. Her escorting frigate, *HMS Chatham*, docked alongside her. And so began the series of farewells to a much loved colony and naval base.

The shore establishment of HMS Tamar was closed down with the lowering of the White Ensign by the First Sea Lord, Sir Jock Slater, and the commander of Hong Kong's departing army garrison, Major-General Bryan Dutton. The latter then moved his headquarters on to *HMS Chatham*, running everything from the warship with its highly sophisticated weapons and communications systems.

All the classified equipment from the stripped down Prince of Wales Building was placed on board the *Chatham*. Other gear, including the sail training yacht, *Vengeance*, was winched on board the Royal Fleet Auxiliary landing ship, *Sir Percivale*, for transport Home. After all, Britain was leaving enough behind in Hong Kong in the form of value added real estate without leaving naval and communications equipment as well.

One of the last acts of the colony's three familiar patrol craft, *HMS Peacock*, *Plover* and *Starling*, was to sail right round Hong Kong island to say good-bye to the people that they – and previous patrol craft – had served for so many years. Since they were at the end of their commissions they were entitled to trail their paying-off pennants – all 150 feet of them – as they steamed from Victoria harbour to Tai Tam Bay and then round the Stanley peninsula and into beautiful Repulse Bay where *HMS Repulse* was once stationed to deter pirates. From there they continued to Aberdeen and up the west side of the island, through the Sulphur Channel and back into the choppy waters of the harbour. As they passed the junks and sampans, on some of which whole families of fisherfolk lived, they received waves and cheers from the normally undemonstrative Chinese, while in the harbour a flotilla of sailing vessels came out from the Royal Hong Kong Yacht Club to give their salute.

From the bridge of *HMS Peacock* the Senior Naval Officer Afloat, Lieutenant Commander Will Worsley, said, "This is a very poignant moment. We have warm memories of and a close relationship with the people of Hong Kong and it is hard to be saying good-bye. We have served Hong Kong faithfully and have served the people with honour." [1]

The whole scene was dripping with emotion, poignancy and historical allusions. There was *HMS Chatham* escorting *Britannia* just as an earlier *Chatham* had escorted George Vancouver's *HMS Discovery* two centuries earlier on the other side of the Pacific while two of the three patrol craft (*HMS Plover* and *Starling*), that circled Hong Kong Island, were the "name descendants" of *HMS Plover* and *Starling* that, taking soundings as they went, led the British naval expedition up the Yangtse in 1841 to bring to an end the First Opium War, one result of which was that Hong Kong – "a barren island with hardly a house upon it" – became part of the British Empire with all the positive things that followed.

On the night itself, 30th June, there was a pageant on the parade ground of HMS Tamar, which was watched by thousands. It was followed by a fireworks display, which lit up the three patrol craft. It was during this parade that the heavens opened up in one of the summer's heaviest downpours – as if the gods themselves were weeping for what was happening on this historic night.

From there Britain's official party, consisting of the Prince of Wales, the Pattens, the newly elected Prime Minister, Mr. Blair, and the Foreign Secretary, went to the harbourside convention centre where a farewell banquet was held. During his speech the Prince reminded China of the pledges she had made to preserve Hong Kong's special freedoms. Several of these "pledges" were soon to be broken, a Chinese government of the twenty-first century being no more trustworthy than the Manchus of the nineteenth century, whose "word" was never worth the paper it was written on. "I would like, on behalf of Her Majesty the Queen and the entire British people to express our thanks, admiration, affection and good wishes to the people of Hong Kong, who have been such staunch and special friends over so many generations," said the Prince.

Then *God Save the Queen* was played at 11.59 p.m. and the Union Jack was brought down for the last time in 156 years by twenty-two year old Nick Tarrant of *HMS Chatham*. Then it was the turn of China's leaders, who had taken time off from murdering Tibetans and imprisoning "dissidents" to attend the ceremony. It was hard not to notice the contrast between the polished prince and the gentlemanly governor who were leaving and the coarse brutes who were taking over.

From here Prince Charles and the Pattens proceeded to the nearby Royal Yacht. On the quay were a large number of the many friends that the Pattens had made during their five years in the colony and the tears flowed freely.

As the royal party walked on board the *Britannia* a band of the Royal Marines on the upper deck played the moving but rather sombre tunes of *Jerusalem* and *I Vow To Thee My Country*. Then, with the Prince and the ex-Governor and his wife at the stern and the three Patten daughters on the bridge deck, all of them waving as they tried to keep back the tears, the *Britannia* slipped her moorings and made her way slowly through Victoria harbour and out to sea.

As she pulled away from her berth the band increased its tempo and thumped out the stirring notes of *Rule Britannia* and *Land of Hope and Glory*. The thousands on the dark quay responded by singing the words at the tops of their voices. They then waved a last, moving good-bye as *Britannia*, followed by the *Chatham*, the three patrol craft and the *Sir Percivale*, headed towards the Lei Yue Mun channel – the same narrow stretch of water across which the last of our troops had withdrawn from the mainland in 1941 and through which the British fleet had sailed when it came to liberate Hong Kong in 1945.

On the banks of the channel thousands more had gathered to wave a tearful good-bye. It seemed that nobody wanted the British to leave – least of all the locals, so many of whom were descended from refugees fleeing China or had been refugees themselves, but they had no say in the matter as the whole dirty deal had been signed by the British and Chinese governments behind the backs of those whose lives and freedoms would be affected. After passing through this emotion packed channel the *Britannia* and her flotilla disappeared into the night.

The sailors were pleased to get away from the ugly scene on shore where the People's Liberation Army, the butchers of Tianamen Square, were already pouring over the border, and an unelected government of kowtowing "anti-democrats" was being sworn in to govern Hong Kong in the interests of Communist China. This ceremony was boycotted by Mr. Blair and the Foreign Secretary as well as by the U.S. Secretary of State but it was enthusiastically attended by the three horrible "Hs" of the Conservative Party – Heath, Howe and Heseltine. The "leader" of this new, puppet government was Tung Che-Hwa, a local lickspittle whose main qualification for the job was that he was in China's pocket, the communist regime having "bought" him some years earlier by bailing out his failing shipping company. It didn't take Hong Kong long to realise that, with the replacement of Patten by Tung, they had swapped a lion for a donkey. No wonder Simon

Jenkins wrote in *The Times*, "Poor *Britannia*. It looks as if it cannot wait to escape". [2]

From the bridge of *HMS Chatham* Commodore Peter Melson, the last Senior Naval Officer in Hong Kong, said, "We have had to say good-bye to a lot of good Chinese friends and there are some very mixed feelings there. They have been very happy under the British, they have made a lot of money and had their freedom respected but they are now facing an unceratin future." [3]

Among those "good Chinese friends" facing "an uncertain future" were seventy-eight year old Jenny Ah Moy and her "girls" of the "side party" who, in their smocks and baggy, black trousers and with their long pigtails, were one of the first and most welcome sights for Royal Navy vessels when they arrived at the Hong Kong dockside.

Working from sampans, Jenny and her girls would wash, scrape and paint the ship's side with the sailors often doing the other side. They never took payment but they earned their keep by selling soft drinks to the sailors, changing their money and taking whatever might be offered to them in the way of old clothes, unwanted stores, etc. In 1938 Jenny had been presented with a Long Service and Good Conduct medal by the captain of *HMS Devonshire* and forty-two years later she was awarded the British Empire Medal in the Queen's Birthday Honours. But with the demise of the Navy's role in Hong Kong after 1997 Jenny and her girls suffered a great fall-off of business.

When *Britannia* and her escorts got outside Hong Kong's territorial waters on this historic night they were greeted by a large fleet of British warships – *HMS Illustrious, Beaver, Fearless, Richmond*, HM Submarine *Trafalgar* and the Royal Fleet Auxiliary's *Fort Austin, Fort George, Olna, Sir Galahad, Sir Geraint* and *Diligence*. These were joined by *Britannia's* escort vessels, and the seventeen ships formed two lines for the Royal Yacht to sail between, all the available hands lining the decks to cheer the Queen's yacht and its precious cargo – the Heir to the Throne and the man who was probably the finest governor of any colony in the history of the British Empire. Hong Kong might have gone but there'll always be a Navy.

EPILOGUE

That the cruise around Hong Kong island by *HMS Peacock*, *Plover* and *Starling*, their long. colourful pennants trailing and White Ensigns flying proudly in the summer breeze, should have attracted the waves and cheers of those they passed, both on their junks and on the coast, is not surprising since the overwhelming sentiment for the Royal Navy in the Pacific is one of goodwill and gratitude for a job well done.

By its constant presence and vigilance off the coast of British Columbia the Royal Navy ensured that Canada would be a nation on two oceans, by establishing and supplying Australia's northern outposts it helped ensure that the southern continent would be a single country, by a subtle combination of persuasion and force it succeeded in eradicating cannibalism from New Zealand, Fiji and other islands, by its vital role in the Maori wars it made New Zealand safe for settlement, by its victory in the First Opium War it enabled Britain to acquire Hong Kong and turn it into the world's greatest and most dazzling free port, by eradicating piracy from the seas around Borneo it secured the safety of honest trade in and out of Singapore and, by compiling thousands of charts of virtually every part of the Pacific, it ensured that the world's greatest ocean was made safe for mariners and known to the world.

With the exception of a few "awkward minorities" such as pirates, Chinese communists, Japanese ultra-nationalists and New Zealand "anti-nuclear" fanatics, the people of the Pacific have positive feelings towards the Navy, that has been in their seas longer than any other and which has used its sea power for the benefit of mankind. In India it was the army that preserved peace and order whereas in the Pacific it has been Britain's navy, and both carried out their long and adventurous missions with pride, dedication, courage and honour.

Just as in India, where a mere 70,000 British soldiers were able to maintain order among the hundreds of millions of Indians of diverse races and religions, so too in the vast Pacific did the Royal Navy keep peace and order with an even smaller number of sailors.

It is not the military or naval force itself that is important but what lies behind it. In the two and a quarter centuries covered ever so briefly in this book the Royal Navy was the spearhead of introducing to other societies Britain's time tested institutions – the rule of law, sound and incorrupt administration and, most important of all, parliamentary democracy under our priceless constitutional monarchy, than which no finer, more stable or more magnificent system of government has ever existed.

The expansion of these institutions to societies that lacked them could not have occurred without the Navy, which has always been at the sharp end, be it chasing pirates and cannibals, storming Chinese forts and Maori pas, or fighting the fleets of Germany and Japan in the twentieth century.

The Pacific has been the graveyard of thousands of men of the Royal Navy, who have been killed in action or died of sickness or accident and who were buried at sea, while around its littoral others are buried in quiet and peaceful cemeteries – usually overlooking the ocean.

With the handover of Hong Kong, Britain, unlike France and the United States, no longer has any Pacific colonies (apart from Pitcairn!) but that is not to say that there is no longer a role for the Royal Navy in the ocean that it discovered, charted and kept free of pirates and hostile forces, and whose waters wash the shores of four of the five English speaking nations.

With the ominous growth of China's navy and all the mischiefmaking by its communist dictatorship throughout the Pacific there is a continuing mission for the Royal Navy which, by tradition, experience and popularity, is uniquely placed to work with the fleets of the United States, Australia, Canada and New Zealand to ensure that the peace, order and good government, which came to the Pacific in the wake of the White Ensign, is not frittered away by either benign neglect or distorted priorities such as Britain's poisonous embrace of the European Union at the expense of its wider and more natural interests.

I can do no better than end this book with the wise words once spoken by that master of international diplomacy and former Prime Minister, Anthony Eden, "If Britain, the United States and the British dominions stick together, there is no problem in the world that we can not solve but, if we don't stick together, there will be no problem in the world that we can solve."

BIBLIOGRAPHY

Albion, Robert Greenhalgh, Forests and Sea Power, The Timber Problem of the Royal Navy 1652-1862. London, 1965

Barber, Noel, The Fall of Shanghai, London, 1979

Beaglehole, John, The Life of Captain James Cook. London, 1974

Bennett, Geoffrey, Coronel and the Falklands. Edinburgh, 1962

Bligh, William, An account of the dangerous voyage performed by Captain Bligh, with a part of the crew of His Majesty's ship *Bounty*, in an open boat over twelve hundred leagues of the ocean, from Tofua to Timor in the year 1789. Dublin, 1817

Bryant, Sir Arthur, The Age of Elegance, London, 1950

Calvert, Rev. James, Fiji and the Fijians, Vol. II, London. 1869

Campbell, Hugh, *HMS Buffalo*, Tasmanian Historical Research Association, Vol. 48, No. 2

Clark, Russell S., An End To Tears. Sydney, 1946

Clowes, William Laird, The Royal Navy: A history from the earliest times to the present. London, 1897.

Colledge, J. J., Ships of the Royal Navy: an historical index. Newton Abbot, 1969

Cook, Captain James, Journals, (ed. John Cawte Beaglehole). Cambridge, 1968

Costello, John, The Pacific War, London, 1985

Cowan, James, The New Zealand Wars. Wellington, 1955

Crabb, Brian, In Harm's Way, Stamford, 1998

Earl, Lawrence, Yangtse Incident, The Story of *HMS Amethyst*, London, 1950

Evans, A. C., The Cruise of *HMS Calliope* in China, Austalian and East African Waters. London, 1890

Flinders, Matthew, A Voyage to Terra Australis 1801-3, London, 1814

Foljambe, Cecil, Three Years on the Australian Station. London, 1868

Hawkins, Clifford, Convicts and Kauri, Whakatane, 1993

Hetherington, Roy, The Wreck of *HMS Orpheus*. Auckland, 1975

Howard, Grant, The Navy in New Zealand. Wellington, 1981

Hughes, Robert, The Fatal Shore. London 1987

Ingleton, Geoffrey, Charting a Continent, Sydney, 1944

Jukes, Joseph Beete, Narrative of the surveying voyage of *HMS Fly*, commanded by Captain F.P. Blackwood, in Torres Strait, New

Guinea and other islands of the eastern archipelago during the years 1842-1846. London, 1847.

Keppel, Henry, A Sailor's Life Under Four Sovereigns. London, 1899, A Visit to the Indian Archipelago in HM Ship *Maeander*. London, 1853, The expedition to Borneo of *HMS Dido* for the suppression of piracy, with extracts from the journal of James Brooke, Esq. of Sarawak. London, 1846

King, Phillip Parker, Narrative of a Survey of the intertropical and western coasts of Australia, 1818-22. Adelaide, 1969

Lindsay, Oliver, The Lasting Honour, London, 1978

Lucas, Sir George, The Pitcairn Island Register Book, New York, 1929

McKillop, Henry, Reminiscences of Twelve Months' Service in New Zealand. London, 1849

McNab, Robert, The Old Whaling Days, Auckland, 1975

Markham, Albert Hastings, The Cruise of the *Rosario* amongst the New Hebrides and Santa Cruz Islands. London, 1873

Middlebrook, Martin and **Mahoney**, Patrick, Battleship, 1977

Morris, James, Heaven's Command, London, 1973

Nautical Magazine, 1838 ff.

Palmer, George, Kidnapping in the South Seas – Narrative of a three months' cruise of *HMS Rosario*. Edinburgh, 1871

Phillip, Arthur, The Voyage of Governor Phillip to Botany Bay. London, 1790

Pitt, Barrie, Coronel and Falkland. London, 1960

Poolman, Kenneth, Illustrious, London, 1955

Reed, A.W. Place Names of Australia. Sydney, 1973

Reid, Frank, The Romance of the Great Barrier Reef. Sydney, 1954

Robson, R. W., Queen Emma, Sydney, 1965

Ross, John, The White Ensign in Early New Zealand. 1967.

Stokes, John Lort, Diary of *HMS Acheron*

Swan, Ernest William, The First Commission of *HMS Calliope*. Newcastle upon Tyne, 1939

Taylor, T.D., New Zealand's Naval Story. Wellington, 1948

Thomas, David, Battle of the Java Sea. London, 1968

Vancouver, George, The Voyage of George Vancouver, Vols I –IV

Walpole, Hon. Fred, Four Years in the Pacific in HM Ship *Collingwood*, 1844-8, Vols. I and II, London, 1850

Winton, John, The Forgotten Fleet. London, 1969

Wiseman, Sir William, Catalogue of Curiosities from the South Sea Islands. Sydney, 1865

REFERENCES

Introduction
1. Four Years in the Pacific in HM Ship Collingwood, 1844-8, Hon. Fred Walpole, Vol. I, P. 78
2. Ibid, Vol. II, P. 394

Captain Cook
1. Chapter 68
2. Journals of Captain Cook, Vol. I, P. 232
3. Ibid, Vol. I, P. 237
4. Ibid, Vol. I, P 508-9
5. Ibid, Vol. I, P. 343
6. Ibid, Vol. I, P. 344
7. Ibid, Vol. III, Part I, P. 263-4
8. Ibid, Vol. II, P. 131

Captain George Vancouver
1. The Voyage of George Vancouver, Vol. I, P. 267
2. The Vancouver Expedition, Peter Puget's Journal of the Exploration of Puget Sound (25 May, 1792)
3. The Voyage of George Vancouver, Vol. I, P. 300
4. Ibid, Vol. II, P. 581
5. Ibid, P. 581-2
6. Ibid, P. 582
7. Ibid, P. 583
8. Ibid
9. Journal of Vancouver's Voyage, Archibald Menzies, Victoria, B.C., 1923, Diary of the 18th August, 1792
10. The Voyage of George Vancouver, Vol. II, P. 179
11. Ibid, P. 280
12. Ibid

Captain Bligh and the Bounty
1. An account of the dangerous voyage performed by Captain Bligh, with part of the crew of H.M. Ship Bounty, William Bligh, P. 12
2. Ibid, P. 13
3. Letter from Bligh to his wife quoted in The Bounty: The True Story of the Mutiny on the Bounty, Caroline Alexander, P. 154-6
4. An account of the dangerous voyage performed by Captain Bligh, with part of the crew of H.M. Ship Bounty, William Bligh, P. 23
5. Ibid
6. Ibid, P. 24
7. Ibid, P. 48
8. Ibid, P. 41
9. Ibid, P. 49
10. Panama Star as reported in Southern Cross, Auckland, 22 February, 1853, P. 4
11. Figures from Doctor Murray Bathgate of Wellington, New Zealand.
12. Panama Star as reported in Southern Cross, Auckland, 22 February, 1853, P. 4
13. Ibid

14. Four Years in the Pacific in HM Ship Collingwood, 1844-8, Hon. Fred Walpole, Vol. II, P. 164

15. Hawera and Normanby Star, N.Z., 14 October, 1901, P. 2

Captain Phillip and the First Fleet to Australia

1. The Voyage of Governor Phillip to Botany Bay, Arthur Phillip, P. 16

2. Ibid, P. 14

3. Ibid, P. 38

4. Ibid

5. Ibid, P. 39

6. Despatch by Governor Phillip, 15 May, 1788, Historical Records of New South Wales, ii. 121-2

7. The Voyage of Governor Phillip to Botany Bay, Arthur Phillip, P. 41

8. An account of the English colony in New South Wales, David Collins, Vo. I. P. 6

9. Ibid, P. 6-7

10. Ibid

11. The Voyage of Governor Phillip to Botany Bay, Arthur Phillip, P. 43.

Surveying and Charting

1. A Voyage to Terra Australis 1801-3, Matthew Flinders, Vol I, P. 226-7

2. Ibid, Vol. I, P. 227.

3. Ibid, Vol. II, P. 280

4. Ibid, Vol. I, P. 235

5. Ibid, Vol. II, P. 279

6. Ibid, P. 12-13

7. Ibid, P. 7-8

8. Ibid, P. 10

9. Ibid, P. 30

10. Journals of Captain Cook, Vol. I, P. 359 (12 July, 1770)

11. A Visit to the Indian Archipelago in HM Ship Maeander, Henry Keppel, Vol. II, P.180-1

12. Narrative of a Survey of the intertropical and western coasts of Australia 1818-22, Phillip Parker King, Vol. I, P. 97

13. Ibid, P. 101

14. Ibid, P. 165

15. Ibid

16. Ibid

17. Ibid, P. 168

18. Ibid, P. 175

19. Ibid, P. 169

20. Ibid, P. 174

21. Ibid, P. 244

22. Ibid, P. 345

23. Ibid

24. Narrative of the Surveying Voyage of HMS Fly, Joseph Beete Jukes, Vol. I, P. 313

25. Ibid, P. 103

26. Ibid, P. 10-11

27. Narrative of a Survey of the intertropical and western coasts of Australia 1818-22, Phillip Parker King, Vol. II, P. 243

28. Narrative of the Surveying Voyage of HMS Fly, Joseph Beete Jukes, Vol. I, P. 13
29. Ibid, Vol. I, P. 18
30. Ibid, P. 98
31. Ibid, P. 110
32. Ibid, P. 112
33. Ibid
34. New Zealand Spectator and Cook's Strait Guardian, 8 September, 1847, P. 3
35. Ibid, 27 May, 1848, P. 3
36. Southern Cross, Auckland, 4 October, 1850, P. 2
37. Ibid
38. Ibid
39. Sydney Morning Herald, 14 March, 1850
40. Southern Cross, Auckland, 9 April, 1850, P. 2
41. 10 April, 1850, P. 2
42. 4 June, 1850, P. 2
43. Naval and Military Gazette reported in the New Zealander, 16 April, 1851, P. 2
44. Ibid
45. Sydney Morning Herald, 3 May, 1850
46. Report of Captain Stanley to Governor Hobson, written at sea on 17 September, 1840, and reported in Evening Post, Wellington, 10 February, 1909, P. 11
47. Diary of HMS Acheron in Evening Star, Dunedin, 1 May, 1926
48. Diary of HMS Acheron in Evening Star, Dunedin, 8 May, 1926
49. Ibid
50. Diary of HMS Acheron in Evening Star, Dunedin, 15 May, 1926
51. Diary of HMS Acheron in Evening Star, Dunedin, 22 May, 1926
52. Diary of HMS Acheron in Evening Star, Dunedin, 29 May, 1926
53. 6 June, 1906, P. 15
54. Evening Post, Wellington, 12 May, 1908, P. 2
55. Diary of HMS Acheron in Evening Star, Dunedin, 5 June, 1926
56. Ibid
57. Diary of HMS Acheron in Evening Star, Dunedin, 19 June, 1926
58. Ibid
59. Ibid
60. 22 September, 1849
61. Diary of HMS Acheron in Evening Star, Dunedin, 26 June, 1926
62. The Independent, Wellington, 16 September, 1849
63. Diary of HMS Acheron in Evening Star, Dunedin, 26 June, 1926
64. Ibid
65. Diary of HMS Acheron in Evening Star, Dunedin, 17 July, 1926
66. Otago Witness, 18 March, 1908, P. 55
67. New Zealand Spectator and Cook's Strait Guardian, 18 June, 1853, P. 4 reporting the Survey of HMS Pandora, November, 1852
68. Ibid
69. New Zealand Spectator and Cook's Strait Guardian, 10 June, 1854, P. 4
70. Ibid
71. Southern Cross, Auckland, 26 August, 1853, P. 2
72. Ibid
73. Ibid
74. Ibid

75. Nelson Examiner and New Zealand Chronicle, 25 November, 1854, P. 2
76. Ibid, 11 October, 1864
77. Ibid
78. New Zealand Heritage, Vol. II, P. 565
79. Evening Post, Wellington, 23 September, 1873, P. 2
80. Narrative of the Surveying Voyage of HMS Fly, Joseph Beete Jukes, Vol. I, P. 290
81. Sydney Morning Herald, 6 February, 1850
82. New Zealand Spectator and Cook's Strait Guardian, 16 March, 1850, P. 3
83. Ibid
84. Ibid
85. North Otago Times, New Zealand, 10 May, 1867, P. 2
86. Ibid
87. Ibid
88. Evening Post, Wellington, 21 October, 1873, P. 2
89. North Otago Times, New Zealand, 16 April, 1872, P. 4
90. 20 August, 1873, P. 2
91. Grey River Argus, New Zealand, 30 March, 1872, P. 2
92. Sydney Morning Herald reported in Grey River Argus, 25 April, 1872
93. Article by Beauford Merlin reported in Tuapeka Times, N.Z., 30 October, 1873, P. 7
94. Ibid
95. Sydney Morning Herald reported in West Coast Times, N.Z., 19 July, 1873
96. Sydney Morning Herald, 6 May, 1873
97. 5 July, 1873, P. 6
98. Article by Beauford Merlin in Tuapeka Times, N,Z., 30 October, 1873, P. 7
99. Evening Post, Wellington, 23 September, 1873, P. 2
100. Nelson Examiner and New Zealand Chronicle, 3 July, 1873, P. 3
101. Discoveries and Surveys in New Guinea, John Moresby, P. 153
102. Ibid
103. Evening Post, Wellington, 23 September, 1873, P. 2
104. Nelson Examiner and New Zealand Chronicle, 3 July, 1873, P. 3
105. Sydney Morning Herald, 19 June, 1873
106. Evening Post, Wellington, 23 September, 1873, P. 2
107. Grey River Argus, N.Z., 20 August, 1873, P. 2
108. 20 August, 1873, P. 2
109. Evening Post, Wellington, 22 September, 1873, P. 2
110. Ibid, 23 September, 1873, P. 2
111. Ibid, 22 September, 1873, P. 2
112. Timaru Herald, N.Z., 8 October, 1873, P. 1
113. Evening Post, Wellington, 18 June, 1874, P. 2
114. Ibid
115. Ibid
116. Nautical Magazine, 1860, P. 423-4
117. The Cruise of HMS Calliope in China, Australian and East African Waters, A.C. Evans, P. 22
118. Grey River Argus, 5th July, 1875, P. 2

The Search for Spars
1. P. 401
2. The Journals of Captain Cook, Vol. I. P. 207
3. Ibid, P. 206
4. Dominion, Wellington, N.Z. 15 December, 1933
5. Southern Cross, Auckland, 15 May, 1875, P. 1
6. Evening Post, Wellington, 18 February, 1911
7. Dominion, Wellington, 16 December, 1931
8. HMS Buffalo, Hugh Campbell, Tasmanian Historical Research Association, Vol. 48, No. 2.

HMS Alligator to the Rescue
1. The Whalers, Felix Maynard and Alexandre Dumas, London, 1937, P. 235
2. The Old Whaling Days, Robert McNab, Appendix C, P. 424
3. Ibid, P. 121
4. Ibid, P. 127
5. Ibid, P. 128
6. Ibid, P. 128-9
7. Ibid, Appendix C, P. 426

The Opium Wars
1. Sydney Morning Herald, 7 January, 1842
2. Ibid
3. Ibid
4. Ibid
5. Letter to The Times by Henry Keppel quoted in The Royal Navy: A history from the earliest times to the present, William Laird Clowes, Vol 7, P. 108-9
6. Ibid, P. 129

Recruitment
1. The Age of Elegance, Sir Arthur Bryant, P. 209
2. Otago Witness, N.Z., 9 April, 1896, P. 40
3. New Zealand Spectator and Cook's Strait Guardian, 3 July, 1847, P. 2
4. Four Years in the Pacific in HM Ship Collingwood, 1844-8, Hon. Fred Walpole, Vol. I, P. 2-3 and 7

Australia's Northern Outposts
1. P. 1-2
2. Narrative of a Survey of the intertropical and western coasts of Australia 1818-22, Phillip Parker King, Vol. I, P. 88
3. Ibid, P. 89
4. Ibid, P. 92
5. A Visit to the Indian Archipelago on HM Ship Maeander, Henry Keppel, Vol. II, P. 152
6. Narrative of the surveying voyage of HMS Fly, Joseph Beete Jukes, Vol. I, P. 350
7. Ibid, P. 351
8. Southern Cross, Auckland, 4 October, 1850, P. 2
9. Ibid

10. A Visit to the Indian Archipelago in HM Ship Maeander, Henry Keppel, Vol. II, P. 192

11. Narrative of the surveying voyage of HMS Fly, Joseph Beete Jukes, Vol. I, P. 349

12. Otago Witness, New Zealand, 15 October, 1864, P. 2

13. Reported in Southern Cross, Auckland, 24 April, 1867, P. 4

Island Depots

1. Narrative of a survey of the intertropical and western coasts of Australia 1818-22, Phillip Parker King, P. 243.

2. Report of Captain W. Darby in New Zealand Gazette and Wellington Spectator, 11 May, 1842, P. 2

3. Reported in Nelson Examiner and New Zealand Chronicle, 20 April, 1844, P. 25

4. Letter from Captain van Rees reported in Southern Cross, Auckland, 26 October, 1863

5. Nelson Examiner and New Zealand Chronicle, 31 March, 1860, P. 4

6. The Old Whaling Days, Robert McNab, P. 95

7. 8 April, 1869

8. The Independent, Wellington, N.Z., 8 April, 1869

9. 8 April, 1869

10. Evening Post, Wellington, 5 April, 1869, P. 2

11. The Independent, Wellington, 8 April, 1869

12. Ibid

13. Ibid

14. Otago Witness, New Zealand, 3 April, 1869, P. 4

15. The Independent, Wellington, 8 April, 1869

16. Otago Witness, New Zealand, 3 April, 1869, P. 4

17. Evening Post, Wellington, 21 March, 1874, P. 2

18. Ibid

19. Ibid, 17 March, 1874, P. 2

20. Otago Witness, New Zealand, 24 May, 1879, P. 9

The Siege of Petropavlovsk

1. Letter from a British officer in Nautical Magazine, 1855, P. 51

2. Ibid

3. Letter from Rev. Holme quoted by Michael Lewis in *An Eye Witness at Petropavlovsk, 1854*, in The Mariner's Mirror, the International Journal for the Society for Nautical Research, Vol. 49, 1963, P. 269

4. Letter from a British officer, Nautical Magazine, 1855, P. 53

5. Michael Laws in An Eye Witness at Petropavlovsk, 1854, in The Mariner's Mirror, the International Journal for the Society for Nautical Research, Vol. 49, 1963, P. 272

6. The Royal Navy: A history from the earliest times to the present, William Laird Clowes, Vol. 6, P. 432

The Wreck of HMS Orpheus

1. The Wreck of HMS Orpheus, Roy Hetherington, P. 9-16

2. Ibid

3. Sydney Morning Herald, 10 February, 1863

4. Southern Cross, Auckland, 28 February, 1863, P. 5

5. Ibid
6. The Wreck of HMS Orpheus, Roy Hetherington, P. 1
7. Sydney Morning Herald, 10 February, 1863
8. Southern Cross, Auckland, 18 February, 1863
9. Ibid, 12 February, 1863, P. 3
10. The Ships of Omaha, Carol and James Ramage, P. 19
11. Southern Cross, Auckland, 28 February, 1863, P. 5

The River War
1. 11 May, 1864
2. Three Years on the Australian Station, Cecil Foljambe, P. 14
3. Ibid
4. Ibid, P. 23
5. The New Zealand Wars, James Cowan, Vol. I, P. 317
6. Three Years on the Australian Station, Cecil Foljambe, P. 23
7. Ibid, P. 26
8. 27 November, 1863, P. 3
9. Three Years on the Australian Station, Cecil Foljambe, P. 29-30
10. The New Zealand Wars, James Cowan, Vol. I, P. 330
11. Southern Cross, Auckland, 27 November, 1863, P. 3
12. 25 November, 1863, P. 3
13. Southern Cross, Auckland, 27 November, 1863, P. 3
14. Three Years on the Australian Station, Cecil Foljambe, P. 31
15. Southern Cross, Auckland, 27 November, 1863, P. 3
16. Ibid
17. The New Zealand Wars, James Cowan, Vol. I, P. 311-2

The Battle of Gate Pa
1. Southern Cross, Auckland, 2 May, 1864, P. 4
2. Ibid
3. Ibid
4. Ibid
5. Ibid
6. Ibid
7. Ibid
8. The New Zealand Wars, James Cowan, Vol. I, P. 429.
9. Southern Cross, Auckland, 2 May, 1864, P. 4
10. Taranaki Herald, New Zealand, 14 May, 1864, P. 1
11. 5 May, 1864, P. 5
12. Southern Cross, Auckland, 5 May, 1864, P. 5
13. Ibid
14. Three Years on the Australian Station, Cecil Foljambe, P. 82
15. Ibid, P. 83
16. The Navy in New Zealand, Grant Howard, P. 15

Gunnery
1. Marlborough Express, New Zealand, 24 June, 1893, P. 3
2. 22 November, 1848
3. Evening Post, Wellington, 15 October, 1909, P. 8
4. New Zealander, 27 October, 1849, P. 2

5. Fiji and the Fijians, James Calvert, Vol. II, P. 294
6. 21 January, 1880, P. 2
7. Evening Post, Wellington, 7 July, 1891, P. 2
8. Ibid, 12 January, 1909, P. 8
9. Ibid, 7 January, 1909, P. 7
10. Ibid, 16 September, 1887, P. 4
11. Ibid

Pomp and Circumstance
1. Commentaries, Book 1, Chapter 13
2. Evening Post, Wellington, 22 October, 1896, P. 5
3. Ibid, 24 October, 1905, P. 5
4. Wanganui Herald, New Zealand, 23 October, 1905, P. 5
5. Ibid
6. Evening Post, Wellington, 17 October, 1905, P. 5
7. Ibid, 18 October, 1905, P. 7
8. Otago Witness, New Zealand, 25 October, 1905, P. 37
9. New Zealand Spectator and Cook's Strait Guardian, 1 July, 1846, P. 2
10. A Sailor's Life Under Four Sovereigns, Henry Keppel, P. 8
11. Southern Cross, Auckland, 21 March, 1862, P. 3
12. Journals of Captain Cook, Vol. III, Part 1, P. 262
13. The Cruise of the Rosario amongst the New Hebrides and Santa Cruz Islands, Albert Markham, P. 196-7
14. Te Aroha News, New Zealand, 6 October, 1888, P. 4
15. Southern Cross, Auckland, 26 October, 1872, P. 3
16. Three Years on the Australian Station, Cecil Foljambe, P. 131
17. A Sailor's Life Under Four Sovereigns, Henry Keppel, P. 314
18. New Zealand Herald, 12 September, 1928, P. 10
19. Sydney Morning Herald, 2 February, 1888, P. 5

Wives and Sweethearts
1. A Sailor's Life Under Four Sovereigns, Henry Keppel, P. 230-1
2. Otago Witness, New Zealand, 30 April, 1886, P. 19
3. Marlborough Express, New Zealand, 14 May, 1891, P. 4,

Raising the Flag
1. 23 May, 1840, P. 3
2. Ibid
3. Nelson Examiner and New Zealand Chronicle, 25 June, 1873, P. 3
4. Evening Post, Wellington, 8 October, 1873, P. 2
5. Grey River Argus, New Zealand, 3 March, 1875, P. 2
6. Ibid
7. Evening Post, Wellington, 8 October, 1873, P. 2
8. Otago Witness, New Zealand, 28 February, 1874, P. 5
9. Grey River Argus, New Zealand, 3 March, 1875, P. 2
10. Ibid, 10 March, 1874, P. 3
11. Ibid, 14 May, 1874, P. 2
12. Fiji Times, 16 October, 1874
13. Ibid
14. Ibid

15. Ibid
16. Ibid
17. Ibid
18. Ibid
19. Ibid
20. Waikato Times, New Zealand, 26 November, 1874, P. 2
21. Southern Cross, Auckland, 19 July, 1875, P. 3
22. Ibid
23. Sydney Morning Herald, 15 November, 1884, P. 9
24. Ibid
25. Ibid
26. Ibid
27. Evening Post, Wellington, 16 May, 1889

Missionaries, Cannibals and Blackbirders
1. Kidnapping in the South Seas – Narrative of a three months cruise of HMS Rosario, George Palmer, P. 63
2. 19 October, 1865, P. 4
3. 31 August, 1867
4. Fiji and the Fijians, James Calvert, Vol. II, P. 291
5. Letter from Rev. James Calvert in New Zealand Spectator and Cook's Strait Guardian, 1 December, 1849
6. Quoted in Fiji and the Fijians, James Calvert, Vol. II, P. 296
7. Ibid, P. 297
8. Kidnapping in the South Seas – Narrative of a three months cruise of HMS Rosario, George Palmer, P. 124
9. Ibid, P. 110
10. Ibid
11. Ibid, P. 150
12. Ibid, P. 57-8
13. Ibid, P. 77
14. Grey River Argus, New Zealand, 1 March, 1872, P. 2
15. The Romance of the Great Barrier Reef, Frank Reid, P. 83
16. Reported in Southern Cross, Auckland, 24 February, 1872, P. 3
17. 13 February, 1873, P. 2
18. Southern Cross, Auckland, 26 October, 1872, P. 3
19. Ibid
20. West Coast Times, New Zealand, 8 December, 1880, P. 2
21. Ibid
22. Ibid, 28 February, 1881, P. 2
23. Grey River Argus, New Zealand, 27 September, 1882, P. 2
24. Otago Witness, New Zealand, 6 August, 1881, P. 11
25. Reported in West Coast Times, New Zealand, 1 November, 1886, P. 2
26 New Zealander as reported in New Zealand Spectator and Cook's Strait Guardian, 29 April, 1854, P. 4

The Death of Commodore Goodenough
1. Waikato Times, New Zealand, 31 August, 1872, P. 2
2. Evening Post, Wellington, 30 August, 1875, P. 2
3. Ibid, 20 September, 1875, P. 2

4. Ibid

5. Ibid, 20 February, 1909, P. 15

6. Ibid

7. Illustrated Sydney News and New South Wales Agriculturist and Grazier, 18 September, 1875

8. 4 September, 1875

9. 31 August, 1875, P. 2

10. Grey River Argus, New Zealand, 26 January, 1876, P. 2

Skullduggery in Samoa

1. New Zealander, 16 June, 1847, P. 2

2. Ibid

3. Queen Emma, R.W. Robson, P. 25

4. Ibid

5. Southern Cross, Auckland, 18 April, 1876

6. Ibid

7. Ibid

8. Ibid

9. 18 April, 1876

10. Evening Post, Wellington, 5 May, 1876, P. 2

11. Southern Cross, Auckland, 1 May, 1876

12. Reported in Southern Cross, Auckland, 2 August, 1876

13. Timaru Herald, New Zealand, 5 April, 1878, P. 4

The Apia Hurricane

1. Otago Witness, New Zealand, 18 January, 1889, P. 16

2. Te Aroha News, New Zealand, 16 February, 1889, P. 5

3. Ibid, 6 April, 1889, P. 3

4. Otago Witness, New Zealand, 12 May, 1898, P. 62

5. Wanganui Herald, New Zealand, 20 March, 1906, P. 4

6. 30 March, 1889, P. 2

7. Wanganui Herald, New Zealand, 20 March, 1906, P. 4

8. Evening Post, Wellington, 30 March, 1889

9. The Cruise of HMS Calliope in China, Australian and East African Waters, A.C. Evans, P. 98

10. Evening Post, Wellington, 5 April, 1889, P. 2

11. The Cruise of HMS Calliope in China, Australian and East African Waters, A.C. Evans, P. 98-9

12. 3 October, 1889

13. 2 April, 1889

14. Marlborough Express, New Zealand, 31 May, 1889, P. 2

Getting There and Back

1. Three Years on the Australian Station, Cecil Foljambe, P. 1

2. Four Years in the Pacific in HM Ship Collingwood, 1844-8, Hon. Fred Walpole, Vol. I, P. 5-6

3. The Cruise of HMS Calliope in China, Australian and East African Waters, A.C. Evans, P. 4-6

4. Journals of Captain Cook, Vol. II, P. 21

5. The Voyage of Governor Phillip to Botany Bay, Arthur Phillip, P. 32-3

6. Heaven's Command, James Morris, P. 416
7. Evening Post, Wellington, 11 October, 1873, P. 2
8. 29 September, 1873, P. 2
9. Public Record Office London, PREM 3 163/3
10. The Cruise of HMS Calliope in China, Australian and East African waters, A.C. Evans, P. 116
11. Four Years in the Pacific in HM Ship Collingwood, 1844-8, Hon. Fred Walpole, Vol. II, P. 391 and 395
12. 16 October, 1873, P. 2
13. 5 May, 1882, P. 2
14. Sydney Morning Herald, 17 June, 1867
15. Southern Cross, Auckland, 3 September, 1867, P. 2
16. Ibid, 16 April, 1867, P. 4
17. Four Years in the Pacific in HM Ship Collingwood, 1844-8, Hon. Fred Walpole, Vol. II, P. 407
18. Ibid, P. 414

Carpenters and Sailmakers
1. Journals of Captain Cook, Vol. I, P. 240-1
2. Ibid, P. 242
3. A Voyage to Terra Australis 1801-3, Matthew Flinders, Vol. II, P. 141-2
4. Narrative of the surveying voyage of HMS Fly, Joseph Beete Jukes, Vol I, P 88-9
5. The Expedition to Borneo of HMS Dido for the suppression of piracy, Henry Keppel, Vol. II, P. 27
6. New Zealand Gazette and Wellington Spectator, 25 April, 1840, P. 3

From Sail to Steam
1. New Zealand Spectator and Cook's Strait Guardian, 12 September, 1846, P. 2
2. Hong Kong Gazette reported in Nautical Magazine, 1844, P. 249
3. Ibid
4. Three Years on the Australian Station, Cecil Foljambe, P. 280
5. The Cruise of the Rosario amongst the New Hebrides and Santa Cruz Islands, Albert Markham, P. 159
6. A Sailor's Life Under Four Sovereigns, Henry Keppel, P. 200
7. Ibid, P. 265

Rowing
1. The Voyage of George Vancouver, George Vancouver, Vol. IV, P. 1355
2. Ibid
3. Letter to the Nautical Club, Nautical Magazine, 1860, P. 671
4. Reported in Dunedin Evening Star, New Zealand, 3 July, 1926
5. Southern Cross, Auckland, 31 January, 1862, P. 3
6. 30 January, 1866
7. Ibid
8. 16 January, 1889
9. 19 March, 1883, P. 3
10. Otago Witness, New Zealand, 18 October, 1879, P. 12
11. 17 February, 1903
12. Ibid

13. Reminiscences of Twelve Months Service in New Zealand, Henry McKillop, P. 200-1
14. Ibid
15. The Independent, Wellington, 1 August, 1846
16. The New Zealand Wars, James Cowan, Vol. I, P. 119
17. The Independent, Wellington, 25 July, 1846
18. Ibid, 1 August, 1846
19. The New Zealand Wars, James Cowan, Vol. I, P. 119

Feeding the Fleet
1. Three Years on the Australian Station, Cecil Foljambe, P. 2
2. Ibid, P. 11
3. Ibid, P. 132
4. Ibid, P. 251
5. The Cruise of HMS Calliope in China, Australian and East African Waters, A.C. Evans, P. 21
6. Narrative of a survey of the intertropical and western coasts of Australia, 1818-22, Phillip Parker King, P. 123
7. A Voyage to Terra Australis 1801-3, Matthew Flinders, Vol. II, P. 274
8. The Endeavour Journal of Joseph Banks, Vol. I, P. 449
9. The Cruise of the Rosario amongst the New Hebrides and Santa Cruz Islands, Albert Markham, P. 134
10. Columbia River Exploration 1792, Edward Bell, October-November, 1792
11. A Sailor's Life Under Four Sovereigns, Henry Keppel, P. 255
12. HMS Acheron Diary reported in Evening Star, Dunedin, 12 June, 1926
13. Three Years on the Australian Station, Cecil Foljambe, P. 251
14. Narrative of the surveying voyage of HMS Fly, Joseph Beete Jukes, Vol. I, P. 116
15. Ibid
16. Ibid
17. Nautical Magazine, 1860, P. 522
18. A Sailor's Life Under Four Sovereigns, Henry Keppel, P. 204
19. A Voyage to Terra Australis 1801-3, Matthew Flinders, Vol. II, P. 145
20. The Cruise of the Rosario amongst the New Hebrides and Santa Cruz Islands, Albert Markham, P. 207
21. Ibid, P. 87
22. Kidnapping in the South Seas – Narrative of a three months cruise of HMS Rosario, George Palmer, P. 67
23. Ibid, P. 71
24. Four Years in the Pacific in HM Ship Collingwood, 1844-8, Hon. Fred Walpole, Vol. I, P. 12.
25. Narrative of the surveying voyage of HMS Fly, Jospeh Beete Jukes, Vol. I, P. 11
26. Ibid
27. Ibid
28. Three Years on the Australian Station, Cecil Foljambe, P. 149
29. Narrative of a survey of the intertropical and western coasts of Australia, 1818-22, Phillip Parker King, P. 120
30. Kidnapping in the South Seas – Narrative of a three months cruise of HMS Rosario, George Palmer, P. 71-2.

31. Quoted in The Voyage of George Vancouver, Vol. I, P. 136
32. Fiji and the Fijians, James Calvert, Vol. II, P. 293
33. Journals of Captain Cook, Vol. III, Part 1, P. 261
34. A Voage to Terra Australis 1801-3, Matthew Flinders, Vol. II, P. 154
35. Three Years on the Australian Station, Cecil Foljambe, P. 20
36. The Cruise of the Rosario amongst the New Hebrides and Santa Cruz Islands, Albert Markham, P. 139-40
37. Narrative of the surveying voyage of HMS Fly, Joseph Beete Jukes, Vol. I, P. 35-7
18. Ibid, P. 95

Collecting Curios

1. Three Years on the Australian Station, Cecil Foljambe, P. 237
2. Catalogue of Curiosities from the South Sea Islands, Exhibited by Commodore W. Wiseman of HMS Curacoa, Sydney, 1865
3. 16 November, 1872
4. Three Years on the Australian Station, Cecil Foljambe, P. 150 and 158
5. Ibid, P. 237
6. Notes of a cruise in the Western Pacific 1862 by T.H. Hood reported in Timaru Herald, New Zealand, 13 August, 1864
7. Ibid
8. A Sailor's Life Under Four Sovereigns, Henry Keppel, P. 122
9. Ibid
10. Ibid, P. 123
11. Kidnapping in the South Seas – Narrative of a three months cruise of HMS Rosario, George Palmer, P. 2-5
12. Evening Post, Wellington, 21 May, 1913, P. 8
13. Southern Cross, Auckland, 18 December, 1862
14. Three Years on the Australian Station, Cecil Foljambe, P. 85
15. A Sailor's Life Under Four Sovereigns, Henry Keppel, P. 275
16. Ibid
17. Ibid, P. 214-5
18. Ibid, P. 317
19. Otago Witness, New Zealand, 24 May, 1905, P. 80
20. The Endeavour Journal of Joseph Banks, Vol. II, P. 62
21. Narrative of a survey of the intertropical and western coasts of Australia, Phillip Parker King, P. 222

Diverse Tasks

1. Grey River Argus, New Zealand, 7 August, 1866, P. 2
2. 11 September, 1849, P. 2
3. Southern Cross, Auckland, 18 August, 1866, P. 4
4. Timaru Herald, New Zealand, 17 December, 1900, P. 3
5. Ibid
6. 19 October, 1844
7. The Pitcairn Island Register Book, Sir Charles Lucas, P. 21
8. Otago Witness, New Zealand, 6 May, 1882, P. 22
9. West Coast Times, New Zealand, 26 June, 1891, P. 2
10. 9 May, 1874
11. Evening Post, Wellington, 7 August, 1879, P. 2

12. Journal of HMS Inflexible on a visit to Formosa in search of shipwrecked seamen by Commander G. Brooker as reported in Nautical Magazine, 1859, P. 7
13. Ibid, P. 8
14. Southern Cross, Auckland, 4 October, 1850, P. 3
15. Ibid
16. New Zealander, 9 October, 1847, P. 3

Jack Ashore
1. Journals of Captain Cook, Vol. III, Part 1, P. 260
2. Four Years in the Pacific in HM Ship Collingwood, 1844-8, Hon. Fred Walpole, Vol. I, P. 11
3. Evening Post, Wellington, 10 May, 1873, P. 2
4. Ibid, 4 October, 1873, P. 2
5. Marlborough Express, New Zealand, 29 April, 1876, P. 5
6. Evening Post, Wellington, 25 May, 1882
7. Grey River Argus, New Zealand, 22 October, 1880, P. 2
8. Otago Witness, New Zealand, 25 December, 1875, P. 21
9. Evening Post, Wellington, 10 December, 1890, P. 4
10. Otago Witness, New Zealand, 14 September, 1904, P. 4
11. Ibid
12. Ibid
13. 16 January, 1889
14. The End of a Chapter, Sir Shane Leslie, P. 201
15. 16 January, 1888
16. Otago Witness, New Zealand, 13 December, 1905, P. 33
17. Evening Post, Wellington, 29 July, 1909, P. 2
18. 3 February, 1880, P. 2
19. Evening Post, Wellington, 11 June, 1892, P. 2
20. Ibid, 12 January, 1888, P. 2
21. 26 November, 1873, P. 3
22. Clutha Leader, New Zealand, 8 March, 1889, P. 3
23. Marlborough Express, New Zealand, 22 May, 1878, P. 4
24. As reported in West Coast Times, New Zealand, 29 March, 1873, P. 2
25. Sydney Morning Herald, 14 July, 1876, P. 5
26. Otago Witness, New Zealand, 25 October, 1873, P. 8
27. Evening Post, Wellington, 15 October, 1873, P. 2
28. Ibid
29. 27 January, 1880, P. 2
30. The Cruise of the Rosario amongst the New Hebrides and Santa Cruz Islands, Albert Markham, P. 122
31. Three Years on the Australian Station, Cecil Foljambe, P. 154
32. Evening Post, Wellington, 26 and 27 May, 1882
33. The End of a Chapter, Sir Shane Leslie, P. 10
34. Evening Post, Wellington, 13 January, 1888, P. 2
35. Ibid
36. Ibid
37. Southern Cross, Auckland, 7 March, 1873, P. 2
38. Otago Witness, New Zealand, 20 May, 1876
39. Grey River Argus, New Zealand, 16 February, 1875
40. Three Years on the Australian Station, Cecil Foljambe, P. 238

41. Ibid, P. 239
42. Ibid, P. 246
43. The Observer, Auckland, 19 November, 1904, P. 10
44. Southern Cross, Auckland, 12 November, 1873, P. 3
45. Otago Witness, New Zealand, 15 November, 1884, P. 23
46. Christchurch Press, New Zealand, 24 April, 1869
47. Ibid
48. Ibid
49. Southern Cross, Auckland, 22 November, 1873, P. 2
50. The Cruise of HMS Calliope in China, Australian and East African Waters, A.C. Evans, P. 5
51. Otago Witness, New Zealand, 19 May, 1898, P. 40
52. The Cruise of HMS Calliope in China, Australian and East African Waters, A.C. Evans, P. 38
53. Journals of Captain Cook, Vol. I, P. 98
54. Southern Cross, Auckland, 13 January, 1871, P. 2
55. As reported in Southern Cross, Auckland, 15 July, 1868, P. 2
56. 20 January, 1886, P. 2
57. As reported in Evening Post, Wellington, 22 October, 1869, P. 2
58. Tuapeka Times, New Zealand, 5 February, 1896, P. 6
59. Three Years on the Australian Station, Cecil Foljambe, P. 72
60. 4 August, 1879, P. 2
61. Otago Witness, New Zealand, 3 April, 1869, P. 4
62. Ibid
63. Ibid
64. New Zealand's Naval Story, T.D. Taylor, P. 118
65. Evening Post, Wellington, 16 January, 1888, P. 2
66. Grey River Argus, New Zealand, 3 October, 1876
67. Otago Witness, New Zealand, 1 April, 1903, P. 71
68. Ibid
69. Ibid
70. 5 August, 1848, P. 2
71. West Coast Times, New Zealand, 2 November, 1872, P. 2
72. Southern Cross, Auckland, 5 November, 1861
73. Evening Post, Wellington, 4 May, 1882, P. 2
74. The White Ensign in Early New Zealand, John Ross, P. 92

Runaway Sailors
1. Before the Mast, Henry Boynham, P. 117
2. New Zealand's Naval Story, T.D. Taylor, P. 118
3. Tuapeka Times, New Zealand, 27 January, 1892, P. 6
4. London Standard reported in Evening Post, Wellington, 21 April, 1906, P. 12
5. Ibid
6. Ibid
7. San Francisco Chronicle, 4 September, 1889
8. Waikato Times, New Zealand, 15 April, 1876
9. 25 July, 1891, P. 6
10. Evening Post, Wellington, 10 July, 1880, P. 2
11. 10th and 11th Vic. cap.62, section 11 as reported in Evening Post, Wellington, 20 Septemer, 1861

12. The Observer, Auckland, 2 January, 1886, P. 3
13. Ibid
14. Southern Cross, Auckland, 9 February, 1872, P. 2
15. As reported in Evening Post, Wellington, 13 February, 1872, P. 2

The Pursuit of Pirates
1. China Mail, 9 August, 1855
2. Ibid
3. Ibid
4. Ibid
5. 9 August, 1855
6. Nautical Magazine, 1858, P. 676-7
7. 25 March, 1927, P. 14
8. Ibid
9. Evening Post, Wellington, 9 March, 1929, P. 30
10. Ibid, 23 December, 1932, P. 8
11. A Visit to the Indian Archipelago in HM Ship Maender, Henry Keppel, Vol. I, P. 127
12. Ibid
13. Ibid, P. 132
14. Ibid, P. 133
15. The Expedition to Borneo of HMS Dido for the suppression of piracy, Henry Keppel, Vol. II, P. 3
16. Singapore Free Press reported in Naval Chronicle, 1843, P. 759
17. The Expedition to Borneo of HMS Dido for the suppression of piracy, Henry Keppel, Vol. II, P. 8
18. Naval Chronicle, 1843, P. 760
19. Ibid, P. 761
20. Ibid, P. 762
21. Reported in A Visit to the Indian Archipelago in HM Ship Maender, Henry Keppel, Vol. I, P. 180

Esquimalt
1. Otago Witness, New Zealand, 9 April, 1902, P. 58
2. Southern Cross, Auckland, 20 April, 1860, P. 3
3. Ibid
4. Evening Post, 5 May, 1865, P. 3
5. The Times, London, 31 December, 1863, P. 10
6. Ibid
7. North Otago Times, New Zealand, 26 November, 1895, P. 3
8. Montreal Gazette, 1 April, 1889
9. George Pickett and the Pig War Crisis, Mike Vouri
10. Wanganui Herald, New Zealand, 13 August, 1889
11. New York Times, 24 December, 1897, P. 3

Port Hamilton
1. Evening Post, Wellington, 6 May, 1885, P. 2
2. Ibid
3. Letter in Army and Navy Gazette reported in Evening Post, Wellington, 24 October, 1885, P. 1

4. Ibid
5. The Mercury, Shanghai, 10 June, 1885
6. 16 October, 1885, P. 1
7. Reported in Grey River Argus, New Zealand, 23 July, 1885, P. 2
8. The Gazette, Japan, reported in Te Aroha News, N.Z.,.12 September, 1885, P. 3
9. New Zealand Tablet, 16 October, 1885, P. 1
10. As reported in Evening Post, Wellington, 20 June, 1885, P. 2
11. As reported in Grey River Argus, New Zealand, 16 June, 1885, P. 4
12. The Mercury, Shanghai, 10 June, 1885
13. As reported in Te Aroha News, N.Z., 12 September, 1885, P. 3
14. 4 June, 1885
15. Grey River Argus, New Zealand, 12 December, 1885, P. 1
16. Wanganui Herald, New Zealand, 28 May, 1886
17. Ibid, 27 April, 1888, P. 2

Wei Hai Wei
1. Marlborough Express, New Zealand, 19 May, 1898, P. 2
2. Taranaki Herald, New Zealand, 3 March, 1905
3. Ibid
4. Evening Post, Wellington, 5 September, 1905
5. Poverty Bay Herald, New Zealand, 11 March, 1899, P. 2
6. Hawera and Normanby Star, New Zealand, 5 January, 1905, P. 3
7. The Times, London, 30 September, 1930, P. 11
8. Army and Navy Gazette reported in Evening Post, Wellington, 24 October, 1885, P. 1
9. South China Morning Post, Hong Kong, 4 October, 1996
10. 2 October, 1930, P. 13

Accidents at Sea
1. Evening Post, Wellington, 29 January, 1874, P. 2
2. Ibid
3. Ibid, 20 January, 1874, P. 2
4. Otago Witness, New Zealand, 13 September, 1894, P. 13
5. Ibid
6. Evening Post, Wellington, 28 September, 1894, P. 2
7. Kidnapping in the South Seas – Narrative of a three months cruise of HMS Rosario, George Palmer, P. 5-6

The Fall of Hong Kong
1. The Lasting Honour, Oliver Lindsay, P. 22
2. Ibid, P. 106
3. Ibid

The Prince of Wales and the Repulse
1.   Battleship, Martin Middlebrook and Patrick Mahoney, P. 279-80

The Rise and Fall of the Singapore Naval Base
1. The Pacific War, John Costello, P. 41
2. Ibid, P. 42
3. The Times, London, 15 February, 1938, P. 14

4. Ibid
5. 11 February, 1942, P. 4
6. Ibid

The Battle of the Java Sea
    1.   Page 90

A Daring Submarine Raid
1. Independent, London, 4 September, 2006

The Navy is Back
1. Manchester Guardian, 1 September, 1945
2. An End To Tears, Russell Clark, P. 29-30
3. Manchester Guardian, 1 September, 1945
4. An End To Tears, Russell Clark, P. 35
5. Ibid, P. 33
6. Ibid, P. 45
7. Ibid, P. 44
8. Ibid, P. 100
9. Ibid, P. 175
10. Irish Times, 17 September, 1945
11. An End To Tears, Russell Clark, P. 176
12. Ibid, P. 177
13. 18 November, 1945
14. Manchester Guardian, 30 August, 1945
15. 7 September, 1945, P. 3
16. Sydney Morning Herald, 7 September, 1945, P. 3
17. 7 September, 1945, P. 3

HMS Amethyst on the Yangtse
1. Nelson Examiner and New Zealand Chronicle, 6 September, 1862
2. The Times, London, 1 August, 1949, P. 4
3. A Visit to the Indian Archipelago in HM Ship Maender, Henry Keppel, Vol. I, P. 253
4. A Sailor's Life Under Four Sovereigns, Henry Keppel, P. 250
5. Ibid
6. Ibid
7. Ibid
8. Ibid, P. 252
9. The Times, London, 27 April, 1949, P. 4
10. Ibid, 22 April, 1949, P. 4
11. Ibid, 4 August, 1949
12. Ibid, 2 August, 1949, P. 4
13. Ibid, 1 August, 1949, P. 5
14. Ibid, 1 August, 1949, P. 4
15. Ibid
16. 1 August, 1949, P. 5
17. The Times, 1 August, 1949, P. 4
18. 4 August, 1949
19. The Times, 4 August, 1949,

20. Ibid, 10 September, 1949, P. 4
21. 15 September, 1949, P. 3
22. The Times, 15 September, 1949, P. 3
23. 19 October, 1949, P. 4
24. 25 October, 1949, P. 4
25. 17 November, 1949, P. 4
26. Ibid
27. The Times, 4 August, 1949

The Korean War
1. In Harm's Way, Brian Crabb, P. 172
2. Memoirs of Michael Stephens

The Handover of Hong Kong
1. Navy News, August, 1997, P. 19
2. The Times, 30 June, 1997
3. Navy News, August, 1997, P. 21

INDEX

492

493

495

496

499

501

507

508

510

511

515

517